Textbook on Immigration and Asylum Law

Textbook on
Immigration and Asylum Law

Second edition

Gina Clayton BA (Hons), LLM

OXFORD
UNIVERSITY PRESS

OXFORD
UNIVERSITY PRESS

Great Clarendon Street, Oxford OX2 6DP

Oxford University Press is a department of the University of Oxford.
It furthers the University's objective of excellence in research, scholarship,
and education by publishing worldwide in

Oxford New York

Auckland Cape Town Dar es Salaam Hong Kong Karachi
Kuala Lumpur Madrid Melbourne Mexico City Nairobi
New Delhi Shanghai Taipei Toronto

With offices in

Argentina Austria Brazil Chile Czech Republic France Greece
Guatemala Hungary Italy Japan Poland Portugal Singapore
South Korea Switzerland Thailand Turkey Ukraine Vietnam

Oxford is a registered trade mark of Oxford University Press
in the UK and in certain other countries

Published in the United States
by Oxford University Press Inc., New York

British Library Cataloguing in Publication Data

Data available

Library of Congress Cataloging in Publication Data

Data available

Typeset by RefineCatch Limited, Bungay, Suffolk
Printed in Great Britain
on acid-free paper by
Ashford Colour Press, Gosport, Hampshire

ISBN 0–19–928973–5   978–0–19–928973–8

3 5 7 9 10 8 6 4 2

OUTLINE CONTENTS

DETAILED CONTENTS

Introduction   1

SECTION 1 Laying the foundations   3

1 History and nature of immigration law   5

2 Nationality and right of abode   45

3 Immigration law and human rights   72

SECTION 2 European law and migration   129

4 The European context   131

16 Deportation 544

17 Removal 572

PREFACE

Behind the continuing rapid changes in the law of immigration and asylum there is a sense that the landscape itself is changing. Not only do legislation and case law multiply, and immigration rules and policies churn out at an alarming rate, but behind these specific features there is change in the nature of the field itself.

The context is an enlarged Europe, and the European Community's new and increasing legal competence in relation to immigration and asylum. European governments including the UK are embracing new technology as a form of control over population movements, and the UK's new managed migration policy envisages more routinized and efficient decision-making at entry clearance posts, beginning with an applicant making an on-line assessment of their own eligibility for entry. In conjunction with the removal of the right of appeal against refusal of entry clearance effected by the Immigration Asylum and Nationality Act 2006, these developments indicate the UK's government's vision of a system in which people do not arrive at these shores unless they have legal authority to enter, and problems about whether they should have such authority are dealt with bureaucratically abroad, rather than judicially here.

This connects with the present domestic institutional context of ongoing tension between the executive and judiciary in which the judiciary's constitutional role is in question, prompting Lord Bingham in the case of *A v SSHD* [2004] UKHL 56 to say:

The function of independent judges charged to interpret and apply the law is universally recognised as a cardinal feature of the modern democratic state, a cornerstone of the rule of law itself. The Attorney General is fully entitled to insist on the proper limits of judicial authority, but he is wrong to stigmatise judicial decision-making as in some way undemocratic. (para 42)

The picture of judicial involvement is a mixed one. On the one hand recent decisions of the House of Lords stand as eloquent and learned expositions of human rights law which already have a place in history, for instance in the case quoted of the Belmarsh detainees and of the question of the admissibility of evidence which may have been obtained by torture (*A v SSHD* [2005] UKHL 71). In the lower courts too a number of highly significant decisions have asserted human rights as a powerful form of law. Recent examples are *R (Baiai, Bigoku and Tilki) v SSHD, JCWI intervening* [2006] EWHC 823 (Admin) on the illegality of new marriage rules for foreign nationals and *R (on the application of S, S, M , S, A, S, K, G v SSHD* QBD 10 May 2006 – Sullivan J in the Afghan hijackers case.

On the other hand a relentless succession of judicial decisions in one form or another seeks to exclude foreign nationals from the protection of human rights law. In an almost grotesque reversal of the universal principles which underly the great international human rights treaties of the twentieth century, human rights law is developing within the immigration and asylum context as a special clause which may, in rare cases, be invoked to assist in the most exceptional situations. This does not necessarily mean in the situations of most humanitarian need (*N v SSHD* [2005]

UKHL 31) but rather suggests something legally unusual (*ZT v SSHD* [2005] EWCA Civ 1421). In such cases the judiciary has accepted the arguments of the government, which, through case law as well as legislation, seeks to minimise judicial involvement and contain immigration and asylum decisions within a bureaucratic framework. This is evidenced not only in the managed migration polices but also in the new asylum model, whereby all asylum claims are assigned to a stream within the system aimed at fast processing, and the maximum number will be dealt with in some form of detention. The tendency to create categories and systems of exclusion is buttressed also by policies which prioritise security against terrorism.

The media too plays an important role: on the one hand, exposing alleged corruption in the immigration system, for instance the 'sex for asylum' scandal (Observer May 21 2006), on the other, disseminating misunderstanding about legal decisions, for instance the grant of leave to Afghanis who had hijacked a plane to obtain safety in the UK. A thought-provoking alternative view was offered by Sheena York, interviewed on Radio 4 on 13 May: it's not a desirable action, and they have apologised, but if these people had been escaping Nazi Germany they would have been treated as heroes.

In this climate, it continues to be a daunting task to write a textbook for law students that will relevantly and accurately reflect the law and impart an understanding both of detail and principle. This edition brings together the two chapters on European law, to make a coherent European section. There is a new chapter on asylum process and appeals, and a section on criminalization has been added to take account of the increasing ways in which migrants may be subjected to criminal prosecution, including in particular through the provisions of the Asylum and Immigration (Treatment of Claimants etc) Act 2004. The historical section of chapter one has been extended to include the legislative developments of the last two years and some comment on welfare support for asylum seekers, which is otherwise outside the scope of this book, but important in understanding the development of government policy.

Like other authors in this field, I have had to give up the idea that the book could be up to date even at going to press. In general I endeavour to state the law as at 16 February 2006, though in some specific and important respects, later developments are included. References are given to the Immigration Asylum and Nationality Act, which received Royal Assent on 30 March. The Citizens Directive 2004/38 on the rights of citizens of the European Union and their family members, due to be fully transposed into UK law by 30 April 2006, is treated as though in force and references to UK regulations are to the 2006 regulations which give it effect. It has also been possible to note briefly some later judicial decisions of significance, though fuller treatment of these is reserved for the online resource centre.

Once again, thanks are due to many people, including all those who would have liked me to be more available during the time of writing this second edition. In particular I would like to thank Prakash Shah for his encouragement, Valsamis Mitsilegas for comments on the European chapters, Mahmud Quayum for his generous answers to my questions, and Arlene Audergon for inspired supervision during the final weeks of writing. Thanks are also due to Kate Whetter for her guiding hand, and to the team at OUP for supporting this second edition. And finally once again thanks to my husband Mike Fitter for his continued unstinting patience, support and encouragement in the face of the absence and obsession that this writing entails.

Gina Clayton
May 23 2006

TABLE OF CASES

TABLE OF STATUTES

TABLE OF STATUTORY INSTRUMENTS

TABLE OF EC LEGISLATION

TABLE OF INTERNATIONAL CONVENTIONS

TABLE OF IMMIGRATION RULES

LIST OF ABBREVIATIONS

AIT	Asylum and Immigration Tribunal
API	Asylum Policy Instructions
ARC	asylum registration card
BDTC	British dependent territories citizenship
BIOT	British Indian Ocean Territory
BNA	British Nationality Act
BN(O)	British national (overseas)
BOC	British overseas citizen
BOTA	British Overseas Territory Act
BOTC	British overseas territories citizen
BPP	British protected person
CAT	Convention Against Torture
CEDW	Convention on the Elimination of All Forms of Discrimination Against Women
CERD	Convention on Ending Racial Discrimination
CO	Crown Office
CRC	Convention on the Rights of the Child
CRE	Commission for Racial Equality
CUKC	citizen of the UK and Colonies
ECHR	European Convention on Human Rights
ECtHR	European Court of Human Rights
EESC	European Economic and Social Committee
ELR	exceptional leave to remain
EWCA	England and Wales Court of Appeal
FGM	female genital mutilation
HLR	Housing Law Reports
HRLR	Human Rights Law Reports
IANL	Immigration, Asylum and Nationality Law
IAT	Immigration Appeal Tribunal
ICCPR	International Covenant on Civil and Political Rights
IDI	Immigration Directorate Instructions
ILR	indefinite leave to remain
IND	Immigration and Nationality Directorate
INLP	Immigration and Nationality Law and Practice
INLR	Immigration and Nationality Law Reports
JCWI	Joint Council for the Welfare of Immigrants
NI	Nationality Instructions
SEF	Statement of Evidence Form
SIS	Schengen Information Systems

INTRODUCTION

The notion of a textbook might be taken to imply that there is a standard body of legal knowledge which can be imparted with neutrality and understood in isolation from its context. Nowhere is this less true than in immigration law. To use the words of Legomsky, 'Ensconced as it is in sensitive and controversial policy considerations, immigration law is an area in which the need to place legal doctrine within its larger social and political context is especially acute' (*Immigration and the Judiciary* 1987:5).

As a legal textbook, although this book does not examine in detail the historical and political circumstances, it does introduce the historical and political context in which the law arises. It gives the historical context of many of the topics covered, and includes references to political debates and some of the current research into the social dimensions of migration. This is not comprehensive, but is an encouragement to the reader to pursue some of these matters further using the wealth of literature in this area, and reference should be made to reading lists at the end of each chapter.

One social phenomenon that has influenced the content of his book greatly is the increase in the number of asylum claimants in the UK over the last 20 years. The response of the government to this has been a massive acceleration of lawmaking and a proliferation of statutes and procedural rules. An important aspect of this has been the increasing integration of immigration control and asylum claim determination. Although it is possible to write books purely about asylum law, which is strictly speaking a branch of international humanitarian law, it is not really possible to write a book about immigration law in the UK without also discussing asylum. This book deals with both these issues, and it will become apparent that asylum policy has become the driver behind legal change in many areas of immigration law, which affects all migrants.

Another reason for addressing both asylum and immigration law in one book is that the distinction between asylum seekers and other migrants is not always as sharp as may be supposed. This is not to say, as the press sometimes does, that one is masquerading as the other, but rather that the reasons that people move or are forced to leave their country are complex and not always easy to classify.

The essential political context of these developments is the European Union. European freedom of movement has already radically affected UK immigration law by creating a class of privileged travellers who may enter the UK as of right. The next step is the creation of a Common European Asylum System which, under powers granted by the Treaty of Amsterdam, has now completed its first stage with the UK as an active partner. The influence of European developments is apparent not only in asylum law itself, but also in the UK's rapidly changing border control systems. The Treaty of Amsterdam has as yet had little effect on substantive immigration law as the UK has not opted into the immigration provisions. However, in every area except immigration entitlements, the development towards co-ordination with Europe is apparent.

The Human Rights Act 1998 marked a new era in UK law, and the approach of this book is to look at the law through the prism of that Act. Chapter 3 provides extended discussion of the way that the Act affects immigration law, and the human rights dimension is addressed in each chapter as it arises. Most human rights claims arise where a person faced with removal fears ill-treatment in their destination country, and/or their family or private life will be damaged by the removal. Such considerations are reflected in the emphasis in this book.

Section 1 deals with the areas of law that need to be understood as a foundation for the rest of the book. Chapter 1 gives an outline of the historical development of immigration law in the UK, and an introduction to the nature of immigration law as an exercise of executive power. The immigration rules and sources of immigration law are covered in this chapter. Chapter 2 explains who is subject to immigration control by looking at who has the right of abode in the UK and at key aspects of British nationality law. Chapter 3 deals with the application of the Human Rights Act to immigration and asylum law.

Section 2 covers the European dimension. Chapter 4 sets the out some of the framework issues arising from European membership, explaining how Europeans and non-Europeans are treated differently in the legal structures. Chapter 5 describes the rights of entry of European nationals and others through European free movement provisions.

Section 3 deals with the system of immigration control. Chapter 6 follows the process of entering the UK by examining the legal hurdles encountered before and on arrival, discusses the powers of decision-making held by immigration and entry clearance officers, and concludes with an explanation of the kinds of leave that can be obtained. Chapter 7 examines the way in which the UK is extending its borders into other countries as part of the changing nature of immigration control, which is becoming more akin to policing. It also examines the way in which other public and commercial bodies and even private individuals have become involved in immigration control, particularly by the development of carriers' liability. Chapter 8 examines the control of decision-making, both the structure of the appeals system and some of the standards such as protection from race discrimination which can be used to call decision-makers to account.

Section 4 examines the commonest legal bases for obtaining entry to the UK in immigration law. There is a chapter devoted to family settlement, one to entry for work and business, and one to entry for temporary purposes such as study or holidays.

Section 5 is concerned with asylum claims. Chapter 12 considers the process of making an asylum claim and the special procedures such as fast tracking and certification of claims which enable claims to be decided in a minimum time and with minimum opportunity for challenge. It also examines the issues which are special to refugee appeals. Chapter 13 is devoted to an examination of the criteria which must be fulfilled in order to attain refugee status. Chapter 14 considers criminalization particularly of asylum seekers, and the laws which allow them to be excluded from protection because of what they have or are alleged to have done.

Section 6 is about enforcement. Chapter 15 concerns the grounds for immigration detention and the means of challenging it. Chapters 15 and 16 concern deportation and removal. Removal ends the book as it is the end of the process. In a sense, however, it brings us back to the beginning, as the capacity to remove those with no claim in law to stay is currently seen as a key to the credibility and power of the executive to carry out its policy.

SECTION 1
Laying the foundations

1

History and nature of immigration law

SUMMARY

This chapter divides into two parts. The first gives a brief history of immigration law in the UK, focusing on key legislative developments and noting the themes which arise in that history. The second part discusses immigration law as an exercise of executive power. In so doing it introduces the reader to the sources of immigration law, the immigration rules and concessions, and considers the dominant role of the executive in recent legislation.

1.1 Introduction

One of the reasons for having at least a passing acquaintance with the history is that themes repeat themselves over time, and it is possible to gain a greater perspective and understanding when we know that the current trend is not new. Particular kinds of legal provisions are created, abolished, and then recreated. For instance, sanctions on airlines for carrying passengers who do not carry full documents were introduced in the latter part of the twentieth century by the Immigration (Carriers Liability) Act 1987, but in 1905 the Aliens Act had provided for fines to be levied on carriers of unauthorised passengers.

Bevan identified nine themes in UK immigration policy: lack of planning, the Commonwealth, the importance of the European Community, international law, bipartisan policy, concern for civil liberties, race relations, the question of assimilation or diversity and the use of language (1986:22–28). These themes are still visible and important in the twenty-first century, though the balance has changed since 1986. We would now need to add the preoccupation with deterring false asylum claims and terrorism. Each of these will emerge to varying degrees in the course of this book. In enabling us to see that the issues of today are not new, a historical perspective creates the possibility of learning from history.

1.1.1 Attitudes to immigration

Every history of immigration shows that in Britain each new group of arrivals has been regarded with suspicion and hostility. Allegations against Jews at the turn of the twentieth century, West Indians in the 1950s, people from the Asian sub-continent in the 1960s, and in the 1990s, and at the turn of the twenty-first century, against asylum seekers, are all remarkably similar: 'every mass immigrant group was liable to be pronounced unconventional, unclean, unprincipled and generally unwelcome' (Jones in Juss 1993:71). To this we can add that they are accused of being inveterate liars and scrounging from, or alternatively taking the jobs of, native British people, sometimes even the last two at the same time.

A linked phenomenon is the assertion that the issue is not one of race but of numbers. This is strongly correlated with a political objective of assimilation rather than diversity. If an immigrant group gains sufficient strength in numbers it is thought that it will have more capacity to retain an identity distinct from that of the host population. Interestingly, while denying that the control of entry is to do with race, it is generally said that it is to do with race relations. Politicians often justify a curb on immigration by saying that it is good for race relations. The basis for this is the numbers idea again, and the goal of assimilation. Immigrant groups are thought to be assimilable in small numbers (see for instance the report of Political and Economic Planning discussed in Dummett and Nicol 1990:174). In larger numbers they are said to generate resentment in the host population. Established immigrant groups have also sometimes supported this line of argument though others have opposed any form of immigration controls. Examples of the latter are the action of Jewish trade unions in the nineteenth century and the Indian, West Indian and Pakistani Workers' Association in the twentieth century, (see Cohen, Humphries and Mynott 2002).

The link between immigration and race relations was enshrined in government in the former Home Affairs Select Committee on Race Relations and Immigration. Just by way of example, this Committee's report of 1990 asserted that 'the effectiveness and fairness of immigration controls affect both the maintenance of good race relations at home and Britain's standing in the world'. The European Court of Human Rights did not accept this argument for the maintenance of immigration rules that discriminated against women (*Abdulaziz, Cabales and Balkandali* (1985) 7 EHRR 471). The Commission did not accept that the restriction on the entry of husbands was justifiable on the grounds advanced by the Government, which included the protection of employment opportunities for the indigenous population and the maintenance of 'public tranquillity'. The numbers involved were so small that the effect on the employment situation was insignificant, and no link had been demonstrated between excluding such men and 'good race relations'. The effect could equally be the reverse, in that although the rules addressed the fears of some members of the population, they could create resentment in others, particularly the immigrant population which would regard the rules as unfair (para 77). The Court endorsed the Commission's view (para 81).

Protection of race relations is often advanced as a reason for government policy. However, Lester and Bindman say that this thinking is an expression of 'the ambivalence of public policies. One face confronts the stranger at the gate; the other is turned towards the stranger within' (1972:13–14). Roy Hattersley discovered that he was wrong to make the connection between race relations and immigration:

Good community relations are not encouraged by the promotion of the idea that the entry of one more black immigrant into this country will be so damaging to the national interest that husbands must be separated from their wives, children denied the chance to look after their aged parents and sisters prevented from attending their brothers' weddings. It is measures like the Asylum and Immigration Bill — and the attendant speeches — which create the impression that we cannot 'afford to let them in'. And if we cannot afford to let them in, then those of them who are already here must be . . . doing harm. (The Guardian 26 February 1996)

1.2 **History of immigration law**

In studying immigration we are focusing on movement *into* a country, in this case the UK. However, this is only one small part of a worldwide movement of peoples which has gone on since time immemorial. Until at least the late 1980s Britain was a country of net emigration; in other words, more people left the UK than entered it. Many of the people who have come to the UK have been from areas with a long history of migration, and in paying attention to their arrival in the UK we are only selecting a tiny portion of history.

A complex body of statute and case law governing entry into the UK is a twentieth century phenomenon. Before this there was not a developed body of law, but there were numerous provisions controlling the movement of aliens. Aliens are defined as people who do not owe allegiance to the Crown; in other words they are not citizens of the UK nor of any territory in the control of the UK. Sometimes sweeping measures have been employed; for example, in 1290 Edward I, following an increasing campaign of hatred against Jews, expelled all Jews from England. Some of those expelled would have been aliens, and some British subjects. The latter, according to Magna Carta, had a right to remain in the kingdom and travel freely in and out; the royal decree was illegal as well as immoral, but there was no remedy.

Measures controlling the movement of aliens were often connected with hostilities with other countries. In the sixteenth century, when England was at war with Spain, Ireland gave assistance to the Spaniards, and Ireland and England were in continual conflict. There were by this time a significant number of Irish people resident in England. As Dummett and Nicol comment, regardless of the individual views or affiliations of these people, Queen Elizabeth I issued a proclamation that 'no manner of person born in the realm of Ireland . . . shall remain in the realm' (1990:45). The Irish were either expelled from England or imprisoned. Again in 1793, a statute was passed to control the entry of aliens, this time directed towards travellers from France; following the French Revolution it was feared they might stir up similar fervour in England. While some echoes of these earlier practices may be detected in modern law, by and large the immigration law of the last 100 years is a very different creature from the Royal Proclamations of Edward and Elizabeth.

The beginning of modern-day immigration control can be traced to the persecution of Jews in Eastern Europe at the end of the nineteenth century. From being an envied and romanticized minority as they had been in the nineteenth century, Jews once again became a target of violence and hostility. Many took refuge in Western Europe, including England. However, such movements of hatred are not generally confined within national boundaries, and the new arrivals found themselves also the subject of a campaign in Britain. They were concentrated in areas of poor housing and working conditions, and popular prejudice could regard them as having created these conditions rather than suffering from them alongside other workers. Here is an instance of the characteristics identified by Jones and many other writers as linked with immigrants. As mentioned earlier, both in former times and later in the twentieth century, immigrants are associated with overcrowded housing, disease, crime, and either taking jobs and keeping down wages, or refusing to work and taking up welfare provision.

A campaign against alien workers followed, and the government responded by setting up a Royal Commission to investigate the effect of immigrant workers upon housing and employment conditions and upon public health and morals, the allegations being that they were unclean and spread disease and crime.

The conclusion of the Royal Commission was that there was no threat to the jobs and working conditions of British workers, and immigrants did not create poverty, disease, and crime. There was a slightly higher rate of crime among some alien groups, though Dummett and Nicol suggest that 'the figures were crude and took no account of social class' (1990:101), and immigrants were living in overcrowded housing. The balance of the report was not obviously in favour of immigration control; nevertheless, the Royal Commission recommended control. The result was the Aliens Act 1905, the first major piece of modern immigration legislation. This Act marked the inception of the immigration service and the appeals system. It set up an inspectorate which operated at ports of entry to the UK. It was called the Aliens Inspectorate and its officers (the first immigration officers) had the power to refuse entry to aliens who were considered 'undesirable'. Undesirability was defined as lacking in the means to support oneself and dependants, and lacking in the capacity to acquire such means; mentally ill; likely through ill health to become dependent on the public welfare system or to endanger the health of others; or as having been previously expelled or convicted abroad of an extraditable non-political crime. As a result of successful argument in Parliament, those opposed to controls on aliens had managed to limit the inspectorate's powers to those who travelled on the cheapest tickets (steerage class) on immigrant ships, which were defined as those carrying more than twenty aliens. These categories bear a striking similarity to the requirements for entry in modern-day immigration rules. Under present rules, all categories of entrant are required to show that they will not be reliant on public funds, long term entrants are required to undergo a medical examination (HC 395 para 36) and the commission of criminal offences may give grounds for deportation (Immigration Act 1971 s 3(5)(a)). Note also that the standards in the Act do not clearly correspond to the findings of the Royal Commission; instead they compromise between averting real problems which had been identified and pandering to fears which had been shown to be unfounded. The overall effect is somewhat mitigated by the arguments in Parliament of those concerned with civil liberties. Here we see a reflection of Bevan's themes of lack of planning and bipartisan policy, the latter meaning that political parties would tend to take opposing positions on immigration (though it would also be true to say that it is an issue which does not always split on party lines). The combination of these two factors led to legislation with a confused purpose.

The Act also marked the beginning of an appeals system, by providing for Immigration Appeals Boards. They were set up in every major port of entry and immigrants refused leave to enter had a right of appeal to them.

As we have seen in relation to earlier conflicts with France and Spain, war has been used to impose severe restrictions upon foreigners. During the First World War, the Aliens Restriction Act 1914 s 1 gave the Secretary of State a great deal of power to regulate the entry, stay, and deportation of aliens, and even to pass regulations 'on any other matters which appear necessary or expedient with a view to the safety of the realm'. The Aliens Restrictions (Amendment) Act 1919 extended these wartime powers to apply at any time, subject to a yearly review. This was the pattern also with Prevention of Terrorism Acts, introduced in 1974 as an emergency measure subject to annual review, but culminating in a permanent Terrorism Act in 2000. The effects of the 1919 Act were far reaching. Not only did the wide powers given to the Secretary of State for wartime now also apply in peacetime, the Act also set the pattern, as Bevan describes, for the legal structure of immigration control. The legislation, like many modern statutes, was skeletal in form, having few substantive provisions but giving wide powers to the Secretary of State to make rules.

The 1919 Act was followed by the Aliens Order of 1920, which laid out the more detailed control of aliens and initiated today's system of work permits. Both passports and work permits grew out of wartime controls, as before 1914 it was possible to travel between a number of countries without a passport.

The Second World War had a very significant effect upon patterns of immigration to the UK. War was declared at a time when the Commonwealth was a strong bond which held together a number of nations in allegiance to the monarch of the UK. The UK was regarded by many as the 'mother country'. The fact that British and Commonwealth soldiers were fighting alongside one another contributed to the development of the idea of family, a sense of partnership, and belonging. Additionally, some Commonwealth service people had contributed to the war effort by doing essential work in the UK and so developed real familiarity with Britain. The media talked in terms of loyalty and gratitude to other Commonwealth citizens. This sense of belonging was not a thought-out policy based on a concept of rights enforceable by individuals, but more of a pleasing sentiment which was not expected to have any legal effect.

The reality of post-war entry to the UK was somewhat different. Spencer (1997) describes the deliberations of an interdepartmental working party set up in 1948, and also the later work of a committee of the Ministry of Labour, to consider where there were labour shortages and whether citizens from Commonwealth countries could or should be recruited to make up any shortfall. Writers differ as to the extent of any labour shortage and of recruitment policies aimed at remedying such shortage. The main focus was on the West Indies, and the question of whether workers should be recruited from there. Spencer reports negative conclusions as far as the recruitment of West Indians was concerned; they were not considered suitable workers or acceptable to the unions in the UK. Spencer also reports a refusal by the unions to co-operate with a recruitment scheme, and a preference by the government committees for workers from the continent of Europe. The reasons for this preference were that European workers would be easier to integrate and easier to return when no longer needed. The latter is in part because European workers would not have any claim as British subjects whereas Caribbean workers would. That Europeans would be regarded as easier to integrate could be surprising in view of the fact that English would be a native language for Caribbean workers though not for any European. However, Spencer's analysis of the Cabinet papers of the time, now released under the 30-year rule, strongly suggests that colour was at the root of the government's objection to West Indian workers. An analysis of Cabinet papers of the following few years relating to attempts to restrain immigration in the early 1950s reveals the same concerns (Carter, Harris, and Joshi 1987).

All the authors mentioned above, whose work is based on Cabinet papers, recount obstructive practices that were instituted in the Caribbean, West Africa, India, and Pakistan, making it more difficult for citizens of those countries to travel to Britain despite their being Commonwealth citizens. Examples of tactics employed were the delay in issuing passports and the omission of the reference to British subject status on travel documents, even though the holder was entitled to such a reference.

The passage of the British Nationality Act in 1948 did not affect right of entry into the UK; it dealt with nationality rather than immigration. However, it did so in a rather theoretical sense, being more a matter of labelling than of delivering enforceable rights. Indeed it was not within the contemplation of those who produced this legislation that the millions of Commonwealth citizens and citizens of the UK and Colonies would attempt to use their theoretical right to enter the UK. This Act will be considered in more detail in the chapter on nationality. In terms of this brief history, it both expressed the rather theoretical and symbolic idea that legislators had of the meaning of British subject status, and began the division between citizens of independent Commonwealth countries and other British subjects, which laid the foundation for the later development of immigration control.

Despite the disincentives mentioned above, immigration into Britain continued. There were opportunities for work, and these were attractive. By far the largest number of entrants was from Ireland and the countries known as the Old Commonwealth, i.e., Australia, Canada, and New Zealand. Immigration from the Caribbean was also rising, though not keeping pace with Ireland and the old Commonwealth. Until the release of the Cabinet papers relating to the 1950s, it was widely believed that there was a disproportionate rise in that period of immigration from the Caribbean and of social problems associated with this immigration. The popular account also entailed that the government was dedicated to retaining the rights of British subjects from the Caribbean to enter the UK, but then as social problems escalated, reluctantly they were forced to legislate in the form of the Commonwealth Immigrants Act 1962 to restrict the right of some Commonwealth citizens. Political speeches of the time focused on the familiar theme of numbers. A certain number of immigrants, it was asserted, could be assimilated — in other words absorbed — into the majority culture in Britain without noticeable impact or making demands. Beyond that number they became unassimilable. The studies mentioned above suggest a contrary view, namely that in working parties established specifically to consider the role of 'coloured' workers, the link of immigrants with social problems was not proven, and immigrants from the West Indies were far outnumbered by those from Ireland and the old Commonwealth. The initiative to control black immigration seemed to come, not from the identification of a social problem, but from an independent agenda within the Home Office and Cabinet Office. The Government moved to impose a quota system on immigrants from the West Indies. However, official descriptions of them became more favourable after arrivals increased from India and Pakistan. Those who were formerly lazy were now industrious and English-speaking, and it was the South Asians who were 'unassimilable'. The British Government succeeded in obtaining co-operation from West Indian, Indian and Pakistani Governments to restrain migration, and Paul comments:

The range of administrative methods used by territories of origin and the United Kingdom to prevent colonial migration was so extensive that one might suggest that those migrants who did succeed in obtaining a passport, completing an English language interview, bearing up to scrutiny and accepting the propaganda at its true value were indeed hardy souls. (1997:153)

After years of political debate and manoeuvring the Commonwealth Immigrants Act was finally passed in 1962. The significance of the Act was immense. For the first time there was a restriction on the rights of certain Commonwealth citizens to come to the UK.

The Act distinguished between Commonwealth citizens based on parentage. Those who were born in the UK or Ireland or who held a passport issued by the Government of those countries would not be subject to immigration control; others would. The immigration control consisted of conditions that a Commonwealth citizen would have to satisfy to gain entry. Whether these conditions were satisfied was to be determined by an immigration officer who was given a wide measure of discretion.

One of the peculiar features of British immigration law, to which we shall return time and again, is the heavy reliance on formerly unpublished instructions, guidelines, and concessions. These less formal sources in practice determine the outcome of applications. In the course of the implementation of the Commonwealth Immigrants Act 1962, it was made clear by internal guidance that the discretion given to immigration officers to refuse entry on the basis that requirements were not met, would not be applied in practice to immigrants from Canada, Australia, or New Zealand. The system of control that was established therefore discriminated at two levels against black would-be entrants. Initially, the terms of the Act itself, while neutral on their face as regards race or colour, were based on a requirement of birth in the UK or possession of a passport issued by the UK government, both of which would be satisfied more often in practice by white people. At the second level of internal instructions, the discrimination was closer to being explicit. As with the Jews in the thirteenth century, though more subtly, the distinction was made on the basis of ethnicity, not nationality.

For the Commonwealth citizens subject to immigration control, a three-tier system of work vouchers was instituted. Dummett and Nicol comment that this founded a bureaucratic system for processing immigration rather than a method of controlling it. The actual effect of the Commonwealth Immigrants Act was very different from the Government's intention. There was a substantial rise in immigration from the Indian sub-continent in particular around the time of the 1962 Act. The Act has often been presented as the response to this increased immigration, but as Spencer (1997) and Bevan (1986) recount, it is more likely to have caused it. Spencer suggests four ways in which the Commonwealth Immigrants Act actually encouraged immigration, as follows.

First, the build-up to the legislation had taken years. The proposal to restrict immigration was therefore known long in advance and during the years 1960–62 this created a rush to 'beat the ban'.

Second, prior to the 1962 Act, those who had come from the Indian sub-continent to Britain were mainly men who had come for a temporary period to work, and to send money back to their families. Often this was in a tradition in their original locality, and they came to Britain because at that time there was a good chance of employment particularly in the textile industry in the north. These men's travels were therefore not immigration as it is sometimes understood forty years later, i.e., they had not come to settle. The 1962 Act made it less likely that men retiring from this role could be replaced by younger relatives as the work voucher system would not have favoured their entry. The tendency of the Act therefore was to encourage those men to apply for leave to remain in the UK.

Following on from the last point, the Act permitted unification of families, and so for the men who had come as sojourners, the provisions of the Act combined to make remaining in the UK and being joined by their families the more viable option. It might be said (though Spencer does not make this point) that the Act encouraged and established the growth of an immigrant population modelled on British assumptions of working and family life, rather than an understanding of what migration meant to those who were doing it.

Spencer's final point is made also by Dummett and Nicol (1990): that the Act established a regime that regulated and therefore to a degree allowed people to enter the UK, namely the system of entry control and work vouchers.

The 1962 Act was formative in that it laid the foundation of the distinction between entry as a right and entry subject to the fulfilment of conditions, and did so by using the criterion of connection with the UK. The particular history of this Act reminds us not to take at face value assertions of cause and effect in relation to legislation; it also introduces the role of internal guidance in the operation of immigration law.

The history of the Commonwealth Immigrants Act 1968 is discussed by many writers including Shah, P. (2000), Bevan (1986), and Dummett and Nicol (1990). It provides a stark illustration of the difference between immigration policy based on loyalty to those whom the Empire and then the Commonwealth gave the status of British subject, and immigration policy based on fear of admission of numbers of non-white people. The key events were the independence of, first, Kenya and, later, Uganda and Tanzania. Each of these countries at independence had an established minority population which had come from the Indian sub-continent, some of whom had been introduced into East Africa by Britain which, as colonial power, had employed them on construction projects. Many had left India before its independence and before the creation of Pakistan, and their only citizenship was that of the UK and Colonies. The East African countries, on attaining independence, pursued a policy of Africanization that required residents to demonstrate their allegiance to the new state. Many Asians either did not fulfil the conditions for acquiring the new citizenship or did not register within the time limit, preferring to wait and see how their fortunes were likely to go in the new regime before committing themselves. Some may have been reluctant to lose their British connection. For many of those who did not acquire the new citizenship, serious consequences ensued. They lost their employment or their livelihood, and sought to use whatever protection their citizenship of the UK and Colonies could offer them. Their passports had been issued by the British High Commission and, therefore, under the 1962 Act they were not subject to immigration control. They had, as British subjects, right of entry into the UK. Inflated figures of likely entrants were quoted in the media, and the Commonwealth Immigrants Act 1968 was rushed through Parliament. The new Act provided that British subjects would be free from immigration control only if they, or at least one of their parents or grandparents, had been born, adopted, registered, or naturalized in the UK. The issue of a passport by a

British High Commission thus ceased to be a qualification for entry free of control. For those subject to control, another voucher system was introduced. This one was based on tight quotas, reflecting the government's contention that numbers were the problem.

The story of the East African Asians illustrates how a British Government was prepared to mix together issues of nationality and immigration. This is one of the themes identified by Bevan. While the East African Asians retained their CUKC (citizen of the UK and Colonies) status, it was in effect worthless as it no longer conferred a right of entry to their country of nationality.

The issue of colour (which was the terminology then used, and which was quite accurate) continued to dominate public debate about immigration. When the Immigration Act 1971 was passed, the racial definition of those with rights of entry and those without was complete. While the Immigration and Asylum Act 1999 and Nationality Immigration and Asylum Act 2002 have made substantial changes to the immigration process and the rights of immigrants, the 1971 Act remains the source of Home Office and immigration officers' powers to make decisions on entry, stay, and deportation. Its significance in terms of the history we are now tracing is its division of the world into patrials and non-patrials. Previously, UK law had divided the world into British subjects and aliens. This was the fundamental category which determined whether a person had right of entry into the UK. Legislation then, as we have seen, restricted the rights of some British subjects to the extent that these rights became practically worthless. The Immigration Act 1971 gave right of abode in the UK to those it defined as 'patrials'. These were:

(i)   citizens of the UK and Colonies who had that citizenship by birth, adoption, naturalization, or registration in the UK;

(ii) citizens of the UK and Colonies whose parent or grandparent had that citizenship by those same means at the time of the birth of the person in question;

(iii) citizens of the UK and Colonies with five years' ordinary residence in the UK;

(iv) Commonwealth citizens whose parent was born or adopted in the UK before their birth;

(v)   Commonwealth citizens married to a patrial man.

Commonwealth citizens who had been settled in the UK for five years when the Act came into force (1 January 1973) also had the right to register and thus possibly the right of abode. More detail is given of these provisions in chapter 2. Others, including British citizens without the necessary tie of parentage, would be subject to immigration controls. Apart from the five-year residence qualification, the right to live in the UK and to enter free from immigration control was determined by birth or parentage, not by nationality. The British Nationality Act 1981 carried this classification into British nationality law, and it is still the case that there are some, though a dwindling number, of British nationals who do not have a right of entry to the UK.

On the same day that the Immigration Act 1971 came into force, the UK entered the European Community. One of the cornerstones upon which the EC is built is freedom of movement, not only of goods but also of workers and their families. Despite this timing, the Immigration Act made no reference to European membership or the principle of freedom of movement. It continues to be the case up to the present that UK immigration law has developed quite separately from European law on freedom of movement (*R v IAT and Surinder Singh ex p SSHD* [1992] Imm AR 565) and that, at the same time that immigration restrictions were confirmed for Commonwealth citizens with a traditional allegiance to Britain, a new category of privilege was created for European nationals. It was not until January 2006, with the full implementation of the European Council Directive on the status of long-term residents (2003/109) that third country nationals (i.e., non-Europeans including Commonwealth citizens) acquired any kind of security of residence in European law independently of their association with an EU national (see chapter 4).

Primary immigration, that is of people coming to establish a life on their own rather than to join family members, virtually ceased with the Acts of 1968 and 1971; nevertheless in the 1980s the general trend in immigration provisions remained towards increasing restriction. Attention switched from primary immigration to family settlement, and more demanding rules for the entry of spouses were introduced. These raised such a political storm that, most unusually, there was a debate in Parliament concerning new immigration rules (see discussion in chapter 9).

On the whole, however, toward the end of the twentieth century, immigration policy (as distinct from asylum) did not play such a prominent part in the political life of the UK as it did previously. The Labour Government's abolition of the infamous primary purpose rule in 1997 was a reversal of one of the most punitive provisions on family settlement (again see chapter 9) and the reduced tension around immigration and increased awareness of rights made this possible. The increasingly restrictive nature of immigration law did not arise from concerns about immigration as such, but from concerns about increased asylum claims. The rapid growth of a visa regime, now affecting travellers from potentially any country in the world, is an example of this (see chapter 6). The Immigration and Asylum Act 1999 made significant inroads into the rights of appeal of those alleged to be in breach of immigration law, but this was to address the backlog of cases at the Home Office and to expedite the removal of unsuccessful asylum seekers. The backlog, rather than issues of entry and entitlement, became the immigration scandal of the late 1990s in its own right.

The other major development in immigration law in the last twenty years has been the introduction of internal controls. This entails the devolution to housing officers, benefits officers, employers, registrars of births, marriages, and deaths, and airline officials of decisions concerning immigration status. These decisions then determine entitlement to a civil benefit such as housing or employment. Juss dates the introduction of these provisions from the first report of the Select Committee on Race Relations and Immigration in 1978. The effect has been to exclude from social benefits those people who have, or who may have, or who may be thought to have, a questionable immigration status. These provisions are predicated on the idea that there is a negative impact on Britain's housing and welfare system from immigrants who have deceived their way into the system — an idea we have seen at work earlier in the twentieth century.

Both the development of internal controls and the reduction of appeal rights ride on the back of the issue which has attracted public attention in the 1990s — that of asylum. The bulk of the case law reported in the Immigration Appeal Reports has for some years concerned asylum rather than immigration issues. Recent years have seen an escalation of legislation principally aimed at controlling asylum seekers: the Asylum and Immigration Appeals Act 1993, Asylum and Immigration Act 1996, Immigration and Asylum Act 1999, Nationality Immigration and Asylum Act 2002, the bizarrely named Asylum and Immigration (Treatment of Claimants etc) Act 2004, and the Immigration, Asylum and Nationality Act 2006. However, although the target group is different, the themes are recognizable.

The 1993 Act introduced an appeal right for asylum seekers, but also the concept of a claim 'without foundation' (Sch 2 para 5). Again, this is based on the concept of a potential entrant as dishonest. Claims so certified would attract only limited appeal rights, the government's avowed intention being to speed through the system claims which could be identified at an early stage as unmeritorious. This provision is based not only on the idea of the deceptive applicant but also on addressing the backlog. Juss gives a stinging account of the origins of the 1993 Act in which he suggests that the problem of the backlog was self-inflicted, resulting from a recruitment freeze in the Immigration and Nationality Department (IND). Opportunities for applicants to manipulate the system arose as a result of increasing delays, and these manipulations in turn extended the delays. His account may be borne out by the fact that the backlogs were effectively tackled in the year 2000 by recruiting extra personnel in IND.

Delay and cheating the system, and the relationship between the two, became the political issues of the 1990s. The alleged cheating was both at the point of entry (the concept of the 'bogus' asylum seeker) and after entry (the concept of the 'scrounger'). These ideas underlie further provisions in the Asylum and Immigration Act 1996 such as, for instance, the creation of a new offence of obtaining leave to remain by deception (s 4). The kinds of claims that would be subjected to restricted appeal rights (known then as the short procedure) were extended to include those from a designated country of origin. Designation, according to the promoting minister in Parliament, would be on the basis that there had been a high number of applications and a high number of refusals from that particular country and that there was, in general, no serious risk of persecution in that country (HC Col 703 (11 December 1995)). This provision has a similar basis to the 'without foundation' provision, that of expediting applications on the basis that they may be identified without full examination as being unmeritorious. Similar provisions followed in the 1999 Act ('manifestly unfounded') and in the 2002 Act ('clearly unfounded'). The list of designated countries became known as the White List. It was abandoned after a successful challenge, in *R v SSHD ex p Javed and Ali* [2001] Imm AR 529, to the inclusion of Pakistan because of known widespread discrimination against women and against Ahmadis, which had been accepted in the higher courts in the UK (*Shah and Islam v IAT and SSHD* [1999] Imm AR 283 and *Ahmed (Iftikhar) v Secretary of State for the Home Department* [2000] INLR 1). Where sectors of society could be said to be at risk, it could not be reasonable to say there was, in general, no serious risk of persecution. A new 'white list' was produced in the 2002 Act and has been extended by ministerial orders.

Section 2 of the 1996 Act also introduced a power to remove asylum seekers before their appeal is heard (a 'non-suspensive appeal') if they had travelled through a country which can be regarded as a 'safe third country'. These provisions, as mentioned earlier, arose from concern in Europe about asylum seekers being 'bounced around' Europe, i.e., shuttled from one country to another, each one declining to hear their asylum application but finding a reason to return them to another member state. The UK was a signatory to the Dublin Convention, the treaty by which EC countries sought to find a way of determining which state should hear an asylum application. However, as international law, this treaty was not binding in the UK directly in tribunals. It has now been superseded by a regulation, discussed in chapter 12.

Other provisions of the 1996 Act continued the dual themes of deception and internal controls. More criminal offences were devised, targeting the racketeering of those who arrange entry to the UK for gain (s 5), and more internal controls were set up, denying welfare benefits to many asylum seekers and also recruiting employers into the system of detection of residents with potentially irregular immigration status (ss 8 and 9).

The Immigration and Asylum Act 1999 continued the trend by, according to Statewatch, 'hugely increasing surveillance, monitoring and compulsion.' Registrars of births, marriages, and deaths were brought into the internal control system (s 24). Penalties for carrying passengers without full documentation increased once again, being extended to include trains, buses, and coaches to cover entry via the Channel Tunnel (Part II of the Act). There were also provisions for penalizing private car and lorry drivers who carried clandestine entrants. Material support for asylum seekers was converted into a voucher system and a dispersal system which would distribute asylum seekers around the country (Part VI). Appeal rights were further curtailed, both for asylum seekers and other deportees (Part IV). Limited appeal rights for family visitors were reinstated. The 1990s had seen a massive increase of asylum seekers detained in detention centres and prisons. One of the anomalous features of immigration detention generally, including that of asylum seekers, is that it is not subject to any form of supervision by the courts, and there is no presumption of a right to bail, as there is when someone is charged with a criminal offence. In the 1999 Act the government took the opportunity, partially, to address this issue by introducing a routine bail hearing (Part III). However, these provisions were never implemented, and were repealed by the Nationality, Immigration and Asylum Act 2002.

The 1999 Act was proclaimed as a radical overhaul of the immigration and asylum system. It expressed the political agenda of its day — suspicion that there is a large volume of unmeritorious asylum claims; the cost of welfare benefits obtained by people who made such claims; the progressive extension of internal controls; the problem of backlog and delay in the system both before dealing with claims and before removal from the country of those who did not succeed; and the shifting of blame to the morally more acceptable targets of 'racketeers' rather than the obviously vulnerable asylum seekers. There was another influence at the time of debates on the 1999 Act, namely, the Human Rights Act 1998 (HRA), which had received Royal Assent but was not yet in force. The 1999 Act removed some rights to have an appeal heard in the UK. The counterbalance was to provide an in-country appeal on human rights grounds. The 1999 Act provided the first statutory right of appeal against immigration decisions on human rights grounds (s 65, now in the Nationality, Immigration and Asylum Act 2002 s 84). Further discussion of the implications of the introduction of the HRA is reserved for chapter 3.

1.2.1 **Twenty-first century**

Three immigration statutes have been passed already in this century, in an atmosphere of 'gathering storm in relations between the executive and judicial branches in the national constitution' (Rawlings 2005:380). There have also been two terrorism statutes with another on the way, one of which (Prevention of Terrorism Act 2005) consists entirely of the most severe statutory curtailment of civil liberties seen in Great Britain since wartime internment. This came into existence to replace earlier even more restrictive measures applied to foreign nationals through a misuse of immigration powers (Anti-terrorism, Crime and Security Act 2001, Part IV).

Two major cases in the House of Lords arising from the same issue were heard by chambers of nine and seven Lords respectively, indicating the constitutional importance of the matters addressed. Without doubt they have reasserted the place of the judiciary as protectors of fundamental constitutional values. *A and others v SSHD* [2004] UKHL 56 concerned the direct challenge to the detentions under the Anti-terrorism, Crime and Security Act, and *A v SSHD* [2005] UKHL 71 the question of whether evidence which could have been obtained by torture could be used in cases before the Special Immigration Appeals Commission.

At the same time as the 2004 judgment, the executive was proposing to stop all immigration and asylum issues from being heard by the courts, whether on appeal or review, by means of a far-reaching ouster clause in the Asylum and Immigration (Treatment of Claimants, etc) Bill 2003 (AITOC). Such a move was unprecedented. Rawlings refers to it as part of a 'revenge package' from a government frustrated that the judiciary continued to develop and maintain the rights of asylum seekers in the face of government attempts to restrict them (2005:378).

This atmosphere of constitutional tension between the executive and judiciary is the background for the immigration statutes and non-statutory legal developments of the twenty-first century.

At the time of the passing of the 1999 Act it was widely predicted there would be another immigration statute within three years, and so it turned out (see for this point and generally Mckee). The Nationality, Immigration and Asylum Act 2002 was preceded by a White Paper: *Secure Borders, Safe Haven; Integration with Diversity in Modern Britain* (Cm 5387). The publication of the White Paper was announced by Home Secretary David Blunkett in the following terms:

> The White Paper takes forward our agenda by offering an holistic and comprehensive approach to nationality, managed immigration, and asylum that recognises the inter-relationship of each element in the system. No longer will we treat asylum seekers in isolation or fail to recognise that there must be alternative routes to entry into this country. (HC col 1028 7 February 2002)

The Act deals with changes to nationality law, the provision of accommodation centres for asylum seekers, restrictions on the asylum support system, the provision of removal centres and expansion of powers of detention and removal, extension and amendment of the carriers' liability scheme, and the introduction of further criminal offences. At least as much as the 1999 Act, this Act was dominated by objectives concerning the asylum system. A continual problem for the government, through the 1990s and into the current decade, is that the asylum system is said to lack credibility. The difficulty in proposing and implementing solutions is that there are radically different diagnoses of the problem. By simplifying in order to make a point we can say that on one view, the lack of credibility of the system is signalled by a perceived failure to remove unsuccessful claimants, deter new ones, and reduce the numbers of claims overall. This view is promoted by certain politicians and some sections of the media. On another view, the lack of credibility of the system arises from the lack of independent and well-informed decision-making at the initial stage. This view is supported by organizations of migrants and representatives. Analyses of phenomena observable in the system flow from these positions. Frequent challenges of asylum decisions are interpreted from the first perspective as abuse by undeserving claimants determined to spin out their stay; from the second as necessitated by the poor quality of initial decision-making. The increasing complexity of legal challenges is interpreted from one perspective as abusive claimants and their lawyers manipulating the system, and from the other as necessitated by the continual reduction in appeal rights and the absence of a straightforward process to protect fundamental rights.

Numerous Parliamentary committee reports have been produced, identifying the reasons for the system not being satisfactory, but following their recommendations has political and financial implications. At the time of writing the Home Affairs Committee has launched a new inquiry into immigration control.

In relation to the 2002 Act, McKee refers to 'divergent and contradictory goals', specifically:

- to keep asylum seekers out, but to provide a welcome for genuine refugees;
- to integrate refugees and ethnic minorities into mainstream British culture, but to celebrate cultural diversity;
- to include a raft of authoritarian and repressive measures under the same anodyne umbrella of 'modernisation' as liberal measures to allow economic migration and facilitate easier travel. (2002:181)

Within the broad purposes identified by McKee, the Act and the White Paper have a number of underlying policy themes which may be characterized as:

1. developing an all-pervasive control system for asylum-seekers;
2. a controlled development of the possibility of entry for work;
3. the creation of a class of people without rights or status;
4. development of extra-territorial immigration control;
5. combating terrorism; and
6. the strengthening of executive power, considered in the next section of this chapter.

The White Paper's proposals for ensuring credibility rested on the belief that it is important to control asylum seekers. End-to-end credibility translated into end-to-end monitoring. Accommodation and removal centres were elements in this development. Restrictions on welfare support which made it conditional on reporting or residence also tightened the level of continuous control that the government is able to exercise over asylum seekers. Increased powers of detention and removal served the same purpose.

The second policy underlying the 2002 White Paper was a cautious encouragement of economic migration. This was the first evidence for decades that immigration policy might be directed towards encouragement of entry, and received a general welcome. Shah, R. (2002:315), for instance, saw this as evidence of 'a new dynamism' in the Home Office. However, this apparent shift in policy was not reflected in the 2002 Act. Extensions of various schemes permitting entry of workers were implemented by concessions and developments in administrative practice which, in some cases, resulted in changes to the immigration rules. The retention of government control over entry into the UK is presaged in the White Paper, para 12: 'We have taken steps to ensure that people with the skills and talents *we need* are able to come to the UK on a sensible and managed basis' (emphasis added). The retention of control and the words emphasized lend support to the argument of Cohen that such proposals represent nothing new; rather, they replicate a historical tendency to manipulate overseas labour, 'labour which can be turned on and off like a tap' (2002). Bevan made the same comment in relation to earlier provisions (1986:278). Scepticism it seems was warranted. A further White Paper in 2005 announced a tiered system of managed migration that seems to bring entry for work and study into a more routinized, bureaucratized system, dominated by immigration control. But this is to anticipate. Schemes for entering the UK for work and their relationship to economic conditions are discussed further in chapter 11.

The growth of a class of people without rights or status can be identified from a number of disparate current developments, and three provisions of the 2002 Act in particular are part of that development. Section 4 substantially extends the power of the Secretary of State to deprive a person of their British nationality. In the case of people who acquired their British nationality by naturalization or registration, there is no requirement to have regard to whether doing so will leave them stateless. In the case of others, although they may not strictly speaking be left stateless, as the Joint Parliamentary Committee on Human Rights pointed out:

deprivation of British citizenship would entail loss of British diplomatic protection; loss of status; loss of the ability to participate in the democratic process in the United Kingdom; and serious damage to reputation and dignity. The Home Office argument assumes that the real threat to human rights would derive from any subsequent decisions taken as part of the immigration control process. In that process, there would usually be adequate opportunity to ensure that effect is given to Convention rights, and that other rights are given appropriate weight. However, we are concerned about the wider implications of loss of British citizenship. (Joint Committee on Human Rights Parliamentary Session 2001–2 Seventeenth Report para 26)

While recognizing that there is no right to a nationality, the Committee was concerned about the consequences of statelessness, and that if the other country refused a passport, the alternative nationality would be 'an empty shell' (para 26). The Committee's report reveals that the civic limbo in which persons would find themselves was not recognized by the Home Office. The dangers of being left in a condition of no status or rights were sadly demonstrated after the case of *Ahmed v Austria* 24 EHRR 62. The European Court of Human Rights decided that the applicant could not be removed from the country as this would breach his human rights. However, the Austrian Government did not issue him with a residence permit, and eventually, without any support or security, Mr Ahmed took his own life. There is further discussion of s 4 in the next chapter.

Section 76 of the 2002 Act enables the Secretary of State to revoke a person's indefinite leave to remain if the person 'is liable to deportation but cannot be deported for legal reasons'. The legal reasons which would prevent deportation are likely to be that the person would face a serious violation of their human rights in their country of origin and no other country is willing to accept them. Without indefinite leave to remain, a person may neither work nor claim benefits. They are without status and without means.

The 2002 Bill was amended in the House of Lords so that citizenship by birth (though not by application) could only be removed in reliance on acts committed after s 4 came into force (1 April 2003). However, indefinite leave to remain may be revoked in reliance on anything done before s 76 came into force (10 February 2003) and leave granted before that date may be revoked, giving the section retrospective effect.

Finally, s 67(2) in combination with its interpretation in *R v SSHD ex p Khadir (Appellant)* [2005] UKHL 39 means that a person who is granted temporary admission — a status without rights — may remain in that position for years, even though there is no possibility of being removed (see chapter 15).

The status of temporary admission, on which many asylum seekers remain for years, is a bar to rights of many kinds. The government has maintained that people on temporary admission are not 'lawfully present' for the purpose of social security rules and housing rules. Arguments on this and other issues have even led to the legal fiction that people temporarily admitted are not present at all, let alone lawfully. This has been scotched in *Szoma v Secretary of State for the Department of Work and Pensions* [2005] UKHL 64, in which their Lordships held that the appellant was lawfully present. As a consequence, he was one of a small minority of those on temporary admission who are able to claim income support.

The concern with undocumented migrants both throughout Europe and further afield is marked by this paradox. Ever-increasing control measures are developed alongside measures to exclude some people from the system altogether.

The development of extra-territorial immigration control is strongly signalled in the 2002 White Paper but barely appears in the Act. Most measures taken for this purpose are administrative arrangements whose statutory support appears elsewhere (e.g., the Channel Tunnel Act 1987). They include the posting of immigration officers abroad as airline liaison officers, and alongside their counterparts at European ports. They are aimed at deterring asylum claims and in policy terms are important. To these measures could be added the extension and amendment of provisions relating to the liability of carriers (lorry drivers, rail companies, and so on) for clandestine entrants hidden in their vehicles. These developments constitute a significant change in the nature of immigration control, and are discussed fully in chapter 7.

Combating terrorism is a thread which runs throughout legislation and government policy much more strongly since 11 September 2001. The Anti-Terrorism Crime and Security Act 2001 contains significant provisions affecting refugee claims, discussed in chapter 14, but the connection with prevention of terrorism is not explicit in the Immigration Acts. There are not, for instance, sections headed 'terrorism'. Nevertheless, in the 2002 Act, the strengthened and extended border controls, the new offences created, and the intensive monitoring of asylum seekers all have security as a background theme and objective (see Mckee and Shah, R. 2002). A radical interpretive provision in the 2006 Act (discussed in chapter 14) has the same objective, as do the proposals to work the Prime Minister's 2005 set of 'unacceptable behaviours' into immigration and nationality law (see chapters 2 and 16). This trend is the 'Secure Borders' aspect of the 2002 White Paper's title. More directly, as discussed in chapter 14, s 72 enables members of organizations proscribed under the Terrorism Act 2000 to be excluded from refugee status. For a discussion of the effect of the 2001 Act on immigration and asylum see Blake and Hussain, *Immigration, Asylum and Human Rights* (2003, Chapter 7).

The welfare support provisions of the 2002 Act were among its most contentious provisions. Despite research suggesting that welfare policies are not an effective deterrent (Home Office Research Study 243, 2003), the Government was dedicated to a path of reducing welfare provision. As welfare support is not covered as a subject in its own right in this book, the main issues will be outlined here. The crucial provision in the 2002 Act was s 55 which provided that the Secretary of State has no obligation to provide welfare support (money or accommodation) where a claim for asylum has not been made 'as soon as reasonably practicable' unless this is necessary to avoid a breach of the claimant's human rights. Challenges to denial of benefit multiplied in the High Court. In the first year of the Act judges made over 800 emergency orders for the payment of interim benefit (Sedley LJ annual Legal Action Group lecture November 2003). After people were refused support even when they claimed asylum on the day of their arrival in the UK, the case of *R (on the application of Q) v SSHD* [2003] EWCA Civ 364 considered the meaning of s 55. The Court of Appeal accepted that the asylum seeker's circumstances should be taken into account in determining what was 'as soon as reasonably practicable' and this could include advice given by someone arranging their passage. In January 2004 the government was obliged to introduce fairer procedures and a three-day period to allow people to find their way to relevant government offices (Macdonald and Webber 2005:868).

The government still pursued to the House of Lords the question of whether actual or imminent destitution would amount to a breach of Article 3 — the right to be free of inhuman or degrading treatment. The House of Lords found that it did (*R v SSHD ex p Adam, Limbuela and Tesema* [2005] UKHL 66; see further in chapter 3). After the High Court judgment in *Limbuela* the Secretary of State issued a policy instruction that support would no longer be denied under s 55 to people who had recently arrived in the country unless they clearly did have other means of support (see The Guardian 26 June 2004).

Despite the inroads which court decisions at all levels have made into the operation of s 55 the Parliamentary Joint Committee on Human Rights reiterated their concern that

the levels of homelessness and destitution which reliable evidence indicates have in practice resulted from section 55 are very likely to breach both the obligation of progressive realisation of rights under Articles 9 and 11 International Covenant on Economic Social and Cultural Rights (since they represent a regression in the protection of these rights for asylum seekers), and the obligation to ensure minimal levels of the Covenant rights to the individuals affected by section 55. (JCHR Eighth Report session 2005–06 HL paper 104 HC 850 para 121)

At the time of the passing of the Human Rights Act there was concern that its provisions would be hijacked by those with money for relatively trivial ends. In these House of Lords decisions, *A v SSHD 2004*, *A v SSHD 2005* and *Limbuela*, the government was challenged on breaches of the most basic rights, to physical liberty and to be free of torture, inhuman and degrading treatment and punishment. These battle lines on fundamental constitutional issues drawn around the rights of foreign nationals reveal the lack of a fundamental principle of equality of treatment (see Singh 2004).

Welfare support continued to be a major preoccupation in the 2004 Act. The proposal in the consultation letter which preceded the Act which provoked the most opposition was that welfare support and accommodation should be withdrawn from failed asylum seekers with families. The 1999 Act had already withdrawn support from asylum seekers whose claim had failed, but it was not thought appropriate then to inflict destitution on children. In 2003 the Government had a different solution — take the children into care. Section 9 enables support to be withdrawn once a claim has failed and appeals are exhausted in a case where the Secretary of State certifies that the claimant 'has failed without reasonable excuse to take reasonable steps to leave the UK voluntarily' (s 9 of the 2004 Act, inserting para 7A into Sch 3 of the 2002 Act). Section 10 drew almost as much criticism as it enables the Secretary of State to make regulations making continuation of accommodation for a failed asylum seeker dependent upon performing community service.

The Parliamentary Joint Committee on Human Rights noted that an asylum seeker 'who has exhausted their rights of appeal, cannot return to their country for reasons beyond their control and who has no other means of support is in an analogous position to a UK citizen or any other person in the UK who is entitled to emergency state assistance to prevent destitution' (Fourteenth Report 2003–04 HL 130/HC 828 para 18). An obligation to perform community service as a condition of receiving emergency social assistance was not, as claimed by the Government 'a normal civic obligation'. On the contrary, it was 'without precedent or even analogy' (para 15). There was a significant risk of breach of Article 4(2) ECHR through forced or compulsory labour (para 16). Singling out asylum seekers would breach Article 14 as it was unjustifiably discriminatory (para 21), and a withdrawal of support if someone did not perform the labour could breach Article 3 by subjecting them to inhuman and degrading treatment (para 24).

In the event, s 10 has proved impossible to implement as no community organizations could be found who were willing to provide the community service in question. The YMCA, which considered it, was persuaded to change its mind.

A similar fate may be in store for s 9. The operation of s 9 was piloted in East London, Manchester and West Yorkshire. Organizations representing social workers lobbied against it as their members baulked at taking asylum seekers' children into care when this would not be in the children's best interests. The Joint Committee on Human Rights considered that it would be difficult to implement s 9 without breaches of Articles 3 and 8 (Fifth Report session 2003–04 HL Paper 35 HC 304 para 45). Reports of children's charities and refugee organisations concluded that the pilot of s 9 had caused enormous distress and destitution. Many families' support had been wrongly ended when they still had the possibility of appeals. Families were at low risk of absconding, but some did disappear when faced with the prospect of parents being separated from children (Refugee Action and Refugee Council 2006).

The Immigration, Asylum and Nationality Bill 2005 was amended by the House of Lords on 7 February 2006 to include a clause enabling the Secretary of State by order to repeal s 9. The intention was that the minister would be able to do this once the pilot study was over (HL Debs 7 Feb 2006 cols 587–8). The opposition of unions, professions and elements of civil society to the implementation of ss 9 and 10 may have neutralized these provisions.

The consultation letter that preceded the 2004 Act did not generate much heat on the subject of the proposed ouster of the jurisdiction of the courts, because this fundamental measure was barely trailed in it. It was hinted at by 'we are looking at ways to restrict access to the higher courts' (27 October 2003). When the Bill was published in November 2003 it contained a clause which would prevent all higher courts from hearing any immigration or asylum case whether by way of appeal or review. The Government had taken the views of senior judiciary on the unwork-ability of the clause as legal advice on how to make it watertight, contrary to the judges' intention which was tactfully to object to it in principle (Lord Woolf, *The Rule of Law and a Change in the Constitution* Squire Centenary Lecture, March 2004). The decisions that would be affected were all those which came before the Asylum and Immigration Tribunal. These might be, for instance, refusal of a visa for a married partner to enter the UK, or a determination of free movement rights under European Union law. The Government's stated reason was to streamline the appeals process and end unmeritorious appeals, but the measure contained no means of separating the meritorious from the unmeritorious, and that decision is precisely the one the courts can make. In addition to the plain injustice to foreign nationals the development of international refugee law would be denied the contribution of the British House of Lords.

There was unanimous opposition from the legal establishment. The Law Society, Bar Council, Joint Parliamentary Committee on Human Rights and senior judiciary including two former Lord Chancellors agreed the ouster clause violated the rule of law. Matrix Chambers published an opinion quoting Lord Denning: 'If tribunals were at liberty to exceed their jurisdiction without any check by courts the rule of law would be at an end' (*ex p Gilmore* [1957] 1 QB 574 at 586). The government was forced to concede, and on introducing the Bill for its second reading in the House of Lords the Lord Chancellor Lord Falconer accepted that the ouster clause could not stand (HL Debs 15 March 2004 col 51).

The Bill contained other reforms of the appeals system which, after reformula-tion, gained acceptance in Parliament. The principal one was collapsing the former two-tier system of immigration appeals into one. This and the other features of the new system are discussed in chapter 8.

In the course of 2003, another battleground developed in immigration and asy-lum policy; a curious parallel developed between advisers and their clients as the government proposed a series of measures to cut legal aid. With reference to the two views identified earlier of the cause of the system's lack of credibility, the Home Secretary appeared to espouse the view that the system was exploited by lawyers as well as their clients and funding for this should be removed. Legal aid was cut radically, and in the 2004 Act the court was given the power to order that costs be paid retrospectively if the legally aided claimant succeeded. This is referred to by Rawlings as an aspect of the Government's 'revenge package' and is considered further in chapters 7 and 8.

The 2004 Act added a number of enforcement powers. It is a fairly short miscel-lany of mainly punitive or enforcement measures, the Bill being referred to by Lord

Lester as 'mean spirited and reactionary' (2004:263) It received Royal Assent on 22 July 2004.

In February 2005 the White Paper entitled *Controlling our Borders: Making migration work for Britain* (Cm 6472) was announced as a 'five year strategy for asylum and immigration'. Whether that means a five-year moratorium on new legislation is yet to be revealed. The Immigration, Asylum and Nationality Act 2006 was said to provide the legislative base for implementing the proposals, but includes fresh initiatives not raised in the White Paper, so the signs are that the White Paper is not a five-year plan in any comprehensive sense. Much of its content referred to changes that had already been agreed or made. New proposals included:

- the introduction of a points system encompassed in four tiers for all migration for work or study, privileging the most skilled and ending settlement rights for the low skilled;
- detaining more failed asylum seekers;
- giving recognised refugees only temporary leave (five years);
- abolishing appeals against work and study immigration decisions;
- increasing use of new technology and intelligence co-ordination at borders, and re-introducing exit monitoring.

Most of these did not require legislation, and the majority of the 2006 Act provisions concern tightening enforcement powers, whether through immigration officers' powers or sanctions on employers.

The most radical and far-reaching proposals of *Controlling our Borders* are those to end appeal rights and to institute a comprehensive points system for work and study. The two proposals run together. At the time of writing full details of the points system are still awaited. However, the consultation paper envisages that all applications to enter for work will be made at overseas posts instead of through the current specialised system at Work Permits (UK) (see chapter 11). There will be no appeal against refusal for entry clearance for any purpose except family-related applications. The minister, challenged in Parliament about taking away appeal rights from an untried system replied that criteria would be objective and their application verifiable and accurate. The longstanding critique of the entry clearance system is discussed in chapter 6. Suffice it to say here that there are 'indicators of low quality of decision-making and arbitrary fluctuations in refusal rates' (Lindsley 2004). The 2006 Act continues some policies of the 2002 Act including the plan for end-to-end monitoring. Remarkably, the five-tier system extends this policy to all who enter for work and study. A feature of the system, set out in 'Framework for Managed Migration' available on the Home Office website, is 'compliance checking'. This will involve checking with sponsors that migrants are here and are doing what their terms of entry permitted them to do and checking on whether people have left the UK at the end of their permitted period of stay. The new system of 'e-borders' which involves more extensive use of biometric information and computer records to create an all-pervasive system of information on migrants will be used to effect this tracking. In particular, the Government aims to introduce a biometric residence card which will be necessary to obtain work or access to services (2005 Consultation on Managed Migration para 1.11). The proposed new system is discussed in chapter 11.

Continuing the control theme, *Controlling our Borders* introduced a 'new asylum model,' an administrative system designed to streamline applications and make greater use of detention. Two induction centres are already in place. The accommodation centres proposed in the 2002 Act did not prove viable, and this is another attempt to process as many asylum claims as possible while keeping the claimant in some form of detention or controlled accommodation.

The Government proposed in the 2005 Bill to remove the right of appeal against decisions to vary or refuse to vary leave to enter or remain in the UK. This curtailment of in-country appeal rights did not appear to have been the subject of even minimal consultation. It would have affected, for instance, a married partner applying for indefinite leave to remain in the UK, or a student applying for an extension to stay on their course. Opposition from the House of Lords Constitution Committee, the Immigration Law Practitioners Association (ILPA) and the Immigration Advisory Service (IAS) pointed to the success rate of about one third of existing appeals, the increase in illegally resident population that would result and the disadvantage to employers and universities. In the House of Lords the Government agreed to withdraw the clause.

The right of appeal for visitors was removed by the 1993 Act, but s 4 of the 2006 Act is a far more radical step. It removes the right of appeal against refusal of entry clearance in all but specified visitor and dependant cases. Those who will retain the right of appeal are not defined in the statute but will be by regulations and will include family visitors. So far as is known at the time of writing, the change will affect students and all those who apply under the rules for reasons such as religious ministry, self-employment, or working holidays. The change is potentially enormous. There was advance warning of this in relation to students and work permit holders in the five-year strategy document, and a swell of opposition ensued, including from University Vice Chancellors and Principals (letter from Universities UK to Financial Times, Tuesday, 5 July 2005) but to no avail.

The Government regards appeal rights as less important in the future because of the claimed quality of the new points system. In its briefing to the House of Lords Committee Stage of the Bill, ILPA quoted the then Shadow Home Secretary Rt. Hon. Tony Blair, MP, during the passage of the Asylum and Immigration Appeals Act 1993:

When a right of appeal is removed, what is removed is a valuable and necessary constraint on those who exercise original jurisdiction. That is true not merely of immigration officers but of anybody. The immigration officer who knows that his decision may be subject to appeal is likely to be a good deal more circumspect, careful and even handed than the officer who knows that his power of decision is absolute. That is simply, I fear, a matter of human nature, quite apart from anything else. (Commons Hansard, vol 213, col 43, 2.11.92)

1.3 Immigration control as an exercise of executive power

There is no doubt that immigration control is an exercise of executive power; that is, it is exercised by the executive arm of government, in this case principally by the Home Secretary, Home Office civil servants, immigration officers, and entry clearance officers. Less clear are the source and limits of that power. Immigration law is, in a sense, all about the exercise of executive power and the limits upon it.

A characteristic that will be encountered over and over again in the study of immigration law is the retention of discretion, which of course is less amenable to control than the application of specific rules. The discretionary nature of immigration law is at the root of much of the criticism that has been directed at it. While challenges to decisions and initiatives towards accountability and openness seek to put limits on the power of the executive, in other ways the scope to use discretion is continually reasserted.

In order to ascertain the extent to which decisions can be challenged, it is necessary to consider the source of the power which is exercised. A purely statutory power is subject to public law constraints and the exercise of appeal rights; something with a more nebulous origin may be harder to control.

1.3.1 Prerogative origins?

The right of nation states to control the entry and expulsion of foreign nationals is often said to be an essential aspect of sovereignty, which some regard as exercised under the prerogative. The prerogative was originally the power of the crown. The Bill of Rights 1689 decreed that the prerogative could not be extended any further and that statute could supersede the prerogative. From this time on, the prerogative had a residual character (see, for instance, Loveland, *Constitutional Law; Administrative Law and Human Rights: A Critical Introduction* 2003). In the present day, relevant prerogatives, if any, are at the disposal of the government, which now holds the authority of the crown for most purposes. There are personal prerogatives of the monarch such as dispensing certain honours, but we are not concerned with these.

The present extent of the prerogative has been a matter of argument even in quite recent times. In *R v Secretary of State ex p Northumbria Police Authority* [1989] QB 26, the Court of Appeal found that there was a prerogative to keep the peace even though it had not been written down anywhere. However, Vincenzi argues that there are specific recognized areas of prerogative power, not an amorphous pool which could be used for purposes convenient to the government (1992:300). Following *CCSU v Minister for the Civil Service* [1985] AC 374 (the GCHQ case) in which the House of Lords decided that the exercise of the prerogative was reviewable, a number of prerogative powers have been considered, and the reviewability of each decided as a separate question (see, e.g., *R v Secretary of State for Foreign and Commonwealth Affairs ex p Everett* [1989] QB 811 CA, *R v SSHD ex p Bentley* [1993] 4 All ER 442). This seems to support Vincenzi's argument. Indeed this approach seems to flow from Lord Diplock's list in the GCHQ case of potentially non-reviewable prerogative powers, and the question was not resolved in *ex p Northumbria Police Authority*.

Those prerogative powers which have been identified include matters such as the conduct of foreign affairs, the power to conduct the internal affairs of the civil service, and the issue of passports (Vincenzi, *Crown Powers, Subjects and Citizens* (1998)). It would be a brave person now who suggested that there was a major prerogative power left undiscovered, and in the area of immigration control it is reasonable to assume that whatever prerogative power exists is known about. Chapter 4 of Vincenzi's book explores the relationship between the prerogative and immigration control, and reference should be made to that for a full account. All the authorities agree that there is a prerogative power to deal with aliens, but there is disagreement over the extent of that power.

Immigration control in the UK is now largely governed by statute and immigration rules made pursuant to the statutory duty to do so (Immigration Act 1971 s 3(2)). The Immigration Act 1971, however, expressly reserves a prerogative power in mysterious terms: 'This Act shall not be taken to supersede or impair any power exercisable by Her Majesty in relation to aliens by virtue of her prerogative' (s 33(5)). In its reference only to aliens, the subsection is in conformity with the established view that the prerogative does not apply to those who owe allegiance to the Crown, that is, British and Commonwealth citizens (*DPP v Bhagwan* [1972] AC 60 and *R v IAT ex p Secretary of State for the Home Department* [1990] 3 All ER 652). However, what power over aliens does the section reserve? The whole Act and all subsequent immigration statutes, deal with those who are subject to immigration control. If there was a prerogative of immigration control, this would, as a normal rule, be in abeyance to the extent of the statutory power (*AG v de Keyser's Royal Hotel Ltd* [1920] AC 508). It would be both superseded and impaired. Section 33(5) is not thought to displace this rule. Immigration control is exercised pursuant to the statute and rules as indeed the rule of law requires. It is not empowered by a mysterious source which somehow lurks behind the rules. Vincenzi suggests that the only non-contentious prerogative in relation to aliens is to imprison enemy aliens, that is, nationals of those countries with whom the UK is at war. Macdonald in his 5th edition (2001:708) suggested there was a power to deport, and as we have seen, Edward and Elizabeth I behaved as though they thought so. However, this was in relation to aliens regarded as enemies, not those regarded as friends. In the 6th edition Macdonald has revised his views (2005:3) and, following the work of Shah and Vincenzi, adopts the view that there was no distinction in common law between the rights of subjects and friendly aliens. The first appearance of a reservation of a prerogative power was in the Aliens Restriction Act 1914, which, at a time of war, can be taken to have been referring to enemy aliens.

There is undoubtedly a power to make immigration decisions outside the immigration rules, but this can more simply derive from the powers in the statute to give or refuse leave to enter or remain (the Immigration Act 1971 ss 3A, 3B and 4), and there is no need to employ the prerogative as an explanation (Macdonald 1995:41). Glidewell LJ in *R v Secretary of State for the Home Department ex p Rajinder Kaur* [1987] Imm AR 278 took the view that this power to make decisions outside the rules is derived from the prerogative. However that case concerned a Commonwealth citizen, and Glidewell LJ cannot have been right in this. Vincenzi argues that immigration control cannot be a prerogative power because the concept of immigration control is a modern one, originating in the Aliens Act 1905. The prerogative, as we have seen, could not be extended after 1689.

If immigration control is seen as a 'prerogative power clothed in statute', its amenability to regulation is that much less. If it is seen as a purely statutory power, it must be exercised in accordance with the power granted by that statute and in accordance with principles of statutory interpretation, and not otherwise. Evans notes an effect of a belief in the prerogative as a source of immigration control:

The reluctance of the courts to challenge the Executive's exercise of statutory powers on matters touching national security may also have been influenced by the Crown's claim that the exclusion and expulsion of aliens were within its prerogative, the scope of which was never definitely established, but which still maintains a shadowy existence alongside immigration control. (1983:422–3)

The conclusion here is that it is unlikely that the prerogative is the source of immigration control, but there has been a tendency in the courts and executive to treat it as though it was. This has enabled them to call upon a supposed reserve of undefined power to supplement explicit provisions.

1.3.1.1 *A modern equivalent?*

It is perhaps less likely now that inexplicable discretion will be attributed to the prerogative (though see chapter 11 for a theory of work permits), but there is an increasing tendency to see behind immigration control, not the prerogative, but two other principles: sovereignty and the judgement of the executive. The first is explanatory and the second is justificatory.

Sovereignty in dealing with foreign nationals is curtailed by treaties to which the state is a party such as, in the UK's case, the European Convention on Human Rights and the 1951 UN Convention Relating to Refugees. In the age of internationalism, globalization, the development of international human rights' norms, and an international criminal court, the nation state can no longer be properly regarded as the ultimate legal authority. It is well recognized that national legal authority must now be tempered by regard for international law, and that international regulation is a fact of life.

Ironically it is through the Human Rights Act 1998, bringing the rights of the European Convention into UK law, that the idea of sovereignty seems to be making something of a comeback. In immigration cases in the ECHR, the court routinely begins its reasoning with the statement that states have the right, as a recognized principle of international law, and subject to their treaty obligations, to control the entry of non-nationals (see *Abdulaziz Cabales and Balkandali* (1985) 7 EHRR 471 para 67). This statement has an understandable place in the judgment of an international court, but has been transposed into the UK courts' and tribunals' reasoning in human rights cases. It is not inaccurate, but is unnecessary in the national context, where the task of the decision-maker is to apply and interpret law which is already made by the sovereign law-maker (Parliament) or is of a lesser status (immigration rules) or is case law which arises or can be argued to have a place in the jurisdiction. Sovereignty, if it arises at all, is being exercised, not challenged, and the reiteration of it in national courts has an effect similar to that noted by Evans in relation to the prerogative. This was demonstrated in *R v SSHD ex p Saadi, Maged, Osman and Mohammed* [2002] 1 WLR 3131 HL, in which the principle of sovereignty prevailed over human rights (see chapter 15). As Dauvergne comments, 'Migration law is transformed into the new last bastion of sovereignty' (2004:588), and correspondingly, sovereignty is invoked to buttress the state's right to control migration.

The second principle, that of deference to the executive, is an important current question. It is not new, but arises in a new form within the context of the Convention rights. The existence, extent, and nature of this principle is a current subject of debate in academic writing and judicial decisions, and has crucial importance in immigration cases. In the case of indefinite detentions of foreign nationals the Court of Appeal deferred to the judgment of the executive that discrimination on grounds of nationality was necessary (*A v SSHD* [2002] EWCA Civ 1502). In the House of Lords, Lord Bingham in particular set out the UK's obligations under international treaties as an important part of the reasons why this deference was not warranted (*A v SSHD* [2004] UKHL 56). Discussion of this issue is mainly reserved for chapter 3.

1.3.1.2 *Statutory origins*

For the avoidance of doubt, the present-day legal source of the power of immigration control is statutory, specifically, the Immigration Act 1971 ss 3 and 4 as amended. The statutory power is given more specific substance by voluminous immigration rules. The prerogative is not a source to which there can be fresh recourse, whatever view is taken of its earlier extent. A number of writers now argue that the territorial notion of sovereignty is also breaking down (e.g., Thomas and Kostakopoulou, Dauvergne). The search for a deeper principle continues, however, and part of the present debate is a re-examination of the rule of law (see, e.g., Dauvergne, Harvey C. 2005; Poole for a range of views).

1.3.2 **Discretion in immigration law**

Even without shadowy principles such as the prerogative or sovereignty, the immigration rules, which form the substance of immigration law, allow considerable scope for individual judgment. The ability of an individual to, for instance, visit their family or join their spouse depends, ultimately, on an exercise of judgement by an official. Some immigration decisions are closer to an exercise of discretion (though not uncontrolled), for instance the decision to deport. More often the decision is an exercise of judgement as to whether the specified criteria are met, for instance whether maintenance for a spouse is adequate and the couple intend to live together as husband and wife. This is not a discretion in a pure sense, but it is a matter on which an entry clearance officer and an applicant could disagree. Consider by way of comparison an application for a welfare benefit. If the claimant's income is less than the applicable amount, the benefit must be paid. There might be a question about whether all assets have been disclosed, but on a given set of figures there is no judgment to be made: the claimant has an entitlement. In the event of being turned down for entry clearance, applicants cannot point to the rules and say 'you are wrong — I am entitled to entry clearance'; they can only argue about the strength of their evidence.

   The other factors which magnify the effect of discretionary decisions are, first, that initial decisions are taken in many cases by officials in another country, whereas appeals take place in the UK. Much mystification and false information has surrounded the entry clearance process, which is discussed further in chapter 6. Second, appeal rights have been somewhat fragile. They have been granted but taken away again, and the latest statutory development is to remove the right of appeal from all entry clearance decisions except those connected with families, apparently because the Government considers that only decisions which are patently an exercise of a fundamental right should be challengeable (promoting minister, the Home Secretary in second reading debate, 5 July 2005, HC Debs col 194). Challenge by judicial review, because of its limitations, will often not result in overturning even a poorly grounded decision.

The repeated formula throughout the body of the rules, and particularly in Parts 3 to 8, which deal with categories for admission, is that the immigration officer *may* give leave to enter if 'satisfied that the requirements are met'. This emphasis should not be taken too far; the wording implies the grant of a power, not an unlimited discretion. The manner of exercise of discretion is considered in more detail in chapter 6 in the context of the grant or refusal of leave to enter the UK.

The early immigration rules were phrased in terms which gave far more scope for the exercise of discretion than do the rules of today. Examples relating to students are considered in chapter 10. The publication of policies and their incorporation into rules, as discussed below, is part of a trend of increasing codification. On one viewing, there is a move towards certainty and openness which is the antithesis of the discretionary culture that has been discussed here. It is increasingly possible for any person to find out the rules that will apply in their case. However, what will become apparent later in this chapter is that as uncontrolled executive power begins to disappear from one area, it reappears in another.

1.3.3 Executive as rule-maker

One of the most potent exercises of executive power by the Secretary of State in immigration law is the making of the immigration rules. They are made pursuant to a duty to do so found in the Immigration Act 1971 s 3(2). Section 1(4) contains the only requirement as to their content. They must

include provision for admitting (in such cases and subject to such restrictions as may be provided by the rules . . .) persons coming for the purpose of taking employment, or for the purposes of study, or as visitors, or as dependants of persons lawfully in or entering the UK.

Section 3(2) provides that this

shall not be taken to require uniform provision to be made by the rules as regards admission of persons for a purpose or in a capacity specified in section 1(4) (and in particular, for this as well as other purposes of this Act, account may be taken of citizenship or nationality).

There is no other statutory requirement as to their content. The rules, however, are now voluminous and run into several hundreds. (Numbering stops at 395 but this is not indicative as many are divided into sub-rules: A to K and so on.) The rules govern almost all immigration cases and also have an impact on asylum cases. They therefore contain the practical substance of immigration law.

The status of the immigration rules has been a subject of much legal argument. For most purposes there is no doubt that they are not subordinate legislation. They are made by the minister pursuant to a statutory duty to do so, and are subject to the negative resolution procedure in Parliament. In these respects they resemble delegated legislation. However, s 3(2) describes them as 'rules . . . to be followed in the administration of this Act', and this is how they have been regarded in case law. *Pearson v IAT* [1978] Imm AR 212 remains the authority that the Rules are not delegated legislation or rules of law, but rules of practice for the guidance of those who administer the Act. Despite this, the rules have a status well beyond that of normal administrative guidelines. *Pearson* also found that the rules, while not rules of law, have the force of law. Previous statutes provided that an adjudicator 'must allow an appeal if he considers that the decision or action against which the appeal is brought was not in accordance with the law or any immigration rules applicable to the case' (Immigration Act 1971 s 19 and Immigration and Asylum Act 1999 Sch 4 para 21). The current equivalent provision is differently phrased. The appeal must be allowed if the decision 'is not in accordance with the law (including immigration rules)' (Nationality, Immigration and Asylum Act 2002 s 86(3)(a)). This seems to represent a shift towards recognizing the rules as a form of law. In either form of words the immigration rules are treated by statute as though they have binding force. In ascertaining what is the law relating to a given situation, for instance, to discover whether an aged mother will be permitted to join her daughter in the UK, the first place to look is the rules. They provide the basic content of legal entitlement, even if they are not themselves of a legal character.

Two present opposing tendencies may be observed. One is the steady absorption of less formal sources such as concessions into the rules, thus increasing accessibility and codification. The other is the removal of the right of appeal from entry clearance refusals by Immigration, Asylum and Nationality Act 2006 s 4. This creates an apprehension that the status of rules relating to entry clearance may begin to unravel as there will be no method of enforcing them.

As mentioned above, the rules are made by the minister subject to the negative resolution procedure. They are therefore subject only to very limited Parliamentary scrutiny, and if Parliament wants to reject them it must reject the rules as a whole: there is no provision for amendment. This has happened on very few occasions, the most notable perhaps being in December 1982 (HC col 355 15 December 1982) when the Labour Party opposition succeeded in defeating the Conservative Government's proposed new marriage rules. These would have introduced a burden on the applicant to show that the marriage was genuine (later introduced anyway) and a two-year probationary period (defeated on that occasion but introduced on 1 April 2003 without Parliamentary debate).

Even though the rules are subject only to a limited Parliamentary scrutiny they are subject to challenge by way of judicial review. The duty to make the rules is derived from statute, and so the minister cannot achieve by the rules anything which is outside the powers given in the Act. The rules are therefore in theory subject to challenge on the grounds of illegality, irrationality, and procedural impropriety (following Lord Diplock's classification in *CCSU v Minister for the Civil Service* [1985] AC 374). Unsuccessful attempts have been made to challenge the rules on the basis that they fetter discretion, this being an aspect of illegality (*R v Secretary of State for the Home Department ex p Rajinder Kaur* [1987] Imm AR 278). For the purpose of a challenge for irrationality, the rules are treated like by-laws, and so may only be struck down if they are 'impartial or unequal in their operation as between classes; manifestly unjust; made in bad faith; or involving such oppressive or gratuitous interference with the rights of those subject to them as could find no justification in the minds of reasonable persons' (*Kruse v Johnson* [1898] 2 QB 91). This has succeeded on one occasion, when the rule on admission of family dependants was challenged for its requirement that the elderly dependent relative, in order to gain entry, must be living at a standard substantially below that in their country. This discriminated against applicants in poor countries, for whom even a small amount of financial help would lift their standard of living above a low level for their country (*R v IAT ex p Manshoora Begum* [1986] Imm AR 385).

The rules are now also subject to challenge on a further ground of illegality, namely that the minister in making them has acted unlawfully under s 6 HRA as the rules breach Convention rights. On and after 2 October 2000 there has been a trend towards removing discrimination from the rules, presumably to avoid such challenges. The rules are also subject to directly applicable EC law, and in *The Queen on the application of Ezgi Payir* [2005] EWHC 1426 (Admin) the High Court made a declaration that rr 92–94 were unlawful insofar as they purported to exclude the right to an extension of stay for a Turkish au pair, contrary to Article 6 of Decision 1/80 of the Council of the Association between the EU and Turkey.

On reading the rules it is apparent that they are the language of the administrator rather than the lawyer. They are practical and descriptive, stating what action should be taken in given sets of circumstances. This being the case, they should not be treated as a legal text in the English tradition, namely as language which has been created with great precision and therefore must be interpreted strictly. The accepted approach (*Alexander v IAT* [1982] 2 All ER 766) to interpretation is to treat the rules in a purposive fashion.

Although for most purposes the rules are not regarded as subordinate legislation, they may be for the purposes of the Human Rights Act. The Act defines subordinate legislation in s 21(1) as including 'rules . . . made under primary legislation'. It appears that this includes the immigration rules, and so the interpretive duty in HRA s 3 will apply. Even without this, those who implement the rules are public authorities under s 6 and their actions must be in accordance with the Convention. In effect, immigration rules must be applied in a way that upholds Convention rights; the only relevance of their being subordinate legislation would be if to uphold rights requires a strained construction of the rules. Section 3 would require this of subordinate legislation, but s 6 may not require it of a public body. Ultimately, as discussed above, if the rule conflicts with rights and cannot be interpreted by whatever means so as to deliver the rights, it may be struck down as being made in breach of s 6.

An important question for applicants and the development of the law is whether the immigration rules already embody human rights standards. If they do, the scope for human rights appeals in cases brought under them will be limited. A Tribunal case, *SS Malaysia* [2004] Imm AR 153, was starred on this question, meaning that the Tribunal decreed it should be treated as a precedent. The Tribunal said it thought the rules did embody human rights standards. This was swiftly followed by Laws LJ in *Huang v SSHD* [2005] EWCA Civ 105, a judgment which has proved influential in subsequent cases. Athough there is no other authority, neither judgment gives reasons for this novel proposition. The majority of the substantive rules predate the Human Rights Act by many years. They are not even subject to the rudimentary safeguard of a Parliamentary declaration of compatibility as is statute (HRA s 19). New rules are most often introduced to set up a new scheme of entry for work or to close a perceived loophole in existing provisions rather than to address a human rights issue. No doubt they are subject to departmental procedures to check for human rights compliance but explanatory memoranda issued with each new set of rules since the beginning of 2005 offer no reassurance about the content of this process. Over the course of that year new rules dealt with a range of subjects including the entry of children, the extension of visa requirements, the entry and stay of civil partners, the extension of non-compliance provisions to human rights as well as asylum claims, new categories of visitors, and some half a dozen amendments to schemes of entry for work and training, including one totally new scheme. In every case the explanatory memorandum states that the European Convention on Human Rights is 'Not applicable'.

Executive statements of intent are a guide but do not entirely dispose of the question. Some rules were revised in October 2000 to coincide with the commencement of the HRA, apparently to ensure they were 'human rights compliant'. The main policy behind these changes seemed to be the elimination of discrimination between the sexes and on grounds of sexuality or marital status. Other areas of discrimination, such as that against maintenance by extended families remained untouched or even strengthened (see chapter 9). The content of the rules themselves would be the surest guide to whether they embody human rights norms. Reading the rules on family entry, it is apparent that there is a balance, as Laws LJ said, between the public and private interests. An individual can apply to join their family (private interest) but will not be able to do so if they have to claim from the public purse to enter (public interest). However, whether this strikes the balance mandated by human rights law can only be a judgement on the particular facts and application of policy to a particular case. Macdonald's view is that the equation of immigration rules with 'policies which balance immigrants' human rights against the economic well-being of the country or the prevention of crime and disorder is highly disputable and totally unproven'. (2005:366)

1.3.4 **Policies and concessions**

Secrecy has been a hallmark of immigration law, but this has changed significantly in recent years. Mention has already been made of the exclusion of black passport holders from the UK by means of internal government instructions which accompanied the Commonwealth Immigrants Act 1962. Internal instructions are highly influential in the implementation of immigration law as they guide immigration officers and Home Office officials in their response to individual cases. Internal instructions as they now exist may be divided into three kinds.

First, there are policy documents which give guidance on the exercise of a discretion. An example is DP3/96, a policy document which sets out situations when it will and will not be appropriate to exercise powers of removal and deportation in relation to people who have families in the UK. It is not comprehensive but it is far more detailed than the statute. The criteria for immigration detention are found entirely in guidance documents of this kind, disclosed on the IND website in the Operational Enforcement Manual.

Second, there is guidance on the application of the immigration rules. There is a comprehensive code of guidance on the application of the immigration rules known as the Immigration Directorate Instructions (IDIs). There is another for dealing with asylum claims, the Asylum Policy Instructions (APIs), which include summaries of the relevant law, and Nationality Instructions (NIs) which give similar guidance for dealing with nationality applications. Frequent reference is made to relevant instructions throughout this book. They are a practical guide to how discretion is exercised.

Third, there are various kinds of concessions. One of the features of immigration law is the extent of provision which has been contained in discretionary practices outside the rules. Although the rules have become more and more comprehensive, they still do not cover every eventuality. In relation to some situations commonly encountered, there is standard practice which is known as a concession. Some concessions have been established for many years but never integrated into the immigration rules. An example of this was the grant of indefinite leave to remain to a person who attains refugee status. This had the appearance of established rule, as it was invariable practice for some years, but when practice was changed in August 2005, this could be done simply by an announcement. Such announcements may be given for instance by notice on the IND website, in Parliament, by letter to interested organizations.

Some concessions are announced in Parliament and devised in terms as detailed as an immigration rule. Examples here have been a concession for entry of unmarried partners, which was announced in Parliament on 10 October 1997 and a concession for spouses subject to domestic violence to obtain indefinite leave to remain, announced in Parliament on 16 June 1999. In these cases the concessions had the appearance of trial rules. They were both amended by later statements in Parliament, following representations about how they operated in practice (17 June 1999 and 26 November 2002 respectively), and incorporated into the immigration rules. The first of these two provisions raises issues of equality of treatment between married and unmarried and between heterosexual and homosexual couples. Strong and conflicting opinions are held about these questions, and it appears that the government was seeking a politically viable rule by experiment in order to achieve some level of equality by 2 October 2000 when the Human Rights Act came into force, though it has since been amended more than once. The trend is for concessions to be incorporated into the rules, and there is a long-term project to incorporate all concessions into a set of consolidated rules.

There are also temporary concessions directed towards periods of upheaval or emergency. An example of such a concession was the Home Office decision in July 1999 temporarily to suspend the return to the Republic of Congo of asylum seekers whose applications had been rejected, because of the civil war. Concessions may also be given in the form of procedural waivers where hardship would arise if strict procedure were insisted upon. For example, following the Humanitarian Evacuation Programme from Kosovo, Kosovan families in Britain were required to travel to Croydon for an asylum screening interview. This involved whole families, who were surviving on minimal resources, paying fares for transport and travelling perhaps with ill family members or small children. In June 2000 the Home Office decided that it would be sufficient for only the principal applicant to attend the asylum screening interview providing certain conditions were met.

What all these forms of guidance have in common is that if an individual comes within their terms they can expect to be treated in accordance with the policy. In *R v SSHD ex p Amankwah* [1994] Imm AR 240 it was held that if the policy was undisclosed, but its existence was known, then a decision which did not take the policy properly into account was unreasonable and unfair. The purpose of a policy was to ensure fairness between applicants. *Amankwah* was the first case in which this principle was successfully used as the existence of a policy on marriage and deportation had become known by accident, having been referred to in a Home Office letter in a previous case.

Since then, policies have been gradually disclosed. At first, selected documents were sent to practitioner organizations. Now the majority of internal instructions of substance are available on the Home Office website. Much of the substantive detail is contained in annexes to IDIs, APIs and NIs, but the majority of these too are disclosed. In 2003 the Government took the further step of putting on the website parts of the Operational Enforcement Manual which deals with detention and removal.

Once the content of policy has been disclosed, if an applicant seems to meet the usual conditions, they may have a remedy using judicial review on the grounds of breach of legitimate expectation (e.g., *R v Secretary of State for the Home Department ex p Khan* [1985] 1 All ER 40). In *R v SSHD ex p B* [2002] EWCA Civ 1797 the Court of Appeal held that when the facts strongly suggested that the concession on domestic violence applied, the claimant should have been given the benefit of it. The Court of Appeal in *Dhudi Saleban Abdi v Secretary of State for the Home Department* [1996] Imm AR 148 made a decision with far-reaching consequences when it held that failure to take into account an established policy or concession rendered a decision 'not in accordance with the law' and so appealable under Immigration Act 1971 s 19(1)(a)(i) (now s 86(3) Nationality, Immigration and Asylum Act 2002). Thus for a time the distinction between the rules and concessions was partly eroded (see also chapter 8).

In *SSHD v the Queen on the application of Rashid* [2005] EWCA Civ 744 the Court of Appeal did away with the distinction in *Amankwah* between whether the policy was known to the claimant or not:

It would be grossly unfair if the court's ability to intervene depended at all upon whether the particular claimant had or had not heard of a policy, especially one unknown to relevant Home Office officials. (Pill LJ, para 25)

The Court of Appeal held that that repeated failure to apply the policy policy which would have resulted in a grant of refugee status to Mr Rashid constituted conspicuous unfairness amounting to an abuse of power (para 34). There was a legitimate expectation that policy on asylum claims would be applied and applied uniformly.

There may still be a question as to which version of a policy applies in a particular case. While policies and instructions are increasingly disclosed on the IND website, there has been a tendency in the last couple of years to no longer disclose their date. In *R (on the application of I and O) v SSHD* [2005] EWHC 1025 (Admin) the Home Office was unable to provide the exact date when a policy came into effect, though Owen J accepted an assurance that there was no material difference from the earlier policy (para 21).

Individual exceptions may be made, and as Macdonald describes (1995: 44–5), may become established concessions as the compassionate circumstances which led to their first being recognized are replicated in other cases. An established concession is a stronger basis from which to argue, as is apparent from above, but if there is no such concession available it is possible to argue that the particular circumstances of the case warrant more lenient treatment than the rules seem to provide. There is no doubt that both the Home Office and immigration officers do on occasion agree to act more leniently than the rules provide. The source of this power has been discussed above, and is the Immigration Act 1971, not the prerogative.

1.3.5 Subject to public law constraints

As indicated above, immigration decisions are subject to judicial review in accordance with usual public law principles, including since 2 October 2000 on the basis that they infringe Convention rights. In accordance with the normal rules of judicial review, any relevant appeal rights must first be exhausted (e.g., *Cinnamond v British Airports Authority* [1980] 2 All ER 368), but the trend of limiting appeal rights has resulted in an increase in judicial review as the only way of challenging decisions.

A number of principles of administrative law have been established in immigration cases. Examples include the court's power to examine the factual basis of a decision-maker's exercise of power where this necessary to see that the decision-maker has jurisdiction (*Khawaja v Secretary of State for the Home Dept* [1983] AC 74 concerning illegal entry); the publication of an express promise or undertaking will lead to a legitimate expectation of its being honoured (*Attorney General for Hong Kong v Ng Yuen Shiu* [1983] 2 AC 629 also concerning the treatment of illegal entrants); the right to reasons for a decision (*R v Secretary of State for the Home Department ex p Fayed* [1998] 1 All ER 228 CA a challenge to refusal of British nationality), and the obligation to hear both sides of a case which affects fundamental rights, even where strict rules of natural justice do not apply (*R v Secretary of State for the Home Department ex p Moon* (1996) 8 Admin LR concerning the issue of entry clearance).

Judicial review cannot be treated as a separate subject. Its principles arise often and will be encountered for instance in chapter 6 in the context of the exercise of discretion and in chapter 8, in the context of natural justice.

1.3.6 Separation of powers

The constitutional rationale for judicial review is to make the executive accountable, not ultimately to the judiciary but to Parliament, as the powers being interpreted are statutory powers. In the era after the Human Rights Act and the European Union the judiciary must also have recourse to international standards and sources, so calling to account also has an international dimension. This accountability is only possible where there is the proper separation between the executive and judiciary which is demanded by the doctrine of separation of powers, and if the executive is effectively scrutinized by Parliament. Executive dominance of Parliament undermines the separation of powers.

Historically immigration laws and structures have contained many instances where the tendency to executive dominance threatens the separation of powers. In the present decade there is a new wave of advances towards executive dominance and of both attacks on and assertions of the independence of the judiciary.

1.3.6.1 *Structural closeness of executive and judiciary*

The most explicit violation of separation of powers in the immigration sphere is now in the past. It used to be the case that immigration adjudicators, who were the first tier in the immigration appeal system, were appointed by the Home Office. However, in 1987 the function of appointing adjudicators was transferred to the Lord Chancellor's Department, bringing them into line with other members of the judiciary.

The most glaring remaining structural deficit in terms of separation of powers in the immigration and asylum system is the lack of an independent determination process for asylum claims. The Home Office both decides claims and enforces the removal of unsuccessful claimants. In many countries an independent body exists to determine refugee claims.

1.3.6.2 *Influence of the Home Office on judicial matters*

This kind of influence, or the appearance of it, appears to be returning. For instance, at the beginning of the British and American military action in Iraq in March 2003, the hearing of Iraqi asylum appeals was frozen at the behest of the Home Office. The normal process in legal proceedings when one party wants to defer the action is that they make an application to the court for an adjournment. It is unthinkable that a litigant would be able to instruct or even request the court to adjourn all their cases without the other side having an opportunity to object.

The Asylum and Immigration (Procedure) Rules 2005 are the second set of procedure rules to provide for service of judicial decisions first on the Home Office who must then serve them on the claimant (see chapter 8 for further discussion). As Luqmani commented about a comparable provision in the Civil Procedure (Amendment) Rules 2003, SI 2003/364: 'This gives the impression that the court is there to serve principally the Home Secretary and not applicants' (Legal Action May 2003 p 24).

Both the 2004 Act and the 2006 Act appear to be the joint proposals of the Home Office and Department for Constitutional Affairs. Proposals for cutting legal aid in 2003 emanated jointly from the Home Office and the Department for Constitutional Affairs. This was open to the constitutional objection that the funding of legal services was not a matter for the Home Secretary (The Guardian 29 November 2003). In immigration and asylum proceedings, the Home Office is the opposite party as far as the individual is concerned. It is a Home Office decision that they wish to dispute which has brought them before the tribunal, whom they must trust to be the independent arbiter of their case. The tribunal is governed by the Department for Constitutional Affairs. Case law and international guidance in asylum cases is to the effect that an asylum claim should be treated as a joint inquiry between all parties to establish the real risks to the claimant. However the spirit of this is that because of the dangers involved and the problems of proof, the bodies entrusted to deal with the claim should work in a co-operative way to reach a proper understanding without intimidating the claimant. This is not at all the same thing as the two state departments involved co-operating in the claimant's absence to restrict their opportunities to make their case. Farbey links this with other joint initiatives to make the case that the Home Office, Department for Constitutional Affairs and the Legal Services Commission have 'become partners in immigration and asylum policy' (2004:199). She cites also the inter-departmental board responsible for delivering the government's target for clearing asylum cases through the system, the fast-track procedure rules, and the joint submissions of the DCA and Home Office on legal aid. The growth of co-operation between the DCA and Home Office has led, she says, to 'the politicization of immigration law' (2004:200).

An indirect influence of the Home Office on the judiciary, and certainly a curb on judicial freedom, is a recent practice of legislating on how the judiciary should interpret facts or a legal provision. Section 8 of the AITOC lists factors which decision-makers are required to take into account as adverse to an asylum claimant's credibility. The decision-makers include Home Office officials and the tribunal. There is a precedent for this in criminal law in which adverse inferences may be drawn from a defendant's behaviour. The judiciary have taken a fairly robust attitude to this attempt to influence their judgement (*SM Iran* [2005] UKAIT 00116; see chapter 12).

They will find it less possible to avoid the constraint of the 2006 Act s 54 as this contains no discretion. The section mandates a wide interpretation of a clause in the Refugee Convention which prevents an applicant from obtaining refugee status, extending to all whose actions may come within the UK's wide definition of terrorism. This provision is discussed in chapter 14.

1.3.6.3 *Open criticism between executive and judiciary*

The immunity of the judiciary from comment by the executive is an aspect of their independence, and almost a sacred principle in the theory of the constitution. In relation to two High Court decisions, each concerning the human rights of asylum seekers (*R v SSHD ex p Saadi, Maged, Osman and Mohammed* [2001] EWHC Admin 670 and *R (on the application of Q and M) v SSHD* [2003] 2 All ER 905), the then Home Secretary David Blunkett made his views known in the media in uncompromising terms, even saying on the second occasion that he would not put up with judges interfering with the democratic process in this way. In each case the human rights of asylum seekers had been upheld by the judge. Both were cases of statutory interpretation. In the first, asylum seekers challenged the power to detain them in Oakington Reception Centre, in the second, the denial of benefits under the Nationality Immigration and Asylum Act 2002. Commenting on Mr Blunkett's response, Geoffrey Bindman in the Independent newspaper in February 2003 pointed out that it is normally seen as the constitutional task of the judiciary to interpret legislation, and judicial review is the essential constitutional check by the judiciary of the executive. Here the judiciary had done just that, though their judgments were interpreted by Mr Blunkett as an attack on government policy.

The executive of course is open to comment from anyone, in a democracy, but the judges' traditional restraint in this matter is another aspect of their independence. Their comment on government policy is seen as an indication that they are not unbiased in their treatment of the issue at hand and therefore by constitutional convention they do not become publicly enmeshed in party politics nor comment upon government policy except when called upon to do so in consultation upon some juridical matter.

The fact that senior judiciary have broken this time-honoured tradition is an indication of the level of tension between the two branches of government, and the force of their remarks is in itself remarkable. The battle over the proposed ouster clause in the AITOC Bill, brought out the senior and retired judiciary in powerful opposition, not only in Parliament but also outside it. Lord Woolf's trenchant criticism in his Squire Centenary lecture marks a new point in executive/judicial relations. Lord Steyn was prepared to count himself out of hearing the challenge to the British Government's role in detention in Guantanamo Bay, which he described as a 'legal black hole' (2004:256), in order to be free to warn publicly against an 'unprincipled and exorbitant executive response' (The Independent 26 November 2003).

1.3.6.4 *Legislative reversal*

The history of immigration law is full of examples of legislation swiftly introduced to reverse higher court decisions. In an earlier instance of the removal of benefits from asylum claimants the Social Security (Persons from Abroad) Miscellaneous Amendment Regulations 1996, SI 1996/30, removed benefits from almost everyone who was subject to immigration control. The regulations were declared *ultra vires* by Simon Brown LJ because they were beyond the tolerance level of a 'civilised nation'. 'Something so uncompromisingly draconian can only be achieved by primary legislation' (*R v Secretary of State for Social Security ex p JCWI* [1997] 1 WLR 275). As Macdonald puts it: 'The government duly obliged, enacting the condemned regulation as section 11 of the 1996 Act', i.e., the Asylum and Immigration Act 1996 (now largely repealed) (2001:9). There was a similar phenomenon in relation to the certification by the Secretary of State of certain countries as safe third countries to which asylum seekers could be returned. This also had its first form in the 1996 Act. However, it was clearly not within the contemplation of the Secretary of State that the certificates he issued would be regularly struck down by the courts. In the Immigration and Asylum Act 1999 s 11, the certificates in relation to European countries were ensured against susceptibility to judicial review by the insertion of a statutory presumption that such countries were deemed safe. This has proved unassailable (*R (Thangasara) v SSHD* [2002] UKHL 36).

The Nationality, Immigration and Asylum Act 2002 Act contained a number of provisions with retrospective effect, in itself an extraordinary exercise of power. One of these was s 67(2), discussed above, which was introduced to reverse a decision in the High Court which had the effect of giving enforceability to a discretionary practice of granting exceptional leave to people whose asylum claims had failed but who could not safely be returned to their home country. It had been used particularly in relation to Iraqi Kurds. The effect of s 67(2) was that such people could be obliged to remain in the insecure status of temporary admission (confirmed in *R v SSHD ex p Khadir (Appellant)* [2005] UKHL 39).

The passage of statutes in the first decade of the twenty-first century has demonstrated other aspects of the retention of executive power.

1.3.7 **Passage of legislation**

The policy objectives preceding the 2002 and 2006 Acts were stated in terms indicating breadth of vision. The 2002 Act concerned citizenship, identity, and 'integration with diversity' and the 2006 Act was said to provide the statutory basis for a new system of managed migration. These are long term goals which warrant measured consideration in Parliament and full participation by organizations concerned with these matters. The objectives of the 2004 Act were not announced in a White Paper, but, as has been described, in a short consultation letter which set out few of the major proposals. In terms of its effect on principles and rights, the Bill was exceedingly draconian, and warranted democratic consideration of the most careful kind.

However, the progress of these extensive and complex pieces of legislation was marked by indecent, or more to the point, undemocratic, haste. McKee's view of the 2002 legislation was that: 'The Bill's objectives have partly been prompted by heightened security concerns about security in the wake of September 11th', additionally by the wish to 'stem the flood of asylum seekers' (2002:181). Shah said the Bill's overall concern was with 'the promotion of a fortress UK' (2002:315). Certainly the progress of this and the 2004 Act had more of the flavour of an emergency. The effect of this was a democratic deficit in the legislative process.

Haste and lack of consultation have come to characterize the process of legislating on immigration and asylum issues. The 2003 AITOC Bill was introduced in November 2003, with minimal consultation and during the currency of a Home Affairs Committee inquiry into Asylum Applications. Their report was published in January 2004. The Committee had to break off its work to provide a response to the Bill, and said:

we have not had the benefit of a draft bill, nor — in common with other interested parties — were we given more than a few weeks' notice of the proposals even in outline. In view of the fact that since March 2003 we have been conducting a major inquiry into asylum applications, we find this regrettable. (Home Affairs Committee second report of session 2003–4 HC 218 para 3)

At the same time the Constitutional Affairs Committee was preparing a report on Asylum and Immigration Appeals, published in February 2004. The Committee noted the contents of the AITOC Bill and said:

The new proposals do little to address the failings at the initial decision making level and the low level of Home Office representation at initial appeals, which must add to the delays in the system. We think it unlikely that the abolition of a tier of appeal can by itself increase 'end to end' speed and achieve improvements in the quality of judicial decisions. We doubt whether many of the proposals contained in the new Bill are necessary to deal with the current issues in relation to asylum and immigration appeals. (Constitutional Affairs Committee session 2003–4 second report HC 211 summary)

With irony equal to the above, the Government has instituted a Home Affairs Committee inquiry into immigration control which began in November 2005, more than half-way through the passage through Parliament of the Bill which was to set the legal framework for the implementing the Government's five-year plan.

Since the inception of the Human Rights Act the Joint Parliamentary Committee on Human Rights has been charged with scrutiny of all legislation, and comments substantively on legislation affecting rights. In the passage of both the 2002 and 2004 Act there were late amendments which gave rise to significant human rights issues. Also on occasions the Home Office did not reply to the Committee's questions until crucial Parliamentary stages had been passed. The Committee commented adversely on this practice in relation to the 2002 Act, (para 4 JCHR 17th report, Session 2001–2) but in relation to the 2004 Act 'we find ourselves once again in the very same position so soon after having made clear that such a practice undermines parliamentary scrutiny of legislation for compatibility with human rights' (JCHR 14th Report session 2003–4 HL130 HC828 para 3). Lord Lester in Parliament commented that an unfortunate effect of this lack of scrutiny is that 'the matter will end up in court' (HL Debs 6 July 2004 Col 722) as has in fact happened on the very matter upon which that comment was made (regulations on marriage, discussed in chapters 7 and 9).

A practice of introducing late amendments on significant matters affects not only human rights scrutiny but also the opportunity for Members of Parliament to debate matters. Farbey (2003) discusses this practice in relation to the 2002 Act, including in relation to a provision which, as she said, became 'one of the most hotly debated in the Bill'. It was the proposal that the Secretary of State should be able to certify asylum claims 'clearly unfounded' and that this certificate should prevent any appeal from taking place in the UK. This late amendment prevented proper Parliamentary scrutiny of the removal of appeal rights for people who, if they have been wrongly refused, may face the most serious human rights violations. This was announced after the end of the Commons Standing Committee, leaving any effective debate only to the House of Lords. A further amendment to this clause was one of many announced even after Committee stage in the House of Lords. This led to the unusual step of the Bill being sent back to the Lords Committee for further consideration.

Late amendments also prevent effective input from concerned and expert groups. Some provisions are on their face dry and obscure, and under pressure of time and without context or interpretation it is difficult to understand their very real impact on the lives of those affected. In another way also this damages democracy. Farbey quotes the Hansard Society Commission on the legal process: 'All citizens directly affected should be involved as fully and openly as possible in the processes by which statute law is prepared'. So governments 'should make every effort to get bills in a form fit for enactment, without major alteration, before they are presented to Parliament'.

These hasty processes 'increase the government's imprint on legislation at the expense of the imprint of citizens and Parliament.'

As has already been detailed, the 2006 Act removes appeal rights from most entry clearance applicants. The points system that would replace the existing system had not been published in any detail at the time of Parliamentary debate on the Bill. Parliament was asked to take on trust that an as yet unseen and untried system would guarantee fair and objective decisions. This made it difficult for Parliamentarians to debate the Bill effectively. Eventually at report stage in the House of Lords the Government agreed that the new tiered migration system would be published before their Lordships went on to the third reading, so that they could assess the safeguards for themselves.

1.3.8 Delegation by Parliament

Not only the process but also the content of legislation shows an increasing tendency to allocate important delivery or denial of rights to the executive.

1.3.8.1 *Enabling provisions*

In her submission to the Joint Committee on Human Rights concerning the 2002 Bill, Dummett made one overriding point: 'the chief threat to human rights in the Bill appears to me to arise from the character it shares with all the immigration legislation of the twentieth century: it is an enabling Bill.' In this vast piece of legislation, consisting of 164 sections and 9 schedules, it seems extraordinary that much should still be left to the executive, but this is the case. Dummett's submission continues: 'Many of its provisions are vague and general, allowing for subsequent, more precise provisions contained in statutory instruments and rules. The nature of these precise provisions is to be to a very large extent discretionary.'

The same is true in the 2006 Act, which leaves determination of who may lose appeal rights to the Secretary of State (s 4) — a remarkable delegation by Parliament of the power to remove the common law right of access to a court. Discretion and lack of scrutiny are the hallmarks of executive power. Even as accountability and openness increase in the disclosure of guidance and policy, the power to actually make the rules is strongly retained by the executive.

Chief among the express reservations in the 2002 Act of power to the executive is the power already discussed to certify a human rights or asylum claim 'clearly unfounded' and so remove the applicant's right to appeal (s 94). The Act also contained further powers for the Secretary of State to certify as 'safe' a claimant's country of origin, and so prevent them from appealing against the (inevitable) refusal of their claim from inside the UK. The 2004 Act extended the Secretary of State's power to certify third countries as 'safe' for asylum claimants (see chapter 12 for the history of these provisions).

1.3.8.2 *Monitoring and management*

The 2006 Act represents an important shift towards executive control of immigration. As discussed above, the Government's response in Parliament to a challenge on removal of appeal rights was that this was part of the tiered system of managed migration in which decisions would be correctly made. There is a plan for an internal administrative review, but no judicial scrutiny of decisions on entry. The Government's reliance in Parliament and in consultation on objective and verifiable criteria correctly applied shows a faith in administrative systems that would not be shared by many who have examined, experienced or appealed against entry clearance decisions in the past. Problems with the entry clearance system are examined in chapter 6. The Government's vision for the new scheme, so far as it is discoverable at present, seems to be for an efficient and self-policing bureaucracy.

The Government has adopted a practice of appointing independent monitors of various aspects of the immigration and asylum system. With a major inroad into rights, seems to come a monitor. With the authorization to discriminate on grounds of nationality, which admittedly replaced the former lack of statutory control on discrimination, came a race monitor; with the restriction of entry clearance appeals came an entry clearance monitor; with the virtual abolition of entry clearance appeals came a full-time entry clearance monitor, and there is a monitor of 'clearly unfounded' certifications. Monitors are monitors of systems not of individual cases, and are not able to take up individual complaints. Unlike a judicial decision in an appeal, there is no compulsion to change anything.

Farbey comments that in the new structure of the Immigration and Asylum Tribunal there are senior immigration judges who supervise others. No doubt they will take a hand in advising on points of law and so on. She questions the effect of this on judicial accountability for decision-making (2004:198): 'in constitutional terms, managerialism cannot pre-empt, or reduce the need for, the oversight of the higher courts'.

1.4 Conclusion

Whether the focus of attention is the Jews in the nineteenth century, West Indians in the 1960s, East African Asians in the 1970s, or more recently asylum seekers: immigration legislation is passed with a target group in mind. The political agenda of the day moulds the law in a very direct way. The British constitutional feature of executive dominance of Parliament is particularly dangerous in this case as the executive is so centrally concerned with the implementation of immigration law. It is no accident, though it was unplanned, that both sections of this chapter, one on the history of immigration law and the other on its nature, end by reiterating the need for effective judicial scrutiny of immigration decisions.

QUESTIONS

1 What themes can you identify arising from the history and development of immigration law? Are these the same as the ones identified by Bevan in 1986?

2 Are there any other mechanisms of democratic accountability that could or should be introduced into the process of dealing with immigration? Is it a matter for the government or the people?

3 Given the use and origin of the immigration rules, it appears that the Secretary of State both makes and implements much of immigration law. Is this a problem?

FURTHER READING

Bevan, V. (1986) *The Development of British Immigration Law* (Beckenham: Croom Helm).

Carter, B., Harris, C., Joshi, S., *The 1951–55 Conservative Government and the racialisation of black immigration* [1987] Policy Papers in Ethnic Relations no. 11 CREC.

Cohen, S. (2002) 'In and Against the State of Immigration Controls', in Cohen, S., Humphries, B., and Mynott, E. (eds) *From Immigration Controls to Welfare Controls* (London: Routledge).

—— (2000) 'Never mind the racism . . . feel the quality' *Immigration and Nationality Law and Practice* vol. 14, no. 4, pp. 223–226.

Dauvergne, C. (2004) 'Sovereignty, Migration and the Rule of Law in Global Times' *Modern Law Review* vol. 67, no. 4 pp. 588–615.

Dummett, A. and Nicol, A. (1990) *Subjects, Citizens, Aliens and Others* (London: Weidenfeld and Nicolson).

Farbey, J. (2003) 'Lobbying Lessons' *Legal Action* January 2003, p. 6.

—— (2004) 'Becoming a subsidiary of the Home Office? Joined-up government in immigration law' *Immigration and Nationality Law and Practice* vol. 18 no. 3 pp. 197–200.

Fryer, P. (1984) *Staying Power: The History of Black People in Britain* (London: Pluto).

Gillespie, J. 'Asylum and Immigration Act 1996: an outline of the new law' *Immigration and Nationality Law and Practice* vol. 10, no. 3 pp. 86–90.

Gilroy, P. (2002) *There Ain't no Black in the Union Jack* (London: Routledge).

Harvey, A. (2002) 'The 1999 Immigration and Asylum Act and how to challenge it', in Cohen, S., Humphries, B., and Mynott, E. (eds), *From Immigration Controls to Welfare Controls* (London: Routledge).

Harvey, C. (2005) 'Judging Asylum' in Shah, P. (ed) *The Challenge of Asylum to Legal Systems* (London: Cavendish).

Hayes, D. (2002) 'From aliens to asylum seekers', in Cohen, S., Humphries, B., and Mynott, E. (eds) *From Immigration Controls to Welfare Controls* (London: Routledge).

JCWI (2005) *Recognise Rights, Realize Benefits* JCWI analysis of the five-year plan

Juss, S. (1993) *Immigration, Nationality and Citizenship* (London: Mansell).

Layton-Henry, Z. (1992) *The Politics of Immigration* (Oxford: Blackwell).

Lester, A. 'The Human Rights Act 1998 — Five years on *European Human Rights Law Review* [2004] Issue 3 pp. 258–271.

Lindsley, F. (2004) Independent Monitor Report.

Macdonald, I., and Webber, F. (2005) *Macdonald's Immigration Law and Practice*, 6th edn (London: Butterworths) chapter 1.

McKee, R. (2002) 'Fitting the bill? A survey of the main proposals in the Nationality, Immigration and Asylum Bill and some related developments' *Immigration Asylum and Nationality Law* vol. 16, no. 3, pp. 181–188.

Moor, R. and Wallace, T. (1975) *Slamming the Door* (London: Martin Robertson and Co.).

Mynott, E. (2002) 'Nationalism Racism and Immigration Control', in Cohen, S., Humphries, B., and Mynott, E. (eds) *From Immigration Controls to Welfare Controls* (London: Routledge).

Paul, K. (1997) *Whitewashing Britain: Race and Citizenship in the Postwar Era* (New York: Cornell).

Poole, T. 'Harnessing the power of the Past? Lord Hoffmann and the *Belmarsh Detainees* Case' *Journal of law and Society* vol. 32 no. 4 pp. 534–561.

Rawlings, R. (2005) 'Review, Revenge and Retreat' *Modern Law Review* vol. 68, no. 3 pp. 378–410.

Refugee Action and Refugee Council (2006) *Inhuman and Ineffective — Section 9 in Practice*

Shah, P. (2000) *Refugees, Race and the Legal Concept of Asylum in Britain* (London: Cavendish).

Shah, R. 'Secure Borders, Safe Haven' [2002] NLJ vol. 152, no. 7021, pp. 315–317.

Spencer, I. (1997) *British Immigration Policy since 1945: The Making of Multi-Racial Britain* (London: Routledge).

Stevens, D. (1998) 'The Asylum and Immigration Act 1996: the erosion of the right to seek asylum' *Modern Law Review* vol. 61, no. 2, pp. 201–222.

—— (2001) 'The Immigration and Asylum Act 1999: a missed opportunity?' *Modern Law Review* vol. 64, no. 3, pp. 413–438.

—— (2004) 'The Nationality Immigration and Asylum Act 2002: Secure Borders, Safe Haven?' *Modern Law Review* vol. 67, no. 4 pp. 616–631.

—— (2004) *UK Asylum Law and Policy* (London: Sweet & Maxwell), Chapters 1 and 2.

Steyn, Lord (2004) 'Dynamic Interpretation Amidst an Orgy of Statutes' *European Human Rights Law Review* issue 3, pp. 245–257.

Thomas, R. 'Asylum appeals overhauled again' [2003] *Public Law* Summer pp. 260–71.

Vincenzi, C. (1992) 'Extra-statutory ministerial discretion in immigration law' *Public Law* Summer pp. 300–321.

—— (1998) *Crown Powers, Subjects and Citizens* (London: Cassell).

Virdee, S. (1999) 'England: Racism, Anti-racism and the Changing Position of Racialised Groups in Economic Relations' in Dale, G., and Cole, M. (eds) *The European Union and Migrant Labour* (Oxford: Berg).

Woolf, Lord (2004) Squire Centenary Lecture: http://www.timesonline.co.uk/article/0,,1-1025111,00.html (accessed 20 February 2006).

2

Nationality and right of abode

SUMMARY

This chapter traces an outline history of British nationality law from 1948 to the present. It explains by reference to particular groups of people the reasons for the development of the present categories of British nationality. The development of these categories is shown to have been largely a history of progressive exclusion, based on views of who 'belonged' to Britain. Recent developments are discussed in which there is a trend towards inclusion in British citizenship, both in that formal discrimination on the grounds of sex and birth status has been reduced, and in that groups of people formerly excluded have now reduced in number and so are included. The bases for obtaining British nationality by registration and naturalization are discussed, and finally, the powers to deprive a person of nationality, which suggest a new basis for inclusion and exclusion.

2.1 Introduction

The purpose of considering nationality law in a book on immigration and asylum is to give some context and meaning to the immigration law question, 'who has the right of abode?'. In other words, who has the right to enter the UK 'without let or hindrance' (Immigration Act 1971 s 1(1))? As will be seen, the answer to the question 'who has the right of abode?' is not the same in UK law as the answer to the question 'who is a British national?'. However, there is a substantial overlap, and some general idea of nationality principles is necessary.

As a result of legislation in 2002, the number of British nationals who do not have the option of right of abode has diminished. The 2002 legislation is itself the culmination of a process which may be summarized as one of gradual exclusion from the most favoured class of British nationality, which carries the right of abode, until the group remaining was so small that steps towards inclusion were finally taken. This brief account of British nationality is therefore also an account of a number of different routes which have led to British citizenship, and of the stories of inclusion and exclusion which have brought about the present situation. It is part of the historical introduction to immigration law, and reveals how immigration considerations have driven the law on nationality.

For greater depth of coverage, reference should be made to *Fransman's British Nationality Law* (2005), the definitive work.

2.1.1 **Nature and definition**

Nationality is a concept arising in international law, because a fundamental defining quality of a state is the power to determine who are its own nationals. The European Convention on Nationality 1997 defines nationality as 'the legal bond between a person and a State'. Nationality is a legal relationship, and nationals of a State can look to that State for protection just as the State is entitled to look to its nationals for allegiance. As noted in the 1997 Convention, nationality does not indicate a person's ethnic origin, as a state may be made up of many ethnicities either from its creation or by the process of immigration or both. An ethnic group, as defined in law for the purposes of the Race Relations Act 1976, involves a shared history and some of the practices we regard as culture, such as language or sometimes religious practice (*Mandla v Dowell Lee* [1983] 2 AC 548 HL). Thus Sikhs are an ethnic group, as are the English, and Roma (also called gypsies). However, the legal relationship with the state which is called British nationality may encompass all these and many other ethnic groups.

The state has the power to determine who are its own nationals. In the European Union, nationality of a Member State also confers the benefits of citizenship of the European Union. However, the power to determine this remains with the Member State, and the European Court of Justice does not take over the state's role in determining who are its nationals. For further discussion of this, see chapter 4 and Case C-192/99 *R v Secretary of State for the Home Department ex p Manjit Kaur*. The State, within international law limits, sets the criteria and procedures for how its nationality is gained or lost.

It is possible to hold dual nationality, providing the law of both states involved permits this, as UK law does.

Nationality law has consequences for immigration law. As explained by Juss (1993:48), 'those individuals who are nationals of a state are deemed . . . to be its citizens . . . and the state uses its immigration law to prevent the entry and residence of non-nationals'. From this we might expect that if we can determine who has British nationality then we can say that immigration law applies to those who are not British nationals. In some states this would be the case, however, British nationality is not one but a number of different statuses each carrying different rights. Some British nationals are subject to immigration law, and European nationals are privileged over some British nationals in terms of rights to enter the UK. The status of British national does not always mean that the holder has a right in UK law to the protection of the UK or to enter the country. In some cases it has been a virtually empty status.

2.1.2 **Human rights and the UK's nationality law**

Protocol 4 Article 3 ECHR says 'No-one shall be deprived of the right to enter the territory of which he is a national'. Paragraph 1 protects nationals against expulsion. Because of the anomaly that not all British nationals have a right to enter the UK, the UK has not, to date, ratified Protocol 4, though there has been gradual progress towards being able to do so. Non-ratification of the provision does not necessarily mean that the standard it protects is irrelevant. Where European law is applicable, all the rights of the ECHR are imported, whether or not the respondent government has ratified them, and Protocol 4 was used (though unsuccessfully) in argument in *Manjit Kaur*. In both international and Parliamentary debates (see, e.g., that on the Commonwealth Immigrants Act 1968) Protocol 4 is a standard towards which the UK is expected to move.

In the White Paper *Bringing Rights Home* which introduced the Human Rights Act the Labour Government which came to power in 1997 acknowledged that Protocol 4 contained important rights, and that it should be ratified 'if potential conflicts with our domestic law can be resolved' (para 4.11). As we shall see, in the process which followed this statement the British Overseas Territories Act 2002 went some way towards resolving injustices, but did not give the right of entry to the UK to all British nationals. The Nationality, Immigration and Asylum Act 2002 has taken a further step, bringing the UK closer to being able to ratify Protocol 4.

Another relevant Council of Europe document is the European Convention on Nationality 1997. This treaty came into force on 1 March 2000, having had the three required ratifications from Austria, Moldova, and Slovakia, though none as yet from the UK. The UK has had no difficulty complying with the terms of this treaty in relation to the class of British nationals which has the most rights, namely British citizens. However as with Protocol 4, significant areas of non-compliance arise in relation to other kinds of British national, and new powers in the Immigration, Asylum and Nationality Act 2006 to deprive British citizens of their nationality may now put compliance in question in relation to British citizens.

There is a potential engagement of human rights not only in the rights accorded to nationals but also in the process of determining who has nationality. In *Harrison v SSHD* [2003] INLR 284 the Court of Appeal held that the right to be recognized as a British citizen was not a civil right within the meaning of Article 6 ECHR; thus the requirement of that Article for a fair hearing did not apply. However, Mr Harrison could apply to the court for a declaration of his citizenship and this hearing would follow normal requirements of fairness, so the finding has more symbolic than practical significance. It illustrates a phenomenon which will be encountered time and time again in this book, namely that in matters seen to be affecting the State's power to control its membership or borders, the courts are reluctant to imply private rights for an affected party. This question concerning Article 6 is considered more fully in chapter 3.

2.1.3 Brief history of the development of UK nationality law

British nationality law is closely bound up with Britain's colonial history, and the law has changed as the former colonial relationships have changed. In order to understand the present categories of nationality status we need to look briefly at their historical development. For a fuller account, see for instance Fransman (2005), Shah, P. (2000), and Dummett and Nicol (1990).

Prior to the British Nationality Act 1948 the theoretical position was that all British subjects enjoyed the same status. Shah (2000:70) describes how the reality was somewhat different, in that non-white British subjects were already subject to restrictions and exclusions without reference to the right of abode which they supposedly enjoyed. In law, however, there was one status, that of British subject, and part of the myth of the Empire was that this status was the same wherever it was held or acquired.

As Commonwealth states gained independence they naturally wished to gain more control over their own citizenship and entry to their territories. In 1946 Canada precipitated legislative change in the UK by passing its own citizenship laws. Rather than have the rug pulled out from under it, the British Government moved to legislate to accommodate both the desire of independent Commonwealth countries to control their own affairs and the myth of seamless equality (see Dummett and Nicol 1990:134–6). The 1948 Act divided British subjects into two main categories: citizens of the United Kingdom and Colonies (CUKCs) and citizens of independent Commonwealth countries. Thus, in independent Commonwealth countries, citizenship would give access to British subjecthood, rather than the other way round. Rather confusingly, all these people were called not only 'British subjects' but also 'Commonwealth citizens' (s 1(2)). There was a third category, that of British subjects without citizenship, for people who were potentially citizens of a Commonwealth country who did not actually gain citizenship when the country in question passed its citizenship laws or whose parent had lost their British subject status (BNA 1948 ss 13 and 16). It was intended to apply as a transitional status but in fact persisted for a dwindling group of people. While they did not become citizens of independent Commonwealth countries on independence, for instance because they did not meet residence conditions, at the same time they could not acquire CUKC status because they did not have the requisite connection with the UK or a colony. The government of Empire also created a distinction in status between those who were born in a colony (British subjects) and those who were born in a protectorate (British protected persons). A protectorate did not in theory fall within the rule of the common law, but in practice the British did not recognize a local ruler and exercized administrative control. The status of BPP was not transmitted to children, and is now held by very few people. However, the distinction had important repercussions for East African Asians in the 1960s (see Dummett and Nicol 1990:125–6 and 196–204 and Shah 2000:71).

CUKCs under the 1948 Act (ss 4 and 12) were people who were born, adopted, registered, or naturalized in the UK or Colonies or whose father was. Citizens of independent Commonwealth countries or of Ireland had a right to register as a CUKC if they had been resident in the UK or a colony for 12 months. These registration rights were gradually eroded, first by the Commonwealth Immigrants Act 1962, then by the 1971 Immigration Act. The 1948 Act made no immediate impact upon the immigration status of either group: CUKCs or citizens of independent Commonwealth countries. All retained a theoretical right to enter the UK. There was also movement between the two groups as citizens of independent Commonwealth countries resident in the UK could register as CUKCs as described above, and CUKCs would, if they met any necessary criteria, become citizens of independent Commonwealth countries when their home country gained independence.

As we have seen in chapter 1, the immigration statutes of the 1960s introduced immigration control for citizens of independent Commonwealth countries. This built upon the distinction created by the 1948 Act between two groups of British subjects. The 1971 Immigration Act used the categories of CUKC and citizen of independent Commonwealth country and the concept of familial connection introduced by the 1948 Act, to create different classes of immigration entitlement. These categories were imported directly into the nationality definitions set out by the British Nationality Act 1981. The 1971 Immigration Act therefore had a significant impact on the development of nationality law. The Act defines who has a right of abode and who does not. Most of those who retained right of abode when the Act was implemented on 1 January 1973 were CUKCs. Those who had the right of abode were referred to as 'patrial'. This was a term previously unknown in immigration law, and which, following the repeal of these provisions, is no longer used. Section 2 set out who were patrials. These were:

(i)   CUKCs by birth, adoption, naturalization or registration in the UK (s 2(1)(a));

(ii) CUKCs whose parents or grandparents were CUKCs by birth, adoption, naturalization, or registration in the UK (s 2(1)(b));

(iii) CUKCs who had been ordinarily resident in the UK for five years (s 2(1)(c));

(iv) Commonwealth citizens with a parent born or adopted in the UK (s 2(1)(d));

(v)   Commonwealth women married to patrial men (s 2(2)).

It may be seen, by comparing paragraphs (iv) and (v) above with the rest, that the ancestral connection for Commonwealth citizens needed to be closer than for CUKCs in order to obtain the right of abode.

At the time of implementation of the 1971 Immigration Act, nationality passed through men to the children of their marriage. A person who was born in the UK and Colonies would acquire that citizenship through their birth. However, a person born outside the UK and Colonies could only acquire CUKC status through their parents if their father had it and their parents were married. The CUKC citizenship so acquired was citizenship by descent, which could not pass to a child. Transmission of nationality outside the UK and Colonies could therefore only occur for one generation, and this is still the position under the 1981 Act, although some rights of registration help to remedy this deficit (see below).

The British Nationality Act 1981 now governs current British nationality law, together with amendments brought about by the British Overseas Territories Act 2002, the Nationality Immigration and Asylum Act 2002 and Immigration, Asylum and Nationality Act 2006. Section 2 of the Immigration Act 1971 as set out above was repealed by the 1981 Act and replaced with the current s 2. This gives right of abode to:

(a)   British citizens;

(b)   Commonwealth citizens who immediately before the commencement of the 1981 Act had a right of abode in the UK under the old s 2.

Currently there are the following categories in British nationality law: British citizens, British Overseas Territories citizens, British Overseas citizens, British subjects, British nationals (Overseas), and British protected persons. We shall consider each of these categories in turn.

2.2 British citizenship under the British Nationality Act 1981

Holding British citizenship carries a right of abode in the UK and is the most privileged class of British nationality.

2.2.1 Acquisition by birth after commencement

Section 1 of the British Nationality Act 1981 (BNA 1981) deals with the acquisition of British citizenship by people born after the commencement of the Act on 1 January 1983. It provides that a person born in the UK after commencement is a British citizen if, at the time of their birth, their mother or father is a British citizen or settled in the UK. This changed the nature of the UK's nationality law in a very substantial way. It abolished the long-standing common law tradition, enacted in the 1948 Nationality Act, of *jus soli*. This Latin name means 'the right from the soil or land', and the common law rule was that anyone born on British soil was a British subject, regardless of their parents' nationality or whether they were just visiting or had lived in the UK all their lives. The BNA 1981 changed all this and gave the UK more in common with those countries which employ the rule not of *jus soli* but of *jus sanguinis*, i.e., 'the right of blood', meaning by inheritance rather than by birth. Parental connection with the UK, of increasing relevance in the earlier part of the twentieth century, from 1983 assumed a vital importance in the determination of a child's nationality.

The British Overseas Territories Act 2002 (BOTA) Sch 1 amended British Nationality Act s 1 so that since 21 May 2002 birth in an overseas territory also results in British citizenship if the child's parents are British or settled in the territory. Their parents are likely now to be British following BOTA s 3 (see below). British Overseas territories are currently: Anguilla, Bermuda, the British Antarctic Territory (so-called, although this is also claimed by Chile and Argentina and has no inhabitants), British Indian Ocean Territory, Cayman Islands, Falkland Islands, Gibraltar, Montserrat, Pitcairn, Henderson, Ducie and Oeno Islands, St Helena and Dependencies, Turks and Caicos Islands, and the Virgin Islands. The Sovereign base areas on Cyprus are British Overseas Territories, but birth there does not give rise to British citizenship. The BOTA is discussed more fully below.

Under BNA 1981 s 1 British citizenship is acquired by birth in the UK if the child's parents are either British or settled. To be settled means to be ordinarily resident in the UK without any immigration restrictions (Immigration Act 1971 s 33). Settlement is discussed more fully in chapter 6 and does not normally imply any particular nationality. However, in the present context it has an additional specialized meaning. European nationals exercising free movement rights in the UK used to be regarded as settled for nationality purposes, i.e., their child born in the UK could have British nationality. This policy was confirmed in a letter to Walthamstow Citizens Advice Bureau on 6 December 1999 (INLP vol 14 no. 1 2000). However, article 8 of and Sch 2 to the Immigration (European Economic Area) Regulations, SI 2000/2326, which came into force on 2 October 2000, limited the definition of European nationals who would be regarded as settled for nationality purposes to those who have remained for four years and had their residence permit endorsed with permission to remain indefinitely, or who have EC rights having remained in the UK after employment or self-employment. Therefore children born to EEA nationals who are exercising EC rights in the UK will be British if born before 2 October 2000, but not if born after that date unless their parents fulfil the conditions mentioned above.

Table 1 Right of abode

Legislative era	Right of abode	Subject to immigration control
Pre-1948	All British subjects	Aliens
British Nationality Act 1948	All British subjects	Aliens
Commonwealth Immigrants Act 1962	Those born in the UK Irish citizens Commonwealth citizens (i.e. British subjects) with passports issued by UK government	Aliens Commonwealth citizens with passports issued by colonial or Commonwealth government
Commonwealth Immigrants Act 1968	Those born in the UK Irish citizens Commonwealth citizens (i.e. British subjects) with passports issued by UK government and whose parent or grandparent was born, naturalised or adopted in the UK	Aliens Commonwealth citizens with passports issued by colonial or Commonwealth government Commonwealth citizens with passports issued by UK government, but without parental connection
Immigration Act 1971	CUKCs born, naturalised or adopted in UK or with parent or grandparent born, adopted or naturalised in UK CUKC resident in UK for five years Other commonwealth citizens without parent born in UK Commonwealth citizens married before 1st January 1973 to a man with right of abode	Aliens CUKCs without parental connection or residence Other commonwealth citizens whose parent was born (only) in UK Irish citizens (in theory subject to control but mainly exempt because of Common Travel Area)
British Nationality Act 1981	British Citizens Commonwealth Citizens who had right of abode at commencement (1st January 1983)	Aliens Citizens of Commonwealth Countries British Overseas Citizens British Dependent Territories Citizens

2.2.2 Acquisition under the Act by those born before commencement

Section 11 of the British Nationality Act gave British citizenship to anyone born before commencement of the Act who was a CUKC with right of abode before the Act. In other words, it gave British citizenship to patrial CUKCs as defined in the old s 2 of the 1971 Act, discussed above. These were the people with a parental or grandparental connection with the UK who were citizens of the UK itself, or a colony, but not Commonwealth countries.

On 21 May 2002 British citizenship was also acquired by existing citizens of the British Overseas Territories listed above (British Overseas Territories Act 2002 s 3), whatever their date of birth.

2.2.3 British citizenship by descent

Where a person is born to British parents outside the United Kingdom, they are a British citizen by descent (BNA s 2). The essential characteristic of this status is that

Table 2 Effect of legislation determining immigration and nationality status

Legislation	Legal principle	Effect
Pre-1948	In theory all British subjects had the right to enter UK	In reality there was less travel than now, and informal means were used to control non-white entry
British Nationality Act 1948	Divided British subjects into CUKCs and Citizens of Independent Commonwealth Countries. British subjects also called Commonwealth Citizens	Laid foundation for distinctions to be made between CUKCs and other British subjects/Commonwealth citizens
Commonwealth Immigrants Act 1962	Introduced first immigration control on Commonwealth citizens	Linking freedom from control to passports issued by UK government or birth in UK meant ex-patriate white British more likely to be exempt than non-white colonial or Commonwealth residents
Commonwealth Immigrants Act 1968	Parental connection with UK more fully established as basis for freedom from immigration control	Developing blood tie as basis of UK citizenship, many UK passport holders, esp. East African Asians, excluded
Immigration Act 1971	Parental or birth connection with UK becomes main means of establishing freedom from control. More generous provisions for CUKCs than for Commonwealth Citizens	Consolidating blood tie and effects of 1968 Act. In simultaneous legislation European Nationals granted rights of free movement.
British Nationality Act 1981	Birth in UK no longer enough for exemption from immigration control. Crucial emphasis on parentage. Citizens of Dependent Territories excluded	British Citizenship finally established, and on basis of earlier immigration law. Immigration law considerations have informed who is deemed fully British
British Overseas Territories Act 2002	BDTCs renamed BOTCs, made BCs and given right of abode	Hong Kong's independence is now established. There are very few overseas territories left and British government grants right of abode to their citizens

it cannot be passed to a child. It therefore means that if a British couple, A and B, go abroad, say to work, and have a child C while they are abroad, but later return, C's children, if born in the UK will be British, and the line of British citizenship continues unbroken. If however C stays abroad, or goes to work abroad herself and has children there, they will not be British unless their other parent is British otherwise than by descent. C's children have an entitlement to register as British if they meet the conditions set out below, but this ends with them, and is not available to their children. The provision maintains a distinction between those who are British and those who are settled. The children of a settled couple are British if born in the UK, but otherwise are not. The exception since 21 May 2002 is that birth in an overseas territory to British parents will now give rise to British citizenship otherwise than by descent (i.e., full British citizenship) regardless of whether the parents are settled in the UK or in the overseas territory where the birth takes place. British citizenship by descent in the overseas territories continues only for those who had that status before 2002.

2.2.4 **British nationality in European law**

For the purposes of EC law Britain has defined 'British nationals' as British citizens, British overseas territories citizens deriving their citizenship from Gibraltar (though since the British Overseas Territories Act 2002 s 3 came into force these people have been British citizens), and British subjects with the right of abode. This excludes British overseas citizens (see *Manjit Kaur*), British protected persons (see *R v SSHD ex p Upadhey* ILU Vol 3 no 13) and Commonwealth citizens with right of abode. For discussion of these issues, see chapter 4.

2.3 **Other categories of British nationality**

The less privileged classes of British nationality were created to answer immigration concerns at particular moments in history, and can best be understood in the context of the UK's relationship with the groups who were the targets of the legislation.

2.3.1 **British Overseas Territories citizens**

In older documentation and in the British Nationality Act 1981 this nationality status is referred to as British Dependent Territories Citizenship; but in recognition that many territories are not dependent but thriving communities, (see White Paper, *Partnership for Progress and Prosperity* (Cm 4264)), they were renamed in s 1 British Overseas Territories Act 2002 as 'overseas' rather than 'dependent'. Since the 2002 Act came fully into force on 21 May 2002, the majority in this citizenship category have become British citizens.

On the face of it there seems to be little reason for retaining BOTC status at all, as most BOTCs became British citizens on 21 May 2002. One remaining function is that the 2002 Act does not amend the British Nationality Act in relation to naturalization. Therefore residence in an overseas territory can only lead to naturalization as a BOTC, not a British citizen. This prevents British citizenship from being attained by going to live in a British Overseas Territory. The Parliamentary debates also reveal another reason. Birth in the Sovereign base areas in Cyprus (Akrotiri and Dhekelia) gives only BOTC status, not British citizenship. Why should such children not be British citizens? The Foreign Office Minister replied, concerning the Cyprus bases, that according to the treaty with Cyprus which established them 'they are for use as military bases only, and not for the establishment of a wider community' (HC 22 November 2001 col 543). This is part of the answer. The rest is to be found in the proceedings of the Standing Committee, in the words of the same minister:

Hon. Members should also bear in mind that Cyprus is at an important crossroads between the middle east and Europe. We have already had difficult experiences with refugees from the middle east landing in Cyprus and claiming asylum in the bases. The potential to acquire British citizenship through the back door could be a huge pull factor and make us, and Cyprus, vulnerable to a large influx of asylum seekers. We want to avoid that if we can, because it would also undermine the military integrity of the bases . . . if we extended the treaty's [sic] provisions to cover the bases, there would not just be a handful of people who might be eligible for British citizenship. The fear is that more people would be attracted to go to Cyprus and make applications for asylum. (6 December 2001 Standing Committee D)

Here we see the development of trends as described in chapter 1. Whereas in the mid-twentieth century, a desire to curb non-white immigration drove immigration law and policy and that of nationality, in the late twentieth and early twenty-first centuries, a desire to curb asylum claims is the driver. This policy shapes not only immigration law, but also, as we see here, an otherwise incomprehensible and some would say, obscure, provision of nationality law.

2.3.1.1 *The status as it was created*

The category originally called British Dependent Territories Citizenship was created by the BNA 1981 for those people who were CUKCs by virtue of a close connection with what would have formerly been called a colony, then called a dependent territory and now an overseas territory. The close connection was birth in the territory and at the time of the birth their father or mother was either a BDTC, or settled there, or in another overseas territory (BNA 1981 s 15). Under BNA s 23 a person became a BDTC on commencement if they were a CUKC before commencement by their birth, naturalisation, or registration in a dependent territory or if their parent or grandparent had CUKC citizenship by one of these means. There are also provisions for naturalization and registration as BOTCs, and for obtaining BOT citizenship by descent if born outside the territories to a BOTC parent.

BOTC status can be passed through generations. It can also be acquired by descent by birth outside the territory in the same way as British citizenship and with the same consequences.

At the time of the passing of the British Nationality Act 1981 the promoting minister made it clear that all BDTCs were to have the same citizenship status, although this did not give them entry to other dependent territories. More significantly, it did not give them entry to Britain as BDTC status did not carry a right of abode. It may appear that the 1981 Act removed the right of abode from this group of CUKCs. However, as discussed earlier, the Commonwealth Immigrants Act 1968 and the Immigration Act 1971 had already restricted the right of abode to those with a British born, adopted, registered, or naturalized parent or grandparent. In practice therefore most CUKCs living in overseas territories would not have had a right of abode, and in relation to this group the 1981 Act did not do much more than crystallize into nationality law what was already the case in immigration law.

2.3.1.2 *Hong Kong*

In the 2002 Act BOTCs from all overseas territories apart from the Cyprus bases have become British citizens, with full rights of abode, with a limited exception in the case of the British Indian Ocean Territory, discussed further below. The reader might feel moved to ask why these rights could not have been accorded in 1983, instead of these British nationals going through twenty years of nationality wilderness. It is not possible to give a full answer to this question. There have been changes of government in the meantime, and the political climate is different in 2002 from that in 1981. The government has stated its wish to advance towards ratification of Protocol 4. Another relevant factor is certainly Hong Kong. During the Parliamentary debate on the 1981 Act, the question was raised of whether each dependent territory should have its own citizenship status. The government was opposed to this. Opposition members argued the case for Gibraltar and the Falklands, but it was noticeable that opposition parties conceded that Hong Kong was a special case, and no one was prepared to argue for concessions for Hong Kong. The anticipated return of the territory to China, due in 1997, gave rise to fears that many Hong Kong CUKCs would want to enter the UK rather than live under Chinese control. Dummett and Nicol's analysis is that: 'No British politician was ready to consider a redefinition of British nationality which would give right of abode in the UK to 2.6 million British Chinese in Hong Kong' (1990: 242). Before 1997 Macdonald said that:

The population of Hong Kong consists of some 3.2 million British Dependent Territories Citizens who will become Chinese nationals after 1997, 10,000 who will not, 2 million Chinese nationals, 17,000 British citizens with the right of abode, 150,000 foreign nationals (ie not British or Chinese) and about 11,000 stateless persons (mainly refugees from Vietnam). (1995:147)

The figures are slightly at variance but the point is clear. The right of abode in the UK would not be given to the people of Hong Kong.

However, the return to Chinese rule also created anxiety on the part of those who wanted to see these former British nationals protected. In anticipation of the return to China, and in response to pressure various legislative measures were brought in to give some possibility of entry to the UK to a limited number of Hong Kong BDTCs.

Article 4 of the Hong Kong (British Nationality) Order 1986 created a new category of citizenship: British national (overseas). This applied only to BDTCs who had that citizenship by virtue of birth, parentage, naturalization, or registration in Hong Kong. This status was not awarded automatically but only on application before a cut-off date.

BN(O) status does not carry any right of entry to the UK. It entitles the holder to a passport which show a form of British citizenship and to registration as a British citizen after five years' lawful residence in the UK, providing the last year is free of immigration restrictions. This is the same right which is held by BOTCs and BOCs. It therefore only retains the registration right which Hong Kong BDTCs would have had anyway under s 4(1) BNA. It seems that most of those who were entitled to register as BN(O)s did so, although the vast majority were ethnically Chinese and therefore obtained Chinese nationality as well.

A more practically significant right was later given in the British Nationality (Hong Kong) Act 1997 to those who were ordinarily resident in Hong Kong immediately before 4 February 1997. If, by virtue of connection with Hong Kong, they held any of the categories of British nationality which do not carry a right of abode, or were a British protected person, and would otherwise be stateless, s 1 gave a right to register as British citizens after 1 July 1997. This would be full British citizen status carrying a right of abode. The effect was that neither ethnic Chinese nor those with a form of British nationality need become stateless as a result of the handover. A discretionary right to register was given to Hong Kong war widows. There was also a scheme for selecting key people in certain occupational classes and awarding British citizenship to them. This was under the British Nationality (Hong Kong) Act 1990, and the scheme is now closed.

The Nationality, Immigration and Asylum Act 2002 s 14 provides that no one may be registered as a BOTC by virtue of a connection with Hong Kong.

2.3.1.3 *Gibraltar and the Falkland Islands*

More favourable terms were granted to citizens of these two overseas territories. Under BNA 1981 s 5 Gibraltarians had a right to register as British citizens. They were also the only group of BDTCs who were included in the UK's declaration of British nationality for EU purposes. When the Falklands war broke out, the British Nationality (Falkland Islands) Act 1983 was passed, providing that anyone born in the Falklands after the date of commencement to a parent born or settled in the Falklands would be a British citizen. Following the British Overseas Territories Act the advantage to Gibraltarians and Falkland Islanders evaporates as all BOTCs become British citizens automatically, and obtain the rights of an EU citizen.

2.3.1.4 *Chagossians*

The story of the Chagossians is one of the more scandalous episodes in British colonial history. The term refers to the inhabitants of the Chagos Islands which form part of the British Indian Ocean Territory. This territory came into existence as a separate dependent territory in 1965, having up to that time been governed as part of the then British colony of Mauritius. Mauritius became independent in 1968. The separation of the BIOT, however, had less to do with Mauritian independence than with the USA's desire for a military base in the Indian Ocean. They identified Diego Garcia, the largest Chagos island, as a suitable site, and the British Government was persuaded that it would be acceptable to give the island over to the Americans for this use, removing those who lived there. They were removed by various tactics including forcible eviction. The majority were displaced to Mauritius, though some to the Seychelles and other locations. This forcible displacement finally faced a legal challenge in the UK's Divisional Court in *R v Secretary of State for the Foreign and Commonwealth Office ex p Bancoult* [2001] 2 WLR 1219. The court found that 'a power to make laws for the "peace, order and good government" of a territory . . . required its people to be governed, not removed', and Mr Bancoult won the right for the Chaggossians to return.

In the Standing Committee debate on the British Overseas Territories Bill the Foreign Office minister stated that 'such treatment would be impossible today' (HC Standing Committee D 6 December 2001). Nevertheless, it took some lobbying, the case of *Bancoult*, and an amendment to the Bill before those Chagose who had lost the opportunity of BDTC status were included in the provisions of the 2002 Act. As nationality prior to the 1981 Act passed only through married fathers, those born to Chagossian (CUKC) mothers but whose father was not Chagossian (say, for instance, Mauritian, as was highly likely in the circumstances) after the enforced exile but before the 1981 Act, did not obtain CUKC status. If they had been born in the Chagos Islands they would have been CUKCs by birth. Section 6 of the British Overseas Territories Act 2002 provides that a person born in these circumstances between 26 April 1969 and 1 January 1983 will obtain British citizenship by descent. This puts them in the same position as they would have been if their citizenship had been transmitted through their mother, but not the same position as if the exile had never happened, as in this case they would have become British Citizens under the 2002 Act like other BOTCs. The Government's justification for this at the time was that they were now free to return to the Chagos Islands. If they did so their children will be British citizens. If they did not, there would be no reason for them to have any more enduring form of British citizenship than any other British citizen who chooses to stay abroad.

Practical plans for their return were slow to materialize, and a government feasibility study suggested the low-lying islands would not be habitable. On 10 June 2004, European and local election day, two Orders in Council were signed by the Queen relating to the Chagos Islands. The British Indian Ocean Territory (Constitution) Order appointed a Commissioner to rule over the territory and stated as a constitutional principle that no person has any right of abode in the territory or has unrestricted access to any part of it. The British Indian Ocean Territory (Immigration) Order provided for a system of permits to visit the islands, decisions being appealable only to the Commissioner. These orders were made under the Royal Prerogative and, in the words of Baroness Symons 'restore the legal position to what it had been understood to be before the High Court decision' in *ex p Bancoult* (HL Debs 15 June 2004 col WS27). The executive had overturned the judicial decision and stopped the repopulation of the islands. This undermined the justification offered by the Government for limiting the nationality entitlement of Chagossian people born between 1969 and 1981, as they have no right of return to enable them to pass British citizenship to their children. The orders were challenged by judicial review and once again found unlawful (*R (Bancoult) v SSFCA* [2006] EWHC 1038 (Admin)).

The announcement of the prerogative orders provoked outrage in a number of quarters including in Mauritius, where the government threatened to withdraw from the Commonwealth to enable it to sue the UK in the International Court of Justice. On 7 July an early day motion secured a debate in the House of Commons at which the Minister had an opportunity to defend the government's reasons. He also took this opportunity to disclose that two days earlier the government had amended its declaration accepting the jurisdiction of the International Court of Justice to exclude not only current Commonwealth countries (an existing exception retained by a number of Commonwealth members) but also former Commonwealth countries. In other words, Mauritius would not be able to sue at any time.

On 16 November 2004 the Parliamentary Under Secretary of State at the Foreign and Commonwealth Office made a statement that 'following consultations with the US authorities' the government had agreed to a fixed number of Chagossians visiting the graves of their relatives on Diego Garcia as well as the other islands. A number of former Chagos Islanders have now come to the UK, using their entitlement under the British Overseas Territories Act 2002.

See minorityrights.org/features/features_diegogarcia.htm for an argument that the government's treatment of the Chagossians amounts to a crime against humanity.

Another curious exception is Ascension Island, which is part of the territory of St Helena, and like Diego Garcia is devoted largely to military use. Here, no one has a right of abode. A Foreign Office promise to grant this was revoked in early 2006, and St Helenian British citizens must leave Ascension Island on retirement.

2.3.2 **British overseas citizens**

This kind of nationality was created by the BNA 1981 s 26. It was to consist of those CUKCs who did not at commencement obtain British citizenship or British Dependent Territories citizenship. It carries no right of abode in the UK, and the number of people holding this status is diminishing as it cannot be transmitted to children.

Those most affected by the creation of BOC status were people of Asian origin living in East African countries. The situation of people from India and Pakistan who had moved to Kenya and Uganda has been briefly described in chapter 1. The legislative history reveals one of the longest-running human rights issues in UK nationality and immigration law.

Following the British Nationality Act 1948, as previously described, British subjects were divided into CUKCs and citizens of independent Commonwealth countries. Some people who came, or whose parents came, originally from Commonwealth countries which became independent did not obtain citizenship of those countries when they passed their citizenship laws because they were not able for instance to meet residence conditions. Such was the situation of people from South Asia living in East Africa, who did not obtain citizenship of their country of origin. Accordingly this group were not citizens of independent Commonwealth countries, although when for instance Kenya and Uganda became independent, they were living in independent Commonwealth countries. They were CUKCs, or British subjects without citizenship, and as such had a right of abode in the UK. Yet others were British Protected Persons if they originated from protectorates rather than what were then colonies. The 1962 Commonwealth Immigrants Act retained CUKCs' exemption from immigration control providing they had a UK passport issued by the UK Government rather than the government of a colony. One issued by a High Commission would suffice for this, so once their country of residence became independent, passports issued by the High Commission in those countries would give the right of abode in the UK.

The independence statutes of East African countries gave Asian people a difficult choice. They had a two-year period in which to decide whether to opt for citizenship of their African country of residence. After this they would lose that option and thus their right to live in that country. Kenya and Uganda began to pursue policies of Africanization, which involved favouring their own citizens in economic and civic matters. In anticipation of increasing discrimination, and in reliance on the possibility of using their right of abode in the UK, the vast majority chose to retain their CUKC or even BPP status, and not opt for Kenyan or Ugandan citizenship.

The 1968 Commonwealth Immigrants Act, however, divided CUKCs into those who could enter the UK without restriction, and those who could not. The line of inclusion was drawn around those who had a British parent or grandparent, born, adopted, registered, or naturalized in the UK. The value of a UK passport for those without such parental connections suddenly diminished. They were subject to a voucher scheme which operated on a quota system, so they might or might not be able to gain entry to the UK. The Act took away the right of abode for the majority of East African Asians. They were thus left with no country in which they had any right to live.

Section 1 of the 1968 Act was the subject of the challenge before the European Commission of Human Rights in *East African Asians v UK* (1981) 3 EHRR 76. The successful basis of the claim was that the Act was racially discriminatory and that such treatment was degrading and thus in breach of Article 3 of the Convention. This decision was of historic importance in firstly, finding as fact that the statute was passed with a racial motive. This was strenuously denied by the government on the basis that requiring a familial connection had nothing to do with colour but only with defining who 'belongs' to the UK. However, the evidence for this emerges clearly from the Cabinet papers and other official records of the time, which refer to 'coloured' immigration (see Lester 2002).

The second significant aspect of the Commission's decision is the finding that racial discrimination can amount to a breach of Article 3 in itself. If it is sufficiently severe it amounts to degrading treatment. This does away with the need to identify another Convention right in respect of which discrimination may be alleged under Article 14 (see chapter 3 for further discussion of these Articles). If the UK had ratified Protocol 4 of the Convention the applicants would have had a virtually unanswerable case under Protocol 4, being nationals denied entry, and also under Article 14 read with Protocol 4. This course was not open to them, and the actual decision could be said to have greater significance because of the use of Article 3.

All this of course is immigration law rather than nationality law, however it is necessary history to understand the category of BOC under the BNA 1981. The decision of the Commission was answered by the UK Government increasing the number of vouchers available under the quota system. This compromise was accepted by the Council of Europe's Committee of Ministers. East African Asian CUKCs thus remained without a right of abode, but with a greater chance of obtaining entry to the UK through the voucher system.

It will be apparent from the foregoing that East African Asians did not have the necessary connection with the UK to obtain British Citizenship on 1 January 1983, nor with an overseas territory to become a BDTC. Accordingly under the BNA 1981 they obtained the residual status of BOC with no right of abode and no transmission to children.

There was a significant lobby to include them in what became the 2002 British Overseas Territories Act, but this failed. A Private Member's Bill was proposed to fill this deficit, but did not receive government support. East African Asians thus remained BOCs without right of abode while citizens of overseas territories attained full British citizenship. The government gave as a reason for not including BOCs in the 2002 Act that many had access to or had acquired dual nationality, or had access to the UK through the voucher scheme. The assertion of dual nationality is generally correct as regards the most numerous group of people who have BOC status, namely those of Malaysian nationality living in Singapore, but not East African Asians, who could only use the discretionary voucher system. However, on 4 March 2002 the voucher scheme was abolished by announcement in Parliament without any prior warning. The reason given was that it was not much used (Angela Eagle, Minister of State for Home Office HC 5 Mar 2002 col 162W).

The matter was finally addressed by a late amendment to the Nationality, Immigration and Asylum Bill 2002. This amended the BNA 1981 to provide that BOCs have a right to register as British citizens if they have no other nationality or have not deprived themselves of such nationality after 4 July 2002 when the provision (s 4B) was announced. In *The Queen on the application of Shah* [2004] EWHC 2733 (Admin) the claimant was a BOC who applied for a BOC passport in 2001, but was erroneously refused by the High Commission. He applied in 2003 for registration as a British citizen under s 4B but was refused on the ground that he had Indian nationality. In Indian law he would have lost his Indian nationality if the High Commission had acted correctly and granted a BOC passport. He renewed his application in 2004. Lightman J refused permission to move for judicial review of the 2004 refusal on the basis that s 4B did not permit any discretion to be exercised on the ground of injustice to the applicant and it was too late to compel a remedy for the 2001 mistake. The Court of Appeal agreed it was too late. If the court now ordered a correction of the 2001 decision, Mr Shah would lose his Indian citizenship, but this would mean that he would have taken a step to divest himself of another citizenship after July 2002 and so be unable to avail himself of British Nationality Act 1981 s 4B (*R (on the application of Shah) v SSHD* CA Civ 21/6/5, unreported).

This is probably the end of the legislative line as far as the East African Asians are concerned. Providing they have not had dual nationality, they now have an option of registration as a British Citizen. Unlike other British citizens, they do not have the option of dual nationality, and the operation of the cut-off date prevents relinquishment of another nationality, so there is a sting in the tail of lack of choice. However, the most serious charge, that people were left without effective citizenship, should at last be laid to rest. For those who entered under the voucher system or can otherwise obtain leave to enter, there is a right to register after five years' residence also for a dual national (see s 4 below). The abolition of the special voucher scheme and creation of a right to register was accompanied by an assertion that no one would be worse off because of the scheme's abolition and that the provisions were intended to right a historic wrong. In *RM (India)* [2005] UKIAT 00067 the tribunal held that these pronouncements did not give rise to a legitimate expectation that someone who had been refused a voucher under the old system but since granted indefinite leave to remain would be treated as a voucher holder (which would be more advantageous) for the purpose of admission of dependants.

The case of *Manjit Kaur* referred to above was brought by a British overseas citizen. Her contention was that she should be treated as a British national for EU law purposes, thereby giving her citizenship of the European Union. However, the ECJ respected the UK's declaration on that point, which excluded BOCs. Therefore BOCs do not, by virtue of that status, obtain citizenship of the European Union, though following the new s 4B, the discrimination inherent in this situation is much reduced.

2.3.3 British subjects under the Act

This name is given by the 1981 Act to the people known under earlier nationality statutes as British subjects without citizenship. If such people acquire any other citizenship they lose their British subject status. In addition to those mentioned in the historical section above, this group includes some Irish citizens who exercised a right to retain their British subject status. They have right of abode in the UK by virtue of the Common Travel Area (see chapter 6) though most others do not. The new right to register under BNA 1981 s 4B applies also to this group.

2.3.4 British protected persons

Earlier reference has been made to this status. Before the majority of countries under British rule obtained independence it applied to millions of people; now there are very few. They too have the new right to register under BNA 1981 s 4B.

2.4 Registration

This is a means of obtaining British nationality by application, rather than by place of birth or parentage. Registration may be an entitlement, unlike naturalization, which is always discretionary, although Immigration, Asylum and Nationality Act 2006 s 58 imports a requirement of good character and thus an element of judgement, except in the case of children under ten.

Those who are entitled to register as British citizens are:

(a) Children of a British citizen by descent, if either the child and both parents have lived in the UK for three years prior to the date of the application (BNA 1981 s 3(5)) or application is made for registration within twelve months of the child's birth, and providing at least one of the parents was a British citizen otherwise than by descent (s 3(2) and (3)). This is the provision referred to above which limits the transmission of citizenship by descent to one generation by birth and a second generation by registration. In the case of the second entitlement, the British parent by descent must also have lived in the UK for at least three years prior to the birth (s 3(3)). In the case of registration under s 3(5), i.e. where the child and parents have returned to live in the UK for three years, both parents must consent to the registration. If the parents are divorced or legally separated or one has died, the three-year residence requirement only applies to one parent. It may be seen that these rules provide a mixture of *jus soli* and *jus sanguinis*. Where a British citizen by descent returns to the UK and lives here with their child, this demonstrates an intention to make the UK their home, which gives the child a kind of restored *jus soli*. They have not actually been born in the UK, but their presence here and that of their family suggests that they should be treated as though they were. Where the child themselves is not resident, a stronger blood tie with the UK is required (s 3(3)).

(b) British overseas Territories citizens, British nationals (overseas), British overseas citizens, British subjects under the 1981 Act, and British protected persons, so long as they have been resident in the UK for five years, are entitled to register as British citizens under BNA 1981 s 4. As mentioned earlier, since the British Overseas Territories Act 2002, the only BOTCs who remain to use the right to register are those who have naturalized in the overseas territories or who are BOTCs solely by virtue of birth in a Cyprus base (unlikely to be the case as the parent's nationality will generally have superseded this). The rest will be British citizens automatically. BOCs, BPPs, and British subjects under the Act who have no other nationality can now register under s 4B without the five-year residence condition, but note that this does not apply to British Nationals (Overseas). Residents of Hong Kong have still not won the rights now attained by the East Africans Asians and the Chagossians.

(c) Gibraltarians used to have a right to register under BNA s 5. This has become unnecessary since BOTA s 3 has come into force.

(d) Children born in the UK whose parent becomes British or settled, providing the application is made while they are still minors (BNA s 1(3)).

(e) Children born in the UK who live here until they are ten years old (BNA s 1(4)).

(f) Persons born stateless in the UK, providing they have lived in the UK for five years at the date of the application and apply before they reach the age of 22 (BNA Sch 2 para 3, as amended by the Nationality, Immigration and Asylum Act 2002).

The Secretary of State has a discretion under BNA s 3(1) to register any minor. A child registered under s 3(1) is a British citizen by descent if one of their parents was British at the time of their birth (s 14(1)(c)). This discretion may be used to fill gaps in the entitlements listed above, for instance where a child has been adopted abroad by British parents. Nationality Instructions Chapter 9 gives guidance on the exercise of the discretion. 9.15.2 says 'the most important criterion is that the child's future should clearly be seen to lie in the UK'. If the child and family seem to have an established way of life in the UK then the Home Office 'should accept at face value that the child intends to live here'.

2.5 Naturalization

This is another process of obtaining British nationality by application, and while there are conditions which must be fulfilled, there is no entitlement to naturalization. It is an exercise of discretion by the Secretary of State. As an exercise of discretion subject to statutory requirements and published criteria, it is open to judicial review on usual administrative law grounds. This is discussed further at the end of this chapter.

The requirements which must be fulfilled in order to qualify to apply for naturalization are found in BNA 1981 s 6 and Sch 1. Applications may only be made by persons of 'full age and capacity'. So, the applicant must be at least 18 years of age.

2.5.1 Capacity

Full capacity is defined in BNA 1981 s 50(11) as 'not of unsound mind'. The Nationality Instructions Ch 18 Annex A says that the question is whether the applicant is sufficiently mentally competent to know that they want to become British citizens. 'Where applicants have lodged their own applications, it should be assumed that they meet the requirement 'unless there is information on the Home Office papers to cast doubt on this.' Such information would include 'a report . . . from an address suggesting that the applicant is an in-patient in an establishment for the mentally handicapped [sic]'. This is a little confusing as 'an establishment for the mentally handicapped' (more often nowadays referred to as 'learning disabled') could include all kinds of residential establishments as well as those for medical treatment which the term 'in-patient' suggests. Additionally it is not clear why people with learning difficulties who require medical treatment should be singled out. Fortunately, para 3.2 is clearer, saying: 'mental illness or handicap, or . . . in-patient or out-patient treatment . . . is not in itself sufficient grounds for refusing the application.' Where enough doubt is cast, professional reports may be called for. By Immigration, Asylum and Nationality Act 2006 s 49, the Secretary of State may waive the capacity requirement 'if he thinks it in the applicant's best interests'.

2.5.2 Period of residence

Naturalization requires a period of residence in the UK. The qualifying period is three years for a person married to or in a civil partnership with a British citizen (s 6(2)) and otherwise it is five years (s 6(1)). Schedule 1 allows certain period of absence from the UK without jeopardizing the application. For a s 6(1) application this is 450 days, providing that not more than 90 of these days are in the last 12 months. For a s 6(2) application the permitted days' absence is 270, again providing not more than 90 of these are in the last 12 months. In addition to this, the Secretary of State has a discretion to waive fulfilment of the residence requirement. However, as the NI says, that discretion cannot be exercised 'in such a way as, virtually, to ignore these requirements'. The Home Office has a tariff, set out in NI Ch 18 Annex B paras 4 and 5 for periods of excess absences which will normally be accepted.

Apart from limited exceptions, the NI says that there is no discretion to waive the requirement for presence at the beginning of the qualifying period. The common sense reason for this is clear: if the applicant was not here at the beginning of the period then it is in fact a shorter period, and it would be difficult to find another suitable marker to start the period running. This is a reasonable, though not necessarily the only interpretation of Sch 1 para 2(a). There is a difficulty where the applicant arrived, say on 10 March 1997, went abroad for the month of May, then lived in the UK continuously and submitted an application for naturalization during May 2002 on the basis that they have now lived in the UK for at least five years. They do not meet the requirement to be physically present on the date five years before the application was submitted. NI Ch 18 Annex B allows for the application form to be returned to the applicant to be re-signed and dated for a date when the requirement will be met, providing the date is only missed by a maximum of two months either way (para 3.3).

2.5.3 Type of residence

Residence during the majority of the qualifying period is only required to be physical presence, not a particular immigration status. However, at the date of application a spouse or civil partner, and for the last year of residence a s 6(1) applicant, must be free of immigration restrictions on their stay (Sch 1 para 1(2)(b)). Residence must also not have been in breach of immigration laws (1(2)(d)), though once again there is a discretion to regard periods so spent as lawful (para 2(d)). NI Ch 18 Annex B para 8.9 gives examples of when the Home Office would normally exercise discretion to disregard a breach, for instance when an application form was submitted in time but incorrectly completed. The discretion would not normally be exercised 'when the breach was substantial and deliberate' or could affect the good character requirement (see below) (para 8.10). Clearly in between these extremes there are countless other situations, and in particular asylum seekers and refugees are affected as they may have been forced to enter illegally and then spend years waiting for their claim to be determined. The Nationality, Immigration and Asylum Act 2002 s 11 defines time spent in breach of immigration laws as including any time when a person 'does not have leave to enter or remain in United Kingdom', which seems to include periods of waiting for the determination of even a successful application. Such an interpretation would breach Article 34 of the UN Convention on Refugees which provides that naturalization procedures for successful refugees should be expedited so that they can be more fully assimilated into the host community. However, by letter to Fiona Mactaggart MP dated 18 July 2002, the Minister of State for the Home Office stated that there was no intention to change policy on this matter and s 11 was intended to codify, not change, the previous position, and the Home Office indicates that it will disregard periods of unlawful presence after an application has been made to regularize stay (NI para 8.9 and 10).

There is a special provision concerning periods spent in detention or on temporary admission (as to which, see chapter 15). BNA 1981 Sch 1 gives a discretion to regard periods of 'technical absence' as residence for naturalization purposes. This is generally used for members of the forces and diplomatic staff. People in detention without leave, and those on temporary admission, are physically present in the UK but in immigration law they are not legally present. NI 9.7 says that if at the end of detention or temporary admission the person was given leave to enter, their time in detention or on temporary admission should count as residence, but not if they are removed or depart voluntarily.

2.5.4 Good character requirement

Schedule 1 para 1(1)(b) requires 'that he is of good character'. The Act gives no further explanation as to how this requirement should be interpreted. Home Office guidance is to be found in NI Ch 18 Annex D. Criminal activity is clearly an indication that the person may be regarded as not of good character, however not all criminal activity will debar an applicant. The Home Office applies the Rehabilitation of Offenders Act 1974 for this purpose, and in Northern Ireland the Rehabilitation of Offenders (Northern Ireland) Order 1978. For offences which can never be spent under the statutory provisions, the Home Office will look for a period clear of offending. The whole issue is discretionary, however, and the question is whether it seems that the person intends to abide by the law (para 2.1).

Deception in relation to the application and immigration offences such as harbouring or assisting illegal entry will count heavily against the applicant. The Home Office confirmed to Bindmans solicitors, in a letter dated 4 September 2001, that homelessness of itself did not put a person's good character in doubt. Other matters which should not be held against the applicant include 'Eccentricity, including beliefs, appearance and lifestyle' (para 5.2). Notoriety may be a reason to refuse an application, taking account of 'anticipated public reaction' (para 5.4).

2.5.5 Language requirement

This requirement came into the public spotlight with the publication, in February 2002, of the White Paper, *Secure Borders, Safe Haven* (Cm 5387). The White Paper proposed that applicants for British citizenship should be required to demonstrate a level of language proficiency in English, Welsh, or Scottish Gaelic, these being regarded as the British languages. The BNA 1981 in fact already required that the applicant 'had sufficient knowledge of the English, Welsh or Scottish Gaelic - language' (Sch 1 para 1(1)(c)). However, as the White Paper observed, this was assumed to be the case unless there was evidence to the contrary. The new proposal was for actual testing of language ability as in other countries cited in the White Paper, for instance Australia, Canada, France, Germany, and the USA. The proposal came into being in the Nationality, Immigration and Asylum Act 2002 as an addition to the rule-making powers in BNA s 41, enabling rules to be made 'for determining whether a person has sufficient knowledge of a language for the purpose of an application for naturalization' (s 1(3)). In particular rules may be made specifying possession of particular language qualifications and providing for attendance on language courses, (see British Nationality (General) (Amendment) Regulations 2004, SI 2004/1726 as amended by British Nationality (General) (Amendment No. 2) Regulations 2004, SI 2004/2109). The level of language qualification has been set at ESOL (English for Speakers of Other Languages) level 3.

Schedule 1 BNA 1981 contains provision for waiving the language requirement if 'because of the applicant's age or physical or mental condition it would be unreasonable to expect him to fulfil it' (para 2(e)). The 2002 Act does not repeal this provision and so exemption may be given to ill or elderly people or those with learning difficulties. The measure has been controversial, not because there is doubt about the value of fluency in British languages, but because of concern about the alienating effects of compulsion.

2.5.6 Knowledge of British society

This was a highly contentious provision in the 2002 Act in s 1(1), adding a require-ment 'that he has sufficient knowledge about life in the United Kingdom', backed up with an addition to the rule-making power to enable this to be assessed as for language. The proposal was a manifestation of the government's policy to make citizenship a meaningful concept, associated with the school education pro-gramme in citizenship which had just started. The controversy surrounding this proposal is related to the lack of a concept of citizenship in the UK. At the begin-ning of this chapter the distinction was made between nationality and ethnicity. Citizenship is another concept again. It has no foundation in British law and is a political idea implying a relationship between the individual and the State, the content of which is undeveloped as yet. The phrase 'life in the United Kingdom' suggests something about habits and practices, usual ways of behaving, and so on. This suggests culture and so raises connotations of ethnicity rather than national-ity. In a state made up of many ethnicities this raises the question of whose life the candidate for naturalization should know about. In the words of Jim Marshall MP in the Second reading debate in the House of Commons, is the measure concerned 'to improve civic participation and awareness' or to 'promote cultural uniformity' (HC 24 April 2002 col 366)? Answers may be found in *Life in the United Kingdom: A Journey to Citizenship*, the handbook produced by the 'Life in the United Kingdom' Advisory Group which was set up to advise the Home Secretary on implementation of these proposals. The group has recommended a programme of studies as well as distribution of the handbook to all applicants for entry to the UK. Knowledge of life in the UK is a requirement for applications for naturalization made after 1 November 2005 when s 1(1) and (2) came into force.

2.5.7 Pledge

Along with the requirement for knowledge of British society was the institution of a pledge to be taken as well as the oath of allegiance, which is the formal moment at which new citizenship is acquired. Contrary to what an observer might glean from much of the media discussion at the time of the 2002 Bill, the oath of allegiance to the monarchy had always been part of obtaining citizenship. However, it was administered by a commissioner for oaths (usually a solicitor) or magistrate, in private and without ceremony.

The additional pledge, in Sch 1 to the 2002 Act, is as follows:

I will give my loyalty to the United Kingdom and respect its rights and freedoms. I will uphold its democratic values. I will observe its laws faithfully and fulfil my duties and obligations as a British Citizen.

This is administered in formal ceremonies for nationality applications made after 1 January 2004.

Part of the legacy of the focus on immigration considerations as a basis for nationality law is that the 'duties and obligations' of a British citizen have never been identified. Most people who are British by birth or descent would have no idea what these are, and in law it would be not a straightforward matter to identify them. It is therefore debatable whether those who acquire their nationality by a formal process should be asked to promise to fulfil them.

2.5.8 Intention to live in UK

The final requirement for naturalization is that the applicant intends to make their future home in the UK (Sch 1 para 1 (1)(d)). Where the applicant has an established home in the UK, or there is no reason to doubt this intention, then it will be regarded as met (NI Ch 18 Annex F para 2). An intention to travel should not debar the applicant unless it appears that they do not intend to return.

2.6 Discrimination

Nationality law has been riddled with inequality on grounds of sex and birth status. Steps have been taken to eradicate this, and the Nationality, Immigration and Asylum Act 2002 makes further moves in that direction.

Prior to the 1981 Act, citizenship could pass only through a married father. The 1981 Act provided for citizenship to pass through the mother also, and this applied to the citizenship of British Dependent Territories as well as British citizenship. This was a substantial move towards equality.

Even following the 1981 Act, children could not obtain British citizenship from their father if their parents were unmarried. This state of affairs was challenged in *R on the application of Montana v SSHD* [2001] 1 WLR 552 CA. The appellant was a British citizen who had a son born in Norway to a Norwegian mother. The couple were not married and the relationship had ended. As the child was born outside the UK he would have been British by descent if his parents had been married, however, s 50 BNA defined 'father' to exclude an unmarried father. The appellant applied to have his child registered as a British citizen under the discretionary power in s 3. When his application was turned down he applied for judicial review of the Secretary of State's decision. The basis for the Secretary of State's refusal was that the child had insufficient connection with the UK. The appellant's argument was that the child would have British citizenship if his parents had been married, so the exercise of the Secretary of State's discretion was in breach of human rights, namely, Article 8, the right to respect for private and family and Article 14, freedom from discrimination in relation to Convention rights. The Court of Appeal held that common nationality was not a requirement of family life, so Article 8 was not engaged. It considered that there was no true comparison between those who obtained citizenship under s 2, by descent, and those who did so by registration under s 3, and therefore there was no discrimination. However, the Nationality, Immigration and Asylum Act 2002 s 9 addresses the disparity between married and unmarried fathers. 'Father' is redefined to include not only married fathers but also those treated as the father of a child under the Human Fertilisation and Embryology Act 1990 and any other person 'who satisfies prescribed requirements as to proof of paternity'. Regulations will be made as to how this is to be done. In other provisions of the BNA, which had previously excluded unmarried fathers from being defined as a parent, the exclusions are removed.

The 2002 Act s 13 also offers a remedy for those born between 7 February 1961 and 1 January 1983 who would have been British citizens if, at the time of their birth, nationality could pass through a woman. They now have a right to register as British.

The 2002 Act brings nationality decisions fully within the ambit of the Race Relations Act 1976. The Race Relations (Amendment) Act 2000 had made a partial exclusion for nationality functions as it did for immigration functions, however the 2002 Act s 6 takes nationality out of that exclusion, and so nationality functions are now included within the general duty on public authorities to avoid race discrimination.

2.7 Deprivation of nationality

The 2002 and 2006 Acts contain significant extensions of the Secretary of State's powers to deprive a person of their citizenship. The BNA 1981 provided in s 40 for citizens who obtained their citizenship by naturalization or registration, to be deprived of it if the Secretary of State was satisfied that the person had been guilty of 'disloyalty or disaffection to Her Majesty', helping an enemy in time of war, or a criminal offence within five years of obtaining citizenship. Additionally, the Secretary of State had to be satisfied that it was conducive to the public good to deprive the person of their nationality and that they would not become stateless as a consequence.

The 2002 Act replaced this section with two new powers. The first is to deprive any person of their citizenship, whether or not this is acquired by registration or naturalization, and all classes of British nationality are included. The basis for so doing is that 'the Secretary of State is satisfied that the person has done anything seriously prejudicial to the vital interests of the UK or a British Overseas Territory' (new s 40(2)). This is the first power granted to the Secretary of State to remove nationality obtained by birth. The implications of this are considerable. There is nothing to govern who decides what are the vital interests of the UK or what this phrase ought to mean. The removal by executive action of citizenship obtained by birth or parentage is an extraordinary exercise of power by the Government. This power is restricted in that it cannot be used if the Secretary of State is satisfied that the order would make the person stateless.

Although this subsection was open to a politicized or subjective interpretation it was in line with the 1961 UN Convention on the Reduction of Statelessness. The standard it represents is certainly higher than that in a new s 40(2) which will replace it (Immigration, Asylum and Nationality Act 2006 s 56). This provides that citizenship may be removed 'if the Secretary of State is satisfied that deprivation is conducive to the public good'. There is no requirement for reasonable grounds, and although administrative law imports a requirement of reasonableness into the Secretary of State's decision this means that an appeal would have the rather limited scope of a judicial review. There is no requirement for any particular kind of behaviour by the person who loses their nationality, nor any specific risk that they must present. The criterion is the same as that for deportation, which means that on the face of the law British citizenship offers little protection against deportation. The Government indicated that the kind of behaviour which could found deprivation of citizenship under this subsection would include that in the 'list of unacceptable behaviours' made public by the Home Secretary on 24 August 2005 (Standing Committee E 27 October 2005 col 254). These were part of the Government's public strategy to counter terrorism after the London bombings of 7 July 2005 (see chapter 16).

The second new power under the 2002 Act retains the power of the old s 40 to deprive a person of nationality obtained by registration or naturalization if this has been obtained by fraud, false representation, or concealment of a material fact (s 40(3)). However, unlike the old s 40, in this case the Secretary of State apparently does not have to have regard as to whether the person will be left stateless.

These powers demonstrates a new attitude to nationality. It has become more conditional upon conduct. In the case of people who have obtained their nationality by registration or naturalization the possibility that they could be left stateless if they have obtained it by fraud conveys a powerful message.

The International Covenant on Civil and Political Rights Art 24 (3) provides a right to a nationality, and avoidance of statelessness is one of the objectives of the European Convention on Nationality 1997, according to its preamble. Its Article 4 provides that the rules of each State Party should be based on the principles that everyone has a right to a nationality and that statelessness should be avoided.

As mentioned in chapter 1, the Parliamentary Joint Committee on Human Rights raised these concerns with the Home Office, particularly 'loss of British diplomatic protection; loss of status; loss of the ability to participate in the democratic process in the United Kingdom; and serious damage to reputation and dignity' (Joint Committee on Human Rights Session 2001–2 Seventeenth Report para 26). The Home Office, somewhat disingenuously, replied that the person would have another nationality and so the harm to them would be limited, but did not mention that this may not be the case where nationality is removed because of fraud.

Deprivation of nationality has in the past been rare. There has been one deprivation order since 1973 and ten between 1948 and 1973. Lord Filkin in Parliamentary debate said that it would continue to be used only in the most serious and flagrant cases (HL 9 October 2002 col 279). The first attempted use of the new 2002 Act power was in relation to Sheikh Abu Hamza, the controversial cleric at the Finsbury Park mosque in London, but this has been delayed pending a criminal case against him

The 2006 Act also carries a new power to deprive someone of their right of abode where this is held without citizenship. This is to be exercised if the secretary of state 'thinks' that the person's deportation or exclusion would be for the public good (s 57), restoring the use of subjective wording that was a feature of the 2002 Act at Bill stage, but defeated then.

2.8 Challenging nationality decisions

Under the old s 40 a proposal to make an order depriving a person of their citizenship could be referred to a committee of inquiry. The 2002 Act introduced a full right of appeal to the Tribunal, but not if the Secretary of State certifies that the decision was taken wholly or partly in reliance on information which in his opinion should not be made public in the interests of national security, or the relationship between the UK and another country, or is 'otherwise in the public interest'. This is a very wide ground, and given the grounds for deprivation in s 40(2) there is potential for it to apply in almost any case. In these cases an appeal will lie to the Special Immigration Appeals Commission. As discussed in chapter 8, the proceedings of this Commission may be closed to the public and evidence may be withheld from the appellant.

Under the BNA there is no appeal against a refusal of naturalization or registration, and this remains unchanged. The Act has however provided some increased rights for aggrieved applicants. It repeals s 44(2) and (3) which provided that no reasons should be given for discretionary nationality decisions. In practice this had already become a discredited provision as in Mohammed Al Fayed's well-known challenge to the Home Secretary's refusal of his naturalization application, the Court of Appeal held that in some cases the Secretary was under a duty to give the applicant notice of the reasons for refusal (*Fayed v SSHD* [1997] 1 All ER 228). The Secretary of State followed this with an announcement in Parliament that reasons would generally be given and this is in accordance with the 1997

Convention. The method of legal challenge to a refusal of naturalization is judicial review on usual administrative law grounds on the basis of reasons given.. In practice if an application fails through not meeting the factual criteria, the remedy would be to re-apply when the criteria were met, or point out the Home Office error if there had been one.

2.9 Conclusion

This chapter has sought to show that the UK's nationality law has been strongly influenced by its relationships with its former colonies and by the desire to restrict immigration from the majority of these. From the early part of the twentieth century, when millions of people could claim the status of British subject and the theoretical right of abode that went with this, we have now come to a time when only the status of British citizen carries the right of abode. Obtaining this by birth is restricted to those with a close connection with the UK or its few remaining overseas territories. The process of changing the basis of entitlement seems to be coming to an end, but some people, particularly British Overseas citizens, have had to fight long and hard not to be entirely left out of the concluding arrangements of the empire.

Currently a new phase is heralded by the Nationality, Immigration and Asylum Act 2002. The Act demonstrates the exclusive power of the State, as noted at the beginning of this chapter, to determine who are its nationals. In earlier legislation the government was preoccupied with the question of who 'belonged' and this was seen in terms largely of birth and parentage. In this and the 2006 legislation, the State's power of determination is turned in a new direction, testing allegiance not by blood line but by conduct and participation as a citizen. As one era ends, a new one is dawning.

QUESTIONS

1 Are the UK's nationality laws closer to a principle of *jus soli* or *jus sanguinis*? Whichever you think, what elements can you find in UK nationality law of the other principle? How do registration and naturalization fit into this?

2 Is it possible to give content to the idea of 'belonging' to a country? How would you do it?

FURTHER READING

Dummett, A., Nicol, A. (1990) *Subjects, Citizens, Aliens and Others* (London: Weidenfeld and Nicolson), Chapter 7.

Fransman L. *Fransman's British Nationality Law*, (2005) 3rd edn (London: Butterworths) — the major authoritative work, for reference on all issues.

JCWI (2006) *Immigration, Nationality and Refugee Law Handbook* 6th edn. (London: JWCI).

Juss, S. (1993) *Immigration, Nationality and Citizenship* (London: Mansell).

Lester, A. 'Thirty Years On: The East African Asians Case Revisited' [2002] *Public Law* Spring 52–72.

Paul, K. (1997) *Whitewashing Britain: race and citizenship in the postwar era*, (New York: Cornell) Chapter 1.

Pilger, J. (2004) Stealing a Nation — documentary film about the Chagos Islanders Sawyer, C. A losing ticket in the lottery of life: expelling British children [2004] PL Winter pp. 750–758.

Sawyer, C. Civis europeanus sum: the citizenship rights of the children of foreign parents, P.L. (2005) Autumn, pp. 477–484.

Shah, P. (2000) *Refugees, Race and the Legal Concept of Asylum* (London: Cavendish, chapter 5).

Shah, R. 'Special voucher scheme abolished' [2003] *Immigration, Asylum and Nationality Law* vol. 16, no. 2, pp. 108–110.

—— 'A Wrong Righted: full status for Britain's "other" citizens' [2003] *Immigration, Asylum and Nationality Law* vol. 17, no. 1, pp. 19–24.

The Overseas Territories White Paper and Protocol 4 of the ECHR — the ILPA response *Immigration, Asylum and Nationality Law and Practice* vol. 14, no. 3, pp. 142–150.

The Stationery Office, 'Life in the United Kingdom: A Journey to Citizenship' (2004).

Tomkins, A. 'Magna Carta, Crown and Colonies' [2001] *Public Law* Autumn pp. 571–585.

White, R. M. (2002) 'Immigration, Nationality, Citizenship and the meaning of naturalisation: Brubaker, the United Kindom EU citizens, third country nationals and the European Union' *Northern Ireland Law Quarterly* 53(3) pp. 288–319.

Woollacott, S. (2005) Persons Granted British Citizenship, 2004, Home Office Statistical Bulletin 08/05.

3

....

Immigration law and human rights

SUMMARY

This chapter discusses the effects of the Human Rights Act 1998 on immigration law in the UK, including the effect on unsuccessful asylum claimants. It begins by noting the relationship between immigration law and human rights, then gives a general introduction to the European Convention on Human Rights and the operation of the Human Rights Act. There is a more detailed discussion of the application of the Act to immigration law and the application of Article 3 and Article 8 to immigration situations, particularly removal from the UK. There is briefer treatment of the remaining Articles, and finally, discussion of the jurisdiction of the Asylum and Immigration Tribunal to decide human rights issues.

3.1 Introduction

3.1.1 Relationship between immigration law and human rights

There is an obvious connection between migration and human rights. In moving between countries fundamental rights are often being exercised, for instance to be reunited with one's family or to be free from torture or discrimination. Some accounts of human rights would include the right to freedom of movement itself, or the right to work. Immigration law enforcement may involve violations of other rights; for instance, people who are not even suspected of crime can be detained under immigration powers. However, there is no human right to move to a particular country. States have the right to a system of law which, within the constraints of international law regulates who may enter. Whatever the origins of that power, which we briefly considered in chapter 1, immigration law is primarily concerned with defining and giving enforceable substance to it. It has been concerned with regulating the numbers, origin, and material and other circumstances of those to whom entry will be granted, not primarily with the protection of their rights.

In the context of migration and human rights, seeking asylum is a special case as an application for asylum is an application for a specialized form of international human rights protection. This chapter is not concerned with making an asylum claim, which is dealt with in section 5 of this book, but is concerned with the application of human rights law in the UK in immigration decision-making, including to a person whose asylum claim has failed. In fact the majority of human rights claims heard by the immigration appellate bodies are made by people whose asylum claims have been unsuccessful.

The commencement of the Human Rights Act on 2 October 2000 marked a new era. From that date onwards, human rights could be relied upon as the basis of legal argument, and this offers the potential to give a greater equality of arms between the executive and the individual. However, human rights are only powerful tools for individuals to the extent that rules of law permit human rights arguments to be fully considered by decision-makers. For instance, it is of limited use to have a right to respect for family life if no appeal body can decide freely for itself whether the right has been violated. As we have seen in chapter 1, challenges on procedural points and to establish rights of appeal have become essential in the sphere of immigration and asylum law. The points at issue may be hard to follow and may seem dry and inaccessible. In the context of human rights cases the real human reasons for these esoteric battles become apparent. In immigration and asylum cases, delivery of human rights, through the legal system at any rate, raises important questions about the jurisdiction of the courts and tribunals and the relationship between the executive and the judiciary.

These questions underlie much of the material in this chapter, and will be discussed specifically in a section at the end. The theme of executive power raised in chapter 1 is still present, and there are indications that the leopard is having difficulty changing its spots.

3.1.2 Development of immigration law and human rights

International human rights law has already played an important role in immigration cases in UK courts. For instance an early example of the use of human rights norms in the UK was *R v Miah* [1974] 1 WLR 683, where Stephenson LJ held that a penal provision of the Immigration Act 1971 could not have retrospective effect as this would violate human rights treaty provisions.

However, immigration considerations, in other words, political positions on immigration matters, have also had a restrictive effect on human rights law. When the UK first ratified the ECHR, it did not immediately grant the individual right of petition to people who were aggrieved because of an infringement of their Convention rights. This meant that although the UK was a party to the Convention in international law, no one in the UK's jurisdiction who suffered an infringement of their rights could actually go to the Court of Human Rights and complain. In 1966, some 13 years after the Convention came into force, the UK granted the individual right of petition. The delay may be attributed to the government's fear of the applications that would arise from overseas territories, of which Britain had 42 in 1953 when the Convention was ratified. Macdonald cites a reply of a minister in Parliament on the question of individual petition: 'among emerging communities political agitators thrive and one may well imagine the use which political agitators would make of the right of individual petition' (Blake and Fransman (1999:vii). By the end of 1966, the number of overseas territories had dropped to twenty-four.

The expectation that relations with non-British citizens would give rise to human rights cases did seem to be borne out; the first case to be taken to the ECtHR from the UK was an immigration case: a challenge to the refusal of admission to a

12-year-old boy who was coming to the UK to join his father (*Alam v UK* Application 2991/66 The Times, 12 October 1967).

Further in relation to the UK's endorsement of the ECHR, as discussed in the previous chapter, the UK has not ratified Protocol 4 of the Convention, because of its inability to comply with Article 3. This was on account of the position of British overseas citizens in particular, and that of citizens of the overseas territories.

Some effects of bringing together immigration law and human rights are illustrated by one of the earliest and most influential cases decided by the European Court of Human Rights (ECtHR) in the field of immigration law, that of *Abdulaziz, Cabales and Balkandali v UK* (1985) 7 EHRR 471. In *Abdulaziz* three women who were settled in the UK challenged the immigration rules then in force (HC 394) on the basis that they discriminated against women. The rules allowed virtually automatic admission of wives of British men, but there were more hurdles to be overcome for the husbands of British women. The ECtHR found that the rules were discriminatory. The British Government's response to this was to alter the rules to make the more restrictive process applicable to wives as well as husbands. The inequality between the sexes was thus rectified, but inequality between British citizens of different ethnic origins was increased as more people who have family connections abroad are likely to want to marry someone from abroad. The Court considered this question in relation to Mrs Balkandali who was a British citizen born outside the UK, but concluded that the Government was not obliged to provide equal rights between citizens of different ethnic origins. They said: 'there are in general persuasive social reasons for giving special treatment to those whose link with a country stems from birth within it' (para 88).

Abdulaziz established the principle that Convention rights, and in this case the right to respect for family life (Art 8), do apply to a State's immigration decisions. The court did not accept the Government's assertion that immigration was catered for by Protocol 4 and so the other articles would not apply. They made the following important statement:

the right of a foreigner to enter or remain in a country was not as such guaranteed by the Convention, but immigration controls had to be exercised consistently with Convention obligations, and the exclusion of a person from a State where members of his family were living might raise an issue under Article 8. (para 59)

Despite the UK Government's conservative response to *Abdulaziz*, this principle remains a crucial foundation of the relationship between immigration decisions and human rights. The ECtHR acknowledged the long-established principle that a state has the right to control the entry of non-nationals, but that this right is *subject to its treaty obligations*. It is not unfettered.

One might then ask, to what treaty obligations is it subject? Primarily, we shall be concerned with the European Convention on Human Rights. However, many other treaties may be relevant in immigration and asylum cases. Examples are the International Covenant on Civil and Political Rights (ICCPR), the Convention on Ending Racial Discrimination (CERD), the Convention on the Elimination of All Forms of Discrimination Against Women (CEDAW), the Convention Against Torture (CAT) and the Convention on the Rights of the Child (CRC). Human rights principles may also be drawn from the deliberations of bodies whose work is to develop human rights, for instance the United Nations Commission on Human Rights.

Case law from other jurisdictions where there are constitutionally enshrined rights is relevant, including in particular from Commonwealth jurisdictions and judgments of the Privy Council.

The UK's constitutional doctrine of the legislative supremacy of Parliament prevents treaties entered into by the executive from automatically becoming part of the UK law. However, even before the Human Rights Act 1998 there was a body of opinion that international human rights norms could be relied upon in argument in UK courts as they formed part of customary international law (see, e.g., Hunt, *Using Human Rights Law in English Courts*, (1998) 29). Since the implementation of the Human Rights Act immigration decisions in the UK are subject to the rights contained in the Human Rights Act, which are derived from the ECHR. Other international human rights instruments may be used to interpret these rights, and this is increasingly the normal practice in the House of Lords. In a European law matter, any relevant human rights treaty to which states are parties should be respected (Treaty on European Union Article 6 ex F).

To summarize, the relationship between immigration law and human rights has been a complex one. Immigration decisions are subject to human rights considerations. In the UK, this means at a minimum implementation of the rights contained in the European Convention on Human Rights through the Human Rights Act.

3.2 European Convention on Human Rights

The European Convention for the Protection of Human Rights and Fundamental Freedoms, better known as the European Convention on Human Rights (ECHR), is an international treaty, entered into after the Second World War by the Member States of the newly formed Council of Europe. This Council is an association of states whose objective is the securing of democracy and human rights in Europe. The dissolution of the Socialist bloc has had a major impact on its membership as, having embraced democracy rather than Communism as an ideal, the states of the former Eastern Bloc became eligible to join. The Council of Europe now encompasses nearly all the countries of Europe, and currently has forty-five members.

In the reports of some ECHR cases there are two stages of decision: that of the Commission and that of the Court. Commission decisions carry less weight than those of the Court, and since reforms in 1998, the Court has become full time and the Commission has been abolished. All cases that are found to be admissible are heard by a chamber of seven judges. Those which are judged to have the greatest significance can be referred to a grand chamber of seventeen judges (Articles 27 and 30).

The particular importance of the ECHR for the development of human rights protection is that, unlike most international treaties, it provides for a right of individual petition. This means that an individual who claims that their human rights have been violated may apply directly to the Court for a remedy, although they must first have tried all the remedies available to them in their domestic legal system.

The rights which are included are classic civil rights, and the ECHR does not explicitly include social and economic rights, though these may occasionally be indirectly addressed through another right. For instance the Nationality, Immigration and Asylum Act 2002 s 55 allows the Secretary of State to refuse all support to asylum seekers who do not claim 'as soon as reasonably practicable' after arrival in the UK, with the possible consequence that asylum seekers could be left destitute. The interpretation of this provision was challenged in *R v SSHD ex p Adam, Limbuela and Tesema* [2005] UKHL 66 in which the House of Lords held that it would be possible in particular cases for the system to give rise not to a breach of a right to welfare support, which would be an economic right, but degrading treatment in breach of Article 3.

The substantive rights, with the exception of Article 13, have become part of UK law in the Human Rights Act, though the Convention as a whole is not incorporated. The UK courts pay attention to general principles which have been developed by the ECtHR as guidance in the interpretation of the Convention rights and so a brief account is given here of the main principles. For a full account reference should be made to the many books on the Convention itself, some of which are listed at the end of this chapter.

3.2.1 **ECHR principles**

The Court encourages the development of rights which are 'practical and effective' (*Artico v Italy* (1980) 3 EHRR 1), not just theoretical. This approach is also apparent in the HRA in the long title to the Act, which is said to be 'to give further effect to' the rights and freedoms of the European Convention.

Linked to this principle is the idea of the Convention as a living instrument (*Tyrer v UK* (1978) 2 EHRR 1 and *Loizidou v Turkey* (1995) 20 EHRR 99). In other words, its decisions are intended to be appropriate for the times and conditions in which they are made, and to adapt to developing understandings and changing opinions within the Council of Europe. Consistently with this concept, the Strasbourg Court does not operate the doctrine of precedent. Although the Court has an interest in developing coherent case law, and does use and often follow earlier decisions, it is not bound to do so. A clear example of how decisions are affected by the growth of knowledge in social and scientific spheres has arisen in the court's judgments in relation to transsexualism. This passage from *I v UK* (2003) 36 EHRR 53, which concerned violations of Articles 8 and 12 in relation to a transsexual, expresses these points.

54. While the Court is not formally bound to follow its previous judgments, it is in the interests of legal certainty, foreseeability and equality before the law that it should not depart, without good reason, from precedents laid down in previous cases (see, for example, *Chapman v. the United Kingdom* [GC], no 27238/95, ECHR 2001–I, § 70). However, since the Convention is first and foremost a system for the protection of human rights, the Court must have regard to the changing conditions within the respondent State and within Contracting States generally and respond, for example, to any evolving convergence as to the standards to be achieved . . . It is of crucial importance that the Convention is interpreted and applied in a manner which renders its rights practical and effective, not theoretical and illusory. A failure by the Court to maintain a dynamic and evolutive approach would indeed risk rendering it a bar to reform or improvement (see the above-cited *Stafford v. the United Kingdom* judgment, § 68). In the present context the Court has, on several occasions since 1986, signalled its consciousness of the serious problems facing transsexuals and stressed the importance of keeping the need for appropriate legal measures in this area under review . . .

55. The Court proposes therefore to look at the situation within and outside the Contracting State to assess 'in the light of present-day conditions' what is now the appropriate interpretation and application of the Convention (see the *Tyrer v. the United Kingdom* judgment of 25 April 1978, Series A no 26, § 31, and subsequent case-law).

Notable in the remainder of the judgment, as also in *Abdulaziz*, is the court's readiness to examine information from other disciplines in order to inform itself of the weight of the relevant scientific or social arguments.

The idea of the Convention as a living instrument should not be taken to imply that the Court changes with every wind that blows, or is open to political pressure. Many judgments use and stress another principle, namely that the terminology of the Convention is autonomous. This means that the Court gives a certain meaning, e.g., to the word 'criminal', as in *Malige v France* (1999) 28 EHRR 578 where penalty points on a driving licence were held to be a criminal sanction for Convention purposes. Governments are therefore not at liberty to impose upon the Court their own interpretation of such crucial phrases.

This realistic, practical, purposive approach to law is different from the stricter approach to interpretation which has hitherto characterized English law.

3.2.1.1 *Margin of appreciation*

An important Convention principle which does not apply in UK law is the margin of appreciation. This principle does not derive from the nature of rights, but from the nature of the ECtHR as an international authority. The margin of appreciation plays a key role in Convention case law. It is most classically defined in this passage from *Handyside v UK* (1979–80) 1 EHRR 737:

By reason of their direct and continuous contact with the vital forces of their countries, state authorities are in principle in a better position than the international judge to give an opinion on the exact content of these requirements [for the protection of morals] as well as on the 'necessity' of a 'restriction' or 'penalty' intended to meet them '. . . it is for the national authorities to make the initial assessment of the reality of the pressing social need implied by the notion of "necessity" in this context. Consequently, Article 10.2 leaves to the Contracting States a margin of appreciation. This margin is given both the domestic legislator ("prescribed by law") and to the bodies, judicial amongst others, that are called upon to apply and interpret the laws in force'. (para 48)

This passage refers to principles which may restrict a qualified right, and some of the terminology will be discussed again later. The reason for the margin of appreciation is clear, however. It is the closer contact which national authorities have with the matters in hand and the considerations which bear upon them. The margin of appreciation is by definition the deference of an international authority to a national authority. It therefore does not apply when there is no international authority in the situation.

For different reasons there may be a place for the national courts when deciding a human rights point to give weight to the views of the executive. However, it is clear that to fall back too readily on the judgement of public authorities would undermine the purpose of the Act and the role which has been assigned to the judges by Parliament. This is a highly contested area of law under the Human Rights Act, and one in which immigration cases have played a crucial role. It is discussed fully below.

3.2.2 **Classification of ECHR rights**

The ECHR rights may conveniently be divided into three groups: non-derogable or absolute rights; derogable rights which are limited in their application; and qualified rights. Non-derogable rights are those from which the State is not allowed to derogate — that is, opt out — even in times of war or public emergency. These are Article 2 (the right to life, except for deaths resulting from lawful acts of war), Article 3 (prohibiting torture, inhuman and degrading treatment, or punishment), Article 4.1 (prohibiting slavery), and Article 7 (retrospective criminal penalties). The derogable and limited rights are Articles 4.2 (forced labour), 5 (liberty), 6 (fair trial), 12 (right to marry), and 14 (non-discrimination in Convention rights). The shared characteristics here are that the right may be derogated from, and carries limitation within it as to its scope. An example is Article 5 which permits a person to be deprived of their liberty, for instance if they have been convicted of a criminal offence. The qualified rights are generally regarded as a group because they all share a two-paragraph structure, which sets out the right in the first paragraph and the conditions when it may be restricted in the second. The implications of this will be considered in detail in the context of Article 8 below.

3.3 **The ECHR in UK law before 2 October 2000**

The conventional understanding in the period immediately preceding the Human Rights Act was that international treaties including the ECHR could not be relied upon unless the statute or other legal provision being applied was unclear or ambiguous (*R v SSHD ex p Brind* [1991] 1 AC 696). However, at an earlier stage the courts had on occasions seemed to assume that Parliament would not legislate in a way that was contrary to its treaty obligations (e.g., *Miah*). Reference could therefore be made to treaty standards without further justification. The courts had also made use of the ECHR to interpret and develop the common law. Well before the HRA, some judges were prepared to give full weight to Convention rights, some regarded them as relevant in judicial review, but a matter for the executive to assess, and some as not relevant at all. Although the Human Rights Act has introduced a new legal order, it will become apparent later in this chapter that it has not overturned these underlying trends. This is no small matter, because, as mentioned in the introduction above, the effectiveness of rights depends upon the extent to which the courts will take or grant jurisdiction to decide rights issues.

3.3.1 **The interim period**

The HRA received Royal Assent in November 1998, two years before it came into force, and the White Paper *Bringing Rights Home* was published in October 1997. There was therefore a substantial period during which there could be speculation about its effect. There was also a period after the Act came into force when appeal cases were being heard on the basis of the law as it stood before the Act, but it was impossible to ignore the Act. Various legal devices were used at this time to enable human rights arguments to be made and to treat the Act as though it was in force.

In *R v DPP ex p Kebilene* [1999] 3 WLR 972 the House of Lords refused to find a legitimate expectation that the executive (in that case the DPP) should apply Convention rights before 2 October 2000. This was because, according to administrative law doctrine, an expectation can be defeated by express statements that a published policy will not be relied on, or a treaty provision will not be followed in certain cases (see also *R v SSHD ex p Ahmed and Patel* [1998] INLR 570). Here, Parliament's express intention was to bring the Human Rights Act into force on a day to be appointed by the minister, not before.

A common route for the ECHR to be used in argument and judgments based on pre-2 October law was that the Convention right had already been taken into account in the Secretary of State's decision which was being challenged. Therefore it was a relevant factor within the principles of judicial review and the court could consider whether it had been interpreted correctly.

The case of *R (Mahmood) v SSHD* [2001] 1 WLR 840 was a key case in immigration law decided during this period. It concerned the removal of someone who had entered the UK illegally, had remained for some time, and was now working, married, and had children in the UK. This is a situation frequently encountered in immigration law and which clearly involves a clash between immigration enforcement and the right to respect for family life. Indeed it is perhaps the most typical encounter between these two conflicting principles, and we shall meet it in many forms in the course of this book. The majority of the Court of Appeal (Laws LJ, with May LJ agreeing) declined to approach the case on the basis that the Act was in force, but said it would have made no difference if they had. The Master of the Rolls said that he approached the matter as though the Act was in force because the Secretary of State had had regard to Article 8 in making his decision. *Mahmood* will be discussed below in the context of jurisdiction to decide human rights questions, and in chapters 9 and 17 where it has its particular impact.

3.3.2 Traditionalist view

The view espoused by Laws and May LJJ, that the common law already embodies the values of the Convention, is referred to as the 'traditionalist' approach by Fenwick (2000). Before the Human Rights Act 1998 came into force there were indeed developments in the common law which protected rights. For instance, creative use was made of the law of tort (see, e.g., *Entick v Carrington* (1765) 19 St Tr 1029 or *Kaye v Robertson* [1991] FSR 62) and of criminal law (see, e.g., *Redmond-Bate v DPP* (1999) Crim LR 998 or *DPP v Jones* [1999] 2 All ER 257). These cases brought before the UK courts many of the classic issues of rights protection which are dealt with by the ECHR; for instance, the liberty of the subject, unwarranted intrusion by the State, or suppression of freedom of expression. However, care should be taken in applying case law from that period to interpret rights after 2 October 2000. The Convention rights have their own structure and logic which may be overlooked if it is assumed that the principles were there all along, and the Human Rights Act introduces new principles of interpretation.

3.4 **The Human Rights Act 1998**

This section explains the main provisions of the HRA, with an emphasis on points of particular relevance to immigration or asylum law. The Act sets out the twelve Convention rights and the Protocols which the UK has ratified in Sch 1, and s 1 refers to these as 'Convention rights'. The key provisions of the HRA are ss 3 and 6.

3.4.1 **Public authorities**

Section 6 makes it unlawful for public authorities to act in a way which is incompatible with a Convention right. An act includes a failure to act (s 6(6)). Section 6 includes 'core' public authorities (including courts and tribunals), whose actions are always regarded as public, and 'hybrid' authorities, who are regarded as public authorities under the Act in relation to public but not private functions (s 6(3) and (5)).

The most vexed questions have arisen where, as is increasingly the case, public functions are contracted out to private service providers; see, for instance, *Poplar Housing and Regeneration Community Association Ltd v Donoghue* [2001] 3 WLR 183, and *R (on the application of Heather) v Leonard Cheshire Foundation* [2002] All ER 936. In the immigration context the identification of a public authority is rarely an issue. Immigration officers, entry clearance officers, and Home Office officials are undeniably public, and are regarded as 'core' public authorities. However, here too contracting to commercial bodies is a growing practice. The question could arise in relation to security firms running removal centres or airline officials who, for instance, prevent a passenger without a visa from travelling.

In the case of *Quaquah v Group 4 Securities Ltd* (No 2) The Times, June 27 2001 the High Court found that duties in the law of tort in relation to a detainee had been fully delegated to the independent contractor who ran the detention centre. This decision was reached by construing the statute which delegated the power, as in the *Leonard Cheshire* case and *R v Servite Housing and Wandsworth Borough Council ex p Goldsmith and Chatting* [2001] 33 HLR 369 where Moses J acknowledged the unsatisfactoriness for claimants of public authorities being able, in effect, to contract out of their human rights obligations. In *Farah v British Airways* The Independent, 18 January 2000 the appellants were prevented from boarding an aircraft. They claimed in contract against the airline and in negligence against the Home Office for the inaccurate advice of the airline liaison officer. The reported case concerns the reinstatement of the negligence claim against the Home Office, and so far as can be extracted from this decision, it weighs against the airline being regarded as a public authority. The decision not to carry the passengers was treated as a decision taken under the terms of the contract, in reliance on the undoubted public authority, the airline liaison officer. Again a commercial company acted as a buffer between a public authority and a person affected.

The *Poplar* and *Leonard Cheshire* cases suggest much will depend on the terms of the contract which delegates the power and how enmeshed the authority in question is with the core public authority. The House of Lords in *Parochial Church Council of the Parish of Aston Cantlow and Wilmcote with Billesley, Warwickshire v Wallbank* [2003] 3 All ER 1213 held that a public authority should be identified in a particular case, bearing in mind the aims of the Human Rights Act. This leaves open the possibility, despite the conclusion in *Quaquah*, that in the case of an allegation of breach of Convention rights an independent contractor running a removal centre may be regarded as a public authority.

Section 6(3) excludes Parliament from the definition of 'public authority', so Parliament's actions in legislating or failing to legislate are not challengeable. The inclusion of courts and tribunals as public authorities means that courts and tribunals in their decision must uphold Convention rights. The combination of this and the interpretive obligation in s 3 means that where the law can be interpreted so as to uphold the applicant's rights, the court must do it.

3.4.2 Duty of interpretation

Section 3 creates a principle of interpretation which has far-reaching consequences. By s 3(1), so far as it is possible to do so, primary and subordinate legislation must be read and given effect in a way which is compatible with Convention rights. The phrase 'and given effect' makes it clear that the purpose is to uphold rights and echoes the principle of ECHR case law that human rights law should be practical and effective. The duty is to read statute and secondary legislation so as to protect rights whenever possible. This is a powerful principle, changing the normal rules of statutory interpretation. It may be compared with the purposive approach in European law, as applied, for instance, by the House of Lords in *Litster v Forth Dry Dock Engineering* [1990] 1 AC 546, and suggests that the courts must be ready to push statutory language as far as it will go in order to give it a meaning which would uphold the rights of the applicant.

This duty of interpretation overrides the duty to follow a superior court where the precedent predates the Act and would lead to a conflict with human rights. A case under the HRA can be heard in any court or tribunal, and this means that an Asylum and Immigration Tribunal is not bound by a pre-HRA interpretation of statute by the House of Lords. This was illustrated, albeit at a higher level in the court hierarchy, by the Court of Appeal's judgment in *Ghaidan v Godin-Mendoza* [2003] 2 WLR 478. The Court of Appeal was called upon to construe Sch 1 para 2 of the Rent Act 1977 compatibly with Convention rights. The authority on the interpretation of the paragraph was the House of Lords case, *Fitzpatrick v Sterling Housing Association* Ltd [2001] 1 AC 27, decided on the basis of pre-2000 law. The Court of Appeal in *Ghaidan*, using the s 3 duty of interpretation, ruled that the House of Lords' interpretation was not compatible with Convention rights. It was not bound by it and could interpret the statute differently.

In *R v A* (No 2) [2001] 2 WLR 1546 the House of Lords interpreted the Youth Justice and Criminal Evidence Act 1999 s 41 so as to permit the inclusion of evidence which was so relevant to the defence that to exclude it would endanger the fairness of the trial under Article 6. The section was quite clear and unambiguous, and the House of Lords' judgment involved a radical reading inserting words and in effect putting a gloss on the statute.

Immigration rules and statutes should therefore be interpreted so far as possible to uphold Convention rights, as illustrated in *R (on the application of Amirthanathan) v SSHD* [2003] EWHC 1107 Admin, in which Singh J interpreted powers of detention so as to uphold human rights. Despite this clear lead by the House of Lords, in

Radhika v ECO New Delhi [2005] EWCA Civ 89 the Court of Appeal took a more conservative view of s 3, holding that it did not empower it to regard a natural parent who was unwilling to look after their child as being unable to do so. This meant that the child's adoption could not come within the immigration rules that would have enabled her to live with her adoptive parents. The count held that inability and unwillingness were 'quite distinct' and one could not be read so as to encompass the other, even to ensure respect for the appellant's family life.

3.4.3 Use of ECtHR case law in UK courts

In human rights cases, HRA s 2 obliges courts and tribunals to 'take into account' the judgments and opinions of the European Court of Human Rights and the other Strasbourg decision-making bodies which operate the Convention. This raises the question of what weight the court or tribunal should give to the jurisprudence of the ECtHR. The UK courts are not bound by the Strasbourg court, and ECtHR judgments are not precedent setting. The tendency is to follow ECtHR case law where there is, in the words of Lord Slynn, 'a clear and constant jurisprudence' on a particular matter *(R (Alconbury Developments Ltd) v Secretary of State for the Environment* [2001] 2 WLR 1389 at para 26). Indeed, in the same passage, Lord Slynn suggested that 'in the absence of some special circumstances' that would be the proper course of action. A positive direction of growth is suggested by Singh J in *Amirthanathan*, towards 'an autonomous human rights jurisdiction by reference to principles to be found animating the Convention rather than an over-rigid approach' (para 59). A less liberal approach by the UK courts would invite an application to Strasbourg, and should be carefully justified. Despite this, as we shall see, in immigration matters some UK decisions have followed some of the most restrictive strands in ECtHR jurisprudence.

Reference has already been made to the doctrine of the margin of appreciation and its international character. Where UK courts take into account ECtHR case law, caution is needed to ensure that an international margin of appreciation is not imported into a UK decision.

The practice followed in this book is to use both ECtHR and UK cases when interpreting the Convention. In the course of discussing one topic we may move from ECtHR case law to UK case law and back again. The following points summarize the status of the decisions.

1. The ECtHR is not a precedent-setting court. Nevertheless, the Court does attempt to create a consistent jurisprudence, so ECtHR case law will give an indication of how the ECtHR might approach an issue. If a decision is old, and the subject matter is one in which there have been significant developments, then the decision may provide less reliable guidance as to how the court may approach a similar matter now.

2. Decisions of the ECtHR are not binding on UK courts. However, since 2 October 2000, where UK courts are deciding a question of Convention rights, they are obliged to take Convention jurisprudence into account. They must use the ECtHR case law as guide to interpretation of the Convention, and will follow a 'clear and constant' line of cases, but in suitable circumstances may differ from it.

3. Since 2 October UK courts have been called upon to interpret Convention rights directly for the purpose of the case before them. In doing so they become a source of authority on the interpretation of the ECHR as on any other question of law. A House of Lords or Court of Appeal decision on the meaning or application of the Convention therefore binds lower courts, whereas an ECtHR decision on the same point does not. In the Asylum and Immigration Tribunal therefore, a decision on a Convention right made by the House of Lords or Court of Appeal is binding; a decision made by the ECtHR must be taken into account.

4. In decisions on Convention rights made by the UK courts before 2 October 2000, or made after 2 October on the basis of pre-Act law, the strictest interpretation would make reference to the ECHR *obiter* except where the Convention was used to clarify an ambiguity in UK law. In practice, UK courts' pronouncements on the meaning of the Convention in the context of pre-Act law are often treated as having persuasive value in the development of rights jurisprudence.

5. The exception to all this is EC law. The Treaty on European Union 1992 Article 6 (ex F) provided that the ECHR must be respected as a principle of EC law. Following this, EC law questions, whether in UK courts or elsewhere, must be decided compatibly with the Convention.

3.5 Scope of human rights claims

Immigration, by its nature, raises questions of the scope of the human rights jurisdiction. It does so in terms of those who can make a human rights claim, and where, geographically, liability for breaches of human rights begins and ends.

3.5.1 Who may make a human rights claim?

Anyone present in the jurisdiction may make a human rights claim. There is no requirement of lawful presence. Article 1 ECHR provides that the rights and freedoms of the Convention must be secured to everyone within the state's jurisdiction. This Article was not included in the HRA, but the statute contains no exclusions of people on grounds of their status, and anyone may apply who claims that their Convention rights have been violated, 'if he would be a victim for the purposes of Article 34 of the Convention if proceedings were brought in the ECtHR' (HRA s 7). This requires that the applicant be directly affected by the act or omission in question. The effect may be actual, as, for instance, in *Berrehab v Netherlands* (1988) 11 EHRR 322, where the applicant's right to have contact with his child was interfered with by the order to remove him from the Netherlands. Alternatively, the effect may be prospective, as, for instance, in *Campbell and Cosans v UK* (1982) 4 EHRR 293 where two children attended a school which permitted corporal punishment. They themselves had not been punished in this way, but by being at the school they were at risk of being so.

Appeals against immigration decisions on the basis that the decision infringes a human right are made not using the HRA directly but the appeal provisions of the

Nationality, Immigration and Asylum Act 2002. An immigration decision listed in s 82 may be appealed on the ground that the decision, or a removal consequent upon it, 'is unlawful under s 6 of the Human Rights Act 1998 . . . as being incompatible with the appellant's Convention rights' (s 84(1)). The substance of the human rights appeal proceeds just as if it were brought under the HRA, using the Convention rights, duties under ss 3 and 6, and so on. The main differences between s 84 and action under the HRA are that the appeal under the 2002 Act relates only to the immigration decisions listed in s 82, and that the appeal can only be brought by the person to whom the immigration decision is addressed.

In this respect both s 84 of the 2002 Act and s 65 of the Immigration and Asylum Act 1999 which preceded it draw the test of standing more narrowly than the HRA. The case of *SS Malaysia* [2004] Imm AR 153 was starred on a number of questions including the relevance of the interests of third parties. Departing from ECtHR judgments which considered the effect on all family members (*Boultif v Switzerland* (2001) 33 EHRR 50 and *Amrollahi v Denmark* Application no 00056811/00) and steering a course between earlier tribunal decisions, the tribunal held that the interests of third parties could only be taken into account as far as they impacted upon the appellant. It rejected the argument that if a decision defeated the human rights of third parties it would be 'not in accordance with the law', a ground of appeal under what was then Immigration and Asylum Act 1999 Sched 4 para 21. This followed an earlier line of reasoning represented by *Kehinde** 01/TH/02688, and appears to depart from *R (AC) v IAT, SSHD as interested party* [2003] EWHC 389 Admin. Tribunals have followed *SS Malaysia*, as they are bound to do, for instance in *HR Serbia and Montenegro* [2004] UKIAT 00088, noting that the rights of others are irrelevant 'save insofar as they relate to the human rights of the appellant'. In this sense Article 8 claims are more limited that the provisions of the immigration rules in relation to some removals and deportation as these require the effect on others to be taken into account (HC 395 para 364: see chapters 16 and 17).

Where the human rights claim is made through judicial review, the test of standing is that of 'sufficient interest'. For an affected or at risk individual this is easily met. Neither s 7 nor the 2002 Act allow for human rights challenges by interested pressure groups, as has been increasingly allowed in judicial review, for instance *R v SSHD ex p Joint Council for the Welfare of Immigrants* [1997] 1 WLR 275; *R v Lord Chancellor Ex p Child Poverty Action Group* [1999] 1 WLR 347; *R (on the application of Greenpeace Ltd) v Secretary of State for the Environment, Food and Rural Affairs* [2002] 1 WLR 3304. However, it is possible for public interest organizations to appear as intervenors in either appeals or judicial review, and since the implementation of the Human Rights Act there have been a number of immigration and refugee law cases in which this has been done. For instance in *R (on the application of Q) v SSHD* [2003] EWCA Civ 364, a challenge to withholding benefits from asylum seekers, both Liberty and the Joint Council for the Welfare of Immigrants were represented. The United Nations High Commissioner for Refugees sometimes intervenes in asylum cases of particular significance.

3.5.2 Immigration decisions

The Nationality, Immigration and Asylum Act 2002 covers the majority of immigration decisions. The most contentious exception is the decision to carry out a removal. This is discussed in chapter 17. In the event of an action or decision not covered by s 82, for instance a decision to detain, the decision-maker as a public authority is still bound by the Human Rights Act itself. In this case an alleged breach of a Convention right is not heard by the Asylum and Immigration Tribunal, but in any court or tribunal in which a Convention right arises (HRA s 7). In the case of a decision to detain, human rights points could be made in a bail hearing. By HRA s 8 each court in which a human rights matter is heard may only deliver the remedies that are normally within its jurisdiction. Therefore applications under the 2002 Act are limited to the remedies which the tribunal can normally award. It can, for instance, allow an appeal against refusal of leave to enter, but not grant damages.

3.5.3 **Geographical scope —expulsions**

Many human rights decisions in the immigration and asylum context are concerned with the effect of removing a person from the country, and this includes both the damage to their life here and what may happen to them abroad. In the case of expulsion the expelling state carries out a positive act which results in the risk of ill-treatment. This act (the expulsion) takes place within the jurisdiction. Expulsions only engage the question of geographical scope in the sense that the consequence may be experienced outside the UK. This has generated some important questions which were clarified by the House of Lords in *R v Special Adjudicator ex p Ullah and Do* [2004] UKHL 26.

The case of *Soering v UK* (1989) 11 EHRR 439 was the first to establish that where a state expelled a person to face treatment in breach of a Convention article, the expelling state could be held to be in breach. This is not vicarious liability for the actions of the other state, but because the expulsion itself amounts to a breach. In *Soering* a German national challenged extradition to the US state of Virginia to face the death penalty on a charge of murdering his girlfriend's parents. The threat to his life could not be challenged because Article 2, the right to life, permits the death penalty and at that time the UK had not ratified Protocol 13 which outlaws it. However the ECtHR decided that expulsion to face the phenomenon of being on death row was a breach of Article 3 because of the inordinate delays and suspense, during which the condemned person might wait for years to know whether they would be killed or not. *Cruz Varas v Sweden* [1991] 14 EHRR 1 confirmed that expulsion itself may amount to a violation in the case of deportation as well as extradition. The principle is expressed in *Soering* as follows:

A decision by a contracting State to expel a fugitive may give rise to an issue under Article 3, and hence engage the responsibility of that State under the Convention, where substantial grounds have been shown for believing that the person concerned, if extradited, faces a real risk of being subjected to torture or inhuman or degrading treatment or punishment in the requesting country. The establishment of such responsibility inevitably involves an assessment of conditions in the requesting country against the standards of Article 3 of the Convention. Nonetheless, there is no question of adjudicating on or establishing the responsibility of the receiving country, whether under general international law, under the Convention, or otherwise. Insofar as any liability under the Convention is or maybe incurred, it is liability incurred by the extraditing Contracting State by reason of its having taken action which has as a direct consequence the exposure of an individual to proscribed treatment. (para 91)

This phenomenon is referred to loosely as 'extra-territorial' application of the Convention right. This is inaccurate, as the extract from *Soering* shows, as the liability is incurred in the expelling state by the expelling state. It is a convenient shorthand as the expulsion is a breach because of what is likely to happen elsewhere.

Soering and *Cruz Varas* put the application of Article 3 to expulsions beyond doubt. By extension of Article 3 it would be difficult rationally to exclude Article 2, and despite some case law to the contrary, this is now established (see account of Article 2 below). *Soering* itself seems to suggest there may be scope for extra-territorial application of Article 6. In *Bensaid v UK* (2001) 33 EHRR 205 the applicant failed in his challenge to removal on the ground of a feared breach of Articles 3 and 8, but the ECtHR considered his case on its merits, and found no obstacle to his arguing a feared breach of Article 8.

In the early days of the Human Rights Act, a number of cases, without deciding the point, assumed the possibility of extra-territorial application of qualified rights, that is, those which allow the state to interfere with the right when necessary for the protection of listed public interests. For instance, *Nhundu and Chiwera* 01TH00613 and *SSHD v Z, A v SSHD, M v SSHD* [2002] Imm AR 560 assumed that Article 8 could be breached by an expulsion as a result of conditions in the receiving country. The point was considered by Collins J in *Kacaj* [2002] Imm AR 213:

We therefore see no reason to exclude the possible application of any relevant Article (. . .) in deportation cases, but it will be virtually impossible for an applicant to establish that control on immigration was disproportionate to any breach. (para 26)

This was put in doubt by the Court of Appeal in *Ullah and Do* [2003] 1 WLR 770 but restored by the House of Lords who held that:

- theoretically, a real risk of breach of *any* Convention right on return may make the expulsion a breach of the UK's obligations (overturning the CA that only Article 3 could be engaged in an extra-territorial case);

- such a feared breach would need to be flagrant, or in the case of a qualified right, amount to a fundamental denial of that right in order to engage the responsibility of the UK (departing from CA in which a breach of any other right would only be regarded if it amounted to a breach of Article 3);

- it is not the case that the Convention rights were not intended to interfere with the state's sovereign rights in relation to foreign nationals (refuting the CA's *obiter* comments in this respect);

- the expelling state cannot relieve itself of responsibility by saying the breach happens elsewhere. The action of expulsion takes place within the jurisdiction;

- *Soering* and *Cruz-Varas* clearly stated the law and may be followed. They are not exceptions.

The third point above was the argument made for the UK Government in *Abdulaziz* and which did not find favour with the ECtHR in that case. Indeed, 20 years of ECtHR case law since Abdulaziz has proceeded on the basis that immigration decisions are subject to human rights considerations. This was *obiter* in the Court of Appeal but had already been followed in *N v Secretary of State for the Home Department* [2003] EWCA Civ 1369.

In *R v SSHD ex p Bagdanavicius (FC) & another* [2005] UKHL 38 the House of Lords explained that the assessment of risk on return does not mean that the court is making a decision in law about that receiving country, which after all is not represented in the court. It only means there has to be an assessment of risk to the appellant (para 22).

Although the House of Lords held in *Ullah and Do* that expulsions may engage qualified rights as a result of anticipated treatment in the destination state, this is not a straightforward matter to assess. The appeals in *SSHD ex p Razgar* [2004] UKHL 27 concerned claims based on Articles 3 and 8, that the claimants would suffer deterioration in their mental health if returned to France or Germany. The House of Lords held that the right to respect for private life can be engaged by the foreseeable consequences for health or welfare of removal from the UK when removal does not violate Article 3, if the facts relied on by the appellant are sufficiently strong. The threshold is said to be a high one. Such a claim could not be successfully made simply by showing relative disadvantage in care between the sending and receiving state (para 9). It is settled law that removal can engage Article 8 because of the consequences for family or private life in the UK, and this is dealt with extensively below and in chapters 16 and 17.

Where the consequences of removal for family or private life are felt in the UK, the House of Lords called this a 'domestic' case. Where the consequences are feared abroad, they called it a 'foreign' case. The difference between these two is perhaps best expressed by Baroness Hale:

42. . . . In a domestic case the state must always act in a way which is compatible with the Convention rights. There is no threshold test related to the seriousness of the violation or the importance of the right involved. Foreign cases, on the other hand, represent an exception to the general rule that a state is only responsible for what goes on within its own territory or control . . . the Strasbourg court has not yet explored the test for imposing this obligation in any detail. But there clearly is some additional threshold test indicating the enormity of the violation to which the person is likely to be exposed if returned.

43. . . . Lord Bingham also refers to a third, or hybrid category. Here 'the removal of a person from country A to country B may both violate his right to respect for private and family life in country A and also violate the same right by depriving him of family life or impeding his enjoyment of private life in country B' . . . On analysis, however, such cases remain domestic cases. There is no threshold test of enormity or humanitarian affront. But the right . . . protected by Article 8 is a qualified right, which may be interfered with if this is necessary to pursue a legitimate aim. What may happen in a foreign country is therefore relevant to the proportionality of the proposed expulsion.

In *BK Serbia and Montenegro* [2005] UKIAT 00001, the tribunal held that it was a foreign case because the appellant was not settled in the UK. If this were so the effect of the distinction would be to deny equal protection of fundamental rights to people present in the UK but without a secure immigration status. It is doubtful whether Baroness Hale had this in mind.

3.5.4 Geographical scope — entry decisions

In the first edition of this book it was confidently stated that 'there is little doubt' that the Human Rights Act applies to decisions of entry clearance officers. This has proved to be too optimistic a view. The application of human rights to entry clearance cases has become contentious, and this touches on issues which are at the heart of the application of human rights to immigration law.

Article 8 is relied on in entry cases, for instance where someone is refused leave to join their husband or wife in the UK or leave to remain as an elderly parent with their son or daughter. In reality, this ground of challenge will continue, but the question is: on what legal basis does it do so? This has consequences for the exercise of other qualified rights, for the form of proceedings used and for the chances of exercising rights under Article 8.

There are two possibilities: firstly, Nationality, Immigration and Asylum Act 2002 s 82 provides for an appeal against refusal of entry clearance. Section 84 says that a ground of appeal is 'that the decision is unlawful under s 6 Human rights Act 1998 . . . as being incompatible with the appellant's Convention rights'. Thus, entry clearance decisions can be appealed on a human rights basis. As we have seen above, the human rights appeal may only be made by the person to whom the decision is addressed, in this case, the applicant overseas. The second possibility is that Convention rights are not intended to apply to those outside the jurisdiction, and applicants abroad are outside the jurisdiction. The application of Article 8 is an exception which arises because there are family members in the UK whose rights may be infringed. There is a third possibility, which is that Convention rights only apply to those within the jurisdiction, but that ECOs exercise that jurisdiction and applicants for entry clearance thus come within it. This at the moment is speculative, having not been developed in case law.

At first, matters appeared to proceed on the basis of the first possibility and without comment, but the second possibility is being gradually introduced in case law. The decision in *SS (Malaysia)* was starred on this issue and endorsed the earlier decision in *H (Somalia)* [2004] UKIAT 00027 that the protection of UK human rights law did not extend to those outside the territory of the UK, and that use of Article 8 in entry cases was by way of special extension, relying on the existence of family members in the UK. Both cases relied on comments in the Court of Appeal's decision in *Ullah and Do*. As these were *obiter* and not dealt with by the House of Lords, the question of whether they have been overruled is problematic.

Much of the growing case law on the jurisdictional reach of the ECHR outside the respondent state derives from conflict situations and does not translate directly to entry clearance. See, for instance, *Bankovic v Belgium* (2001) 11 BHRC 435, *Al-Skeini v Secretary of State for Defence* [2005] EWCA Civ 1609 and *Issa v Turkey* (31821/96) 17 BHRC 473.

Somewhat closer to our entry clearance situation, in *The Queen on the application of B v Secretary of State for Foreign and Commonwealth Affairs* [2004] EWCA Civ1344, the Court of Appeal considered a wealth of ECtHR authorities, none conclusive, on the question of whether the Convention applied to the actions of consular officials who gave temporary protection to asylum seekers in Australia. Being unable to reach a concluded view, the court was content to assume that the applicants were sufficiently within the jurisdiction of the UK.

The case of *Rev Sun Myung Moon v ECO Seoul* [2005] UKIAT 00112 was an appeal against the refusal of entry clearance by the Rev Moon under Articles 9, 10, 11, and 14. The tribunal was concerned particularly with whether the actions of ECOs come within a 'consular exception' referred to in *Bankovic* to the territorial limit of jurisdiction. It followed *H(Somalia)* closely, and quoting its reasoning did not place much weight on *B*, despite the volume of authorities it considered, because the decision on Article 1 was assumed. It also did not place much weight on the House of Lords' references to *Abdualaziz* in *Ullah and Do*. As in *SS (Malaysia)*, the tribunal held that to apply the ECtHR jurisdiction to ECOs would be a 'remarkable extension' of the scope of the ECtHR (para 38) as it would 'create a right of entry based on Article 3'. The line of reasoning followed by the tribunal has greater consequences because it has decided that the rights do not apply, rather than that they are not breached in this case. It drew on an *obiter* comment of Lord Bingham in *R v Immigration Officer at Prague Airport ex p European Roma Rights Centre and others* [2004] UKHL 55 in which he doubted that functions of immigration officers abroad constituted a relevant exercise of jurisdiction over foreign nationals (para 21). It concluded that the 'ordinary work of the ECO considering applications to enter from non-nationals' could not possibly be subject to ECHR rights (para 59).

Clearly, this question is ripe for further consideration. It is puzzling, for instance, that the actions of immigration officers in Prague were subject to judicial review and race discrimination law (see chapter 8) but not, if one takes Lord Bingham's *obiter* comment a perhaps unwarranted step further, the Human Rights Act. No doubt these questions will be the subject of further litigation.

3.5.5 Margin of discretion

The Human Rights Act preserves different roles for the judiciary and the executive. Nevertheless, it is inescapable that decisions under the Human Rights Act involve the judiciary to a greater extent than previously in political areas of decision-making. A doctrine sometimes known as the margin of discretion preserves the constitutional roles, and arises particularly in the context of judicial review. When a case arises in judicial review, the job of the court is to review its lawfulness, and in so doing the court may defer to the judgment of the executive in certain areas. It is evident that if too much leeway is allowed the human rights protection is lost, see, for instance Singh, Hunt, and Demetriou (1999). Attrill suggests the principled basis for it is found in four factors:

- decision-makers should be accountable to a democratic body;
- a decision-maker may have more expertise in the relevant matter;
- the primary decision-maker will have evaluated the facts;
- the allocation of a kind of decision to a particular decision-maker is the will of Parliament (e.g., the Home Secretary is entrusted by Parliament with immigration control) and so to undermine that interferes with the will of Parliament (Attrill 2003).

One might also say that Parliament has made the judiciary the guardian of rights through the Human Rights Act, a matter in which it, as the traditional arbiter of justice, also has expertise (see *Huang v SSHD* [2005] EWCA Civ 105 para 55). That the judiciary is not answerable to Parliament for the outcome of those decisions is in itself a constitutional safeguard (the separation of powers) and judicial review is in any event not concerned with facts unless they go to jurisdiction (*Khawaja v SSHD* [1985] 1 All ER 765). Lack of expertise is perhaps the commonest reason used by the judiciary for deferring to the executive. A common example is in judging risk to national security (e.g., *Rehman v SSHD* [2001] 3 WLR 877 HL). However, as Lord

Steyn said in *Daly*, 'in law, context is everything', and this reason falls down where the judiciary is as well placed as the executive to judge the matter. This was endorsed by Laws LJ in *International Transport Roth GmbH v SSHD* [2002] EWCA Civ 158, seeing the distinction between branches of government in terms both of constitutional responsibility and expertise (paras 83–87). The separation of powers requires both independence in the branches of government and the power to check and balance each other. Lord Hoffmann considers that the margin of discretion is a rule of law contained in the doctrine of separation of powers and should not be referred to as 'deference' because of its 'overtones of servility' (*R (on the application of ProLife Alliance) v BBC* [2003] UKHL 23).

Others see the discretion referred to as that of the court in determining when it is appropriate not to intervene (e.g., Lester 2004:265). This makes it a voluntary practice of restraint, exercised on the basis of the courts' respect for the constitutional functions of other branches of government, not something that can be demanded because of the subject matter (Steyn 2005). This chimes with the views of R. Clayton who points out that 'routine decision-making by civil servants' should not be elevated to a constitutionally protected act just because a minister somewhere up the chain of command was put in post by an elected government (2004:40).

Lord Bingham in *A and X v SSHD* [2004] UKHL 56 adopts the idea of 'relative institutional competence', rather than suggesting that one branch of government gives way to the other (para 29). The judiciary, rather being somehow anti-democratic because not elected, and therefore liable to defer to the executive, was a 'cardinal feature of the modern democratic state, a cornerstone of the rule of law itself' (para 42).

The margin of discretion is a key doctrine in which the respective jurisdictional limits of the executive and judiciary are delineated. This is of great importance in day-to-day immigration and asylum decision-making in the tribunals.

3.6 Convention rights

Not all the Convention rights will be examined in detail here. This section will concentrate on those rights which are most commonly encountered in the immigration and asylum contexts.

3.6.1 Article 3

3.6.1.1 *Absolute right*

This Article provides that:

No-one shall be subjected to torture or inhuman or degrading treatment or punishment.

This is an absolute right, the breach of which cannot be justified by any interest of the State. This is a settled principle of law, and the ECtHR confirmed in *Chahal v UK* (1996) 23 EHRR 413 that this means that even a person who may be a danger to national security cannot be expelled to face torture. This simple assertion has now become the focal point of an international debate, in which states bent on defeating terrorism seek ways to circumvent the absolute nature of this prohibition.

In the UK, both the Government and the Opposition have talked of withdrawing from the whole European Convention, and then re-ratifying without Article 3 (e.g., British Prime Minister on television's 'Frost Programme' on 26 January 2003). Legal opinion, unsurprisingly, was that 'it is strongly arguable that the ECHR does not permit a contracting state to use the power of denunciation . . . as a device to secure a reservation which could not otherwise validly be made, and therefore the proposal floated by the Prime Minister would be invalid and unlawful' (29 January 2003, Blackstone Chambers, D. Pannick and S. Fatima, for Liberty).

The main difficulties for government have been the prohibition on sending someone to a country where they face a risk of torture (this so-called extra-territorial liability was discussed at 3.5.3 above), and the possibility (some would say the probability, e.g., C. Murray, speech at Chatham House, 8 November 2004) that evidence used in national security cases may have been obtained by torture.

As to the first, the Government has attempted to obtain assurances from receiving governments that returnees would not be subject to torture. The reliability of these assurances has been seriously doubted (see 2005 Human Rights Watch). Indeed, reliance on assurances of the Indian Government was not sufficient protection, according to the ECtHR in *Chahal* (para 105) where there was evidence of torture uncontrolled by the Government. Memoranda of understanding that returnees will not be tortured have now been signed with Jordan, Libya, and Lebanon. The Joint Committee on Human Rights says that 'it will be for the courts to determine the factual question of whether an individual faces a substantial risk of torture on his return, and in reaching that decision the courts will properly take into account the assurances given as part of all the relevant evidence, including evidence about the likelihood of those assurances being delivered in practice' (Counter-Terrorism Policy and Human Rights Third Report of sessions 2005–06 HL 75-I, HC 561-I para 145).

As to the second problem, in *A and others v SSHD* [2005] UKHL 71 a committee of seven Law Lords unanimously rejected the Secretary of State's argument that evidence which might have been obtained by torture could, as a matter of law, be admitted before the Special Immigration Appeals Commission. Their uncompromising affirmation of the unacceptability of torture may, as Lord Brown said, 'spill over into other court proceedings designed to provide a judicial check on the exercise of other executive powers to place constraints of one sort or another on terrorist suspects in the interests of national security' (para 168).

The prohibition on the use of evidence obtained by torture was a principle going back many centuries, now buttressed by international agreements such as the ECHR, the Universal Declaration of Human Rights 1948, the International Covenant on Civil and Political Rights 1966, and the UN Convention Against Torture 1987. The International Criminal Tribunal for the Former Yugoslavia, in *Prosecutor v Furundzija* [1998] ICTY 3, 10 December 1998, even said that prohibition and prevention of torture: '. . . enjoys a higher rank in the international hierarchy than treaty law . . . [and] . . . has now become one of the most fundamental standards of the international community' (quoted by Lord Bingham, para 33).

In an interim report to the UN General Assembly on 1 September 2004, the UN Special Rapporteur on Torture criticized attempts by governments to circumvent the absolute nature of the prohibition on torture and other inhuman treatment on the ground of combating terrorism. A similar warning was issued by the Council of Europe's Committee for the Prevention of Torture in its 14th report on 21 September 2004.

The debate about extra-territorial liability in expulsion cases needs to be seen in the light of these developments, and of the recently uncovered practice of 'extraordinary rendition' — that is, transporting people to extra-territorial locations for interrogation 'in circumstances that make it more likely than not that the individual will be subjected to torture or cruel, inhuman or degrading treatment' (All Party Parliamentary Group on Extraordinary Rendition, December 2005). These locations include US bases and countries known for their record of torture (Amnesty International 2005:4). A legal opinion prepared for the All Party Parliamentary Group was unequivocal that the UK's obligations in international law were independent of those of the US, and that such renditions engaged the international obligations of any state implicated (Crawford J. and Evans K., 9 December 2005).

3.6.1.2 *What 'treatment' is included*

Treatment must pass a certain threshold of severity in order to come within Article 3, and what constitutes torture or inhuman or degrading treatment or punishment is influenced by current understandings. The Convention moves with the times, and it is likely that the interrogation techniques (hooding, exposure to noise, deprivation of food and drink, deprivation of sleep, and enforced standing against a wall) found to be degrading and inhuman in *Ireland v UK* (1978) 2 EHRR 25 would now be found to be torture (see *Selmouni v France* (1999) 29 EHRR 403). This is the case even if some local public opinion lags behind in this respect. In the case of *Tyrer v UK* birching a schoolboy on the Isle of Man was held to be a violation of Article 3, as this form of punishment, once considered acceptable, was now generally regarded as degrading. The Court's conclusion was not affected by evidence of belief by the public on the Isle of Man in the deterrent effect of such treatment. This arises from the absolute nature of the Article. The police force cannot, for instance, say that such treatment is necessary to extract a confession.

Within the jurisprudence of the ECtHR the understanding of the Convention as a living instrument seems to point towards lowering the threshold of what is considered degrading, inhuman, or torture. However, the international climate of the war against terrorism and the political concern in some countries such as the UK to increase the numbers of unsuccessful asylum claimants removed also prompt a countervailing trend in cases of expulsion.

Whether treatment is degrading will depend on the circumstances of the individual. Adverse treatment on grounds of race may amount to degrading treatment if it is institutionalized, as in the *East African Asians cases* (1981) 3 EHRR 76. Here, the European Commission on Human Rights found that the refusal of entry to the UK to the British passport holders resident in Uganda, Tanzania, and Kenya (discussed in chapter 2) amounted to institutionalized racism. Such consistent adverse treatment of people on account of their race was degrading, and passed the threshold of severity to amount to a violation of Article 3.

A breach of Article 3 normally requires actual or threatened physical or psychological ill-treatment which is deliberately applied. There must be 'treatment'; an omission will not breach the Article. In *Q and M* there was argument as to what might constitute treatment. The Court of Appeal found:

57. The imposition by the legislature of a regime which prohibits asylum seekers from working and further prohibits the grant to them, when they are destitute, of support amounts to positive action directed against asylum seekers and not to mere inaction.

The denial of benefits was therefore 'treatment' for the purposes of Article 3, and this was endorsed by the House of Lords in *R v SSHD ex p Adam, Limbuela and Tesema* [2005] UKHL 66. If the asylum seeker has, by some other means, for instance friends or a charity, obtained shelter, sanitary facilities, and some money for food, the denial of benefit does not reach the threshold to be regarded as degrading (*R (on the application of S, D, T) v SSHD* [2003] EWHC 1951 (Admin)). The House of Lords' judgment in *Adam, Limbuela and Tesema* explores individual circumstances to assess whether the threshold for a breach of Article 3 has been reached: 'section 55 asylum-seekers . . . are not only forced to sleep rough but are not allowed to work to earn money and have no access to financial support by the state. The rough sleeping which they are forced to endure cannot be detached from the degradation and humiliation that results from the circumstances that give rise to it' (Lord Hope, para 60).

When Article 3 is applied to general living conditions it raises extremely difficult questions. In *N (Burundi)* [2003] UKIAT 00065 the claimant said that the ravages of civil war in her country were such that it would be inhuman to return her. However, the Tribunal disagreed. The standards were general in that country and did not apply specially to her. This raises the question of whether human rights law can or should be used to equalize living standards, and which standards from the country of origin the Convention country is prepared to call acceptable.

3.6.1.3 *Inadequate medical treatment*

Where there is torture or other severe physical or psychological ill-treatment then there is little doubt that the treatment will cross the high threshold necessary to amount to a breach of Article 3. Other kinds of ill treatment are more controversial. The case of *D v UK* (1997) 24 EHRR 423 broke new ground in this respect, although it has generally been distinguished in subsequent cases where applicants have sought to rely on it. The Secretary of State sought to deport D after he had served a long prison sentence for supplying prohibited drugs. He was by this time in an advanced stage of AIDS. He was receiving terminal care in a hospice. The treatment he had been receiving had slowed down the progress of the disease and relieved his symptoms, and he was receiving support as he faced death. His life expectancy was short in any event, but if he was deported to St. Kitts the treatment upon which he depended would not be available at all, and he had no family or social network to support him. The end of his life would be marked by much greater suffering. The ECtHR held that to return him in these circumstances would breach Article 3.

In subsequent cases it has generally been difficult to show that an acceptable level of treatment would not be available in the destination country. In *Bensaid v UK* (2001) 33 EHRR 205 the applicant was suffering from schizophrenia, and argued both that the upheaval would aggravate his condition, and that suitable treatment would not be available in Algeria. He failed on the second point. There may be scope for arguments under Article 8 in relation to loss of medical care, as indicated in *Razgar* and discussed further below.

The case of *N v SSHD* [2005] UKHL 31 was one of an AIDS sufferer facing deportation to Uganda. In the UK where she had been living for five years her condition
had stabilized on medication. This medication would not be available to her in
Uganda. Her brothers and sisters had died of AIDS and her life expectancy would be
reduced to a year or two. The House of Lords unanimously and carefully distinguished *D v UK*. It held that in *D* the removal was a breach of Article 3 because it
would mean that his death, which was imminent, would take place in far more
distressing circumstances. Here, death was not imminent, although their Lordships
acknowledged there could be no real difference in humanitarian terms between
removing someone to face imminent death and removing someone to face death
within a year or two. The difference came in that the Convention could not be
taken to have imposed upon the parties an obligation to provide medical treatment. Lord Brown identified *D* as concerning a negative obligation — not to deport
D to 'an imminent, lonely and distressing end' (*N v SSHD* [2005] UKHL31 para 93).
N he thought concerned a positive obligation — to provide N with medical treatment. To allow N to remain but not give her medical care would not answer her
needs.

All their Lordships expressed strong sympathy with N, and distaste for having to
make this decision. Lord Brown came very close to suggesting that the Secretary of
State should exercise discretion to let N stay (para 99). In the end, social policy
considerations had to be overt in order to make sense of this case. Lord Nicholls and
others acknowledged 'If the appellant were a special case I have no doubt that, in
one way or another, the pressing humanitarian considerations of he case would
prevail'. However, given the prevalence of AIDS in Africa in particular and the
shortage of treatment, her case was 'far from unique' (para 9). Their Lordships saw
the issue as being outside their capacity to resolve. The problem arose from 'Uganda's lack of medical resources compared with those available in the UK' (para 8) and
the better answer than migration and human rights claims was, in the words of
Lord Hope 'for states to continue to concentrate their efforts on the steps which are
currently being taken, with the assistance of the drugs companies, to make the
necessary medical care universally and freely available' (para 53).

In terms of institutional competence or judicial restraint the message of this case
is clear. It may, if one agrees with the decision, illustrate Gearty's point that 'sometimes it will be right for the judge to hesitate, to say — against his or her own moral
intuitions — that bad though the case is it does not call for his or her intervention'
(2004:6).

The application of *N* to other health risks and conditions is not yet established. In
CA v SSHD [2004] EWCA Civ 1165 the appellant was HIV positive, and the adjudicator found that she would not necessarily lack the requisite treatment on return to
Ghana. However, her baby, who at the time of the hearing had not yet been born,
would have little chance of staying well as he or she could not be breastfed, and
dried formula milk would be mixed with unsafe water. There was a reasonable
likelihood that the baby would die, therefore it was a breach of Article 3 to return
the mother. Laws LJ, giving the leading judgment, said 'It seems to me obvious
simply as a matter of common humanity that for a mother to witness the collapse
of her new-born child's health and perhaps its death may be a kind of suffering far
greater than might arise by the mother's confronting the self-same fate herself.' *JB
Ghana* [2005] UKIAT 00077 was a pre-*N* decision concerning AIDS treatment. The

tribunal held that if the appellant could not afford the treatment this was the same as it not being available at all. This point is now presumably subsumed within *N*.

An increasing number of cases are dealing with the question of suicide risk in the context of Articles 3 and 8; this arises in particular where the applicant has already made suicide attempts and there is a real risk that they will take their life if they are returned to their home country. In *J v SSHD* [2005] EWCA Civ 629 the Court of Appeal said that in a case where suicide is anticipated on return, relevant questions for the court include whether there is a causal link between the removal and the risk of suicide, and whether the applicant's fear of ill-treatment is objectively well founded. An Article 3 claim could in principle succeed in a suicide case, but the threshold would be high because it is a 'foreign' case (i.e., the feared risk would materialize abroad) and higher still because the harm feared would not be directly caused by the authorities but as a result of an illness (following *D v UK* and *Bensaid v UK*).

Where the risk arises in the UK when someone is told of their impending removal, the question still is whether there is a real risk of suicide. In *R (on the application of Kurtolli) v SSHD* [2003] EWHC 2744 Admin the Article 3 and 2 risks arose from the claimant's likely suicide or suicide attempt if removed. Whether the treatment in Germany would be adequate or even better than that in the UK was not the point. The claimant's mental state was such that notice of removal was in itself a danger to her. Her situation was analogous to that of Ms Soumahoro, one of the co-appellants in *Razgar*. In theory, a case of suicide risk might meet the threshold for Article 8 but not Article 3. Tribunals since *N* have differed on whether the risk of suicide in itself is an 'extreme and exceptional' circumstance as required by *N* in order to meet the criteria for a breach of Article 3 (e.g., *MK (Pakistan)* [2005] UKIAT 0075), and there is a difference in the Court of Appeal as to whether this test in itself is appropriate in cases of suicide risk. *J*, referred to above, suggests not, but the test was employed in *KK v SSHD* [2005] EWCA Civ 1082.

3.6.1.4 *Relationship with asylum claims*

There is a substantial overlap between the treatment which might form the substance of an asylum claim and treatment which would breach Article 3. If the elements of an asylum claim are made out then refugee status will be granted, and Article 3 adds nothing. However, where an asylum claim fails then there is need for an inquiry into whether expulsion of the asylum seeker will breach Article 3. This is only relevant where the asylum claim has failed because an element of the refugee definition has not been established which has no bearing on the severity of the treatment feared or the risk of its occurring. The case of *Kacaj* established that the standard of proof is the same for a refugee claim and for a human rights claim. The standard to be applied is to enquire whether there is a real risk of the feared treatment occurring. This was further explained by Sedley LJ in *Batayav v SSHD* [2003] EWCA Civ 1489: 'If a type of car has a defect which causes one vehicle in ten to crash, most people would say that it presents a real risk to anyone who drives it, albeit crashes are not generally or consistently happening' (para 38). The Administrative Court in *The Queen on the application of Kpangni* [2005] EWHC 881 (Admin) reiterated that the test of real risk as described in *Batayav* is the one that should be used.

Kacaj also established that the approach in the asylum case of *Horvath v SSHD*

[2000] 3 WLR 370 to the question of state protection applies in Article 3 cases. In that case the Roma applicant had been subjected to attacks by skinheads, and the case in the House of Lords turned on whether the system of criminal law in Slovakia gave him adequate protection. It was held that where there is a system of criminal law which makes violent attacks punishable, and a reasonable willingness by the enforcement agencies to enforce that law, then the state is held to protect its citizens sufficiently. Therefore when treatment contrary to Article 3 is feared from people who are not part of the state machinery themselves, if there is such a system in place there will be no sustainable claim under Article 3. This was confirmed by the ECtHR in *HLR v France* (1997) 26 EHRR 29 in which a Colombian drug trafficker feared reprisals from drugs barons in Colombia. The Court said:

40. Owing to the absolute character of the right guaranteed, the Court does not rule out the possibility that Article 3 of the Convention (art 3) may also apply where the danger emanates from persons or groups of persons who are not public officials. However, it must be shown that the risk is real and that the authorities of the receiving State are not able to obviate the risk by providing appropriate protection.

This was confirmed in the UK by the House of Lords in *Bagdanavicius*. The House went further and said (in the only reasoned judgment) that serious harm without a failure of State protection did not amount to inhuman or degrading treatment or punishment. Only the State was capable in law of inflicting these, and the prospect of a brutal attack by non-State agents where there was a reasonable system of protection did not constitute the treatment proscribed by Article 3 (para 24).

Scope may arise for an Article 3 claim where the asylum seeker is unable to prove that the ill-treatment they fear is for a reason laid down by the Refugee Convention (see chapter 13). The Jamaican case of *A v SSHD* [2003] EWCA Civ 175, discussed below, was one such, where violent reprisals were feared from a criminal gang. *R (on the application of Islam (Samsul)) v Immigration Appeal Tribunal* [2002] EWHC 2153 was another where the asylum claim had failed because the adjudicator had not accepted that Biharis were a persecuted minority in Bangladesh. This case importantly establishes that where an asylum claim has been turned down, but a claim is made under Article 3, there must be a reasoned decision on the Article 3 claim also. The applicant argued that he would face inhuman and degrading conditions in the refugee camp to which he would be returned. On the evidence his claim did raise issues under Article 3, and the court on judicial review held that these must be considered. It is not enough for a decision-maker to dismiss an asylum claim and then dismiss the human rights claim without proper consideration. The principle of separate reasoning for Article 3 was endorsed by the Court of Appeal in *I v SSHD* [2005] EWCA Civ 886.

3.6.1.5 *Who can assess the evidence?*

R v SSHD ex p Turgut [2001] 1 All ER 719 established an important principle in relation to Article 3 claims even though it proceeded on the basis of the law before the commencement of the Human Rights Act. The applicant was a Turkish Kurd whose asylum claim had failed and who challenged the refusal of the Secretary of State to grant him exceptional leave to remain. He argued that any young Kurdish man whose asylum claim had failed would be at risk on return to Turkey. He lost on this point. However, one of the questions arising was the jurisdiction of the court on judicial review to decide this question for itself. The challenge was to the rationality of the decision following *Wednesbury* principles. The Court of Appeal had this to say:

The domestic court's obligation on an irrationality challenge in an Article 3 case is to subject the Secretary of State's decision to rigorous examination, and this it does by considering the underlying factual material for itself to see whether or not it compels a different conclusion to that arrived at by the Secretary of State. Only if it does will the challenge succeed. All that said, however, this is not an area in which the Court will pay any special deference to the Secretary of State's conclusion on the facts. In the first place, the human right involved here . . . is both absolute and fundamental: it is not a qualified right requiring a balance to be struck with some competing social need.

Secondly, the Court here is hardly less well placed than the Secretary of State himself to evaluate the risk once the revealed material is placed before it.

Thirdly . . . we must . . . recognise the possibility that he has (even if unconsciously) tended to depreciate the evidence of risk and . . . maintain his pre-existing stance rather than re-assess the position with an open mind. In circumstances such as these . . . the area of judgment within which the Court should defer to the Secretary of State . . . is a decidedly narrow one.

This conclusion was partly induced by a rule of evidence concerning human rights and asylum claims that all evidence is admissible up to the date of the hearing, because the assessment is of future risk, not historical liability. The court must therefore be in a position to assess the evidence. This decision is a very remarkable one which has remained unchallenged. It deals with the margin of discretion to be left to the executive in making human rights decisions and concludes that in relation to Article 3, very little margin is required. What is required in an Article 3 case is an objective assessment of risk.

This approach in the ECtHR is demonstrated by the case of *Hilal v UK* (2001) 33 EHRR 2. It was originally an asylum claim, and shows that treatment which could found an asylum claim may also found a claim under Article 3. The applicant had been tortured in Tanzania, but did not mention this in his initial interview which he was told was not for the purpose of giving detail, but just to lodge his claim. He gave full details at the second interview, but his credibility was then doubted because he had not mentioned these matters at his first interview and because he had no corroborating evidence. He later produced a hospital report which verified precisely the injuries he claimed to have suffered, but his asylum claim was refused at all stages through the UK legal system, mainly because of doubts as to his credibility and the authenticity of the various documents he produced. The ECtHR commented, *inter alia*:

Though the Government have expressed doubts on the authenticity of the medical report, they have not provided any evidence to substantiate these doubts or to contradict the opinion provided by the applicant. (para 63)

This is a very different approach from that employed in UK asylum decision-making at all levels, where doubts as to credibility are a major reason for refusal of claims. Blake and Hussain express the difference in the following way:

Clear evidence of past torture in a country where continued torture is still prevalent may speak louder as to the objective nature of risk than the usual distracting minutiae of asylum decisions as to why a person should have so suffered, why he did not claim protection elsewhere, and why there was delay or inconsistency in setting out his account. (2003:96)

3.6.2 **Article 2**

Article 2(1) provides that:

Everyone's right to life shall be protected by law. No-one shall be deprived of his life intentionally save in the execution of a sentence of a court following conviction of a crime for which this penalty is provided by law.

Article 2 does not outlaw the death sentence. This is done by Protocol 13, which the UK ratified on 10 October 2003. The inclusion of Protocol 13 in the rights in Sch 1 to the Human Rights Act means that there are substantial constitutional problems in the way of any future government which might wish to re-introduce the death penalty, including in time of war.

Article 2(1) entails both that the State must take some positive steps to prevent life being taken and that the State must not itself take life.

3.6.2.1 *Positive obligation*

The positive duty to protect life is of a limited kind. In *Osman v UK* (2000) 29 EHRR 245 the police were aware that a schoolteacher who had developed an obsession with his pupil was harassing him. The European Court of Human Rights held that there was no breach of Article 2 in their failure to apprehend him and to prevent the killing which he committed, because there was no decisive stage at which the police knew or ought to have known that the lives of the applicant family were at real and immediate risk. The corollary of this is that if, in another case, there were such a decisive stage at which the risk was real and immediate then there could be a breach of Article 2. More generally, the court interpreted the duty of protection in Article 2 to mean that the state has a general duty to establish and maintain an effective system of criminal law to deter, detect, and punish offenders. Such a duty would be fulfilled by the maintenance of a police and criminal justice system such as that in the UK.

3.6.2.2 *Negative obligation*

The negative obligation not to take life is qualified by Article 2(2), but this does not set out circumstances in which deliberate killing may be justified. It sets out possible defences which the state may be able to maintain where death results accidentally from the use of force which is no more than absolutely necessary:

(a) in defence of any person from unlawful violence;

(b) in order to effect a lawful arrest or to prevent the escape of a person lawfully detained; and

(c) in action lawfully taken for the purpose of quelling a riot or insurrection.

The terms of this paragraph are strictly construed by the Court, and in determining whether the use of force was no more than absolutely necessary attention may be paid to whether adequate guidelines for the situation were in place and followed. This was demonstrated in the case of *Mcann v UK* (1996) 21 EHRR 97 (the 'deaths on the Rock' case) where the lack of training in shooting to wound rather than to kill was one of the reasons that the UK Government was found in breach of Article 2 for the killing of IRA suspects in Gibraltar.

The negative aspect of the duty will generally have less relevance in the spheres of immigration and asylum, except where immigration enforcement involves policing functions. For instance, in 1993 a woman called Joy Gardner suffocated to death when she was bound and gagged by the police Alien Deportation Group. They were arresting her in order to deport her as an overstayer. Prosecution and complaints failed. What Article 2 may add to these existing legal routes is a further element of state responsibility. If the individuals were exonerated because sufficient justification was found for their actions at the time, given their training, responses, and state of knowledge, this does not exonerate the state from providing a level of training that would prevent such incidents from occurring. In the case of *Mcann* the SAS officers were not trained to shoot to wound rather than kill. They were not held individually to blame but the state was in breach of Article 2. In the case of Joy Gardner, it seems that the officers were insufficiently aware of the effect of binding someone's head with 13 feet of surgical tape. This could suggest a similar level of state responsibility. The positive obligation also requires diligent and prompt investigation of a death at the hands of the state (*Kaya v Turkey* (1999) 28 EHRR 1).

3.6.2.3 *Article 2 and expulsions*

Article 2 is relevant in the case of threatened expulsion of someone from the UK to a risk of death. In general this refers to deliberate killing, and not to the circumstances in *N*. Earlier case law suggested that the risk of death must be 'near certain' in order to engage the responsibility of the expelling state, following a Commission decision, *Dehwari v Netherlands* (2001) 29 EHRR CD 74. The Tribunal in *Hane* [2002] UKIAT 03945 in August 2002 used this standard. However, in *A v SSHD* [2003], decided in January 2003, the Court of Appeal applied the same standard to a risk of violation of Article 2 as to Article 3, namely that there was a 'real risk'. The risk to the appellant in that case came from gang members seeking revenge for her giving a name to the police of the person she thought killed her son. There was substantial other evidence of reprisals her family had already suffered and of the risk to her life should she return to Jamaica. Note here an example of the effect of the Human Rights Act on the doctrine of precedent. Prior to a decision of the Court of Appeal there was no binding authority on the level of risk to be proved where Article 2 was applied to an expulsion because of risk of death in the receiving state (so-called 'extra-territorial application'). The Tribunal in *Hane* (for example) was obliged under HRA s 2 to take into account decisions of the Strasbourg bodies though not necessarily to follow them. They did not in fact quote *Dehwari*, but could have done, and accepted the principle from it as established. Since the UK Court of Appeal has decided the matter this is now binding on subsequent tribunals, and *Dehwari* ceases to have effect.

The case of *A* illustrates that it is immaterial whether the danger comes from the State or, as here, criminal gangs, if there is a real risk that the applicant will not be protected. This confirms the approach in *Kacaj*, referred to above, in relation to State responsibility.

3.6.2.4 *Death penalty*

If the danger to life comes from the State this may be by way of extra-judicial killing, or by the death penalty. The imposition of the death penalty raises different legal questions, which are changed and possibly simplified by the inclusion of

Protocol 13 in the Human Rights Act. The Protocol says 'The death penalty shall be abolished. No one shall be condemned to such penalty or executed'. Although this refers to the actions of the state which carries out the execution, it is also arguable that the act of expulsion 'condemns' the person to the penalty in the same way that it 'subjects' a person to treatment in breach of Article 3. A minister in a Parliamentary written answer (WA 40 28 November 2001) confirmed that there would not be expulsions to face the death penalty.

The way in which the death penalty is carried out may involve an expelling state in a breach of Article 3. This is a small extension of the outcome of *Soering*, and is demonstrated in cases such as *Jabari v Turkey* [2001] INLR 136. Here, the applicant was granted refugee status by the UNHCR in Turkey, but because she had not made her application within five days, under Turkish law she was still vulnerable to expulsion from Turkey. There was a real risk that if returned to Iran she would face death by stoning for adultery. Returning her to face this was held to be a breach of Article 3.

3.6.3 **Article 6**

3.6.3.1 *Content of the right*

Article 6, the right to a fair hearing, is one of the most litigated Articles in the Convention. It sets out minimum requirements of a fair hearing which apply to the determination of 'civil rights and obligations' and criminal trials and provides further minimum rights for a person charged with a criminal offence, for instance to have information of the charge, facilities and time for preparing a defence, and so on.

In addition to the express rights set out, Article 6 also imports a general requirement of fairness into trials, which is open to interpretation by the court. It has been held to require access to a court (*Golder v UK* (1979–80) 1 EHRR 524), the right to put one's case on equal terms with one's opponent, which may, depending on the circumstances entail the right to legal representation and the right to participate effectively in proceedings (e.g., *Goddi v Italy* (1984) 6 EHRR 457).

3.6.3.2 *Defining a 'civil right'*

Where an immigration offence such as illegal entry is charged, then Article 6 applies as to any other criminal matter. However, the vast majority of immigration issues only come within the ambit of Article 6(1) if they are regarded as civil rights. The case law to date suggests that they are not so regarded. The Court of Human Rights interprets the word 'civil' in Article 6 as equivalent to 'private' in the sense of private rather than public law. So if a matter is considered to be a public law matter it will not be regarded by the Court as civil for Article 6 purposes.

The dividing line between public and private is not clear, and the ECtHR does not necessarily take the same view as a domestic authority of what constitutes a private and what a public matter. For example, in *Salesi v Italy* (1993) 26 EHRR 187 the Court found that payment of a social security benefit falls within Article 6. In *Adams & Benn v UK* (1996) 23 EHRR 160 CD the Commission referred to personal, economic, or individual aspects as characteristic of a private law and thus a civil right. It could be argued that immigration matters have these as well as other characteristics. However, the Commission tended to focus on the administrative character of immigration matters, and thus deem them public and so not civil rights. In *Uppal v UK* (1979) 3 EHRR 391 the Commission found that decisions to deport were of an administrative nature and so not covered by Article 6(1). Extradition (*Farmakopoulous v Greece* (1990) 64 DR 52), nationality (*S v Switzerland* (1988) 59 DR 256) and entry for employment (*X v UK* 1977 9 DR 224) have all been found not to qualify as civil rights for Article 6. However, the matter was not settled by these decisions as they are all decisions of the Commission and not of the Court.

The case of *Maaouia v France* (2001) 33 EHRR 42 concerned the question of whether Article 6 applied to the rescission of an expulsion order against a foreign national. This was considered to be sufficiently important to warrant hearing by the full court. The background to the case was as follows.

Mr Maaouia was unaware of a deportation order made against him as it was not served on him. The following year he went to the Nice Centre for Administrative Formalities to regularize his immigration status and was served with the deportation order. He refused to leave the country in compliance with the order, and was sentenced to one year in prison and ten years' exclusion from French territory. He appealed through the French system against his exclusion, but his appeals were finally dismissed in 1994 on the ground that he had not challenged the deportation order in the lower courts, though it was eventually quashed because it had not been served. Mr Maaouia then applied for rescission of the exclusion order, which clearly could not stand as the deportation order on which it was based no longer existed. Rescission is a remedy available on mainly humanitarian grounds. He continued to take steps to regularize his immigration status. Eventually in 1998 the exclusion order was rescinded and he obtained a residence permit.

Mr Maaouia claimed in the ECtHR that the four-year delay in rescinding the exclusion order was unreasonable and thus a breach of Article 6 as he had not had a fair hearing within a reasonable time in determination of his civil rights (6:1).

The Court, by a majority of 15 to 2, decided that Article 6:1 did not apply. Rescission of the exclusion order was not a criminal matter because the original merits of the criminal charges were not examined. The majority also thought that the exclusion order was not a penalty but an administrative measure particular to immigration control. It was also not 'civil' within the meaning of Article 6, for two principal reasons. The first was the view which the majority took of the existence and rationale of Protocol 7 Article 1, which provides procedural safeguards relating to the expulsion of aliens. They considered that the purpose of this Protocol was to fill a gap by making provision for the protection of aliens which had not previously existed. If there had been no previous protection then it must be the case that Article 6 did not apply to aliens faced with expulsion.

The Court's second main reason was that the Commission had previously expressed a consistent view that the rights of aliens faced with expulsion were not within Article 6. This reasoning is rather disappointing. Given that the matter was referred to a full court because of its importance and the lack of previous decisions of the Court, for the Court to follow the less authoritative earlier decisions rather than to look at the matter afresh seems something of a missed opportunity.

Personal and economic effects of rescission were not considered sufficient to bring the matter within Article 6. The Court said 'the fact that the exclusion order incidentally had major repercussions on the applicant's private and family life and on his prospects of employment cannot suffice to bring those proceedings within the scope of civil rights'.

There were powerful dissenting judgments from Judges Loucaides and Traja. They suggested that insufficient attention had been paid to the history of Article 6 and to Article 31 of the Vienna Convention on the Law of Treaties. This Article requires that if a term is capable of more than one interpretation, the meaning which enhances individual rights should be preferred. Their view of the history of Article 6 was that the phrase 'civil rights and obligations' was meant to catch all non-criminal matters, rather than to develop a new and specialized meaning. The result of limiting its application to private law matters is that the individual has less protection against the power of the State than against other individuals, which is 'absurd' and flouts the purpose of the Convention. Their view of Protocol 7 was that it was designed to furnish 'additional special protection' for people liable to be expelled. It refers to administrative safeguards rather than judicial safeguards, and it is the latter which are the realm of Article 6.

The case is an interesting and important one even though its practical effects in the UK are limited. As the sole judgment on this matter of a full court, it is an important statement of the interpretation of Article 6 and reveals significant trends in judicial reasoning. In the UK *Maaouia* was applied in the starred tribunal case of *MNM v SSHD* [2000] INLR 576 and the non-applicability of Article 6 to immigration matters is treated as settled law. The majority of procedural issues which would affect a fair hearing in the immigration appeal tribunals are covered in the tribunal's procedure rules. However, its non-applicability to immigration procedure does not mean that it does not apply in related matters which may have a different claim to be called civil rights.

In the previous chapter we have already noted the case of *Harrison v SSHD* [2003] INLR 284 in which the court of Appeal held that the right to be recognized as a British citizen was not a civil right for Article 6 purposes. In *AM (Upgrade appeals: Article 6) Afghanistan* [2004] Imm AR 530 the tribunal held that an appeal by which a person with exceptional leave to remain could upgrade his status to that of refugee was not a 'civil right' and thus did not engage Article 6.

In the Court of Appeal in *A, X & Y v SSHD* [2002] EWCA Civ 1502, Woolf LJ thought that proceedings before the Special Immigration Appeals Commission were civil proceedings for the purposes of Article 6. In the House of Lords (*A and others v SSHD* [2005] UKHL 71) the question was not fully considered and so is not resolved.

3.6.4 **Article 8**

Article 8 is discussed at length here because of its central relevance to immigration and asylum cases. Its application raises all the difficult questions about proportionality and jurisdiction. Applications to enter to join family members and challenges to a removal or deportation which would break up a family are the substance of much immigration law. They may also follow unsuccessful asylum claims where a person has built up a life in the UK while waiting for their case to be determined.

Article 8 paragraph 1 provides that 'Everyone shall have the right to respect for his private and family life, his home and correspondence'.

In an immigration context the issue is rarely of interference with home or correspondence. Interference with private or family life is usually the question. These are ECHR concepts which are given their meaning by the ECtHR. In accordance with HRA s 2 the UK courts are obliged to take account of these meanings. In applying Article 8.1, two questions arise. First, is there family or private life in this situation? Second, what does respect for it entail?

3.6.4.1 *Does private or family life exist?*

Private life

The concept of private life in Article 8 is a wide one. The ECtHR in *Niemietz v Germany* (1992) 16 EHRR 97 has said that it is not possible or desirable to define all the situations to which the concept of private life can apply. In *Marckxx v Belgium* (1979) 2 EHRR 330 the Court identified the central purpose of Article 8 is to protect the individual from arbitrary interference by public authorities, and this principle may be used to help determine new situations which may come within the protection of Article 8. The range of circumstances which the Court has accepted as coming within Article 8 includes the right to have one's own body free from invasion or harm (as in, e.g., *Costello-Roberts v UK* 19 EHRR 112 in which the issue, also raised under Article 3, was corporal punishment), and self-determination (*see Pretty v UK* (2002) 35 EHRR 1 where although the court did not find in the applicant's favour, Article 8 was held to be engaged in the question of the applicant's desire to end her life in the way she chose). In *Niemietz* private life was held to 'comprise to a certain degree the right to establish and develop relationships with other human beings.' This includes the most intimate relationships as in *Dudgeon v UK* (1981) 4 EHRR 149 and may include professional relationships, especially where these are not easily separated from the rest of life. The case of *Botta v Italy* (1998) 26 EHRR 241 is one of a number of cases endorsing the principle that private life includes physical and psychological integrity.

In the UK, in the deportation appeal of *B v SSHD* [2000] Imm AR 478, Sedley LJ held that private life could include the network of everyday contacts that made up the life of a Sicilian man who had lived in the UK since the age of seven. In *Razgar* the House of Lords held that the right to respect for private life can be engaged by the foreseeable consequences for health or welfare of removal from the UK, endorsing holistic concept of private life which extends 'to those features which are integral to a person's identity or ability to function socially as a person' (para 9). Following this, where a child with a specific language impairment would have to start all over again in a country where he had no functional ability to communicate in words, it could not be said that a claim under Article 8 was manifestly unfounded (*The Queen on the application of Jegatheeswaran v SSHD* [2005] EWHC 1131 (Admin)).

Family life

Family life includes the society of close relatives. The ECtHR regards a 'lawful and genuine' marriage as amounting to family life, even if the couple have not yet been able to establish a home together (*Abdulaziz, Cabales and Balkandali v UK* and *Berrehab v Netherlands*). *J (Pakistan)* [2003] UKIAT 00167 illustrated that there must either be a valid marriage with a plan to cohabit, or a marriage which the parties believed, even if mistakenly, to be valid, with actual cohabitation. In this case (discussed further in chapter 9) the marriage had taken place by telephone and was not valid in the UK. The wife had gone to live with her mother-in-law, symbolizing the union, but, partly due to the sponsor's health, the husband and wife had not yet lived together. The tribunal held that there was no family life as required by Article 8. Aside from the controversial subject matter, this case is a clear example of an uncomplicated application of Article 8 to an entry clearance case. The parties could not succeed under the rules. The tribunal examined the matter under Article 8 and concluded that they could not succeed on that either.

Children are also regarded as having a relationship of family life with biological or adoptive parents, even if they do not live together, and the ECtHR has repeatedly held that in the absence of exceptional circumstances the parent–child relationship automatically gives rise to family life. In *Berrehab*, the parents were not married and no longer lived together. Nevertheless, the father had contact with the child four times a week for several hours at a time. The court found that family life between father and child had not been broken by the ending of the partnership between the parents. The Court of Appeal in *Singh v ECO New Delhi* [2004] EWCA Civ 1075 had to consider an application for entry clearance following an intra-family adoption which did not and never could meet the requirements of the immigration rules. The case had had a very protracted history, including a decision by the ECtHR that an application was admissible because the refusal to recognize adoptions carried out in India was prima facie discriminatory. The Court of Appeal followed the ECtHR's approach in *Lebbink v Netherlands* (Application no. 45582/99) para 36: 'The existence or non-existence of "family life" for the purposes of Article 8 is essentially a question of fact depending upon the real existence in practice of close personal ties'. It had no doubt that the substantial relationship between the child and adoptive parents amounted to family life. The fact that it did not meet the UK's stringent requirements in the immigration rules should not be allowed to impede the reality of genuine family life and entry clearance should be granted. The concept of family life must be understood in the context of the UK's multicultural society.

In *Soderback v Sweden* (2000) 29 EHRR 95 the relationship between the natural father and seven-year-old daughter was assumed to amount to family life where the parents had never been in a stable relationship and the contact between father and child was minimal for the first four years of her life and intermittent for the next four. This was a family law case, but the Immigration Appeal Tribunal has confirmed this approach to parent–child relationships, for instance in *Majji v SSHD* (01 TH 1352) where the father had had very little contact with his child.

Although the ECHR places a high value on biological fathering as the basis of the family tie, this was not the case where a child was born as a result of a sperm donation to a lesbian couple. Despite baby-sitting for seven months, the sperm donor was held by the Commission not to have established family life with the child (*G v Netherlands* (1993) 16 EHRR CD 38).

The anti-discrimination provisions of Article 14 mean that the marital status of the parents should not make any difference to the degree of respect accorded to the family under Article 8. The case of *Marckxx v Belgium* expounded on this point: 'Article 8 makes no distinction between the legitimate and illegitimate family. Such distinction would not be consonant with the word "everyone" in Article 1 and this is confirmed by Article 14 with its prohibition . . . of discrimination grounded on birth'. It seems therefore that in order to comply with Article 8, immigration law should respect the relationship between parent and child, whatever the family's marital status and whether or not they are living together.

This principle was applied to the relationships of transsexuals in *X, Y, Z v UK* (1997) 24 EHRR 143, a non-immigration case, where family life was held to exist between a woman, her child by artificial insemination by an anonymous donor, and her female-to-male transsexual partner.

Somewhat in contradiction of these principles, Commission cases have not treated couples of the same sex in the same way as married couples. In the case of *Kerkhoven v Netherlands* Application no 15666/89, the Commission found that family life did not exist between unrelated cohabitees of the same sex, but that same-sex relationships amounted to private life and therefore still attracted the protection of Article 8. In the UK the Secretary of State's decision in *R v SSHD ex p Cardoso* [2000] Imm AR 1 was taken before the Human Rights Act came into force in the UK, but taking into account the ECHR. The decision was made on the basis that family life did exist in the 17-year relationship between the applicant and his male partner, although the applicant's relationship was not treated as overriding the defects in his immigration status. There is authority of the House of Lords and Court of Appeal outside the immigration context that same sex couples should be treated as a family and equally with heterosexual couples (*Fitzpatrick v Sterling Housing Association* and *Ghaidan v Mendoza CA*). These cases concerned interpretation of the Rent Act, and are not strictly binding in a different context. However, in such a constitutionally important concept as discrimination it seems unjustifiable to maintain competing concepts of family life.

On the other hand, *dicta* in *SS (Malaysia)* show same-sex relationships treated as private life. On this basis they would still obtain the protection of Article 8, but on occasion respect for private life may not require for instance the opportunity to live together, where respect for family life might do so. Hence, there may be less protection for same-sex relationships.

It can be assumed that family life exists between brothers and sisters who are living together as children. However, in the case of adults the reality of the relationship will be relevant in determining whether there is family life. In *Moustaquim v Belgium* (1991) 13 EHRR 802 family life was held to exist between the applicant and his brothers and sisters and his parents. He was an adult no longer living with the family, but he maintained contact with them. Similarly in *Boughanemi v France* (1996) 22 EHRR 228, family life was engaged in a deportation which separated the applicant from his ten siblings who all lived in France. The Court of Appeal in *Senthuran v SSHD* [2004] EWCA Civ 950 confirmed that family life may exist between adult siblings where the requisite level of connection and dependency is present. The question depends on the facts of each case.

The evaluation of the level of contact between family members, as well as blood ties raises particular difficulties where adult children and parents are living in different countries. The UK case of *R v ECO ex p Abu-Gidary* CO 965 1999 concerned a challenge by way of judicial review to a repeated refusal of entry clearance as a visitor to a daughter who wanted to visit her ailing and elderly father. The case preceded the Human Rights Act, and Richards J did not need to come to a view as to whether the relationship between father and daughter in these circumstances amounted to family life. However, had he needed to decide the question, he 'would be reluctant to hold that the concept of family life under Article 8 does not include contact between a non-dependent and non-cohabiting daughter and her ailing father'. In this we can see that the definition of 'family life' is somewhat circumstantial as the father's illness was relevant. By way of contrast, in *E-Jannath v ECO Dhaka* [2002] UKIAT 02131 the Tribunal did not recognize family life between an 18-year-old daughter and her father in the UK with whom she had had very little contact. She argued that family life arose simply from the relationship, following ECtHR case law such as *Berrehab*. The Tribunal, however, pointed out that the Court in *Berrehab* had held that subsequent events could break the tie, and a long period in different countries with little contact had done that. This does not mean that relatives must live in the same country to enjoy family life, but just that there is 'an irreducible minimum' of actual and effective relationship (*Kugathas v SSHD* [2003] INLR 170 CA). In *Kugathas* the appellant was a man of 38 who had lived away from Sri Lanka for 17 years and had no family there. However, he had a mother, brother and sister in Germany and had lived with them before coming to the UK three years earlier. His sister had visited him and he had maintained contact by telephone. The Court of Appeal held there had been no family life with them since he left Germany. In *R (on application of Mthokozisi) v SSHD* [2004] EWHC 2964 (Admin) the court held that family life required more than the 'normal emotional ties' (following *Kugathas*) between a man of 21 and his foster parents. This seems somewhat harsh given the claimant's relative isolation in the UK, but this context does seem to be taken as relevant in many immigration cases.

In terms of other blood relationships, although they did not directly arise in the case, in *Marckxx v Belgium* the Court expressed the view that 'family life includes at least the ties between near relatives, for example grandparents and grandchildren'. This will, as the cases above demonstrate, depend on the quality of contact. In *Boyle v UK* (1994) 19 EHRR 179 family life was held to exist between an uncle and his nephew as the uncle was a father figure to his nephew, and there was substantial contact between them. In *R (on application of Kitson Locke) v SSHD* [2005] EWHC 2127 (Admin) a young man who came to live with his uncle in the UK at the age of 13 was held not to have family life with him when he was 18, though Crane J accepted that an immigration judge might view that differently.

3.6.4.2 *What does 'respect for private or family life' entail?*

Both case law (e.g., *Marckxx v Belgium*) and the wording of Article 8.1 establish that it entails some positive duty on the part of the State. While the other qualified Articles use the formula 'everyone has the right to freedom' whether of religion, expression, or assembly, Article 8 says, not that everyone has the freedom to have a family life, but that everyone has the right to 'respect for' their private or family life. This has two implications. First, Article 8 does not provide a right to establish a family life. To the extent that this is covered in the Convention it is dealt with in Article 12, the right to marry and found a family according to the laws of the host state. The Tribunal in *ECO Lagos v Imoh* [2002] UKIAT 01967 held that Article 8 cannot be used to establish family life, in that case between a four-year-old girl and her aunt whom she had only visited once. It should be recalled in this context that marriage is regarded as family life even where the couple have not yet lived together. Second, this wording implies a positive obligation on the part of the state to respect existing private and family life. In the case law on the positive obligation under Article 8, the emphasis has generally been on the requirement for the State to have in place an effective legal system and legal provisions which enable people to protect their family life. For instance, in *Marckxx v Belgium* there was no legal measure protecting the status of children in families if their parents were not married, and this was a violation of the positive duty in Article 8.

What a positive obligation of respect requires in the immigration context depends upon the situation. In *Abdulaziz* no breach of Article 8 was found because the Court held that there was no lack of respect for the family life of the applicants. The immigration rules prevented them from bringing their husbands to the UK as of right, but the State was entitled to have an immigration policy which restricted the entry of non-nationals, and the applicants were considered to have been aware of the provisions of the rules when they entered into their marriages. Respect for the right does not prevent the State from establishing provisions which conflict with family life if such provisions maintain an appropriate balance between private and public interests. The Court in *Abdulaziz* found that respect does not necessarily entail enabling a family to establish themselves in the country of their choice. There were no significant obstacles, the Court said, to the applicants establishing family life in the home countries of their husbands.

This leaves open the possibility that in certain factual situations where there are such obstacles that the respect for family life might entail permitting a family to be united in the UK. Such was the case in *R v SSHD ex p Arman Ali* [2000] Imm AR 134, heard before the Human Rights Act came into force, but applying Article 8. For economic reasons, the family could only be together in the UK, thus to deny entry to the applicant's wife and children breached Article 8.

As the Court said in *Abdulaziz*, however, the notion of respect is not clear cut, and what it requires will vary from case to case. The question of whether there are significant obstacles to the family living together outside the UK should not be elevated to a general principle which determines whether there has been a lack of respect for family life. This point was made by Pill LJ in *Husna Begum v ECO Dhaka* [2001] INLR 115, a Court of Appeal case decided after the Human Rights Act came into effect. The case used pre-Act law as the decision appealed was before 2 October 2000, but the Court of Appeal employed Article 8 in its judgment as it had formed part of the reasoning of the IAT. The question of whether the family could have lived together in Bangladesh was inappropriate as most of the family had legitimately gained entry to the UK under the rules. To in effect try to reverse history would punish the appellant (who had not gained entry) for their successful application and was not the right approach to her right to respect for her family life. The appellant's actual circumstances must be the basis of the decision.

Finally, just as the definition of 'family life' does not rely on cohabitation (*Berrehab*), so the respect accorded does not necessarily entail the opportunity of cohabitation, but rather of the level of contact appropriate to the relationship. So in *Abu-Gidary*, what would have been required was the capacity to visit, in *Husna Begum* what was required was the opportunity to live within the sphere of protection of the family. Respect for private life may not entail the opportunity of cohabitation at all.

In *ECO Dhaka v Shamim Box* [2002] UKIAT 02212 the tribunal held that the positive duty of respect is engaged by entry applications and the negative duty, to refrain from interference with family life, is engaged in removal and deportation. This received a tentative endorsement from the Court of Appeal in *Kugathas*. It also said, endorsing *Box* more wholeheartedly on this point, that 'the approach to

Article 8 in the case of an entry decision is different from the approach in a removal case' (para 15). The 'underlying criteria', however, would be the same.

3.6.4.3 *Has there been an interference with the right?*

The next question in applying Article 8 is whether there has been an interference with the right to respect for private or family life. There is normally little doubt about the act of interference in the immigration context. It is likely to be a refusal of entry clearance or a decision to remove or deport. It has also been held that a requirement to move to another town pursuant to the policy of dispersing asylum seekers could be such an interference (*R (on the application of Blackwood) v SSHD* [2003] EWHC 98 TLR 10/2/03). The dispersal was held in that case to interfere with the claimant's psychological integrity and thus her private life.

An important decision was made by the European Court of Human Rights in *Sisojeva v Latvia* Application no. 60654/00. The family had lived in Latvia for some 30 years. Mr Sisojev was a soldier in the Soviet army stationed in Latvia. His wife joined him and their child was born there. Following the break-up of the Soviet Union and Latvian independence in 1991, the family became stateless and there followed a series of conflicting administrative decisions about their rights to remain in Latvia and to be issued with Russian or Latvian passports. The European Court of Human Rights found that prolonged refusal to recognize a family's right to permanent residence in Latvia constituted an interference with their right to respect for their family life. The full judgment is available only in French, but a summary may be read in English in the press release issued by Registrar at press.coe.int/cp/2005/333a(2005).htm

3.6.4.4 *Can the interference be justified?*

This is the main question in the majority of Article 8 cases. It is governed by Article 8.2 which may be regarded, like the other qualified rights, as having the following substantive requirements. The interference with the right, to be permitted, must be:

- in accordance with the law;
- in pursuit of a legitimate aim;
- necessary in a democratic society in the interests of that aim;
- proportionate to the aim pursued.

Finally, the reasons given by the state must be relevant and sufficient (*Handyside v UK*). These are established principles of Convention case law, referred to in almost every ECtHR case decided using the qualified rights. According to the ECtHR in *Smith and Grady v UK* (1999) 29 EHRR 493, these principles 'lie at the heart of the Court's analysis of complaints under Article 8 of the Convention' (para 138). We shall consider each in turn.

In accordance with the law

This has the same meaning as 'prescribed by law', which is the wording used in the other qualified Articles and generally discussed in case law. It requires that the provision which interferes with the right not only complies with domestic law, but also that the law itself is accessible (*Silver v UK* (1983) 5 EHRR 347) and precise enough to enable an individual to regulate their conduct accordingly (*Sunday Times v UK* (1979) 2 EHRR 245). In immigration and asylum cases this requirement is very rarely an issue. The interference normally arises from the application of statute or rules, which easily meet these criteria. A rare case of an immigration provision not being 'in accordance with the law' was *KK (Jamaica)* [2004] UKIAT 00268 which concerned the concession that children under 12 only needed to show adequate accommodation with their parent in order to obtain settlement. The terms of the concession were held to be insufficiently precise as it was not clear whether it only applied to entry clearance cases, nor whether the applicant had to be informed that the concession applied to them.

In pursuit of a legitimate aim

This requirement is rarely the subject of case law, but in immigration cases it plays a significant role. The legitimate aims are listed in para 2 of the qualified Articles. They differ slightly as between the different qualified rights, and in the case of Article 8 are as follows:

National security, public safety or the economic well-being of the country, for the prevention of disorder or crime, for the protection of health or morals, or for the protection of the rights and freedoms of others.

This list of aims is said to be exhaustive. The Court in *Golder v UK* said that the words 'There shall be no interference . . . except such as . . .' left 'no room for the concept of implied limitations' (para 44). Article 18 provides that restrictions on Convention rights cannot be used for any purposes other than those prescribed. Indeed for this to be otherwise would subvert the purpose of the Convention, which is to control the situations in which governments can legitimately interfere with the rights of individuals. The aims listed are quite wide in their coverage, and it is not usually problematic for a Government to bring their action within them. In relation to immigration control, Blake and Husain (2003:190) summarize the position as follows:

Immigration control has consistently been held by the European Court to relate to the preservation of the economic well-being of the country, the prevention of disorder or crime, the protection of health and morals, and the protection of the rights and freedoms of others. Exclusions and expulsions of illegal entrants are therefore likely to fall easily within a permissible competing interest under Article 8(2). It is important to note that immigration control is not of itself a valid end capable of justifying an interfering measure; it is rather the medium through which other legitimate aims are promoted.

The identification of the legitimate aim is a fundamental requirement for considering proportionality. Without identifying the legitimate aim there is nothing to which the interference must be proportionate. This was demonstrated in *Abdulaziz*, in which the government argued that the economic well-being of the country was preserved by having an immigration policy which limited access to the job market. Evidence was presented of unemployment rates. The ECtHR accepted the validity of the objective, but in the light of the evidence held that this did not justify sex discrimination.

In UK case law the matter of legitimate aim has often been neglected entirely. Quite often, immigration control has been cited as a legitimate aim without further discussion. When it has been raised the treatment has often been marked by substantial confusion, for instance, in *SSHD v Vandi* [2002] UKIAT 05755. Here, the Tribunal said 'there can be no doubt that the maintenance of immigration control falls within two of the legitimate aims set out in Article 8.2, the economic well-being of the country and the prevention of disorder or crime' (para 9). The appellant might have been surprised to learn that her removal could be said to be for the prevention of crime, she herself having a strong family life, employment record, connections with the church, and no criminal involvement. In effect the Tribunal treated immigration control as a legitimate aim in itself. It did so explicitly in *Milanovic* 01 TH 01556. Here, the Tribunal overturned an adjudicator's decision on the basis that he had, 'apparently unaware of a long line of European jurisprudence to the contrary before and after *Berrehab v Netherlands* (1989) 11 EHRR 322, held that maintenance of an effective system of immigration control was not within the legitimate objects of interference laid down by Article 8.2'. This is a most unfortunate interpretation of *Berrehab*, where the ECtHR was at pains explicitly to identify the appropriate legitimate aim, correcting the reasoning of the Nether-lands Government and the Commission on this point. The immigration policy in question was concerned with regulating the labour market, and so was for the preservation of the economic well-being of the country (*Berrehab* para 26). There are signs that the tribunal is beginning to take seriously the need to identify the appropriate legitimate aim. The importance of this was recognized in *CW (Jamaica)* [2005] UKIAT 00110 in which the adjudicator

analysed some of the issues which were relevant to the prevention of crime, i.e. the nature and gravity of offending, but his conclusions on the risk of re-offending are not easy to discern. This may be because he focused on the wrong aim. It is difficult to be satisfied that the proportionality balance was weighed appropriately, according to law, if the wrong public interest was put into the scales. (para 26)

The reason that immigration control is not of itself a legitimate aim is illustrated in the case of *SSHD v Mobin Jagot* [2000] Imm AR 414. Article 8 was raised in *Mobin Jagot*, but it was not decided on that basis. Use was made of the policy document DP 069/99 in considering whether removal of a child was justified. The document allowed disruption to the child's family life if 'strong reasons' justified it. The Secretary of State argued that immigration control was just such a strong reason. However, the Court of Appeal pointed out that a breach of immigration control was the basis for invoking the policy. It was inherent in the policy that the person whose family life was under threat was in breach of immigration control. Therefore immigration control in itself could not amount to a 'strong reason'. Similarly, in a case decided on the basis of Article 8, if there were no attempts to enforce immigra-tion control, there would be no interference with family life. To cite immigration control as a legitimate aim in an immigration case is circular and does not assist.

Yet another approach was used by the Court of Appeal in *Ullah and Do*:

44. In *Abdulaziz* as in all similar Article 8 cases, the Court has been astute to recognise the right under international law of a state to control immigration into its territory. This right has been weighed against the degree of interference with the enjoyment of family life caused by the immigration restriction often, as we see it, not because this served a legitim-ate aim under Article 8(2), but because it acted as a free-standing restriction on the Article 8 right.

This proposal for the State's right to control immigration as an unwritten exception to human rights protection was reversed by the House of Lords.

There must be a rational connection between the aim and the means by which it is pursued (*de Freitas v Permanent Secretary of Ministry of Agriculture, Fisheries, Lands and Housing* [1999] 1 AC 69). This means not just that the aim generally is a legitimate one, but that it can be served by interfering with individual rights in this particular case.

Investigating the rationality of the connection between the aim and the measures employed, the Court may consider that the margin of discretion requires it to defer to the judgment of the more expert primary decision-maker. A leading case in point is *Samaroo* [2001] UKHRR 1150 in which there was uncontested evidence that Mr Samaroo was a model prisoner, unlikely to re-offend, with a strong family life, and many years' residence in the UK. It was argued for the appellant that his deportation was not necessary for the prevention of crime, as no future crime would be committed by him. The Court of Appeal, however, accepted the Secretary of State's argument that the deportation was not because he would re-offend, but because it was necessary to deter other people from committing drugs offences. The court is an expert in the question of deterrence as applies to the individual, but the Secretary of State had a greater knowledge of the overall policy matter of deterrence in relation to drug crimes.

Necessity in a democratic society

The question of whether the interference is necessary in a democratic society was said by the ECtHR in *Smith and Grady* to be the core of rights protection. Necessity has been equated with serving a 'pressing social need' (*Sunday Times v UK*). There is a question as to the relationship of this requirement with that of proportionality. Is it the same thing in different words? The approach suggested here is to treat the question of proportionality as additional to the question of necessity. This will sometimes be seen in the judgments of the ECtHR, though sometimes one question seems to flow into the other. The questions to be asked by a decision-maker are, firstly, is it necessary to interfere with this person's rights in order to achieve a legitimate aim? If it is, is the *actual* interference proportionate to this aim? Finally, are the reasons advanced by the state relevant and sufficient to support that interference? For further discussion of this issue, see Fasti (2002).

The question of necessity is considered in the context of a democratic society. The characteristics of a democratic society according to the ECtHR are tolerance, pluralism, broad-mindedness, and willingness to tolerate ideas that shock or offend (*Handyside v UK*). These qualities are derived from the context of freedom of expression cases, and have limited relevance to the immigration sphere. However, it is relevant that a democratic society is evidently not one in which all people think or behave in the same way. Necessity should be distinguished from reasonableness. The priority is given to the right, the interference permitted by paragraph 2 is the exception rather than the rule. This was explicitly stated in *Sunday Times v UK*, but in principle applies to all the qualified rights.

What is proportionality?

Proportionality is a relatively new concept in UK law, though it is established in some other countries and in the ECHR and in European law. It began to play a small part in judicial review, but its use was marginal until the advent of the Human Rights Act 1998. It is therefore appropriate and necessary to look outside the UK's domestic case law for some guidance as to the nature of proportionality.

A classic formulation of proportionality, consistent with the approach used in

European law, may be found in *de Freitas*, which was a Privy Council case from Antigua and Barbuda. Here, Lord Clyde observed, at p. 80, that in determining whether a limitation on a right was arbitrary or excessive the court should ask itself:

whether: (i) the legislative objective is sufficiently important to justify limiting a fundamental right; (ii) the measures designed to meet the legislative objective are rationally connected to it; and (iii) the means used to impair the right or freedom are no more than is necessary to accomplish the objective.

In the context of Convention rights, point (i) here overlaps with the question of necessity in a democratic society. The second and third points are a useful guide in considering the question of whether an infringement of a right is proportionate to the aim pursued. Proportionality requires a rational connection between the interference and the aim pursued, and that the interference is no more than is necessary.

Proportionality is very fact-specific. It is only possible to form a judgement about the infringement of an individual's rights in the light of all the circumstances of a particular case. Often in judgments one sees the phrase 'in all the circumstances'. In the context of proportionality these are not empty words but may actually be the nub of the issue. It may be justifiable policy in general to remove people who have entered the UK illegally, and still disproportionate in a particular case, given that person's situation. This is not to say that proportionality is an opportunity to make an exception to policy. It is the opposite. Where human rights are concerned, even within the context of a policy, the state must justify an infringement on the merits of the individual case.

A common example of the need for proportionality — expulsion and family life
There is a substantial body of case law in the ECtHR applying the principle of proportionality in the expulsion of individuals with a settled family life. In the ECtHR such cases commonly concern the expulsion of people who have been found guilty of criminal offences, though they arise in other circumstances too, *Berrehab* being one such example. The many cases coming before UK courts and tribunals more often concern expulsion of those who have entered illegally and who no longer have any immigration or asylum law claim to stay. Typically there is no criminal involvement and the individual is not considered any threat to public order or safety.

In *Boultif v Switzerland* the Court laid down some guiding principles in cases of actual or threatened expulsion where there are obstacles to a couple or family continuing their family life in another country. The Court set out to identify relevant factors in considering whether the exclusion of Mr Boultif was necessary in a democratic society, and ended by concluding that his exclusion was disproportionate. The particular factors listed in the case are not all applicable where no criminal offence has been committed, but they provide a good example of the fact-specific nature of the proportionality exercise.

. . . the Court will consider the nature and seriousness of the offence committed by the applicant; the length of the applicant's stay in the country from which he is going to be expelled; the time elapsed since the offence was committed as well as the applicant's conduct in that period; the nationalities of the various persons concerned; the applicant's family situation, such as the length of the marriage; and other factors expressing the effectiveness of a couple's family life; whether the spouse knew about the offence at the time when he or she entered into a family relationship; and whether there are children in the marriage, and if so, their age.

Not least, the Court will also consider the seriousness of the difficulties which the spouse is likely to encounter in the country of origin, though the mere fact that a person might face certain difficulties in accompanying her or his spouse cannot in itself exclude an expulsion. (para 48)

There are numerous earlier cases assessing some of these factors, though trends are not always easy to identify precisely because decision-making is so fact-specific. Long residence in the state is often regarded as very important. See, for instance, *Beldjoudi v France* (1992) 14 EHRR 801 in which a life of crime was not sufficient to outweigh the fact that the applicant had spent almost all his life in France, and had a French wife with whom his marriage would probably be destroyed if he were deported. On the other hand, in *Boughanemi v France* the retention of links with Tunisia meant that the deportation was proportionate, though in other respects the facts were quite similar. Warbrick (1998) criticizes the decision on this basis. *Beldjoudi* is probably more indicative of the Court's approach. The seriousness of a crime is a relevant factor, but again it must be weighed against other consider-ations. In *Bouchelkia v France* (1998) 25 EHRR 686 the applicant had lived in France since the age of two, and was living with his family of origin, but the ECtHR held that his deportation following conviction for rape was proportionate. In *Nasri v France* (1996) 21 EHRR 458 the applicant had been involved in a gang rape, and some petty offences. He was deaf and mute, and the ECtHR held that to deport him would interfere with his right to respect for family and private life under Article 8(1). In *Yildiz v Austria* [2003] 2 FCR 182 the court took account of the fact that the applicant's traffic convictions not only were not particularly serious, but also were unlikely to pose a threat to public order.

The approach of the ECtHR ranges between a search for principles respecting the lives of integrated aliens, to that exemplified in the minority judgment of Judge Pettiti in *Beldjoudi* that only Article 3 was capable of interfering with the State's right to deport an alien. There is however a development towards considering the actual harm which would be inflicted by continuing residence, rather than just looking at a criminal history. Rogers (2003) identifies a trend towards a more real-istic assessment of the difficulties facing family members required to relocate and that *Boultif* gives some indication of this. She says: 'The judgement is significant for its recognition that in cases where there are real barriers such as lack of ties for some of the family members or language difficulties, the Court is likely to conclude that the family cannot be expected to follow the deportee' (p. 62).

It is instructive to consider how the tension between immigration control and family life is treated in the context of European free movement law. Here, following the Treaty on European Union, ECHR rights must be applied. In C-60/00 *Carpenter Case* a factual situation similar to many non-European Article 8 claims, the ECJ did not regard the immigration breach as particularly worth dwelling on by com-parison with the disproportionate upheaval in the appellant's family life. The maintenance of immigration control for its own sake, where no other damage was anticipated, was not regarded as important enough to outweigh fundamental rights.

To summarize this and the previous section, the question of whether an infringement with a right is proportionate is answered by balancing the actual effect on the individual against the aim sought to be achieved by expelling them or refusing them entry as the case may be. For the interference to be permitted by the

Convention Article it must be rationally connected with the aim (for instance prevention of crime), and no more invasive of the individual's rights than is necessary to achieve the aim. The question of proportionality involves a close examination of facts but it is not a factual question, it is a judgment based upon an investigation into facts. In *A and X v SSHD* Lord Bingham said: 'The European Court does not approach questions of proportionality as questions of pure fact ... Nor should domestic courts do so' (para 44).

Expulsion and family life — the case of Mahmood

In the first few years following the commencement of the Human Rights Act the application of Article 8 to immigration cases was dominated by the case of *Mahmood*. Although express references to it are now less common, the case has deeply affected the development of the law in this area. It may be recalled that the case concerned the removal of a man who had entered the UK illegally, made an unsuccessful claim for asylum, and while it was being considered had obtained a job, married a British citizen, and had two children. The case came to the Court of Appeal as an appeal against a refusal of an application for judicial review of the Secretary of State's decision to remove Mr Mahmood as an illegal entrant. The Court declined to give judgment on the question of proportionality. Laws and May LJJ made their decision on the basis of the common law, which did not involve a question of proportionality. The Master of the Rolls made his decision on the basis that proportionality was a question for the Secretary of State. However, he reviewed a number of ECtHR cases concerned with conflicts between immigration control and family life, and from these drew some conclusions as to the approach of the Commission and the Court to a conflict between the respect for family life and 'the enforcement of immigration controls' (para 55):

(1) A state has a right under international law to control the entry of non-nationals into its territory, subject always to its treaty obligations.

(2) Article 8 does not impose on a state any general obligation to respect the choice of residence of a married couple.

(3) Removal or exclusion of one family member from a state where other members of the family are lawfully resident will not necessarily infringe Article 8 provided that there are no insurmountable obstacles to the family living together in the country of origin of the family member excluded, even where this involves a degree of hardship for some or all members of the family.

(4) Article 8 is likely to be violated by the expulsion of a member of a family that has been long established in a state if the circumstances are such that it is not reasonable to expect the other members of the family to follow that member expelled.

(5) Knowledge on the part of one spouse at the time of marriage that rights of residence of the other were precarious militates against a finding that an order excluding the latter spouse violates Article 8.

(6) Whether interference with family rights is justified in the interests of controlling immigration will depend on:
  (i) the facts of the particular case, and
  (ii) the circumstances prevailing in the state whose action is impugned.

The Master of the Rolls approached the case as though the Human Rights Act was in force, and engaged in this review of ECtHR case law having noted that HRA s 2 required him to take ECtHR jurisprudence into account. He therefore bore these six points in mind when coming to his decision on the reasonableness of the Secretary of State's decision (para 40).

These points, which draw quite strongly on *Abdulaziz*, a case on entry, were widely followed by tribunals deciding appeals against removals. Despite the Master of the Rolls having expressly disavowed any intention of applying the test of proportionality for himself, in the first few years following the commencement of the Human Rights Act they were often used as 'important and indeed vital guidelines providing the framework for the determination of Article 8 appeals' (*Arslan v SSHD* [2002] UKIAT 00699). It appeared that following *Mahmood* became a substitute for taking relevant ECtHR cases into account and for carrying out an assessment of the proportionality of the interference in the particular case. This question is considered further below in the context of the jurisdiction of tribunals

Delay

Delay in enforcement or in processing an application may have a major effect on the lives of applicants, and the appellant may accrue rights partly because of the time taken in dealing with their claim. There is authority, *Shala v SSHD* [2003] EWCA Civ 233, that delay is a relevant factor in the question of proportionality. Examples from the Tribunal suggest that not only the effect of delay is relevant but also whether the appellant or the Home Office is responsible for it. In *Shala* delay by the Home Office affected the outcome as it meant that the application was not dealt with under an earlier policy that ethnic Albanians from Kosovo would generally be granted asylum. In *Oghenekaro* 00/TH/00682 the tribunal concluded deportation was not proportionate because the Home Office had not taken any enforcement action for eight years until the appellant herself took steps to try to regularize her position. It was disproportionate to support the Home Office's enforcement procedure at great cost to the appellant's family life when the Home Office itself had not taken steps promptly to remove her. A long stay in the UK may of course arise because of persistent evasion of immigration control. The Court of Appeal in *R (on the application of Ekinci) v SSHD* [2003] EWCA Civ 765 held that immigration history was a relevant factor in balancing an interference with private life against the public interest. However, in *ul-Haq v SSHD* [2002] UKIAT 04685 the Tribunal held that despite a 'shocking immigration history', as the Home Office had taken no steps to enforce his departure until his wife was expecting their third baby, it would now be disproportionate to allow them to proceed. In *K (Russia)* [2004] UKIAT 00082 the tribunal held that the appellant should not benefit from the four-year delay by the Home Office because her claim was entirely false, and this was relevant to the question of proportionality. There is an implicit distinction here between an unsuccessful claim and one based on falsehood, but it would be rash to rely on such a distinction in a human rights appeal without clear proof (see *Khawaja*).

The trend since *Shala* has been to distinguish it as turning on its own facts, as in *Janjanin v SSHD* [2004] EWCA Civ 448 where delay was held to be a relevant factor in proportionality, though not enough to change the outcome. In *Alihajdaraj v SSHD* [2004] EWCA Civ 1084 the appellant would have qualified under the same policy as Mr Shala, but in his case of lesser delay the Court of Appeal held that he could not succeed. On the basis of changing policies in relation to return of Croatian Serbs a number of Croatian appellants attempted to follow *Shala* and failed. In *M (Croatia)* the tribunal held that the change in wording in policy from a 'general presumption' in favour of Serbian claims to a 'likelihood' that they could be established had not deprived M of refugee status.

Sometimes delay takes a claim out of the ambit of a policy, but not because the policy itself changes. For instance, in *Mthokozisi* a delay of four years meant that the claimant did not have his claim decided while still a minor and thus lost the opportunity to apply for indefinite leave to remain, which would probably have been granted. The refusal of his claim was quashed.

A striking case of delay is that of *R (on the application of N) v SSHD* [2003] TLR 7 March, in which atrocious delays and the service of a removal notice despite a policy not to return failed asylum seekers to Libya because of the risk of ill-treatment on return, resulted in an award of damages for breach of positive duties under Articles 3 and 8.

The situation may be summarized by reference to *Strbac v SSHD* [2005] EWCA Civ 848 in which the Court of Appeal resisted an attempt to extract a formula from *Shala*. Delay may be a relevant element in assessing proportionality. It depends on all the circumstances.

3.6.5 Other qualified rights

Article 10, which protects freedom of expression, is regarded as one of the most central Articles of the Convention. It protects freedom of expression in written or spoken words, action, and through any medium such as theatre, film, photography, or painting. A rare application to immigration law arose in *Farrakhan* [2002] 3 WLR 481 where it was held that refusal of entry to the Nation of Islam leader Louis Farrakhan for a speaking tour did not breach his right to freedom of expression. An important question was whether Article 10 was engaged at all prior to his entry to the country. The Secretary of State accepted that the fact that Mr Farrakhan 'was neither a citizen of a Member State nor within the territory of a Member State did not of itself preclude the application of the Convention' (para 34). However, the Secretary of State withdrew the concession that had been made in the court below that Article 10 was engaged in this case. The Court of Appeal, relying on the ECtHR cases of *Piermont v France* [1995] 20 EHRR 301, *Swami Omkarananda and Divine light Zentrum v Switzerland* (1997) 25 DR 105 and *Adams and Benn v UK* (1997) 88A DR 137, held that where an immigration decision was made with the purpose of preventing the exercise of Article 10 rights, then the Article is engaged. Where the decision was not for this reason, but, for instance, as in *Farrakhan*, to prevent public disorder, and the right to freedom of expression was indirectly affected, then that Article was 'in play' (para 62). To the extent that the Article was in play the Court of Appeal thought that the Secretary of State had just about justified its restriction.

The Court of Appeal's decision in *Farrakhan* is not easy to understand. The ECtHR jurisprudence relied on concerned the application to immigration decisions of Article 10, but in these cases the applicant was in the Contracting State at the time of the decision. It therefore seems that the Court of Appeal did not decide that

Article 10 applied to entry decisions, because this is what was conceded. This was the conclusion, after argument, of the tribunal in *Rev Sun Myung Moon USA* v *ECO Seoul* [2005] UKIAT 00112 in which the application of Articles 9, 10, 11, and 14 to a refusal of entry fell directly for decision.

The situation therefore now seems to be that an immigration decision, such as deportation, may engage a qualified right such as Article 10 if the reason for exercising the immigration power is to prevent the exercise of that right. This would be, for instance, as in *Piermont v France*, where the detention of the applicant with a view to deportation prevented her from talking with the politicians who had invited her to speak. Without such a connection between the exercise of the immigration power and the right, the qualified right does not protect the applicant's stay in a country (*Agee v* UK (1976) 7 DR 164). This does no more than say that foreign nationals are protected by human rights law and immigration decisions are not exempt from it. Where an expulsion decision threatens a qualified right in the destination country, *Ullah and Do* is authority that in the case of a real risk of a fundamental breach, the qualified right may protect from the exclusion. Where an individual seeks to enter a country to exercise a qualified right, *Moon* suggests that they have no human rights appeal against refusal, aside from Article 8. However, this should be seen in the light of the discussion of the application of human rights to entry decisions above, and the question is not authoritatively concluded.

3.6.6 **Other derogable rights**

Article 12 provides that:

'Men and women of marriageable age have the right to marry and to found a family according to the national laws governing the exercise of this right.'

In *Abdulaziz, Cababales and Balkandali v UK* the right to marry and found a family was considered to encompass the right to live together, otherwise the notion of a family becomes rather meaningless. The Court in the same case, however, held that this did not include the right to live in the country of the applicant's choice, and so the right to live with one's family is regarded as subordinate to the State's right to regulate immigration, and cannot necessarily be used to support a family reunion application in an immigration context. It also cannot be used to establish a right of entry for a spouse married according to traditions regarded as unlawful in the UK, for instance, the marriage of a person under the age of 16. The Article expressly provides only the right to marry 'according to the national laws governing the exercise of this right'. This means according to the national laws of the country where Article 12 is or would be invoked, not the laws of the country where the marriage took place.

Article 13 of the Convention provides a right to an effective remedy and is not included in the scope of the HRA. The Government justified its omission by arguing that the Act itself was the guarantee of a remedy, but its omission may exclude the greater opportunity for judicial creativity which would have been generated by the right to a remedy.

Article 14 is potentially of wide application. The full text of Article 14 is:

The enjoyment of the rights and freedoms set forth in this Convention shall be secured without discrimination on any ground such as sex, race, colour, language, religion, political or other opinion, nationality or social origin, association with a national minority, birth or other status.

Article 14, as discussed above, was successfully used by the applicants in *Abdulaziz, Cabales and Balkandali v UK*. In that case the applicants succeeded in pleading sex discrimination in the application of Article 8 rights, even though no breach of Article 8 was found.

Article 14 guarantees non-discrimination in the delivery of the other Convention rights, but is not a free-standing right. In order to lodge a claim under Article 14 it is necessary that discrimination is alleged in some area that is within the ambit of one of the other Convention rights. For instance, in *Abdulaziz*, the applicants alleged that the immigration rules interfered with their Article 8 rights to family life and discriminated against them as women because it would have been easier for men to bring their spouses into the country. The Court found in their favour on the discrimination issue but not on the family life issue as it was not impossible for them to set up family life in another country. So, while UK immigration law treated men more favourably than women, it did not prevent people from establishing their family as they could do that elsewhere. It was necessary to claim under Article 14 that the Article 8 issue of the interference with family life was involved, but there did not need to have been a violation of Article 8 in order for the applicants to succeed under Article 14.

Discrimination for Article 14 entails a difference in treatment which is not based upon 'an objective and reasonable justification' and is not proportionate to the social objective of that difference in treatment. These principles were established in the *Belgian Linguistics case (No 2)* (1968) 1 EHRR 252. Although the wording of Article 14 makes no reference to any defences or justification, this potential defence is held to be inherent in the concept of discrimination, i.e., it is differential treatment which cannot be justified. The principles of discrimination and its justification are not fully developed in the law of the ECHR, but by analogy with cases in the European Court of Justice the defence must be strictly construed, and the justification must exist independently of any discriminatory reasoning (Case 170/84 *Bilka Kaufhaus GmbH v Weber von Hartz* [1986] ECR 1607).

In UK law a distinction is made between direct discrimination, which entails that one group is treated less favourably than another (e.g., men are paid more than women for the same work) and indirect discrimination, which entails that a requirement or condition is applied equally to all groups but has a disproportionate impact on one group (e.g., part-time workers have fewer rights, but more part-time workers are women, so women are indirectly discriminated against). Neither European law nor the law of the ECtHR expressly distinguishes between direct and indirect discrimination. In Article 14 arguments there is therefore no need to make this distinction.

The most significant decision on Article 14 in recent times concerned not immigration, but why it was discriminatory to categorize an issue as one of immigration. The challenge by those detained under the powers of indefinite detention in the Anti-terrorism, Crime and Security Act 2001 was mounted partly on the basis that the statutory power was discriminatory as it allowed the detention of only foreign nationals (*A v SSHD* [2004] UKHL 56). The Government's case was that the power was not discriminatory because these detainees could not be deported because they faced a real risk of treatment contrary to Article 3, and the relevant comparison was with non-UK nationals who could be deported. The House of Lords accepted the appellants' argument that the appropriate comparator for the purpose of assessing discrimination was a British suspected international terrorist. The difference in treatment between British and non-British suspects (i.e., the detention) had no bearing on the objective of defeating terrorism but was purely immigration or nationality related, an impermissible basis under Article 14. The Home Office's proposed comparator group were not the appropriate ones because they did not share the most relevant characteristics of the appellants, namely non-removability. British nationals did share that characteristic, and to say that they were not comparable because they had a right of abode whereas the appellants could not be removed, as did the Court of Appeal, was to accept the Secretary of State's treatment of the matter as an immigration issue, which it patently was not. The decision is discussed again in chapter 15.

In the actual immigration context, bringing immigration decisions within the ambit of the Race Relations Act 1976 has had significant ramifications. This is discussed in chapter 8.

Article 5 protects the right to liberty and security of person and is discussed in chapter 15. It is the Article from which the UK has derogated on a number of occasions. The first derogations were all in relation to overseas territories during their struggles for independence. Later, there was a derogation from Article 5 in relation to detention in Northern Ireland. This was withdrawn as part of the peace process. In 2001 there was the derogation discussed above in relation to 'international terrorists, also' discussed further in chapter 15.

The UK Government has no plans to sign Protocol 12 ECHR, which provides for a free-standing right not to be discriminated against in any action by a public authority and in delivery of 'rights set forth by law' (see their response to the Parliamentary Joint Committee on Human Rights report on the International Covenant on Economic Social and Cultural Rights, Eighth Report session 2005–06 HC 850 HL paper 104).

3.7 Jurisdiction to decide human rights issues

We now return to the issues of jurisdiction raised at the beginning of this chapter. We have considered some of the substantive human rights law applicable in immigration cases, but we have not yet considered the crucial question — who decides?

The primary decisions are made by immigration officers and Home Office civil servants, and these are public authorities charged with the duty under s 6 HRA to act in a way that upholds human rights. However, what happens when they do not? If an affected applicant can appeal to a body that can consider the whole case and come to a view on whether rights have been upheld, then there is a form of redress, and initial decision-makers will be aware that decisions which infringe rights may be overturned. If, however, the hands of appeal bodies are tied, there is no effective redress for applicants, and even with goodwill on the part of the initial decision-makers, there is less incentive for their decisions to give proper weight to rights.

These questions will be considered in the context of two questions:

- What is the scope of judicial review in a human rights case?
- What is the scope of an appeal body hearing an immigration and human rights appeal?

3.7.1 Scope of judicial review

One of the key issues in post-Human Rights Act jurisprudence, and of great importance in immigration and asylum law, is the question of what impact the Act has
had on the powers of the court in judicial review. Broadly speaking, there are three
possible models of the court's jurisdiction in judicial review in a human rights case.
The first is the conventional *Wednesbury* model, following *Associated Provincial
Picture Houses v Wednesbury Corporation* [1948] 1 KB 223. A decision which is
Wednesbury unreasonable is 'so unreasonable that no reasonable authority could
ever have come to it'. The excesses of language vary, but the key point is that in
using this approach the court asks whether the decision was within the range of
reasonable responses. The underlying rationale of the *Wednesbury* test is that Parliament has entrusted the executive with the particular power of decision-making,
and the role of the judiciary is supervisory.

The second model is known as 'anxious scrutiny' or 'heightened scrutiny' or
'super-*Wednesbury*'. This requires that a greater intensity of review is applied when
fundamental rights are at stake. Its origins can be traced to an asylum case: *Bugdaycay v SSHD* [1987] AC 514 HL. It was recognized by the Court of Appeal in the
pre-Human Rights Act era in *R v Ministry of Defence ex p Smith* [1996] 1 All ER 257,
which challenged the ban on homosexuals in the armed forces. Following this case
the concept gained currency, having not really 'taken off' after *Bugdaycay*. It was
developed in the application for anonymity by soldiers testifying to the Saville
Inquiry on the events of Bloody Sunday: *R v Lord Saville ex p A* [1999] 4 All ER 860,
and was given a formulation there which was repeated in subsequent cases:

it is not open to a reasonable decision-maker to risk interfering with fundamental rights in
the absence of compelling justification. Even the broadest discretion is constrained by the
need for there to be countervailing circumstances justifying interference with human rights.
(p. 872)

This may be seen to be an elaboration and refinement of the *Wednesbury* doctrine as
it is couched in terms of reasonableness. However, it takes away the breadth of
discretion of the executive where fundamental rights are at stake. It also shows the
influence of the ECtHR and of the third approach, the proportionality approach, in
that it introduces the need for specific countervailing factors. In other words, where
the executive proposes to interfere with fundamental rights, for instance the police
to arrest and detain someone, they cannot do so without specific reasons which
justify that action. The more substantial the interference with fundamental rights,
the more the court would require by way of justification before it could be satisfied
that the interference was reasonable (e.g., in *R v Secretary of State for the Home
Department ex p Simms* [2000] 2 AC 115). This approach was espoused by Laws LJ in
Mahmood.

The third approach is the proportionality approach, as we have seen, an established doctrine in European law and as a central principle of the ECHR now an

ineradicable part of UK law. The meaning of proportionality in judicial review was set out by Lord Steyn in the House of Lords in *R (on the application of Daly) v SSHD* [2001] 2 WLR 1622. He first of all noted that there can be an overlap between proportionality and the common law approach. The decision that the rule in issue violated a prisoner's right had already been reached on the basis of the common law; specifically that the infringement of the prisoner's right to conduct legally privileged correspondence had been interfered with *to a greater extent than was necessary* by the policy of opening all mail in a prisoner's absence. The phrase emphasized here shows that the anxious scrutiny test was indeed applied. The House of Lords specifically considered whether the legitimate aim of good order and discipline in prisons could be served by any lesser infringement, and concluded that it could. Lord Steyn said that he thought that although there was an overlap between anxious scrutiny and the proportionality test, and the same result would be achieved by either route in this case, the proportionality test did have distinguishing features. These were as follows:

First, the doctrine of proportionality may require the reviewing court to assess the balance which the decision maker has struck, not merely whether it is within the range of rational or reasonable decisions. Secondly, the proportionality test may go further than the traditional grounds of review inasmuch as it may require attention to be directed to the relative weight accorded to interests and considerations. Thirdly, even the heightened scrutiny test developed in *R v Ministry of Defence, Ex p Smith* [1996] QB 517, 554 is not necessarily appropriate to the protection of human rights. (para 28)

The crucial point here is that in applying the approach of proportionality the court itself assesses the balance which the decision-maker has struck. It considers the factors advanced, and weighs them. It follows that where a reviewing court does not consider the factors weighed in the case, it cannot claim to have properly applied the test of proportionality, whatever the language used. Lord Steyn drew on the formulation of proportionality we have already noted in *de Freitas* at 80:

- Is the legislative objective sufficiently important to justify limiting a fundamental right?
- Are the measures designed to meet the legislative objective rationally connected to it?
- Are the means used to impair the right or freedom no more than is necessary to accomplish the objective?

Although in practice the courts have not always complied, in terms of authority there is little doubt that *Daly* expounded the approach that should be used in judicial review of a decision affecting human rights:

in *Smith* the Court of Appeal reluctantly felt compelled to reject a limitation on homosexuals in the army. The challenge based on article 8 of the Convention for the Protection of Human Rights and Fundamental Freedoms (the right to respect for private and family life) foundered on the threshold required even by the anxious scrutiny test. The European Court of Human Rights . . . *Smith and Grady v United Kingdom* (1999) 29 EHRR 493 . . . concluded, at p 543, para 138:

the threshold at which the High Court and the Court of Appeal could find the Ministry of Defence policy irrational was placed so high that it effectively excluded any consideration by the domestic courts of the question of whether the interference with the applicants' rights answered a pressing social need or was proportionate to the national security and public order aims pursued, principles which lie at the heart of the court's analysis of complaints under article 8 of the Convention. (Lord Steyn in *Daly*, para 28)

In other words, even the 'anxious scrutiny' test, being addressed to the question of reasonableness, may ultimately not protect fundamental rights. Lord Cooke of Thorndon in the same case made another point concerning *Wednesbury*:

I think that the day will come when it will be more widely recognised that *Associated Provincial Picture Houses Ltd v Wednesbury Corporation* [1948] 1 KB 223 was an unfortunately retrogressive decision in English administrative law, insofar as it suggested that there are degrees of unreasonableness and that only a very extreme degree can bring an administrative decision within the legitimate scope of judicial invalidation. (para 32)

The purpose of the Human Rights Act, as set out in its long title, is to 'give further effect' to the rights and freedoms of the Convention. If consideration of fundamental rights does not receive a more intensive scrutiny after the Act, then this purpose is not fulfilled.

The appropriate level of intrusion by the courts on executive acts is now discussed mainly in the context of the margin of discretion, discussed earlier. The true question is probably to what extent the judiciary is willing to embrace the approach of proportionality. This approach is not new in UK law. Hunt traces its use as a form of human rights protection going back decades, and argues:

the true obstacle to the effective use of human rights law will remain so long as English courts remain resistant to overtly recognising the concept of proportionality. (1998:xiii)

3.7.2 Scope of an appeal to Asylum and Immigration Tribunal based on human rights

In the case of *Pardeepan v SSHD* [2000] INLR 447 the Tribunal said it was 'somewhat ironic that this tribunal of all Tribunals should be precluded from considering human rights issues from the inception of the Human Rights Act'. That case concerned the start of the human rights jurisdiction, and a provision which restricted the date of matters that the Tribunal could consider. Five years into the operation of the Act, there is a further irony, that the remit of immigration appeals bodies has been an area of fierce controversy, and many principles of law have been advanced which limit their human rights jurisdiction. These have come from both legislative changes and decisions of the Court of Appeal.

Much of the case law discussed in this section arises from before the introduction of the Asylum and Immigration Tribunal in April 2005, and so concerns the powers of adjudicators who were at that time the first tier of the appeal system. The same principles apply now to immigration judges of the tribunal, but with the proviso that there is no onward appeal to a tribunal on a point of law. The present position can only be understood in the context of the development of case law on this crucial even if apparently technical and esoteric issue.

Ismet Ala v SSHD [2003] EWHC 521 (Admin) was one of the many challenges to the Secretary of State's certificate that an Article 8 claim was manifestly unfounded. If this certificate was upheld, the claimant would be removed and would have no right of appeal in the UK. If on the facts, which were not disputed, the adjudicator could have come to a different decision from the Secretary of State then the human rights claim could not be said to be manifestly unfounded as there would be a point which could be argued. As the facts were not in dispute, the question was whether the adjudicator could differ from the Home Office in their assessment of proportionality. The question of the adjudicator or immigration judge's jurisdiction has arisen very often in this kind of case as it is central to whether the certificate can stand.

The Divisional Court distinguished between the adjudicator's role and the role of a reviewing court (para 32). The appeal to an adjudicator is an appeal, not a review, and the two are distinct. The court established: 'The essential question is whether an adjudicator is entitled to substitute his own decision as to where the balance fairly lies' (para 42). Throughout the case law that has followed, this remains the crucial question. Moses J said, in para 43: 'The answer is to be found, in my view, in the recognition, acknowledged by both by European Court of Human Rights and the Court of Appeal, that the Convention itself, in the context of Article 8, affords the decision-maker a discretionary area of judgment.' He referred to the expertise of the Secretary of State, which indicates that he considered a measure of deference was necessary. The most striking paragraph is 44:

It is the Convention itself, and, in particular, the concept of proportionality which confers upon the decision-maker a margin of discretion in deciding where the balance should be struck between the interests of an individual and the interests of the community. A decision-maker may fairly reach one of two opposite conclusions, one in favour of the claimant, the other in favour of his removal. Of neither could it be said that the balance has been struck unfairly. In such circumstances, the mere fact that an alternative but favourable decision could reasonably have been reached will not lead to the conclusion that the decision maker has acted in breach of the claimant's human rights. Such a breach will only occur when the decision is outwith the range of reasonable responses to the question as to where a fair balance lies between the conflicting interests. Once it is accepted that the balance could be struck fairly either way, the Secretary of State cannot be regarded as having infringed the claimant's rights by concluding that he should be removed.

One does not have to go to the opposite extreme of arguing that proportionality means only one right answer to recognize here the language of *Wednesbury* reasonableness. The court concluded that the Secretary of State had failed to take into account the effect of delay, which took his decision outside the range of reasonable decisions. Therefore there was room for an adjudicator to decide differently from the Secretary of State and so the certificate must be struck down. Failure to take into account a relevant factor is grounds for judicial review under the old *Wednesbury* rules.

Ala was endorsed by the Court of Appeal in *Edore v SSHD* [2003] 3 All ER 1265. Here, the case was an appeal from the Immigration Appeal Tribunal on the application of Article 8, and specifically the question of proportionality. The question addressed in *Ala* arose directly and the Court of Appeal had to decide what was its jurisdiction on appeal. The only previous authority was the fully reasoned tribunal case of *Noruwa* 00/TH/2345 where the Tribunal set itself the task of answering the question of the adjudicator's jurisdiction, and came to the conclusion that proportionality sets limits on discretion, even though it too allows for a range of lawful responses. The Court of Appeal in *Edore* found *Noruwa* a difficult case and only touched on it briefly, which was perhaps unfortunate for the development of this important question as it reviews the relevant authorities in some detail. *Ala* was adopted, at great length and without a great deal of further argument. The Court of Appeal in *Razgar* endorsed *Edore* in terms even more explicitly those of *Wednesbury* review:

41. When it comes to deciding how much weight to give to the policy of maintaining an effective immigration policy, the adjudicator should pay very considerable deference to the view of the Secretary of State as to the importance of maintaining such a policy. There is obviously a conceptual difference between (a) deciding whether the decision of the Secretary of State was within the range of reasonable responses, and (b) deciding whether the decision was proportionate (paying deference to the Secretary of State so far as is possible). In the light of *Blessing Edore*, we would hold that the correct approach is (a) in all cases except where this is impossible because the factual basis of the decision of the Secretary of State has been substantially undermined by the findings of the adjudicator.

This turned rights on their head. Article 8 requires that the right be respected except when there is a pressing social need to do otherwise, but the Court of Appeal gave the weighting instead to the importance of maintaining immigration policy.

Following *Edore*, the tribunal case of *M (Croatia)*, discussed above in relation to delay, was starred on the question of the adjudicator's approach to proportionality. The tribunal followed *Edore* and held that adjudicators should normally hold that a decision to remove is unlawful 'only when the disproportionality is so great that no reasonable Secretary of State could remove' (para 28). This is identical with the *Wednesbury* test in judicial review. The tribunal took this even further, adding 'where the Secretary of State, e.g. through consistent decision-making or through decisions in relation to members of the same family, has shown where within the range of reasonable responses his own assessment would lie, it would be inappropriate to assess proportionality by reference to a wider range of possible responses than he in fact uses' (para 28). This was extraordinary. Not only was the human rights appeal now equated to judicial review, but the Secretary of State and not the judicial body would be the arbiter of what was reasonable, and human rights law translated into common practice of the executive.

Razgar was appealed to the House of Lords on the question, discussed above, of whether Article 8 could be engaged by the consequences for health or welfare of removal from the UK. *Razgar* too was a certification case, so the question of the adjudicator's jurisdiction arose in determining whether the Secretary of State was right to certify Mr Razgar's claim as manifestly unfounded. Lord Bingham set out the proper approach by the adjudicator, using the classic four steps in any assessment of Article 8:

(1) is there an interference with the right to respect for private or family life?;
(2) is it in accordance with the law?;
(3) is it necessary in a democratic society for a legitimate aim?;
(4) is the interference proportionate to that aim?

Lord Bingham also inserted a new stage, asking whether the interference would have such gravity as to potentially engage the operation of Article 8. It is not clear whether this applies only when the feared breach is abroad. It would otherwise be a new departure in Article 8 jurisprudence (para 17). Importantly for our present subject, Lord Bingham said that 'the adjudicator must exercise his or her own judgment' (para 20). This brief reasoning is, strictly speaking, *obiter*.

Following *Razgar*, decision-makers were left with a Court of Appeal decision

(*Edore*) and starred tribunal (*M (Croatia)* in favour of the *Wednesbury* approach, and *obiter dicta* in the House of Lords favouring a full exercise of proportionality by the adjudicator or immigration judge.

Huang Abu-Qulbain and Kashmiri looked set to resolve the matter, being a post-*Razgar* case in the Court of Appeal precisely on the issue of the adjudicator's jurisdiction. The three appeals were brought together for the purpose of deciding what had become known as the '*M (Croatia)* question'. The court found that the earlier decisions of the Court of Appeal, *Edore* and *Ragar*, could not stand in the light of the House of Lords' judgment in *Razgar*. The court applied *Daly*, and contrasted *Wednesbury* review with what proportionality requires, saying: 'the very language … "the range of rational or reasonable decisions" is here *contrasted* with what proportionality will require' (para 45). It decided that the adjudicator must 'decide whether the action appealed against involves a violation of the appellant's Convention rights. Any other approach would in our judgment perpetrate an abdication of his duty and ours, as public authorities, to vindicate and uphold Convention rights' (para 26). On the question of the margin of discretion to be left to the Secretary of State, the court held that in the case of an adjudicator making a human rights decision there was no such margin. This only applied, in accordance with the principles we looked at earlier, where government takes decisions on matters of policy.

In these appeals the adjudicators were not called on to decide whether any *policy* was proportionate to its legitimate purpose, nor, therefore, to pass judgment on government policy at all. Accordingly therefore they were not required to enter into any field which lies within the distinct constitutional responsibility of government. On the contrary, their duty was to see to the protection of individual fundamental rights, which is the particular duty of the courts. (para 55)

This straightforward application of the principle of proportionality and the democratic justification for a margin of discretion stands in direct line with *Daly, Razgar, A & X v SSHD* and much jurisprudence from the ECtHR. However, at paragraph 56 the judgment appears to go into reverse:

The adjudicator has no business whatever to question or pass judgment upon the policy given by the rules. In our judgment his duty, when faced with an Article 8 case, where the would-be immigrant has no claim under the rules, is and is only, to see whether an exceptional case has been made out such that the requirement of proportionality requires a departure from the relevant rule in the particular circumstances. If that is right, the importance of maintaining immigration control is a prior axiom of the debate before him. It is not at all the subject of that debate. There is no basis upon which he should defer to the Secretary of State's judgment of the proportionality issue in the individual case unless it were somehow an open question what weight should be given to the policy on the one hand and what weight should be given to the Article 8 right on the other. (para 56)

In other words, policy is binding and is expressed in the immigration rules. The court goes on to say that a case which does not succeed under the rules should only succeed under Article 8 if it is 'truly exceptional'. There is an ambiguity in para 56 as to whether Laws LJ is referring to people whose claims do not fall within the rules, or those who claim within the rules but fail because a criterion of the rules is not met. This ambiguity arises from the combination of cases in *Huang*. The three appellants were in different positions. Mrs Huang was refused under substantive immigration rules, i.e., rules which refer to the content of what has to be established, in this case the entry of dependent relatives. The other two appellants, as in many Article 8 cases, were failed asylum seekers who faced removal. The immigration rules which govern their case are procedural rather than substantive. As Lord Bingham said in *R v Immigration Officer at Prague Airport ex p European Roma Rights Centre* [2004] UKHL 55, applying for asylum is not a purpose covered by the rules (para 30). The substance of the law affecting whether the individual should be removed is Article 8 itself, and prior to the commencement of the Human Rights Act, people in Mr Kashmiri and Mr Al-Qubain's position could only resort to policies or judicial review as a safety net after the failure of their asylum claim.

Relying on the notion that the immigration rules already embody the democratically approved balance between public interest and individual right, the Court of Appeal held that cases which succeeded outside the rules would be exceptional. Mrs Huang's situation fell within the ambit of the rules but was held to not meet the criteria. The other two appellants did not make applications under the rules and were not in a position to do so. Like many failed asylum seekers, they would not be able to bring themselves within the ambit of the rules, even those which the Court of Appeal thought 'within the territory' of their situation. The consequence of following this aspect of the Court of Appeal's judgment is that cases not decided under the rules (most often removal of failed asylum seekers with a family or private life in the UK) are subject to a requirement that they be 'exceptional' in order to succeed. This begs the question: 'exceptional to what?'. The risk is that the answer becomes: 'exceptional among the group of failed asylum seekers in the UK who have a family or private life here'. The risk is that application of this aspect *Huang* removes much of the substance of human rights appeals, even while its principle concerning the role of immigration judges appears to restore it. As discussed more fully in chapter 1, the equation of immigration rules with a human rights standard is without precedent or authority and, it is suggested, unconvincing.

Nevertheless *Huang* is being followed. In *Betts v SSHD* [2005] EWCA Civ 828 the Court of Appeal employed a loose application of *Huang*, by finding that there was nothing to justify a departure from 'the normal consequence of a failed asylum application', namely, removal. No reference was made to specific rules or policies which were said to embody the balance between public interest and human rights considerations. In a similar vein, the Court of Appeal in *Dbeis v SSHD* [2005] EWCA Civ 584 found that the 'distressing' circumstances of the applicant did not 'constitute an exceptional case, sufficient to override immigration control' (para 26). At its most crude, this may give the appearance that if something happens often, it cannot be a breach of human rights. It gives no weight to the right itself.

A different approach was demonstrated in *The Queen on the application of Lekstaka v IAT and SSHD (interested party)* [2005] EWHC 745 (Admin). In a judicial review of a refusal of leave to appeal to the IAT Collins J held that the case showed real prospects of success. The claimant did not come within the rules or concessions, but Collins J thought that he came within the spirit of the concession or policy concerning family reunion, and that this was the sort of case which might well succeed even though not meeting the terms of the policy. He did not consider that being a 'near miss' went against the claimant, as was suggested in *Huang*. Significantly, Collins J did not think that *Huang* materially affected this case.

3.8 Conclusion

In simple terms, human rights are a counterbalance to the exercise of executive power. Perhaps it is not surprising that the 'new human rights era', rather than simply shifting the balance, seems to have thrown existing tensions into sharper relief. In relation to Article 3 the courts have accepted that they have jurisdiction to judge the matter and therefore the Secretary of State's decisions are subject to a full appeal. Standards of proof have been assimilated to the lower asylum standard, although there is an indication that the threshold of treatment which comes within the article may be raised. On the other hand, first in *Ullah and Do* and then in *Huang* the Court of Appeal find ever new ways to restrict the jurisdiction of appeal bodies even at the first tier, to question to decision of the executive. The application of human rights to entry cases is imperiled, with implications for the ways in which human rights are to be delivered to foreign nationals affected by the UK administration. The 'deference' view on the one hand and the 'proportionality' view on the other were present before the Human Rights Act and remain so after it.

QUESTIONS

1 If the court exercises discretion in not encroaching upon the sphere of another branch of government, when should it do this and why?

2 How would you have decided the case of *N?*

3 Does it or should it make any difference to rights under Article 8 whether family life has been formed while waiting for an asylum claim to be processed or while spending time in the UK as, say, a student?

4 Is proportionality a question of law?

FURTHER READING

All Party Parliamentary Group on Extraordinary Rendition, December 2005, *Briefing: Torture by Proxy: international law applicable to 'Extraordinary renditions'*

Amnesty International (2005) *Cruel, Inhuman, Degrades us all*

Atrill, S. 'Keeping the executive in the picture: a reply to Professor Leigh' [2003] *Public Law* Spring pp. 41–51.

Blake, N., and Fransman, L. (1999) *Immigration, Nationality and Asylum under the Human Rights Act 1998* (London: Butterworths).

Blake, N., and Husain, R. (2003) *Immigration, Asylum and Human Rights* (Oxford: Oxford University Press).

Clayton, R. 'Regaining a Sense of Proportion: the Human Rights Act and the Proportionality Principle' EHRLR [2001] 5, pp. 504–525.

Clayton, R. [2004] Public Law 33–47 *Judicial deference and democratic dialogue: the legitimacy of judicial intervention under the Human Rights Act*

Fasti, M. 'The restrictive approach taken by the European Court of Human Rights: deportation of long-term immigrants and the right to family life, Part 1: integrated aliens and family rights: involution versus evolution' (2002) IANL vol. 16, no. 3, pp. 166–175; 'Part 2:

"Consensus enquiry" and security of residence of long-term immigrants in Europe' vol. 16, no. 4, pp. 224–236.

Frost, T. (2006) *Legal Commentary on the use of Torture Evidence* http://www.campacc.org.uk/Library/legal_commentary_torture_evidence_220106.pdf

Gearty, C. (2004) *Principles of Human Rights Adjudication* (Oxford:OUP)

Gordon, R. 'Legitimate Aim: A Dimly Lit Road' [2002] EHRLR 4, pp. 421–427.

Human Rights Watch (2005) Still at Risk: Diplomatic Assurances No Safeguard Against Torture

Leigh, I. 'Taking Rights Proportionately: Judicial Review, the Human Rights Act and Strasbourg' [2002] *Public Law* pp. 265–287.

Lester, A. 'Universality versus Subsidiarity: a reply' EHRLR [1998] 1, pp. 73–81.

——— 'The Art of the Possible: Interpreting Statutes under the Human Rights Act' EHRLR [1998] 6, pp. 665–675.

——— *The Human Rights Act — Five years on* [2004] EHRLR 3 258 –271.

Liddy, J. 'The Concept of Family Life under the ECHR' EHRLR [1998] 1, pp. 15–25.

Macdonald, I., and Webber, F. (2005) *Macdonald's Immigration Law and Practice*, 6th edn (London: Butterworths), Chapter 8.

Nash, S. and Furse, M. Regular Human Rights updates in the *New Law Journal*.

Ovey, C. 'The Margin of Appreciation and Article 8 of the Convention' *Human Rights Law Journal* vol. 19, no. 1, pp. 10–12.

Pannick, D. 'Principles of interpretation of Convention Rights under the Human Rights Act and the Discretionary Area of Judgment' [1998] *Public Law*, Winter pp. 545–551.

Rogers, N. 'Immigration and the European Convention on Human Rights: are new principles emerging?' EHRLR [2003] 1, pp. 53–64.

Shah, P. 'The Human Rights Act 1998 and immigration law' (2000) INLP vol. 14, no. 3, pp. 151–158.

Sherlock, A. 'Deportation of Aliens and Article 8' ECHR (1998) 23 ELR, pp. 62–75.

Singh, R., Hunt, M., and Demetriou, M. 'Is there a role for the Margin of Appreciation in National Law after the Human Rights Act?' EHRLR [1999] 1, pp. 15–22.

Steyn, Lord (2005) *Deference — A Tangled Story* Public Law 346–359.

Warbrick, C. 'The Structure of Article 8' EHRLR [1998] 1, pp. 32–44.

SECTION 2

European law and migration

4

The European context

SUMMARY

This chapter introduces the law and policy of the European Union towards immigration and asylum. It is concerned with policy towards outsiders: third country nationals who do not take primary benefit from the Union's free movement provisions. The concern of this policy with asylum deterrence is introduced as the context in which UK law on immigration and asylum is currently formed. 'Fortress Europe' is described in terms of stratification of rights according to nationality, and there is discussion of the UK's definition of British national for EU purposes. The chapter briefly charts the progress towards implementing the new immigration and asylum provisions deriving from the Treaty of Amsterdam. The UK's opt-in position is noted, as are its choices to date. Finally, there is an introduction to the EU dimension of human rights.

4.1 Introduction

The previous chapter mainly concerned the application of rights found in the European Convention on Human Rights, the most well-known treaty of the Council of Europe. This chapter concerns a different European system, that of the European Community and European Union. Both the Council of Europe and the European Community had their origins in the desire of states after the Second World War to avoid such a conflict ever occurring again. The European Community (EC) began as the European Economic Community (EEC), one of three associations of states which aimed to build close trading links in Europe. Economic interdependence was seen as a means to promote peaceful co-operation. The EEC became the EC, a supranational institution which has legal powers and a separate existence. It was established by the EC Treaty, also known as the Treaty of Rome. The EC Treaty contains the four freedoms upon which the Community is built, the free movement of goods, persons, services and capital, all of which serve the central purpose, stated in Article 14 EC (ex 7a) as the goal of establishing an area of freedom of movement 'without internal frontiers'.

The Treaty of Amsterdam 1997 extended the EC's competence in areas of social policy, the environment, public health, consumer protection, co-operation in policing and civil and criminal justice, and immigration and asylum. It had become apparent that market issues could not be seen in a vacuum. For instance, the employment of workers raises questions of their rights and health and safety; the establishment of businesses has an impact on the environment; the presence of transient nationals of other states has implications for policing, and so on.

The European Union (EU) is the political union of the Member States of the EC, it encompasses a number of intergovernmental areas of co-operation as well as the institutions of the EC. It was established by the Treaty on European Union 1992 also known as the Treaty of Maastricht. The EU is developing a political vision which far exceeds in scope the economic idea of a free market and EU law is expanding to serve that goal. The creation by the Treaty on European Union of EU citizenship seems to prefigure a political union within which free movement derives from citizenship status rather than economic function. In May 2004 ten more states acceded to membership of the EU, and on 1 January 2007, or at the latest 1 January 2008, Bulgaria and Romania will also accede to membership (Treaty signed 25 April 2005, OJ 2005 L 157).

The next stage of European unity was to be represented by the Treaty establishing a Constitution for Europe (OJ 2004 C 310 16) which consolidates all the treaties and advances the political union of twenty five states in Europe. However, the Constitution was rejected in referenda in France and the Netherlands and other Member States have postponed their referenda, so the Constitution process is now in doubt.

The UK's law on immigration and asylum is formed in the context of the UK's membership of the European Community and the European Union, and its influence both political and legal. At the present stage of development, the UK has not opted into many of the Treaty of Amsterdam implementing provisions concerning immigration, and while it is not impossible that at some point in the future, much of immigration law will be at least partly subject to European law, currently we are a long way from that position. However the UK has for the most part opted into the Common European Asylum System (CEAS), created through a series of directives, regulations and decisions, and the statutory and executive provisions of the UK's asylum system are increasingly not just politically influenced by European developments but subject to them in law. There is a vast body of writing on legal and political developments in Europe, both generally and as they affect immigration law. For a greater understanding, reference should be made to the selected bibliography at the end of this chapter.

4.1.1 Fortress Europe

The first principle to grasp in coming to an understanding of the EU and its law and policy on migration is that it appears very differently depending on whether one is looking from inside or out. The origin of the EC in the idea of an internal market meant dismantling the barriers between member countries to the movement of persons, goods and services. On the other hand the development of the Union has been characterized by measures designed to restrict the entry to Europe of nationals of non-European countries: 'third country nationals'. The hardening of European immigration policies towards nationals of other countries has earned the EU the nickname 'Fortress Europe'. Until recently this took place through the gradual harmonization of the immigration policies of Member States, and immigration and asylum were matters of intergovernmental co-operation, now the treaty of Amsterdam sets legal objectives to be attained by all the Member States, there are legal provisions created by the organs of the EC which have effect in the sphere of immigration and asylum, and the European Court of Justice (ECJ) has competence to make decisions on these matters. A further dimension is the accession of a further ten Member States in May 2004. The perception of where the borders of Europe are drawn has changed with the accession of these States, but not by their immediate inclusion for all purposes.

4.2 **Treaty of Amsterdam**

The Treaty of Amsterdam, which came into force on 1 May 1999, inserted into the EC Treaty a new Title IV which governs immigration, asylum, and the issue of visas. The Title makes the dual purpose of EC law on migration very plain. Article 61(1)(a) says that the Council must adopt:

measures aimed at ensuring the free movement of persons in accordance with Article 14, in conjunction with directly related flanking measures with respect to external border controls.

In other words, member states must open their borders to each other and control their borders to those from outside. As the internal market developed, so, as Guild says, 'one member state's third country nationals become those of the whole unified territory' (in Guild and Harlow (eds) 2001:90). Member States would want to be assured that other member states were admitting third country nationals on similar terms to themselves. The stronger external border could be seen in part as a consequence of the more relaxed internal borders.

The required controls on external borders include 'standards and procedures' for external border checks and rules on visas, including a 'list of third countries whose nationals must be in possession of visas when crossing the external borders' (Article 62). The required asylum measures include minimum standards on a range of matters and, a particular concern of European states: 'criteria and mechanisms for determining which Member State is responsible for considering an application for asylum submitted by a national of a third country in one of the Member States' (Article 63(1)). Measures on immigration policy must include 'conditions of entry and residence' including for family reunion, and measures on 'illegal immigration and illegal residence'.

None of these provisions suggest what the standards or objectives of these measures should be. For instance, is the list of visa countries to be short, and thus permissive, or long, and thus restrictive? European law is interpreted in accordance with its purpose, and the purpose of Title IV is: 'In order to establish progressively an area of freedom, security and justice'.

The meaning of this phrase has been extensively debated (see, for instance, P. Boeles in Guild and Harlow (eds) 2001). In general terms the freedom referred to is the freedom to move within the Union, and security is safety from threats largely seen as external. This makes the question of 'and justice for whom?' an important one in the understanding of the Union objectives. On the whole, justice is understood as criminal justice. The purpose of Title IV, therefore, largely seems to be to replicate the strong external and relaxed internal controls which have already characterized the EU. There is only one requirement to promote the rights of third country nationals in Title IV, and that is that there must be provision for family reunion.

Title IV allowed a period of five years after the entry into force of the Treaty of Amsterdam for the new measures to be adopted, which gave a deadline of 1 May 2004. There were exceptions to this deadline for provisions on the rights of legally resident third country nationals, conditions of entry and residence, and the promotion of balanced effort between Member States in receiving refugees ('burden-sharing').

4.2.1 Tampere conclusions — migration

Shortly after the Treaty of Amsterdam came into force, there was a meeting of the European Council at Tampere, devoted to the development of the 'area of freedom, security and justice'. It was a key opportunity to formulate some objectives for policy on migration. Four main principles emerged:

- partnership with countries of origin;
- moving towards a common European asylum system, which should in time lead towards a common asylum procedure and a uniform status for those granted asylum;
- fair treatment of third country nationals;
- more efficient management of migration flows.

The Tampere conclusions set wide-ranging objectives in terms of partnership with countries of origin. The tone of the conclusions was liberal, although there was also scepticism as to whether this was form or substance (see, for instance, *Statewatch* vol 9 no 5). The Council recognized the need for a 'comprehensive approach to migration addressing political, human rights and development issues in countries and regions of origin and transit'. This would require 'combating poverty, improving living conditions and job opportunities, preventing conflicts and consolidating democratic states and ensuring respect for human rights, in particular rights of minorities, women and children' (Commission of the EC 2001 Conclusions para 11).

A High Level Working Group set up in 1998 was to continue its work to look at the causes of migration, including forced migration. The group's work was concentrated on six countries which were all perceived to produce large numbers of refugees, and action plans were adopted.

The treatment of long-term resident third country nationals was one of the most liberal policy conclusions to come from the Tampere Council. Following Tampere the Commission proposed two Directives: one to enhance and consolidate the rights of third country nationals who are long-term residents in the EU, the second to give rights of entry and residence to their family members. In a number of respects the first draft Directives attempted to harmonize the rights of long-term residents with those of EU nationals. This could have heralded an equalization of rights within the Community based not on nationality but on residence, however, the provisions of the directives were much reduced during subsequent negotiations. It is still the case that lawful residence, not just nationality, became a basis for the acquisition of rights, but of a lesser kind. The watered down Family Reunion Directive 2003/86 EC was finally adopted on 22 September 2003. As with most directives, a period was allowed for Member States to arrange how they would implement the Directive, and it was due for full implementation by October 2005. The reduced nature of the rights given by the Directive drew criticism not only from non-governmental groups but also from the European Parliament which launched a legal action against the European Council on the grounds that the limitations imposed on family reunification for children were incompatible with the right to respect for family life and the principle of equality of treatment, as was the waiting period of up to three years for the issue of a residence permit (Case C–540/03 OJ 2004 C 47/35). The Advocate General presented an opinion on 8 September 2005 that these Articles could not, as the Parliament claimed, be severed from the rest of the Directive. The Advocate General considered that the waiting period and exclusion of those over 15 years old would have had to be annulled as they violated the right to respect for family life. The provision for extra conditions for those above 12 should be applied only in conformity with ECtHR case law on a case-by-case basis. However, because these provisions could not be severed the application must be declared inadmissible.

The Directive on the status of long-term residents 2003/109 was finally agreed after refugees were removed from its ambit, and discretion restored to Member States in a number of respects. Broadly speaking, the Directive gives to third country nationals who have been lawfully resident in Europe for five years security of status and the right to move to other Member States on a limited number of grounds providing the destination state does not restrict the right. It was due to be implemented by January 2006. For an interesting discussion of this Directive, see Belaert-Suominen 2005. Other Commission proposals have borne fruit, for instance concerning the entry of third country nationals for study or voluntary work (Directive 2004/114). A Green Paper has launched a new stage of discussion on entry for work (COM (2004)811), focusing on economic issues.

One result of the focus on partnerships with countries of origin has been to use the EU's political and economic power to conclude readmission agreements, the aim of which is to ensure that illegal entrants to the EU from these countries can be repatriated. Readmission agreements have been entered into with Hong Kong, Sri Lanka, Macao, and Albania. Negotiations have been commenced with Russia, Pakistan, Morocco, Ukraine, Algeria, Turkey, and China. Even without formal readmission agreements, a third country's capacity and willingness to deal with irregular migration is a key factor in the EU's negotiation on migration issues. For instance, in the case of Romania, the removal of a visa requirement for nationals of that country was delayed pending undertakings on irregular immigration and residence and repatriation. The first case brought under Title IV concerned the uncertain position in which this left Romanian nationals. Romania appeared on the list whose nationals do not require a visa for entry to an EU country, but whether this was in force depended on the view taken by the European Council of efforts by Romania to control irregular migration. In Case C–51/03 *Georgescu* the migrant's liability to criminal proceedings in Germany depended on this. Under Title IV references cannot come from a lower national court, as with other EC law matters, but must first go through the national appeals system. This application was declared inadmissible because it was not referred by a final court.

The Commission's initiation of talks with Libya provoked a storm of protest in the light of evidence that Libya was forcibly returning even recognized refugees to their countries of origin (Italian Council for Refugees press release 4 October 2004). Italy itself summarily expelled to Libya about 1,000 asylum seekers who had landed in the Sicilian island of Lampedusa. Ten NGOs filed a complaint with the President of the European Commission (*Statewatch* news online 25 January 2005), and the European Parliament passed a resolution stating that these expulsions were in breach of international obligations (Motion for resolutions on Lampedusa, vote 14 April 2005). Whatever the breadth of vision at Tampere, there is strong pressure to institute means to expel asylum seekers. This was partly due to the increased interest in security during the Tampere period. The European Council developed an Action Plan on the fight again terrorism, which included more stringent exclusion from refugee status, one of many developments making a link in law between terrorism and asylum.

In September 2005 the Commission issued a further communication on integrating migration issues into relations with third countries (COM (2005) 390). A key focus is the economic role of money paid by migrant workers to families back home ('remittances').

See the reading list below for accounts of the five-year period governed by the Tampere objectives.

4.2.2 Hague Programme

In November 2004 the Member States approved a new five-year plan to further the creation of an area of 'freedom, security and justice'. The objectives of the Hague Programme include:

improvement of the common capability of the Union and its Member States to guarantee fundamental rights, minimum procedural safeguards and the access to justice, to provide protection in accordance with the Geneva Convention and other international treaties to persons in need, to regulate migration flows and to control the external borders of the Union, to fight organised cross-border crime and repress the threat of terrorism . . . development of a Common Asylum System . . . the approximation of law and the development of common policies.

The European Council's introduction to the programme reveals an emphasis on security 'in the light of terrorist attacks in the United States on 11 September 2001 and in Madrid on 11 March 2004', and exhorts Member States to 'take full account of the security of the Union as a whole'.

Returning illegal migrants is prioritized in the Hague Programme, and the Commission has proposed a Directive on common policy on returns of those who have stayed illegally (COM (2005) 391 final). It includes a radical new proposal for a re-entry ban that would be valid throughout the EU, reinforcing a European-wide approach to removals.

4.2.3 UK's position

In accordance with protocols appended to the Treaty of Amsterdam, the UK, Ireland, and Denmark have an anomalous position which enables them to remain outside the new immigration and asylum provisions unless they opt in. The UK has not yet opted in to any substantial provisions on legal migration or protection of third country nationals, although it would be fair to say that the UK's immigration provisions on admission of family members for those on short-term visas or for settlement are more generous than those in the ill-fated family reunion Directive (see in particular chapter 9, also chapters 10 and 11). The settlement rights of long-term resident third country nationals as set out in Directive 2003/109 are comparable with those in force in the UK. The major difference is that indefinite leave to remain in the UK does not entitle the holder to travel freely in the EU and, conversely, a beneficiary of third country national rights in Europe may not freely enter the UK. Ryan speculates that the desire to avoid granting such rights of entry is the reason that the UK did not opt into this directive (in Higgins and Hailbronner 2004:443). The UK has opted into many of the provisions concerning irregular migration: Directive 2001/40 on mutual recognition of expulsion decisions, Directive 2001/51 on carrier sanctions, a Framework decision on trafficking in persons (OJ 2002 L 203/1), a Directive and Framework Decision on facilitation of illegal entry and residence (OJ 2002 L 328) and Directive 2004/82 creating an obligation for carriers to communicate passenger data to immigration services. The UK has not opted into the majority of provisions on borders and visas, but has opted into the European common visa format (Reg 334/2002), including the proposal to insert biometric information (see chapter 7) and has opted into the format also for residence permits (Reg 1030/2002). In some cases, the UK, in common with other Member States, has taken no steps to implement a Directive by the required date, but it may be that the present law is believed to be sufficiently compliant. For instance, the UK has taken no explicit steps to implement Directive 2001/40 on recognition of expulsion decisions, but existing powers of deportation could be used to expel someone subject to another Member State's expulsion decision.

The new proposal on returns (COM (2005) 391 final above) presents significant issues for the UK. Currently, re-entry to the UK is examined on a case-by-case basis, except for deportees (see chapter 16) who are few and far between. A fixed period of ban on re-entry, imposed at the time of the removal, raises human rights issues and would undermine the reasoning of tribunals who currently endorse the removal of illegal entrants on the basis that they should join the join queue to come in legally. The proposal provides for returns always to be subject to a fair and transparent procedure, limiting the use of coercive measures including detention, binding these to the principle of proportionality and to protective standards. The standard for justifying detention could be more rigorous than that currently applicable in the UK. Current indications are that the UK will not opt in, but then not introducing five-year re-entry bans would make it a lower risk destination for illegal entry if other states have done so.

Where the UK has not opted in there is not a consistent pattern as to whether the UK or EU provisions are the more generous, and the main reason given by the UK Government for not opting in is to retain control and flexibility.

In terms of asylum policies, the UK is a key player, not swept unwillingly into European co-operation, but in the forefront of promoting deterrent measures. The Common European Asylum System and the UK's participation are discussed below.

4.2.4 Security — the Schengen Agreement

Before the Treaty of Amsterdam, co-operation in law and order and immigration was achieved by entering into agreements between states. Key among these was the

Schengen Agreement 1985, and its implementing convention 1990, entered into by all the then member countries of the EU with the exception of the UK and Ireland, with the objective of achieving the gradual abolition of checks at common borders. The Schengen Agreement also declared an intention to reinforce co-operation between the customs and police authorities of the contracting states 'notably in combating crime, particularly illicit trafficking in narcotic drugs and arms, the unauthorized entry and residence of persons, customs and tax fraud and smuggling' (Article 9). To this end the Schengen Information System (SIS) was established, facilitating exchange of intelligence between the contracting states. The Treaty of Amsterdam brought the Schengen Agreement into the first pillar of the EC, i.e., into the Treaty, making it justiciable by the ECJ. The Schengen provisions are aimed at maintenance of external borders as well as dissolution of borders within the Community. The provisions of the Schengen *acquis* (i.e., the collection of authoritative documents) apply to third country nationals wherever the context so allows.

Under the Treaty of Amsterdam, the UK needs the consent of other Schengen states to opt into elements of the Schengen *acquis*, but where new measures are building on Schengen, then the UK may unilaterally opt in as it can to other Title IV measures. There are limited provisions relating to border control which have effect in the UK. These concern security issues such as protection of personal data and the entry of individuals carrying narcotic drugs (Articles 75–76 and 126–127 of the Convention applying the Schengen Agreement). The UK has also opted into a decision and regulation on funding a new Schengen Information System (Regulation 2424/2001 and Decision 2001/886/JHA). This new system (SIS II) is partly necessitated by the accession of ten new Member States to the EU, but the opportunity is being taken to extend its use and capacities. The new system is now under construction. The SIS works on the basis of records (alerts) being created for five categories of people and for lost and stolen objects. Records suggest that Italy and Germany have been using the category of 'people to be refused entry to the Schengen area' to register all failed asylum seekers (*Statewatch* News Online April 2005: statewatch.org/news/). New categories of alert are being created for SIS II, widening the scope for creating records, and enabling greater data sharing, and this is not only for passport control. The Justice and Home Affairs ministers of the EU at a meeting in June 2003 agreed the addition of new categories of data and the possibility of access to that information being granted for a purpose different from that for which it was originally entered on the system. The main other likely purpose is law enforcement, and this is proceeding in accordance with the UK's proposal that, in the new SIS, law enforcement officers should have access to information that someone has been refused entry because they are believed to constitute a threat to public order, national security, or safety or there are grounds to believe they will commit a serious offence. Previously this information was only made available to immigration officers for the purposes of border control. The UK proposal (Doc 7786/03 March 2003) means that border control will also be used for policing and law enforcement purposes. The new SIS is accompanied by a new Visa Information System, but the UK has not yet opted into this.

4.3 **Europe and asylum**

During 2004, Europe was the region worldwide which received the highest number of individual asylum applications. In absolute numbers, throughout the first years of the twenty-first century, the highest refugee populations in the world by far have been in Pakistan and Iran. Germany has come a close third. If the ratio of refugees to other inhabitants or to gross domestic product is measured, no country in the EU featured in the top ten refugee receiving countries in 2000 nor probably since (UNCHR). Nevertheless, globally, including in Europe, the number of refugees grew during the 1980s and 1990s. Although the number seems to have peaked and now to be declining there is a widespread perception within Europe that asylum is a problem. The refugee determination process in Europe is centred on individuals proving their case in a legalistic framework according to the criteria in the 1951 UN Convention Relating to the Status of refugees. This has in part led to a popular perception that a successful applicant is a 'genuine' refugee and an unsuccessful one is a 'bogus' refugee. Some popular thinking also equates the unsuccessful asylum claimant with an 'economic migrant'. As the EU has not had a migration policy which enables economic entry, this motivation has not been regarded as legitimate.

Europe's more recent recognition of its need for labour has only very marginally penetrated asylum policy for fear that the asylum route will be used by economic migrants. In accordance with recommendations of Tampere and earlier policies there is a volume of research on causes and patterns of migration. Some of the more recent findings, which draw on original data and earlier work suggest:

- Repression and/or discrimination against minorities and/or ethnic conflict exists in all the main refugee-producing countries.
- Conflict seems to be a major cause of refugee movements.
- Poverty or underdevelopment may precipitate conflict but is not of itself apparently a cause of refugee movement.
- Where a country is undergoing rapid change or crisis, the motivations of individuals for leaving may be mixed — it is therefore difficult to distinguish between someone in need of protection (a Convention refugee) and someone seeking economic stability (an economic migrant).
- A reputation for democratic institutions, the rule of law, and developed social systems make Europe an attractive destination for people who decide to leave a situation of conflict and crisis.
- Existing personal, familial or other known links, knowledge of the language, and past colonial links are a strong influence on an individual's choice of a particular European country. (Castles, Crawley and Loughna, 2003)

The above suggests that addressing the causes of forced migration requires addressing the causes of conflict, and that distinguishing between a Convention refugee and an economic migrant may not be simple. The main effort of EU policy however has been concentrated on prevention of illegal migration and the deterrence of asylum seekers. It may be argued that such measures 'make it more difficult for those who are genuinely in need of protection to seek asylum and at the same time have created a "migration industry" of smugglers, facilitators and traffickers' (Castles *et al* 2003:v). Asylum policy then must deal with controlling the smugglers and traffickers, and a further range of penal provisions has been introduced to this end.

The argument between Britain and France over the Red Cross camp at Sangatte may be seen in this light. It came to symbolize the supposed burden of asylum seekers in the context of European practice. Much of the public debate concerning the camp focused on the perceived differences between reception conditions and legal standards in the two countries. Despite the active role played by the UK in promoting common European asylum policy, the effort to remedy the problem of illegal entry to Britain from France did not concentrate on harmonization of standards, but rather on strengthening the border between the two countries. In the short to medium term it has produced a 'race to the bottom', that is, an endeavour by each country to be tougher than the other and therefore appear less desirable. There is a contradiction between this approach and creating a Common European Asylum System. Phuong makes the point that smugglers can capitalize on perceived differences, because legal controls between Britain and the rest of Europe exist. There would be no money to be made out of promising a route to the UK if the UK were part of the Schengen area (Phuong 2003).

The asylum provisions adopted under Title IV, have now completed the first stage of creating a Common European Asylum System and include the following:

- Decision 2000/596/EC on the European Refugee Fund, which concerns exceptional support for the costs of asylum. A second fund is currently under discussion.
- Regulation 2725/2000 on Eurodac, a Europe-wide fingerprint database for asylum seekers, and Regulation 407/2002 implementing it.
- Directive 2001/55 on temporary protection, limiting the obligations of states in the case of a mass exodus.
- Directive 2003/9, setting minimum reception conditions.
- 'Dublin II' Regulation 343/2003, making provision for the criteria for establishing which Member State is responsible for an application. Regulation 1563/2003 gives the detailed rules.
- Directive 2004/83, giving the definition of a refugee or one who may obtain subsidiary protection, and the content of that protection.
- Directive 2005/85 on minimum standards on procedures for granting and withdrawing refugee status.

Council Regulation (EC) 2725/2000 [2000] OJ L316/1, concerning the implementation of the Eurodac system, was the first regulation made using Title IV, adopted on 11 December 2000. It institutes a system for collecting and identifying the fingerprints of all those who seek asylum in the Member States which became operational on 15 January 2003. Fingerprints are retained for ten years in a Central Unit which can compare sets of prints against those in the database at the request of a Member State. The aim is to be able to identify when an asylum seeker has already sought asylum somewhere else, thus giving effect to the central provision of the Dublin Convention (now Dublin II): that an asylum seeker must make their claim in the country through which they enter Europe. The Eurodac system was enlarged to include power to take fingerprints of third country nationals apprehended in connection with an irregular entry into Europe (Article 8). Therefore it would be possible to say of an asylum claimant in France that they previously entered Germany illegally. However, it is not clear what would be the incentive of the first state to take such prints and then release the subject into their territory. This would be the equivalent of giving that person an entitlement to return to make their asylum claim.

Guild's conclusion, confirmed in the first annual report of Eurodac, is that the Eurodac system is only effective as regards one category of persons — asylum seekers who have already applied for asylum in one Member State and then move, after having made that application, to another Member State where they again apply for asylum (ILPA European Law Update March 2001).

It is apparent that legal provision concerning the minimum standards for dealing with asylum claims has taken longer to complete than the more explicitly deterrent and burden-sharing aspects of the Common European Asylum System. There are still outstanding issues concerning the procedures Directive (2005/85). Negotiations on a common list of safe countries of origin were shelved in order to complete the Directive (see chapter 12 for further discussion), and the Standing Committee of Experts on International Immigration, Refugee and Criminal law has recommended that the European Parliament commence a legal challenge, particularly with reference to safe countries of origin as the directive says that Member States 'shall' consider an application from a list state as unfounded, thus removing the state's discretion and the individual's capacity for challenge. Here as elsewhere the debate on asylum provisions is dominated by the tension between on the one hand an attempt to tighten borders against asylum claims and on the other hand the need for protection of individual rights.

4.4 **UK implementation**

The UK has opted into all the provisions on asylum. This means that where asylum regulations are in force (for instance 'Dublin II'), the UK is bound by the regulation and must give effect to it (EC Treaty Article 249). Where directives are in force, the UK must adopt its own legal provisions which bring its law into compliance with the Directive by the date set for this purpose.

The Directive on reception conditions (2003/9) was given legal force in the UK on 5 February 2005 by the Asylum Support (Amendment) Regulations 2005, SI 2005/11; the Asylum Seekers (Reception Conditions) Regulations 2005, SI 2005/7, and a new Part 11B of the immigration rules HC 395. SI 2005/7 provides for rudimentary minimum standards, for instance, in accommodating families to have regard to family unity and 'so far as . . . reasonably practicable' to accommodate families together (reg 3), and to take into account the needs of a vulnerable person, but not to assess for such needs (reg 4). SI 2005/11 deals mainly with discontinuation or suspension of asylum support. The new immigration rules deal mainly with obligations to give written information to asylum seekers. They also give the right to apply to the Secretary of State for permission to take up paid work if the asylum decision is still outstanding after one year.

The Directive on minimum standards for procedures in assessing an asylum claim (2005/85) is discussed in the context of the asylum claim process in chapter 12, and the Directive concerned with the conditions for qualifying as a refugee (2004/83) is discussed where that subject is treated in depth in chapter 13.

Dublin II (reg 343/2003), governing criteria and mechanisms for determining the Member State responsible for examining an asylum application, is considered more fully in chapter 12 in the context of the development of so called 'safe third country provisions'.

The UK did not need to bring in further measures to ensure compliance with the Eurodac regulation as the power to collect fingerprints from asylum seekers had already been granted in the Immigration and Asylum Act 1999 s 141. This is part of the development of the use of biometric information in UK immigration control. See chapter 7.

At a policy level, the creation of a Common European Asylum System proceeded more briskly than other Title IV measures, although practical effects may have lagged behind legal and policy measures. Concern with asylum deterrence has been to the fore in the early years of giving legal form to Title IV, however this is but one aspect of the strong external borders of Europe. The system of border control, both internal and external, rests upon a stratification of rights.

4.5 Stratification

The EU's political agreements and legal provisions produce a stratified system in which free movement rights, discussed in the next chapter, apply fully at the most privileged level and only in a limited way at the least privileged, whereas immigration and asylum provisions under Title IV apply not at all at the most privileged level but fully at the least. This stratification is largely dependent upon nationality. The directive on third country nationals marks a move away from this traditional position by creating some rights at a European level on the basis of residence rather than nationality, though it did not go as far as recommended by the Opinion of the European Economic and Social Committee (EESC) on Access to European Union citizenship (OJ 2003 C 208/76) who proposed that European citizenship should be open to long-term resident third country nationals. The EC's stratification of rights co-exists with Member States' own system of immigration control, but as European law takes precedence where it applies, European membership has changed previous legal relationships.

4.5.1 Europeans in UK immigration law: shifting allegiances, freedom, and restriction

In UK immigration law European nationals are foreign nationals, as European countries are not and were not part of the British Empire or the Commonwealth. As we have seen, twentieth-century development of British immigration policy and law has been formed with the Commonwealth in mind, and particularly the New Commonwealth. The development of immigration law has by and large meant the development of immigration control, and so those who were the target of that law have become the target of control. Thus, Commonwealth citizens, in the middle part of the twentieth century Britain's allies in the world, also from that time became subject to more stringent immigration control.

The second target group of policy, particularly in the last twenty years, has been asylum seekers, and the imposition of visa regimes has been used to deter travellers from countries which are considered to produce a high number of refugee claims. Some of the new members of the European Union are countries from which there have in the past been significant numbers of asylum claims, for instance the Czech Republic and the Slovak Republic. Asylum applications between EU member states are so rare as to be almost unknown, and anyway would normally be unnecessary as a potential claimant may exercise rights of free movement. We can see, however, that the boundary between who is an asylum seeker and who is exercising European free movement rights is movable.

Since the Second World War European countries have been for the UK not only neighbours but also allies. European countries are not visa national countries, and could not be so because of the Treaty of Rome with its foundational principle of freedom of movement. In European law European citizens have freedom to come and go, and Commonwealth citizens, who before 1962 had the right of abode in the UK, are 'third country nationals'. This term also encompasses nationals of the main refugee-producing countries. However, while the aim of UK immigration law is immigration control, the aim of the European Treaties and their implementing legislation is to promote freedom of movement within Europe.

4.5.2 **European system of stratification of rights**

Until recently, very broadly speaking, the EU's stratification has been into three groups: EU nationals, nationals of countries with which the EC has association agreements, and third country nationals. A number of factors indicate change in these groupings. Firstly, there is differentiation within the category of 'favoured EC nationals' (a phrase occasionally used in case law). By the European Economic Area Agreement, and the Swiss Agreement, the specific, free movement rights are extended to nationals of Iceland, Liechtenstein, Norway, and Switzerland in addition to the Member States of the EU. There is also a debate as to whether the establishment of European Union citizenship by the Treaty of Maastricht carries with it a general right to freedom of movement over and above specific rights under the primary and secondary legislation. If this were the case, nationals of Iceland, Liechtenstein, Norway, and Switzerland would not benefit as the agreements do not make them EU nationals. Furthermore, with the accession of ten new Member States in 2004, not all rights were automatically acquired on accession. Therefore within the category of EU nationals there are some with more rights than others. The rights which accompany EU citizenship are discussed further in the next chapter.

4.5.2.1 *The favoured group: EU nationals*

Currently, the most extensive rights in freedom of movement attach to EU nationals, and on the face of it those who qualify for this status are simply 'nationals of EU Member States'. The Member States upon entering into the Treaty on European Union declared that in cases of disputed nationality status the question should be settled solely by reference to the national law of the Member State concerned. The jurisprudence of the Court has tended to follow this approach with the proviso that in making its determination the Member State must have due regard to

Community law. This proviso gives some jurisdiction to the ECJ on a question affecting entitlement under EC law.

In Case 21/74 *Airola v Commission* [1975] ECR 221 the question of the nationality of a female Commission staff member arose in the context of the application of the staff regulations relating to expatriation allowances. These would be paid to officials 'who are not and have never been nationals of the state in whose European territory the place where they are employed is situated'. The staff member in question was Belgian, but Italian law automatically naturalized her as Italian when she married an Italian man, thereby giving her dual nationality. Recognition of her Italian nationality would deprive her of the expatriation allowance. The application of the provision in the staff regulations would be discriminatory on grounds of sex, as men would not automatically acquire a new nationality on marriage. Combating sex discrimination is a principle of law of the European Community; the Court had jurisdiction on the interpretation of the regulation and was faced with a choice between upholding fundamental Community principles and respecting a State's view on nationality. It chose the former, and for the purpose of the staff regulations accepted the applicant's contention that it was necessary to define nationality 'as excluding nationality imposed by law on a female official upon her marriage with a national of another state when she has no possibility of renouncing it'.

The Court may also have a role when there is a difference in law between Member States as to whether a person is a national of one of them. This arose in Case C–369/90 *Micheletti v Delegacion del Gobierno en Cantabria* [1992] ECR I–4329. Mr Micheletti had dual Italian and Argentinian nationality. He obtained recognition of his dental qualification in Spain, and went to live there from Argentina. The Spanish authorities, however, refused to grant him permanent residence as they did not recognize his Italian nationality and so would not grant him rights under European law. They followed a rule that where a person had nationality of more than one country, neither of which was Spain, then he would be regarded as a national of the country where he had last lived.

As in *Airola*, the ECJ set a limitation upon a Member State's right to determine conditions of acquisition and loss of nationality. It was, they said, within the competence of each Member State to define such conditions, but this competence 'must be exercised with due regard to Community law. Directive 73/148 (now 2004/38) provided that Member States must admit Community nationals into their territory, merely upon production of a valid identity card or passport'. On producing his Italian passport Mr Micheletti should have been granted residence. It was not open to Spain to subject his Italian nationality to further scrutiny under their own domestic law, or to set a residence requirement in order to grant recognition.

UK nationals for EU purposes

A number of Member States, including the UK, have made declarations, appended to the Maastricht Treaty, as to whom they regard as their nationals for EC purposes. The UK's Declaration ([1983] OJ C23/1) defines as nationals for EU purposes British citizens, British subjects with the right of abode in the UK, and British dependent territories citizens who acquire that citizenship from connection with Gibraltar. This appears to exclude Commonwealth citizens with right of abode in the UK, unless the Immigration Act 1971 definition of 'British citizens' can be implied into the declaration. Such people are treated by the Immigration Act 1971 as British citizens, indeed their right of abode in the UK is the same as that of a British citizen. However, it appears they do not obtain freedom of movement rights in the EU, even though they may well have lived in the UK all their lives, have the right to vote, and are in every other respect the equivalent in law of a British citizen. The exclusion of British dependent territories citizens who are not from Gibraltar no longer has any significance: as British overseas territories citizens they now have become British citizens by virtue of the British Overseas Territories Act 2002. It may be noted that the Act did not give other European nationals the right to enter the British Overseas Territories (see Standing Committee D). Other categories of British national remain excluded, namely British overseas citizens, British nationals (overseas), and British subjects under the Act or British protected persons.

A challenge to this declaration and its exclusion of British overseas citizens arose before the ECJ in February 2001 in Case C–192/99 *R v Secretary of State for the Home Department ex p Manjit Kaur*. The case was an attempt to reverse the under-privileged immigration status of British overseas citizens, as discussed in chapter 2, and was important for the further reason that the applicant argued that funda-mental rights were involved. The application to the British High Court was brought by Manjit Kaur, who was born in Kenya in 1949 of a family of Asian origin. She was at birth a citizen of the United Kingdom and Colonies. As such, she had a right of abode in the UK. After the immigration statutes of the 1960s she became subject to immigration control and after the commencement of the British Nationality Act 1981 in 1983, she became a British overseas citizen with no right of abode. In 1990 she claimed a right to enter and remain in the UK as an EU national, but her claim was denied on the basis of the UK's declaration defining UK nationals for EU purposes as excluding British overseas citizens.

Article 6(2) of the Treaty on European Union, as amended by the Treaty of Amsterdam, made fundamental rights a principle of Community law. Ms Kaur argued that her right of abode in the UK was a fundamental right, as recognized by Article 3, Protocol 4 of the European Convention on Human Rights which says that nationals shall not be deprived of the right to enter their country of nationality. The UK's failure to ratify this Protocol, at least in part because of a wish to avoid obligations to British overseas citizens, had no bearing on the decision in Ms Kaur's case, as under Article 6(2) the Convention is used as a source of principle for EU law rather than being directly applied. The ECJ, however, reaffirmed the pre-Maastricht principle that it was for Member States, with due regard to Community law, to determine who would be their nationals and thus nationals of the Union. The court would therefore not interfere with Ms Kaur's status as determined by Britain. The High Court in *ex parte Zaunab Upadhey* 31 January 2000 (unreported) ILU Vol 3 no 13 confirmed that a British protected person was also not a British national for EU purposes.

It is possible to summarize the current position on nationality in the following way. Although the determination of who is a national is primarily that of the State whose nationality is being claimed, this competence must be exercised within the principles of Community law; there is scope therefore for the Court to inter-vene. It is arguable that as the benefit of Community law and in particular of Union citizenship is dependent upon being a national of a Member State, that deprivation of nationality is a matter of Community law as it operates to exclude a person from those benefits. However this has yet to be tested in the courts. Currently the definition of who may be a 'Union citizen', the prime category of privilege within the Union legal system, is largely in the hands of individual states.

4.5.3 Association agreements

The next layer of rights is a broad and mixed one, applying to nationals of those countries with which the EC has entered into agreements of association. These agreements with non-EU countries give rights to nationals of those countries to engage in economic activity in the EU. These are less than the rights available to EU nationals, but they provide a legal basis for workers. Each agreement provides for the establishment of a Council which has the responsibility for the development and implementation of the Agreement.

The first of the current agreements was with Turkey, and this remains the most advanced in terms of the rights available. Many of its provisions have direct effect and Articles 12–14 of the Agreement provide that the contracting parties are to be guided by the relevant articles of the EC Treaty in progressively securing freedom of movement for workers, freedom of establishment, and provision of services. As in all the Association agreements there is not a right of entry as it is expected that a Turkish national will enter in accordance with the national law of the host country. However, once they have entered there is a principle of non-discrimination as between Turkish and EU nationals. Council Decision 1/80 Article 6 sets out the specific rights for a worker:

(i) after one year's legal employment, to renewal of the work permit to work for the same employer;

(ii) after three years' legal employment, to respond to an offer of employment from another employer; and

(iii) after four years' legal employment, to any paid employment of the worker's choice.

Article 7 of Decision 1/80 provides that members of a Turkish worker's family who have been authorized by national law to join them may take up offers of work although they must first have three years of lawful residence. Children may enter education once one of their parents has been working for a period, and if they have been in vocational training in the host state are then free to enter employment, providing their parent has been legally employed for three years.

The Turkey Agreement has a protective effect which ensures that the movement is towards the integration of Turkish workers, not against it. In C–37/98 *Savas* [2000] All ER (EC) 627 the ECJ held that the standstill provision in Article 41 EC meant that the UK could not apply provisions on establishment to Turkish workers that were more restrictive than those which obtained at the time of the commencement of the Turkey Agreement. For the UK this was 1 January 1973 when the UK joined the EU. Immigration rules on self-employment were then more favourable to the individual than they are now. Consequently the old rules must be applied to Turkish workers. The question of the scope of the standstill clause has been referred by the House of Lords to the ECJ from the Court of Appeal in *Tum and Dari v SSHD* [2004] EWCA Civ 788. In that case unsuccessful Turkish asylum seekers were not debarred from benefiting from *Savas* and the standstill clause, and the Court of Appeal held that the Secretary of State was wrong to apply current immigration rules to them and thus deny them leave. Woolf LCJ indicated in an obiter remark that this might have been different if they had committed fraud. Following this indication, Beatson J in *Yilmaz v SSHD* [2005] EWHC 1068 (Admin) held that a Turkish national who had attempted but failed to gain entry by means of false endorsements in his passport could not take advantage of the Turkish Association Agreement. He rejected an attempt on Mr Yilmaz's behalf to argue that this fraud exception should be construed narrowly so as to exclude unsuccessful fraud.

The Turkey Agreement has a developing case law and is of importance as Turkish accession to the EU is still some way off.

There were association agreements (the CEEC, Central and Eastern European Agreements) with Bulgaria, the Czech Republic, Estonia, Hungary, Lithuania, Poland, Romania, Slovakia, and Slovenia. These countries apart from Bulgaria and Romania became Members of the EU on 1 May 2004. The CEEC agreements are relevant still for the new Member States as a minimum standard for their rights to work in the old Member States during the transition period. Bulgaria and Romania are due to join the EU on 1 January 2007. The CEEC agreements are less far reaching than the agreement with Turkey. They set out some anti-discrimination provisions for employed workers, and rights of establishment (that is, to set up business) and provide services. The rights of establishment are given effect in the UK in the Immigration Rules HC 395 paragraphs 213–219, as amended.

A number of cases decided in late 2001 established principles on the effect of these agreements on the treatment of entry of nationals from these states. In C–63/99 *Gloszczuk* [2002] 2 All ER (EC), C–235/99 *Kondova* [2001] ECR I–6427, and C–257/99 *Barkoci and Malik* [2001] All ER (EC) 903, all referred from the UK, the ECJ held that the right of establishment has direct effect and so can be relied upon directly by individuals in national systems. This presupposes a right to enter and reside in the Member State (*Kondova*); however, this can be limited by proportionate national rules on entry and residence which have a relevant purpose. A visa or entry clearance requirement does have a legitimate purpose insofar as it makes it possible to restrict the rights of entry and stay to those who are establishing themselves. However, such a system should not be applied so as to force people already lawfully resident to leave the country to make a fresh application. This is disproportionate and a change of status while lawfully in the country should be allowed. Mr Gloszczuk was a Polish builder who came to the UK lawfully as a visitor and then stayed in self-employment. He sought to do so under the Poland Agreement, and the ECJ agreed that he did not need to return to Poland. Those resident unlawfully can be required to return to their country of origin to make an application for entry clearance, but when they apply, their previous breach should not be held against them. There is a contrast here with the immigration rules applicable to non-EU nationals in respect of whom a previous breach is a ground for refusal of leave to enter or entry clearance (HC 395 para 320). The visa or entry clearance requirement also cannot be employed in a way that defeats the purpose of the Agreement. If someone arrives with sufficient evidence of their capacity and intention to establish themselves, they should be admitted without the requirement for a visa, and applications for such entry may not be refused on economic grounds. The UK's immigration rules are now however written in a way that appears to conflict with this case law as they make entry clearance mandatory (HC 395 paras

215 and 217). The ECJ has also moved in this direction in Case C 327/02 *Panayotova v Minister voor Vreemdelingenzaken en Integratie*, holding that a requirement for entry clearance did not conflict with the Agreements providing there is a prompt, transparent, objective and accessible system for obtaining it.

There are less advantageous co-operation agreements with Algeria, Morocco and Tunisia, the so-called 'Maghreb agreements'. These provide for equality of treatment for employed workers only.

4.5.4 New Member States

Under the Act of Accession old Member States have an option for the first two years until 1 May 2006 to continue to apply their national law. There follows a three-year period during which old Member States have agreed to introduce greater freedom of access to labour markets. The transition period should then end (i.e., after five years), but an old Member State which has not achieved full access to the labour markets for new Member State workers may, in case of threatened or actual 'serious disturbances to its labour market', have a further two years in which to achieve full access. While full rights do not apply, the Association Agreements will continue to have effect and so, following *Kondova*, these same economic reasons cannot be used for refusing those entering as self-employed. The option to restrict access only applies to employment and does not apply at all to nationals of Malta and Cyprus. Full integration must be achieved after seven years.

The UK granted to new entrants from the new Member States a right to work from 1 May 2004, providing that they register with the Home Office within one month of obtaining employment (Accession (Immigration and Worker Registration) Regulations 2004, SI 2004/1219 as amended) Existing workers from new Member States retain access to the labour market. Under the Accession Regulations the UK does not allow someone who is seeking work to be given the status of worker with its associated benefits (which they may be under full EC free movement provisions) and there is no entitlement to claim social security benefits. Early reports showed that 96 per cent of the new arrivals were in full-time work (Accession Monitoring Report 10 November 2004). On 16 February 2006 the UK passed the European Union (Accessions) Act 2006 which enables the making of regulations to bring nationals of Bulgaria and Romania into the Workers' Registration scheme at a time to be determined.

4.5.5 Third country nationals

In many respects, those who are called 'third country nationals' have fewer rights than the nationals of non-European countries with Association Agreements. However, this assertion must be qualified in the light of another Title IV provision, the Common Visa List (Council Regulation EC 539/2001 as amended). The regulation lists those countries whose nationals require a visa to enter Europe and those whose nationals do not require a visa. The UK has not opted into this provision as the European list includes a number of Commonwealth countries which the UK has not yet included on its own visa list, for instance Trinidad and Tobago and Mauritius and would require the lifting of visa requirements in relation to some other countries, e.g., Croatia and Ecuador

While nationals of countries on the European list not requiring visas, e.g., citizens of the USA, Japan, or Singapore, do not gain European rights of free movement, they may gain entry for a short visit without obtaining a visa. Nationals of countries on the first list require visas for any purpose. Nationals of Bulgaria and Romania do not require visas, however those of Turkey, Algeria, Morocco, and Tunisia do.

Aside from visits of up to three months for non-visa nationals (Regulation EC 539/2001 Article 1), nationals of third countries have only been able to enter a European country by virtue of a European freedom of movement provision if they benefit from it by virtue of their connection with a European exercising free movement rights. For instance a third country national might enter if they were employed by a European business exercising its right of establishment in another Member State, or if they were a family member of a European citizen who was moving between Member States. Note that European free movement rights do not allow a third country national family member to enter Europe unless the European upon whose right they rely is exercising European treaty rights. For instance, the Cameroonian wife of a German business man may move to Italy with him when he sets up business there, but European law will not enable her to enter Germany from Cameroon in the first place. For primary entry to a European country, third country nationals have been reliant on the immigration law of the individual country they seek to enter.

This situation is in theory in the process of change, as Title IV enables European law provision to be made for the entry of third country nationals. However, as previously described, this aspect of implementation of Title IV has been proceeding extremely slowly. The position of third country nationals under specific European freedom of movement provisions is discussed in the next chapter.

4.6 Human rights in the EU

The EC is steadily increasing its competence in the field of human rights. The Treaty of Amsterdam gave the ECJ, in the course of exercising its normal powers under the Treaties, jurisdiction to examine the compatibility of actions of the institutions of the EU with fundamental rights. The source of these fundamental rights may be the legal traditions of the Member States, the ECtHR, or other international treaties to which member states have contributed or to which they are parties (see, e.g., Case 4/73 *Nold v Commission* [1974] ECR 491).

4.6.1 Charter of Fundamental Rights

In an initiative separate from the main Treaties, there is also a new European Charter of Fundamental Rights (OJ 2000 C 3641). This was formally adopted at the Council of Nice in December 2000 and it forms part of the Constitution for Europe. It recognizes a wide range of fundamental rights, but has a declaratory, non-binding status. It may be used by the ECJ as a source of reference for the nature of rights which should be respected in the Union, but so far the ECJ has not made a great deal of use of it. The relationship between the Charter and the ECHR is not fully resolved. The two documents are intended to be compatible, though the scope of the Charter is wider. Concerning the relationship between the two documents, the Charter's Article 52(3) says:

In so far as this Charter contains rights which correspond to rights guaranteed by the Convention for the Protection of Human Rights and Fundamental Freedoms, the meaning and scope of those rights shall be the same as those laid down by the said Convention. This provision shall not prevent Union law providing more extensive protection.

There is a contradiction here, but a plausible interpretation is that the Charter may be interpreted so as to be more protective of rights than the ECHR, but not less, and the principle of consistent interpretation cannot be used to defeat rights granted in Union law. An interesting relevant example of where the Charter could extend protection is in Article 47(2), which extends the scope of the right to fair hearing to 'rights and freedoms guaranteed by the law of the Union'. This would include any rights arising from the immigration and asylum provisions under Title IV, which as we have seen in chapter 3, are excluded from the right to a fair hearing under the present case law of the ECHR.

It is apparent from the extension of the EC's competence in the Treaty of Amsterdam that the ECJ and other EC institutions increasingly see themselves as concerned with rights in a broad and non-legalistic sense. The extension of the EC's competence and the introduction of the Charter of Fundamental Rights raise a number of issues concerning the scope of EU's competence in human rights issues.

4.6.2 Limited human rights competence

First, it does not seem to be the case that the EU has acquired a general human rights competence. In other words, it is not yet the case that the EU independently promotes human rights, but rather that it upholds human rights when these are potentially violated in defined circumstances within the existing bounds of EU law. The Constitution for Europe would not change this.

4.6.3 Relationship of human rights and Community law

Second, there are case by case issues of how European Community law and human rights principles interrelate. The idea of human rights as important principles in EC law is not new. In 1977 the European Commission, European Parliament, and Council of Ministers adopted a Joint Declaration stressing the importance that these institutions attached to fundamental rights (OJ 1977 C 103). The ECJ has on many occasions stated that fundamental human rights are a foundation of EC law, and is not a stranger to independent application of fundamental rights to the cases that come before it. For instance, in Case C–63/83 *R v Kirk* [1984] ECR 2689 the question was of the validity of the Sea Fish Order 1982 which prohibited fishing in UK waters by Danish fishing vessels. This, of course, is discriminatory. Council Regulation 170/83 Article 6(1) purported to allow Member States to derogate from the non-discrimination principle in relation to sea fishing, and to do so retroactively. The ECJ held that this would amount to retroactive imposition of a penalty which was equivalent to a criminal penalty. The Court said at para 3:

The principle that penal provisions may not have retroactive effect is one which is common to all the legal orders of the member states and is enshrined in article 7 of the European Convention for the Protection of Human Rights and Fundamental Freedoms as a fundamental right; it takes its place among the general principles of law whose observance is ensured by the Court of Justice.

Before the TEU Art F (now 6(2)) made fundamental rights a principle of EU law, the Court can be seen here employing a principle of fundamental rights by reference both to 'all the legal orders of the Member States' and to the ECHR. In Case C–5/88 *Wachauf v Bundesamt für Ernährung und Forstwirtschaft* [1989] ECR 2609 the ECJ referred to general principles of fundamental rights as enshrined in numerous international instruments to which the Member States were parties. Without naming any particular treaty or any particular right, the Court found that rules which, on the expiry of an agricultural lease, had the effect of depriving the tenant of the fruits of his labour, would breach such fundamental rights. The Court, at para 18, enunciated the following principle:

The fundamental rights recognized by the Court are not absolute, but must be considered in relation to their social function. Consequently, restrictions may be imposed on the exercise of those rights, in particular in the context of a common organization of a market, provided that those restrictions in fact correspond to objectives of general interest pursued by the Community and do not constitute, with regard to the aim pursued, a disproportionate and intolerable interference, impairing the very substance of those rights.

The Court's first assertion here must be qualified as the ECHR, and in many cases criminal law, makes some rights absolute which in theory might be interfered with in the name of free movement of workers. The right to be free from slavery is an example of such a right. The principle of free movement of workers could not be advanced to promote for instance abusive domestic labour or sex-trafficking. The Court's statement is also contentious in implying that fundamental rights may be subject to free market rights, although not so as to 'impair the[ir] very substance'. This implies a kind of sandwich structure in which, at the first level, fundamental rights may be asserted as a principle of EU law, but then interfered with in the interests of the common market, then re-asserted if that interference is too severe. *Kirk* and *Wachauf* pre-date the TEU.

After the TEU, the comparison of *Manjit Kaur* with *Airola* suggests that the ECJ did not see its role as promotion of traditional fundamental human rights above other interests. In *Airola* it appears that the Treaty's explicit commitment to eliminating sex discrimination was a stronger basis for challenging a national provision on nationality than was the principle of fundamental rights derived from the ECHR in *Manjit Kaur*. The two cases cannot however be compared as being like for like as in *Airola* the national provision was not challenged directly. The Court simply interpreted a Commission staff regulation so as to disapply the Italian law within a limited context. In *Manjit Kaur* the Court was being invited to make a declaration that the UK's own declaration appended to a treaty was invalid. This is a much more direct challenge to national sovereignty. However, in *Airola* the non-discrimination principle was treated as paramount. The Court did see its role as to further the elimination of inequality between the sexes. These rights are derived from the original economic purposes of the Community, i.e., they relate to creating equality and favourable social and economic conditions among the work force, rather than, as in *Manjit Kaur*, to the protection of life and liberty or the rights of minorities.

The relationship between human rights law and EC law is complex. For further analysis, reference should be made to works in the reading list below. We have already noted some interactions between Article 8 ECHR and freedom of movement as developed by the ECJ. For instance we have seen the bold use of Article 8 by the Court in *Carpenter*, and *Gloszczuk* and *Kondova* which were the first ECJ cases to refer to the right to respect for family life held by third country nationals. As we saw, the cases were not decided on this basis, but Court of its own motion added the rider that any removal of the applicants would have to be carried out in accordance with Article 8, i.e., with due respect for their right to family life and only if necessary in a democratic society in the interests of a legitimate aim. The unofficial aim of protecting immigration control would be the only available one, and the Court's approach to this in *Carpenter* suggests that such an aim would not be sufficient to support removal.

Case C–112/00 *Eugen Schmidberger, Internationale Transporte und Planzüge v Austria* [2003] 2 CMLR 34 broke new ground in its explicit reasoning weighing an interference with an EC right against the exercise of a fundamental right protected by the ECHR. Here a transport firm challenged the decision of the Austrian Government to permit a demonstration by environmental protesters which blocked the Brenner highway, a major international route, for 30 hours. There had been forewarning and advertising of alternative routes. The Austrian Government took its decision bearing in mind the protesters' right under Article 11 ECHR to demonstrate peacefully. The ECJ held that although the Community law 'right to free movement of goods' was engaged, the State's decision to uphold the Article 11 right, given all the measures that were taken, was not disproportionate and did not infringe EC law. Finally, fundamental rights arose in an interesting way in Case 36/02 *Omega Spielhallen und Automatenaufstellungs- Gmbh v Oberburgermeisterin der Bundesstadt Bonn* in which the German public authority had prohibited the parts of Laserdrome activity which were 'playing at killing' or simulated homicide, in the interests of public order and the protection of human dignity. In upholding the prohibition the ECJ reiterated that fundamental rights play an integral part in Community law, and then said that Community law also 'strives to ensure respect for human dignity as a general principle of law'. This being the case, it was 'immaterial' that respect for human dignity has a constitutional status in Germany. The protection of it is part of Community law anyway. A restriction on policy grounds need not be endorsed by the systems of other Member States, but it must be necessary to protect the right and no more than is required to achieve that end (i.e., proportionate).

This case is of particular interest in upholding the protection of human dignity as a fundamental legal principle, and illustrates that human rights principles in EC law come from 'the constitutional traditions common to the Member States' (*Omega* para 33) and not just the treaties such as the ECHR.

4.6.4 Challenging EC primary legislation

The third question concerning the ECJ's jurisdiction in human rights matters is: what happens if the EC's own primary legislation appears to conflict with fundamental rights? In the normal course of things the ECJ does not have power to examine the validity of primary EC legislation, and human rights do not function in the EC as a constitutional standard which would give the ECJ any special jurisdiction in this respect. This limitation on the jurisdiction of the ECJ was revealed in

Matthews v UK (1999) 28 EHRR 361. The case could not be heard in the ECJ but was considered by the European Court of Human Rights. The Court held the Members of the European Parliament, the UK, and the other Member States to be in breach of the ECHR by entering into a decision and primary legislation which excluded the people of Gibraltar from voting in European Parliamentary elections. This breached their rights under Article 3 of Protocol 1 to the ECHR which guarantees free and fair elections. Secondary legislation which is alleged to breach fundamental rights could have been challenged within the Community's own legal order, but primary legislation could not. The ECHR but not the ECJ could judge the matter.

4.6.5 **EU as a signatory to the ECHR**

This raises the further question of whether the EU could itself accede to the ECHR. This would then give the ECHR a clear jurisdiction over any matter of Convention rights which involved the EC institutions. *Matthews*, it may be noted, was brought against the UK as the EU was not a party. In 1994 the Council of the EU had asked the ECJ for an opinion on whether the EC could accede to the ECHR. At that time the ECJ ruled that it could not answer the question, though the tenor of the opinion was that the EC did not have a legal personality such that it could accede to a treaty (Opinion 2/94 [1996] ECJ 1–1759). However, on 23 June 2003, the Council of Europe voted to invite the EU to become an associate member of the Council of Europe and to sign the ECHR. The proposed Constitution for Europe gives the EU a legal personality which would enable it to do this and provides that the EU would accede to the ECHR. This would mean that an application could be made to the ECHR about any Convention right involved in an EC law matter.

This prospect of accession with or without this particular Constitutional framework raises further issues. It would be counterproductive for the ECJ to lose its human rights jurisdiction to the ECHR, and for the ECHR to become a court of last resort could make legal proceedings unduly protracted. The relationship between the two courts would need to be resolved so as to further the delivery of rights and not obstruct them.

4.7 **Conclusion**

This chapter has raised some of the policy issues which dominate immigration and asylum law in Europe, and the UK's negotiated opt-in arrangement to the provisions arising under Title IV of the Amsterdam Treaty. To date the UK has taken a leading part in discussions on asylum and has opted in to all provisions on that subject. It has also chosen to opt in to some of the increased security measures in the Schengen *acquis*, which now forms part of Community law. However, the Community as a whole has been slow to implement provisions creating rights for third country nationals, and the UK shows no inclination to opt into these. Increasing political and economic integration in Europe means that while certain historical and geographical differences will mean that aspects of the UK's immigration law will remain distinct, the influence of European provisions is ultimately irresistible.

QUESTIONS

1   Why do you think the UK negotiated an opt-in arrangement to the Treaty of Amsterdam?

2   What are the benefits to the UK of opting in to the EU measures on asylum?

3   What do you think motivated the EC to enter into the Association Agreements?

FURTHER READING

Bank, R. (2000) 'Europeanising the reception of asylum seekers', in Bommes, M., and Geddes, A. (eds.) *Immigration and Welfare: Challenging the Borders of the Welfare State* (London: Routledge).

Biondi, A. (2004) 'Free Trade, A Mountain Road and the Right to Protest: European Economic Freedoms and Fundamental Individual Rights' [2004] EHRLR 1, pp. 51–61.

Boelaert-Suominen, S. (2005) 'Non-EU Nationals and Council Directive 2003/109 EC on Status of TCNs who are long term resident: 5 paces forward and possibly 3 paces back' (2005) *Common Market Law Review* 42: 1011–1052.

Boeles, P. (2001) 'Freedom, Security and Justice for All', in Guild, E., and Harlow, C. (eds) *Implementing Amsterdam* (Oxford: Hart).

Castles, S., Crawley, H., Loughna, S. (2003) *States of Conflict: Causes and patterns of forced migration to the EU and policy responses* (London: IPPR).

Currie, S. (2006) ' "Free" movers? The post-accession experience of migrant workers in the UK', (2006) European Law Review, April, pp. 207–299.

Dale, G., and Cole, M. (1999) *The European Union and Migrant Labour* (Oxford: Berg).

Drzemczewski, R. 'The Council of Europe's Position with Respect to the EU Charter of Fundamental Rights' *Human Rights Law Journal* vol. 22, no. 1–4, pp. 14–31.

Dutheil de la Roche, J. (2004) 'The EU and the Individual: Fundamental rights in the Draft Constitutional Treaty (2004) *Common Market Law Review* 41: 345–354

European Commission (2004) Area of Freedom, Security and Justice: Assessment of the Tampere programme and future orientations, COM (2004) 4002, final, 2 June

European Council on Refugees and Exiles (2004), *Broken Promises — Forgotten Principles: An ECRE Evaluation of the Development of EU minimum standards for Refugee Protection Tampere 1999 — Brussels 2004*

Facenna, G. (2004) *Eugen Schmidberger, Internationale Transporte und Planzüge v Austria*: Freedom of Expression and Assembly vs Free Movement of Goods [2004] EHRLR 1, pp. 73–80.

Guild, E. (2001) 'Primary Immigration: The Great Myths', in Guild, E., and Harlow, C. (eds) *Implementing Amsterdam* (Oxford: Hart).

—— (1999) 'Free movement of persons in Europe: the Amsterdam Treaty and its implications for the UK' *Immigration and Nationality Law and Practice* vol. 13, no. 4, pp. 128–132.

Guild, E., and Harlow, C. (eds) (2001) *Implementing Amsterdam: Immigration and Asylum Rights in EC Law* — generally, and see specific chapters below referenced in this chapter (Oxford: Hart).

Hailbronner, K. (1998) 'European Immigration and Asylum Law under the Amsterdam Treaty' *Common Market Law Review* (1998) 35 CML Rev 1047–1067.

Hall, S. (1996) 'Loss of Union Citizenship in Breach of Fundamental Rights' *European Law Review* (1996) 21 EL Rev 129–143.

Higgins and Hailbronner, (2004) *Migration and Asylum Law and Policy in the EU* FIDE 2004, National reports, Cambridge; Cambridge University Press.

Langrish, S. (1998) 'The Treaty of Amsterdam: selected highlights' *European Law Review* (1998) 23 EL Rev 3–19.

Lenaerts, K. (2000) 'Fundamental Rights in the European Union' *European Law Review* (2000) 25 EL Rev 575–600.

Lyasky, O. 'Complementing and Completing the CEAS: a legal analysis of the emerging extraterritorial elements of EU refugee protection policy'. (2006) EL Rev. April, 230–235.

Mitselegas, V. 'The Directive on the Reception of Asylum Seekers and its Implementation in the UK', (2006) IANL Vol. 20, no. 1, pp. 42–45.

O'Keeffe, D., and Twomey, P. (1999) *Legal Issues of the Amsterdam Treaty* (Oxford: Hart) (All the above are collections of essays.)

O'Leary, S. (1999) 'Putting Flesh on the Bones of European Union Citizenship' *European Law Review* EL Rev 1999 24(1) pp. 68–79.

Peers, S. (1998) 'Building Fortress Europe: The Development of EU Migration Law' *Common Market Law Review* (1998) 35(6) 1235–1272.

—— (2002) 'Human Rights Judgments of the European Court of Justice' *Human Rights Law Review* vol. 2 (1 and 2).

—— (2002) 'EU immigration and asylum law after Seville' *Immigration Nationality and Asylum Law* IANL vol. 16(3), pp. 176–180.

—— (2003) 'Key legislative developments on migration in the European Union' (2003) 5 *European Journal of Migration and Law* 107–141.

Phuong, C. (2003) 'Closing Sangatte: the legal implications of the asylum dispute between France and the UK' IANL vol. 17(3), pp. 157–169.

Rollason, N. (2002) 'Free movement of persons: citizenship and the expanding European Union' *Immigration Asylum and Nationality Law* IANL vol. 16 (4), pp. 237–245.

Shah, P. (2002) 'Why some British nationals are not European Union Citizens' *Immigration Asylum and Nationality Law* IANL vol. 16(2), pp. 82–96.

Stevens, D. (2004) *UK Asylum Law and Policy* (London: Sweet & Maxwell), Chapter 9.

—— (2005) 'Asylum Seekers in the New Europe: Time for a rethink?' in Shah, P. (ed.) *The Challenge of Asylum to Legal Systems* (2005) London: Cavendish.

Tayleur, T. (2001) 'Schengen: opting in — but how far?' *New Law Journal* vol. 151, no. 6978, pp. 484–493.

5

European freedom of movement

SUMMARY

This chapter gives an introduction to freedom of movement for work in the European Community. The focus is on the rights of employed workers, and there is a summary also of provisions relating to the self-employed. There is discussion of the public policy reasons for excluding these rights; the relationship between UK and European law as it affects the entry of family members, particularly third country nationals; and the limits and possibilities of free movement following the introduction of European Union Citizenship.

5.1 Introduction

This chapter concerns the law of the European Community (EC) which governs the free movement of people within the European Union (EU), and the effect of European membership on the immigration law of the UK. As it is a study of European law, which guarantees freedom of movement to nationals of the European Economic Area (EEA), it is principally about the movement of European nationals, but it is also about the movement of non-European nationals as governed by Community law.

For the most part this chapter does not deal with movement into Europe from outside the boundaries of the EU. As discussed in chapter 4, the EC's new competence in law governing immigration to the Union has only a limited impact in the UK. The UK's law on entry is still principally its domestic law, but when European free movement law applies the entry of people to the UK is affected. The asylum provisions have impact in the UK in the ways discussed in chapters 4, 12, and 13.

The bulk of the law discussed in the rest of this book concerns those known in European law as third country nationals (TCNs). In this chapter the position is reversed, and most of the legal provisions concern European nationals. However, it also fleshes out the picture as regards TCNs, who may benefit from European free movement rights as a result of their connection with European nationals, for instance as a spouse or employee. While the aim of UK immigration law is immigration control, the aim of the European Treaties and their implementing legislation is to promote freedom of movement within Europe. It may therefore be advantageous for a TCN to establish a right in European law if this is available.

For a full account of the law of freedom of movement reference should be made to textbooks devoted to EC law, as mentioned at the end of this chapter.

5.2 **The two systems: free movement provisions in UK law**

European law on freedom of movement of persons is given effect in UK law by statute and rules which apply to European nationals. In the unlikely or rare event of a European provision not being given effect by these mechanisms, European law, the main relevant provisions of which are directly effective, takes precedence over any inconsistent national provision (Case 6/64 *Costa v ENEL* [1964] ECR 585). The effect is that European nationals are subject, in English law, to a different regime of control from other immigrants, although appeals against decisions made under the European provisions are made to the same appellate bodies as other UK appeals (Immigration (European Economic Area) Regulations 2006, SI 2006/1003 part 6).

5.2.1 **The implementing provisions**

Section 7 of the Immigration Act 1988 provides that those who have an 'enforceable Community right' shall not require leave to enter under the Immigration Act 1971. This means that although they are technically subject to immigration control, within that system of control they have a right to enter to exercise their freedom of movement. This may be seen at any port of entry to the UK where there is a channel for European citizens who are normally waved through on presentation of proof of right to travel. Those with an enforceable Community right are nationals of the European Economic Area (EEA), that is, EU countries, Iceland, Norway and Liechtenstein, and Swiss nationals (see below). The definition of EU nationals has already been discussed in chapter 4, to which reference should be made.

The entitlements to Community rights are set out in delegated legislation, now the Immigration (European Economic Area) Regulations 2006, SI 2006/1003. Regulation 2(1) defines EEA nationals as 'nationals of an EEA State'. Therefore in UK law the status of nationals of Norway, Iceland and Liechtenstein is equivalent to that of other EU nationals. In the 2006 regulations the definition is extended to apply the EEA regulations to Swiss nationals. The Immigration (European Economic Area) and Accession (Amendment) Regulations 2004, SI 2004/1236 and the Accession (Immigration and Worker Registration) Regulations 2004, SI 2004/1219 apply the European freedom of movement provisions to workers from the new Accession states, but with some limiting provisions as discussed in chapter 4.

The EEA Regulations use the concept of the 'qualified person'. This is a person who is an EEA national and is in the UK as a worker, a self-employed person, a provider of services, a recipient of services, a self-sufficient person, a retired person, a student, or self-employed person who has ceased activity. These are the main categories of EC freedom of movement which we consider in the body of this chapter. By Regulation 6, these terms are given the meaning that they are given in relevant EC legislation, and so the main categories of EC freedom of movement, the case law, and legislation of the EU are incorporated into English law through these regulations.

In addition to the EEA regulations a number of European rights of entry and matters under Association Agreements between the EU and third countries (see chapters 4 and 11) are incorporated into the Immigration Rules.

Although the doctrine of direct effect would, where necessary, prevent UK law from failing to deliver an EU right, it does not prevent UK law from giving greater rights to EEA nationals than are contained in EU law. Paragraph 255 of HC 395 does just this by granting the right to remain in the UK indefinitely to people (other than students) who have been issued with a five-year residence document or permit under the EEA Regulations, and been resident in the UK for four years.

5.2.2 European law: introduction and terminology

The Treaty of Amsterdam (ToA) amended the EC Treaty and renumbered most of the Articles. This chapter follows a common practice of using the new number with the old number in brackets, e.g., 'Article 39 (ex 48)' so that the connection can be made with older cases and materials.

The system of European law is not described here. For this, reference should be made to one of the many textbooks on the subject, for instance from the reading list at the end of this chapter. Knowledge of that system is useful but not essential to the reading of this chapter. EC law is founded on the principle of the free movement of goods, persons, services and capital. These four freedoms are the traditional basis of EC law, however since the creation of the political union, the European Union, a new question has arisen. The Treaty on European Union created EU citizenship, and Article 18 EC Treaty (ex Article 8a) provides:

1. Every citizen of the Union shall have the right to move and reside freely within the territory of the Member States, subject to the limitations and conditions laid down in this Treaty and by the measures adopted to give it effect.

This raises the question of whether this Article gives a freestanding right of free movement over and above the existing four freedoms. If so, what is the content of that right? This question will be addressed later when the conventional EC law free movement of persons has been considered.

5.3 Freedom of movement for workers

Free movement of persons is set out in Article 3(c) EC Treaty as one of the four fundamental freedoms of the EC. Consonant with the original purpose of the Treaty, the free movement of persons was linked to economic activity. However, as we shall see, even without consideration of Article 18, this is not limited to actually carrying out work, as the Community institutions, including the ECJ in interpreting Community law, take a liberal and purposive approach to the Community's legal provisions in order to make the free market effective. Case law and secondary legislation flesh out the content of the free movement right, but it begins with Article 39 (ex 48) of the EC Treaty, which reads as follows:

1. Freedom of movement of workers shall be secured within the Community.
2. Such freedom of movement shall entail the abolition of any discrimination based on nationality between workers of the Member States as regards employment, remuneration, and other conditions of work and employment.
3. It shall entail the right, subject to limitations justified on grounds of public policy, public security, or public health:

(a) to accept offers of employment actually made;
(b) to move freely within the territory of Member States for this purpose;
(c) to stay in a Member State for the purpose of employment in accordance with the provisions governing the employment of nationals of that State laid down by law, regulation, or administrative action;
(d) to remain in the territory of a Member State after having been employed in that State, subject to the conditions which shall be embodied in implementing regulations to be drawn up by the Commission.
4. The provisions of this Article shall not apply to employment in the public service.

Paragraph 1, setting out the objective of the Article, may be regarded as an agenda for the Court in its decisions and for the other Community bodies in making secondary legislation. Unlike UK legislation which usually prohibits a certain sort of activity, or sets out a power that may be exercised in defined circumstances, EC Treaty articles, which are the EC's primary legislation, are often phrased in terms of a purpose. The court's interpretive task is to promote that purpose within the framework of EC law.

In terms of achieving the purpose set out in para 1 of Article 39 (ex 48), the listed rights a, b, c, and d within para 3 may be regarded as the minimum content of the freedom. Paragraph 2 expresses one of the key policies of the EU, the abolition of discrimination based on nationality. Paragraph 4 on the other hand represents a concession to the sovereignty of states, permitting them, for national security or related purposes, to retain some posts specifically for their nationals. In a series of cases Article 39 has been held to be sufficiently clear, precise, and unconditional to be directly effective, see for instance Case 167/73 *Commission v French Republic* [1974] ECR 359. It may therefore be relied upon directly by a worker to protect their freedom of movement, which means it may be used as a basis for argument in national courts.

5.3.1 Personal scope — to whom Article 39 applies

For economic conditions to be rich and varied so as to provide flexible opportunities and a vibrant economic environment, it is necessary for a broad approach to be taken to the definition of who is a worker. This definition has been consistently held by the Court to be a matter of Community law, not domestic law, so Member States cannot subvert the purpose of Article 39 (ex 48) by using their own definition.

5.3.1.1 *People in work*

The term 'worker' refers to someone who is or has been employed. The rights of self-employed people are dealt with separately by the provisions on the rights of establishment and provision of services. Case C–66/85 *Lawrie-Blum v Land Baden Wurttenburg* [1986] ECR 2121 held that a worker in Community law was someone who, for a period of time, performs services under the direction of another in return for remuneration. This definition seems straightforward but is not always easy to apply. In Case C–53/81 *Levin v Staatssecretaris van Justitie* [1982] ECR 1035 a part-time worker had been refused a residence permit by the Dutch authorities on the grounds that she was not in gainful employment. The reason they gave was that she earned less than Dutch law regarded as a subsistence level of income, i.e., the minimum on which someone could live. The ECJ took account of the contribution low part-time wages can make to a family. The need to engage in such work was a real economic need. Concerning part-time work which paid less than subsistence wages, the ECJ said that it:

constitutes for a large number of persons an effective means of improving their living conditions'. Freedom of movement should not be restricted to full-time workers who were earning more than the minimum wage.

However, there would have to be some lower limit on the amount of work which would qualify. The ECJ held that the Article guaranteed freedom of movement only for those 'who pursue or are desirous of pursuing an economic activity' and that that activity had to be 'genuine and effective'. It would exclude activities 'on such a small scale as to be marginal and ancillary'.

Case 139/85 *Kempf v Staatssecretaris van Justitie* [1986] ECR 1741 established that low paid work may be supplemented not only by the earnings of other family members, but also from other sources including public funds. In *Kempf* the applicant was a music teacher who taught twelve lessons per week and supplemented his income by a claim on public funds. The court held that:

It is irrelevant whether those supplementary means of subsistence are derived from property or from the employment of a member of his family, as was the case in *Levin*, or whether, as in this instance, they are obtained from financial assistance drawn from the public funds of the Member State in which he resides, provided that the effective and genuine nature of his work is established.

Remuneration is crucial to worker status, as found originally in *Lawrie-Blum*, however the remuneration need not be in the form of a wage. This was established in Case 196/87 *Steymann v Staatssecretaris van Justitie* [1988] ECR 6159. The applicant was a German national and a plumber who lived and worked in the Netherlands. He joined a religious community in which he did plumbing and other necessary work for the community in return for his keep and pocket money. In order for him to be considered a worker, this would have to be defined as economic activity. The ECJ found that work 'which aims to ensure a measure of self-sufficiency for the Bhagwan community constitutes an essential part of participation in that community'. The services which the community provided in return for his work were regarded as payment for that work and thus Mr Steymann could be regarded as a worker.

The economic nature of the work is the key. In Case 344/87 *Bettray v Staatssecretarais van Justitite* [1989] ECR 1621 the applicant did not convince the ECJ that he was a worker as the work that he did was rehabilitative in purpose, and not economic. This was so even though he was paid a wage for his work. The work was selected because of its suitability for him rather than he for the work. The wage however does not have to be the full rate for the job. In *Lawrie-Blum* the applicant was regarded as a worker while working as trainee teacher. The wage was less than the full rate for a qualified teacher but the court noted that a trainee was giving lessons to pupils and thus providing a service of economic value to the school.

In Case 413/01 *Ninni-Orasche v Bundesminister für Wissenschaft, Verkehr und Kunst* the ECJ held that the fact that the employment contract was for a fixed short term and that she knew that in advance did not affect Ms Ninni-Orasche's claim to receive the benefits of a worker. The question is an objective one as to whether the employment is effective and genuine. Note though that since the implementation of Directive 2004/38 in April 2006 the status of worker is only retained for six months after the end of a short fixed-term contract, if the person remains unemployed.

In *The Queen on the application of Payir* [2005] EWHC 1426 (Admin) Stanley Burnton J held that there was no doubt that an *au pair* qualified as a worker. This would not often arise, as EEA nationals have no need of using the *au pair* scheme under the UK's immigration rules. However the claimant in this case was a Turkish national who had obtained leave to enter as an *au pair* under the immigration rules and applied for an extension of stay, relying on Article 6 of the Turkish Association Agreement. This she could do if she was a worker in EC terms and the High Court had no doubt that she was. The UK immigration rules were thus unlawful to the extent that they purported to limit the stay of a Turkish worker to a greater extent than the Turkey Agreement.

5.3.1.2 *People seeking work*

Article 39 itself does not mention freedom of movement for people seeking work, but neither are they excluded. Arguably for the freedom of movement for workers to be fully meaningful, it is necessary for that freedom to be extended to those who have not yet secured a job offer in another European country but wish to work there. The expectation that job-seekers will also benefit from freedom of movement provisions is implicit in Council Regulation 1612/68 Article 5, which says:

A national of a Member State who seeks employment in the territory of another Member State shall receive the same assistance there as that afforded by the employment offices in that State to their own nationals seeking employment.

In Case 316/85 *Centre Public d'Aide Social de Courcelles v Lebon* [1987] ECR 2811 the ECJ held that those who were seeking work should be entitled to equality of treatment in access to employment under Article 39 and under Article 2 and 5 of Regulation 1612/68.

Case C–292/89 *R v Immigration Appeal Tribunal ex p Antonissen* [1991] ECR I 745 considered more fully the position of unemployed job-seekers. Mr Antonissen, a Belgian national, had entered the UK, but did not find work. The UK Government proposed to deport him following his conviction for drugs offences. Part of his challenge was to the immigration rule then in force, para 143 of HC 169, which limited to six months the stay of an EC national seeking work. The Court held that an EC national should be allowed a reasonable period within which to become acquainted with the job opportunities available in the country to which they had moved, and that, in the context of that case, six months was a reasonable period. However, at the end of that time the person could still not be deported if they could show that they were genuinely seeking work and had a chance of obtaining work.

In *Lebon* and *Antonissen* a job-seeker was not treated as a worker for all purposes. The right to remain to seek work was simply a necessary corollary of Article 39, required to give effect to the freedom of movement for workers, but not in itself giving entitlement to all the rights which attach to a worker. In Case C–85/96 *Martinez Sala v Freistaat Bayern* [1998] ECR I 2691 the Court said that there was no single definition of 'worker' in Community law: 'it varies according to the area in which the definition is to be applied'. In the context of Article 39 (ex 48), 'a person who is genuinely seeking work must . . . be classified as a worker'. It is arguable on the basis of *Martinez Sala* itself that rights arising from Union citizenship under

Article 18 mean that it is no longer necessary to come strictly within the definition of worker in order to rely on a right arising from that status. The Court drew the conclusion that as Ms Martinez Sala was lawfully resident in Germany, as an EU citizen she should not be discriminated against in respect of a child-raising benefit which was found to come within the scope of Regulations 1408/71 and 1612/68. This case left open whether Article 18 gave a right to reside in another member state, but it did use the article to eliminate discrimination between Community nationals when residence was already lawful.

5.3.1.3 After work has ended

Article 39 (3)(d) accords the right to 'remain in a Member State after having been employed in that State, subject to conditions which shall be embodied in implementing regulations'. Since implementation of Directive 2004/38 in April 2006, the definition of circumstances in which this right applies is less important, as Article 16 of the Directive gives a right to remain after five years of lawful residence to all Union citizens who have sufficient resources and sickness insurance not to be a burden on the state.

Even before 5 years residence is completed there is right to remain permanently for three groups: those who have reached pension age; those who, having lived in that Member State continuously for two years or more have ceased work through permanent incapacity, and those who, after three years continuous employment and residence in a state, obtain employment in another Member State, but who return at least weekly to the first Member State (Directive 2004/38, continuing the rights implemented in Commission regulation 1251/70). An early judgment, that in Case 75/63 *Hoekstra (nee Unger) v Bestuur der Bedrijfsvereniging voor Detailhandel en Ambachten* [1964] ECR 177, held that the Treaty 'tends logically to protect also the worker who, having left his job, is capable of taking another'.

One question is whether a worker may stay in the member State after work has ended, another is whether they may retain the status of worker, with its attendant benefits.

The Court in Case C–39/86 *Lair v Universität Hannover* [1988] ECR 3161 considered that a Community national who had ceased work in order to pursue higher education would retain their status as worker if there was a link between their course and their previous employment. Alternatively, if the worker had become unemployed involuntarily, that link would not be required if they needed to retrain in order to find other work.

Case C–197/86 *Brown v Secretary of State for Scotland* [1988] ECR 3205 limits the application of *Lair*. In *Brown* the applicant was employed for eight months in work that was described as 'pre-university industrial training'. He could be regarded as a worker, but not so as to benefit from social and tax advantages under Article 7(2) of Regulation 1612/68. In the UK the Court of Appeal did not regard EC nationals who had stayed in the UK after ceasing to look for work, as 'not lawfully here' for the purposes of housing entitlements (*R v Westminster City Council ex p Castelli and Garcia* [1996] 3 FCR 383).

Council Directive 2004/38 Article 7(3) provides for the situations in which a worker who is involuntarily unemployed in a Member State may retain the status of worker. These include that he or she is temporarily unable to work because of illness or accident; he or she has been in employment for more than one year and is now registered as unemployed and seeking work; he or she has completed a fixed term contract of less than a year, though in this case the status is only retained for a further six months, and under certain conditions he or she embarks on vocational training.

Article 18 may also have a role to play here. In Case C–413/99 *Baumbast v SSHD* [2002] 3 CMLR 23, the court considered the situation of a German man who had been running a business in the UK but, when that failed, left his Colombian wife and children in the UK while he worked outside the EU. He considered the UK his family home. Directive 90/364 provided for residence to be granted to people who are self-sufficient, 'provided that they themselves and the members of their families are covered by sickness insurance in respect of all risks in the host Member State and have sufficient resources to avoid becoming a burden on the social assistance system of the host Member State'. Directive 2004/38 has replaced it in very similar terms (Article 7(1)(b)). He was refused leave to remain in the UK on the basis that his German health insurance did not cover emergencies in the UK and that therefore he did not fulfil the requirements of the Directive.

For separate reasons, Mr Baumbast's wife and child could establish a right to remain in the UK. Here, the ECJ used Article 18 in a way which demonstrates the potential of that Article to enhance greatly the scope of freedom of movement in the EU. The ECJ held that Article 18 confers directly effective rights of residence on all EU citizens. These may be curtailed, but only if conditions and restrictions are proportionate and authorized by Community law. Preventing Mr Baumbast from having a right to remain in the country where his wife and children lived, given that he supported them financially and there was nothing weighing against him apart from the terms of his health insurance, was strikingly disproportionate.

5.3.2 Material scope — the content of free movement rights for workers

Because the rights derive from a statement of principle it is impossible to give an exhaustive list of the free movement rights of workers. They are capable of expansion in accordance with situations brought before the court. However, it is possible to give an account of some of the rights found so far by the court, and of those set out in the treaty and in the secondary legislation which is designed to give it further effect. Council Directive 2004/38 on the rights of citizens of the Union and their families to move and reside freely within the territory of Member States consolidates and enhances rights in this area and was due to be fully transposed into national law by 30 April 2006. It replaces a number of earlier directives, builds on Commission Regulation 1251/70 concerning the right to remain after employment and amends Council Regulation 1612/68 concerning eligibility for employment, equal treatment, and the rights of workers' families.

5.3.2.1 *Entry and residence*

Article 39(3) (ex 48(3)) provides the right to enter the territory of another Member State and to reside there in order to take up an offer of employment. Directive 2004/38 provides that Member States must allow Community nationals entry simply on production of such identity card or passport, and no entry visa requirement or similar may be imposed (Article 5.1). Where a Union citizen or family member does not have the necessary travel documents, they must be given every opportunity to obtain them or have them brought before they are turned back at a border between Member States (Article 5.4). On production of an identity document or passport and confirmation of employment a Community national must be issued with a residence permit (Article 8.3). The residence permit is proof of the existing entitlement to free movement rights, and so possession of such a permit cannot be required as a condition of exercising the rights (*Martinez Sala*). Lawful residence for five years gives rise to a right to permanent residence (Article 16). There are also special provisions for temporary permits for seasonal workers, those on short-term temporary contracts, and frontier workers.

Member States must, 'acting in accordance with their laws,' issue identity documents or passports to their own nationals (Article 4.2). A failure to issue a passport in the UK would be more effectively challenged as a breach of this Directive, which may only be permitted on the restricted grounds allowed by Article 27, than as an unreasonable exercise of the prerogative (*R v Secretary of State for Foreign and Commonwealth Affairs ex p Everett* [1989] QB 811).

5.3.2.2 *Working conditions*

One of the fundamental principles of the Treaty is the abolition of discrimination between nationals of Member States. Article 39(2) (ex 48(2)) requires the abolition of discrimination between workers of Member States as regards 'employment, remuneration and other conditions of work and employment'. The provision has been held to apply to obvious working conditions such as the length and security of employment contracts; see, for instance, Case C–272/92 *Maria Chiara Spotti v Freistaat Bayern* [1993] ECR I–5185. It applies also to matters not within the direct province of the employer such as the refund of tax deductions. In Case C–175/88 *Biehl* [1990] ECR I–2779 these were held to be a matter affecting remuneration and so within the ambit of Article 39(2), even though the provision in question was a national tax rule rather than a condition of employment.

Regulation 1612/68 Article 7 which governs equality in relations to social and tax advantages may be interpreted to give effect to the right of non-discrimination in relation to working conditions. See for instance Case C–195/98 *Österreichischer Gewerschaftbund, Gewerkschaft Öffentlicher Dienst v Austria* [2000] ECR I–10497.

5.3.2.3 *Access to employment*

The most fundamental right relating to work is of course the opportunity to obtain a job in the first place. Article 39(3) (ex 48(3)) provides that the worker has the right to 'accept offers of employment actually made'. In addition to this, domestic legal systems must not put in place provisions which discriminate against other Member State nationals in being able to obtain such an offer of employment (Article 39(2) (ex 48(2)). Regulation 1612/68 gives further effect to these Articles:

Any national of a Member State shall . . . have the right to take up an activity as an employed person, and to pursue such activity, within the territory of another Member State in accordance with the provisions laid down by law, regulation or administrative action governing the employment of nationals of that State. He shall, in particular, have the right to take up available employment in the territory of another Member State with the same priority as nationals of that State. (Article 1)

This prohibits indirectly discriminatory provisions i.e. those which apply both to foreign and home state nationals but which would deter other Member State nationals, in addition to directly discriminatory provisions, i.e., those which discriminate between home and foreign workers. This is made explicit in Article 3 of the regulation which makes 'provisions laid down by law, regulation or administra- · tive practices of a Member State' of no effect if they

limit application for and offers of employment, or the right of foreign nationals to take up and pursue employment or subject these to conditions not applicable in respect of their own nationals; or

though applicable irrespective of nationality, their exclusive or principal aim or effect is to keep nationals of other Member States away from the employment offered.

One of the best-known cases dealing with this principle, though in the application of Article 39 (ex 48) rather than the regulation, comes from the world of football, and is Case 415/93 *Union Royale Belge des Sociétés de Football Association v Bosman* [1995] ECR I–4921. Bosman was a goalkeeper with the Belgian team, RC Liège, and after refusing an unfavourable new contract was put on the transfer list. His transfer to the French club, US Dunkerque, fell through when RC Liege failed to complete the formalities, having doubts about the solvency of the French club and therefore their ability to pay the transfer fee. Bosman challenged two provisions of the rules governing football clubs, the transfer rules inasmuch as they required a fee, and the nationality rules, which limited the number of foreign players a club could field in official matches. Both of these rules limited the possibilities for a player of moving between countries. The ECJ ruled in his favour on both counts. The clubs argued that the nationality rules did not limit employment, only the matches in which a player would appear. However, the Court said that as playing in such matches was the whole point of the contract, a limit on foreign players obviously discouraged a club from employing them. The transfer fee provisions were not directly discriminatory in that they applied without distinction to a player of any nationality. However, the Court ruled that the objective of what was then Article 48 (now 39) was not only to eliminate discrimination but also to eliminate obstacles to workers' movement between Member States. The fee was an obstacle and therefore breached the Article.

The decision in *Bosman* did not affect transfer fees charged for transfers during a player's contract, which was the reason that fees could continue to be charged if a player transferred before their contract ended. However, the Commission considered this also to be an obstacle to freedom of movement. Negotiations between the EU and football's governing bodies resulted in an agreement, but the lawfulness of this agreement has still to be tested.

One of the arguments used by the Belgian Football Association was that the rules promoted cultural identity and thus were supported by Article 151(1) (ex 128(1)) which was one of the measures introduced by the TEU 'to contribute to the flowering of the cultures of the Member States'. The TEU marked a move away from the strictly economic base of EC law and began the process of increasing the Community's competence in educational and cultural areas. The Court rejected this argument as applied to Bosman. It said that sport and culture should not be confused, and that the case concerned the freedom of professional sportspeople to move between Member States. Later intergovernmental discussions on the place of sport have not yet exempted it from freedom of movement provisions, though the sporting bodies have continued to promote that view (see McAuley 2003). The Court has restated that sportspeople are protected by Article 39 (ex 48) in Case C–176/96 *Lehtonen v Fédération Royale Belge des Sociétés de Basketball ASBL* [2001] 1 All ER (EC) 97, though accepting rules to ensure the regularity of sporting competitions, subject to a test of necessity.

There are requirements for employment which may have a genuine cultural purpose which would be protected by the Treaty, even though they are discriminatory in their effect. One of the most obvious is language, and explicit provision is made for this in Article 3 of Regulation 1612/68. This Article and its effect was considered in Case 379/87 *Groener v Minster for Education*. Groener was a Dutch national who had been working in Ireland as a part-time art teacher. After two years she applied for a full-time post and was recommended for the job. However, she was not appointed as she failed a test in Irish language. A level of Irish was required for all appointees even though the lessons would be given in English. Groener argued that as Irish would not be required for the lessons it could not be required, as provided in Article 3(1) of Regulation 1612/68, 'by reason of the nature of the post to be filled'. However, the Court supported the lawfulness of the Irish Government's policy which was that the use of Irish was being promoted in schools as a means of expressing national culture and identity. The requirement was not disproportionate to this objective, and could be upheld within Article 3(1).

5.3.2.4 *Social and tax advantages*

This provision of Article 7 of Regulation 1612/68 has been the subject of imaginative use by the Court and applicants, and is one of the major instruments in creating a legal basis for equality of social condition and opportunity. The social advantages covered by the Article are not confined to those arising from employment, as a result of Case 207/78 *Ministère Public v Even* [1979] ECR 2019. Even was a French national working in Belgium. He took early retirement, and his pension was reduced on the basis of the number of years early he had received the pension. This was the usual practice, but it did not apply to Belgian nationals who received a war service pension. Even received a French war service pension and so argued that his pension should not be subject to the early retirement reduction. Like nationality, war service is regarded as a quasi-personal relationship between the individual and the State, and the Belgian provision was to give the country's own nationals 'an advantage by reason of the hardships suffered for that country'. Therefore, Mr Even lost his claim. However, the statement of principle made by the Court in the case has wider impact:

The advantages which this regulation extends to workers who are nationals of other Member States are all those which, whether or not linked to a contract of employment, are generally granted to national workers primarily because of their objective status as workers or by virtue of the mere fact of their residence on the national territory.

This principle has been built upon in succeeding cases, of which the following are only examples. In Case 65/81 *Reina v Landeskreditbank Baden-Württemberg* [1982] ECR 33 an Italian couple living in Germany applied for a discretionary childbirth loan. The loan could only be granted where one member of the couple was German. It was means tested, and based on a policy of promoting population growth in

Germany. The Landeskreditbank refused the Reinas' application, and defended their claim in the ECJ on the basis that the political objective meant that the loan was not a social right within the meaning of Article 7(2). The ECJ looked at the question from the point of view of the impact upon workers. The actual effect of denying the loan to non-German families was that families from other Member States would be living with less material support than German families. This flew in the face of the purpose and the wording of Regulation 1612/68. Article 7(2) could include benefits granted on a discretionary basis, and the ECJ was not debarred from making decisions on social advantages which might have a political effect.

In Case 137/84 *Ministère Public v Mutsch* [1985] ECR 2681 the Court employed the *Even* formula to endorse the right of a Luxembourg national to use the German language in certain court proceedings, as Belgians were allowed to do. This social advantage had no connection with employment, and was unlikely to influence nationals of other Member States in their desire or otherwise to travel to Belgium for work. However, the Court recognized that the ability to conduct court proceedings in their own language 'plays an important role in the integration of a migrant worker and his family into the host country, and thus in achieving the objective of free movement for workers'. It may be seen from this that the objective of the law relating to freedom of movement is not only to ensure equality in working conditions, but also to remove obstacles to the social integration of workers in pursuit of a vision of a European Community in which people are genuinely free to live wherever their occupation takes them.

The judgment in Case 249/83 *Hoeckx v Openbaar Centrum voor Maatschappelijk Welzijn Kalmthout* [1985] ECR 973 showed that Article 7(2) of Directive 1612/68 may be used to fill a gap left by another provision, in this case regulation 1408/71 on social security benefits. The minimum income allowance, the 'minimex', was granted to people who could show five years' residence in Belgium, which the applicant could not as her residence in Belgium had been interspersed with periods in France. The Court found that the benefit was not one of those covered by Regulation 1408/71, but that it did constitute a social advantage in accordance with Article 7(2). Moreover, the residence condition discriminated against nationals of other Member States in access to this social advantage. It did not apply to Belgian nationals, but even if did it would still be indirectly discriminatory as non-nationals would be less likely to be able to fulfil it.

5.3.2.5 *Social security benefits*

However, Regulation 1612/68 does not give open access to the welfare benefits system of another country. In *Lebon* the Court held that a work seeker did not qualify for equal social and tax advantages under Article 7 of that regulation. This was also the view taken by the ECJ in *Collins* Case C–138/02 [2005] QB 145. The worker there was in a similar position to Mr Antonissen, having come to the UK to seek work but not yet found it. Although he would have a right under Articles 1–6 of Regulation 1612/68 to equal treatment in job opportunities, unlike Ms Martinez Sala, he had not made any economic contribution in the EU for 17 years. The Court held that his status as worker did not, for all purposes, remain intact for that period. It was relevant that his current search for work was unrelated to his casual employment 17 years earlier. He could not return to the UK and claim means-tested benefits.

This is consistent on principle with the approach in Case C–184/99 *Grzelczyk v Centre Public D'Aide Sociale D'Ottignies-Louvain-La-Neuve* [2002] 1 CMLR 19 in which the denial of a student's claim for benefit was held to be discriminatory. The situation would have been different if he had arrived in Belgium and made a claim, but he was in his fourth year of study, had worked and supported himself so far, and thus had a claim to be accorded the benefits that a Belgian student would be able to obtain in this situation.

The ECJ in these cases emphasizes that the objective of the secondary legislation on social security and social and tax advantages is not to provide a Europe-wide system of welfare support, but to co-ordinate the systems of different countries so that people do not lose out by moving. This, however, implies an engagement in the economic system.

5.3.2.6 *Education*

Education is a social advantage which is the subject of specific provisions in secondary legislation which will only be briefly described here. Access to the educational system of a host state can be obtained through three routes: (a) as a worker (b) as a student (c) as a dependant of a worker.

Article 7(3) of Regulation 1612/68 gives workers access to vocational schools and retraining on the same basis as national workers. As we have already seen, in the cases of *Brown* and *Lair* the status of worker is retained where training following work was either linked to the former occupation or was necessary re-training after the worker had become involuntarily unemployed. According to *Lair*, a grant awarded for maintenance and training constitutes a social advantage within the meaning of Article 7(2) of Regulation 1612/68. A worker would be entitled in the country where they worked or had worked to such financial advantages where these were available to a home student. Mr Brown's case must be regarded as anomalous. He was not entitled to funding for his subsequent university education, as the purpose of the work was preparation for university rather than an economic purpose.

Students have a specific right of residence for vocational education by virtue of Directive 2004/38 Article 7(1)(c) provided they can satisfy the relevant national authority: (a) that they have sufficient resources to avoid becoming a burden on the social assistance system of the host member state; (b) they are enrolled in a recognized educational establishment for the principal purpose of following a course of study and (c) they are covered by sickness insurance in respect of all risks in the host state. This does not entitlement to the payment of maintenance grants by the host state (Article 24); however, *Grzelczyk*, above, established that social security payments may be available for students where they are to host state nationals.

By Article 12 of Regulation 1612/68, children dependent on a worker have the same right of access to the education system of the host country as do nationals of that state.

5.3.2.7 *Families*

Third country nationals may benefit from European free movement law, as family members of EU migrant workers, and the right to be accompanied by family members is one of the most significant and litigated rights accorded to workers. Directive 2004/38 from 30 April 2006 supplements Regulation 1612/68, and the two must be read together with the case law on Regulation 1612/68. Directive 2004/38 replaces Regulation 1612/68 in respect of family members' right of entry, residence and employment, and Articles 10 and 11 of the Regulation are accordingly repealed. The Directive increases the rights which the family member acquires and diminishes their dependence on the Union citizen for these. Initially, family members acquire the right to enter a Member State because they are accompanying a Union citizen (Article 6). The right to reside there for longer than three months also arises by accompanying a Union citizen who is a student, worker, or self-financing (Article 7.1 and 2). This right is *evidenced*, not established, by a residence card which must be issued to the family member within six months of application and is valid for five years or such shorter period as the Union citizen anticipates staying (Article 10).

In establishing the position of third country national family members, there is a tension between underlying principles. The origin of the right of family members is the right of the worker to be accompanied by their family, and this is intended to facilitate the movement of workers in the Community and their integration in the host state. However, when the Union citizen dies, or there is a divorce, and in other situations too, the derivative aspect of the rights of family members has caused difficulties for the family members themselves. The common market principles no longer require that their residence is supported, but respect for their fundamental rights may well do so. The 2004 Directive goes some way to resolving some of these tensions.

Rights under the 2004 Directive apply to the worker's spouse, their registered partner if the *host* Member State treats such partnerships as equivalent to marriage (bringing into legislation the judgment in *Netherlands v Reed* [1986] EDR 1283), children or grandchildren under 21, dependent children or grandchildren if over 21, parents or grandparents if they are dependent, in each case of either partner. According to Article 3 Member States must also facilitate the admission of other dependants of the Union citizen, including where health grounds strictly require personal care by them, and of an unregistered partner with whom the Union citizen has 'a durable relationship, duly attested'. Family members in the Directive on family reunion for third country nationals (2003/86) are more restrictively defined.

In case law applying Reg 1612/68, dependants were treated as those who are in actual fact dependent upon the worker. There should not be an assessment of the need for support, but simply of whether the worker is actually providing support for that person (Case 316/85 *Centre Public d'Aide Sociale de Courcelles v Lebon* [1987] ECR 2811). This approach was recently confirmed in the UK in the Asylum and Immigration Tribunal in *LS (Sri Lanka)* [2005] UKAIT 00132 where no more sophisticated analysis was required than actual dependency.

Children are those who have been treated as children of the family, not only biological children. This is in keeping with the purpose of European secondary legislation and family life as defined by Article 8 of the European Convention on Human Rights, which takes account not only of biological relationships but also of the actuality of relationships. In *Baumbast* the worker's stepchild benefited from Regulation 1612/68.

Zu and Chen v SSHD [2004] Imm AR 333 broke new ground in establishing the right to be accompanied by a parent. The claimants were a mother and her child. The mother and her husband were Chinese nationals who worked for a large chemical production company which exported to various parts of the world. In the course of the husband's work he frequently travelled to the EU including the UK. The couple wished to have a second child, which was against China's one child policy. They decided to have the child in Northern Ireland. The effect of Irish law is that if a child who would otherwise have no nationality is born on the island of Ireland, that child acquires Irish nationality. The baby was an EU citizen and so had free movement rights within the EU. This meant that subject to Directive 90/364 she had a right of residence in another member state. As she had adequate sickness insurance and sufficient resources, she had a right of residence for an indeterminate period of time (para 78).

The mother and daughter sought to exercise this right in the UK. The mother was not the daughter's dependant, but she had a right to reside with the child in order to give effect to the child's right. The child was too young to live alone and her right of residence was otherwise meaningless. This was supported by Article 8 ECHR. The right to reside was also derived from the anti-discrimination provision of Article 12 EU Treaty. If the daughter had been a British Citizen her mother would have been entitled to reside with her. She should therefore not be treated less favourably because of her Irish nationality. The conscious use by the couple of Community law was not an abuse because it did not distort the purpose and objectives of Community law, but rather 'took advantage of them by legitimate means to attain the objective which the Community provision sought to uphold; the child's right of residence' (para 122). This was so even though the necessary economic self-sufficiency derived entirely from the parents, the child being too young to provide this. In the UK new immigration rules HC 395 paras 257C–E give effect to *Chen* by allowing a self-sufficient minor to live in the UK with their primary carer and other non-EEA national family members.

Chen was distinguished in *RI* [2005] UKAIT 125 where the child's Ugandan mother could not establish a right to remain in the UK on the basis of her baby's Italian nationality as they were dependent on benefits. The baby's parents were not married, and so the father did not qualify as a family member under the EEA regulations.

A family member who is an EU national may acquire EU worker status on their own account. They will be entitled to residence, equal treatment, social benefits, and all the other advantages of an EU worker. A family member from a non-EU country on the other hand would be subject to full immigration control if they were not related to the EU citizen who holds the primary right of entry. Prior to the Directive, the dependent nature of their rights caused difficulties in a number of situations.

While a couple was still married, the non-EU spouse retained their rights of residence (Case 267/83 *Diatta v Land Berlin* [1985] ECR 567). This was so whether or not they continued to live under the same roof. The regulation could not require couples to live together permanently, particularly as it gave spouses a right to work. They could not be obliged to exercise this close to where the migrant worker was employed so that they could live together, and the Court would not get involved in the reasons for physical separation. However, on divorce the non-European national lost their right of residence (*Secretary of State for the Home Department v Sandhu* TLR 10 May 1985 HL). When there were children of the relationship the harshness of this position was mitigated as Article 8 ECHR would prevent the separation of children from their parent if there was regular contact (*Berrehab v Netherlands* (1989) 11 EHRR 232), but this would have to be argued. Now, Article 13 Directive 2004/38 makes provision for retention of rights of residence on divorce, annulment or termination of registered partnership in the following situations:

- Where the relationship lasted three years including one year in the Member State.
- Where the non-EU partner has custody of their children.
- Where 'particularly difficult circumstances' such as domestic violence require it.
- Where the non-EU partner must have contact with a child in the Member State, for as long as this continues to be the case.

Article 12 of Regulation 1612/68 gives a right to children of a national of a Member State 'who is or has been' employed to be admitted to education and training on the same basis as national children and 'under the best possible conditions'. This was interpreted in *Baumbast* as meaning that where the EU worker was working away, his children could stay in the host state in education, and that the requirement for the 'best possible conditions' entailed the non-EU parent staying with them even though she could not obtain her own independent right to do so. This was also the case in the joined case of *R*, in which the parents were divorced. This has now been formalized in Article 12 of the new Directive which provides that where the EU citizen leaves the country, their children retain their right of residence while they are in education, and their custodial parent retains that right for the same period.

Article 12 of Directive 2004/38 also deals with the death of the EU citizen. Where the EU citizen dies, family members who were living with them for a year in the Member State prior to the death do not lose their rights of residence.

This is of course very beneficial, but does not remedy a situation such as that in Case 131/96 *Romero v Landesversicherungsanstalt Rheinprovinz* in which the applicant's father had died when he was a child. However he was unable to claim the benefit of what was then Regulation 1612/68 as the dependant of a worker as his father, although a Spanish national working in Germany, died before Spain acceded to the EC and so never acquired EC rights. Nevertheless, the Directive represents an increase in rights by comparison with the earlier provisions on death of the EU national spouse contained in Regulation 1251/70.

The new Directive, Article 16, provides that family members acquire permanent residence after five years, as do EU citizens. The Long Term Residents' Directive provided that third country nationals could acquire long term resident status after five years of lawful residence, and there was an opportunity to change status from family member to long-term resident. Following Directive 2004/38 there will be no apparent advantage in doing that.

The rights granted to family members of EU workers do not necessarily tackle discrimination between EU and non-EU nationals in the host country, as illustrated in Case C–243/91 *Belgium v Taghavi*. The Italian worker's Iranian wife was not entitled to a disability allowance. The entitlement was assessed on the individual claimant and was only paid to Belgians living in Belgium. She would not have received it had she been married to a Belgian. The benefit was therefore not a social advantage to a worker and was not denied to her because her husband was Italian but rather because she was Iranian. This illustrates clearly that freedom of movement provisions do not operate as pure non-discrimination rights. The fact that she lost out because of her status as a third country national was not in the first instance the result of EU law but of Belgian law. Her rights to a remedy for that in EU law were subsidiary to her husband's worker status and this did not have a bearing on the grant of the benefit. If she herself had been Italian she could have argued her case directly as an EU national suffering discrimination in provision of a social benefit.

It can happen that the derivative nature of family members' rights can work in their favour. Case C–60/00 *Carpenter v SSHD* is a significant case concerning the rights of family members. Mr Carpenter was a UK national living in the UK from where he ran a business which involved a significant amount of travel to other Member States, where most of his clients were based. Mrs Carpenter was a Phillipine national who had overstayed her visitor's visa and married Mr Carpenter. She was refused leave to remain in the UK because of her irregular immigration status at the time of her marriage. She challenged the decision that she should return to the Philippines to apply for entry clearance and a residence permit on the basis that she had Community law rights. The fundamental question in the case is whether Community law rights are engaged at all. The ECJ concluded that they were. Mr Carpenter was exercising his rights under Article 49 (ex 59) to provide services in another Member State. His capacity to do this was hindered if his wife had to return to the Phillipines and so could not look after the children during his absences, and if she could not travel freely with him because she would not gain re-entry to the UK.

The ECJ placed great emphasis on the infringement of Article 8 ECHR which was entailed by separating Mr and Mrs Carpenter. Deportation was disproportionate as although she had infringed immigration law there was no other complaint against her. Therefore, Mr Carpenter's Article 49 rights were infringed by requiring his wife to leave the country. It may be seen here that Mrs Carpenter could have established no independent right to stay in the UK either under EU or national law. Her right derived from the nature of her husband's business.

Entry as a family member

In order to obtain a residence card in a Member State, in addition to showing the document with which they entered (passport or identity document) the family member may only be asked to produce evidence of their relationship or dependency. The right of entry of the non-EU partner may be subject to a visa requirement, but it is disproportionate and therefore prohibited to send them back at the border for lack of a visa provided they are able to prove their identity and marriage and there is no evidence to suggest they present a risk to public policy, etc. (Case C–459/99 *Mouvement Contre Le Racisme, L'Antisemitisme et la Xenophobie Asbl (MRAX) v Belgium* [2002] 3 CMLR 25). This decision is important for the movement of third country nationals in Europe in confirming that the harsh effects of domestic immigration laws should not be visited on those who are married to European nationals. This was affirmed in C–157/03 *Commission v Spain* in which Spain was not allowed to require a visa for a family member that entailed a long process of decision-making. Furthermore, when it kept a particular applicant waiting more than six months Spain violated Directive 64/221 which sets a six-month limit on processing such applications. This time limit is reproduced in Directive 2004/38 and now incorporated by amendment in the UK's implementing regulations (SI 2006/1003 reg 17).

Social and tax advantages

If a worker obtains the right to remain after the end of work in accordance with Article 17 (see 5.3.1.3 above), their family members obtain the right to remain permanently also.

Article 24 provides that family members who obtain a right to remain are entitled to equality of treatment as are workers. An illustration of equal treatment in relation to social advantages is found in the case of Case 32/75 *Fiorini v SCNF*. Here an Italian woman and her children were resident in France. She was the widow of an Italian man who had worked in France and died in an industrial accident. During his life he had been entitled to a fare reduction card for large families, but when she claimed this after his death it was refused on the grounds that she was not French. She claimed discrimination in breach of what was then Article 7 of the EEC Treaty, now Article 12 (ex 6) and of Article 7(2) Regulation 1612/68. This case predated *Even*, but the ECJ still took the view that the social advantages referred to in Article 7(2) did not have to arise from a contract of employment. The Article was intended to refer to all social and tax advantages. As the family had a right to remain in France after Mr Fiorini's death, pursuant to Regulation 1251/70, they also had a right to equal treatment in relation to these social advantages. Combining the effects of Article of Regulation 1251/70 and Article 7(2) of Regulation 1612/68 they were entitled to the fare reduction card as would be any French family in a comparable situation.

The right to social advantages for family members is illustrated in a different way by Case C–261/83 *Castelli v ONPTS*. Here, an Italian woman went to live with her son in Belgium after her husband died. Her son had retired in Belgium and had a right to stay there permanently, pursuant to Regulation 1251/70. As his family member she was entitled to install herself with him under Article 3 of Regulation 1251/70. She claimed the guaranteed income which was paid to all elderly people in Belgium, but was initially denied it. The ECJ ruled that the guaranteed income was a benefit paid to workers primarily because of their objective status as workers or by virtue of their residence on national territory and the extension of which to workers would facilitate their mobility within the Community. It therefore came within the definition of a social advantage as laid down in *Even*. The grant of such a social advantage to dependent relatives could not be on a discriminatory basis. The Court in *Lebon* commented that the grant of benefit in *Castelli* was because it could be construed as an advantage to the worker. His mother was dependent on him, and so a financial advantage to her benefited him. In *Lebon* the child of the worker was no longer dependent and so there was no social advantage to the worker in his child receiving the minimex. Therefore an erstwhile dependant who has become independent can no longer qualify for such social advantages.

An important right for families established in Regulation 1612/68 Article 11 and continued in Directive 2004/38 Article 23 is to 'take up any activity as an employed person throughout the territory of that same state'. If the worker moves to another Member State (unless for a short temporary period), the right of a third country national partner to remain in their job depends on Article 13, discussed above. An

EU partner however would have the status of worker in their own right, providing they are engaging or can engage in meaningful economic activity.

As mentioned earlier, the worker's children's right to education is the same as that of host state nationals, and continues after their parent has ceased work. In keeping with the spirit of the Article and the Treaty, admission to education is interpreted to include provisions such as grants which facilitate admission (Case 9/ 74 *Casagrande v Landeshauptstadt München* [1974] ECR 773 and Cases 389/87 and 390/87 *Echternach and Moritz v Minister van Onderwijs en Wetenschappen* [1989] ECR 0723).

5.3.2.8 *Relationship with UK law*

UK law on the entry and settlement of spouses differs in material ways from the rights of spouses to accompany EU workers pursuant to Regulation 1612/68 or 1251/70 or Directive 2004/38. At the point of initially gaining entry, a spouse coming to join their UK husband or wife must have proved that they can be supported and accommodated without recourse to public funds (HC 395 para 281). There is in effect a means test in UK law to gain entry of a spouse. No such test applies to a spouse of an EU worker accompanying them. They only need show valid travel documents and prove the marriage. Conversely, after two years of marriage and residence, a spouse who entered through UK law can apply for settlement (HC 395 para 287). They will then have the right to live in the UK, to claim benefits, and not be tied to any particular employment or employment status. A spouse entering with an EU worker obtains the same entry entitlement as the worker, i.e., usually a residence card for five years. They can only apply for settlement after four years (HC 395 para 255).

In EU law there is no test of intention to live permanently together as is found in the UK immigration rules. A spouse is held not to qualify as a spouse for the purpose of the Treaty or secondary legislation if the marriage is one of convenience. By a non-binding resolution of 4 December 1997, the European Council defines a 'marriage of convenience' as one entered into between an EU national or legally resident third country national and a third country national 'with the sole aim of circumventing the rules on entry and residence'. This is a much more stringent test than the old primary purpose rule in UK law. Evasion must be the *sole* aim of the marriage, rather than one motive among many. The resolution sets out a list of factors which may provide grounds for believing that the marriage is one of convenience. They include for instance that the parties do not live together after the marriage, that they do not speak a language understood by both, and they are inconsistent about details such as each other's nationality and job. These provisions are directed at obvious subversion of the rules, are more objective, and have not given rise to the invasions of privacy and voluminous case law that have accompanied national marriage rules.

In Case C 370/90 *R v Immigration Appeal Tribunal and Surinder Singh ex p Secretary of State for the Home Department* [1992] ECR I–4265 the ECJ considered the position where a British national entered the UK with her Indian husband, after they had both been living and working in Germany. If she had never left the UK she would have had to use UK law to bring her husband in. However, as she had exercised her Community right of freedom of movement by going to work in another EU country her husband had the right of entry with her under EU law. The Immigration

(EEA) Regulations 2000 incorporated this judgment in reg 11 and the right of a spouse returning to the UK with a UK national now derives from the Regulations.

In *Sahota v Secretary of State for the Home Department* [1998] 2 WLR 626 the English Court of Appeal expounded on the issue by holding that the spouse entered on the same terms as their sponsor. This much is clear from Community law as we have already seen. Mrs Sahota argued that this meant that as she was a British national with the right of abode, her husband should obtain immediate settlement. However, the Court of Appeal said that there are two different systems of law and the entrant must choose which to use. If Mr Sahota wanted to enter using EU law then he could only obtain the most advantageous kind of entry available in that system, namely a five-year residence permit. If he used the UK system, with its means testing, he could apply for settlement after a year (as the rules then provided). The two systems could not be blended to produce instant settlement. In *Kungwegwe v SSHD* [2005] EWHC 1427 (Admin) the court seemed to accept some blending of the two systems. Mrs Kungwengwe had lived lawfully in the UK from 1992 to 2004, and applied to be granted indefinite leave to remain in the UK on the basis of the long residence rules (see chapter 6), which required ten years' lawful residence. Lawful residence was defined in the immigration rules as either exemption from immigration control or having leave to enter or remain. Mrs. Kungwengwe had spent her last four years of residence on a residence permit following her marriage to a Portuguese national. That marriage had broken down and her husband's whereabouts were unknown. As she was unable to show that he was a qualifying person under the EEA regulations she was unable to apply for indefinite leave to remain after four years' residence as his spouse. Wilkie J held that she was not lawfully resident for the purposes of the long residence rules as she was not exempt from immigration control, and did not have leave to enter or remain, because, as a holder of a residence permit and the spouse of an EEA national she did not need it. The Home Office said they would be prepared to accept her lawful residence if she could show she remained a family member of a qualifying person, and Wilkie J agreed that would be right, though in that case she could have applied for ILR under para 255 anyway.

The difference in treatment between spouses of UK nationals and spouses of other EU nationals entering the UK was upheld by the ECJ in Case 356/98 *Kaba v Secretary of State for the Home Department* [2000] ECR I–2623. Mr Kaba was a Yugoslavian national in the UK who married a French woman who was working in the UK. He became entitled to remain as the spouse of an EU worker. After some 18 months in the UK Mr Kaba applied for indefinite leave to remain. If he had married a UK national he would by then have been entitled to make this application and to succeed in it under para 287 HC 395. His application was refused, as under para 255 of the Immigration Rules an EEA national and their spouse are only entitled to apply for indefinite leave to remain after four years' residence. Mr Kaba claimed in the ECJ that this was discriminatory contrary to Article 7(2), the social advantage in question being the right of the spouse to become settled after one year. The Court did not find in his favour, saying that

Member States were entitled to rely on any objective difference there might be between their own nationals and those of other Member States when they laid down the conditions under which leave to remain indefinitely in their territory was to be granted to the spouses of such persons.

In so saying they did not make any pronouncement on whether the right of a spouse to apply for indefinite leave to remain should be construed as a social advantage, although following *Reed* it seems that it should be.

The UK Government had successfully argued that the position of the spouse of an EC worker was not comparable with the position of the spouse of a UK citizen because the right of nationals of other Member States to reside in the UK is not unconditional whereas the right of a UK national is. Furthermore, to give the spouse the right to apply for indefinite leave to remain after one year would give them a right greater than that of the migrant worker on whose status they depended.

The ECJ's judgment proceeds on the basis that it is the applicant, Mr Kaba, who is making the claim of discrimination. However, the distinction, accepted by the ECJ for justifying a difference in treatment is a distinction between the status of the EU national and the UK national. The 'objective difference' found by the ECJ and relied upon by the UK government is the difference in status between a sponsoring UK spouse and an EU worker bringing a spouse to the UK. This basis for the decision demonstrates the difference between the right being that of the entrant spouse and the right being derived from the EC migrant worker's status. Mr Kaba attempted to re-open the case on the basis that the difference between a UK principal and another EU principal was not as great as alleged because the UK principal had only to be settled, i.e., to have indefinite leave to remain, and this status is entirely comparable with that of an EU national resident in the UK. The difference was not actually one of nationality. This argument failed however in a brief judgment in which the Court restated its earlier position (Case C–466/00).

Further exploration of the application of *Surinder Singh* took place in Case C–109/01 *SSHD v Akrich*. Here, the non-EEA spouse was the subject of a deportation order from the UK and as such had no right to reside in the UK. He and his British wife moved to Ireland and then sought to return to the UK some months later, claiming to exercise their Community rights. The ECJ held that in order to benefit from Regulation 1612/68 a non-EEA spouse must be lawfully resident in the country from which they move, which Mr Akrich was not as his residence was in breach of a deportation order. However, even in this situation, the Member State must have regard to the right to respect for family life under Article 8 ECHR when the couple seek to return. Mr Akrich could therefore not be refused entry without a proper consideration of the reasons for refusing him entry and the proportionality of so doing (see chapter 3). The court also held that the reasons for the couple's attempting to exercise treaty rights were irrelevant. They rejected the idea advanced by the UK Government that because this application was an abuse of Community rights it should not succeed. This contention reflected the UK's regulations then in force which provided that family members could not exercise their rights of entry if the EEA national left the country 'in order to enable his family member to acquire rights under these Regulations and thereby to evade the application of UK immigration law' (Immigration (European Economic Area) Regulations 2000, SI 2000/2326 reg 11(2)(b)). As a consequence of *Akrich* this form of reg 11(2)(b) was deleted and replaced by a requirement only that the family member is lawfully resident in the other EEA country (now Immigration (European Economic Area) Regulations 2006, SI 2006/1003 reg 12). This is an objective rather than a subjective requirement.

UK regulations were also amended in 2003 to give effect to *Baumbast and R*. The regulations which give effect to Directive 2004/38 include the concept of a 'family member who has retained the right of residence' (Immigration (European Economic Area) Regulations 2006 SI 1003 reg 10. This status may be obtained by the widow(er) of a qualified person who had been living with them for a year, a direct descendant of a deceased qualified person or their partner who is in full time education, the custodial parent of such a person, and the partner of a qualified person after termination of a marriage or civil partnership under conditions as set out in the Directive, including that they have custody of a child.

The new regulations also effect the implementation of Directive 2004/38 by including registered partnerships and an expanded definition of students to include students on vocational courses.

5.4 **Internal effect**

In a number of cases applicants have sought to use rights granted by European law in situations which have not involved the crossing of national borders. The ECJ has held that these situations must be regarded as internal to Member States and thus not involving freedom of movement. The doctrine of internal effect began with Case C–175/78 *R v Saunders* [1979] ECR 1129. Ms Saunders was a British national from Northern Ireland who was convicted of an offence in England and bound over to return to Northern Ireland and keep out of England and Wales for three years. The ECJ declined to interfere with this. They took the position that the state was entitled to impose restrictions within the Member State upon its own nationals where this was done in the course of criminal law. This kind of restriction had no European law dimension, and the Court had no mandate to interfere.

Cases 35 & 36/82 *Morson and Janjan v Netherlands* [1982] ECR 3723, show that this principle prevents European law from being used to extend domestic law on family reunion. The applicants in this case were nationals of Surinam, and went to the Netherlands to visit their children who were Dutch nationals and upon whom they were dependent. They applied for residence permits to live with their children using Article 10 of Regulation 1612/68. However the Dutch nationals had not exercised freedom of movement rights. They simply lived and worked in the Netherlands. Therefore, the Court found that there was no external or European element in this case, and the parents could not use European law to enable them to live with their children. This may be contrasted with the case of *Surinder Singh*, discussed above, where because Mrs Singh had travelled to work in Germany, she was able to use her European right to bring her husband back with her to the UK. The Commission in *Morson and Janjan* commented that this approach was necessary to prevent nationals from abusing Community law in order to avoid more stringent national law. However, as we have seen in relation to *Akrich* above, the Court has now found motivation to be irrelevant.

As Arnull comments in *The European Union and its Court of Justice* (1999), such abuse would be hard to differentiate from a genuine use of Community law and such an inquiry could distort the proper development of the freedom of movement provisions. Whether the 'internal effect' limitation on the reach of EC law can be sustained in the light of Article 18 (ex 8a) is open to question. A number of commentators have suggested that if borders within the EU are to be removed, the requirement of movement across borders in order to trigger family reunion rights is artificial. In *Carpenter v SSHD*, discussed above the Court was invited by the UK Government to find that the situation was purely internal as Mrs Carpenter did not cross EU borders. However they declined to do so. The artificiality was recognized by the Commission in early drafts of the Family Reunion Directive in proposing that discrimination between EU nationals who exercise their right of freedom of movement and those who do not should be abolished in respect of family reunion. This proposal did not survive to the final version of the directive, and discussions on the subject were finally abandoned and the Commission proposal withdrawn (COM (2004) 542 final 3).

It is interesting that the ECJ in *Chen* rejected the argument that the situation was purely internal. The fact that she had not made use of freedom of movement did not, the court thought, make the situation entirely an internal one. Although she was exercising her right to live in the Member State in which she was born (the UK), she was doing so as an Irish national.

5.5 Rights of establishment and provision of services

These two rights concern self-employment, defined by the ECJ in a case under the CEEC agreements as economic activities carried out by a person outside a relationship of subordination concerning the choice of activity, working conditions, and conditions of remuneration; under that person's own responsibility; in return for remuneration paid directly to that person and in full (Case C–268/99 *Jany v Staatssecretaris van Justitie* [2001] ECR I–8615 para 70).

These rights are only very briefly dealt with here for the sake of completeness, and to show that the general principles of free movement for the self-employed are similar to those for workers, though the specific provisions and details may differ. Once again, for a fuller account, reference may be made to a textbook on EC law.

5.5.1 Characteristics of establishment and provision of services

Self-employed nationals who work in another Member State are protected by Article 43 (ex 52) and its associated secondary legislation if they take up the right of establishment, i.e., they work from a base within the host Member State. If, however, they work in the host state without becoming established there then the relevant legal provisions are those governing the right to provide services under Article 49 (ex 59). The difference between these two categories is not always clear cut. At the time of the Treaty the distinction was probably clearer, but nowadays electronic communication opens up modes of operating in business that were unknown then. Such factors as the physical base of a business are less relevant, and its geographical scope of operation is harder to identify. The reason for the difference is that the rules on establishment envisage the business will be integrated into the economy of the host state. It is therefore reasonable to expect the business to be subject to the relevant rules in that state. In the case of provision of services, the degree of integration into the host state is less and the business is subject to the laws of the state where it is based. It would be an impediment to freedom of movement to make the business subject to a second set of legal provisions in the host state also.

As an example of the way the Court approaches this distinction, Case C–55/94 *Gebhard v Consiglio dell'Ordine degli Avvocati e Procuratori di Milano* [1995] ECR I–709 concerned the right of a German lawyer to practise in Italy and call himself a lawyer there. The ECJ decided that his practice came within the right of establishment. He practised 'on a stable and continuous basis', his services were available to nationals of the host state, and he maintained premises there from which he operated.

Where the Court considers that a self-employed person is keeping their place of establishment outside a Member State, even though most of their services are actually provided there, it may regard this as an evasion and deem the undertaking to be established in the state where work is carried on, for instance Case 404/98, *Josef Plum v Allgemeine Ortskrankenkasse Rheinland, Regionaldirektion Köln*.

To be covered by Article 49 (ex 59) the services must be paid for. This payment need not come from the recipient of the services (Case C–352/85 *Bond van Adverteerders v Netherlands* [1988] ECR 2085) but must, however, have the character of a commercial arrangement. An educational course taught under the national education system and paid for by the state did not qualify as provision of services under Article 49 (ex 59) as the nature of the activity was unaffected by whether pupils or parents paid anything towards it. The state was seeking to fulfil its social, cultural, and educational duties to the population rather than to make a profit (Case 263/86 *Belgium v Humbel* [1988] ECR 5365). Private educational services are in a different category. The many ventures which now have mixed state and private funding may throw up some difficult questions in this context.

The Court in Cases 286/82 and 26/83 *Luisi and Carboni v Ministero del Tesoro* [1984] ECR 377 found that the Treaty Article covers recipients of services for instance, 'tourists, persons receiving medical treatment and persons travelling for the purposes of education or business'.

5.5.2 Restrictions on freedom of establishment or provision of services

There is some debate as to whether the protection against discrimination is the same for Articles 43 and 49. The right of establishment under Article 43 is certainly protected against direct discrimination on the grounds of nationality, and the provision of services under Article 49 is protected against any obstacle unless it can be objectively justified. This means that the obstacle must be:

- adopted in pursuance of a legitimate public interest which is not incompatible with Community aims;
- equally applicable to persons established in the state and would be avoided if the person providing the services were established in another state;
- objectively justified as necessary and proportionate to the aim (Case 33/74 *Van Binsbergen v Bestuur van de Dedrijfsvereniging voor de Metaalnijverheid*).

The case of *Gebhard*, however, suggests that any disincentive to establishment, even if it is not express and direct discrimination on the ground of nationality, will also be prohibited.

Article 43(1) (ex 52(1)) prohibiting restrictions on the freedom of establishment has direct effect (Case 2/74 *Reyners v Belgium* [1974] ECR 631), as has Article 49 (ex 59), in relation to restrictions on provision of services. The positive aspect of the rights is to take up self-employment in another Member State under the same conditions as are laid down for nationals of that Member State.

One of the issues raised here is recognition of qualifications. Directive 89/48 replaces earlier specific directives with a general system for the recognition of higher education diplomas awarded on completion of professional education and training of at least three years' duration. Directive 92/51 covers recognition of other diplomas in relation to regulated professions. Where qualifications are not covered by a specific Directive there should be an examination of their merit rather than dismissing them (Case C–234/97 *Fernandez de Bobadilla v Museo Nacional del Prado and others* [1999] ECR I–4773).

5.5.3 The morality of services

Lotteries have been the subject of ECJ judgments on provision of services, as the extent to which they are lawful varies from State to State. The Court has held that 'even if the morality of lotteries is at least questionable, it is not for the Court to substitute its assessment for the legislature of the Member State where activity is practised legally. 'Providing the activity is lawful in some Member States, the Court will not on grounds of immorality deem it not to be a service. Restrictions may be placed upon such services providing they are not discriminatory on grounds of nationality' (Case C–275/92 *Customs and Excise v Schindler* [1994] ECR 1039).

In Cases 115 and 116/81 *Adoui and Cornouaille v Belgium* [1982] ECR 1665 the ECJ held that prostitution could not be restricted for non-nationals when it was not restricted for nationals. *Jany* (above) confirms that the same principles apply under the CEEC agreements.

5.5.4 Internal situations

As with workers, the Court does not consider that freedom of establishment provisions can apply in a 'purely internal' situation but is not quick to identify a situation as purely internal. For instance, in Case 115/78 *Knoors v Secretary of State for Economic Affairs* [1979] ECR 399 the Court held that the article could not be interpreted to exclude a Dutch national who had lawfully resided in Belgium, obtained a plumbing qualification and worked there, and then returned to the Netherlands. It was discriminatory to prevent Mr Knoors from practising on his return to the Netherlands.

As mentioned above, the cross-border nature of services is harder to identify now than when the Treaty was drawn up. However, in Case C–384/93 *Alpine Investments BV v Minister van Financien* [1995] ECR I–1141 the ECJ held that the offer of financial services by telephone to potential recipients in another State contained the necessary cross-border element.

5.5.5 Other rights comparable to workers

Rights of residence for the self-employed, whether establishing or providing services, are now contained in Directive 2004/38, replacing 73/148, and thus are on a par with those of workers that we have already discussed.

The self-employed, whether using the right of establishment or of provision of services, are also entitled to non-discriminatory provision of certain social benefits. For instance, in Case C–63/86 *Commission v Italy* [1988] ECR 29 access to reduced-rate mortgages and to social housing. In Case C–186/87 *Cowan v Le Trésor Public* [1989] ECR 195 a British tourist who was attacked and robbed on the Paris Métro was entitled to receive the social benefit of the French criminals injuries compensation scheme. The ECJ held that the corollary of freedom of movement was 'the protection of that person from harm in the Member State in question, on the same basis as that of nationals and persons residing there'.

5.6 Public service exceptions

The EC Treaty recognizes that some kinds of work may require a particular affiliation to the State, and where this is the case it may be legitimate for the state to restrict work to its own nationals. Each of the three treaty Articles we have considered, Article 39 (ex 48), 43 (ex 52), and 49 (ex 59), includes an exception in relation to public services. The way this works in each Article is to provide that those who are employed in public service are exempt from the other provisions of the Article. This gives the state the right to discriminate on the basis of nationality in opportunities to be admitted to public service.

The first question is what kind of work counts as public service? This is one of those issues, like the definition of a 'worker', which the ECJ regards as a matter of Community law, and thus within its provenance to determine. The definitions of Member States will not be conclusive as this would give them power to define the terms of their own exemption, which would not be appropriate. Two approaches to the question have been identified, the 'institutional approach' and the 'functional approach'. The institutional approach would say that because a person is employed by a particular body, say, a national railway, this employment is defined as employment in the public service. The functional approach would look at what is entailed in the work and determine whether this should qualify as public service. The ECJ tends to prefer the latter approach, while Member States have attempted to argue for the former.

In Case 149/79 *Commission v Belgium* the Court set out some characteristics which could bring employment within the definition of public service. First, the post presumes on the part of the employee and employer a 'special relationship of allegiance to the State'. Second, there is a reciprocity of rights and duties which form the foundation of the bond of nationality. Third, the post must involve the exercise of powers conferred by public law and duties designed to safeguard the general interests of the State.

There is no secondary legislation to clarify the concept of employment in the public service, but the Commission has published guidance which suggests when the exception might apply. It includes certain functions within the armed services, police, judiciary, tax authorities, and certain public bodies engaged in preparing or mounting legal actions. It would generally not include nursing, teaching, and non-military research (1988 OJ C 72/2). This guidance is not legally binding.

When a non-national is actually employed in public service, the Article 39(4) exception cannot be used to treat them less favourably than national workers. The exemption allows states to restrict employment to their own nationals where special duties or allegiance are required, it does not give them freedom to discriminate against non-nationals where there are no such objections to employing them. This was illustrated in Case C–195/98 *Österreicher Gewerkschaftbund, Gewerkschaft Öffentlicher Dienst v Austria*. The case concerned the union's challenge to the practice of discounting periods of service spent in other Member States when reckoning periods of service for the purposes of pay and promotion. Part of the government's defence was that the employment of teachers was employment in the public service and therefore exempt under Article 39(4). This argument clearly fell right within the principle just mentioned; the non-recognition of earlier periods of service was not a matter connected with access to employment but to conditions of employment once in post. The government could therefore not claim the exemption under Article 39(4).

The exception in Articles 45 (ex 55) and 55 (ex 66) takes effect in relation to 'activities which in that state are connected, even occasionally, with the exercise of official authority'. In Case 2/74 *Reyners v Belgium* [1974] ECR 631 a Dutch lawyer had obtained his legal education in Belgium, but was refused admission to the Belgian bar on the grounds that he was not of Belgian nationality. The Court said that the extension of the exception to the whole profession was not permissible where activities connected with the exercise of official authority were separable from professional activity as a whole. The exercise of official authority in the legal profession was the exercise of judicial authority by judges, and not contact with the courts by advocates.

5.7 Public policy exceptions

The discussion of freedom of movement in this chapter so far has shown that questions of Community law are approached generally from the point of view of whether the person or situation comes within the scope of the right. There is not the examination of counterbalancing factors which is entailed in applying the qualified Articles of the ECHR. However, there is what is known as a public policy exception to the freedoms we have been considering. This is the only basis for deportation of an EEA national, and it is the most visible and significant means of immigration control exercised in relation to EEA nationals. The grounds for deportation should be compared with those for other foreign nationals, discussed in chapter 16. Freedom of movement may be curtailed by refusal of entry or deportation on grounds of public policy, public security, or public health, known collectively as the 'public policy exception'. Directive 2004/38 replaces Directive 64/221 in implementing this exception. The basic grounds are the same, but there is enhanced protection for the individual in the later Directive, as we shall see.

5.7.1 **Public health**

This may be dealt with briefly. Article 29 of the Directive says:

1. The only diseases justifying measures restricting freedom of movement shall be [those] with epidemic potential as defined by . . . the World Health Organization and other infectious or contagious parasitic diseases if they are the subject of protective provisions applying to nationals of the host Member State.
2. Diseases occurring after three months from the date of arrival shall not constitute grounds for expulsion from the territory.

Article 29.1 represents a tighter policy than its predecessor, as Directive 64/221 listed specific diseases in addition to those listed by the World Health Organization. Article 29.2 allows for some possibility of expulsion as opposed to refusal of entry; Directive 64/221 did not.

Medical examinations may only be required 'where there are serious indications that it is necessary' within the first three months after arrival. By way of comparison, UK immigration law may require a medical examination of any applicant for settlement.

5.7.2 **Public policy**

This is the more contentious and frequently used ground. It encompasses public security, which is not treated as a separate ground. There is no definition of 'public policy' in the Directive or by the ECJ, but the court interprets the Directive restrictively in order not to interfere with the purposes of the Treaty.

Article 27.2 of the Directive provides:

Measures taken on grounds of public policy or public security shall comply with the principle of proportionality and shall be based exclusively on the personal conduct of the individual concerned.

Previous criminal convictions shall not in themselves constitute grounds for the taking of such measures.

The requirement for proportionality is new in the 2004 Directive, the other wording being identical in the earlier Directive.

The first of the issues in Article 27.2, that of personal conduct, has been important in many cases. The requirement has been elaborated in uncompromising terms in the 2004 Directive, as follows:

The personal conduct of the individual concerned must represent a genuine, present and sufficiently serious threat affecting one of the fundamental interests of society. Justifications that are isolated from the particulars of the case or that rely on considerations of general prevention shall not be accepted.

To appreciate the radical nature of this paragraph comparison needs to be made with grounds for UK deportations discussed in chapter 16, where it will be seen that a general policy of deterrence is often accepted by the courts as justifying an individual deportation. This new element in Article 27.2 sharply illustrates the social objectives of EU law, and shows the legislature reiterating its intention where it was not followed sufficiently on earlier occasions.

Accordingly, it is clear if it was ever in doubt that one of the earliest and foundational decisions on the application of the public policy exception, would not be decided the same way today. Case 41/74 *Van Duyn v Home Office* [1974] ECR 1337, concerned whether association with an organization could amount to personal conduct. Ms Van Duyn was a member of the Church of Scientology and was refused leave to enter the UK to work for the Church because the UK government considered its activities to be socially harmful. The ECJ concluded that a decision of this kind was within the permissible range of discretion for a Member State, and this was the case even if (as was the case here) the organization had not been made unlawful in that Member State, and its nationals could participate in it without legal sanction. It would be an undesirable distortion of social policy to require a government to outlaw an activity so that it could prevent people from entering the country to take part in it. The Court would however expect to see some administrative measure taken against the activity. In the *Van Duyn* case a statement in Parliament sufficed for that. Arnull (1999) suggests that the political background of Britain's renegotiation of its terms of European membership may have encouraged the ECJ to be lenient to the UK in this case.

The judgment in *Adoui and Cornouaille* referred to above takes a different approach, and suggests a more likely approach if *Van Duyn* were heard again today. The ECJ would be concerned to see that effective measures were taken against nationals who engaged in the activity in question before regarding it as a suitable basis for excluding a non-national. In *Adoui and Cornouaille* the Belgian authorities were not permitted by the ECJ to derogate on grounds of public policy from the obligation to issue prostitutes with residence permits. Prostitution was not illegal in Belgium and there was not a strong enough policy reason to prevent non-nationals from engaging in an activity that was not prohibited for nationals.

Parity with nationals is also suggested by Case 36/75 *Rutili v Minister for the Interior* [1975] ECR 1219. In this case an Italian national residing in France was subject to restrictions which prevented him from residing in certain French territories. When he obtained a Community law residence permit this was made subject to the same restrictions. The ECJ held that public policy considerations could not justify exclusion from only part of the territory. The exclusion must be from the whole territory or not at all. An exclusion from part of the state's territory could not be made using Directive 64/221. It could only be made under domestic law, and then in such a way as to treat the non-national in the same way as nationals. The later case of C–100/01 *Ministre de L'Intérieur v Olazabal*, however, held that a partial restriction of this nature could be justified if public order or security considerations warranted it, and if the alternative was deportation.

EU nationals should not be deported as a sanction for administrative lapses or irregularities. In Case C–215/03 *Oulane* it was disproportionate to detain and deport a French national who did not produce identity on two occasions when requested.

5.7.2.1 *Criminal convictions*

The most common basis for derogation using public policy is criminal conduct. The ECJ has reinforced on a number of occasions that previous convictions do not in themselves constitute grounds for exclusion or expulsion. However, such convictions may be taken into account in determining whether someone should be deported or denied freedom of movement rights on the grounds of public security or public policy. The proper approach is identified in the leading case of Case 30/77

R v Bouchereau [1977] ECR 1999. Here, the defendant, a French national working in the UK, was convicted for a second time of unlawful possession of drugs. The sentencing court wished to recommend that he be deported. Two questions were referred to the ECJ. First, whether the recommendation for deportation was a 'measure' in the terms of Directive 64/221 Article 3(1) ('measures taken on grounds of public policy or public security shall be based exclusively on the personal conduct of the individual concerned'). Second, if it was, in what circumstances could criminal convictions be taken into account in deciding to recommend deportation?

On the first question, the Court ruled that a recommendation for deportation was a 'measure' within Article 3. On the second, the Court ruled that 'the existence of previous criminal convictions can only be taken into account in so far as the circumstances which gave rise to that conviction are evidence of personal conduct constituting a present threat to the requirements of public policy'. Elaborating, the Court went on, 'recourse . . . to the concept of public policy presupposes . . . a genuine and sufficiently serious threat to the requirements of public policy affecting one of the fundamental interests of society'. However the court also issued a caveat that in sufficiently serious cases conduct alone would warrant deportation. Directive 2004/38 adopts the wording of *Bouchereau*.

By way of illustration, the personal conduct of the applicant in Case 67/74 *Bonsignore v Oberstadtdirektor der Stadt Köln* [1975] ECR 297 could not be said to pose any threat to public policy affecting one of the fundamental interests of society. He was an Italian worker resident in Germany who purchased a gun. While he was handling the gun it went off and killed his younger brother. The incident was a tragic accident, and there was no reason to deprive Mr Bonsignore of his German residence on the grounds of public policy.

The more explicit wording in Directive 2004/38 means that cases such as Case C–348/96 *Donatella Calfa* [1999] ECR I–0011 should no longer need to come before the ECJ. Here, an Italian national was excluded from Greece under a rule which provided for exclusion in the case of certain offences. This rule was not based on the conduct of the individual as it was applied simply on the basis of the conviction. It was therefore not a permissible restriction on freedom of movement under Directive 64/221. This must mean, as Macdonald suggests, that para 320 (18) of the Immigration Rules HC 395 cannot be applied to EEA nationals. This paragraph provides that entry clearance or leave to enter the UK should normally be refused where the applicant has committed an offence punishable in the UK with imprisonment of 12 months or more. The presumption of refusal is another such blanket rule, now conflicting with Directive 2004/38.

We can usefully compare the EC public policy proviso with the UK law concept of a deportation being 'conducive to the public good'. Theoretically, the emphasis in both is not on what the individual has done but on the effect of their continued presence on society. The European law standard, however, makes more demands on the state than the UK law standard. Although the Home Secretary in UK law has the burden of proving that the deportation is conducive to the public good, until the Human Rights Act 1998, the decision only needed to be weighed against compassionate circumstances, not justified as an infringement of fundamental rights. The Court of Appeal in *R v IAT ex p Al-Sabah* [1992] Imm AR 223 rejected an attempt to apply the European approach more widely than EEA nationals. In EC law the state's argument must be sufficient to outweigh the right of freedom of movement, within a system in which this freedom is the primary purpose, and the Court has repeatedly stated that this power of derogation must be interpreted restrictively. Even following the Human Rights Act the UK courts have been ready to find deportation necessary in a democratic society for the prevention of crime, even when the evidence suggests that the proposed deportee will not re-offend (e.g., *Samaroo v SSHD* [2001] UKHRR 1150).

In UK courts and tribunals the caveat in *Bouchereau* permitting deportation when past conduct is sufficiently serious has been applied in offences involving Class A drugs, for instance the case of *Marchon* [1993] Imm AR 384 in which a Portuguese doctor had been convicted of importing 4.5 kilos of heroin. The Court of Appeal found that this conduct by a doctor showed a disregard for the fundamental moral tenets of society. As such it would justify deportation following *Bouchereau* without any evidence of a likelihood of re-offending.

In cases where the proposed deportee has a family or private life in the UK, the disruption to this must be proportionate to the public interest pursued in accordance with Article 8 ECHR. In *B v Secretary of State for the Home Department* [2000] 2 CMLR 1086 Sedley LJ took the view that the protection of private life requires an even stronger justification for its infringement than the protection of free movement rights. However, comparison between cases concerning European and non-European nationals does not suggest that this approach is always followed.

Comparison may be made in this respect between the case of *Carpenter*, discussed above, and the case of *Mahmood v SSHD* [2001] 1 WLR 840, discussed extensively in chapters 3, 9, and 17. Both cases concerned a non-European national with an irregular immigration status. Mrs Carpenter had overstayed and Mr Mahmood had entered illegally, but both were liable to the same sanction: namely, removal. Both were married to British citizens settled in Britain and both had children. Both, apart from their illegal status, met the requirements for leave to remain as a spouse. Both claimed that their removal would breach their right to family life under Article 8 and in both cases the Secretary of State replied that they could leave the country and apply for entry clearance from their home state. In each case to do so would cause difficulties. For Mrs Carpenter this would cause disruption to her husband's business as he would be unable to travel while she was away, for Mr Mahmood, he would lose his job, thereby jeopardising his chances of entry clearance and destroying his family life altogether. The claim in *Carpenter* was made under Article 49, and as discussed above, the ECJ readily concluded that Mr Carpenter's freedom to pursue his business would be interfered with by Mrs Carpenter being required to leave the country. The court concentrated though on the breach of Article 8. It concluded that the requirement to leave was disproportionate to the aim of enforcing immigration law. There was no examination of Mr Carpenter's knowledge of his wife's faulty immigration status or any enquiry as to whether he could be expected to follow her to the Phillipines (the answer to this would have been that he could not, but the question was not even raised). By contrast, the Court of Appeal in *Mahmood* considered Mrs Mahmood's state of knowledge relevant, and concluded that she could follow him to Pakistan, as she had come from that country originally. Her right of abode as a British citizen did not enter the picture at all.

Recent judicial consideration of the deportation of the partner of an EU national may be found in *Machado v SSHD* [2005] EWCA Civ 597 where the Court of Appeal said that the Tribunal's obligation was to stand back from the evidence and address the legal questions: 'does the appellant's conduct manifest a real and sufficiently serious threat to a fundamental interest of society, and if it does is it proportionate in all the circumstances to deport him?'. His immigration history could come into the consideration of whether it was proportionate to deport him as it could be relevant to whether he would be likely to respect the law, and thus part of whether his presence presented a danger to public policy. Mr Machado married after a notice of intention to remove was served upon him, and his wife then took advantage of her entitlement to Irish nationality, thereby introducing EU rights. Following the rule change consequent upon *Akrich*, his EC rights were valid in law, even if they had been obtained in order to rely upon them, and the Home Office dropped its contention that the marriage was one of convenience.

Directive 2004/38 Article 28 introduces a new set of protections against expulsion. Firstly, it sets out counterbalancing personal factors which should always be considered. Equivalent to the widest possible interpretation of the ECHR Article 8, it includes 'social and cultural integration into the host Member State'. Secondly, where the individual has a right of residence, an expulsion decision may not be taken except on 'serious grounds of public policy or public security'. Thirdly, where a Union Citizen has more than ten years residence, an expulsion decision may only be taken on 'imperative grounds of public security'. It is clear that expelling an EU national is intended to be a rarity.

5.7.2.2 *Procedural rights*

Article 8 of Directive 64/221 provided that a person excluded or denied entry should have the same legal remedies in respect of that decision 'as are available to nationals of the State concerned in respect of acts of the administration'. Case C–65/95 *Shingara and Radiom* [1997] ECR I–3343 determined that the right to seek judicial review would fulfil this requirement in a national security case where a non-European would have no right of appeal. However, Directive 2004/38 provides for a right to judicial procedures for all expulsion decisions. Furthermore, it provides for appeals to have suspensive effect, i.e., to stop the removal, where an application is made for an interim order to suspend enforcement, with limited exceptions for repeat cases and where expulsion is based on 'imperative grounds of national security'.

In the UK, the right of appeal to the Special Immigration Appeal Commission in national security cases, provided for in the amended EEA regulations was made non-suspensive by SI 2005/47, now Immigration, Asylum and Nationality Act 2006 s 7.

An important decision in terms of European law's impact on rights in UK law was C–357/98 *R v SSHD ex p Yiadom* [2000] ECR I–9265. Here, the ECJ held that a decision refusing leave to enter after the applicant had been in the UK for seven months on temporary admission was in reality a decision to remove her, not a decision on entry. This would therefore attract a right under Article 9 Directive 64/221 to have an appeal before removal, which was not available to a non-European. As mentioned in chapter one, one of the sub-themes of immigration and asylum law in the UK at present is the creation of a kind of non-status; a condition of being present in body but not in law. Here the European Court of Justice takes a very realistic approach. It is not appropriate to give someone a temporary status in the country, then make a decision which means they must leave, but to label it a decision on entry rather than removal and so deprive them of appeal rights (compare *Khadir*, discussed in chapter 15).

5.8 A general right to freedom of movement? Article 18

All the rights we have considered in this chapter are specific rights dependent upon certain conditions being fulfilled. They do not amount to a general right to reside in other Member States without being, at the very least, say, a work seeker. At the beginning we noted that there is an outstanding question as to the effect of the status of EU national, introduced by the TEU. Article 18 EC Treaty (ex Article 8a) provides:

1.   Every citizen of the Union shall have the right to move and reside freely within the territory of the Member States, subject to the limitations and conditions laid down in this Treaty and by the measures adopted to give it effect.

On the face of it this Article could give a general right to reside, but it is expressed to be subject to other Treaty provisions and secondary legislation. The scope and effect of Article 18 is in the course of being explored in the courts.

The exploration began when this provision first appeared in the Treaty on European Union.

Case C–378/97 *Wijsenbeek* [1999] I–6207 was an attempt to test directly the ambit of Article 8a (now 18) and reveals the view of the Commission on the direct effect of the Article. Mr Wijsenbeek, a Dutch national, refused, when entering the Netherlands through Rotterdam airport, to present his passport to establish his nationality. He maintained that the only scheduled flights into Rotterdam airport were from other Member States, and that therefore national provisions compelling production of a passport were contrary to the EC Treaty. Specifically, they infringed Article 7a (now Article 14) of the Treaty which provided for the progressive establishment of the internal market and the consequent abolition of frontiers, and of Article 8a (now 18) giving EU citizens freedom of movement throughout the Union. The Spanish, Irish, and UK Governments, who all made representations in this case, argued that Article 8a was not capable of having direct effect. The Commission on the other hand argued that the direct effect of Article 8a was 'uncontestable'. Most strikingly, 'the Commission states that the right to move and reside freely constitutes an autonomous and substantive right subject to the specific limitations and conditions laid down in the Treaty and its implementing provisions. This new right conferred on citizens of the Union should be interpreted broadly and its exceptions and limitations should be interpreted strictly'.

The case was decided on a point which was agreed upon by all parties, namely that the provisions to harmonize external borders had not in fact come into effect and therefore the internal market was not yet perfected. This being the case, Member States were entitled to request proof of a traveller's entitlement to travel. The Court therefore did not give a judgment upon the effect of Article 8a (now 18) or the content of any rights it imported.

In *Manjit Kaur* the English court referred to the ECJ the question of whether

Article 18 (ex 8a) has direct effect, but as we have seen, the Court did not comment on Article 18, restricting its opinion to the capacity of Member States to determine nationality questions. As Ms Kaur was not, by this definition, an EU national, the question of the effect of Article 18, they said, did not arise.

The development of the effect of Union citizenship is indicated in Case C–85/96 *Martinez Sala v Freistaat Bayern* ECR [1998] I–2691. Here the ECJ said that a Member State cannot require a discriminatory condition to be fulfilled by a Community national who 'has authority to reside' in another Member State. It left open for the referring court the question of whether she was a worker or a self-employed person for the purposes of Regulation 1612/68 or 1408/71, not having sufficient information to determine that question. However, *quite apart from any such designation*, Ms Martinez Sala was still entitled to protection against discrimination as a lawfully resident EU citizen. The ECJ said that in a case such as *Martinez Sala*

> it is not necessary to examine whether the person concerned can rely on Article 8a of the treaty in order to obtain recognition of a new right to reside in the territory of the Member State concerned, since it is common ground that she has already been authorised to reside there . . . As a national of a Member State lawfully residing in the territory of another Member State, the appellant . . . comes within the scope . . . of the provisions of the Treaty on European citizenship. Article 8(2) of the Treaty attaches to the status of citizen of the Union the rights and duties laid down by the Treaty . . . It follows that a citizen of the European Union, such as the appellant . . . lawfully resident in the territory of the host Member State, can rely on Article 6 of the Treaty [which prohibits discrimination on grounds of nationality].

In this passage the Court rejected the view that Article 8a (now 18) provides any new right of residence, however it regarded Ms Martinez Sala's status as Member State national and lawful resident as sufficient to give her the protection of the Treaties, whether or not she came within the definition of worker or any other specifically protected category. To the extent that Ms Martinez Sala did not have to fit precisely within an existing category, the decision seems to point in the direction of Article 18 (ex 8a) enhancing existing rights, but without giving a right to reside. The effect of this is not entirely clear, but the case points in the direction of developing the potential of Article 18.

The English Court of Appeal after *Martinez Sala* and the Treaty of Amsterdam has continued to reject any direct effect of Article 18 (ex 8a), as illustrated in the case of *Ahmed and Barrow v Secretary of State for the Home Department* Imm AR [2000] 370, where the Court took the view that Article 18 could not authorize entry of TCN relatives where the UK residents had not exercised freedom of movement. The rejection of direct effect goes hand in hand with the rejection of the application of freedom of movement to situations characterized as purely internal, as demonstrated in *R v SSHD ex p Adams* [1995] All ER (EC) 177. Nevertheless, this does not seem to be the direction of change.

In the ECJ the developments hinted at in *Martinez Sala* are unfolding. In *Grzelczyk* the Court held that a condition requiring students to be of Belgian nationality before they could claim the minimex social security payment breached the principle of non-discrimination read in the light of Article 17 (ex 8). 'The prohibition of discrimination on grounds of nationality was to be read in conjunction with the right to move and reside freely within member states.' While it was acceptable for states to require that students should not be a burden on the social assistance system of the state, the concept of Union Citizenship and the freedom of movement that went with it meant that students studying in another Member State should not be penalized. The scope of the Treaty provisions on freedom of movement was thus extended to students in a new way by use of Article 17 (ex 8).

The effect of Articles 17 and 18 is taken a step further in the joined cases of *Baumbast and R*, the family rights implications of which we have considered above. The ECJ held that to exclude Mr Baumbast on the basis of possible shortcomings of his private health care scheme was disproportionate, and found so on the basis of Article 18. Article 18, it said, conferred *directly effective* rights of residence on all EU citizens. These rights could be constrained, as the text of the Article provides, but such constraints must be proportionate.

This decision gives an indication that a right of residence for all EU nationals is developing. However there are caveats to this. One is the slightly later case of *Olazabal* in which the Court did not consider it necessary to rely on Mr Olazabal's rights of residence as an EU national because these were subsidiary to his existing rights as a worker. The case concerned public order and security, and so it is understandable that the restrictions were upheld. However, if the court is developing a consistent view of EU citizenship as a basis for the exercise of rights, it might be expected that they would say that in this case such rights would not assist him, rather than regarding them once again as subsidiary (see Toner, H., ILPA European Update December 2002).

The ECJ did not accept an argument in *Collins*, although this was supported by the Commission, that Article 18 entailed that he should qualify for benefits on arrival. The judgment is interesting in its treatment of Mr Collins' status. He was American-born, and had in recent years additionally acquired Irish nationality. However he had spent relatively little time in EU countries. The Court was uncompromising in its maintenance of Union citizenship as the criterion for benefiting from EU rights. They held that in view of the establishment of Union citizenship and the right of union citizens to equal treatment 'it is no longer possible to exclude . . . a benefit of a financial nature intended to facilitate access to employment in the labour market of the Member State'. This did not mean however that the State could not set a period of residence in order to qualify for such a benefit.

The ECJ in *Chen* built upon *Baumbast* to develop the notion of the child's right of residence. *Baumbast* had recognized the right of residence of an adult carer for a child in education. *Chen* took this a step further by recognizing the right of a carer in order to allow the child to exercise their right of residence at all. This right of residence was buttressed by Article 18. Providing she was financially self-sufficient, the child had a right to residence on account simply of her EU citizenship.

Directive 2004/38 is another step in the direction of development of free movement. The recitals indicate that it is intended to 'simplify and strengthen the right of free movement and residence of all Union citizens'. As we have seen, it does this in various ways, though not without limit. It reiterates the earlier principle that free movement applies on the basis of citizenship, but 'subject to the limitations and conditions laid down in the Treaty and the measures adopted to give it effect'. It repeats the important limitations of previous legislation that those who reside in a Member State for longer than three months must have sufficient resources not to be an economic burden on the host state. The result of the ECJ judgment in Case C–456/02 *Trojani v Centre public d'aide sociale de Bruxelles* was that Article 18 could not save Mr Trojani from this requirement, in fact at worst a claim for benefit might persuade the national authorities that he had ceased to fulfil his conditions of residence.

A further caveat concerns European enlargement. The nationals of the new Member States have a chequered collection of rights, depending on which country they seek to enter, and their full status will only accrue after seven years. It will be interesting to see how the ECJ approaches the question of Article 18 in relation to these EU citizens.

5.9 Conclusion

The ECJ has developed the rights of freedom to move for work, often in very creative ways, and at the same time has safeguarded against excessive demands being made on the welfare systems of Member States. The focus is on economic activity or the potential for it. The area of change is particularly now in the way that the use of Article 18 develops. It suggests a vision of a united Europe which is truly an area of free movement at least for its nationals. Directive 2004/38 is a significant development enhancing rights of free movement. In the area of family reunion EC law not only concerns the mobility of workers, but also human rights and the immigration policies of individual Member States. *Carpenter* shows that in the context of the objective of free movement, taking Article 8 into account can have a profound effect. There is a gradual development of human and economic rights hand in hand, and EU enlargement provides an enormous challenge for this process.

QUESTIONS

1   Was the ECJ right to refuse entitlement to benefit to Mr Collins? Do you have any sympathy with the Commission's view that Article 18 requires that the mobility of citizens of the Union should not be impeded by being unable to claim benefits while they look for work? After all, Mr Collins would only have qualified for income-based job-seeker's allowance if he was genuinely seeking work.

2   Do you agree with the Court in *Akrich* that motivation is irrelevant when a couple relies on the rights arising from *Surinder Singh*?

3   The mother in *Chen* had no right of residence in the UK prior to the birth of her child. Is the case consistent with *Akrich*?

FURTHER READING

Carlier, J-Y. (2005) Case Note on *Chen, Common Market Law Review* (2005) 42: 1121–31

Guild, E. (ed.) (1999) *The Legal Framework and Social Consequences of Free Movement of Persons in the European Union* (London: Kluwer Law International).

Daniele, L. (1997) 'Non-Discriminatory Restrictions to the Free Movement of Persons' *European Law Review* (1997) 22 EL Rev 191.

Fairhurst, J. (2006) *Law of the European Community*, 5th edn (Oxford: Longman).

Hall, S. (1991) 'The European Convention on Human Rights and Public Policy Exceptions to the Free Movement of Workers under the EEC Treaty' *European Law Review* (1991) 16(6) 466–488.

Hall, S. (1999) 'The European Convention on Nationality and the right to have rights' *European Law Review* (1999) 24 EL Rev 586–602.

Handoll, J. (1988) 'Article 48(4) EEC and Non-National Access to Public Employment' *European Law Review* (1988) EL Rev 13(4) 223–241.

Hansen, J. L. (2000) 'Full Circle: Is there a difference between the Freedom of Establishment and the Freedom to Provide Services?' *European Business Law Review* (2000) EBL Rev 11(2) 83–90.

Hilson, C. (1999) 'Discrimination in Community free movement law' *European Law Review* (1999) 24 EL Rev 445–462.

Jacqueson, C. (2002) 'Union Citizenship and the Court of Justice: Something New under the Sun? Towards Social Citizenship' *European Law Review* (2002) 27(3) 260–281.

McAuley, D. (2003) 'Windows, Caps, Footballs, and the European Commission. Confused? You Will Be' *Competition Law Review* [2003] 24(8) 394–399.

O'Keeffe, D. (1992) 'The Free Movement of Persons and the Single Market' *European Law Review* (1992) 18 EL Rev 3–19.

Oosterom-Staples, H. (2005) Case note on *Collins Common Market Law Review* (2005) 42: 205–233

Peers, S. (2001) 'Dazed and Confused: Family Members' residence rights and the Court of Justice' *European Law Review* (2001) EL Rev 26(1) 76–83.

Rogers, N., and Scannell, R. (2005) Free Movement of Persons in the Enlarged EU (London: Sweet & Maxwell).

Spaventa, E. (2005) Case note on *Akrich Common Market Law Review* (2005) 42: 225–239

Steiner, J., and Woods, L. (2006) *Textbook on EC Law*, 9th edn. (Oxford: Oxford University Press).

Toner, H. (2001) 'Community law immigration rights, unmarried partnerships and the relationship between European Court of Human Rights jurisprudence and community law in the Court of Justice' *Web Journal of Current Legal Issues* [2001] 5 Web JCLI.

Toner, H. Chen — judgment of the ECJ *IANL* vol. 18, no.4 (2004), pp. 265–266.

SECTION 3

The system of immigration control

6

Entry, stay, and decision-making

SUMMARY

This chapter is concerned with the legal process by which a person enters the UK, the status they may acquire in immigration law after their arrival, and the institutions which are involved. The Common Travel Area is introduced. The chapter describes the role and powers of entry clearance officers and immigration officers in granting entry clearance and leave to enter, and considers the general grounds for refusal of leave or entry clearance. Finally, there is discussion of the consequences of a decision to grant leave, and of how the most secure immigration status of settlement may be achieved.

6.1 Introduction

The legal processes described in this chapter apply to all those who are subject to immigration control (Immigration Act 1971 s 3(1)). To obtain entry it is necessary to bring an application within a specific category in the immigration rules, e.g., spouse, dependent child, work permit holder, or to make a successful asylum claim. The law relating to the various categories of entry is dealt with in the fourth part of this book and asylum claims in the fifth part. The provisions discussed in this chapter apply throughout, in other words, to those whose applications are discussed in part four, and, where relevant, to asylum seekers. The power to give or refuse leave to enter is the foundation of immigration control, and to understand the system it is necessary to study the grant and refusal of leave to enter and remain in their own right. The study of these powers and of their interpretation by civil servants and judicial bodies reveals more about the nature of immigration control and the way that it is changing.

6.1.1 Changing nature of immigration control

The development of immigration control from the Aliens Act 1905 up to the end of the twentieth century was increasingly complex in detail but quite simple in concept. Immigration control was the very visible exercise of sovereignty by an island nation. At the borders, whether sea or air, immigration officers determined whether a passenger needed leave to enter, and if so whether and on what terms to grant it. The exception to this was the Common Travel Area (see discussion later in this chapter) which expressed a recognition that the land border between Britain and Ireland required a more flexible approach.

At the end of the twentieth and beginning of the twenty-first century this traditional model has begun to dissolve. A principle reason for this is the UK's increasing involvement in the European Union, as discussed in chapter 4. Although the UK has not yet opted into many immigration provisions made under the Treaty of Amsterdam, it is actively participating in the effort to harmonize European asylum policy, and has begun to participate to an extent in security measures such as the Schengen information system and the Eurodac fingerprinting system. Among the European Union member states who share land borders, there is a tradition of internal security, for instance the compulsory use of identity cards. The UK's gradual movement towards harmonization with the rest of Europe, increasingly sophisticated international intelligence networks, increasingly sophisticated communication media, and the dominance of immigration policy by the objective of deterring asylum claims have combined to extend border control further than the geographical edges of the UK and make it a more dispersed process. Immigration control is becoming a matter of interception, policing, and internationally coordinated restriction of movement and not just of granting leave by a stamp in a passport at a port of entry.

At the beginning of the twenty-first century the system could rightly be said to be in transition. It still bears some of the features of geographical border control, but at the same time it bears features of a new and more dispersed system, mainly introduced by the Immigration and Asylum Act 1999. Both these kinds of characteristics will be identifiable in the account of the system which follows. In the traditional model, which still applies for the vast majority of passengers, immigration control is exercised principally at two points. One is the port of entry, the other is an entry clearance post at an Embassy, High Commission, or diplomatic post overseas. Immigration control at the port of entry is administered by the immigration service, a branch of the Home Office Immigration and Nationality Directorate (IND). Asylum applications and applications for leave to remain in the UK after initial entry are dealt with by the IND.

In this chapter we shall be looking at the central structures and processes of control, noting the changes to a more diffuse control as they arise. Chapter 7 describes some elements of the wider distribution of immigration control.

6.2 Scope of immigration control

6.2.1 Who is subject to immigration control?

People who are subject to immigration control must go through immigration control in order to enter the UK lawfully. The question of who is subject to immigration control has been answered more fully in the chapter on nationality and right of abode. The answer may be summarized as follows. British citizens and Commonwealth citizens with right of abode are not subject to immigration control (Immigration Act 1971 s 3(1)). The following groups are, strictly speaking, subject to immigration control but do not need leave to enter: nationals of the European Economic Area (Immigration Act 1988 s 7); air and sea crews making a lawful stop within s 8(1) of the 1971 Act; servicepeople, diplomats, and their households;

people arriving from another part of the Common Travel Area (1971 Act s 8); and prisoners brought to the UK to give evidence in drug-trafficking cases (Criminal Justice (International Co-operation) Act 1990 s 6). Certain representatives of governments and those benefiting from immunities conferred by Orders in Council referring to international tribunals and other international bodies are exempt from immigration control under the Immigration (Exemption from Control) Order 1972, SI 1972/1613, as amended. All other passengers need leave to enter. Visa nationals need entry clearance which must be obtained at an entry clearance post overseas. The list of visa national countries is appended to the Immigration Rules and is updated (usually lengthened) frequently. There were 106 such countries at the time of writing. To put that number in perspective, the United Nations currently recognizes 191 countries. Since 13 November 2005 there is less difference between visa nationals and non-visa nationals as all non-EEA nationals need entry clearance for stays of more than six months, bringing the UK's visa provisions closer to those of the European common visa list.

Prior entry clearance was introduced by the Immigration Appeals Act 1969 for applications to join family members in the UK. This control was aimed at limiting entry from the New Commonwealth. The expansion of that system by the introduction and expansion of the list of visa national countries is directed towards controlling and reducing asylum claims, and visa national countries tend to be those which are perceived to produce the majority of asylum claims. This is an example of the influence on immigration law of government policy to deter asylum claimants. Countries are added to the list when circumstances suggest that asylum claims from there will increase. For instance, during the three months of July to September 2002, a total of 2,105 Zimbabweans sought asylum in the United Kingdom, almost as many as in the whole of 2001. In November 2002 the Secretary of State announced that Zimbabwe would become a visa national country.

Although asylum claimants need leave to enter, this cannot be granted until their asylum claim has been processed. This cannot be done at the port as the investigation is too complex, and by the nature of the claim cannot be done before arrival. Asylum claimants are therefore normally given a status called temporary admission pending determination of their claim (Immigration Act 1971 Sch 2 para 21); alternatively they may be detained. Detention and temporary admission are discussed in chapter 15.

For recognized refugees, the issue of a travel document pursuant to the obligation in the 1951 UN Convention Relating to the Status of Refugees was until recently all that was necessary. So if a person was granted refugee status in Germany, they could present their travel document to enter the UK. However, from 11 February 2003 the UK suspended its participation in the 1959 Council of Europe Agreement on the Abolition of Visas for Refugees 'on public order and security grounds'. All holders of refugee travel documents now therefore require a visa before coming to the United Kingdom.

6.2.2 Common Travel Area

6.2.2.1 *Common Travel Area — introduction*

Entry from another part of the Common Travel Area is an exception to the requirement for leave to enter. Agreements on absence of immigration controls between the UK and Ireland have existed in various forms since the founding of the Irish Free State in 1922. Although there were restrictions on travel during and for a short while after the Second World War, these were relaxed after an exchange of letters between the two governments in 1952 proposed a similar and mutually enforced immigration policy. This laid the foundation for the present day Common Travel Area (see Ryan 2001). The UK implemented this by repealing the requirement for aliens to obtain leave to land from Ireland (Aliens (No 2)) Order 1952, SI 1952/636. The arrangement for an absence of immigration control between the two countries and mutual assistance with enforcement included passing information between governments about the movement of aliens. In particular there was and still is a sharing of intelligence about those who appeared on the other country's list of undesirable aliens.

The present-day Common Travel Area consists of the United Kingdom of Great Britain and Northern Ireland, the Channel Islands, the Isle of Man, and the Republic of Ireland. It was established by Immigration Act 1971 s 1(3) which provides that journeys which are purely between any of these places (i.e., they do not start or end outside the CTA) are free of immigration control. This does not mean, however, that the whole of the immigration law of the CTA is entirely harmonized or that it is subject to the same laws. The UK, Islands, and Ireland remain different jurisdictions. Neither does it mean that no individual travelling is subject to any restriction, as there are exceptions to this freedom of movement. The effect of the CTA is to create an area somewhat similar to the Schengen system, in which there is mutual enforcement of each other's immigration laws but which does not facilitate entry to the area from outside.

6.2.2.2 *Common Travel Area — operation*

The Isle of Man and Channel Islands, while their inhabitants have British nationality, in theory have their own immigration laws. In reality, British immigration statutes are applied in the Islands with slight modifications. Because there is one nationality, Islanders are not subject to British immigration control, and vice versa. Immigration Act 1971 Sch 4 gives effect in the UK to the immigration laws of the Islands. The result is that limited leave granted in the UK or Islands has effect with the same limitations throughout the UK and Islands. Similarly, deportation orders made in the UK or Islands are given effect in each other's jurisdiction and illegal entry into one is illegal entry into the others.

Citizens of the Republic of Ireland on the other hand, are subject to British immigration control (and vice versa). The Common Travel Area means that British and Irish citizens may enter Ireland and Britain respectively without leave and without having to present a passport to establish their status, but like other EEA nationals they may be deported. There is an additional provision for the exclusion of Irish citizens if the Secretary of State personally directs that their exclusion is conducive to the public good (Immigration (Control of Entry through Republic of Ireland) Order 1972, SI 1972/1610 article 3(1)(b)(iv) and (2)).

The CTA effects mutual enforcement of immigration controls. An illegal entrant to Ireland for instance is not permitted by the CTA to enter Britain, and requires leave to do so. The UK and Ireland enforce each other's deportation orders, though not without question. The IDI Ch 9 s 2 para 3.4, June 2004, advises that an Irish deportation order is a relevant consideration, but an application for entry should still be considered on its merits. Visa nationals who do not, on entering another part of the CTA, have a valid visa for the UK, do not have this omission wiped out on entering the UK. They still need a visa. The Immigration (Control of Entry through Republic of Ireland) Order 1972, SI 1972/1610 article 3(1)(b) makes this plain in relation to entry through Ireland. The mutuality provisions mentioned above give effect to this in relation to the Islands. There are restrictions on some lawful travellers as well as those who are in breach of immigration law on entry.

SI 1972/1610 article 4 restricts the stay in the UK of certain people entering through the Republic of Ireland. This restriction applies to those who are neither British nor Irish nor visa nationals on short-stay visas nor EEA nationals, and either their leave to remain in the UK has expired while they were in Ireland or they have entered Ireland from outside the CTA. In this case they may only remain in the UK for three months and may not take paid work. The case of *Kaya v SSHD* [1991] Imm AR 572 confirmed that the three months' permission granted under this Order is granted by the Order directly and is not leave to enter, which can only be granted by designated officers (at that time just immigration officers). This, however, did not prevent the Tribunal in *Kaya* (and later the Court of Appeal) from finding that the appellant, a Turkish national, had overstayed and was liable to the sanctions, even though there was no leave for him to overstay.

For more detail on the operation of the Common Travel Area, reference should be made to the IDIs and a practitioner work such as *Macdonald's Immigration and Nationality Law and Practice*.

6.2.3 Institutional basis of immigration control — an overview

The fundamental legal authority for the power to control immigration is found in the Immigration Act 1971 s 4(1), which says:

The power under this Act to give or refuse leave to enter the United Kingdom shall be exercised by immigration officers, and the power to give leave to remain in the United Kingdom, or to vary any leave under section 3(3)(a) (whether as regards duration or conditions), shall be exercised by the Secretary of State

The Secretary of State also has the power set out in s 3(2) to make the immigration rules and holds the power to make delegated legislation under the immigration statutes. The main ones are the Immigration Act 1971, the Immigration and Asylum Act 1999, the Nationality, Immigration and Asylum Act 2002, the Asylum and Immigration (Treatment of Claimants etc) Act 2004, and the Immigration, Asylum and Nationality Act 2006.

The immigration legislation does not specify which Secretary of State this is, but as a matter of long-standing government policy and practice the Secretary of State with responsibility for immigration is the Home Secretary, immigration officers are part of the Home Office, and the Home Office is the government department with responsibility for immigration control. In *Pearson v IAT* [1978] Imm AR 212 the Court of Appeal held that the Secretary of State, referred to throughout the immigration statute, must 'by reason of the subject matter' be the Home Secretary. The Home Office itself has internal divisions of responsibility. The immigration, nationality, and asylum work of the Home Office is carried out by the Immigration and Nationality Directorate (IND), which has its main office in Croydon and regional offices in Liverpool and Leeds. The immigration service, originally a separate service based at ports, is now part of the Home Office, and immigration officers are appointed by the Secretary of State (Immigration Act 1971 Sch 2 para 1). Immigration officers are still based mainly at ports and airports, now not only in the UK but sometimes overseas. In June 2001, Work Permits (UK), which handled work permit applications, transferred from the Department of Education and Employment to the Home Office, and is based in Sheffield. The National Asylum Support Service, which was set up by the Immigration and Asylum Act 1999 to take the major part of the responsibility for welfare support of asylum seekers, is also part of the IND and is based in Croydon. The work of this service is outside the scope of this book. Entry clearance officers, who make immigration decisions in British posts abroad, were historically responsible to the Foreign and Commonwealth Office rather than the Home Office. In 2000 the Home Office and Foreign Office have set up a joint unit to manage entry clearance; initially called the Joint Entry Clearance Unit, now known as UK Visas.

This is the institutional outline of those involved in the process of immigration control. The remainder of this chapter will follow through the immigration process from the beginning, dealing with the powers of officials in order as they are encountered.

6.3 Before entry — entry clearance

An entry clearance application is the earliest point in time at which an intending immigrant might encounter UK immigration control. Where entry clearance is required it must be obtained before setting out for the UK (HC 395 para 28). As mentioned earlier, it is now mandatory for all non-EEA passengers coming to the UK for more than six months, and for nationals of visa national countries also for shorter stays. Those people for whom entry clearance is not mandatory may apply for entry clearance as a precaution (HC 395 para 24) to establish their eligibility for entry and so avoid the risk of being turned away at the port. The visa requirement does not apply to British nationals without a right of abode.

6.3.1 Decisions on entry clearance

Entry clearance applications are granted or refused by entry clearance officers (ECOs) based in 166 British posts abroad, that is, in Embassies, High Commissions, and Consulates. Entry clearance officers perform a vital function in the implementation of immigration control. Given this it is surprising both that entry clearance officers are not mentioned in any of the legislation, and that until the creation of the Joint Entry Clearance Unit in June 2000 they were answerable to the Foreign and Commonwealth Office rather than the Home Office. The defining reference to entry clearance officers in the immigration rules is in para 26, which says that where appropriate the term 'entry clearance officer' should be substituted for 'immigration officer'. The UK Visas website (ukvisas.gov.uk) gives ready access to the guidance notes for ECOs, called Diplomatic Service Procedures (DSPs).

The operation of the entry clearance system and the quality of decision-making by entry clearance officers is of primary importance in the immigration system. As noted above, all non-EEA travellers to the UK apart from non-visa nationals coming for less than six months now require entry clearance; ECOs therefore play a key role. The Asylum and Immigration Appeals Act 1993 removed the right of appeal against refusal of entry clearance for visitors. It was reinstated for family visitors by the Immigration and Asylum Act 1999 but, very radically, the Immigration, Asylum and Nationality Act 2006 s 4 removed the right of appeal for all entry clearance decisions except dependants and family visitors to be defined in an order by the Secretary of State. The material here on entry clearance should therefore be read with the awareness that, except in family cases or on human rights grounds, there will not be a right of appeal. It is then even more important that the initial decision is of a high quality, but the lack of appeal right removes an incentive to produce good decisions.

ECOs work under severe pressure. The increased numbers of people requiring entry clearance are swelled by the increase in global travel generally. Delay in making entry clearance decisions has been a notorious source of complaint over the years, people sometimes waiting years to visit relatives or join their spouse, missing deaths, weddings and funerals. Now, performance targets require higher speeds of processing. Streamlined systems are resulting in greater speed but not necessarily better quality of decisions.

Underlying all this is the inescapable power of discretion. While an applicant who fulfils the requirements for entry clearance may reasonably expect to have it granted, the decision as to whether the requirements of the rules are met is a judgment made by the ECO, and there is considerable scope for discretion to be exercised outside the rules, which is more difficult to challenge. The Entry Clearance Monitor has encouraged the use of more objective measures of for instance whether a visitor has enough money for their visit. In student cases there is a rough tariff applied, and she has advocated the same be done for visitors using, say, figures from the *Lonely Planet Guides* or *Rough Guides*, but this suggestion has been resisted. The belief in the importance of discretion is deeply embedded in the practice of decision-making. While with good training and support and time to make considered judgments, there is nothing invidious in discretion as such, the reports of the Entry Clearance Monitor reveal that in conditions where these elements are lacking, decisions are often made on a basis not permitted by the rules.

Major studies in the early 1980s, later work for instance by Juss (1997), research conducted into the reinstated family visitor appeals and the revised working holidaymaker scheme all revealed concerns with the quality of entry clearance decisions. These are repeated in government-sponsored reviews — the annual review of the Entry Clearance Monitor, and reports in 2004 by the National Audit Office and FCO.

A contentious feature of the decision-making process has been the entry clearance interview. Modern processes have moved towards dispensing with the interview, and there are arguments that it is time-consuming, unnecessary, burdensome for the applicant and contributes to subjectivity. However, the review of the entry clearance process which followed alleged abuses in relation to business applications from Romania and Bulgaria recommended that interviews be reinstated for these applications under the European Association Agreements.

Traditionally, applications for entry clearance were made in person, and the majority of applications are granted after a short discussion at a counter. These are known as tier 2 interviews. Settlement applications entail a lengthier interview (known as tier 4). The importance of the interview for people who seek to join their family in the UK can hardly be overestimated, but this first experience of the UK immigration system has often been traumatic. The answers that are given in such interviews play a crucial role in determining the outcome of the application. However, these answers may be affected by the conditions in which the interview was carried out, or may be of dubious value in determining the application because the questions are not relevant to the central purpose of establishing the family connection to the requisite standard of proof. The background reading listed at the end of this chapter is recommended to develop an understanding of the conditions in which applications may be conducted. However, examples from the studies will give an indication of the reasons for concern. For instance, there are few entry clearance posts, and so in any particular country an applicant may face a long and arduous journey in order to arrive at the interview. A research report by the UK Immigration Advisory Service describes a common journey as follows:

The train journey from Sylhet to Dacca alone takes 13 hours, added to that, of course, the cumbersome boat, bus journey, including miles of walking to reach Sylhet town from the village. [Most wives were also] carrying an infant and other children of very young age through the long journey. (p. 11, as quoted by Juss, p. 73)

On arrival after such a journey, an applicant, who would not have the resources to rest in a hotel before attending the interview, would be exhausted and not really fit for an important interview. Despite this, researchers reported that applicants would never answer in the negative the standard question asked by the ECO as to whether they were fatigued, nervous, or unwell. The reason uncovered by the researchers was the fear that if they were unfit for interview on arrival the interview would be postponed for a long period (CRE p. 36).

In addition to adverse conditions of interview, a long journey, and interminable waits, the conduct of interviews has attracted criticism, and in particular the operation of the so-called 'discrepancy system'. This is the process whereby ECOs would interview different members of the same family, and then turn down claims to be related from people who differed in minor detail in their accounts of events or circumstances. Examples given by Juss include the colour of a sari worn by the wife at the wedding, the materials of which a house was built, the length of time the family had had their buffalo, and the names of a family member's barber and tailor (pp. 65–66). These questions are not addressed to establishing the relationship on the balance of probabilities, but seem more likely to be intended to catch out applicants. Because of the delays in the system the events in question could be years in the past, thereby increasing the likelihood of difference in memories in *bona fide* applicants.

In the case of delay, there may be a breach of natural justice and this may, as discussed in chapter 3, also involve human rights. In the case of *R v SSHD ex p Phansopkar* [1975] 3 WLR 322 CA Lord Denning propounded the principle that 'justice delayed is justice denied'. In this case the Home Office had adopted a rule of practice that women who were entitled under Immigration Act 1971 s 2 as then in force to come to the UK, must apply for the certificate to prove this in their country of origin. This entailed a wait of 18 months, as they were in the same queue as those who needed leave to enter. The Court of Appeal granted mandamus to compel the Secretary of State to determine their applications. They had an entitlement, and there was no justification for compelling them to wait, other than an illegitimate form of immigration control.

6.3.2 Monitoring entry clearance applications

Informal interviews with powerful officials far away from the system of redress are a fertile ground for abuse of power and lack of transparency. Tribunals have repeatedly criticized the use of discrepancies in irrelevant matters. This criticism continues to be seen, but less often, and it seems that poor practice in entry clearance posts has been gradually on the wane. The removal of the right of appeal against the majority of entry clearance decisions, which came about in Immigration, Nationality and Asylum Act 2006 s 4, is, according to the Government, partly on the basis of this improvement in practice. However, there is still room for much more change, and without the safeguard provided by appeals, there are concerns that the system will deteriorate.

In 1993 the first monitor of the entry clearance system was appointed to oversee refusals of entry clearance where there was no right of appeal. Section 23 Immigration and Asylum Act 1999 required that this monitor be independent of the Home Office. The Reports of the Independent Monitor suggest improved standards but that there is still cause for concern. The most recent report published in February 2005 relates that the global refusal rate has risen steadily since 2000 (the first year of monitoring) reaching 15.4 per cent by the end of the year 2003–4, compared with 6.5 per cent in 2000. This disguises the fact that refusal rates vary greatly around the world. In Canberra for instance the refusal rate was 0.2 per cent, whereas in Accra it was 51.7 per cent.

The same statute which removes the appeal right also allows the Secretary of State to set the terms upon which the monitor will report (Immigration, Asylum and Nationality Act 2006 s 4(2)). The post has been made full-time and the new monitor, appointed in January 2006, will make two reports a year. The increased role for the monitor is in recognition of the vastly increased numbers of entry clearance applicants without a right of appeal, but as the Monitor cannot make recommendations in individual cases and her systemic recommendations are not enforceable it is doubtful whether this is adequate recompense for the loss of appeal rights.

Against this background, we now consider the legal effect of entry clearance once granted. The grounds upon which entry clearance may be refused are almost identical to reasons for refusal of leave to enter, and are discussed later in that context.

6.3.3 Effect of entry clearance

Entry clearance is called a 'visa' for visa nationals and an 'entry certificate' for others (HC 395 para 25). Each of these is a vignette which is stuck into the passport and so entry clearance is shown when the passport is shown.

Before the changes introduced by the Immigration and Asylum Act 1999, entry clearance and leave to enter were two distinct stages of the entry control process.

Although possession of entry clearance made it highly likely that leave to enter would be granted, it was not in itself a grant of leave. That stage still had to be passed at the port of entry. The Immigration (Leave to Enter and Remain) Order 2000, SI 2000/1161 enabled entry clearance to have effect as leave to enter provided it meets the conditions in article 3. These are, that it specifies the purpose for which the holder wishes to enter the UK, and is endorsed with any conditions to which it is subject or a statement that it is to have effect as indefinite leave. In most cases now, therefore, entry clearance will function as leave to enter. Entry clearance granted before the effective date of this article, i.e., before 28 April 2000, will not have the effect of leave to enter as it will not comply with the conditions. Gradually, however, these old-style entry clearances will die out.

Where there is entry clearance there will also be leave to enter granted prior to the passenger's arrival in the UK. The role of immigration officers at the port of entry has therefore changed from being border guards who have power to decide whether the passenger enters to more of a policing function, checking the validity of existing documents. Immigration Act 1971 Sch 2 para 2A says that in the case of a passenger who arrives with leave, the powers of the immigration officer are to examine that person to ascertain whether any grounds exist to cancel that leave. However, there is no obligation to exercise these powers. The Diplomatic Service Procedures (DSP) for entry clearance officers describe in the following terms the role of the immigration officer where the entrant holds entry clearance which functions as leave to enter:

The focus for the IO switches from examination to verifying the bearer's identity and the validity of the entry clearance/leave to enter and ensuring that there has been no change of circumstances since the entry clearance was issued. Under certain circumstances the IO has authority to refuse entry to anyone holding an entry clearance (paragraph 321 of the Rules). (*Entry Clearance* Ch 1 para 1, 9 May 2002)

Clearly, where the entrant holds leave to enter the legal focus of the immigration officer's examination must shift. However, as the grounds for refusing leave to enter to passengers with entry clearance were already limited before 2000 it may be doubted whether, in practice, the intensity of examination of such passengers has changed substantially. The key difference in law is that there is no longer any obligation to examine a person with entry clearance.

The grant of entry clearance which has effect as leave to enter has further practical implications in which, ironically, an individual's fate becomes once again a matter of the way in which administrative discretion is exercised. Leave to enter granted at the port of entry takes effect from the date of entry. If it is limited in time, say for a year, then the year will run from that date. Entry clearance which functions as leave to enter bears two dates, one when the entry clearance becomes effective, 'valid from . . .' and one which marks its expiry, 'valid until . . .'. The passenger may travel once the entry clearance/leave to enter is effective. The 2000 Order in article 4(3) states that the period of limited leave starts with the date on which the holder arrives in the UK. Entry clearance officers are advised to ask the passenger when they are planning to travel, and are permitted to make the entry clearance/leave to enter valid from a date up to three months after the date when they granted it (DSP Ch.1 1.4). If a person arrives before the 'valid from . . .' date the immigration officer on arrival has a discretion to cancel the entry clearance (HC 395 paragraph 30C). This discretion must of course be exercised reasonably. So far so good, as the entry clearance takes effect on entry for a limited period. However, article 4(3) goes on to say that the period of limited leave ends on the expiry date of the entry clearance. This gives rise to a risk that if a person's departure is further delayed, although they travel while the entry clearance/leave to enter is valid, they may travel after the expiry of part of the period of limited leave. The consequences of this could be serious. For instance, a person may be given one year's leave to enter, but not travel perhaps for six months after the 'valid from' date. In this case, after just six months in the UK the person may unwittingly become an overstayer and subject to removal, all the while assuming that they had a full year in which to stay.

There is a discretionary remedy for this problem. HC 395 para 31A permits a person who arrives with leave to enter to apply for a variation of that leave on arrival. This gives the immigration officer an opportunity to extend an initial period of leave to ensure that the passenger benefits from the full period of leave they were originally given. The IDI Feb 2002 Chapter 1 Section 4 Annex V advises the immigration officer to grant a short extension in such a situation. Paragraph 31A, however, states that the immigration officer is not obliged to consider any such application. An application for a short extension should not reasonably be refused, but this paragraph protects the immigration officer from having to deal with more complex applications for variation. The absence of an automatic extension of the 'valid until . . .' date seems to create unnecessary obstacles in the way of the applicant, and a risk that well-intentioned people will go through the ordeal of being treated as overstayers and open up grounds for yet more challenges by judicial review.

To summarize, in almost all cases now entry clearance will function as leave to enter, thereby in theory removing the two-tier system of immigration control. In reality there are some practical difficulties, and as is often the case in immigration law, a development which appears to be advantageous to all concerned, incidentally opens up a new area of discretion with its attendant potential for injustice and confusion.

6.4 Immigration officers' powers on arrival

On arrival at a UK port, a passenger with or without entry clearance will encounter an immigration officer. As mentioned at the beginning of this chapter, the immigration service is part of the Home Office. By s 4(1) of the 1971 Act, immigration officers have specific statutory responsibility for giving or refusing leave to enter. Although this responsibility is no longer exclusive to them, as discussed below, in non-asylum cases leave to enter is still granted by immigration officers where it has not already been granted by way of entry clearance.

The grant or refusal of leave to enter is, in a sense, the visible expression of sovereignty in the immigration sphere. There may be no entry to the territory without permission. Until April 2000 leave to enter was only granted at the port of entry. Some of the changes made by the Immigration (Leave to Enter and Remain) Order 2000, SI 2000/1161 have already been discussed and others will be discussed below. Until the implementation of that order, leave was granted only by means of a date stamp in the passport. For travellers receiving leave to enter at the port it may still be granted by this method. Leave to enter could, and still can, be refused on any of the grounds discussed below.

The extensive powers of immigration officers contained in Sch 2 of the 1971 Act are largely geared towards giving them the necessary scope of action in determining applications for leave to enter. Powers of examination, search, detention, and so on have all been granted and developed to lead ultimately to being able to make the decisive judgment — whether or not a person should have leave to enter the UK. Even the power to issue removal directions, now a complex matter involving judicial process, began as an administrative power to enforce a refusal of leave to enter.

The most widely applicable of the immigration officer's power is to examine any person arriving (Sch 2 para 2). This includes where entry clearance has been granted (Asylum and Immigration Act 2004 s 18) and even where leave to enter is not required, as Immigration Act 1971 s 1(1) provides that freedom to come and go, enjoyed for instance by British citizens, may be hindered 'to enable their right to be established'. Immigration Act 1971 Sch 2(1) provides that any person arriving may be examined to ascertain whether they need leave to enter, and para 4(2) requires such a person to produce 'either a valid passport with photograph or some other document satisfactorily establishing his identity and nationality or citizenship'. Therefore a British passport holder must show their passport to gain entry, even though they do not need leave to enter, and without such proof they may be refused entry (see also Immigration Act 1971 s 3(9) and HC 395 para 12). A 'valid' passport means a current one. The case of *Akewushola v Immigration Officer Heathrow* [2000] 2 All ER 148 CA established that an expired passport plus other proof of identity was not sufficient. Case C 378/97 *Wijsenbeek* [1999] I–6207 established that a European passenger could be required to prove their entitlement despite the fact that EC law aspires to the removal of border controls. However, in the case of EEA nationals a valid identity card is all that is necessary to establish the right to travel. In the case of other nationals, passports or refugee travel documents will be required.

The legal process called examination is at minimum an inspection of a passport, and may go on from there to involve an interview or a series of interviews. These may be on different dates so that the whole examination may be spread over a considerable period of time. The examination also includes other investigations carried out by the immigration officer which may not involve the passenger directly (*Thirukumar* [1989] Imm AR 270). In between interviews the applicant may be in detention or released in the UK on a status known as temporary admission (Sch 2 para 21). Paragraph 4 imposes a duty on people who are undergoing examination to provide all information required for the examination including documentation. There is however no 'duty of utmost good faith' to disclose everything which might conceivably be relevant (*Khawaja* [1984] AC 74 HL). Documents so produced may be retained by the immigration officer until the examination is over (para 4(2A) and (4)). This power has been extended by Immigration, Asylum and Nationality Act 2006 s 27 to allow retention of documents including a passport from arrival until the person 'is about to depart or be removed'. In other words, the passport can be retained throughout a person's stay in the UK. The immigration officer also has power to search the passenger and their luggage (para 3).

6.4.1 Extended powers in relation to terrorism

Immigration officers have powers under Sch 7 to the Terrorism Act 2000 to stop, detain, search, and question any person at a port for the purpose of determining whether that person appears to be concerned or to have been concerned in the 'commission, preparation or instigation of acts of terrorism' (s 40(1)(b)). A person at a port may have arrived in the UK from anywhere. There is a wider power in relation to journeys into Northern Ireland from the Republic of Ireland when a person may be stopped not only at the port, but also within the border area. This is defined as any place up to a mile from the border with the Republic, or, if the journey is by train, the first train stop in Northern Ireland (Sch 7 para 4). This places a limit on the freedom of movement given by the Common Travel Area, and consistently with current trends these constraints on movement are not immigration restrictions but are security restrictions entailing policing activity.

However, the 2000 Act contains no equivalent of the exclusion powers which were part of earlier anti-terrorism legislation. Under the Prevention of Terrorism (Temporary Provisions) Act 1989 and its predecessors, it was possible for individuals to be restricted to living in either Great Britain or Northern Ireland. These exclusion orders affecting British citizens did not appear in the 2000 Act, the omission being an aspect of the peace process in Northern Ireland.

Powers under the schedule do not require a basis of reasonable suspicion. They may be exercised 'for the purpose of determining whether' the person may have terrorist involvement, in other words, simply in order to find out. These powers are also given a wide scope by the broad definition of terrorism used in s 1 (discussed more fully in chapter 14). The exercise of these powers is subject to the usual administrative law restraints and to the Race Relations Act 1976 as amended, as discussed in chapter 8. However, this places the burden on the complainant to show that the powers were unlawfully exercised, rather than on the immigration officer to show that there was a reasonable basis for their actions.

In similar vein, an immigration officer may search a ship, aircraft, or anything on or which he reasonably believes to have been or be about to be on a ship or aircraft (e.g., a container) 'for the purpose of satisfying himself whether there are any persons he may wish to question under paragraph 2' (para 7).

The maximum period of detention for these powers to be exercised is nine hours (Sch 7 para 6), although the person may be detained for longer by the police if there are grounds for suspicion.

6.4.2 Immigration (Leave to Enter and Remain) Order 2000, SI 2000/1161

The Immigration (Leave to Enter and Remain) Order 2000 was made pursuant to a widely phrased power, introduced by Immigration and Asylum Act 1999 s 1 in the following terms:

(1) The Secretary of State may by order make further provision with respect to the giving, refusing or varying of leave to enter the United Kingdom.

(2) An order under subsection (1) may, in particular, provide for—

    (a) leave to be given or refused before the person concerned arrives in the United Kingdom;

(b) the form or manner in which leave may be given, refused or varied;

(c) the imposition of conditions;

(d) a person's leave not to lapse on his leaving the common travel area.

(3) The Secretary of State may by order provide that, in such circumstances as may be prescribed—

(a) an entry visa; or

(b) such other form of entry clearance as may be prescribed

is to have effect as leave to enter the United Kingdom. (s 3A Immigration Act 1971)

This was the first time since the 1971 Act that there had been a substantive change in the power to grant or refuse leave to enter. It should be noted that the power in s 3A is simply to 'make further provision with respect to the giving, refusing, or varying of leave to enter' (emphasis added). The specific powers which follow in subsection 2 are not necessarily an exhaustive account of how this power will be exercised.

The power granted to the Secretary of State by s 3A was first exercised in the Immigration (Leave to Enter and Remain) Order 2000, SI 2000/1161. By article 7 of that order, 'an immigration officer *whether or not in the United Kingdom*, may give or refuse a person leave to enter the United Kingdom *at any time before his departure for, or in the course of his journey to*, the United Kingdom' (emphases added). This means that neither the immigration officer nor the grant of leave are fixed to the port of entry any longer. Leave may be given before or during travel and the immigration officer need not be based at the port. Article 8 provides that notice giving or refusing leave to enter, instead of being given in writing as required by s 4(1) of the 1971 Act, may be given by fax or e-mail, or, in the case of visitors, orally including by telephone. Leave to enter may also be given to responsible third parties, not just to the passenger directly (article 9). This flexibility in the means of communicating a grant of leave to enter may have drawbacks if, for instance, a question of proof arises at a later date (see Luqmani, Randall, and Scannell 2000: 12). However, it was intended to be for the convenience of those regarded as 'low risk' passengers, for instance those on school trips or other organized tours. In these cases a passenger list may be presented and endorsed with leave to enter, even before setting out on the trip, and this is intended to minimize delay at the port of entry.

In addition to grant by entry clearance as discussed above, and advance clearance for groups of 'low risk' passengers, the power to grant or refuse leave to enter before travel is designed for schemes established abroad to deter unauthorized passengers and in particular asylum seekers. These schemes are discussed in chapter 7.

6.5 **The decision**

6.5.1 **Making the decision on leave to enter**

If satisfied that the passenger meets the requirements then the immigration officer (or in practice now often the entry clearance officer) may grant them leave to enter. This simple statement conceals a wealth of legal meaning. This decision by the immigration officer is a discretion exercised in public law. It is therefore subject to all the constraints of public law and to appeal, where available, on grounds listed in Nationality, Immigration and Asylum Act 2002 s 84. Since the amendment of s 89 by the 2006 Act there has been no appeal on arrival for a passenger who does not have entry clearance except on grounds of race discrimination, human rights or asylum claim. An immigration officer must act in accordance with the immigration rules and instructions given by the Secretary of State (Immigration Act 1971 Sch 2 para 1 (3)). There is fuller discussion of these legal constraints in the next chapter on appeals and constraints.

An immigration officer or entry clearance officer may grant leave to enter if satisfied that the passenger meets the requirements of the particular rules which apply to the kind of entry they want to achieve; that is, if they meet requirements for entry as a spouse, working holidaymaker, visitor, etc. The applicant is required to bring their application within the rules. This was illustrated in *Abid Hussain v ECO Islamabad* [1989] Imm AR 46 where the appellant failed because his answers were insufficiently clear for the entry clearance officer to be able to decide whether he was planning to visit the UK to marry his fiancée and then return to Pakistan, or whether he intended to settle with her in the UK.

6.5.2 Refusal of leave to enter

There are no general requirements for entry, but there are general grounds for refusal, which apply to decisions on the grant of leave to enter or entry clearance. The grounds for refusal in HC 395 para 320 are divided into those upon which leave to enter or entry clearance 'is to be refused' and those upon which leave to enter 'should normally be refused'. Before considering some of the grounds individually we shall consider their standing in administrative law.

The wording indicates that when a reason in the first group applies, refusal of leave is mandatory and when a reason in the second set applies, refusal is discretionary. However, although 'is to be refused' clearly implies an intention for refusals to be mandatory, the administrative law principle against fettering discretion does not permit prescription of a set of circumstances in which there must always be a refusal. The power to grant or refuse leave arises in statute, (s 4(1) Immigration Act 1971) and administrative provisions such as the immigration rules may not lawfully restrict the statutory power, though they may guide it. The principle against fettering discretion, or, it may be said, against having a rigid policy, arises from cases such as *R v Port of London Authority ex p Kynoch Ltd* [1919] 1 KB 176 and *British Oxygen Co Ltd v Minister of Technology* [1971] AC 610 in which it was held that an authority acted lawfully in having a policy as long as it was prepared to listen to someone who had something new to say which might justify dealing with them in a different way. This principle was applied to the immigration rules by the Court of Appeal in *Pearson v Immigration Appeal Tribunal*. Paragraph 5 of the immigration rules then in force, HC 80, provided that if the Department of Employment did not approve an extension of leave for work then the application 'should be refused'. The Court of Appeal said, at 225 that in making such a rule:

The Home Secretary did, in our opinion, make a rule as to how he would in future, as a matter of general policy, exercise his discretion, but not how he would exercise it in every case without considering the circumstances of a particular case and whether to make an exception to that policy.

The rule was therefore not a fetter on discretion and not *ultra vires*.

In *R(P) and R(Q) v SSHD* [2001] EWCA Civ 1151 the Court of Appeal held that the prison service was entitled to have a policy that when mothers were in prison, children should be separated from them at 18 months old. Schedule 1 Article 8 to the Human Rights Act 1998 (the right to respect for family life) would not prevent such a policy from existing, but it would require that the application of the rule to the individual case should be examined. Article 8 therefore goes further than the existing administrative law rule in that it requires a decision-maker to show that infringement of the right to respect for family life caused by adherence to the policy was proportionate to the aim sought to be achieved. The result of this for the application of mandatory grounds for refusal is that they may be regarded as a legitimate statement of policy and therefore of what will normally happen, but that the immigration officer or entry clearance officer must be prepared to act outside the policy if individual circumstances warrant doing so. When a qualified Convention right is infringed by the refusal then the infringement must be proportionate to the public interest which the officer seeks to protect.

In the case of refusal of leave to enter or entry clearance, however, the courts will not readily find that a Convention right is at stake. On this issue generally reference should be made to chapter 3. In the context of para 320 an indication as to the courts' approach is given by *SSHD v Farrakhan* [2002] Imm AR 447 CA. Louis Farrakhan, the controversial leader of the Muslim sect, The Nation of Islam, had been refused entry to the UK under a mandatory ground in paragraph 320. His application was as a visitor to conduct a week's speaking tour. The refusal was challenged by judicial review, contending, *inter alia*, that it breached his Article 10 right to freedom of expression. The Court of Appeal held that the Secretary of State's reason for excluding Farrakhan was a justifiable one relating to public order and a legitimate exercise of his statutory power to control immigration. It only incidentally affected Farrakhan's freedom of expression in that he would not be able to exercise that freedom in the territory from which he had been excluded. The decision to exclude was prior to the possibility of establishing any freedom of expression, which would only occur once the speaker was in the UK. This distinction does seem rather thin; nevertheless, the exclusion was upheld.

The indication from this case is that the courts will not readily override the Secretary of State's discretion to exclude someone who seeks to enter, and after entry to exercise a Convention right. The situation is different where the arrival itself constitutes the fulfilment of the right, as in a family reunion case where the right to respect for family life is recognized by the person being allowed to enter the UK. It is the geographical separation which caused the breach. These situations are discussed fully in chapters 3 and 9.

The existence of so-called mandatory reasons for refusal is considered lawful, and not an unlawful fetter on discretion according to the principles of administrative law, because there exists a power to act outside the rules. This is acknowledged in the Immigration Directorate Instructions (IDI) Chapter 9 Section 2 para 1 June 2004, which says, referring to the mandatory grounds, '[I]n practice, however, entry clearance or leave to enter, as applicable, is *normally* refused on these grounds'. Guidance is provided in that section for 'occasions when refusal is *not* appropriate'.

At this point reference may be made back to the discussion in chapter one of the exercise of discretion in immigration law. It may be recalled that the power to act is wider than the rules as the power to grant or refuse leave to enter derives ultimately from statute which does not constrain the manner in which this discretion is exercised. Furthermore, there are many established concessions outside the rules, and an applicant who does not meet the requirements of the rules may nevertheless be admitted under an established concession. The applicant may expressly apply for discretion to be exercised outside the rules but may not appeal if it is not (Nationality Immigration and Asylum Act 2002 s 86 (6)). It is only when neither of these exercises of discretion is possible or judged appropriate that refusal is appropriate under this paragraph (IDI Ch 9 s 2 para 2 June 2004).

6.5.2.1 *Immigration officer is satisfied*

A number of the reasons for refusal in paragraph 320 entail the immigration officer being satisfied that something is the case. This is a formula commonly encountered in statute and rules, and requires that the officer approaches the enquiry in a reasonable manner. *Secretary of State for Education v Tameside MBC* [1977] AC 1014 established that even though the statute said that the minister could exercise his powers if he was 'satisfied that' the local authority was acting unreasonably, this was not just a matter of his subjective judgment but of assembling all the relevant information and making a rational decision based on that evidence. He was required to act reasonably, and this requirement is implicit in any immigration rule using a similar phrase.

6.5.2.2 *Reasons for refusal*

The first reason given in para 320 is that 'entry is sought for a purpose not covered by the rules'. As mentioned previously, the reason for entry must generally be brought within the categories provided for by the rules. This sub-paragraph gives the clearest example of when, although the rule might appear to mandate refusal, discretion could be exercised outside the rules. The application might be within the general scope of a category, for instance dependent relatives in exceptional compassionate circumstances (HC 395 para 317), but the particular applicant does not actually qualify because the family relationship to the sponsor is not one of those for which the rule provides. For instance, the applicant, although in exceptional compassionate circumstances, may be a nephew, which is a relationship not provided for in the rule. Refusal is possible under para 320(1), but so also is a grant of entry exceptionally outside the rules if the circumstances seem to the officer sufficiently compelling to make this an appropriate exercise of discretion.

The grounds in full are set out in Table 1.

6.5.2.3 *Grounds relating to public good*

There are three reasons for refusal relating to the public good. The mandatory reason in para 320(6) and the discretionary one in para 320(19) are similarly worded except that the mandatory one is a personal direction of the Secretary of State and the discretionary one is the decision of the immigration officer. Paragraph

Table 1 Grounds for refusal of entry

Mandatory grounds

Entry is sought for a purpose not covered by the rules	Prima facie, categories in rules are exhaustive
Currently subject to deportation order	Deportation order prevents entry during its currency — see chapter 15
Failure to produce a valid national passport or other document satisfactorily establishing nationality and identity	As discussed, this applied to everyone, even those with right of abode
In case of person intending to travel to another part of Common Travel Area, failure to satisfy immigration officer (IO) that passenger will be acceptable to immigration authorities there	Implementing the Common Travel Area
In case of visa national: failure to produce valid and current entry clearance for purpose for which entry is sought	Implementing visa regime
Secretary of State's personal direction that exclusion is conducive to public good	See discussion

Discretionary grounds

For medical reasons, entry undesirable	See discussion
Failure to give IO information required for purpose of deciding whether leave to enter is needed and if so whether and on what terms it should be given	The IDI advises that this ground should be used only if the passenger continues not to provide the information so that it is impossible to proceed
Outside UK: failure to supply information, documents, medical report required by IO	Equivalent to the preceding ground for outside UK post 2000 applications
Failure by a returning resident to meet the requirements of para 18 of the rules	Discussed below
Presenting a passport of a government not recognized by the UK	IDI Dec 00 lists these as Turkish Republic of Northern Cyprus, Taiwan, and Palestine.
Failure to observe a time limit or condition attached to a previous grant of leave	Note this consequence of a breach of immigration law for future applications
Obtaining a previous leave to by deception	As above
Failure to satisfy IO that passenger will be able to return to another country	Though where this is because e.g. a passport may expire, limited leave may be given to avoid refusal (HC 395 para 21)
Refusal by sponsor to give undertaking	See chapter 8
Making false representation or material non-disclosure to obtain a work permit	Self-explanatory
In case of a child, failure to provide parent's consent to travel	Also self-explanatory
Refusal to undergo medical examination	See discussion
Criminal convictions	See discussion
IO believes exclusion is conducive to public good	See discussion

320(18) referring to criminal convictions has an overlap with grounds of public good.

What is conducive to the public good is evidently a matter of judgement, and the discretion granted here by the rules suggests that it is a matter which both the Secretary of State and immigration and entry clearance officers are competent to judge. Such an exercise of discretion raises the question of to what extent this judgement may be challenged in what is after all a public law matter which may affect Convention rights.

Personal directions such as that permitted by para 320(6) are not common. As discussed in chapter 5 on European law, this power was used in relation to a member of the Church of Scientology following statements in Parliament that Scientology was considered harmful to the public (Case 41/74 *Van Duyn v Home Office* [1974] ECR 1337). Commentary on that case has suggested that this was not an adequate foundation for the use of the power to exclude, and that in more modern times the court would be unlikely to support such an exclusion. More recently the power was used to prevent the leader of the Nation of Islam, Louis Farrakhan, from coming to the UK for a speaking tour. As discussed above, a human rights challenge to this exclusion failed. The Secretary of State gave his reasons for the decision as being a concern that, because Mr Farrakhan had expressed anti-Semitic views, and because two members of the Nation of Islam had been arrested for public order offences outside the Stephen Lawrence Inquiry, his presence in the UK might give rise to disorder. The Court of Appeal considered that the Secretary of State was in a better position than they were to reach an informed decision as to the likely consequences of admitting Mr Farrakhan (*SSHD v Farrakhan*). As a personal decision of the Secretary of State, a decision under para 320(6) is not open to appeal (Nationality, Immigration and Asylum Act 2002 s 98). The Court of Appeal referred to this lack of appeal right as indicating that Parliament had taken the view that in this area of decision-making the courts should accord the Secretary of State's opinion a significant degree of deference. They perhaps rather disturbingly compared this case with that of *SSHD v Rehman* [2001] 3 WLR 877. The subject matter of that case was national security in relation to which the courts generally accord the decision-maker considerable deference, partly because of the secrecy of much of the evidence. In Mr Farrakhan's case representations had been received from numerous groups both for and against his exclusion, but there was no suggestion that the security of the country was at risk.

The *Farrakhan* decision may be placed within the spectrum of post Human Rights Act 1998 cases concerning a margin of discretion exercised by the higher courts in relation to the Secretary of State's judgment (see chapter 3). If the Court of Appeal had accepted that freedom of expression was in issue, they would have needed to engage in the balancing exercise required by para 2 of Article 10. This is not to say that the outcome would have been any different, but it would have involved the judiciary more deeply in the merits of the decision. The route that they took, relying on the Secretary of State's right to control the entry of aliens, and the personal and unappealable nature of decisions under para 320(6), avoided the Court itself becoming more engaged. This reflects a similar approach to that found in cases such as *Samaroo* [2001] UKHRR 1440, as well as *Rehman*, (both discussed in chapter 16) where the higher courts have deferred to the executive in matters affecting public order and immigration policy. It may be contrasted with the approach for instance in *R v SSHD ex p Turgut* [2001] 1 All ER 719, where, on an issue of risk of ill-treatment, the Court of Appeal considered that it was as well placed as the minister to judge the situation.

The second ground for refusal on the basis that exclusion is conducive to the public good is that 'from information available to the immigration officer it seems right to refuse leave to enter on the ground that exclusion from the UK is conducive to the public good'. The information available would not be a criminal conviction, as this would be either dealt with under the preceding sub-paragraph or too trivial to warrant exclusion. The sub-paragraph gives some idea of the kind of information intended, as it continues 'if for example, in the light of the character, conduct or associations of the person seeking leave to enter it is undesirable to give him leave to enter'. The IDI elaborates on this, saying 'the immigration officer must specify what past or future action of the person makes his exclusion conducive to the public good. Vague generalisations . . . will not suffice' (Ch 9 s 2 para 21 June 2004). The case of *Ramanathan v Secretary of State for the Foreign and Commonwealth Office* [1999] Imm AR 97 gives an example of the kind of activities which might found refusal under this paragraph. Here the appellant was suspected of facilitating unlawful immigration. The appellant remained outside the UK and no criminal charges were brought, but suspicions expressed in communications between British High Commissions in Sri Lanka (his country of origin) and Singapore (his country of residence) were sufficient to support a refusal on this ground.

The information founding the decision might be prior information, such as a prohibition of a group of which the passenger is a member, for instance the ban on scientologists challenged in *Van Duyn*. It might be information gathered then and there at the port of entry, for instance if the passenger is found to be in possession of illegal drugs or quantities of pornography sufficient to suggest that they are intending to sell it rather than use it personally. The IDI at para 21.2 suggests that a similar principle would be applied in the case of drugs. If the passenger is only carrying a small amount and has sufficient money to pay any likely fine, then entry should not be refused on this basis.

The phrase 'it seems right' in this sub-paragraph is another way of expressing a discretion. As elsewhere, this discretion must be exercised fairly and reasonably (*R v SSHD ex p Moon* [1996] COD 54, *Secretary of State for Education v Tameside MBC*). 'Conducive to the public good' is also grounds for deportation, and arguably a person should not be excluded under this paragraph if they would not be deported on the same facts.

Paragraph 320(18) provides for the refusal of leave to enter or entry clearance on the basis of a criminal conviction 'save where the immigration officer is satisfied that admission would be justified for strong compassionate reasons'. The conviction must be for any offence which would be punishable in the UK by at least 12 months' imprisonment. It therefore includes all but the most trivial offences. The exclusion however is discretionary; discretion must be exercised fairly, and in a case where the right to respect for private or family life is interfered with by a refusal of leave, discretion must be exercised proportionately in accordance with Article 8. As 'strong compassionate reasons' often relate to private or family life, the arguments in pre-October 2000 case law about what would amount to 'strong compassionate reasons' are now largely superseded by human rights arguments and the requirement for proportionality.

The admission of the boxer Mike Tyson to the UK gave the occasion for the Divisional Court to consider the nature of the discretion given to the immigration officer in this sub-paragraph (*R v SSHD ex p Bindel* [2001] Imm AR 1). As Mike Tyson had been convicted of rape he would have been liable for exclusion under this sub-paragraph as rape carries a sentence of more than 12 months and in fact he had been sentenced to six years imprisonment. Exercising his power to issue instructions to immigration officers, the Secretary of State directed that Mike Tyson should be admitted. A group called Justice for Women argued in judicial review proceedings that the Secretary of State was not entitled to give such an instruction, however, as we have seen (chapter 1), the Secretary of State is not bound by the rules and may direct immigration officers to act more generously towards an applicant. Sullivan J, however, went further than this. He held that the discretion to admit Tyson was exerciseable within the rule, and the instruction by the Secretary of State was thus not inconsistent with the rule. There were reasons of public interest for admitting Tyson, such as the economic benefit that the boxing match would bring, the fact that tickets for the fight had already been sold, and business interests were depending on it. As Justice for Women argued, these are clearly not 'strong compassionate reasons', they are economic reasons. However, Sullivan J held that the reference to 'strong compassionate reasons' in the sub-paragraph was not an exhaustive description of the basis for exercising discretion, the sub-paragraph was a discretionary reason for refusing leave to enter, and this discretion could not be constrained. This does seem to make the reference to compassionate reasons redundant, which is probably consistent with the Human Rights Act where a Convention right is involved. Where Convention rights are not involved, as they were not in the Tyson case, it leaves this area of discretion rather open to argument. Macdonald refers to it as 'distressingly vague' (5th edn 2001, p. 84). It is clear that EEA nationals are in a better position as in EC law exclusion interferes with a Treaty right to freedom of movement, which puts the burden on the immigration officer to demonstrate the need for exclusion (see chapter 5). The opposite is the case in this rule, where the burden is on the applicant to show why discretion should be exercised in their favour.

The Rehabilitation of Offenders Act 1974 applies to entry to the UK, so that a person should not be refused entry on the basis of a conviction which is 'spent' under the Act. Returning residents are not exempted from this sub-paragraph, so in theory a settled person could be refused re-entry on the basis of a conviction (see below). In practice Article 8 rights are almost certain to be engaged in such a case, and a conviction would, it is suggested, have to be of a nature which was particularly threatening to the public interest in order to warrant exclusion of a settled person. Arguments about the rights of long-term residents to remain despite criminal convictions are considered more fully in the chapter on deportation.

Travel bans
Increasingly there are international interests involved in restricting certain people from travelling between countries. These centre around the prevention of crime, particularly terrorist and drugs offences, and restriction of the movements of war criminals and national leaders upon whom groups of nations wish to bring pressure to bear. This latter power was given effect in UK law by s 8 of the Immigration and Asylum Act 1999, inserting a s 8B into the Immigration Act 1971. The section provides for a new category of 'excluded persons'. These are people named or

referred to in a resolution of the United Nations Security Council or Council of the European Union which is designated for this purpose by an Order made by the Secretary of State. Since s 8B came into force the Secretary of State has made a number of Immigration (Designation of Travel Bans) Orders designating European resolutions concerning for instance former President Milosevic of Yugoslavia, and President Mugabe of Zimbabwe, and UN resolutions concerning Angola and Sierra Leone. The effect of these designations is, according to s 8B, that the excluded person 'must be refused' leave to enter or leave to remain in the UK. It is apparent that these resolutions and orders are targeted upon particular figures and will not often be encountered. Their significance lies not in their effect upon the individuals concerned or in the scope of their application, but in the fact that they demonstrate the increase in concerted international action on issues which are seen as relating to violations of human rights on a large scale, or to the spread of criminal activity.

6.5.2.4 *Medical reasons*

HC 395 para 36 states that a person who intends to remain in the UK for more than six months should normally be referred to the medical inspector for a medical examination. This applies to anyone who is coming to the UK to settle with family members. Referral to the medical inspector may also be made if the person seeking entry 'mentions health or medical treatment as a reason for his visit or appears not to be in good health' (para 36). An immigration officer may also refer a person for further medical examination after entry 'in the interests of public health' (Immigration Act 1971 Sch 2 para 7). The medical inspector is a doctor employed by the Home Office to make reports on potential immigrants and asylum seekers (Immigration Act 1971 s 4(2) and Sch 2 para 1(2) and medical officers attached to British posts abroad carry out examinations there.

Refusal to undergo a medical examination is a discretionary reason for refusal of leave to enter or entry clearance (para 320(17)) and so is failure to supply a medical report when an application is proceeding outside the UK (para 320 (8A)). The effect of this is that when an immigration officer or ECO (HC 395 para 39) refer a person for a medical examination, that person is compelled to attend the medical examination if they want leave to enter. The IDI makes it clear that it is only in the most exceptional circumstances that a passenger who refuses to undergo a medical examination will be given leave to enter (Ch 9 s 2 para 19 June 2004). The Immigration (Leave to Enter and Remain) Order 2000, SI 2000/1161 article 7(3), referring principally to applications decided outside the UK prior to arrival, provides that immigration officers have the power to require the passenger to supply an up to date medical report. Article 7(4) adds that failure to supply requested documents including a medical report shall be 'a ground, in itself, for refusal of leave'. This may suggest a lack of consistency between the immigration rules and the Order. The rules apply to immigration officers and entry clearance officers, but the Order does not appear to apply to ECOs. The Order does not make clear whether this is a mandatory or discretionary ground for refusal of leave, though in the rules it is clearly discretionary. This illustrates how the boundary between 'mandatory' and 'discretionary' has become blurred, and it may no longer be necessary to make the distinction.

All the above refers to undergoing a medical examination and providing a report. However, the content of the report may be fatal to an application. If the medical inspector reports that 'for medical reasons it is undesirable to admit the person' this is a mandatory ground for refusal of entry clearance or leave to enter. There are broadly speaking two kinds of grounds upon which a medical inspector might come to such a view. These are firstly that the applicant suffers from a disease which is highly infectious or contagious and thus there is a risk to public health. There is a strong argument that refusal on these grounds should be restricted to those diseases which are listed as grounds for refusal in the case of EEA nationals as there seems to be no justification for treating non-Europeans less favourably than Europeans (see chapter 5). Note that people suffering from AIDS or who are HIV positive may not be refused admission on the grounds of this diagnosis alone (IDI Ch 1 s 8 para 2.5 Mar 2004). The second kind of ground for refusal for medical reasons would be the anticipated economic consequences of the applicant's ill health. There is provision to enter the UK for private medical treatment, and this is discussed in chapter 10. However, if a person in substantial need of medical treatment applied to enter as a spouse, for instance, there might be concerns that they would never be well enough to be financially self-supporting; alternatively there might be suspicion that National Health Service treatment was the real reason for entering the UK. These grounds reflect the same arguments against accepting immigrants which go back to the Aliens Act 1905 or even earlier, namely that people should not be admitted who appeared likely 'from disease or infirmity' (Aliens Act 1905 s 1) to become reliant on public funds. The March 2004 IDI perpetuates the inconsistency of earlier IDIs on this subject, as Ch 1 s 8 para 2.1 says that there could be refusal on this ground 'if the nature of the person's condition would interfere with his ability to support himself or his dependants'. Paragraph 2.2, on the other hand, says 'medical inspectors only certify that it is undesirable to admit a passenger to the UK when satisfied that a passenger's condition represents a significant risk to public health.' There must be doubt as to the lawfulness of a medical inspector certifying in the terms suggested in para 2.1, as this is an economic rather than a medical reason for refusal, para 2.2 says that this more restricted ground is on legal advice. It would however be possible for the immigration officer, not the medical inspector, to refuse on grounds of likely inability to maintain without recourse to public funds (see chapter 9). This of course would only be if there were genuine doubt about the passenger's being maintained. Where there are other sufficient sources of financial support, this reason for refusal could not be used. The National Health Service is not defined as 'public funds' for people entering to settle with family (HC 395 para 6 as amended) and so refusal on the grounds of likely demand on the National Health Service would not be lawful.

The position of the medical inspector may be seen to be a curious one. Trained as a doctor to make a diagnosis leading to treatment for the benefit of the patient, they are in this instance a servant of the Home Office required to screen the patient, not for the patient's benefit, but in order to implement immigration policy. Indeed, in para 320(7) there is something of a role reversal. The medical inspector, according to the wording of the rule, makes an immigration decision. The rule provides an exception to following the medical inspector's recommendation, when 'the Immigration Officer is satisfied that there are strong compassionate reasons justifying admission.' Here the medic makes the immigration decision and the immigration official decides on the compassionate circumstances. The medical inspector must not take their non-therapeutic role too far. The IDI stresses in Ch 1 s 8 para 2 that medical inspectors should not be asked to examine passengers to discover whether they have borne children or had sexual relations nor to X-ray them to determine their age. The prohibition in the IDI is worded more strictly here than is common, and this is because precisely these practices were carried out in the 1970s. The former refers to the virginity tests carried out on the claimed basis that a good Muslim or Hindu woman would not engage in sexual relations before marriage, nor would a respectable man of those faiths marry someone who had. Therefore genuine fiancées could be detected by their virginity. The ensuing scandal prompted the Commission for Racial Equality's investigation into immigration control and is not something that the Home Office would wish to repeat.

Tribunal decisions suggest that the medical inspector's opinion may not be challenged on its own merits, and that the immigration officer may only override it if, following the rule, there are 'strong compassionate circumstances' (*Al-Tuwaidji v Chief Immigration Officer Heathrow* [1974] Imm AR 34 followed in *Mohazeb v Immigration Officer Harwich* [1990] Imm AR 555). This illustrates a continuing difference between the mandatory and discretionary grounds, in that because the medical inspector's refusal is said to be mandatory there is no appeal on its merits but only the possibility of judicial review for failure to exercise the residual discretion. Indeed the now exclusive grounds for appeal in Nationality Immigration and Asylum Act 2002 s 84 do not seem to give scope for challenging the medical inspector's report on its merits (see chapter 8). However, following the decision in *ex p Bindel* discussed earlier, it may be doubted whether grounds other than 'strong compassionate circumstances' can any longer be excluded. There is still arguably an unauthorised delegation of the immigration decision-making function to the medical inspector which seems to be less open to judicial review than the immigration officer's exercise of discretion.

This ground for refusal does not apply to people with settled status who, having travelled abroad, may not be refused re-entry on medical grounds.

6.5.2.5 *Exercise of discretion*

Following the so-called mandatory grounds for refusing leave to enter or entry clearance, para 320 sets out thirteen grounds on which leave to enter 'should normally be refused'. As we have seen, this phrase is used in the IDI to describe the mandatory grounds and the discretionary grounds which suggests that the distinction between these two may be blurring. It could be seen as being less difficult for the applicant in relation to the so-called discretionary grounds to displace the presumption that entry clearance or leave to enter should be refused, but the presumption is still there. The discretion must be exercised fairly (*R V SSHD ex p Moon*) and based on evidence, taking into account relevant and excluding irrelevant factors (*Associated Provincial Picture Houses Ltd v Wednesbury Corporation* [1948] 1 KB 223). An example of this arose in the case of *SSHD v Mowla and Patel* [1991] Imm AR 210 in which the Court of Appeal held that the difference in rights of appeal accorded to those refused leave to enter and those refused a variation of leave in the UK was not a factor which the immigration officer should take into account in deciding whether to grant leave to enter. The detriment to the applicants in this respect was therefore not regarded as relevant. Any such decision taken since 2 October 2000 must take into account any Convention rights affected by the decision, and where qualified rights are affected, any infringement of the right must be proportionate to the aim pursued.

Scope for the exercise of discretion is found particularly in sub-paras 11 and 12, which both concern previous breaches of immigration law. The previous breach in question need not have been during the most recent visit to the UK, according to *Ofoajoku* [1991] Imm AR 68. In this case a student had been refused leave to enter on the basis of previous breaches of immigration law even though in the intervening period he had had a further period of leave which had been granted without knowledge of the earlier breaches. The IAT held that this intervening leave did not wipe the slate clean, nor did it give rise to the legal doctrine of estoppel whereby the Secretary of State would be prevented from taking account of the earlier breaches. His discretion could not be limited in that way. These principles apply equally to failure to observe a time limit or condition and obtaining previous leave by deception. In a case such as this the refusal of leave to enter could be seen as more punitive than preventative, and where the right to respect for private and family life is involved, in accordance with Article 8, the immigration officer would need to identify which legitimate aim in Article 8.2 is served by the refusal (see chapter 3). The IDI makes it plain that refusal under sub-para 11 should not be used where previous breaches were trivial, and in a punitive way. It should be used where the passenger has shown that they have 'contrived in a *significant* way to frustrate the purpose of the rules'.

6.5.3 **Cancellation of leave to enter**

Leave to enter may be cancelled on arrival, or refused, even for a person who has prior entry clearance (HC 395 para 321 and 321A). On the same grounds entry clearance may be revoked before travel (para 30A) but this is very rare. Since the implementation of the Immigration (Leave to Enter and Remain) Order 2000, SI 2000/1161, there will be few entrants who have entry clearance and not leave to enter, so cancellation of existing leave to enter is now the most likely form. The effect of cancellation and the old-style refusal is very similar, namely, at the port the passenger is not allowed to enter, although they may be admitted temporarily to pursue an appeal.

Leave to enter may be cancelled on the following grounds: (a) the leave or entry clearance was obtained by false representations; (b) the leave or entry clearance was obtained as a result of material facts not being disclosed; or (c) there has been a material change of circumstances since the leave or entry clearance was obtained.

6.5.3.1 *False representations and non-disclosure of material facts*

In *Akhtar* [1991] Imm AR 326 CA the Court of Appeal held that false representations were simply representations that were inaccurate, they did not necessarily have to be fraudulent. The effect of this is that the falsity does not have to be deliberate. In the case of cancellation of leave to enter, the rule requires that the applicant themselves must have made the false statement (para 321A(2)). In the case of refusal of leave to enter or revocation of entry clearance, the false representation may have been made by someone else 'whether or not to the holder's knowledge'. The representations, whether oral or in writing, need only have been made in order to obtain entry clearance or leave to enter (*Akhtar*). They need not have been decisive of the application. There is a question of degree here. An irrelevant representation, such as for instance that the bride wore a red dress, could not be said to being made in order to obtain entry clearance as nothing turned on it (or nothing should have turned on it — see the earlier discussion about the discrepancy system). However, in *Sukhjinder Kaur* [1998] Imm AR 1 CA, a representation that her husband was at a certain address, whereas he was in prison, was relevant and false and so resulted in a refusal of leave to enter even though entry clearance had been granted. His imprisonment however was not necessarily fatal to his wife's application for entry, demonstrating that the factor about which the false representation is made does not have to be one which is decisive of the application in order to deprive the applicant of leave to enter.

This is related to the question of materiality of facts not disclosed. Again for leave to enter to be cancelled the non-disclosure must have been by the applicant, though refusal of leave to enter and revocation of entry clearance can be based on non-disclosure by third parties. Facts are held to be material if they would have influenced the outcome of the application but similarly they need not be facts upon which the whole application would stand or fall. So in Sukhjinder Kaur's case, her failure to disclose her husband's actual whereabouts was a material non-disclosure, even though she might still have been granted entry had the truth been known. The applicant, however, is not permitted to make that argument. They cannot oppose the cancellation of leave to enter on the basis that if the true facts had been known they would have gained entry anyway (*Bugdaycay* [1987] AC 514 HL).

6.5.3.2 *Change of circumstances*

A change of circumstances, in order to warrant refusal or cancellation of leave to enter, or revocation of entry clearance, must be so fundamental that it undermines the basis upon which the original application was made. In the case of a visitor who changes their itinerary or their sponsor, the change would not normally be regarded as fundamental. It is in each case a question of fact and degree (*Immigration Officer Heathrow v Salmak* [1991] Imm AR 191). Changes in visitors' plans are discussed further in chapter 10. However, each case under this rule turns upon its facts. In *Chakrabarty* 01/TH/1939 the Tribunal found that considering the change of circumstances was a purely objective exercise, comparing the circumstances now with the circumstances at the time of the grant of entry clearance. It was not necessary to engage in speculation as to what decision the entry clearance officer would have reached if the present circumstances had been known then. The Tribunal also confirmed that the onus is on the immigration officer to show that there has been a change of circumstances, and that as an adverse decision will deprive the individual of a benefit (i.e., leave to enter), the change of circumstances must be 'substantial and relevant'.

The rule can have harsh consequences, as in *Angur Begum* [1989] Imm AR 302, in which the Divisional Court held that there was a change of circumstances removing the basis for admission when the sponsoring father and husband of the applicants had died since the application was made.

6.5.3.3 *Further grounds for cancellation*

Where leave is in existence at the date of arrival, it may be cancelled under para 321A on additional grounds over and above those on which leave may be refused to a holder of an old-style entry clearance. These grounds are parallel to some of the original reasons for refusal under para 320. They are the two public good grounds, both the Secretary of State's personal direction and the immigration officer's judgement and, save in relation to a settled person, medical grounds. The medical grounds here are different in that although compassionate reasons may override the medical undesirability of entry, there is no necessary involvement of a medical officer in the decision. The rule (para 321 A(3)) simply says 'where it is apparent for medical reasons', and this may include that it is apparent to the immigration officer, which suggests a judgment made on the basis of a person's appearance and behaviour. Additionally, while a person is still outside the UK, leave to enter may be cancelled for non-production of documents, information, etc., in parallel with para 320(8A).

6.5.4 Leave to enter after living in the UK

Entry to the UK is a legal, not a physical, event. When a person disembarks from their ship, aircraft, or lorry, whether legally or illegally, they have arrived in the UK but not entered. Immigration Act 1971 s 11 defines entry as taking place only after a person has passed through immigration control and been granted leave to enter. So a person may be being questioned at immigration control, in detention in the UK, or living in the UK for a period of months or even years on temporary admission, but still not treated as having entered.

Referring back to s 4(1), it is apparent that in 1971 the statute contemplated a clear division of function between immigration officers and other Home Office civil servants. Immigration officers were to have the power to give or refuse leave to enter, and the Secretary of State, in practice the IND, had power to give leave to remain or to vary leave. Decisions on leave to remain or varying leave are the 'in-country' decisions, the decisions that are taken once a person is in the UK. These may be contrasted with the border control decisions allocated by s 4 to the immigration service. Decisions on asylum claims are made by the Home Office. The effect of this division of powers was that at the end of a claim for asylum, the papers related to the claim went back to the immigration service to grant or refuse leave to enter. This added to the administrative complexity of dealing with asylum cases.

However, the power in s 3A Immigration Act 1971 includes the following:

The Secretary of State may, in such circumstances as may be prescribed in an order made by him, give or refuse leave to enter the United Kingdom. (s 3A(7))

In other words, the power previously reserved to the immigration service may now be exercised by the Secretary of State, to the extent that an order of the Secretary of State provides for this. The Immigration (Leave to Enter) Order 2001, SI 2001/2590, made under the power in s 3A, provides that the Secretary of State may give or refuse leave to enter to an asylum or human rights applicant. Following the growth in asylum claims, it may now often be the case that a person lives in the UK with a status such as temporary admission for a substantial period of time before their application for leave to enter is determined. They are physically present, but in law they have not yet been granted leave to enter. There is something nonsensical about the applications of such people, once they are finally determined, being passed back to immigration officers for grant or refusal of leave as though the applicant had just arrived.

The trend towards eroding the distinction between immigration officers and Secretary of State powers exercised by other IND civil servants has continued in the Nationality, Immigration and Asylum Act 2002. Section 62 envisages the power in Immigration Act 1971 s 3A being used to enable the Secretary of State to examine a person in order to decide whether to give leave to enter, to issue removal directions, to detain pending examination. In other words, all the powers formerly reserved to the immigration service are in the process of becoming Secretary of State powers also.

6.6 The leave obtained

In this section there is discussion of the possible kinds of leave that a person may have acquired as a consequence of passing through immigration control, and of the effects of such leave.

6.6.1 Non-lapsing or continuing leave

A further change made by the Immigration (Leave to Enter and Remain) Order 2000, SI 2000/1161 is the introduction of so-called 'non-lapsing' or 'continuing' leave. Before 30 July 2000, when article 13 of the 2000 Order was implemented the position was governed entirely by Immigration Act 1971 s 3(4), which provides: 'A person's leave to enter or remain in the United Kingdom shall lapse on his going to a country or territory outside the Common Travel Area . . .' There were a few exceptions to this rule, but in general what it meant was that people on limited leave, such as students, could go away from the UK for a weekend break, and be refused entry on their return.

From 30 July 2000, s 3(4) remains in force, but its effects are considerably modified. Article 13(2) of the 2000 Order provides that leave will not lapse on the holder's leaving the Common Travel Area if 'it was conferred by means of an entry clearance . . . or for a period exceeding six months'. This does not apply where the leave has been varied by the Secretary of State and 'following the variation the period of leave remaining is six months or less' (art 13(3)). The effect of this is that most people with limited leave will be able to come and go during the currency of that leave without fear of being refused entry on return. The reasons for cancellation of leave discussed in the last section of this chapter apply to a person returning who holds non-lapsing leave. The immigration officer is therefore entitled to examine them to discover whether any such reason applies (Immigration Act 1971 Sch 2 para 2A).

The non-lapsing provisions do not apply to leave to enter as a visitor, however the 2000 Order contains another provision which has a very similar effect. Article 4 provides that a visit visa 'during its period of validity, shall have effect as leave to enter the United Kingdom on an unlimited number of occasions' for six months if the visa has at least six months of validity remaining, or its remaining period of validity if this is shorter. Visit visas may be granted for periods of up to five years, on the basis that any stay as a visitor is limited to six months, but permitting multiple entries during the five-year period. These visas are used particularly by business people. The leave to enter lapses on the visitor leaving the Common Travel Area (2000 Order art 13(2)) but on their return within the period of validity of the visa it operates as leave to enter again (art 13(2)). The visitor who does not benefit from the 2000 Order is the non-visa national visitor who obtains leave to enter at the port which lapses on their departure (art 13(2)), but who does not possess a visa which can operate as leave to enter on their return. Therefore they must re-apply for leave to enter on arrival at the port on each occasion.

6.6.2 **24-hour rule**

The 24-hour rule is briefly discussed here as it gives a form of deemed leave to enter. It applies to people applying at the port for leave to enter for a limited period. This is now restricted to non-visa nationals wishing to enter as a visitor or student for less than six months. After examination of the passenger is concluded (and as we have seen above this can be an extended process) the immigration officer has 24 hours in which to give notice of their decision to the passenger. If the officer fails to do so, Immigration Act 1971 Sch 2 para 6(1) gives the passenger six months deemed leave with a prohibition on working. This is very similar to the leave that a visitor would be granted routinely. The Immigration (Leave to Enter and Remain) Order 2000, SI 2000/1161 article 12 deals with the giving of notice after an examination has been adjourned for further enquiries or where there has been a further examination. This article envisages that the individual is no longer at the port but their application for leave has not yet been determined. In this situation, where the immigration officer decides that they do not need to interview the applicant again (art 12(1)(c)), the article provides that

any notice giving or refusing leave to enter which is on *any date thereafter* sent by post to the applicant (or is communicated to him in such form or manner as is permitted by this Order) shall be regarded, for the purposes of this Act, as having been given within the period of 24 hours specified in paragraph 6(1) of Schedule 2. (emphasis added)

The words in brackets refer to the possibility of notice being given by fax or e-mail, as mentioned earlier. The words 'on any date thereafter' in effect extend the 24-hour period and override an earlier body of case law concerning the calculation of the 24-hour period. The 2006 Act gives power to make further provision about when an application is treated as being decided. The 24-hour rule applies to lawful applicants for leave, not those treated as illegal entrants on arrival.

6.6.3 **Limited leave to enter**

Leave to enter may be for an indefinite or a limited period of time. Most leave is limited, and may be subject to conditions (Immigration Act 1971 s 3(1)(c)). The conditions may be of three kinds: restricting or prohibiting employment, requiring the holder to maintain themselves and any dependants without recourse to public funds, or requiring the holder to register with the police. No other conditions are possible. If and when the time limit is lifted on the holder's stay in the UK, any conditions will also be lifted as indefinite leave may not be subject to conditions (s 3(3)).

If the holder of limited leave does not intend to leave the country on the expiry of the leave, an application to extend or vary the terms of leave must be made before it expires, otherwise the person becomes an overstayer and is liable to removal (Immigration Act 1999 s 10).

6.6.4 Indefinite leave to enter

For a minority of entrants to the UK, leave to enter is indefinite. This is the case for adult dependent family members coming for settlement. When leave is indefinite there may be no further contact with the Home Office and there is no further stage to pass through in terms of immigration status. For such a person leave to enter and leave to remain are one and the same. A person with indefinite leave to remain has full access to the National Health Service and may freely change employment as no conditions may be attached to indefinite leave (Immigration Act 1971 s 3(3)(a)). As no conditions may be attached it might appear that such a person will also have full access to the welfare benefits system. However, in most cases adult dependent relatives will only gain indefinite leave straight away if their sponsor has signed an undertaking to support them for a fixed period of perhaps five years. During this period no claim for welfare benefits may be made by them or on their behalf. Residence without immigration restriction is one of the qualifications to apply for naturalization as a British citizen (British Nationality Act 1981 Sch 1 paras 1 and 3), and so a person who gains indefinite leave straight away may begin to count time towards qualifying to naturalize as British if they so wish.

6.6.4.1 *Returning residents*

A person with indefinite leave has no immigration restrictions on their stay in the UK, but they are still subject to immigration control in that if they leave the country they may be examined by an immigration officer on their return and refused entry on limited grounds. Prior to the Immigration (Leave to Enter and Remain) Order 2000, SI 2000/1161, the position of such people was governed by the so-called returning resident rules, found in HC 395 paras 18–20. These rules were based on the fact that indefinite leave lapsed when the holder left the UK, but enabled the holder to be readmitted provided they met the requirements of the rules. These were that they had not been absent for more than two years, that when they last entered they had indefinite leave, that they now returned for settlement and that they did not leave the UK with the assistance of public funds (i.e., using a government repatriation scheme). These rules are still in existence, but must now be read together with SI 2000/1161. The effect of the 2000 Order is that leave does not lapse during an absence of less than two years. So a person with indefinite leave who returns within two years no longer has to re-apply for leave. The effect of the change removes the basis for confusion and distressing refusals of leave to enter provided the person returns within two years. The continuing existence of the requirement to prove that they had indefinite leave when they last left and that they now enter for settlement does not really make sense in the light of the fact that they have no application to make at the port. They may only be examined at the port to see if the leave should be cancelled, for the reasons discussed in the earlier section on this subject. Rather bizarrely, following the 2000 Order, the returning residents' rules seem to place a greater burden on a person with indefinite leave than is placed on a person with limited leave.

After two years, even so-called non-lapsing leave actually lapses (Immigration (Leave to Enter and Remain) Order 2000, SI 2000/1161 article 13(4)). Outside the two-year period re-entry is a matter of discretion, but if the only factor preventing return is that the person has been away too long, they should be admitted if, for example, they have lived in the UK for most of their life (HC 395 para 19). This is a wide discretion, and the example of when it should be exercised is no more than an indication of a basis for exercising it. Reference may be made to the IDIs for more examples. Visa nationals returning after more than two years will need a new entry clearance.

Returning residents may be refused readmission on grounds under para 320, in the limited situations where these are relevant, but not on medical grounds. Refusal is possible on grounds of exclusion being conducive to the public good, and para 320 (9) gives the basis for refusal of leave where the requirements of para 18 are not met.

6.6.4.2 *New limits on indefinite leave*

The security of indefinite leave to remain is somewhat undermined by the new power in Nationality, Immigration and Asylum Act 2002 s 76, discussed in chapter 1. Under this section the Secretary of State may revoke a person's indefinite leave to enter or remain if the person is liable to deportation but 'cannot be deported for legal reasons'. In a similar vein, under s 76(2) indefinite leave can be revoked if it was obtained by deception but the person cannot be removed for legal or practical reasons. A person whose leave is revoked will not be able to work or claim benefits and therefore will have no basis for economic support unless they are detained or work illegally. Their children will not be British, and depending on the laws of their country of nationality may be born stateless. They will have no right to be joined by other members of their family. This raises the prospect of a new group of people forced into destitution. There is no exemption in the section for children. Section 76 does not require that national security is in issue and the application of this section may raise issues under Human Rights Act Sch 1 arts 3, 8, and 14.

6.6.5 **Grant of leave to remain**

Leave to remain for a person already in the UK is granted by the Secretary of State under the power in Immigration Act 1971 s 4(1). The power includes giving further limited leave to remain, either by way of extending the existing leave or by varying it to a different immigration category, or giving indefinite leave to remain. Where limited leave is extended or varied the Secretary of State may also vary or continue any conditions attaching to the earlier leave (Immigration Act 1971 s 3(3) and HC 395 para 31).

Most people who obtain leave to enter the UK initially obtain limited rather than indefinite leave. This may later be made indefinite on an application made to do so. It does not happen automatically. For instance a partner will obtain an initial two-year period of leave. At the end of that time they must apply to the Home Office, who, if requirements of the rules continue to be met, will lift the time restriction together with any conditions lifted and grant indefinite leave to remain

Table 2 Types of leave to enter

Indefinite leave to enter	Limited leave to enter Non-lapsing	Visitor
No limit on stay	Fixed period, according to immigration category	6 or 12 or 60 months, multiple entry, maximum stay 6 months
Return within two years to retain status		

(paras 287 and 295G). A number of categories of entry under the rules may lead to settlement after some years of residence, although these entitlements are subject to change under the new five tier system for economic migration (see chapter 11). Once indefinite leave is granted, there is no further control (short of any allegations of illegal entry) on the person's activity, and there is no continuing obligation to remain in for instance, the work permit employment.

6.6.6 No-switching rules

Some categories of entry do not lead to indefinite leave. For instance, the immigration rules concerning leave as a student do not make any provision for indefinite leave to be granted. If therefore a person who is in the UK as a student wants to make the UK their permanent home, they must change the category of the immigration rules under which they are staying. They may then encounter the 'no-switching' rules, which restrict the categories between which such changes may be made. These restrictions are mainly apparent from the immigration rules. However, there are certain changes which, although not provided for or even prohibited by the rules, are permitted either exceptionally or as a matter of policy ascertainable through the IDIs. Until 2003, all categories could change to spouse, though not fianc(é)e. Rule changes following the 2002 White Paper *Secure Borders, Safe Haven*, Cm 5387 now prevent visitors from staying in the UK for marriage (see HC 395 para 284 (i)). Visitors may only change to student status, only if they are not visa nationals (HC 395 para 60(i)) and only if their studies will be at degree level or above. The rules relating to students have been relaxed and students may now apply to stay for work experience or in certain cases, work permit employment (see chapters 10 and 11). For full details of current permitted and prohibited switches, reference should be made to the immigration rules and the latest edition of JCWI Immigration, Nationality and Refugee Law Handbook, which provides a useful chart. Where the change of category is permitted, under the terms of the Immigration Act 1971, there must be an application for a variation of leave.

6.6.7 Variation of leave

The power to vary leave is granted to the Secretary of State by Immigration Act 1971 s 4(1). This is in accordance with the traditional division of function discussed earlier according to which the Secretary of State grants variation of leave and leave to remain whereas the immigration officer grants leave to enter. Some aspects of the way this distinction is breaking down have already been discussed. It may be recalled that the new Immigration Act 1971 s 3A enables the Secretary of State to 'make further provision with respect to the giving, refusing or varying of leave'. Two changes have been introduced using this power with respect to variation of leave. The power to vary remains with the Secretary of State, but the Immigration (Leave to Enter and Remain) Order 2000, SI 2000/1161 article 13(6) extends the scope of that power by providing that it may be exercised while the holder of leave is outside the UK. This is introduced into the rules in para 33A.

The other new power concerning variation is one we have already noted, the power of an immigration officer to vary leave of someone who already has leave when they enter. This power is exercised on behalf of the Secretary of State (HC 395 para 31A), and so is not given to immigration officers in their own right. It is a corollary of the power to grant leave outside the UK as entry may be precisely the occasion when variation of existing leave is needed. This could arise for instance in the situation already discussed when the holder's initial leave is, at the time of entry, no longer enough to enable them to qualify for settlement at the end of that leave.

Section 3C of the Immigration Act 1971 provides a statutory extension of leave where an application for variation of leave is made within the currency of existing leave. It is quite likely that, for reasons outside the control of the applicant, such as Home Office delays, existing leave may expire before the application for variation is decided. This would result in an injustice if a person were then treated as an overstayer simply because their application had not been heard. Section 3C extends the existing leave, on the existing conditions if any, until the decision has been taken.

6.7 **Settlement**

The terms 'settlement' and 'settled' are used widely in immigration law, and it is important to grasp their meaning. Settled status must be distinguished from right of abode, indefinite leave to remain, and ordinary residence. 'Settled' is a term of art, defined by statute. 'Settlement', despite its wide colloquial use, is not.

The Immigration Act 1971 s 33(2)A defines a person who is 'settled' as subject to no immigration restrictions on length of stay and ordinarily resident in the UK. These two components of the definition are both important. Someone who has no immigration restrictions on their length of stay may be in that position either because they have indefinite leave to remain or because they have right of abode. Right of abode, it may be recalled from the chapter on nationality, is the right to come and go 'without let or hindrance' (Immigration Act 1971 s 1) and is held only by British citizens and the relatively few Commonwealth citizens with right of abode. Settlement includes indefinite leave to remain but carries the additional requirement of ordinary residence.

The meaning of the term 'ordinary residence' was considered by the House of Lords in *Shah v Barnet London Borough Council* [1983] 2 AC 309, not an immigration but an education case, concerning a student's entitlement to a grant, which also, under statute, depended upon 'ordinary residence.' The House of Lords held that it was possible to have more than one ordinary residence. The country of ordinary residence was the person's home, chosen as part of a settled way of life for the time being. It could be of long or short duration and did not imply permanence. The reason for being present was irrelevant providing it was voluntary, and immigration status had no bearing on the matter, providing the person was not in breach of immigration law. This meant that someone with limited leave could be ordinarily resident. In the context of defining 'settled status' it means that there is no need to prove that the person intends to be in the UK for the rest of their life. The case of *Chugtai*, [1995] IAR 559 developed *Shah* in holding that a person could be ordinarily resident in two countries at the same time. In *AB Bangladesh* [2004] UKIAT 00314 ILU vol. 8, no. 2 the Tribunal held that this could include where the appellant intended to spend six months of each year in each country. He could therefore be said to be coming to the UK 'for settlement'.

The point in *Shah* about illegality was *obiter*, as none of the students in that case were present illegally. This was taken up by the House of Lords in *Mark v Mark* [2005] UKHL 42 who considered that whether illegal presence in immigration law affected ordinary residence would depend upon the context. Where a statute requiring ordinary residence confers a benefit from the state then it might be relevant to require lawful presence. However, where, as in *Mark*, it was only relevant to the question of which jurisdiction governs divorce proceedings, then legality of residence was not relevant. This decision, while being careful and restricted in its scope to the civil matters in hand, also offers a welcome counter to the trend of excluding foreign nationals without immigration status from the usual benefits of the law.

Colloquially, it is often said that when a person obtains indefinite leave to remain they 'get settlement', as for instance when a work permit holder has lived in the UK and obtains indefinite leave to remain, or a spouse whose restrictions are lifted after their probationary period. The words 'settlement' and 'indefinite leave to remain' are often used interchangeably and for practical purposes this is quite valid. However the two are not exactly the same. Though settled status may be acquired at a particular date, it may not be. It is not awarded by the Secretary of State explicitly, and the term 'settlement' will not be found in the immigration rules. It is a description of a state of affairs rather than an immigration status awarded.

Although the word 'settlement' is not used in the immigration rules, the word 'settled' is. It is necessary to be able to identify when a person is settled as important rights accrue to someone with settled status. Children born in the UK to a settled person will be British (British Nationality Act 1981 s 1), and in the immigration rules a settled person is qualified to sponsor a partner or relative to come to the UK (HC 395, e.g., paras 281, 317).

In practical terms, settlement and indefinite leave to remain are virtually coterminous. As we have seen, a person with indefinite leave to remain who stays away from the UK for more than two years may lose that leave. Therefore an ordinary residence requirement is implied in retaining indefinite leave to remain. The practical result is that it equates to being settled. Although it is technically accurate to refer to a British citizen ordinarily resident in the UK as 'settled', these entitlements are of greater real significance to people who are not British. In general, therefore, the word 'settled' is used to refer to people who have indefinite leave to remain and are ordinarily resident in the UK.

Settled status in this usual sense does not carry full rights of citizenship. A settled person can be deported on the ground that deportation is conducive to the public good (Immigration Act s 3(5)(a)) and does not have the right to vote or stand for Parliament. In these respects as well as the possible loss of status after two years' absence, settled status is less secure than right of abode.

6.7.1 Acquiring settled status

As suggested above, settled status may be acquired after a period laid down in rules relating to particular categories of entrant. So for instance a spouse may obtain settlement after two years, and there are other usual policies leading to settlement.

UK practice was to grant immediate settlement to people on acquisition of refugee status, but since 31 August 2005 a grant of five years has been normal practice. Acquisition of settled status after periods of discretionary leave is now not automatic. Under the policy which prevailed until 1 April 2003, it was common for a person who had been granted exceptional leave to remain (ELR), i.e., leave outside the rules, for whatever reason, to obtain settlement after four years' residence. On 1 April 2003 three new kinds of leave replaced ELR: for asylum and human rights claimants whose asylum claim had failed, humanitarian protection and discretionary leave (HP and DL), and for other people, leave outside the rules (LOTR). The conditions for grant of the first two are discussed in chapter 12. Either may still lead to settlement, HP after three years and DL after six, but only if a continuing need for protection is shown. LOTR may be granted in the kinds of situations we considered in relation to grounds for refusal, where the precise requirements of the rule are not met, but the ECO or immigration officer exercises their discretion to grant leave. Details have not yet been published of whether and how LOTR can lead to settlement.

There are other concessions entailing grant of settlement, for instance a British overseas citizen may be granted settlement after seven years of lawful residence. The final and important provisions relating to grant of settlement are those based on long residence.

6.7.1.1 *Long residence*

It is appropriate that people who have been living for a long time in a country should have some security of residence, when they have not otherwise obtained a secure immigration status. This principle has been given effect in the UK by a concession, which in April 2003 became part of the immigration rules. It gives effect to Article 3(3) European Convention on Establishment, which the UK ratified on 14 October 1969, and which provides that nationals of any contracting party who have been lawfully residing for more than ten years in the territory of another party may only be expelled for reasons of national security or for particularly serious reasons relating to public order, public health, or morality. The IDI Dec 2000 Chapter 18 points out that the Home Office has extended this provision by means of the concession in three respects:

to include all foreign nationals, not just contracting states;

to grant indefinite leave rather than simply refrain from removing such a person; and

to allow those who have been in the UK illegally to benefit also.

It could be misleading to set this provision in the context of the Convention article if it implies that once a person has ten years' lawful residence that they will be safe from expulsion. This is not the case. What it does is to give some security of immigration status to people whose status is insecure. It does not give immunity from deportation or removal. Cases considered in the chapter on deportation make this abundantly clear, for instance the appellant in *B v SSHD* [2000] Imm AR 478 was a settled resident who had lived in the UK for 35 of his 42 years before a deportation order was made, the respondent in *Dinc* [1999] Imm AR 380 had indefinite leave to remain and had been resident for 13 years.

The long residence provisions provide a presumption for the grant of indefinite leave, thus giving peace of mind to someone who has been unsure about their future. The terms of the concession were:

Where a person has 10 years or more continuous lawful residence or 14 years or more continuous residence (of any legality), indefinite leave to remain should normally be granted in the absence of any strong countervailing factors.

Strong countervailing factors are such things as an extant criminal record (not spent under the Rehabilitation of Offenders Act) apart from minor non-custodial offences, and 'deliberate and blatant attempts' to circumvent immigration control, for example by using forged documents, absconding, contracting a marriage of convenience (IDI para 2).

The presumption has been weakened in the rule which replaced the concession, which instead of requiring strong countervailing factors says that indefinite leave may be granted if 'having regard to the public interest there are no reasons why it would be undesirable'. The words 'should normally' have been removed. The rule also introduces consideration of the individual circumstances which are normally considered in a deportation case, and this may have the effect of weakening the presumption also (para 276 B (ii)).

Short absences of up to six months will not break continuity. Sometimes longer ones also will be accepted as part of the period of residence, depending on the intention shown. The question is whether the absences can be said to disrupt or sever ties with the UK (IDI para 5). The approach is similar to that for establishing ordinary residence as set out in *Shah v Barnet London Borough Council*. Similarly, short breaks in legality, as where, for instance, an application was filed late, but then granted, will not break continuity. In *Kungwengwe v SSHD* [2005] EWHC 1427 (Admin) Wilkie J did not accept that residence pursuant to a residence permit issued under EEA regulations amounted to lawful residence for the purposes of this rule. See chapter 5.

The 14-year rule enables overstayers, people in breach of condition and illegal entrants to declare themselves to the Home Office and obtain a status which enables lawful working, an application to be joined by relatives, entitlement to welfare benefits, and so on. However, they cannot count time after enforcement proceedings have been commenced against them (HC 395 para 276B(i)(b)). The way this works was illustrated in the case of *R v SSHD ex p Ofori* [1994] Imm AR 581. Here, the applicant had six years' leave, then overstayed for five. He then applied for indefinite leave to remain but was refused. At the date of decision he had been in the UK for 12 years. A decision was made to deport him and he appealed. At the (unsuccessful) end of the appeal process he had been in the UK for 14 years. He

applied again for indefinite leave to remain, relying on the long residence concession. However, the High Court supported the Secretary of State's decision that
he could not rely on time spent during the appeal process towards his 14 years.
Therefore his application failed.

There was a practice, which has now been abandoned, of serving notice of intention to deport 'on the file', i.e., where a person could not be traced, the notice was
issued but left to lie on the file. There are still people in relation to whom this was
done at some point in the past. *Popatia* [2001] Imm AR 46 establishes that this does
not count as service for the purpose of the long residence provisions and service on
the file does not commence enforcement proceedings.

6.8 Conclusion

This chapter has considered some of the legal provisions relating to crossing the
UK's borders and obtaining an immigration status here. The focus has been on
entry rather than on control after entry, although leave to enter and remain is
increasingly a personal status awarded by a diffuse, intelligence-led governmental
system, rather than permission to cross a border which is granted at the geographical boundary. There has been some discussion of the way in which discretion
is exercised within this system, as despite the complex of rules and policies, the
judgement of officials is still at the heart of immigration control. The ways in which
this discretion can be restricted or challenged are discussed in the next chapter.

QUESTIONS

1 How do you think the Immigration (Leave to Enter and Remain) Order 2000 changes the
   substance and nature of immigration control?

2 What would you consider to be appropriate medical grounds for refusal of leave to enter and
   who do you think should make that decision? How does your idea compare with the present
   law?

3 What do you think are the reasons for limiting the categories of leave to and from which a
   person can switch?

FURTHER READING

Bevan, V. (1986) *The Development of British Immigration Law* (Beckenham: Croom Hill),
   Chapter 3.

Commission for Racial Equality (1985) *Immigration Control Procedures: Report of a Formal
   Investigation* (London: Commission for Racial Equality).

Guild, E. (2000) 'Entry into the UK: the changing nature of national borders' (2000) INLP vol.
   14, no. 4, pp. 227–238.

JCWI (2006) *Immigration, Nationality and Refugee Law Handbook*, 6th edn. (London: JCWI).

Juss, S. (1997) *Discretion and Deviation in the Administration of Immigration Control* (London:
   Sweet & Maxwell).

Luqmani, J., Randall, C., and Scammell, R. (2000) 'Recent Developments in Immigration Law'
   Legal Action July 2000, 11–17.

Macdonald, I., and Webber, F. (2005) *Macdonald's Immigration Law and Practice*, 6th edn (London: Butterworths), Chapters 3, 5, and 6.

Reports of the Entry Clearance Monitor 2000–2005.

Ryan, B. (2001) 'The Common Travel Area between Britain and Ireland' *Modern Law Review* vol. 64 November 2001, pp. 855–874.

Sondhi, R. (1987) 'Divided Families: British Immigration Control in the Indian Subcontinent' (London: Runnymede Trust)

7

The extension of immigration control

SUMMARY

This chapter discusses the extension of immigration control beyond the borders of the UK, in particular the role of immigration officers outside the UK in the context of immigration policy as an instrument of deterrence for asylum claims. There is also discussion of the extension of immigration control to commercial and private bodies, particularly carriers, to other public and private organizations, and the development of new technology for detection and surveillance. The chapter gives a picture of immigration control developing from border management to a diffuse activity more akin to policing.

7.1 Introduction

It is apparent that immigration control has been and is being extended to include far more than the traditional model of border control at a port. There are two dimensions of extension, one is geographical and the other in terms of the personnel involved. The geographical extension is both outward, beyond the borders of the UK, and inward, involving elements of immigration control within the territory also. The extension in terms of personnel involves an extension of the role of the conventional figures of immigration control, immigration officers, and those carrying out similar work, and the inclusion of others not previously engaged. This has taken place through the development of practices and legal provisions which involve local authorities, other public bodies, commercial bodies, and even private individuals in the control of immigration. There is also another dimension, the enhancement of control by new technology which measures, identifies and detects human characteristics.

This chapter deals with all these dimensions. First, the outward extension beyond the border is considered, then the extension of immigration control at the point of crossing the border, and finally the extension of immigration control inside the territory.

7.2 **Outwards — immigration control outside the UK**

This section is concerned with developments in which immigration officers and others doing similar work are positioned in other countries, and some of the work of immigration control is carried out there. In chapter 6, there was discussion of the effect of the Immigration (Leave to Enter and Remain) Order 2000, SI 2000/1161. It provided, among other things, that leave to enter could be granted outside the UK, and the applications of this power were noted. In particular, it enables entry clearance to have effect as leave to enter, and may be used for convenience for groups of passengers considered to be at low risk of immigration infringements, e.g., school tours. The power to grant or refuse leave to enter from abroad was not only granted for convenience of some travellers, but also for deterrence of others, namely asylum seekers. The judgment of Simon Brown LJ in *European Roma Rights Centre and Others v Immigration Officer, Prague Airport and SSHD* [2003] 4 All ER 247 gives a confirmation and summary of this:

There are difficulties, however, of a political nature in imposing a visa regime on certain friendly states and so Parliament in 1999 authorized the Home Secretary to introduce in addition a scheme enabling the immigration rules to be operated extra-territorially rather than simply at UK ports of entry. Intending asylum seekers would in this way be refused leave to enter the UK by immigration officers operating abroad and so be unable to travel to the UK to claim asylum here. (para 2)

Three recent initiatives in which immigration officers have been placed abroad need to be seen in that context.

7.2.1 **Juxtaposed control**

The first of these initiatives considered here is known as 'juxtaposed control'. This involves British immigration officers working at a port abroad alongside the immigration service of that country, sharing information and intelligence, and refusing to allow improperly documented passengers to board transport for Britain.

Juxtaposed controls have only been set up in Europe, and they may be seen as a form of European co-operation; alternatively, as a symptom of the need for a Common European Asylum System or as a failure of the attempt at harmonization to date (see Phuong 2003, discussion in chapter 4 and below). The arrangement when fully implemented is a mutual one, enabling the immigration services of the other country to operate also in UK ports.

A main source of impetus for the establishment of juxtaposed controls was the furore surrounding the Red Cross refugee camp at Sangatte in northern France. There were daily illegal entries to the UK by asylum seekers waiting in the camp, and this combined with the associated breaches of security, danger and injury to individuals, and delays to freight and other traffic created a three-year dispute over causes and responsibilities between the two governments. Accordingly the first juxtaposed controls were set up in 2002 in France, initially at the Eurotunnel site at Coquelles and Eurostar stations at Paris Nord and Calais Fréthun. After the establishment of these controls and the closure of Sangatte at the end of 2002, there was a concern that other routes would then be used, so juxtaposed controls have now spread to Eurostar stations at Lille Europe and in Belgium, the Gare du Midi, Ostend, and Zeebrugge. Controls on channel tunnel trains may all be made under powers granted by the Channel Tunnel Act 1987 and implemented in various orders. The Channel Tunnel (Miscellaneous Provisions) (Amendment) Order 2004, SI 2004/2589 for stopping trains from Belgium is the most recent. It gives effect to an agreement between the British, French, and Belgian Governments and completes the move of UK immigration controls on Eurostar trains from London to continental Europe. Home Office Minister Des Browne said that moving control to France on the trains from there had cut asylum applications at Waterloo by 90 per cent (HO press release 309/2004).

The legal arrangements with France are contained in the Treaty between the Government of the United Kingdom of Great Britain and Northern Ireland and the Government of the French Republic concerning the implementation of frontier controls at the sea ports of both countries on the Channel and North Sea, Cm 5832, in force on 1 February 2004. The powers granted by the treaty are wide. The treaty provides for the designation of control zones, which are the areas of the port within which the authorities of the other country may exercise their powers. It gives operational control, including power to change the control zones if necessary, to the responsible authorities of the two countries. The powers which may be exercised there are 'all the laws and regulations of the Contracting Parties concerning immigration controls and the investigation of offences relating to immigration' (Article 2). The law and regulations of the destination state have the same effect in the state of departure as they would in their own state. So the laws of the UK have effect in French control zone as they would in the UK and should be applied 'in the same manner and with the same consequences' (Article 3). There are similar provisions in the Protocol on rail travel between Belgium, France and UK, given effect by SI 2004/2589.

Article 5 provides that the authorities of the destination state may 'arrest and hold for questioning' anyone who is subject to examination, including, but not limited to, those who are suspected of a breach of immigration law. The use of the word 'arrest' with its connotations of criminal charge raises questions about the rights of those arrested and detained and whether their detention will be subject to the PACE Codes of Practice. In its reply to concerns raised in the consultation process on juxtaposed controls the Home Office said that passengers would be able to contact their Embassy at any time, and 'those passengers refused entry who have a right of appeal from abroad will be served with a notice of refusal which will include information about the Refugee Legal Centre and Immigration Advisory Service' (Juxtaposed Control Implementation, Dover–Calais, Consultation Process Report, Response 1). This does not deal with the situation of, even more importantly, someone who would have had a right of appeal in the UK, although the possibilities of this are extremely limited for the reason given below. It also does not take account of the possibility that judicial review might have been warranted, but without legal advice the detainee will be unlikely to be able to identify or pursue this option. Detention will be limited to 24 hours, or in exceptional circumstances, 48 hours.

The treaty and the whole system of juxtaposed controls are on the face of it aimed at preventing illegal entry. However, the broader context is the deterrence of asylum claims and the prevention of 'asylum shopping' in Europe, i.e., people seeking asylum in the state of their choice. This is particularly clear in Article 9 of the Frontier Control Treaty, which provides that if a person makes an asylum claim, or any other claim for protection which could be available in the state of departure, before the vessel in which they travel leaves the port, they must make that claim in the State of departure. This is the exception to the provision in the treaty that otherwise, once the state of arrival has commenced its enquiries, the state of departure has no further part to play. For this reason, a right of appeal in the UK is unlikely to arise. A person who asserts their human rights would be breached by returning them to their home country would have a right of appeal in the UK if they were there, but if they make such a claim in France the application must be heard by the French authorities. The Protocol with Belgium does not refer to asylum claims, but says that the controls of the state of departure must normally be carried out before those of the state of arrival (Article 5).

The Frontier Control Treaty is given effect in UK law by the Nationality, Immigration and Asylum Act 2002 (Juxtaposed Controls) Order 2003, SI 2003/2818, made under the power in the Nationality, Immigration and Asylum Act 2002 s 141. This section is of interest for constitutional reasons. It allows for the order to provide for 'a law' of England and Wales to have effect in a specified area which may be outside the UK. The old Imperial view that there was no geographical limit to Parliamentary sovereignty has been thought ridiculous by more modern Constitutional lawyers, but this provision, which of course is mutual between the UK and France, may raise some interesting questions about the limits of one country's jurisdiction. The width of the term 'a law' is endorsed by the terms of the Frontier Control Treaty, apparently to include not only statutes and statutory instruments, but also case law and immigration rules. The Orders made using powers in the Channel Tunnel Act 1987 only concern train travel and not port areas, although they do involve immigration officers being posted at railway stations abroad.

It is interesting to consider the justification for juxtaposed controls. Home Office commissioned research assessing the impact of asylum policies in Europe from 1990 to 2000 (Home Office Research Study 259) found that it was difficult to attribute particular movements of asylum seekers to the adoption of particular policies. To the extent that it was possible, pre-entry and on-entry controls had perhaps the greatest impact on the number of asylum claims (p. 120). The researchers cited for instance visa regimes and pre-flight checks and noted these were most effective in combination with carrier sanctions (p. 25). A Home Office press release 172/2003, 23 June 2003, welcomed the publication of the research, saying that its finding of the effectiveness of pre-entry controls was an endorsement of the tight border controls being developed by the UK, and citing particularly juxtaposed controls. It is necessary to see this debate in a European context. Juxtaposed controls operate only at borders with EU member states. They were not in place during the period of the research. The pre-entry controls discussed in the research take place in the country of origin. It is debatable whether juxtaposed controls may be placed in the same category, or whether they are a matter of regulation between the UK and France or Belgium. Phuong's work suggests that the Sangatte debacle, paradoxically, demonstrates the need for the UK to join the Schengen area and open its borders to other Member States (2003:168; see discussion in chapter 4). The Home Office researchers point out that it is not possible to say what would have happened if states did not make their intervention (RDS 259 p. xi).

In summary, juxtaposed controls are playing an increasing role in the UK's border management. On one viewing, they are an essential and effective tool in deterring asylum claims, though note that no distinction would be made between well-founded and other claims in this respect (RDS 259:120). From another viewpoint, they are a temporary local measure between Britain and its neighbours, indicating the failure of harmonization in Europe, and the need for it.

7.2.2 Airline liaison officers

The second kind of role taken abroad by immigration officers is as airline liaison officers to advise airlines on the validity of documents presented to them for travel to the UK. These immigration officers do not grant or refuse leave to enter, but advise airlines who may then refuse to allow the passenger to board. In 2001 about 2,500 passengers were prevented from travelling following such advice (McKee 'Fitting the Bill?' IANL vol. 16, no. 3 2002, p. 183), rising to 33,000 in 2003. Although this is not at present an actual refusal of leave to enter, the power granted in the Immigration (Leave to Enter and Remain) Order 2000, SI 2000/1161 gives scope for expanding the role of these officers. The liability of the officers for wrong advice is a matter of concern, given that there is no appeal against what is in formal terms advice to the airline rather than an immigration decision (see discussion of *Farah v British Airways & Home Office* TLR 26 January 2000 below and in chapter 3). The main objective of these schemes is once again to limit asylum claims. Asylum seekers may often travel on false documents as this may be the only way to leave their country. If they are at risk they are not in a position while still in their own country to make an asylum claim. For obvious reasons, the effect on asylum seekers turned away from flights after such advice is unknown.

As part of its five-year strategy *Controlling our borders: making migration work for Britain*, February 2005 Cm 6472, the Government committed itself to increasing the number of ALOs. A Home Office press release 031/2005 22 February 2005 stated that there were at that date twenty-seven ALOs based in twenty-five posts across Europe, Asia and Africa and these would increase to forty-two. The Independent Race Monitor in her report of July 2005 says that the intervention of ALOs had resulted in 'fewer refusals at UK terminals, which was in the interests of all parties' (2.11). She also comments that improved co-ordination between UK staff, UK Visas and airlines 'enabled a more strategic approach'. There is now an EU regulation establishing a network of immigration liaison officers who are stationed abroad and collect information on illegal activities connected with migration in order to help prevent illegal migration into the EU. As an aspect of the development of the Schengen acquis, the UK has opted into the regulation (Regulation 377/2004).

7.2.3 Pre-clearance

Successive Home Secretaries have asserted that it would be desirable to pre-sift asylum claims abroad, and the third initiative discussed here is an example of an attempt to do this. The Home Office research discussed in connection with juxtaposed controls (RDS 259) suggests that this is the most effective way of limiting asylum claims, if any policy can be said to have an effect. The pre-clearance scheme at Prague in the Czech Republic was an experiment in this form of overseas activity of the British immigration service aimed at deterring unauthorized passengers from travelling. In this case, leave to enter *was* granted or refused before embarkation on a flight for the UK. In *European Roma Rights Centre (ERRC) v Immigration Officer at Prague Airport and SSHD* [2002] EWHC 1989 (Admin) the evidence of the Secretary of State confirmed that 'the Prague operation is not a pre-screening which is a prelude to a subsequent consideration of eligibility at a United Kingdom airport. Rather it takes the place of that consideration of that eligibility' (para 25). The judgment in the Court of Appeal [2003] 4 All ER 247 and House of Lords [2004] UKHL 55 confirmed what critics and the UK Government had agreed upon, namely that the effect of such a scheme was to prevent asylum claims being made. The difference between the parties was whether this was lawful or not. This dispute is one of the clearest illustrations of the changed nature of immigration control implied by the power to grant or refuse leave to enter outside the UK, and of the potential of that new power to affect asylum claims. Where an asylum claim is made at a UK port of entry there is an obligation implied by the 1951 UN Convention Relating to the Status of Refugees to consider it. However, the courts in the *ERRC* case found there was no obligation to allow the claimant to reach the UK in order to make that claim. As discussed in chapter 8, the House of Lords found this scheme to be discriminatory on racial grounds and therefore unlawful. Lord Bingham made the *obiter* comment that he doubted whether the decisions of immigration officers operating this scheme were subject to the ECHR, and this, as discussed in chapter 3, has had as yet unconcluded consequences for the question of the scope of human rights protection for immigration decisions which take place abroad.

The Prague scheme ran from 18 July 2001 to 26 February 2003. Following the Czech Republic's accession to the European Union in 2004 the scheme would have no basis.

Where such a pre-clearance system exists, a passenger has no option as to whether to use it. By contrast, para 17A HC 395 says that the immigration officer 'is not obliged to consider an application for leave to enter from a person outside the United Kingdom'. A passenger therefore cannot compel the immigration officer to afford them the convenience of an early decision, but the immigration officer can impose an early decision on the passenger, even if it means denying their access to asylum.

7.2.4 **New technology abroad — e-borders 1**

Technological developments are a key part of the Government's 'e-borders' scheme, announced in the five-year strategy (Cm 6472). Part of this is to take place abroad, and part at UK ports. A 'pre-entry screening trial' announced for Madrid and Miami in April 2003 was not a scheme like the one in Prague, but involved the use of very advanced scanners to read passports and other documents. The system linked with police records to identify people listed as immigration or security risks and assisted in identifying stolen or forged documents.

Again as part of developing the Schengen area, the UK has opted in to EC Directive 2004/82, which is to be transposed into national law by 5 September 2006. This entails that Member States have systems requiring carriers to transmit passenger data to immigration authorities. The Immigration and Asylum Act 1999 amended the Immigration Act 1971 to require carriers to provide to immigration officers 'such information relating to the passengers carried, or expected to be carried . . . as may be specified' (Sch 2 para 27(2)). An additional power was inserted into this paragraph by the Asylum and Immigration (Treatment of Claimants etc) Act 2004 to require provision of 'a copy of all or part of a document that relates to the passenger'. The 2006 Act has amended these powers further, and added powers for the police to require passenger and freight information (ss 32 and 33). 'Controlling our Borders' says that passenger information will be provided electronically and will be checked against 'multi-agency watchlists' prior to boarding (Cm 6472 Annex 1).

Entry clearance applications in certain posts are now also buttressed by technology. Section 126 Nationality, Immigration and Asylum Act 2002 granted power to require biometric information such as fingerprints with applications for entry clearance. The scanned fingerprints are compared with records held by the IND in the UK. This power has been applied to applications made in Democratic Republic of Congo, Djibouti, Eritrea, Ethiopia, Kenya, Netherlands, Rwanda, Sri Lanka, Tanzania, Uganda and Vietnam (Immigration (Provision of Physical Data) Regulations 2003, SI 2003/1875 and amending SIs 2004/474, 2004/1834 and 2005/3127). It explicitly applies also to applications made by those who already have refugee status, whose entry clearance would be endorsed on their Convention travel document. Fingerprints may be compared with records on the Eurodac database (see chapter 4). Without fingerprints where requested, an entry clearance application may be treated as invalid. The Government aims to apply this requirement to all applications for entry clearance by 2008 (Cm 6472 para 51).

Another form of new technology in use is so-called NDT, new detection technology. This consists of a range of detection devices which may be applied to vehicles to detect human beings inside. This technology is employed in conjunction with immigration control as part of the juxtaposed system in France and Belgium. It is a means of enforcement of the system of carriers' liability, the next subject to be discussed.

7.3 Trans-border controls — carriers' liability

One of the features of the extension of immigration control is the spread of responsibility from the Home Office and immigration service to people in many walks of life. Liability placed on those who transport people and goods is not a new phenomenon in immigration control, but until the 1980s it was relatively unimportant. Its use has expanded enormously in the UK since 1987 and it now represents a major plank in the Government's policy to control asylum claims.

7.3.1 International context

Germany, Belgium, the USA, Canada, and Australia have all introduced measures imposing liability on carriers for the transport of passengers who either hide themselves and gain entry without being detected ('clandestine entrants') or who do not have the appropriate documents for travel, for instance their passport is forged or stolen or does not show the requisite entry clearance ('inadequately documented' passengers). Furthermore, the Schengen Convention, which became part of EC law following the Treaty of Amsterdam, requires the imposition of carrier sanctions by means of legislation. Articles 26 and 27 contain obligations to impose penalties on carriers and in relation to assisting entry, implemented by Directive 2001/51 effective on 11 February 2003. The UK has been active in these measures and in developing carrier sanctions even in advance of the Directive.

7.3.2 Summary of legislative history

As we saw earlier, liability for bringing certain passengers to the UK is not new. Under the Aliens Act 1905, a shipping company committed an offence punishable by a fine if a person subject to immigration control disembarked without leave to enter. If an immigrant who needed leave was admitted to the UK but expelled within six months, the Home Office could recover the cost of the return journey from the shipping company which had brought that passenger. Similar provisions persist to the present day in relation to removals. Under the Immigration Act 1971 Sch 2 paras 8 and 9, where a person is refused leave to enter, or is an illegal entrant, the removal directions issued by the immigration service may be addressed to the owner or captain of the ship or aircraft in the which the passenger arrived, with the result that the shipping company or airline bears the cost of removal. Immigration Act 1971 Sch 2 para 26 and 27 set out various supplementary duties of shipping companies and airlines, which show how closely these commercial bodies are required to co-operate with the immigration service. For instance, if they carry passengers who require leave the enter, ships or aircraft may only call at designated ports of entry, and must ensure that passengers disembarking pass through designated control areas.

These potential liabilities could be imposed without any implication of fault on the part of the carriers. The offences of harbouring and assisting illegal entry (Immigration Act 1971 s 25) could be used where a criminal state of mind could be proved, but this was rarely done in relation to carriers.

Although all these provisions gave an incentive to carriers to check the documentation of passengers and refuse passage where they had doubts as to someone's status, there was no statutory obligation to do so until the Immigration (Carriers' Liability) Act 1987. This marked an acceleration of developments in carriers' liability. The Act imposed fines on airlines and shipowners or their agents of £1,000 for each person carried by them who entered without a valid passport, and, where required, visa. This was increased to £2,000 in 1991 by the Immigration (Carriers' Liability Prescribed Sum) Order 1991, SI 1991/1497. This amount was per passenger, not per journey. Therefore, if fifty inadequately documented passengers were found on one ship, the fine imposed on the owner or agent would be £50,000, or, after 1991, £100,000. In 1993 the Asylum and Immigration Appeals Act 1993 s 12 amended the carriers legislation to include liability for carrying people who did not have the required transit visas. In 1998 legislation was introduced to include trains following the opening of the Channel Tunnel (The Channel Tunnel (Carriers' Liability) Order 1998, SI 1998/1015).

In 1999 the Immigration and Asylum Act substantially increased penalties on carriers by introducing liability for clandestine entrants as opposed to just passengers with improper documentation and by increasing the scope of legislation to cover road transport. Later amending regulations have included rail freight (Carriers Liability (Clandestine Entrants) (Application to Rail Freight) Regulations 2001, SI 2001/280). These provisions represented an enormous extension of liability. Whereas a professional passenger carrier such as an airline would have in place procedure for checking documentation, the extension to clandestine entrants and road transport meant that other commercial organizations and individuals, who had no professional expertise in transporting passengers, could be held liable to a penalty for people who had hidden in their car or lorry. The Immigration (Carriers' Liability) Act 1987 was repealed. Current law is governed by the 1999 Act, as amended by the Nationality, Immigration and Asylum Act 2002 Sch 8 and the Carriers' Liability Regulations 2002, SI 2002/2817, amending regulations and codes of practice. The major provisions are considered further in the next section.

7.3.3 The statutory scheme of carriers' liability

7.3.3.1 *Liability for clandestine entrants*
Section 32(5) of the 1999 Act imposed liability for clandestine entrants arriving in the UK on the owner or captain of the ship or aircraft, the owner, hirer or driver of another vehicle, including, if the vehicle is a detached trailer, its operator. Since amendment by the 2002 Act liability is imposed on each of these people for each clandestine entrant, the maximum penalty being £2,000 (Carriers' Liability Regulations 2002, SI 2002/2817 reg 3). This means that in respect of each clandestine entrant there may be an aggregate penalty collected from more than one responsible person. In this case there is a maximum aggregate penalty of £4,000 (reg 3). If the driver is an employee of the vehicle's owner or hirer, the employer is jointly and severally liable for the penalty. The maximum applies to the passenger, not the carrier. So up to £4,000 may be paid by a number of different carriers for the one clandestine entrant, but if a carrier carries several clandestine entrants, the maximum penalty is £2,000 per passenger.

The definition of 'clandestine entrant' in s 32(1) as amended is striking. There are two aspects to it, first of all the concealment. A person is a clandestine entrant if they arrive concealed in a vehicle, ship, rail freight wagon, or aircraft or pass or attempt to pass through immigration control concealed in a vehicle. Arrival includes in a control zone as prescribed for the purposes of juxtaposed control (Carriers' Liability (Amendment) Regulations 2004, SI 2004/244). The definition catches both a person who stowed away on a ship, but disembarks on foot, and someone who continues or attempts to continue through immigration control hidden in a vehicle. The second part of the definition is that the concealed person is a clandestine entrant if they evade, or attempt to evade, immigration control, or, which is more surprising, they claim, or indicate that they intend to seek asylum in the UK. There can be no doubt that this provision catches a genuine asylum claimant. Indeed, what seems to follow from these provisions is that the more desperate the traveller's situation, the more likely they are to be faced with legal deterrence. The penalty here is on those who transport them rather than the clandestine entrants themselves, but of course the effect of this is to make carriers more wary of carrying clandestine entrants. Before the 1999 Act there was a non-statutory scheme of refunding penalties that had been paid for carrying inadequately documented travellers where the passenger ultimately succeeded in an asylum claim, but this did not find its way into the Act, and although the scheme has continued, it does not apply when the passenger is granted humanitarian protection or discretionary leave (see Charging Procedures — a Guide for Carriers, Appendix B). A successful asylum claim might of course be years down the line and therefore in any event of small comfort to the carrier.

There is a defence in s 34 to liability for the penalty if the carrier can show that they were acting under duress, or:

(a) he did not know and had no reasonable grounds for suspecting, that a clandestine entrant was, or might be, concealed in the transporter;

(b) an effective system for preventing the carriage of clandestine entrants was in operation in relation to the transporter; and

(c) that on this occasion the person or persons responsible for operating that system did so properly; or

(d) he knew or suspected that a clandestine entrant was concealed in a rail freight wagon which formed part of the train for which he was responsible, there was a proper system in place, but he could not stop the train safely.

In (a) to (c) a simple lack of knowledge by itself will not suffice without a proper system being in place. In determining whether a system is to be considered effective under s 34, account will be taken of the Immigration and Asylum Act 1999: Civil Penalty: Code of Practice for Vehicles issued by the Secretary of State under s 32A. The Code contains detailed provision for road haulage and other commercial vehicles concerning the sealing of containers and repeated inspections. It also contains provisions for buses and coaches concerning the locking of doors and inspections and even for private vehicles such as cars and caravans, making equivalent provision.

Following the extension of liability to rail freight operators by the Carriers' Liability (Clandestine Entrants) (Application to Rail Freight) Regulations 2001, SI 2001/280, a Code of Practice for securing rail freight has also been adopted, and a further code for rail freight shuttle wagons.

The penalty for carrying a clandestine entrant must be paid within 60 days of the date of being served with the notice (s 32(3) and Carriers' Liability Regulations 2002, SI 2002/2817 reg 4). The carrier may serve a notice of objection to the penalty and on receiving notice of objection, the Secretary of State must consider whether to uphold the penalty notice. Under the 2002 Act there are also options to reduce or increase the penalty (1999 Act s 35(6), as amended). If the notice is upheld, the Secretary of State may sue to recover the amount of the penalty. Importantly, following the *Roth* case discussed below, the 2002 Act introduced a right of appeal to a court against the imposition of the penalty (1999 Act s 35A; *International Transport Roth GmbH and Other v SSHD* [2002] 3 WLR 344).

The penalty is backed up by the power in s 36(1) for a senior officer to detain vehicles pending payment of the charge. To authorize such a detention, an officer must believe that 'there is a significant risk that the penalty will not be paid' and there must be no offer of satisfactory alternative security. This power was extended by the 2002 Act to detaining a vehicle, if the driver is the owner or hirer or their employee, pending a decision whether to issue a penalty notice, the issue of the notice, and even pending a decision whether to detain (1999 Act s 36(2A) and (2B)).

The court may order the release of a transporter if it considers that there is satisfactory security, or there is no significant risk that the penalty will not be paid. Under Immigration and Asylum Act 1999 s 37(3)(c) the only other basis for the court to order the release of the transporter was the 'compelling need' of the applicant. This did not give any scope for disputing liability to the penalty. Following the *Roth* case (see below) the court was given more discretion to order the release of a transporter including where it considered that the penalty was not payable (s 37(3A) and (3B)).

If the court does not order the release of the transporter and the penalty is not paid within 84 days, the transporter may be sold (s 37(4)). This power is also amended following introduction of a right of appeal in that a transporter may not be sold while an appeal is pending or may still be brought (s 37(5A)), and the power of sale lapses if not exercised within a prescribed period (s 37(5B)).

7.3.3.2 *Improperly documented passengers*

The 1999 Act continued the provision of the 1987 Act in that a £2,000 charge is also applied by s 40 for each person carried who is improperly documented. The Nationality, Immigration and Asylum Act 2002 amended this section so as to remove bus, coach, and train operators from liability and s 40 now only applies to owners of ships or aircraft. The penalty is payable on demand to the Secretary of State like an 'on the spot' fine. Section 40(4) provides a defence for any carrier if they can show that the passenger embarked with the proper documentation.

7.3.3.3 *Effect of scheme*

The new carrier provisions in the 1999 Act came into effect between 6 December 1999 and 18 September 2000. Simon Brown LJ, in the case of *International Transport Roth GmbH & Others* at para 10, described the effect as follows:

By June 2001, 988 penalty notices had been served in respect of 5,433 clandestine entrants. 249 vehicles had been detained, of which 190 were subsequently released on payment of the penalty or a substantial security. In some 25% of cases where clandestine entrants were discovered, either no penalty notice was served or, following the carrier's notice of objection, the Secretary of State decided, under section 35(8), that the penalty was not payable. The average penalty payable is some £12,000 (in respect, therefore, of six clandestine entrants). The bulk of the penalties are paid by companies, but some 10% are paid by individuals including occasional car drivers. By October 2001 the value of the penalties paid or agreed to be paid was £2,432 million. In some cases instalment payments have been agreed, in the most extreme case at the rate of £40 per month for 12.5 years (£6,000).

In the *Roth* case, three of the appellants only discovered clandestine entrants when they were travelling up the motorway to London. They 'would never have been penalized had they not themselves alerted the police'.

The effect on small businesses of these penalties may be imagined, and the scheme generated an outcry. It was subject to a number of challenges.

7.3.3.4 *Redress for carriers*

One of the first issues to be litigated under the Act was the question of how liability to the penalty could be challenged. As mentioned above, if the carrier believes that they are able to maintain a defence under s 34, they may serve a notice of objection to the penalty under s 35. The Secretary of State must then decide whether to proceed with the penalty. After the expiry of the fixed period, the Secretary of State may sue for recovery of the amount of the penalty. In *R (Balbo B & C Auto Transport Internazional) v SSHD* [2001] 1WLR 1556 the Secretary of State had decided to uphold the penalty and the claimants applied for judicial review of that decision. The Administrative Court held that the appropriate legal forum for deciding a dispute on liability was when the Secretary of State began enforcement proceedings for the penalty. Judicial review was not the appropriate method of challenge. The positive aspect of this for the carriers was that it confirmed that liability could at least be judicially considered in the enforcement proceedings, but it did not give them any way to challenge their liability directly in court. Following the *Roth* case a right of appeal against the penalty was introduced by the 2002 Act. The application in *Balbo* was made shortly before the Human Rights Act came into effect. The claimants therefore were not able to raise any issue under Article 6, the right to a fair trial. However, this was the main substance of the challenge in *Roth*.

The claimants in *Roth* challenged the harshness of the scheme, which they regarded as a disproportionate response to the problem of clandestine entrants. Under the 1999 Act the penalty was fixed, not flexible with a maximum. They challenged the lack of discretion and flexibility in the penalty and the lack of provision for a fair hearing or a right of appeal. The carriers alleged a breach of Article 6 and of Protocol 1, Article 1 to Schedule 1 to the Human Rights Act 1998. The harshness of the scheme was said to be demonstrated by such factors as the fixed penalty, also that carriers bore the burden of establishing that they were not blameworthy and that there was no compensation for loss of business during the period that a vehicle was detained, even if the carrier was determined not to be liable in the end.

It was important, though not necessarily crucial, to the carriers' case that the penalty scheme should be seen as a criminal and not a civil proceeding. The specific procedural requirements of a fair trial in Article 6 apply only to a criminal matter, though the general principle of fairness applies also to the determination of civil rights and obligations. The requirements of fairness would therefore be greater if the proceedings were regarded as criminal. In the Act the charge levied is referred to as a 'civil penalty', there is no criminal charge and the penalty is recoverable as a civil debt. However, what a proceeding is called by the domestic authorities is not conclusive of whether it will be regarded as criminal or civil for the purposes of Article 6 ECHR. The Court of Appeal agreed (by a majority) with the carriers on this point, and held that the penalty scheme should be regarded as criminal, mainly because the carriers were in fact being punished, and the punishment meted out was severe.

It was a small step from this conclusion to decide that the scheme violated Article 6, though not necessarily for the reasons advanced by the carriers. Simon Brown LJ held: 'The hallowed principle that the punishment must fit the crime is irreconcilable with the notion of a substantial fixed penalty' (para 47). He accepted the claimants' characterization of the scheme as 'harsh', and this was his main reason for finding a breach of Article 6. In a similar vein, he concluded that the heavy burden on the carriers violated the principle of proportionality inherent in Protocol 1, Article 1, and that even if there was no violation of Article 6, then there was of this article.

Jonathan Parker LJ found the scheme incompatible with Article 6 for a different reason, namely that the Secretary of State had an exclusive role in determining liability, and the role of the courts was subsidiary. 'Accordingly, for the simple yet fundamental reason that the scheme makes the Secretary of State judge in his own cause, the scheme in my judgment is plainly incompatible with Article 6' (para 157).

As referred to at various points above, following the Court of Appeal's decision in *Roth*, amendments were made to the scheme to provide a right of appeal and flexible penalty.

The other main challenge to the penalty scheme by carriers has been that it breaches European law. This argument failed in *Roth* and in relation to the 1987 Act in the earlier case of *R v SSHD ex p Hoverspeed* [1999] INLR 591. It was alleged in *Hoverspeed* that the scheme infringed free movement rights. The company argued, first, that the scheme constituted an unlawful restriction on their freedom to provide services, contrary to Article 49 EC (ex 59). Second, they argued it constituted an unlawful restriction on the freedom of movement of EEA nationals and their families contrary to Article 3 Immigration (European Economic Area) Regulations 1994. The argument was lost on both counts. The administrative measures might be an inconvenience but not a restriction. If they were a restriction this was proportionate and justified in the interests of the immigration control system which was targeted at visa nationals, not EEA nationals. As carrier penalties were required by the Schengen Convention they were in principle endorsed by EC law.

7.3.3.5 *Redress for travellers*

While the carriers' liability scheme, particularly in relation to clandestine entrants, has clearly caused great problems for carriers, the scheme also carries particular hazards for potential passengers. The greatest hazard of the scheme is to an asylum seeker, who, by reason of their situation, may lack proper documents, and who is turned away from a flight, or discovered and removed from a lorry, perhaps directly into the hands of the authorities whose persecution they seek to escape. There has been considerable criticism of carrier penalties for the risks they may create for undocumented asylum seekers. There is also a potential problem for any traveller whose documents are not correctly understood.

This problem arose in *Farah v British Airways & Home Office* The Times 26 January 2000. In this case the Somali appellants had been prevented from embarking on a flight from Cairo to London. One had a passport. The other four appellants, all members of the same family, had declarations of identity documents issued by the British Embassy in Addis Ababa. The immigration liaison officer advised the airline that the passengers were incorrectly documented and should not be allowed to travel. As a consequence they were detained in Cairo airport for five days, then deported to Ethiopia. The Times report is of the Court of Appeal's judgment that the judge should not have struck out the part of the particulars of claim which claimed negligence. This was held to be an arguable matter which would turn on the particular facts and should be heard. The question of the duty of care here referred to the immigration officer who was working with the airline, and the standard of that duty is not yet ascertained. The question would need to be addressed again in relation to a decision of the airline staff.

The Council of Europe's Parliamentary Assembly considered the issue of sanctions against airlines in 1991 and commented:

Airline sanctions ... undermine the basic principles of refugee protection and the rights of refugees to claim asylum, while placing a considerable legal, administrative and financial burden upon carriers and moving the responsibility away from the immigration officers.

Although the airline in turning away an improperly documented passenger may be performing a public function and therefore liable to action under Human Rights Act s 6 (see discussion in chapter 3) the complainant is not in the UK jurisdiction at the time of the decision and not in a position to bring an action. The Race Relations (Amendment) Act 2000 includes the decisions of immigration officers abroad (see *ERRC* case discussed earlier) in the scope of the Act. However, it is not apparent that this can be extended to a commercial body carrying out a public function under a different statute.

Research on people illegally resident in the UK shows that different routes of entry are more likely to be taken by people of different nationalities. It would suggest that airline controls impact more on travellers from West and Sub-Saharan Africa, and carrier sanctions would bite more on travellers from Albania, Ukraine and Sri Lanka (Home Office 20/05 Chapter 4).

7.4 **Authority-to-carry scheme**

A further development in carriers' liability was introduced in the Nationality, Immigration and Asylum Act 2002 s 124 by the authority-to-carry scheme. The section is not yet in force. The details of the scheme will be almost entirely in regulations. The statute gives an outline of what is entailed, and as it stands the power is one of alarming breadth. The scheme is defined in s 124(2) as one 'which requires carriers to seek authority to bring passengers into the United Kingdom'. The scheme must specify both 'the class of carrier to which it applies' and 'the class of passenger to which it applies' (s 124(3)). It may, for instance, specify that authority is required for airlines to transport citizens of Bangladesh. The submission of the Immigration Law Practitioners Association (ILPA), referring to this clause of the Bill during its passage through Parliament, points out that this scheme is 'akin to imposing a visa regime without any safeguards, such as a duty to give reasons in accordance with the immigration rules, and rights of appeal against refusal'. Section 124(3)(b) also provides that the class of passenger 'may be defined by reference to the possession of specified documents or otherwise'. The explanatory notes to the Bill suggest that authority to carry will be sought by 'checking details of passengers travelling to the United Kingdom against information held on a Home Office database to confirm that they pose no known immigration or security risk and to confirm that their documents are in order'. This could entail for instance airlines obtaining information about criminal convictions which had no bearing on the passenger's journey. Although s 124 is not yet in force, this is very similar to the process piloted in Madrid and Miami. The two schemes operated only with two named airlines, Virgin Atlantic and Easyjet, and had the hallmarks of a prototype authority-to-carry scheme. In *Controlling our Borders* the Government promises the use of the authority-to-carry scheme in association with the electronic checking of passenger lists referred to above (Cm 6472 Annex 1).

Carrying passengers in breach of such a scheme will attract penalties similar to those for improperly documented passengers (s 124(1)).

7.5 Biometrics — e-borders 2

There are a number of dimensions to the Government's plan to establish 'e-borders'. In broad terms, this is the idea that personal details will be recorded and checked electronically and that this will become the paramount form of immigration control. We have already considered some ways in which this may be implemented outside the UK. Here we consider the changes taking place at passport control.

The Council of the European Union has adopted a regulation laying down new minimum security standards for European passports, including biometric fingerprint and facial data (2252/2004) but this is part of the Schengen *acquis* which does not apply to the UK. The UK has opted in to discussions about a proposed regulation to insert biometric information into the uniform format visas. However, implementation was interrupted by technical problems, not only of reliability but also that the EU data chip could clash with other chips already in the document under national systems. In the absence of agreed EU competence, France, Germany, Italy, Spain and the UK have committed themselves to making their travel documents technically compatible (Evian meeting 4–5 July 2005). In the absence of agreement on legislation, an intergovernmental group has adopted proposed minimum standards for national identity documents. Although the UK at present does not have an identity card system, and although the UK is not bound by the regulation on passport format, the G5 agreement and the UK's wish to achieve compatibility and common security systems with its European partners mean that the initiatives towards the e-borders scheme will be designed to be compatible with documentation in other Member States so far as possible.

The UK Government's aim is that from late 2006 there will be personal interviews to process passport applications, at which facial features will be scanned and fingerprints taken (UK Passport Service Corporate and Business Plan 2005–2010). The Home Office plans to have the whole e-borders system fully operational by 2008, but there are doubts about the reliability of scanning irises, fingerprints and facial images (e.g., Howarth 2005). Experimental schemes are in place for frequent travellers, for instance a voluntary iris recognition system at Heathrow, promoted by the Home Office as a quick way to get priority in immigration control.

7.6 Immigration control inside the UK — devolved responsibilities

In the final section of this chapter we consider what we might call the inwards direction, taking immigration control inside the borders of the UK. This involves the attribution of powers and liabilities to bodies not traditionally involved in immigration control. We refer to this as devolved immigration control, as even though actual legal responsibility for status decisions has not passed out of the hands of the Home Office, the effect of these practices and provisions is that the action of other bodies has power to affect an individual's legal entitlements.

7.6.1 Police

There is nothing new about the involvement of the police in immigration control. As may be seen from all that has gone before, internationally their role is on the increase. The powers of the police are twofold in relation to immigration matters. First, they have all the powers relating to investigation of criminal offences connected with immigration, for instance they, like an immigration officer, may arrest for the offences of illegal entry or harbouring an illegal entrant (Immigration Act 1971 s 28A). The new powers granted to immigration officers by the Immigration and Asylum Act 1999 are held in parallel with the police, to whom of course the Police and Criminal Evidence Act 1984 Codes apply directly to govern their actions in carrying out arrests, searches, seizure of documents, and so on. Second, they have some specific immigration powers which are not connected with criminal law detection and enforcement. They have a statutory power to deal with the registration of people who are required as a condition of entry or leave to remain to register with the police (Immigration Act 1971 s 4(3)). They also may be given the responsibility for service of documents such as notice of intention to deport.

7.6.2 Local authorities

This book does not deal with welfare provision for asylum seekers and others subject to immigration control, except for some brief discussion in relation to the asylum process in chapter 12. The field of welfare entitlement, meaning broadly health care, housing, and social security benefits, is a vast and complex one, which must be studied in its own right. Systems for the support of asylum seekers are complex, and the reader is referred to *Support for Asylum Seekers*, Sue Willman, Stephen Knafler, and Stephen Pierce (2004), 2nd edn (Legal Action Group) for an understanding of this subject.

Local authorities are involved in welfare provision for asylum seekers in numerous different ways, and in connection with the devolution of immigration control it is essential to mention them, even without examining their obligations in detail. By statute they may be responsible for interim support for asylum seekers who are not eligible to be supported by the National Asylum Support Service. They have responsibilities towards children, and may be liable to provide community care. They may also be involved in a number of local refugee support schemes. All of these may require some assessment of immigration status. However, the main capacity in which local authorities are required to assess immigration status is as housing providers. The Immigration and Asylum Act 1999 s 119 excludes asylum seekers and other persons subject to immigration control from entitlement to assistance as homeless persons under the Housing Act 1996 Part VII. There are complex provisions resulting in the exclusion of asylum seekers and most people subject to immigration control from allocation of social housing under Housing Act 1996 Part VI. This means that if a person applies as homeless to their local authority, or applies to go on the Council housing waiting list, their immigration status must be ascertained. With some exceptions, if they are asylum seekers or otherwise subject to immigration control, they cannot be housed. By way of example, in *R (on the application of Burns) v London Borough of Southwark* [2004] EWHC 1901 Admin Ms Burns claimed asylum, while her claim was outstanding she married an Irish national, subsequently separated but did not divorce him, and the Home Office refused an EEA residence permit. The claimant was challenging this refusal but got into rent arrears because her housing benefit stopped and she was evicted. Gage J held that the homelessness department was entitled to rely on the current state of the Home Office's judgement of her immigration status and deny her accommodation.

The role of local authorities came to the fore in the pilot schemes for implement- ation of s 9 of the 2004 Act, discussed in chapter 1, in which the opposition of social workers to taking children into care was instrumental in bringing the whole scheme into question.

Even though no immigration entitlements, such as leave to enter or remain, flow from local authority decisions, the requirement that they engage in monitoring and restrictive allocation of social benefits is an aspect of what is referred to as internal immigration control, a practice once more common in Continental Europe but now spreading to the UK.

7.6.3 **Employers**

Employers have been recruited into immigration control in a way which touches their own interests. The Asylum and Immigration Act 1996 s 8 created an offence of employing a person subject to immigration control who is not permitted by their terms of stay to work in the UK or who does not have valid leave to be in the UK. The offence is one of strict liability, that is, it is simply to employ the person who does not have permission to work, and the employer does not need to have any knowledge of their immigration status to be liable. This section is repealed by the Immigration, Asylum and Nationality Act 2006 and replaced by a similar offence but which importantly requires knowledge of the employee's immigration status or at least that it prohibits them from working. The 2006 Act also institutes a system of civil penalties for employing someone who does not have permission to work. Here, no knowledge of status is required. The penalty system is similar in structure to those for carriers in that there will be a penalty, an opportunity to object, and to appeal. There is a statutory defence for the employer, which is that they took one of a list of actions which will be prescribed by statutory instrument, but will include requesting sight of specified documents relating to the employee in question. Under the 1996 Act these included documents issued by a previous employer giv- ing the National Insurance number, for instance a P45, and regulations under the 2006 Act are likely to be similar. When the 1996 Act offence was introduced, con- cern was expressed by employers at this responsibility and by representatives of immigrants and minority ethnic groups that the section would give rise to increased racial discrimination. A predicted scenario was that employers would be reluctant to employ people if they thought that there might be an immigration issue involved, especially as the fine for the offence was £5,000. This kind of deci- sion would be more likely to be made in relation to a minority ethnic applicant.

The Home Office issued a code of practice for employers on how to avoid race discrimination while complying with the Act. This came into force on 2 May 2001 and is available on the Home Office website. It is clear that in the simple case a request for a P45, which is standard in most employment, met the requirements of the Act and avoided discrimination. There were very few prosecutions under the 1996 Act.

The Nationality, Immigration and Asylum Act 2002 empowers the Secretary of State to make orders concerning the production and retention of documentation by employers. For instance, by s 134 the Secretary of State may require an employer to supply information about an employee whom the Secretary of State reasonably suspects of having committed an offence under the Immigration Act 1971 such as illegal entry or obtaining leave by deception or of having committed fraud in relation to asylum support. The information must be related to the employee's earnings or history of employment or be required in order to establish where the employee is (s 134(2)). Under s 137 it is an offence to fail to supply the information without reasonable excuse. It may happen that information provided by an employer for instance about earnings shows an offence committed by the employer, such as failure to deduct National Insurance or tax. Section 139 provides that information provided pursuant to a request under s 134 may not be used as evidence in criminal proceedings. This is consistent with the ECHR's interpretation of Article 6 in the case of *Saunders v UK* (1997) 23 EHRR 313 in which the Court held that it was a breach of Article 6 to use information gathered under compulsion against the defendants in the Guinness trial. These provisions are unaffected by the 2006 Act.

It is a criminal offence to employ a worker from the new EU Member States if they are not authorized to work for the employer, that is, registered or in the process of registration (Accession (Immigration and Workers Registration) Regulations 2004, SI 2004/1219).

7.6.4 Marriage registrars

The Immigration and Asylum Act 1999 also imposed a new duty on marriage registrars. From 1 January 2001 when people give notice of marriage to the registrar, this must be reported to the Secretary of State 'without delay' if the registrar has reasonable grounds for suspecting that the marriage will be a 'sham marriage' (s 24). The Civil Partnership Act 2004 Sch 27 para 162 inserts into the 1999 Act s 24A which applies all these provisions, *mutatis mutandis*, to civil partnerships. A 'sham marriage' or partnership is one entered into by a non-EEA national 'for the purpose of avoiding the effect of one or more provisions of United Kingdom immigration law or the immigration rules' (s 24(5)). For the purpose of carrying out this obligation, registrars have powers under Marriage Act s 28A, inserted by s 162 of the 1999 Act, to ask for specified evidence of the name, age, marital status, and nationality of persons giving notice, and Marriage Act s 27 is amended so that each person to be married must give notice. This results in something like the entry clearance discrepancy system being applied at the registry office, in that each member of a couple will be asked separately for the required information, and an apparent lack of knowledge about each other may give rise to suspicion that the marriage is being entered into for immigration reasons. Sections 19–25 Asylum and Immigration

(Treatment of Claimants etc) Act 2004 introduced stringent new requirements for the marriages of non-EEA nationals.

These provisions are discussed fully in chapter 9 in relation to their significance for marriages.

Cohen (2003) discusses the history of the discretionary power of the registrar which preceded what is now a duty, although there is no statutory sanction for breach of such duty. Through this provision, marriage has become another point in life at which internal immigration control may be exercised.

7.7 Conclusion

The machinery of immigration control may no longer be simply described. It is a constantly changing and growing web of executive control over those who do not have the right of abode in the UK. The involvement of civil society in that control, by means of carrier sanctions and so on, illustrates the deeper penetration of immigration control into the everyday business of life, not just for those who have traditionally regarded that as their job, but also, potentially, for any of us. This absorption of immigration control into wider society does not bring with it the engagement of the communities upon whom it impacts, as the widening scope of control is accompanied by its transformation into an intelligence and technologically driven policing and deterrence system. The dominance of executive discretion in immigration law has been problematic, and difficult for the individual to challenge, but a machine reading which tells the operative that the passenger is denied entry cannot be argued with. Issues of technological reliability and data protection will enter into immigration law. It is debatable which is more transparent as befits a democracy. It is apparent that the integration of various levels of control mechanisms is not mirrored by integration of those subject to control who, as shown for instance by the power to require information from employers, may be singled out by the state for an increasing number of reasons.

QUESTIONS

1 How do you view Phuong's suggestion that the abolition of border controls between the UK and other EU Member States might be a more effective way of combating people smuggling and illegal entry?
2 How do you view the openness of the objective of deterring asylum claims which lies behind carrier sanctions, visa regimes, and external placement of immigration officers?
3 Should basic social goods such as housing depend on immigration status?

FURTHER READING

Black, R., Collyer, M., Skeldon, R. and Waddington, C. (2005) *A Survey of the illegally resident population in detention in the UK* (Home Office Online Report 20/05).
Cohen, S. (2003) 'Do you take this man to be your lawfully wedded immigration officer?' in

Cohen, S. (ed.) *No-one is Illegal: Asylum and immigration control past and present*, (Stoke on Trent: Trentham Books).

Howarth, F. (2005) *Technological barriers to the take up of biometrics* IT-Analysis.com 17 Feb.

Nicholson, F. (1997) 'Implementation of the Immigration (Carriers Liability) Act 1987: Privatising immigration functions at the expense of international obligations?' *International and Comparative Law Quarterly* vol. 46 July 1997, pp. 586–634.

Phuong, C. (2003) 'Closing Sangatte: the legal implications of the asylum dispute between France and the UK' IANL vol. 17, no. 3, pp. 157–169.

Schuster, L. (2003) 'Asylum seekers: Sangatte and the Tunnel' *Parliamentary Affairs* 56(3) 506–522.

Statewatch News Online, *EU: Biometric visa policy unworkable* 5 January 2005.

8

Appeals and constraints

SUMMARY

This chapter describes the structure of the appeals process and some other external standards and principles which constrain Home Office and Immigration Service decisions, specifically, general legal standards of fairness, provisions on race discrimination, and codes of practice. Particular points concerning asylum appeals are reserved for chapter 12. The chapter ends with a section on those who represent immigrants and asylum seekers and the regulation of their services.

8.1 Introduction

Immigration law is unlike, say, criminal or tort law in that the possible grounds for appeal are set out in statute. This means that the interpretation of those grounds has become the subject of legal controversy in its own right. Additionally appeal rights have been reduced often by legislation, and obtaining or retaining a right of appeal has in itself become a major reason for litigation. The result is a complex body of law about the scope and availability of rights of appeal. The majority of this is outside the scope of this book. The first part of this chapter describes the structure of the appeals system and gives a general outline of the grounds for appealing immigration decisions.

8.2 Immigration appellate authorities

The Asylum and Immigration (Treatment of Claimants etc) Act 2004 abolished the previous two-tier system of immigration appeals, which had been in place since 1969 for Commonwealth citizens and since 1973 for all immigrants. The two-tier system was of an initial appeal to an adjudicator with a second appeal from that decision to an Immigration Appeal Tribunal (IAT). Following the Nationality, Immigration and Asylum Act 2002 this appeal was on grounds of error of law only. The 2004 Act instituted a new, single-tier, Asylum and Immigration Tribunal (AIT), with effect from 4 April 2005. Members of the AIT are called Immigration Judges, and adjudicators and legally qualified members of the IAT transferred immediately to this role and title (2004 Act Sch 2 paras 27 and 28). Non-legally qualified members of the IAT became non-legally qualified members of the AIT (para 28).

Immigration judges may sit in panels of one, two, or three. A practice direction issued by the President of the Tribunal gives guidance on the composition of panels for different kinds of cases (Directions under the Nationality, Immigration and Asylum Act 2002 Sch 2 para 7: see www.ait.gov.uk). The Tribunal is headed by a President, and there is a structure under his direction of two Deputy Presidents, Senior Immigration Judges, who have judicial management and legal responsibilities, Designated Immigration Judges, who support teams of about ten Immigration Judges, and finally Immigration Judges.

The proceedings of the tribunal are governed by the Asylum and Immigration Tribunal (Procedure) Rules 2005, SI 2005/230. The overriding objective of the rules provides a principle by which they can be interpreted and which may guide discretionary decisions. In the 2003 Procedure Rules the overriding objective was to 'secure the just, timely and effective disposal of appeals and applications'. This was changed in the 2005 Rules to handling proceedings 'as fairly, quickly and efficiently as possible' (r 4), suggesting that expediency may take precedence over fairness. The UNHCR had recommended that the rule be 'amended to reflect more clearly the emphasis that should be given to the fundamental concern of correctly identifying those who are in need of international protection' (UNHCR December 2004 para 2). While speed and efficiency are generally desirable for all concerned, the main purpose of a refugee determination and appeal procedure is to make accurate decisions about those in need of protection and not to put claimants at risk.

The rules allow short time limits for appealing (ten days, or five for someone who is in detention: r 7). This can create severe problems in a situation where legal advice is hard to come by, public funding for cases equally scarce (see later section on representation), and the appellant's first language may well not be English. They contain features which cast doubt on the perceived impartiality of the system and its capacity to protect those in danger. Specifically, in asylum cases, the tribunal's determination is served on the Home Office who must then serve it on the appellant (r 23(4) and (5)). In non-asylum cases it is served by the Tribunal on both parties within ten days (r 22). Notice of appeal must be filed by the appellant on the AIT, who must then serve it on the Home Office 'as soon as reasonably practicable' (r 12). This is intended to prevent the delays which used to ensue after the appellant had lodged their appeal with the Home Office and then had to wait for lengthy periods before the tribunal was informed (see McKee 2005:99). However it also opens up the possibility that the Home Office, having no notice of the appeal, may arrest, detain and even remove the appellant before the appeal is heard.

Despite the terminology, from the appellant's point of view the tier of appeal that has disappeared is the second tier. The grounds of appeal set out in the 2002 Act are now the grounds of appeal to the AIT. The changes to the appeals structure are in the later stages. If an appellant loses at the AIT, i.e., the first appeal stage, what happens then? The 2004 Act changes the system of onward appeals.

The system of challenging the AIT's decision is quite complex, and some commentators have doubted whether the single tier system is actually simpler or more streamlined (Shaw 2005; McKee 2005). The route for challenge depends on the composition of the panel at first hearing. If there were three legally qualified members and the appeal is dismissed, the appellant may apply to the AIT for permission to appeal to the Court of Appeal, on a point of law only. If the AIT refuses permission, an application may be made to the Court of Appeal.

If fewer than three legally qualified members heard the first appeal, the appellant can apply to the High Court for a reconsideration order, which compels the tribunal to look at the case again on the basis that it has made an error of law. The application for a reconsideration order is made on paper only, i.e., there is no hearing. On receiving an application for a reconsideration order, the High Court can of its own motion refer a question of law of importance to the Court of Appeal. This may not be initiated by the parties. The reviewing court may direct the tribunal to reconsider its decision '*if it thinks* the tribunal may have made an error of law' (Nationality, Immigration and Asylum Act 2002 s 103A: emphasis added). This suggests a low threshold.

Currently, applications for a reconsideration order are considered first of all by a member of the AIT. This is described as a filter mechanism (e.g., Shaw 2005: 92). The tribunal member decides whether the tribunal should reconsider the initial decision, and their decision is sent to the parties. The parties then have the option to renew the application for reconsideration, and if it is renewed, the application goes to the High Court, as mentioned above. This arrangement is described as transitional (s 26(7)), but nearly one year on, it is still in force.

At the reconsideration hearing the tribunal must first of all decide whether there has been an error of law. If it decides there has, then it must go on to hear the case again and make fresh findings. After a reconsideration hearing there is an opportunity to appeal to the Court of Appeal, with permission, on a point of law.

Initial appeals to the AIT are rehearings of the whole case, and the tribunal may 'consider evidence about any matter which it thinks relevant to the substance of the decision' (Nationality, Immigration and Asylum Act 2002 s 85(4)). In entry clearance and certificate of entitlement cases, i.e., those where the applicant is outside the UK, evidence is limited to matters arising before the date of the decision (s 85(5)). The tribunal may adopt an inquisitorial style, asking questions of the Home Office representative and the applicant, but the proceedings are in most respects adversarial in nature.

The burden of proof is on the appellant, and the standard of proof in immigration cases is the balance of probabilities (confirmed in *ECO Dhaka v Shamim Box* [2002] UKIAT 02212). Juss discusses the application of this standard (1997 Chapter 4) and makes a compelling argument that it is often not applied. For instance, in an unreported case *Walayat Begum v Visa Officer Islamabad* TH/13561/75 the Tribunal had before it the passport of the appellant's first wife, whom he claimed had died. The passport was endorsed: 'The holder of this passport has died. Passport has been cancelled and returned'. There was other evidence also. The Tribunal held 'There is no really direct or solid evidence that Manzoor Begum has died' (1997:129). This seems to be an application of a standard of proof higher than the balance of probabilities. This is an old case, but in non-asylum cases decisions are often still made without a reference to the standard of proof. It is more important of course to observe not only whether a standard is referred to, but whether it is in practice applied. In asylum cases the standard of proof is different because what is to be proved is the likelihood of a future risk. See chapter 13.

8.3 **Special Immigration Appeals Commission**

There is a separate system for appeals involving national security. This used to be a secret procedure before a panel of advisers, known as the 'Three Wise Men', but the conduct of these proceedings was very restricted. The panel was required to make the case against the person known to them as far as they considered national security would allow, but there was no obligation to disclose evidence or identify witnesses. The individual could make representations to the panel, but had no right to legal representation, and perhaps most strangely of all, no right to see the decision in their case.

Article 5(4) of the ECHR requires that someone who is detained should have the right to challenge their detention in a court. The applicant in the case of *Chahal v UK* (1997) 23 EHRR 413 was detained for several years following a decision to deport him on national security grounds. The ECtHR held that there was a violation of Article 5(4) of the Convention in that there was no provision for him to challenge his detention before a court as the 'Three Wise Men' procedure could not be called a court. The ECtHR recognized that there may be a necessity for national security matters to be heard in a private forum as disclosure of some issues to the public could cause harm to national security. Nevertheless, some countries, Canada for example, had devised procedures which gave more protection to the rights of the individual while still taking account of the state's need for security. The procedure was also found to breach Article 13 of the Convention, as the panel of special advisers did not provide an effective safeguard for Mr Chahal against removal from the UK to a place where he could suffer torture or inhuman or degrading treatment or punishment in breach of Article 3.

In response to the judgment of the ECtHR the UK replaced the 'Three Wise Men' with the Special Immigration Appeals Commission (SIAC), set up by the Special Immigration Appeals Commission Act 1997(SIACA). The Commission must consist of one member who has held (or holds) high judicial office, one member who either is or has been a legally qualified member of the AIT and a third member who would normally be someone with experience of national security matters (SIACA 1997 Sch 1). The Commission has power to exclude anybody from a hearing, including the appellant and their representative if the Commission accepts a submission from the Secretary of State that it is necessary to rely on 'closed' material — that is, material which it would be against the public interest to disclose, even to the appellant. If the Commission decides to hold a closed hearing, the interests of the appellant are represented by a Special Advocate, appointed by the Attorney General (or in Scotland the Lord Advocate) for that purpose. The Special Advocate is not at liberty to discuss those proceedings with the appellant. This procedure is intended to comply with Article 5 ECHR, while still providing some protection for government concerns about national security.

8.3.1 **Jurisdiction**

The jurisdiction of the SIAC is to hear appeals against immigration-related decisions involving national security, usually exclusion, refusal of entry as an asylum seeker, deportation or appeals against deprivation of nationality (see chapters

2, 6 and 16). In the Anti-Terrorism, Crime and Security Act 2001 the Commission had jurisdiction in relation to the indefinite detention of foreign nationals. This jurisdiction lapsed in March 2005 after the Law Lords had declared the detentions unlawful (*A v SSHD* [2004] UKHL 56: see chapter 15). The Commission can hear human rights and race discrimination arguments raised by the appellant (s 2(2)(e)-1997 Act, as substituted by the 2002 Act Sch 7 para 20), and appeals generally are on similar grounds to those which may be raised in the AIT. The Commission has similar powers to those of the tribunal on appeals, in that it must allow the appeal if it considers that the decision appealed is not in accordance with the law or the immigration rules, or that a discretion should have been exercised differently (SIACA 1997 s 2(3)(b), as substituted by the 2002 Act Sch 7 para 20). In *SSHD v Rehman* [2001] 3 WLR 877, the first case to come before SIAC, the House of Lords agreed with the Court of Appeal and the Commission that its role was to review the merits of the case in full, which could include reviewing the Secretary of State's findings of fact. Note that despite the serious effects of losing a case, the standard of proof is the civil one. The House of Lords in *A and others v SSHD* [2005] UKHL 71 held that SIAC could not admit evidence which could have been obtained by torture (see chapter 3 for full discussion).

8.3.2 Review of SIAC

The extension of SIAC's role to hearing appeals against detention under the 2001 Act was thought by some to push its procedures beyond what they could deliver in the way of the elements of fairness. The Constitutional Affairs Committee conducted an inquiry into the workings of SIAC and identified a number of important reservations with respect to the work of the Special Advocates

The Special Advocate sees the evidence and is required to make representations and conduct cross-examination upon it, but without instructions as they are not permitted to discuss any closed material with the appellant. They lack the resource of an ordinary legal team to conduct a defence, and have no access to expert opinion or research assistants to help them to interpret intelligence information on which they have no expertise. They cannot call witnesses, and have no capacity to interview any. If they have already acted in a case in which they have seen closed material which has relevance to other cases, they may not act in the later cases. Alternatively, they would have to deal with a later case without seeing the appellant at all. This tends to mean they are always dealing with issues for the first time, exacerbating their lack of capacity to challenge government evidence, produced with the whole panoply of state security and intelligence resources. Even if evidence in closed material shows that the case in the open material is flawed, they may not deal with this in an open hearing or take further instructions on inconsistencies (Constitutional Affairs Committee Seventh Report 2004–5, and Rick Scannell, address at ILPA: One Hundred years of Immigration Law, 7 November 2005). The Constitutional Affairs Committee recommended that these issues be addressed.

We now move from the appeals system to the content of appeals.

8.4 **Scope of appeals**

8.4.1 **Appealable decisions**

The Nationality, Immigration and Asylum Act 2002 has simplified the statutory basis for immigration appeals, although the procedures have become ever more complex. Sections 82 and 84 of the Act set out the decisions against which appeals may be brought and the grounds upon which appeals may be made. The appealable decisions are all the major decisions made in relation to a person's stay in the UK, without reference as to whether this decision is made by the Immigration and Nationality Directorate of the Home Office (IND) or by the immigration service. These include for instance refusal of leave to enter, refusal of entry clearance (only in family cases since the 2006 Act), refusal to vary leave, a decision to remove, and a decision to deport. The simplification by bringing the decisions and grounds together in this way is welcome, but the appealable decisions do not include the issue of removal directions, i.e., the actual implementation of the decision to remove. This was a subject which exercised the courts after the implementation of the Human Rights Act and before the 2002 Act, as there might be a considerable delay between a decision being made to remove a person and their actual removal. During this time their situation could have changed substantially, in particular by the establishment of a family. This would give rise to an argument that the right to respect for family life was breached by the removal. The Court of Appeal in *Kariharan v SSHD* [2002] EWCA Civ 1102 held that a human rights appeal should be allowed against removal directions, but the 2002 Act reverses this. The implications of this are discussed more fully in the chapter on removal.

8.4.2 **Grounds of appeal to Asylum and Immigration Tibunal**

The permissible grounds of appeal all involve reference to standards which could make the decision unlawful. Human rights appeals are made on the grounds already explored in chapter 3. Breach of the Race Relations Act 1976 is discussed below. Breach of the Refugee Convention forms the subject of the chapters on asylum law. European Community rights are fully explored in the chapter on European freedom of movement, but note that breach of such a right is a ground for an immigration appeal within the UK system, just as any other breach of rights. The other three grounds are discussed here:

(a) that the decision is not in accordance with the immigration rules;

(e) that the decision is otherwise not in accordance with the law;

(f) that the person taking the decision should have exercised differently a discretion conferred by immigration rules.

Section 86 provides that the tribunal must allow the appeal 'in so far as it thinks that' one of the above is the case. This largely repeats an earlier provision found both in the Immigration and Asylum Act 1999 (Sch 4 para 21) and in the Immigration Act 1971 (s 19).

The status of the immigration rules and of concessions and policy statements made outside those rules has already been discussed in chapter 1, and reference should be made back to that discussion. The status of rules and concessions or policies and the difference between them has implications for appeals.

8.4.2.1 *Rules and policies or concessions*

The effect of s 86 and its predecessors is to give binding force to the immigration rules. Immigration officers, Home Office officials, and entry clearance officers are bound to act in accordance with the rules in the sense that if they do not their decisions are appealable. This means that at the appeal stage, if the tribunal considers that requirements for entry are met, the appeal must be allowed and entry granted. Although the applicant, as we saw in chapter 1, cannot at the beginning insist on obtaining entry if they consider they meet the requirements, at the stage of appeal, the rules have the force of law.

The ground that the decision is not in accordance with the law has played an important part in the development of immigration appeals. Where the decision is said not to comply with statute or common law, this ground may be used. It is also a ground for appeal where a decision is not in accordance with a policy or concession. It may be recalled from chapter one that a basis for entry may be contained in policies and concessions outside the immigration rules, and that failure to apply a published policy could result in the decision being quashed in judicial review proceedings (*R v SSHD ex p Amankwah* [1994] Imm AR 240). However, judicial review as a remedy is limited in that it only compels the decision-maker to take the decision again properly. It is expensive, and subject to strict time limits and the hurdle of the permission stage. In the case of *Abdi v SSHD* [1996] Imm AR 148, the Court of Appeal decided that a failure to take into account a published policy was contrary to established principles of administrative law, and therefore not 'in accordance with the law' as required by Immigration Act 1971 s 19, the relevant section then in force. The decision would therefore be subject to appeal. This was a major breakthrough for immigration appeals. In effect it made failure to implement a policy appealable. This ground of appeal is retained in the 2002 Act, but its effect is limited by the exclusive prescription of appealable decisions in s 82. Where a concession directly affects an appealable decision, such as leave to enter, then its seems it is appealable under s 84(1)(e). Where it does not, for instance, a procedural waiver concerning the application process as applied to Kosovan families in 2000, then there is no appeal, only judicial review. Macdonald puts it that there is still room for argument that a decision is not in accordance with the law where 'the *purpose* of the stay is recognized by the rules, although waiver of part of the rule's requirement, or an extension of its application, is sought in accordance with Home Office policy' (2005:1196).

Schedule 2 para 1(3) to the Immigration Act 1971 provides that immigration officers must act in accordance with the law and the rules and instructions given to them by the Secretary of State, provided these are not inconsistent with the rules. However, the purpose of instructions is often to supplement or supersede the rules. This purpose could not be achieved if officers strictly obeyed statute and refused to obey instructions where they were inconsistent with the rules. A case in point is the IDI July 2004 Ch 4 s 5 para 2.3, providing that leave to enter the UK on an initial work permit for training may be given for five years. For some considerable time before amendment, para 117 of the rules said that the limit was three years. If in a suitable case an immigration officer refused to consider granting leave for five years, their decision would be open to judicial review for failure to take into account the published policy (e.g., *R v SSHD ex p Khan* [1985] 1 All ER 40). This is an example of where failure to follow the policy would not be appealable following the 2002 Act as the decision would not be an appealable immigration decision under s 82, just a grant of a shorter period of leave than anticipated. In avoiding judicial review the immigration officer must flout the rules.

Another basis for arguing that officers act lawfully when they follow an instruction rather than the rules was discussed in chapter 1, namely that as the statutory power to give leave to enter is not made subject to the immigration rules, the power in the Act to give leave remains wider than that specified in the rules. There is therefore a residual power in the Act to make decisions which are more favourable towards the applicant than the rules permit. As Vincenzi (1992) discusses, this does not do away with the problem of Sch 2 para 1(3). It results in a complete contradiction.

8.4.2.2 *Exercise of discretion*

The power to allow an appeal if the tribunal considers that a discretion should have been exercised differently is a wide power, but is limited by the Nationality, Immigration and Asylum Act 2002 s 86(6), which replicates earlier similar provisions. The subsection says that a refusal to depart from the rules is not to be regarded as an exercise of discretion. This means that a where for instance leave has been refused in accordance with the rules, an applicant cannot appeal on the grounds that they asked for discretion to be exercised outside the rules but were refused. The only appeal in this situation would be that the decision was not in accordance with the law if a relevant policy had not been applied. In this case the tribunal cannot substitute its own decision but must send it back to the Secretary of State to make the decision in accordance with the law. If, by contrast, they consider a discretion should have been exercised differently, they can substitute their own decision.

A failure to exercise a discretion can also be treated as not in accordance with the law. Here again, the tribunal is not the primary decision-maker and therefore cannot make a decision, but only send it back to the Secretary of State for the discretion to be exercised.

The detailed rules on jurisdiction, powers and procedures on appeal are outside the scope of this book, and the reader is referred to practitioner works such as Macdonald or the JCWI Handbook for a full account.

8.4.3 **Error of law**

The Nationality, Immigration and Asylum Act 2002 restricted appeals from the adjudicator to the tribunal to an error of law. A body of case law grew up on the question of what is an error of law, some of which has ceased to have relevance following the repeal of ss 100–103 of the 2002 Act by s 26(5) of the 2004 Act, but some of which now applies to orders for reconsideration of tribunal decisions.

An important question of continuing relevance is: what if the factual basis of the decision was wrong? Is that not an error of fact and therefore unappealable where the basis for an appeal (the term 'appeal' is used broadly here to include reconsideration) is only an error of law?

In *E v SSHD and R v SSHD* [2004] EWCA Civ 49 there was a delay of some months between the hearing and the tribunal decisions being promulgated. During that period human rights reports were produced on the country to which the appellants would be sent. These reports significantly affected the factual basis on which the decisions had been made. The Court of Appeal held that the IAT could have reviewed its decision. They made the further important statement that:

It was time to accept that a mistake of fact giving rise to unfairness was a separate head of challenge in an appeal on a point of law, at least in those statutory contexts where the parties shared an interest in cooperating to achieve the correct result. Asylum law was such an area. For a finding of unfairness there must have been a mistake as to an existing fact, including a mistake as to the availability of evidence on a particular matter. The fact or evidence must have been 'established' in the sense that it was uncontentious and objectively verifiable. The appellant must not have been responsible for the mistake and the mistake must have played a material part in the tribunal's reasoning

See further chapter 12.

8.5 Principles which constrain immigration decision-making

In this part of this chapter we shall consider some further legal principles and external structures which set standards that must be met in immigration decisions. We have already noted that discretion must be exercised in accordance with the usual principles of administrative law, that is, fairly and reasonably, having regard to relevant factors and disregarding the irrelevant. This section discusses the application of additional standards and constraints which arise because of the particular nature of immigration law decisions.

8.5.1 *Natural justice or fairness*

Administrative law recognizes a distinction between the performance of a judicial function and the performance of an administrative function. A judicial function is one which decides between competing arguments on the basis of evidence, and determines an outcome which will be decisive of rights or entitlements (e.g., *Ridge v Baldwin* [1964] AC 40). This may be either by taking away such rights or entitlements, as in a criminal case, where a sentence may be imposed which curtails a person's liberty, or by granting them, as in, for instance, compensation for a personal injury claim. An administrative function is to process an application or otherwise follow a procedure according to the rules and principles governing that action. This may include the use of discretion where the rules permit. So, for instance, issuing a driving licence is an administrative matter. While administrative decisions must be made fairly and in accordance with relevant procedures, a judicial decision must be made in accordance with the principles of natural justice, giving both sides a fair hearing and acting without bias. Sometimes fairness and natural justice are equated, for instance in *Lloyd v McMahon* [1987] AC 625.

There is not always a clear distinction between administrative and judicial decisions, and it may be readily apparent that it is not easy to determine whether immigration decisions are administrative or judicial. They have qualities of each. In *Re HK* [1967] QB 617 Lord Parker CJ held that in making inquiries to ascertain the age of a child seeking to enter the UK the immigration officer should act fairly, 'only to that limited extent do the so-called rules of natural justice apply, which in a case such as this is merely a duty to act fairly'. The role of immigration officers in deciding applications was considered in *R v SSHD ex p Mughal* [1973] 3 All ER 796 not to be a judicial but an administrative one. The same goes for entry clearance officers and Home Office officials. Strictly, this means they are not bound by the rules of natural justice, but they are bound to act fairly. This means making all proper enquiries to obtain all relevant facts of the case, but not necessarily notifying the applicant of further information which confirmed the immigration officer's view, and so not necessarily giving the applicant an opportunity to reply to every point. This may be compared with a criminal trial to see the effect of deeming immigration decisions to be administrative. However, in *R v SSHD ex p Moon* The Times, 8 December 1995 the Divisional Court held that in dealing with an application for entry clearance the entry clearance officer should give the applicant an opportunity to deal with objections to their application. The way in which this is achieved may give rise to further questions of fairness. The power held by ECOs and the difficult conditions in which applications are conducted, often involving long queues and sometimes inadequate premises, make even-handedness more difficult to achieve. In practice, advice given by ECOs before a formal application is made may be seen as a refusal, and because the application has not been formally made, there would be no appeal — a complete reversal of natural justice (see practice of 'pre-sifts', Report of the Entry Clearance Monitor 2000 and 2001).

The distinction between fairness and natural justice can be pressed too far, and the development of asylum law in the UK has begun to bring the two together. The distinction made between forfeiture and application cases in public law is based partly on the extent of the effect on the person whose rights to fairness have been infringed. It is said that full rules of natural justice do not apply to 'mere applicant' cases but they do to forfeiture cases. One might say that all immigration and asylum cases are those of a 'mere applicant' (*McInnes v Onslow-Fane* [1978] 3 All ER 211). However, the importance of the matter to an asylum seeker could hardly be overstated, and this has a bearing on the standards of fairness which must be applied. The Court of Appeal in *R v SSHD ex p Thirukumar* [1989] Imm AR 270 held that asylum decisions were of such importance that only the highest levels of fairness would be sufficient, and this would include providing a copy to the applicant of their answers at previous interviews. *Ex p Moon* suggests that this asylum standard is permeating immigration decisions also. The Court of Appeal in *R (Dirshe) v SSHD* [2005] EWCA Civ 421 held that where the applicant had no public funding either for a representative or for their own interpreter, the overall fairness of the process required that the applicant be able to tape record the asylum interview, although there is not necessarily a principle of equality of arms, as there would be between private litigants.

The current state of case law is to the effect that Article 6 of the Human Rights Act provision on fair hearings does not apply in immigration matters (see discussion on *Maaouia v France* in chapter 3). Currently, therefore, the Human Rights Act does not make up any difference in standards between the principle of fairness in administrative law and a fair trial under Article 6. However, as Lord Steyn said in *R v SSHD ex p Anufrijeva,* 'the Convention is not an exhaustive statement of fundamental rights under our system of law' (para 27) and fundamental principles may still be found and applied. In *Anufrijeva* the appellant's asylum claim had been turned down but she was not informed. Shortly after that, the welfare benefits she had received as an asylum seeker (90 per cent of the usual income support rate) were stopped as her asylum claim was no longer current, but she was not given a reason. She argued that the asylum decision could not be treated as effective because she had not been notified. Her case was not isolated as this practice was part of Home Office policy at the time. Lord Steyn said:

The arguments for the Home Secretary ignore fundamental principles of our law. Notice of a decision is required before it can have the character of a determination with legal effect because the individual concerned must be in a position to challenge the decision in the courts if he or she wishes to do so. This is not a technical rule. It is simply an application of the right of access to justice. That is a fundamental and constitutional principle of our legal system (para 26).

He referred to the view that an uncommunicated administrative decision could bind an individual as 'an astonishingly unjust proposition' (para 30).

It seems, though, that in a rare case an uncommunicated statute can do so. This strange point arose in one of the first asylum cases to be certified 'clearly unfounded' under the Nationality, Immigration and Asylum Act 2002. The Act received Royal Assent on 7 November 2002. ZL and VL arrived from the Czech Republic on 8 November and sought asylum. Their claims were rejected and certified clearly unfounded on 14 November and they were issued with removal directions, but the Act had not yet been promulgated. It was not printed and available until 28 November, three weeks after it had taken effect. ZL and VL sought judicial review of the certificates. The principles of the ECHR require that law is accessible in order to be effective (see, e.g., *Silver v UK* (1983) 5 EHRR 347), and the Act was not accessible. If a Convention right had been at stake then the certificates might not have been upheld. However, no Convention right was at stake and the question was whether it was fair of the Secretary of State to use the provision before it was promulgated, given that he was not obliged to do so. The Court of Appeal would have held that it was not fair if it were not for the fact that the appellants could bring judicial review proceedings. This gave the opportunity to produce material concerning risks in the Czech Republic which could have been considered on an appeal and so no injustice had resulted. The court considered itself, even on judicial review, as well placed as the Secretary of State to consider whether the claim was clearly unfounded (*ZL and VL v SSHD and Lord Chancellor's Department* [2003] 1 All ER 1062).

In *SSHD v Rashid* [2005] EWCA Civ 744, discussed in chapter 1, persistent failure over a period of years to apply the appropriate policy in favour of an asylum seeker was so conspicuously unfair as to amount to an abuse of power.

In conclusion, even though full rules of natural justice entailing equality of arms may not yet be applicable in immigration and asylum cases, a high degree of fairness and openness is required, consistent with the importance of the matters at stake and fundamental principles of access to justice and the rule of law.

8.5.2 **Human rights**

Entry clearance officers (though see discussion in chapter 3), immigration officers, and officials in the Home Office are all public authorities for the purposes of the Human Rights Act 1998 s 6, and therefore bound not to act in breach of a person's Convention rights. This obligation is confirmed in HC 395 para 2 and a breach of it was the basis for an appeal under the Immigration and Asylum Act 1999 s 65. This specific provision for a human rights challenge to an immigration decision, offered during the passage of the 1999 Act as a balance to the removal of rights elsewhere in the Act, was the first statutory recognition of human rights in the immigration sphere. It has been repealed by the 2002 Act and replaced by the inclusion of breach of human rights as one of the permissible grounds of appeal under s 84.

(c) that the decision is unlawful under s 6 Human Rights Act 1998 . . . as being incompatible with the appellant's Convention rights.

The continuing provision of an explicit right of appeal on human rights grounds establishes beyond doubt that tribunals have jurisdiction to hear human rights arguments in immigration cases, and these are not reserved for judicial review.

The application of human rights principles is discussed fully in chapter 3 and elsewhere as they arise throughout this book.

8.5.3 **Race discrimination**

Paragraph 2 of the HC 395 also requires immigration officers, entry clearance officers, and Home Office staff to carry out their duties 'without regard to the race, colour or religion of persons seeking to enter or remain in the UK'. The immigration service, Home Office, and entry clearance officers are bound by the Race Relations Act 1976, following the implementation of the Race Relations (Amendment) Act 2000 on 2 April 2001. The Act was passed after the Mcpherson Inquiry into the death of Stephen Lawrence, and the public disquiet that followed at the fact that the police were not bound by the Race Relations Act. As a consequence all public bodies are now brought within the Act's provisions, both as regards the obligation not to discriminate on racial grounds, and to have a positive policy to promote racial equality. For the purposes of the Act racial grounds are grounds of 'colour, race, nationality or ethnic or national origins' (Race Relations Act 1976 s 3).

Section 19B Race Relations Act 1976 19B(1) provides:

It is unlawful for a public authority in carrying out any functions of the authority to do any act which constitutes discrimination

and this is a listed ground of appeal in 2002 Act s 84.

8.5.3.1 *Ministerial authorizations*

Immigration and asylum matters are subject to exceptions under the Race Relations Act. The exceptions are so far as permitted by ministerial authorizations under Race Relations Act 1976 s 19D, and allow decisions to be taken on grounds of nationality or ethnic or national origin, but not on grounds of race or colour. Nationality decisions are no longer part of this exception following their removal from s 19D by Nationality, Immigration and Asylum Act 2002 s 6.

The first authorization was made on 27 March 2001. There have been regular reviews since that time, and a number of further authorizations. There is now an accumulated set of powers in force which may be grouped as follows:

- Powers to discriminate in immigration decision-making

Where a person is subject to examination under Immigration Act 1971 Sch 2 an immigration officer may

(a) subject the person to a more rigorous examination than others in the same circumstances;

(b) subject the person to further examination to ascertain if existing leave should be cancelled, request production of documents, search for and seize them, grant temporary admission;

(c) detain the person pending examination;

(d) decline to give notice of grant or refusal of leave to enter by fax or e-mail as is permitted by SI 2000/1161;

(e) impose a condition or restriction on temporary admission.

These powers may be exercised on the basis of a person's nationality where the minister is satisfied that:

there is statistical evidence showing that in the preceding month the total number of adverse decisions or breaches of the immigration laws by persons of that nationality exceeded 50 in total or 5 for every 1,000 admitted persons of that nationality (Race Monitor, Annual report 2004–5 para 1.6). Adverse decisions are defined as any refusal of an application for leave to enter or remain in any category, including refusals of asylum.

A person may also be refused leave to enter, or documents or information may be requested from them or priority may be given to setting removal directions.

The power to subject a person to more rigorous examination than others in the same circumstances has no other basis in law, though the rest are existing powers under the Immigration Act 1971. Since July 2003 authorisations of this kind have been made monthly so that, in order to comply with the decision of the High Court in the *Tamil Information Centre* case (see below), they may be made in accordance with latest information and under the minister's personal direction.

Narrower authorizations are made from time to time, for instance on 16 January 2006 for more rigorous examination of applications from Zimbabweans for indefinite leave to remain, made on the grounds of UK ancestry. The authorization was to last for a six-month period and was based on evidence of fraudulent applications made before 25 October 2004. In 2004 additional examination was authorized of nationals of Somalia, Turkey, Iran, Iraq, and Sudan, the five nationalities which statistics showed would be most likely to be subject to return to a third country (see chapter 12).

- Prioritizing asylum claims

Asylum claims may be given priority for consideration if the asylum seeker comes from a country from which a large number of 'unfounded' applications are made or which raise similar issues under the Refugee Convention. The implication here is that the application is judged not to merit or require extensive examination (authorization 27 March 2001). The fast-track schemes discussed in chapter 12 are authorized by this power.

- Language analysis

Following disputes about nationality in individual cases, the third authorization on 26 October 2001 provided that applicants from Afghanistan, Somalia, and Sri Lanka who seek asylum could be required to submit to language analysis testing if the immigration officer or Secretary of State 'has reason to doubt that a person is of the nationality he claims to be'. In March 2003 Iraq was added to the countries of origin for language testing, but this power is no longer used.

- Permission to work

The authorizations also provide for some positive discrimination. The first authorization provides that permission to work when the rules would not normally allow this may be given to

(a) participants in the British Universities North America Club Programme; and

(b) participants in the Japan Youth Exchange Scheme.

Priority of this kind was also given to British overseas territories citizens from St Helena or Tristan da Cunha, but since the implementation of the British Overseas Territories Act 2002 this will generally not be necessary (see chapter 2). Authorisations were also used in the scheme for sectors-based work permits, discussed in chapter 11.

Criticism of authorizations
The second authorization, which was revoked by a statement in Parliament on 11 June 2002, (col 1228W), permitted discrimination in examination on the basis of ethnic origin. This had been found to be unnecessary. Also in response to sustained criticism the Home Office removed the power to attach conditions to leave to enter on the basis of nationality. Once a person has been granted leave, suspicion does not attach to them, and discriminatory conditions of this sort are unnecessary.

The lawfulness of the first authorization was tested *in R (Tamil Information Centre) SSHD* TLR 30/10/2002. As the actions permitted by the authorizations are acts of discrimination which would otherwise be unlawful, on principle they should be construed narrowly. This conclusion is supported by the principle that the Race Relations Act 1976 should be construed purposively so as to enable and not defeat its object (*Jones v Tower Boot Co* (1997) ICR 254 and *Anyanwu v South Bank Student Union* [2003] All ER (D) 285 Nov, followed in the *Tamil Information Centre* case). Section 19D which gives the power to make the authorization says explicitly that the permitted discrimination, may be carried out only by a Minister of the Crown acting personally, or in accordance with 'a requirement imposed or express authorization given with respect to a particular case or class of case by a Minister of the Crown acting personally' (s 19D (3)(a)).

In the original version of the first authorization, the basis for discrimination allowed for grounds of intelligence information and that 'there is statistical evidence showing a pattern or trend of breach of the immigration laws by persons of that nationality'. There was no requirement to maintain statistics of any particular type, nor for anyone other than the immigration officer to take a view on the meaning of them. Forbes J found for the claimant in holding that these terms of the authorization 'delegated the essential task of actually identifying and defining any such case or class of case entirely to the decision-making of immigration officials, and what is more, by reference to their standards and/or thresholds rather than his own' (at para 19). Forbes J held the statute required that the minister personally made the actual decision. A licence to discriminate should be strictly controlled, and this the authorization did not do as it left too much in the hands of immigration officers. The amended authorization, as has already been noted, in addition to setting out a more detailed basis for the statistical information, requires that the minister is satisfied that the statistics show the basis as claimed.

Finally, a Race Monitor was appointed, in accordance with Race Relations Act 1976 s 29E, to monitor the likely effect of the authorizations and their operation. In her annual report for 2003–4, she commented that although the authorizations were necessary, as without them 'all people arriving from outside the EU would have to be examined equally, leading to inordinate delays and waste of resources' they may lead to self-perpetuating restrictive attitudes to certain nationalities (para 19).

In the following year she repeated this concern, and commented that basing selection on previous adverse decisions means that passengers of the identified nationalities are less likely to be given the benefit of the doubt, and so more likely to receive a refusal, and thus the authorization can be self-fulfilling (Annual Report 2004–5 paras 2.31–2.35).

The immigration service has often been charged with acting in a discriminatory fashion. The framework of regulation is initially startling as the concept of permitted discrimination seems to reverse the process of bringing public authorities within the anti-discrimination framework. However, as illustrated by the *Tamil Information Centre* case, it also opens up the possibility of challenge and judicial consideration.

As discussed below in relation to the ERRC case, discrimination without an authorization is unlawful.

8.5.3.2 *EU Race Equality Directive*

The EU Council Directive (EC) 2000/43 of 29 June 2000 requires states to implement the principle of equal treatment between persons irrespective of racial origin. The scope of the Directive is mainly in areas of social provision and employment. However, it includes the category of 'social advantages'. In the case of C–356/98 *Kaba v SSHD* [2000] 2 All ER (EC) 537 social advantages were held to include indefinite leave to remain, which suggests a viable argument that social advantage includes immigration status. However, Article 3.2 of the Directive says:

This Directive does not cover difference of treatment based on nationality and is without prejudice to provisions and conditions relating to the entry into and residence of third-country nationals and stateless persons in the territory of Member States, and to any treatment which arises from the legal status of the third-country nationals and stateless persons concerned.

The Directive is not intended to change the substance of immigration entitlements and restrictions in Community law. It seems for these reasons that the additional impact of the Directive in immigration law will be limited (although see Bell 2004).

The Directive was given effect in UK law on 19 July 2003 by the Race Relations Act 1976 (Amendment) Regulations 2003, SI 2003/1626.

8.5.3.3 *Race discrimination and the ECHR*

As discussed in chapter 3, Article 14 of the European Convention prohibits discrimination on grounds of race in relation to the other Convention rights. Therefore where for instance it is claimed that an alleged breach of an Article 8 right affected one racial group more severely or even exclusively and a complaint of discrimination may be made under Article 14. Race discrimination was found in itself to be capable of amounting to a breach of Article 3 in the *East African Asians Case* (1973) 3 EHRR 76, it being a 'special affront to human dignity' to single out a group of people for differential treatment on racial grounds. This does not mean that in all circumstances race discrimination can be regarded as a free-standing breach of Article 3. The level of severity to cross the threshold for Article 3 would have to be met in each case.

8.5.3.4 *Race discrimination as a ground of appeal*

Complaints of race discrimination in the course of carrying out immigration functions found a specific ground of appeal against immigration decisions under the Nationality, Immigration and Asylum Act 2002 s 84(1)(b) and may also be made to the Special Immigration Appeals Commission in cases arising under that Commission's jurisdiction.

An appeal on race discrimination grounds is unlike other appeals because the grounds refer to how the decision was taken, and success on that point may not in itself be enough to decide the claim in the appellant's favour (see Quayum and Chatwin 2004:97). For instance, it may be alleged that an entry clearance officer has made sweeping generalizations about people of the appellant's nationality. A finding that this was the case casts doubt on the reliability of their refusal of entry clearance, but does not establish that without this discrimination the requirements for entry clearance would have been fulfilled. A race discrimination appeal is also unique in that it permits a claim for damages for injury to feelings (Quayum and Chatwin p. 98).

The relationship between race discrimination and other grounds of appeal has been explored in the tribunal, High Court and Court of Appeal. The authoritative position is expounded in *Emunefe v SSHD* [2005] EWCA Civ 1002. Here, the appeal against the initial refusal of entry clearance was on the merits and on the ground of race discrimination. The adjudicator allowed the appeal on the merits but made no finding on the discrimination issue, regarding it as unnecessary as entry clearance would now be granted. The appeal predated the 2002 Act which would now require a finding on the discrimination issue (s 86(2)(a)). The appellant contended that without this he could not go to the county court for damages. Section 57A of the Race Relations Act 1976 provides that no claim for damages can be made in the county court if, inter alia, the challenge to the allegedly discriminatory act 'could be raised in proceedings on an appeal which is pending' in the immigration tribunal. The appellant had appealed the failure to decide the race discrimination ground, but by the time this came before the tribunal the appellant had been granted entry clearance and so by statute (now s 104 2002 Act) the tribunal was bound to treat the claim as abandoned. Ouseley J referred to this is as a 'particularly unfortunate consequence of the abandonment provisions' (*VE Nigeria* [2005] UKIAT 00057 para 21).

The Court of Appeal held, approving *R (on the application of) Bibi v IAT* [2005] EWHC 386 (Admin), that s 57A did not oust the jurisdiction of the county court where the matter had not been determined. Therefore Mr Emunefe could have brought his claim for race discrimination in the county court, providing he did so within the usual limitation period of six months. The remaining disadvantage to an appellant would arise when there is an adverse finding on race discrimination by the tribunal, which would bind the county court, and then a grant of leave to enter so that the appeal is treated as abandoned. The Immigration, Asylum and Nationality Act 2006 rectifies this by preventing an appeal from being treated as abandoned in the event of a grant of leave where the appeal was brought on race discrimination grounds.

8.5.3.5 *Where a whole immigration scheme is racially discriminatory*

The leading discrimination case to date since the Race Relations (Amendment) Act 2000 brought immigration decisions within protection from race discrimination was not an individual complaint using the appeals procedure, but a judicial review of a whole operation in *European Roma Rights Centre and other v Immigration Officer, Prague Airport and SSHD* [2004] UKHL 55. A pre-clearance scheme was operated (discussed in chapter 7) which entailed immigration officers stationed at Prague Airport refusing leave to enter to passengers before they boarded the plane. The scheme was located in Prague because there was a high number of asylum claims refused from the Czech Republic and the scheme was to deter claims that were held to be not well founded. The great majority of claims were made by people of Roma ethnicity, and they generally failed because the applicant was considered to be experiencing discrimination rather than persecution, or the treatment they feared was not at the hands of the state (*Horvath v SSHD* [2000] 3 All ER 577 HL). Perhaps surprisingly, the Secretary of State did not use an authorization under s 19D to operate the scheme, but rather said that it was not discriminatory at all. When it was challenged, the Court of Appeal found that although Roma were selected for more intensive questioning and were more likely to be refused passage, they were not refused as Roma, but as potential asylum claimants. This fine distinction was explained by Simon Brown LJ saying that the higher refusal rate for Roma was not because they were being stereotyped, but because 'they are less well placed to persuade the immigration officer that they are not lying in order to seek asylum' (para 86).

The House of Lords looked at the matter quite differently. Baroness Hale gave the leading judgment on the issue of discrimination:

> The Roma were being treated more sceptically than the non-Roma. There was a good reason for this. How did the immigration officers know to treat them more sceptically? Because they were Roma. That is acting on racial grounds. If a person acts on racial grounds, the reason why he does so is irrelevant. (para 82)

As Baroness Hale pointed out, direct discrimination cannot, in law, be justified, and this was direct discrimination.

There was in existence an authorization under s 19D which permitted more intensive examination of Roma. Although the Secretary of State decided it had no application in this case and did not rely on it, Baroness Hale found that it was not irrelevant.

The combination of the objective of the whole Prague operation and a very recent ministerial authorization of discrimination against Roma was, it is suggested, to create such a high risk that the Prague officers would consciously or unconsciously treat Roma less favourably than others that very specific instructions were needed to counteract this. (para 89)

This is very similar to the point made by the Independent Race Monitor. Authorisations, while intended to limit discrimination to particular cases, may in themselves contribute to an atmosphere of discrimination which needs to be positively countered. 'It is worth remembering that good equal opportunities practice may not come naturally' (Baroness Hale, para 90).

The Prague scheme was found to be discriminatory in its operation, contrary to Race Relations Act 1976 s 1, and a declaration made to that effect.

8.6 Police and Criminal Evidence Act Codes

In accordance with the increased preoccupation with enforcement as a priority in immigration policy, the Immigration and Asylum Act 1999 gave enhanced powers to immigration officers very similar to those possessed by the police in the investigation of crime and the apprehension of suspects. The enhanced powers apply both to dealing with people suspected of immigration offences (Part III Immigration Act 1971) and to the carrying out of immigration functions under Sch 2. Powers of entry, search of people and premises, seizure of documents, and fingerprinting apply in relation to investigation of immigration status and to investigation of criminal offences.

Section 145 provides that in exercising any power to

(a) arrest, question, search or take fingerprints from a person,

(b) enter and search premises, or

(c) seize property found on such person or premises,

an immigration officer must have regard to specified codes of practice. These are the Codes of Practice issued in relation to the Police and Criminal Evidence Act 1984, as modified and specified by the Immigration (PACE Codes of Practice) Direction 2000 and the Immigration (PACE Codes of Practice No 2 and Amendment) Directions 2000. PACE codes of Practice were revised with effect from 1 January 2006 by the PACE Codes of Practice Order 2005, SI 2005/3503.

8.7 Representation

The subject of this chapter is the structures and standards external to the decision-making process which affect the way decisions are made. Essential players in this process are non-governmental organizations and those who represent immigrants and asylum seekers. Non-governmental organizations of course have a leading role in lobbying. In such a politically controversial area, this is important, but political activities are not part of this book. However the work of those who represent immigrants and asylum seekers has given rise to a new set of legal provisions. There are a number of interrelated aspects to the role of representatives in the system.

First, in such a complex and powerful system, effective, knowledgeable and affordable representation is essential. As we have already seen, procedural points are often essential to the outcome of an immigration case, and many issues can only be tested on judicial review, which is a virtually impossible task for an unrepresented applicant. The importance of the matter to the individual also may often mean that representation is highly desirable.

Second, immigration and, to a greater extent, asylum are fields in which political battles are fought with legal tools. There is a rapid and almost continuous flow of legislation and rule and policy-making. Organizations of experienced representatives are in a better position than most to assist government in consultation on these issues.

Third, immigration and asylum law are unusual branches of legal work in that until recent reforms it was possible for unqualified people to represent clients both in dealings with the Home Office and at adjudicator hearings and Tribunals. In addition, prior to 1 January 2000 no legal aid was available for representation. The combination of lack of public funding and the freedom given to unqualified and unregulated advisers gave scope for unscrupulous individuals to set themselves up as immigration practitioners and charge high fees for work of dubious quality and sometimes of no value at all. It would be wrong to suggest that poor practice was the preserve of the unqualified. It was also the case that, due perhaps partly to the absence of immigration law from most legal professional training, bad work for high prices was done by legal professionals. Added to this was the vulnerability of immigration and asylum clients due to the profound importance to them of the matter, the scarcity of sound knowledge of the subject, and the possibility that they may not be fluent in English.

A regulatory system was set up to control so-called 'unscrupulous immigration advisers', but although the reasons for taking action were clear, the terms of the regulatory system have been contentious.

8.7.1 Regulatory system

Part V of the Immigration and Asylum Act 1999 provided the first statutory controls of the provision of immigration advice and representation by prohibiting such work from being done by an unqualified person (s 84(1)). A qualified person is, broadly speaking, an authorized member of a legal professional body (the Law Society, Institute of Legal Executives, or General Council of the Bar), or someone registered with the newly created Immigration Services Commissioner. Voluntary organizations such as citizens' advice bureaux, and other publicly funded organizations providing immigration advice are exempt from the requirement for individual workers to be registered, but the organization must comply with the requirements of the scheme. It is possible for independent organizations, rather than applying for their own exemption, to undertake all of their immigration work under the supervision of a solicitor, providing the supervision is active (Law

Society Gazette vol. 99, no. 33, p. 16). To provide immigration advice outside these provisions is an imprisonable offence under s 91.

The Immigration Services Commissioner's role is (s 83) to promote good practice in immigration advice and representation and to maintain a register of qualified advisers (s 85). Their powers and duties include preparing a code setting standards of conduct which applies to registered individuals and exempt bodies, i.e., all except legal professionals and government employees (Sch 5). The Commissioner's Rules and Codes of Standards allow for registration at a number of different levels, depending on the scope and level of competence of the organization or registered individual. This does not include representation in immigration offences as these are a branch of criminal law. The 2004 Act amended and increased the OISC's powers, introducing a power of entry and search of premises and seizure of documents including a power to seize materials that are subject to legal privilege (s 38). The 1999 Act also makes provision, in s 87, for an Immigration Services Tribunal which may hear complaints from those aggrieved by a decision of the Commissioner, or disciplinary matters referred by the Commissioner.

As mentioned earlier, bad work was done by legal professionals as well as by unqualified people. There was a lobby for all immigration advisers to be liable for individual registration, but the government's policy in the 1999 Act was to allow the professional bodies to regulate themselves. However, now both the Law Society and the Bar Council have set up voluntary panel and accreditation schemes. Non-practising barristers must apply for regulation with the Office of the Immigration Services Commissioner (OISC news April 2002).

Later developments have had a far-reaching impact on the availability of legal services.

8.7.2 Accreditation for publicly funded work

The Law Society and Legal Services Commission together instituted a compulsory accreditation scheme for all advisers working in immigration and asylum law who do publicly funded legal work. The provisions of the scheme are complex (see 'Immigration accreditation scheme explained' Everett, K. and Arnold, N. (2004) *Legal Action* June, pp. 10–12). Since 1 April 2005 all advisers must be accredited. There is evidence that the new system, combined with further legal aid restrictions discussed below, is having a devastating effect on the availability of legal advice (see for instance 'Asylum advisers face axe' The Guardian 11 October 2004, 'Open and shut case' Law Gazette 10 February 2005).

8.7.3 Funding

In early 2004 the allowable amount of public funding for each asylum case was radically reduced, as was legal aid firms' capacity to authorize their own expenditure. As discussed in chapter 1, these proposals emanated jointly from the Home Office and Department of Constitutional Affairs. Rawlings (2005) sees them as part of the 'revenge package' of ministers for the courts having been active in developing asylum seekers' rights in judicial review. Also with effect from 1 April 2004, Home Office funding which had provided free advice for immigrants and asylum seekers through the Immigration Advisory Service and the Refugee Legal Centre was ended, with the result that their clients have to be means-tested.

Legal aid for a reconsideration application and hearing is retrospective, and the tribunal and High Court have acquired powers to decide whether the appellant's legal advisers should be paid. Lawyers therefore take a financial risk with every reconsideration application.

The parameters for exercise of this power are set by the Community Legal Service (Asylum and Immigration Appeals) Regulations 2005, SI 2005/966. These include that if the appellant loses, there must only be a public funds costs order if the judicial body is satisfied that at the time when the application was made there was a significant prospect of success. In the case of an application to the court to order reconsideration, this must also involve a change of relevant circumstances or law since the application.

The House of Commons Constitutional Affairs Committee thought that the test of a 'significant' prospect of success was set too high, but it remained in place (Fifth Report 2004–5).

8.7.4 Independent bodies

The Wilson Committee in 1967 recommended that there be an independent organization, set up jointly by existing voluntary bodies, to give advice and representation in immigration matters. Dummett and Nicol describe the unsuccessful attempts of the Joint Council for the Welfare of Immigrants (JCWI) to become that body (1990:209). JCWI continues as an independent organization offering advice, training, and publications.

There are now numerous national and local bodies devoted to supporting asylum seekers in practical ways, and advising on the law associated with welfare support.

8.8 Conclusion

The procedural rules for appeals have not been discussed here, and neither have many of the rules on evidence and jurisdiction. These may instead be found in works for practitioners. We have seen that standards from increasingly diverse legal sources regulate immigration decisions, the work of those who take them, and those who represent the people who go through the system. Despite this, it was possible in 1998 for Ms Anufrijeva and others not to receive notice of the decision that their asylum claim had failed. Perhaps this case demonstrates that rules and standards, although complex, are necessary.

QUESTIONS

1   Is it appropriate to limit an appeal on the merits of the case to one tier? Consider the arguments for and against this proposal.

2   Is it appropriate to use discrimination on the grounds of nationality in making immigration or

asylum decisions? What about ethnic group? How does this differ from making decisions on the basis of colour?

3   Who should decide whether legal advisers are abusing the system?

FURTHER READING

Coussey, M. (2004 and 2005) Annual *Reports of the Independent Race Monitor*.

Dummett, A. (2001) Ministerial Statements — the immigration exception in the Race Relations (Amendment) Act 2000, ILPA.

Henderson, M. (2003) *Asylum and Human Rights Appeals (best practice guide)* ILPA and Refugee Legal Group — very full and practical guide to appeals. (Much guidance still relevant even though out of date.)

Juss, S. (1997) *Discretion and Deviation in the Administration of Immigration Control* (London: Sweet & Maxwell).

Lee, D. (1999) 'Give me shelter' The Guardian 9 March 1999, Supplement, p. 17.

Macdonald, I., and Webber, F. (2005) *Macdonald's Immigration Law and Practice*, 6th edn (London: Butterworths) Chapter 18, for a full account of procedure and jurisdiction on appeals).

McKee, R. (2005) Highlights of the 2005 Procedure rules, IANL vol. 19, no. 2, pp. 98–108.

Mitchell, H. (2005) The Roma case in the House of Lords and the question of the 2001 authorisation IANL vol. 19, no. 1, pp. 34–38.

Paraskeva, J. (2003) 'Keeping up standards' *Law Society Gazette* vol. 100, no. 16, p. 16.

[—— (2003) 'Protecting legal aid' *Law Society Gazette* vol. 100, no. 23, p. 20.

Quayum, M. and Chatwin, M. (2004) For whites only? Does the working holidaymaker scheme still discriminate? IANL vol. 18, no. 2, pp. 94–99.

Rawlings, R. 'Review, Revenge and Retreat', *Modern Law Review* [2005] vol. 68, no. 3, pp. 378–410.

Shaw, M. (2005) The Asylum and Immigration tribunal IANL vol. 19, no. 2, pp. 86–97.

Singh, R. (2004) Equality: the Neglected Virtue EHRLR 2 141–157.

Vincenzi, C. (1992) 'Extra-statutory ministerial discretion in immigration law' *Public Law* Summer 300–321.

www.oisc.org.uk website of the Office of the Immigration Services Commissioner for codes and standards, press releases, annual reports.

SECTION 4

Entry to the UK

9

Family life

SUMMARY

This chapter deals with the subject of joining family members in the UK for settlement. The emphasis is on applications related to marriage, that is, applications to join a married partner in this country, to come to the UK in order to marry, or to be with a partner in an established relationship akin to marriage. The rules relating to adult family members are then considered, and finally there is discussion of some issues raised by the rules relating to children. The chapter sets these issues of family settlement in the context of the human rights they represent and the political controversies that these policies have generated.

9.1 The context

9.1.1 Human rights context

The right to a private and family life is a universally recognized fundamental human right. It is included in the Universal Declaration of Human Rights 1948 (UDHR) and the International Covenant on Civil and Political Rights 1966 (ICCPR), both of which forbid arbitrary and unlawful interference with family life. The International Covenant on Economic, Social and Cultural Rights 1966 says, in Article 12, that 'the widest possible protection and assistance should be accorded to the family, which is the natural and fundamental group unit of society'. In domestic law, the Human Rights Act 1998 provides remedies for a breach of Article 8 of the European Convention on Human Rights 1950, which contains the right to respect for private and family life. In immigration law, the breach of Article 8 gives grounds for appealing against an immigration decision including a refusal of entry clearance or leave to remain (Nationality, Immigration and Asylum Act 2002 s 84(1)(c)).

The UK has entered blanket immigration reservations to the 1966 Covenant on Civil and Political Rights and the United Nations Convention on the Rights of the Child (CRC). These reservations state that the UK Government reserves the right to apply such immigration legislation as it deems necessary. In relation to the ICCPR it reserves the right not to recognize freedom of movement and voting rights and in relation to the CRC, immigration authorities are exempted from the duty to give primary consideration to the welfare of the child. These reservations restrict the possibilities for developing rights to a family life in an immigration context. Article 8 is in a different category, being part of UK law, while Article 8 jurisprudence, discussed here and in chapter 3, determines the development of the right to family life for those entering the UK.

9.1.2 Political context

The primacy of the right to family life has not been apparent historically in UK immigration law governing marriage-related applications. The settlement of families raises issues of cultural difference far more sharply than for instance the entry of students or workers. Marriage and child-rearing practices, concepts of the family, and family duties are all raised by family settlement applications. Much contention surrounds family settlement applications as a result of differences and perceived differences between the practices of immigrant and host communities. The law governing marriage- related applications has been created in a climate of suspicion, and as we shall see, this has affected the content of the immigration rules. In the area of marriage in particular, the rules reveal an overriding concern with preventing abuse of the system. While it is legitimate for the state to seek to ensure that marriage is not used as a means of evading immigration control, the marriage issue has, as Bevan puts it, 'offered an opportunity to vent a gamut of powerful and well rehearsed emotions' (Bevan 1986:253). These emotions have not been dominated by a concern for human rights. Specifically in the marriage rules, the concerns reflected are for the economic independence of the migrant, the 'genuineness' of the marriage, its compliance with UK domestic law, and establishing a connection with the UK. The legal expression of these concerns has now extended to regulation of the work of marriage registrars, this drawing strong criticism from the Parliamentary Joint Committee on Human Rights (see 9.3.7). A former President of the Immigration Appeal Tribunal has commented that the provisions directed towards the abuse of the system 'have an effect on the system of arranged marriages among the Asian communities' (Pearl, 1986:24), and Jackson, that marriage has 'attracted the most controversial immigration rules' (Jackson, *Immigration Law and Practice* 1996:395).

9.1.3 Legal context

It is perhaps surprising that there is no enshrined right in law for a British citizen to be joined in the UK by their married partner. This is not to say that entry for a married partner cannot be achieved through the legal system, as of course it can and frequently is. However, the process is that the married partner from abroad must fulfil certain requirements laid down in the immigration rules and if these are fulfilled the rules say that the married partner 'may' be admitted. We have already seen in chapter 8 that the Nationality, Immigration and Asylum Act 2002 s 86(3) provides that an appeal must be allowed where an initial decision was not in accordance with the rules. The effect of this is that if the requirements of the rules are met then the applicant must be given leave to enter. In practical terms, therefore, a qualifying applicant, who is able and willing to overcome the obstacles to entry as a married partner, has a legal basis upon which they can expect to secure entry.

This state of affairs is not the same as a right of a British citizen or settled person to be joined by their married partner, which could be enforced by such a person in the UK. First, the applicant is the person from abroad whose case is conducted in reality at appeal stage by the sponsor in Britain. A major source of evidence is the interview with the entry clearance officer, which takes place abroad and as discussed in chapter 6 is in itself a notorious source of difficulty (see Juss 1997 and Sondhi 1987).

Second, the requirements for entry are contained in the immigration rules, not in any Act of Parliament. As we have already seen, the immigration rules are made by a minister after, usually, the most cursory scrutiny by Parliament. The requirements concerning marriage change approximately every two or three years and their content is therefore neither stable nor secured by democratic scrutiny and not comparable with a statutory right.

Finally, there is very little statutory requirement as to the content of the immigration rules, and such as there is (Immigration Act 1971 s 1(4)) does not include a requirement that rules be made for the entry of married partners. In reality it is unthinkable that rules would be made which did not provide for married partners as such rules could be struck down as being in contravention of Convention rights.

Under the Human Rights Act 1998 it is not open to an individual to sue directly for the omission to provide an enshrined right to be joined by their married partner, as this is an omission of the legislature and as such immune from action under s 6 (3)(b).

Another curious aspect of the admission of married partners is the interaction with EC law. Where a British citizen has lived and worked in another EU country, they may re enter the UK with their non-European married partner, the married partner entering as of right (see chapter 5). Where a British citizen has lived and worked only in the UK, their non-European married partner is subject to UK immigration control and required to fulfil the rules whose provisions we are about to examine.

9.2 Application of Article 8

The scope and application of Article 8 (Human Rights Act 1998 Sch 1) is discussed fully in chapter 3. In this section we consider the application of Article 8 to family settlement applications in the context of two questions: first, to what extent does Article 8 support the right of a family member to enter the UK, and second, does Article 8 have anything to offer on the question of cultural differences?

The Article provides:

1. Everyone has the right to respect for his private and family life, his home and his correspondence.
2. There shall be no interference by a public authority with the exercise of this right except such as is in accordance with the law and is necessary in a democratic society in the interests of national security, public safety, or the economic well-being of the country, for the prevention of disorder or crime, for the protection of health or morals, or for the protection of the rights and freedoms of others.

9.2.1 **Entry cases**

As a caveat to the material which follows, it may be useful to refer back to the discussion in chapter 3 of whether the Human Rights Act applies at all in entry cases. This section proceeds on the basis that it does, even if it has to go by the tortuous route of an application by family members in the UK.

The application of a family member to enter the UK engages the positive obligation in Article 8 to 'respect' private and family life. This positive obligation has in effect been interpreted by the ECtHR to give discretion to the state to determine whether any obligation arises or not (see *Rogers* [2003] EHRLR 1 at 59). The starting point for considering what this may mean is the leading case of *Abdulaziz, Cabales and Balkandali v UK* (1985) 7 EHRR 471 in which the ECtHR held that 'article 8 does not oblige states to respect the choice by married couples of the country of their matrimonial residence' (para 67). This may result in the state saying, in effect, 'even though you are married, and we accept this means you have a right to live together, you do not have to exercise that right in the UK'. These principles apply not only to marriage but to all family settlement applications. They have been widely applied, and the absence of a positive obligation to respect a couple's choice of residence is now routinely cited in UK case law.

There are two caveats in the *Abdulaziz* judgment whose influence has been significant in the ECtHR and the UK courts. The first, that if the family was established before the first member migrated to the UK, the considerations might be different, is implied rather than explicit in the judgment.

9.2.1.1 *Established family*

This principle was used by the ECtHR in *Sen v Netherlands* (2003) 36 EHRR 7 where the ECtHR found that the right to respect for family life was violated where the Netherlands refused entry to a 13-year-old girl who had been left behind in Turkey by her parents at the age of three. One factor referred to by the court was that the family was established before the separation. This principle has not been often identified or relied on in UK case law, but in an amendment to the UK rules there is an implicit acceptance that established families should not have to cross major obstacles. From 1 April 2003 the non-British married partner of a couple who have been established outside the UK for four years may gain immediate settlement once leave is granted (HC 538). This provision is discussed below.

9.2.1.2 *Obstacles or special reasons*

The second caveat in *Abdulaziz* is the question of whether there were obstacles to establishing family life elsewhere or 'special reasons why that could not be expected of them' (*Abdulaziz* para 68). In *Arman Ali* [2000] Imm AR 134 Collins J regarded the absence of such obstacles in *Abdulaziz* as of 'fundamental importance' (at 145) in the outcome. Applying that to the case of Arman Ali, he found that the family's inability to live together in Bangladesh was 'crucial'. In the context of judicial review it was 'at least a factor which must be given its appropriate weight in considering whether Article 8 is breached' (at 146). *Arman Ali* predated the commencement of the Human Rights Act, but because the Secretary of State purported to have regard to Article 8 in making his decision, Collins J, on application for judicial review, was able to consider whether the Article had been correctly interpreted. He concluded that failure to have regard to the family's inability to live together elsewhere was a failure to have regard to a material consideration.

In *Husna Begum v ECO Dhaka* [2001] INLR 115 CA Pill LJ held that it 'would be contrary to the statements of general principle in . . . the judgment of the European Court of Human Rights' (para 18) to extract from *Abdulaziz* a generally applicable principle that it is crucial whether the family could reasonably be expected to live together in the other country. Accordingly, in *Husna Begum*, in interpreting HC 395 para 317, the Court of Appeal simply took that factor into account.

In the ECtHR, more recent cases on refusal of admission weigh the factors which indicate whether the family could live together elsewhere and regard this as an important question but not necessarily crucial (see, for instance, *Gul v Switzerland* (1996) 22 EHRR 93, *Ahmut v Netherlands* (1996) 24 EHRR 62, and *Sen v Netherlands* (2003) 36 EHRR 7). Without necessarily determining the precise weight to be attached to the matter, tribunals also consider whether there are obstacles to establishing family life in another country. For example, in the case of *Hussein v ECO Nairobi* [2002] UKIAT 01408 the appellant was a refugee from Somalia, living in Kenya. He applied to join his wife who was also a refugee from Somalia. She had six children by his deceased brother, and he had married her according to tradition. The tribunal found that there were obstacles to the establishment of family life in Kenya. Somalia was clearly not an option. The children had been in the UK for some years, and it would be 'unduly harsh' (borrowing a phrase from refugee law) to expect the children to relocate to Kenya.

The question of whether refusal of entry, when there are obstacles to establishing family life elsewhere, amounts to a failure of respect for family life depends on the circumstances of the case. The question should not be elevated into a rule of law. If there is a failure to respect family life, the question moves on to whether such an interference is necessary in a democratic society for a reason permitted in Article 8.2. These tests have been discussed fully in chapter 3.

9.2.2 Article 8 and cultural diversity

The second question concerning Article 8 is its contribution, if any, to cultural diversity. The Human Rights Act and ECHR are of limited assistance in this respect. The Convention rights do not include a free-standing right to cultural identity such as is found for instance in the Canadian Charter of Rights and Freedoms 1982. The jurisprudence of the Court has developed a little in the area of using Article 8 to protect an individual's right to respect for their identity. For example the Court accepted that an application could be made by transsexuals, objecting to the forced disclosure of their birth gender (e.g., *Sheffield & Horsham v UK* (1998) 27 EHRR 163 and *I v UK* (2003) 36 EHRR 53). The matter of self-definition in something as fundamental as gender was held to be within the ambit of Article 8. In *Chapman v UK* (2001) 33 EHRR 18 the Court accepted that the occupation of caravans by gypsies was an integral part of their ethnic identity. Although the applications were lost because the Court found that the state's interests in Article 8.2 prevailed, nevertheless, ethnic identity was a matter which could be considered as an aspect of private life under Article 8.

However, the European Court does not necessarily rule against differential impact between racial groups. In the unpublished case of *Bibi v UK* 19628/92,

29 June 1992 the Commission accepted that the UK could exclude, as matter of policy, further wives of the same man. The preservation of a Christian-based monogamous culture could be included in the protection of morals and thus a legitimate aim. A counter argument could be advanced that if a culture is dominant it will not be threatened by the existence of minority practices. Furthermore, the Court in the leading case of *Lingens v Austria* (1986) 8 EHRR 407 emphasized that 'in a democratic society' there must be space for ideas which 'disturb, shock or offend'. This case was brought under Article 10, the right to freedom of expression, and cultural practices which might come within the ambit of Article 8 and which might 'disturb, shock or offend' are regarded differently from ideas.

The question of the extent to which society can or should tolerate difference is a fundamental one in immigration law. The role of immigration law in a pluralist democracy arose once again explicitly in the 2002 White Paper, *Secure Borders, Safe Haven* (Cm 5387), whose subtitle was *Integration with Diversity in Modern Britain*. In relation to polygamy the White Paper said this: 'a marital partnership should be formed of only one man and only one woman — we do not recognize polygamous households' (para 7.2). The decision in [2003] UKIAT 00167 *J (Pakistan)*, discussed at 9.3.2.8, reveals a concept of marriage underlying the rules, which does not accord the same importance to the family dimension as did the parties in that case. The tribunal gave short shrift to the idea that they should respect the Muslim perspective on the matter, although the case is not decisive in this respect as there was no independent evidence before them of relevant Muslim practice. See also discussion of *AB Bangladesh* [2004] UKIAT 00314 at 9.3.2.6 where a monogamous view appears to affect the interpretation of the rules. In *Abdulaziz* the ECtHR found 'persuasive social reasons' for treating more favourably people whose link with a country stemmed from birth. Differential impact therefore, even when intentional, will not always be a breach of Convention rights, but it must be proportionate to a legitimate aim in order to comply with Article 14. Again, the crucial context is the democratic society, an idea which itself contains the problem, implying both pluralism *and* the rule of the majority.

9.3 Married partner rules

9.3.1 Application of rules

From 5 December 2005, when the Civil Partnership Act 2004 came into effect, same sex couples have been able to register their relationship as a union under law. Immigration rules on married partners have been amended to include civil partners, and the rules are the same for the two groups so far as the content allows. The term 'married partner' is used here to include both groups. Anyone who is subject to immigration control (i.e., is not an EEA national and does not have right of abode) who wants to come to the UK as the married partner of someone settled here, must obtain prior entry clearance. This is so even if they do not come from a visa national country. The requirements for obtaining entry clearance are set out in para 281 of the current immigration rules. The paragraph is headed 'Requirements for leave to enter', and since the implementation of the Immigration (Leave to

Enter and Remain) Order 2000, SI 2000/1161, entry clearance obtained under this rule will operate also as leave to enter providing its duration and any conditions are endorsed on it.

If entry clearance/leave to enter is given, for most married partners this will be for a limited period. From 1977 to March 2003 the period granted was one year. From 1 April 2003 this was amended (by HC 538) to two years (para 282). At the end of this so-called 'probationary period' the applicant may obtain indefinite leave to remain (para 287). HC 538 also introduced a new basis for entry as the married partner of a person with right of abode or indefinite leave to remain in the UK who has been living abroad with that person as their married partner for at least four years (para 281(i)(b)). A married partner who can apply in this category may obtain immediate settlement.

The requirements to apply for leave to remain as a married partner for someone who is already in the UK in another capacity include all those required for entry clearance (para 284). The cases on meeting the requirements are therefore sometimes concerned with a situation where the married partner is already in the UK. In discussion of entry clearance, cases concerning the similar requirements for leave to remain are used where appropriate.

9.3.2 Entry clearance requirements

9.3.2.1 *Present and settled sponsor*

The first requirement is that 'the applicant is married to a person present and settled in the UK or who is on the same occasion being admitted for settlement'. This person is referred to as the 'sponsor'. Mole (*Immigration: Family Entry and Settlement* 1987:xxiv) defines the sponsor as a:

> UK relative who confers eligibility to enter the UK on an overseas national
>
> or
>
> UK relative or friend who assumes financial responsibility for an overseas national.

At present we are referring to the UK married partner as the first of these alternatives, a sponsor who confers eligibility for entry.

Paragraph 281(i)(a) says that the sponsor must be 'present and settled or on the same occasion being admitted for settlement'. The alternative is the new basis of a four-year relationship. As discussed in chapter 6, a 'settled' person includes both a person who has acquired indefinite leave to remain under immigration law, and one who has right of abode. Settled immigrants, Commonwealth citizens with right of abode, and British citizens therefore all qualify as sponsors, providing they are ordinarily resident in the UK (Immigration Act 1971 s 33(2)(A)). Note that under 281(i)(a) the requirement of ordinary residence or admission at the same time for settlement applies to British citizens just as to others. This flows from the definition of settlement and was confirmed in *Zarda Begum* [1983] Imm AR 175, the Tribunal taking the view that the rule was intended to provide a basis for an applicant to join a partner ordinarily resident in the UK, not to be installed here while their partner lived elsewhere. This does not prevent a settled person, including a British citizen, from having a home in the UK where their partner lives, and another outside the UK, providing they can be said to be ordinarily resident in their UK home.

The time when the sponsor must be physically present or entering is not specified in the rules. While most requirements must be fulfilled at the time of the decision, in this case physical presence would be impractical and arbitrary, as the sponsor has no idea when the decision will be made and there is no reason why they should be in the UK at that date. The most practically workable timing is the date when the applicant married partner will be entering the UK, and this interpretation of the rule was confirmed in *Angur Begum v Secretary of State for the Home Dept* [1990] Imm AR 1. Although the Court of Appeal in *Angur Begum* was not referred to in an earlier Court of Appeal case which took a different view, the principle seems to hold, and the currently accepted time for the sponsor to be present is the time of the applicant's arrival.

At the time of the application, so long as the sponsoring married partner is ordinarily resident in the UK with a right to return, then the condition is met (*Mokbul Bibi* (4954) INLP vol. 2(2) 1987: 50). This was confirmed in *Rourke v ECO Pretoria* [2002] UKIAT 05666, in which the sponsor was regarded as present and settled although he had been living and working abroad since 1992. This gives the opportunity for the sponsor to accompany the applicant to the entry clearance interview, but ECOs are advised as a general rule to see sponsors separately from applicants if at all, both to check for inconsistencies and to protect reluctant applicants (DSP 8.13).

Since October 2000 para 281 of the rules has deemed a member of the forces, diplomat, or staff member of the British Council or Department for International Development to be present and settled in the UK for the purpose of the married partner rules.

The further alternative basis from 1 April 2003 is that the applicant is the married partner of a person with right of abode or indefinite leave to remain in the UK who has been living abroad with that person as their married partner for at least four years. This would apply to the married partner of a British citizen and someone who has lived in the UK for most of their life, as in accordance with the returning residents' rules (paras 18 and 19: see chapter 6), a person with indefinite leave who stays outside the UK for more than two years will have to reapply for settlement unless they have lived in the UK for most of their life. The married partner rules therefore now in this sub-paragraph distinguish between the married partners of settled immigrants and the married partners of British citizens or others with right of abode. The new rule does not enable a man who has lived in the UK for forty years to gain immediate settlement for his wife of 20 years' standing from Bangladesh, but it does enable a British man who has worked abroad for ten years to bring his wife of five years' standing back with him to gain immediate settlement.

Married partners may still be admitted together for settlement under para 281(i)(a). This is most likely when one of them has a right of abode, as in *Rourke*, but the difference where they do not have four years of marriage behind them is that the applicant married partner will only get two years' leave initially, instead of immediate settlement.

9.3.2.2 *That the parties have met*

The second requirement, that the parties have met, would rarely have any impact for applications based on a marriage which has taken place, as in almost every case the couple will have met at the marriage ceremony, if not before. It is possible in the Muslim tradition for a marriage to take place by proxy, providing there is an offer and acceptance before witnesses (e.g., as in the case of *Akhtar* 2166). However, this is extremely rare. The provision may be in issue in applications by fiancé(e)s, to whom this requirement also applies. The impact of this provision is on fiancé(e)s entering very traditional arranged marriages, and while it is increasingly the norm that engaged couples will meet, it may not always be the case. The guidance to ECOs (DSP 13.11) states that relationships developed over the internet will not fulfil the requirement to have met. It entails a face-to-face meeting.

The requirement that the parties have met was introduced into the rules at the end of 1979, as part of the programme of the new Conservative Government. It was one of a number of proposed changes which were so far-reaching that the rules (HC 394) were introduced by a White Paper and thus were debated in the House of Commons. The introduction of these rules marked an important stage in the development of immigration law in the UK. The debate reveals precisely the clash of values which was discussed at the beginning of this chapter. The opposition accused the government of equating marriages of convenience with arranged marriages. Alex Lyon MP went on: 'it is intended to hit the genuine arranged marriages of Asian girls, whether or not they were born in this country' (HC (14 November 1979) col 1336). The Home Secretary in his response did not deny that this was the case, but revealed another objective for the rule:

I remember the hon. Member for Ealing, Southall telling me that in the future it will increasingly be the practice that Asian girls in this country will wish to marry Asian boys in this country. I should have thought that was a position that we should encourage.

This position re-emerged 23 years later in the White Paper *Secure Borders, Safe Haven* (Cm 5387) in which the Home Secretary was more prescriptive than his predecessor:

We also believe that there is a discussion to be had within those communities that continue the practice of arranged marriages as to whether more of these could be undertaken within the settled community here. (para 32)

Here, immigration policy is used to encourage adoption of the practices of the host community and to discourage immigration which occurs for reasons which reinforce the distinctive characteristics of the immigrant community.

HC 394 was challenged in *Abdulaziz, Cabales and Balkandali*, but the European Court of Human Rights found that the requirement for the parties to have met was not racially discriminatory under Article 14 of the Convention. It considered that the changes in the rules were mainly to limit primary immigration in order to protect the labour market at a time of high unemployment, and that this fell within the legitimate aim of 'protecting the economic well-being of the country' (Art 8.2). The greater impact on people from the New Commonwealth and Pakistan (which at that time was not in the Commonwealth) was because it was from there that the greater number of applicants came. The requirement for the parties to have met was directed towards preventing abuse of this system. The Government's argument concerning the economic well-being of the country related to conditions prevailing at the time of that case, but the persistence of these rules at a time of labour shortage has not been subjected to legal challenge.

So much for the rationale and origins of the requirement that the couple should have met. Where there has not been a recent meeting the requirement is fulfilled by meeting the test in *Meharban v ECO Islamabad* [1989] Imm AR 57. In that case the sponsor and her fiancé had played together as children, but she could not recall what he looked like, nor any of his other characteristics. His application for entry clearance was refused. The Tribunal laid down guidance that there was no need for the parties to have met each other in the context of marriage or marriage arrangements, provided they had an appreciation of each other in sense of appearance or personality. In this case they did not, as neither seemed to have any knowledge of the other. In *Hashmi* (4975) the families found a way to satisfy both the immigration rules and their religious tradition. The fiancé and his parents stayed for a few days at the same house as the sponsor and her mother. This was arranged in order to comply with the rule, but because of religious tradition they did not speak to each other. The Tribunal accepted that there had been a 'meeting' within the rule.

9.3.2.3 *Maintenance*

The requirement in para 281 is that 'the parties will be able to maintain themselves and any dependants adequately without recourse to public funds'. This means that their financial position is sufficiently strong that they will not need to claim from a list of state benefits. Paragraph 6 of the rules defines 'public funds', and the list has gradually become longer since 1985 when 'public funds' were first specifically identified. They now include virtually all means-tested and disability benefits apart from emergency provision. Public funds are not limited to cash benefits but include housing. Housing provided under homelessness provisions was included from 1985, but from April 1996 Part II housing was included, i.e., council housing provided to people on the waiting list. National Health Service treatment and state education are not classified as public funds. The anticipation that a married partner will make use of the National Health Service therefore has no bearing on meeting this requirement of the rules, although where they are in a serious and chronic state of ill health, this may have other repercussions as discussed in chapter 6.

Until 2 October 2000, there was a thorny legal issue as to what constituted recourse to public funds. The problem was this: where a family had saved money from benefits to support the incoming family member, or would continue to live on their existing benefits without making an extra claim or receiving any increase on that person's arrival, could the incoming person be said to be having recourse to public funds? Following the approach to policy propounded in *Dhudi Saleban Abdi v Secretary of State for the Home Department* [1996] Imm AR 148, discussed in chapter 6, it was resolved that only an additional claim on arrival would count as recourse. This was put beyond doubt by the October 2000 rule changes, inserting paragraph 6A, as follows:

For the purpose of these Rules, a person is not to be regarded as having (or potentially having) recourse to public funds merely because he is (or will be) reliant in whole or in part on public funds provided to his sponsor, unless, as a result of his presence in the United Kingdom, the sponsor is (or would be) entitled to increased or additional public funds.

Adequacy

The rules require that the parties can maintain themselves 'adequately'. There is potential unfairness or even discrimination here if the rules are interpreted so as to exclude married partners of people with low incomes. According to the case of *Momotaz Begum* (18699) INLP vol. 13 (2) (1999), p. 77 this cannot mean that their standard of living may be allowed to fall below the minimum considered acceptable in general in the UK.

In the case of *D Kamral Islam* (13183) the Tribunal found that the income support figures could offer a 'helpful yardstick' in determining whether the income which the couple would have could be considered adequate, and many other tribunal decisions have used this measure, including *Momotaz Begum*. However, income support is not intended to cater for every event, so the couple need to show that they can also meet unexpected demands.

Another line of cases rejected the comparison with income support, but this debate seems to have been settled, as set out in *Uvovo* 00/TH/01450 in the following way:

3. Income support is what would be provided for the family if they were British residents of the United Kingdom with no other resources: it is not suggested in the rules that family members seeking immigration should be better maintained than those who are already here; and the government can hardly say that the level of support it provides for its destitute citizens is not adequate. What the recipient or holder of the funds spends money on is his own business. We would in general take the view that if the appellant can show a level of income at the income support level or higher, that will be enough.
4. It is, however, essential to maintain comparability. Income Support carries entitlement to a number of other benefits and, in particular, a family on Income Support will be able to obtain Housing Benefit. The appropriate comparison is therefore between the Income Support level on the one hand and the family income net of accommodation costs on the other. (There are other Benefits to which Income Support is a 'gateway', such as free school meals and free prescriptions. These are not always to be ignored, particularly where those seeking entry are of school age or have some medical condition.) It follows that, although we should be slow to enquire into the Sponsor's spending habits, we need to be satisfied that, at the date of decision, his income after paying his rent was sufficient to maintain himself and his wife.

This approach has been followed by the tribunal, more recently in *Choudhury v ECO Dhaka* [2002] UKIAT 00239, and may be regarded as the current standard, confirming income support levels as a yardstick but making allowance for other benefits to which a couple on income support would be entitled. *Uvovo* also clarifies that detailed evidence of outgoings is not generally required. In particular where the sponsor runs a small business it is unwarranted to demand fully audited accounts (*Rafiq* (G0049) INLP vol. 13(1) (1999), p. 21). In a line of tribunal cases also noted in INLP vol. 13(3) (1999), p. 110 where the income seemed reasonable to the IAT, the appeal was allowed, without further enquiry

Disabled sponsor
This approach does not solve all the problems which arise where the sponsor is disabled. In this case the sponsor receives higher benefits than income support, but these are paid because of the sponsor's greater needs. There is no general rule in such cases. In *Shabir v ECO Islamabad* 01/TH/2897 the sponsor, who was severely disabled, received £115.20 per week, 'substantially in excess' of £80, which was the figure deemed necessary for two people living together according to income support rules. The tribunal said that the mere fact that her income was more than the income support level was not enough; they must consider whether all the disability

living allowance would be used up by the sponsor's own needs. She had in fact been saving from her benefits. Her main disability was limited mobility. It was a matter for her how she used the extra money which was paid to deal with this. On the facts, there would be enough to maintain her husband as well.

In *ECO Islamabad v Nazia Bi* [2002] UKIAT 05214 on similar figures it was held that maintenance would not be adequate. The tribunal considered that the sponsor's needs would absorb all the benefits and noted that there was nothing to spare in the family finances generally — accordingly, entry clearance was refused. The decision in this case illustrates the importance of meeting the maintenance requirement and the lack of flexibility in the rules, even in the light of compelling compassionate circumstances. There was substantial evidence that the sponsor, who suffered from paranoid schizophrenia, would have been much better with his wife present and he might well have stabilized sufficiently in order to be able to work. However, this consideration does not feature in the rules. An attempt was made before the Tribunal to use Article 8, but no Article 8 claim had been made in the original application and the argument was summarily dismissed. It seemed that the only route for this couple would have been an exercise of discretion *outside* the rules. Even so, this decision is not necessarily the last word in relation to flexibility. Blake and Husain (2003:203) suggest that where the sponsor has settled status in the UK but cannot meet the public funds requirements in the rules, for refusal to comply with Article 8 there should be consideration of whether, in the particular case, the harm to that family is proportionate to the aim of protecting the economic well-being of the country. In order to reach this point it would have to be established that respect for family life in that case under Article 8.1 required the admission of the family member(s) to the UK.

The Immigration Advisory Service commentator on *Nazia Bi* noted that there had been a number of Home Office policy reviews in which there had been a promise to consider a relaxation of the rules for disabled sponsors, but nothing had ever come of this. Another Article 8 challenge can be anticipated on this issue.

The couple do not need to prove that they will have enough money to support themselves indefinitely. In the case of *Ishtiaq Ali* (11568) the tribunal commented:

> to require some certainty that the parties to the marriage will at all times in the future be able to support and accommodate themselves would make it virtually impossible for a young couple with modest means to meet the requirements of the rule.

In *Shakila Kauser* (17428) INLP vol. 13(2), p. 78, the Tribunal considered there was no need to look further ahead than six months after the appellant's arrival to ascertain whether the couple could maintain themselves adequately. This approach is commonly taken also at the point of applying for indefinite leave at the end of the probationary period and is confirmed in subsequent case law (see, for instance, *Adesegun v ECO Lahore* [2002] UKIAT 02132).

Third party support

The rules say that the parties must be able to 'maintain themselves,' and this has in the past been taken literally. In other words the resources which maintain the couple must be their own. However, this interpretation is no longer supportable. It may be recalled that where there is doubt about the meaning of an immigration rule, a purposive approach should be taken (*Alexander v IAT* [1982] 1 WLR 1076). In the case of *Zabeda Begum* (16677) the Tribunal thought that 'the principle behind the rule is that a married couple should be self sufficient and self sustaining'. Accordingly, it disallowed long-term third party support as a way of meeting the maintenance requirement. A fortnight later, in the case of *Janat Bi* (16929), the Tribunal referred to the purpose behind the maintenance requirement as being to avoid reliance on public funds. Increasingly, the tribunal began to give recognition to support from a third party, such as an older relative, as a valid short term way of meeting the maintenance requirement. In *Balvinder Kaur* (12838) the tribunal were prepared to accept even long-term third party support, provided it could be proved to an adequate standard. A similar view was expressed in *Nguyen* (18738) INLP vol. 13(2) (1999), p. 79. The view of the purpose of the rules expressed in *Janat Bi* is to be preferred. The view in *Zabeda Begum* imposes an idea of the self sufficiency of a couple as a family unit that excludes the concept of close knit extended families. The reliability of support in an extended family was recognized in the case of *Ali* (19736) INLP vol. 13(2) (1999), p. 79 where the family was a prosperous one which had no history of recourse to public funds. After the birth of twins the sponsor and her husband would naturally be maintained by the rest of the family until she could return to work. A similar approach was taken in *Syeda Shabli Begum* (18771) INLP vol. 13(2) (1999), p. 79.

There is now authority for the acceptance of third party support whether short or long term, deriving from the High Court decision in *Arman Ali*.

In this case the applicant's wife and six children were all refused entry clearance as in order for them to be maintained and accommodated without recourse to public funds two of the children would need to accept accommodation with their uncle, and the eldest son would have to work. Work was available for him, but the Home Office decided that he could not be both a dependant and working.

An Adjudicator recommended that they be given entry clearance because although they could not meet the strict requirement of the rules, they fulfilled the purpose behind the rules which was to avoid reliance on public funds. The Secretary of State did not follow this recommendation, and there was an application for judicial review of the Secretary of State's decision. Collins J held that to comply with both Article 8 and the accepted purposive approach to the rules it would be appropriate to interpret the rules on accommodation and maintenance to mean that they were intended to avoid reliance on public funds. It was not necessary to insist that the accommodation must be provided by a parent and that a dependent child must have no income of their own:

If a rich relation or a benefactor is willing and able to maintain a family in this country so that there is no need to have recourse to public funds, I see no reason in principle why that family should be kept apart. The purpose of the rules is quite clearly met and the natural meaning of the language used is consistent with the construction I have espoused. (at 147)

Collins J accepted that a rule which prevented reliance on public funds was consistent with Article 8 as being an interference necessary 'for the economic well-being of the country' (Art 8.2). A rule requiring nuclear family self-sufficiency has no such legitimate aim.

On the facts of *Arman Ali* the main question was of maintenance of the applicant's children rather than his wife. The married partner rule requires that the parties can maintain themselves '*and any dependants*' and so non-fulfilment of the maintenance requirement for children has a direct effect on fulfilling the terms of the married partner rule. Collins J referred to the married partner rule as follows: 'The wording of rule 281(vi) does not in terms suggest that the ability to maintain must be from the parties' own resources.' There seems to be no reason to attribute different underlying purposes to the rules concerning married partners and children, and the reasoning in *Arman Ali* has been applied to married partner cases. In the starred decision in *Amjad Mahmood v ECO Islamabad* [2002] UKIAT 01819, the tribunal spoke in strong terms about a repeated refusal of entry clearance to a husband where there was adequate short-term third party support. The adjudicator had applied the old idea of the rule, that the couple should be financially self-sufficient, and this was held by this tribunal to be wrong in law, following *Arman Ali*.

Collins J also said that 'it will be rare for applicants to be able to satisfy an entry clearance officer, the Secretary of State or an adjudicator that long term maintenance will be provided so that there will be no recourse to public funds' (at 148). This has been misinterpreted to mean that there must be long-term third party support in order for it to be adequate. *Nasreen Akhtar v ECO Islamabad* [2002] UKIAT 02818 clarified the point: *if* it was necessary in the long term to rely on third party support, the reliability and adequacy of that source of funding would need to be proved, and that would not often be easy. This did not mean that there was a *requirement* for third party support to be long term. If the evidence suggested that it would last as long as it might be needed, whether for a few weeks or a few years, that would satisfy the rule.

The immigration rules were amended in October 2000, one year after the judgment in *Arman Ali*, among other reasons to ensure compliance with the Human Rights Act which came into force on the same day. Pursuant to Collins J's interpretation of third party support in the light of Article 8, one might have expected to see an insertion of the possibility of third party support in the married partner rules. However, the amendments had the reverse effect. There was no change to the married partner rules, but there was an amendment to para 297 governing maintenance and accommodation for children which *removed* the scope for third party maintenance and accommodation. In *AA Bangladesh* [2005] UKAIT 00105 ILU vol. 8, no. 12, the Asylum and Immigration Tribunal accepted the ECO's argument that the rule had been changed explicitly to overrule *Arman Ali* in relation to third party support for children. That case therefore cannot be used to interpret the current rule for children. Somewhat unsatisfactory reasons given on behalf of the ECO for amending the rule include that it was overused and evidence inadequate. There is a passing reference to human rights, though this is not explained, except for implication that it may support child protection (*AA* paras 28–1).

An amendment to the equivalent rule for adult dependent relatives adds nothing of substance. Third party accommodation was already ruled out and remained so. The rule contained no bar on third party maintenance, and, like the married partner rule, still did not do so after amendment.

Rather unusually, the IDIs on this subject are at odds with law. Chapter 8 Annex F para 5.1 April 2004 says:

A couple who are unable to produce sufficient evidence to meet the maintenance requirement, may provide an undertaking from members of their families that they will support the couple until they are able to support themselves from their own resources. *This is not acceptable* as the Rules require the couple to be able to support themselves and any dependants *from their own resources*. Nevertheless, such an arrangement *may* be accepted exceptionally if it is clear that it would only be in effect for a limited period and the couple have a realistic prospect of supporting themselves thereafter.

9.3.2.4 *Accommodation*

In addition to financial maintenance para 281 requires that 'there will be adequate accommodation for the parties and any dependants without recourse to public funds in accommodation which they own or occupy exclusively'. This requirement contains a number of elements which may be considered in turn.

The base line is a standard represented by the case of *Mushtaq* (9342), that accommodation would be 'adequate' as long as occupation of it would not be an offence. This means that it is not statutorily overcrowded according to the standard laid down by the Housing Act 1985 s 326. Reports from independent Environmental Health Officers are often prepared to establish that standards are met, however the tribunal in *Thompson v ECO Kingston* (17926) observed that this is not always necessary, in particular because the standard of proof is the civil standard. Compliance with statutory housing standards is therefore to be proved on the balance of probabilities. Where it had proved impossible to gain access to the flat in which the sponsor had lived at the time of the decision, the tribunal were prepared to say that they found it highly unlikely that main living rooms in a local authority flat would measure less than 10 by 11 feet. On the balance of probabilities, therefore, the overcrowding standard was satisfied.

On the other hand, compliance with the overcrowding standard does not in all cases automatically mean that the accommodation is adequate. In [2004] UKIAT 00006 *S(Pakistan)* ILU vol. 7, no. 5 the tribunal held that a small terraced house, although it would not be statutorily overcrowded, was not adequate for two adult couples and four small children. There were three bedrooms and a through living room from which the stairs went up.

HC 395 para 6A applies equally in the case of accommodation. Consequently the provision of accommodation without recourse to public funds simply means without additional recourse. If the sponsor is already living in a council house and the married partner will be able to live there too, this is not recourse to public funds. The case of *Rahman* (14257) INLP (1997) vol. 11(4), p. 135 illustrates that the principle applies to a housing benefit claim. Here a husband was applying to join his wife in the UK. She lived in her parents' house and was not working. The housing costs were met by housing benefit. The tribunal held that the question it had to consider in relation to accommodation was whether there would be any additional claim as a consequence of his arrival. As there would not, his appeal was allowed on the accommodation issue.

The accommodation must be owned or occupied exclusively by the parties. Ownership may be of any form of legal interest in land, freehold or leasehold. Occupation must be by virtue of some legal right to occupy, but this can be as a licensee or a lodger. Exclusive occupation need be of no more than a bedroom (*Saghir Ahmed* 8260).

The requirement for the couple to own or occupy exclusively was introduced into the immigration rules in 1994. At the time of its introduction there was concern that it would discriminate against people living as an extended family. A letter written in October 1994 by Nicholas Baker MP, Minister of State for the Home Office, to Giles Shaw MP gave the interpretation of the rule which was approved by the tribunal in *Saghir Ahmed:*

Arrangements whereby the applicant joins his or her married partner in an established household with other residents are therefore still acceptable providing these requirements are fulfilled, and that the applicant and their married partner have at least a small unit of accommodation e.g. a bedroom for their exclusive use.

It is a feature of this area of immigration law that there are relatively few cases at appeal court level, and that Tribunal decisions are not binding on each other. Add to this that officers on the ground may not always be aware of decisions of appellate bodies, and the situation is ripe for inconsistency and confusion. At approximately the same time as *Saghir Ahmed* another Tribunal decision, that of *Shahida Kauser* (8025), held that the accommodation for exclusive use must be an independent unit. Later cases have tended to follow *Saghir Ahmed,* and the Minister's letter makes it clear that this is the better authority. However, as late as 1998, in the case of *Parkar v ECO Bombay* (17948), the case got as far as the Tribunal because the adjudicator had found that it was necessary to show exclusive occupation of all parts of the house. The Tribunal accepted that this argument was 'simply wrong'. Again it is characteristic of immigration law that a principle of interpretation of the rules is settled and now practically incontrovertible, without a decision of a higher court. In case of doubt, the principle in *Abdi* (see chapter 6) could be used to adduce the minister's letter as settling the meaning of the rule.

9.3.2.5 *Time when requirements must be met*

Clearly, when accommodation *is* an independent unit, it is unlikely to be empty and waiting for the applicant at the date of the application. This is all the more the case because of the long waiting time which many applicants experience. *Prima facie*, the date when the accommodation must be available is the date of the decision, but this has been mitigated in practice by an approach typified in *ECO Islamabad v Younis* (17469), approving:

the question as to whether or not at the date of the decision, which is the material date, the accommodation was adequate and whether or not it could be made adequate within a reasonable time of that decision. A reasonable time has been held by the tribunal in other cases to be six months.

A subject of ongoing contention has been whether, if an application was refused, but accommodation or maintenance later became available, evidence of this could be admitted in an appeal. Following the Court of Appeal judgment in *R v IAT ex p Kotecha* [1982] Imm AR 88 account could be taken of arrangements which were positively and reasonably foreseeable at the time of the decision. The current position is given by the Nationality, Immigration and Asylum Act 2002 s 85 which provides that evidence available up to the date of the hearing should be considered in all immigration and asylum appeals except refusal of entry clearance or certificate of entitlement (s 85(5)). In these cases the adjudicator 'may consider only the circumstances appertaining at the time of the decision to refuse'. The reviewer in ILU vol. 8, no. 5 suggests that this grammatical error should be corrected by reading the section as 'circumstances obtaining', i.e., in existence at the time of the decision to refuse. Therefore evidence which arose after the date of the decision will not be admissible except to the extent that it sheds light on the situation at the date of the decision. This does not allow for evidence of events that were reasonably foreseeable. This interpretation was confirmed in a starred decision, *DR Morocco* [2005] UKIAT 00038 ILU vol. 8, no. 5 where intense correspondence between a couple after refusal of entry clearance was admissible evidence that at the date of the refusal they did in fact have an intention to live permanently together.

The subsection would also still encompass evidence in a case such as *Hashim v ECO Karachi* [2002] UKIAT 00928 in which the sponsor was awarded a significant and backdated increase in benefit by the Social Security Appeal Tribunal after the ECO's decision but before the hearing before the adjudicator. This made his income indisputably adequate. The adjudicator felt unable to take account of this increase because the ECO could not have had it in contemplation at the time of the decision. The Tribunal held that this was the wrong approach. The decision of the SSAT meant that the sponsor at the time of the decision had a legal entitlement to the increased income, therefore it should be taken into account on appeal.

The effect is to exclude post-decision facts, with the above exception where light is shed on the state of affairs at the time of the decision, in appeals where the appellant is outside the UK, such as refusal of entry to a married partner. This is in keeping with a policy which seems to underlie recent immigration legislation of relating entitlements to the perceived level of a person's connection with the UK. It does not apply to a refusal of indefinite leave to remain to a married partner at the end of their probationary period, but McKee reports that for some two years after this section came into force, in-country appeals of this kind were decided on the incorrect basis that post-decision facts were not admissible (Legal Diary, ILU vol. 8, no. 11).

9.3.2.6 *Intention to live permanently with each other*

When Alex Lyon said in the House of Commons that there were other provisions which were intended to prevent marriages of convenience, one of those he may have had in mind was the requirement to show the intention to live permanently together.

Conflicting commitments

A couple may intend to live permanently together even though present circumstances prevent them from cohabiting. In *Kumar* (17779) INLP vol 13(3) p. 109 (1999) the wife stayed with her parents during the week as her stepmother needed her care and attention. The couple were together at weekends and made every effort to see each other when they could. This arrangement was accepted by the tribunal not to conflict with an intention to live permanently together. In the case of *Janat Bi* (16929) the couple had been together for the first 11 years of their marriage, and then apart for most of the following 40, because of the wife's family commitments. Their intention to live together was not questioned. In *Barlas* TH/03975/2000 there were four years of separation before the appellant applied to come to the UK. The tribunal did not regard this as preventing intention to live together being established, particularly in the context of an arranged marriage.

Not only family commitments but also working patterns may interfere with cohabitation. Immigration and appellate authorities need to take into account the demands of the global economy, including particularly employers' demands for workers to be mobile. For instance, in *Niksarli* (21663) (INLP Vol 14 no 2 p. 110) the wife had to stay in Glasgow where she had a job and medical treatment while her husband had to go to London to find work. Shift patterns too may affect actual cohabitation without rupturing the intention to live together. In *Satnam Singh* (19068) INLP vol 13(2) (1999) p. 78 a man who was seeking indefinite leave to remain after his first 12 months was refused because he had not been sleeping with his wife. She and her parents lived above a shop. The appellant was working night shifts. In order to have a better chance of sleeping during the day, instead of joining his wife he slept next door in a friend's flat. The Tribunal allowed his appeal, saying that the couple's intention to live permanently together had 'nothing to do with sleeping in the same bedroom every night'. Restricted actual cohabitation in the past or present therefore will not jeopardize the intention to live together, provided the reasons are compelling. On the other hand, where a sponsor had at the time of the marriage committed an offence which resulted in his receiving a nine-year prison sentence, the tribunal held that no intention to live together could be formed. When the application was made he was in prison. An intention was more than a wish. The tribunal did not focus on the physical impossibility of their living together at that time, but on the fact that this would not be lawful (*Shabbana Bibi v ECO Islamabad* [2002] UKIAT 06623).

In *AB Bangladesh* [2004] UKIAT 00314 ILU vol. 8, no. 2 the Tribunal held that the appellant's intention to live six months of each year with his British wife and the other six months with his wife in Bangladesh could not amount to an intention to live permanently together. Behind this appears to be an idea of intention determined by a view of marriage as monogamous. The appellant argued that not recognising his obligations to divide his time between his two wives amounted to religious discrimination contrary to Article 14. However, the Tribunal disagreed, holding that so far as it had evidence, the Quran did not require cohabitation of equal time with each wife, only that each be treated equally.

Relationship difficulties

A troubled period in the marriage is not fatal to an intention to live together. In *Bryan* (14694) INLP vol 11(3) (1997) immigration officers apparently caught the sponsor on a bad day. When they called he expressed his doubts about the appellant, thought she might be having a relationship with another man, that the marriage was just being used to enable her to stay in the UK, and so on. She was not interviewed. The tribunal allowed her appeal, saying that the whole intention to live together did not turn upon the credibility of what was said or done on a particular day, but rather on the position 'in the light of the whole evidence relating to cohabitation and living together since the marriage took place'.

The level of investigation in which a tribunal may engage in deciding this question is illustrated in the case of *Noisaen* (18213) heard in April 1999. Here, the tribunal considered the couple's behaviour during a period of separation, the extent and quality of the contact they had in that time, and speculated about the emotional states and motivations of the sponsor. The marriage of this couple, some two years after it was entered into, was subjected to a scrutiny as to its viability which most couples would hope to avoid, and which is reminiscent of the family court. Fortunately for the appellant the tribunal took a humane approach which respected the particularity of the situation, and endorsed the view advanced by the appellant's representative that 'relationships are . . . complex and unique in nature and the weight of the evidence in this case suggests that the intentions are genuine'.

9.3.2.7 *Primary purpose, intention to live together, and credibility*

This level of scrutiny of a relationship with a view to establishing the intention to live together would have been almost unknown before 5 June 1997. On that date the new Labour Government, in accordance with its manifesto commitment, abolished (by HC (26)) the infamous 'primary purpose' rule. This rule required the couple to prove that 'the marriage was not entered into primarily to gain admission to the UK' (HC (395) para 281 before amendment). A moment's thought will reveal that there are many reasons for getting married and that these vary between individuals, between cultures, between social groups, and at different stages of life. An examination of them is probably a subject more fit for psychology than law. Where the intended married partner lives may be a factor entering into the decision.

Applicants were faced with the impossible task of proving a negative, that any motivation in relation to where the sponsor lived was *not* the primary one. In order to show that entry to the UK was not the primary purpose, a couple was expected to show evidence of what was called 'intervening devotion'. This required production of letters, and evidence of telephone calls and visits. In an arranged marriage the intentions of the families would be relevant (*R v IAT ex p Hoque and Singh* [1988] Imm AR 216). Investigation of primary purpose was marked by intensive and intrusive questioning. As the matter in issue was so subjective, great weight was placed by entry clearance officers on their findings as to the credibility of the applicant. A key method of determining credibility was the so called 'discrepancy system', in which different family members would be asked questions which might have little bearing on the central matter in hand, but if their answers differed, this would be used to cast doubt upon their credibility in relation to the central issue, the marriage, and its purpose. The assumptions of entry clearance officers about traditional (and therefore predictable and credible) practices in effect meant that the correct civil standard of proof could not be applied (as demonstrated by Juss 1997). It is hardly surprising that Macdonald refers to the 'primary purpose' rule as one which 'generated more anger and anguish than perhaps any of the other Immigration Rules' (1995:343).

Disturbingly, since the abolition of the 'primary purpose' rule the discrepancy approach does not seem to have entirely disappeared. In *ECO Islamabad v Nasir Mahmood* [2002] UKIAT 01034 the ECO had refused the application principally because of discrepancies between the parties. The Adjudicator and Tribunal both disapproved this approach as it did not focus on the central question of intention. Even if the parties had been less than frank, this did not mean that they did not intend to live together as husband and wife. This conclusion on credibility is similar to the approach used in asylum cases and is regarded as correct. Even if some matters are not as stated, the question is whether this affects the core of the claim. The same approach was taken in *Anju Malik v ECO New Delhi* [2002] UKIAT 00738. Here the point was made that discrepancies do not have the same significance in an arranged marriage as in a love match. This point was also made in the case of *Sabar Gul v ECO Islamabad* TH/5118/99 and in *Choudhuryv ECO Dhaka* [2002] UKIAT 00239. In both these cases the adjudicator had looked for evidence of personal knowledge of each other's circumstances which should not be expected where the marriage had been arranged and the parties had little prior direct knowledge of each other.

When the primary purpose rule was current, intention to live together was hardly ever regarded as a free-standing factor. It was treated, along with 'intervening devotion', as evidence towards establishing the primary purpose. For instance, in the case of *Kari Shahjad Miah v ECO Dhaka* [2002] UKIAT 02533 the original refusals were on the basis of primary purpose, maintenance, and accommodation. Intention to live together was not raised. In a later refusal of the same married partner it became a ground. A development which may be seen in the case of *Noisaen* and a number of others, *Chowdhury* (16080), *Hanif* (17561) both INLP vol. 12, (4), p. 146 (1998) and *Iqbal* (17293) in June 1999, is to make credibility again a central issue. An examination of credibility as it relates to intention should be confined to whether the surrounding circumstances and the whole context suggest that the intention exists. This is demonstrated by the tribunal's comments in *Bryan, Sabar Gul,* and *Chowdhury.* Where the application is for entry clearance the parties' statements and practical plans, such as the existence of accommodation, are probably the limit of necessary enquiry. The parties' motives for living together permanently are not a relevant matter. However, there seems to be a tendency to enquire into that motivation, and to raise other matters which are only relevant to primary purpose. For example, in *Chowdhury* there was enquiry into whether the couple had discussed before marriage where they should live. They had accommodation in the UK and so the existence of a home where they would live together was not in issue. In the case of *Hanif,* 'intervening devotion' was used to establish the credibility of the parties with regard to their intention. The investigation of 'intervening devotion' should have lapsed together with the requirement it was used to prove, that of primary purpose. It is not relevant to the intention to live together which may be formed, as was said in *Hoque and Singh,* 'after only a short acquaintance'. In so commenting the Court of Appeal was referring to the context of arranged marriages, which were most often the target of this rule. The same however might be said of a whirlwind romance in the western tradition. By examining motivation, decision makers open the way to limited conceptions of what is a valid motivation. As McKee points out (1999:5) 'money can be a more durable bond than romance in holding a marriage together, but there persists a notion that a marriage cannot be genuine if it does not fit into the Western convention of being entered into for love rather than money'.

Even within a single culture views of a valid motivation will vary. For instance, the Home Office has written to advisers, saying that sexual relations are not an essential component of a genuine marriage. At the same time too much sexual enthusiasm may also fall foul of what is considered a proper motivation for living together. McKee (1999:4) discusses a case in which there was fairly clear arrangement that the young woman would gain material advantages and the older man considerable sexual gratification. Both parties had an obvious motivation to live together permanently, but the adjudicator disapproved of it and upheld the refusal of entry clearance on the issue of intention to live together.

Aside from illustrating the futility and irrelevance of the search for a proper motivation there is a further point of importance in this case, which is that it would have failed the 'primary purpose' test, although the intention to live together is present. The point was made explicitly in the case of *Canas* (20557) INLP vol. 13(3) (1999) p. 109 that there can be intention to live together even when the primary purpose is to live in the UK. In such a case, entry clearance should be allowed. In *Alaezihe v ECO Dublin* [2002] UKIAT 01168 the tribunal overturned the adjudicator's decision because he had placed too much reliance on the appellant's adverse immigration history, from which he had gleaned an intention to come to the UK. This however was not the question. The appropriate question was, given that the parties were married, whether they had the intention to live together permanently. In so saying the tribunal followed the approach of the tribunal in *Gill v ECO New Delhi* 01/TH/02840 in which the adjudicator in considering motivation had moved close to applying the 'primary purpose' rule.

9.3.2.8 *Legal issues concerning marriage and divorce*

The final issue in relation to establishing marriage applications is the validity of the marriage, contained in the rules simply by the phrase in para 281 'is married'. This entails that the marriage be valid according to law and meet the requirements of the Immigration Rules. The validity of the marriage is adjudged at the date of the marriage. It is established by showing that both parties had the legal capacity to marry and that the celebration took place in accordance with appropriate formalities. The second of these requirements is the more straightforward to apply in law, although there may be practical difficulties in obtaining evidence. If the marriage is properly conducted according to the law of the country in which it is celebrated, its formal validity is accepted in English law. This means that in a country where same sex marriage is recognized, a properly conducted same-sex marriage will be recognized for immigration purposes.

The country in which the marriage is celebrated is usually where both parties are physically present. The only exception may be where the marriage is conducted by telephone. The guidance to ECOs DSP 13.10 says that in countries where marriage consists of an offer by a man accepted by a woman, a telephonic marriage is celebrated in the country where the woman is. Therefore where the wife is resident in the UK and the offer made from overseas, the marriage is considered as having been celebrated in the UK and so not valid in UK law.

This does not mean that if the husband were in the UK the marriage would be recognized, as although it may accord with the formalities of the country where it was celebrated, it may still fall foul of the rules on domicile (see below).

Aside from such rare situations, a marriage certificate is normally enough to prove formal validity. In *Babul* (16466) it was held that where a marriage certificate is produced which provides *prima facie* proof of a valid marriage, the party asserting that the marriage is not valid has the burden of proof to a high standard. If a finding were made that the marriage was not valid, this would raise the unresolved question of the effect of such a decision. It cannot be the case that an immigration judge has power to undo a marriage which has been entered into, whether lawfully or not. The appropriate course is surely to regard the marriage as invalid just for immigration purposes. This would have no bearing, for instance, on the couple's tax, benefits, or the legitimacy of their children. There would need to be a separate declaration under the Family Law Act 1986 to affect the marriage for any purpose other than immigration.

The issues which have a greater effect on the recognition of marriages in the UK are the questions of the legal capacity to enter into the marriage in question and the recognition of previous divorces.

Capacity

The capacity to marry is determined for each individual separately, and is governed by the law of the country which is their domicile. *Halsbury's Laws* (vol. 8(1) para 680) explains domicile in this way:

A person is domiciled in that country in which he [sic] either has or is deemed by law to have his permanent home. Every individual is regarded as belonging, at every stage in his life, to some community consisting of all persons domiciled in a particular country. . . . Although a person may have no permanent home, the law requires him to have a domicile.

Domicile differs from ordinary residence, in that a person may have more than one ordinary residence but not more than one domicile. Domicile may also differ from nationality and the personal civil law which applies to an individual is the law of their domicile. Domicile of origin is acquired at birth and is the domicile of the father for a child born inside marriage, of the mother for a child born outside marriage. *Cramer v Cramer* [1986] Fam Law 333 CA confirms an old rule that there is a strong presumption in favour of retaining one's domicile of origin. A domicile of choice is acquired by residence in a country where one intends to stay permanently. This intention must be proved by objective criteria. Statements of intention will not suffice. The House of Lords in *Mark v Mark* [2005] UKHL 42 held that if a person's presence is illegal in immigration law, this does not affect their domicile. The House of Lords made the distinction between a status which would give some benefit against the state, when illegality ought not to benefit an individual, and domicile, which is a private law matter and a question of fact. Domicile does not give an advantage against the state, but simply determines which legal system will govern private law matters, in this case, divorce proceedings.

The burden of proving that the domicile of origin has been lost rests on the person making this assertion. If they do not succeed in discharging the burden of proof, the domicile remains the domicile of origin.

To say that the law of a person's domicile governs their capacity to marry means that conditions for entering into a marriage, such as age and existing marital status, are according to that country's law. In *J (Pakistan)* [2003] UKIAT 00167 it was conceded that a telephonic marriage where the man was present and domiciled in the UK was not valid as the law of the UK governed his personal capacity to marry and does not recognize telephonic marriages. The claim under Article 8 also failed. The tribunal considered it settled law that an invalid marriage followed by a period of cohabitation may amount to family life attracting the protection of Article 8. Here, however, the sponsor was seriously disabled and could not travel to Pakistan. His mother did so, and his new wife went to live with his parents in Pakistan for three weeks. This, said the tribunal was 'of symbolic significance and reflects the fact that both the families regarded the couple as married' (para 4). However, this practice was not accepted by the Home Office, adjudicator or Tribunal as establishing family life.

The law of the UK requires that a person must be 16 years old and not married to anyone else in order to enter into a valid marriage. Although married partners need to be over 16 in order for the marriage to be valid, the age at which someone may sponsor their married partner was raised in 2002 to 18, and at which someone may enter as a married partner in 2004, also to 18 (HC 395 para 277). These changes were introduced as part of the Government's programme to prevent forced marriage (see, e.g., HO press release 330/2004). The Government's stated intention was to allow young people more time to mature and be able to resist family pressure to enter into a marriage they don't want. Of course, it does not actually prevent the marriage, which can take place at whatever age is allowed by law in the country where the marriage is celebrated. It only means that a married partner cannot enter the UK until they are 18, and a young person taken abroad to marry against their will cannot sponsor their married partner to come to the UK until they themselves are 18. In the February 2005 White Paper Cm 6472 the Government announced its willingness to rise the age further to 21 'if necessary' (para 38).

There is a longer history of cases concerning second wives.

Polygamy

Where a polygamous marriage has been validly entered into in another country, English law does not recognize it as valid where one party to the marriage is domiciled in the UK (Matrimonial Causes Act 1973 s 11(d)). *Hussain v Hussain* [1982] 3 All ER 369 CA found that this applied to the marriages of British women to men domiciled in countries that permitted polygamy and celebrated in that country, as they were potentially polygamous. The Private International Law (Miscellaneous Provisions) Act 1995 s 5 simplified the application of s 11(d) by providing that it only applies to *actually* polygamous marriages. The effect of this is that where the practical reality of the marriage is that it is monogamous it will be treated as such by UK law, wherever it is celebrated.

Where a marriage is in fact polygamous, if one of the parties is domiciled in the UK the marriage is void under s 11(d). If neither party is domiciled in the UK the validity of the polygamous marriage is recognized if it was recognized in the country where the parties are domiciled. However, this does not mean that a second wife will be able to join her husband in the UK. Paragraph 278 of the immigration rules prevents entry clearance from being granted to a wife where another wife of the same man has, since her marriage to him, visited the UK or been granted entry clearance or a certificate of entitlement. The rule is wider than Immigration Act 1988 s 2(2) which first removed rights of entry from second wives. The Act provided that women who had the right of abode by virtue of their marriage to a British citizen would not be able to exercise that right where there was another wife alive who had been to the UK since the marriage or had been granted entry clearance or a certificate of entitlement. Paragraph 278 applies whether or not the second wife has a right of abode. In *R v IAT ex p Hasna Begum* [1995] Imm AR 249 an earlier identical rule was challenged on the basis that it was ultra vires the 1988 Act. The challenge failed. Tucker J did not find any problem in the rules being wider than the Act, and rejected the idea that the 1988 Act was the source of the power to make the rules. This must be right, as the source of the power remains the principal Act, the 1971 Act. Also, rights of abode were statutory and could only be taken away by statute, whereas conditions of entry are set by the rules and can be changed by them.

These provisions illustrate the point made at the beginning of this chapter, that immigration law does not focus on the right of the settled person to be joined by their family, but on the status and circumstances of the proposed entrants. The passage of the 1988 Act caused a storm of criticism as the statutory rights of women abroad were taken away. The rules and case law exhibit a mixture of perspectives on the rights of women in these situations. In the case of *Bibi*, which endorsed the UK's prohibition on entry of a second wife, a further legitimate aim was identified in the case, that of 'the protection of rights of others', namely the first wives.

In the rule changes of October 2000, para 278 was amended to apply to both sexes. The prohibition is therefore now on the entry of further husbands as well as further wives.

Recognition of divorce

Because the UK does not recognize polygamy for people domiciled in the UK and does not permit entry of further married partners, no entry clearance will be granted where an earlier divorce is not recognized as the person will be regarded as still married to the previous married partner. The law in relation to recognition of divorces obtained in other countries is set out in the Family Law Act 1986 ss 44–54. A divorce obtained in a foreign jurisdiction will be recognized if it complies with the legal requirements of the country in which it was obtained, if it was obtained by proceedings, and provided either party was habitually resident, domiciled in or a national of the country in which it was obtained (Family Law Act 1986 s 46(1)). The majority of divorces obtained abroad are therefore recognized.

In an immigration context issues may sometimes arise as to the recognition of Islamic talaq divorce. Talaq pronounced in the UK will not be regarded as valid in the UK as within the jurisdiction divorce may only be granted by a civil court (see, for instance, *ECO Islamabad v Tanzeela Imran* [2002] UKIAT 07383). Talaq pronounced in an Islamic country is recognized in the UK if it is obtained by means of proceedings, or, if obtained without proceedings, neither party was habitually resident in the UK for one year before the divorce (Family Law Act 1986 s 46(2)). In an immigration case, however, usually one party has been resident in the UK, and so a divorce without proceedings is generally not recognized. Talaq may be validly obtained in Azad Kashmir without proceedings. Here, a 'bare' talaq, whereby a husband obtains dissolution of the marriage by making repeated declaration of divorce in the presence of witnesses, is recognized. Although this is permitted under Sharia (religious) law, the civil system of most countries imposes an additional requirement of legal proceedings. In Pakistan generally the Muslim Family Law Ordinance of 1961 requires proceedings, but this does not have force in Azad Kashmir. A requirement of the Muslim Family Law Ordinance is registration of the talaq with the Union Council. The divorce then becomes effective in Pakistani civil law after a period allowed for reconciliation. A talaq so registered will then be recognized in UK law but not otherwise (for a dispute on evidence of this see *Niaz Parveen v ECO Islamabad* 01/BH/0061). This should be distinguished from the situation in *Naseem Akhtar* (15412) INLP vol. 12(1) (1998), p. 30 where there had been ancillary proceedings carried out after the divorce. These could not convert a bare talaq into a talaq by proceedings.

The tribunal in *Baig v ECO Islamabad* [2002] UKIAT 04229 gave a starred decision in which it laid down guidance as to the proper approach to be taken to ascertaining whether a divorce was obtained by proceedings. In so doing the tribunal made an important distinction between tradition and proceedings. The talaq in question in this case was not a bare talaq, but a talaq al-hasan, which entailed formal declarations of divorce at monthly intervals. The appellant argued that this was by way of proceedings as it entailed more ritual and process than a bare talaq. The tribunal said, however, that talaq al-hasan

lacks any formality other than the ritual performance. It lacks the invocation or assistance of any organ of the state. It does not even require an organ of the state to act as a registrar or recorder of what has happened. (para 39)

Accordingly, it was regarded as a purely personal act and not a divorce obtained by proceedings. The tribunal's decision to give the case a starred status was no doubt influenced by a perception of its particular contemporary relevance, which arose from a trend in Pakistan towards recognition of a bare talaq as fully effective. This trend had been noted in argument for the appellant as a reason to recognize the talaq al-husan. The tribunal gave this argument a rather startling twist. If Pakistan developed the recognition of divorce without proceedings this would not influence English law. Rather, the opposite would be the case, and English law would become reluctant to recognize Pakistani divorces. In this rather forceful response it is possible to see a significant underlying debate about increasing Islamic influence in civil matters and the limits and possibilities of pluralism.

If a person is not free to marry another, their application to enter as a married partner cannot be treated as an application to enter as a fiancé(e) and granted on that basis (*ECO Islamabad v Mohammad Rafiq Khan* 01/TH 2798 and *ECO Islamabad v Shakeel* [2002] UKIAT 00605). These cases were distinguished from the earlier authority of *Ach-Charki* [1991] Imm AR 162 as in that case the parties had been free to marry by the time of the tribunal hearing.

These questions of the recognition of marriage and divorce have consequences for the recognition of the legitimacy of children born to those marriages and consequently their entitlement to come to the UK. This will be the final subject considered in this section.

Legitimacy

Where a marriage is valid at the time of a child's conception, the child is legitimate wherever the marriage was celebrated. So the child born in Bangladesh of a couple domiciled in Bangladesh and married according to the laws of that country is legitimate, including when the marriage is polygamous (see, e.g., *Taslima Begum v ECO Dhaka* [2002] UKIAT 06644 where the father was a British citizen and as a consequence of that, his children acquired British citizenship by descent and so a right of abode in the UK (see chapter 2)).

Where a marriage is considered void in English law, the children of that marriage are not regarded as legitimate unless, at the time of their conception, one of their parents believed that the marriage was valid (Legitimacy Act 1976 s 1). In *Azad v ECO Dhaka* [2001] Imm AR 318 the Court of Appeal held that this must mean a belief in its validity in English law. In that case the father, who was domiciled in the UK, was aware that his marriage was not recognized, but there was no evidence as to the state of mind of the mother. Therefore it was held that there was no evidence of a 'belief' as that was a positive state of mind, not just an absence of belief in the marriage's invalidity. The effect for children born after 4 April 1988 was mitigated by the introduction of a presumption of a belief in the validity of the marriage. This may be displaced if lack of belief is proved (Family Law Reform Act 1987 s 28). This was the argument advanced by counsel for the appellant in *Azad* and is surely a more satisfactory situation. The result of *Azad* is to require people to hold positive beliefs about legal provisions in another country, not something to which most people would naturally pay attention.

The effect of the provisions above is that where a man is domiciled in the UK, his children by later marriages are not regarded as legitimate and so are not British citizens by descent and have no right of abode in the UK. This has the perverse consequence that a man who intends to make the UK his permanent home may not, as of right, bring in his children by later marriages, whereas one who intends to return to his country of origin may do so. This effect is mitigated by the amendment to the Legitimacy Act, and all minors now benefit from this presumption.

The Nationality, Immigration and Asylum Act 2002 s 9 makes a further welcome reform in this area, inserting into the British Nationality Act 1981 a new s 50(9)A which provides that a child's father includes 'the husband, at the time of the child's birth, of the woman who gives birth to the child'. This means that nationality law moves into conformity with family law, treating such a child as a child of the family, even if it turns out that the child actually has a different natural father. When this section comes into force it will remove the stigma for children such as Taslima Begum in the case of that name, who could not obtain entry to the UK when her siblings could, as DNA tests showed she was not her father's daughter.

9.3.3 Limited leave to enter

If all the above conditions are met, a married partner is given leave to enter the UK (or remain) for two years (HC 395 paras 282 and 285). As this is a period of limited leave it may be subject to conditions, and since 8 November 1996 it is routinely subject to the condition not to have recourse to public funds. The power to impose this condition was inserted by Asylum and Immigration Appeals Act 1996 Sch 2, para 1(1) into Immigration Act 1971 s 3(1) and is in theory a substantial power which the Home Office has over a newly arrived entrant. Breach of a condition is a criminal offence and potentially a basis for removal. However, a policy statement by the Home Office made in a letter from David Waddington MP to Max Madden MP states: 'We would not use this power if a person had become dependent on public funds for a short time through no fault of his own.' Although this statement was made in December 1985 in relation to complying with the requirements for entry rather than as a condition, in practice it is also followed where the condition is attached.

Additionally, the Social Security (Persons from Abroad) Miscellaneous Amendment Regulations 1996 removed entitlement to non-contributory benefits from people with limited leave, such as married partners in their first two years.

9.3.4 Indefinite leave to remain

At the end of the two-year period, the married partner must apply for indefinite leave to remain. The requirements to be met to qualify for indefinite leave are set out in para 287 of the rules. Since 1 September 1996 (Cm 3365), this includes that they can be accommodated and maintained without recourse to public funds. It follows that they may not rely substantially on public funds for long periods after the married partner's arrival as this would undermine their case for meeting this requirement, unless there was a dramatic change in circumstances.

The remaining conditions are that the marriage is subsisting and that they still intend to live permanently with one another as their married partner. The married partner who is settled is required to confirm that this is the case and must be present in the UK when the application is made, although a necessary temporary absence may be explained.

Once indefinite leave is granted the married partner from abroad is free to claim benefits in their own right. They are free of immigration restrictions on their stay, and may come and go freely, subject to the requirements of para 18 of the rules (see chapter 6). Note that having indefinite leave to remain is not the same as citizenship. After three years of residence as a married partner they may apply to become a British citizen (British Nationality Act 1981 s 6 and Sch 1, amended by Civil Partnership Act 2004 Sch 27 para 72) but until they acquire that citizenship the married partner with indefinite leave may, if they fall foul of the criminal law, be recommended by a court for deportation (Immigration Act 1971 s 3(5)) and may not vote unless they are a commonwealth citizen (Representation of the People Act 1983). See chapters 2 and 6 on naturalization and settlement.

9.3.5 Extending leave

As mentioned earlier, a person with limited leave under some other categories of the immigration rules may apply to stay after the end of that leave as a married partner (para 284). The White Paper *Secure Borders, Safe Haven* (Cm 5387) expressed doubts about the genuineness of marriages entered into by people who had been in the UK for less than six months (para 7.11). Consequent rule changes ended the possibility of extending leave to stay as a married partner for those granted six months' leave or less. This affects visitors and prospective students (though not actual students). In addition to the conditions for entry clearance, and the condition of having limited leave, a person wishing to remain as a married partner must not have remained in breach of immigration laws. Where a person who is an illegal entrant or has overstayed, marries in the UK and wishes to stay, their application may be considered in accordance with Article 8 and Home Office Policy document DP 3/96. For a full account of this policy, see chapter 17. In a similar vein, the marriage must not have taken place after a decision to deport or remove or after a recommendation for deportation has been made.

Paragraph 285 provides that an applicant for an extension of stay as a married partner may be granted two years in the first instance, placing them on a similar footing to a married partner who comes directly from abroad. Immigration Act 1971 s 3(1)(c) also applies, giving a power to impose a condition that there be no recourse to public funds during the probationary period.

The grant of indefinite leave after an initial two years, whether following leave to enter or leave to remain, is expressed to be a discretion. In practice indefinite leave will be granted where the conditions are met. The discretion however gives scope to grant a further extension where there may be some doubt about the fulfilment of conditions, instead of refusing the application.

9.3.6 Domestic violence and bereavement

On the basis of the rules above an incoming married partner would have no claim to remain where the marriage broke down in the first two years or their partners died. This has caused particular anguish to those bereaved and to women who were subject to violence from their husband in the probationary period. The latter group could safely neither stay in their marriage nor leave it, particularly if return to their country of origin might be financially or socially impossible. On 16 June 1999 concessions were announced in Parliament which permitted applicants in this position to apply for indefinite leave to remain, if the violence or bereavement occurred whilst the marriage was subsisting and if specified evidence was produced. From 2 October 2000 the concession on bereavement was incorporated into the rules at para 287 (b), and from 18 December 2002 (HC 538) the substance of the concession concerning violence was included at para 289A.

The domestic violence concession has been applied quite strictly. For instance where there was a delay in applying for indefinite leave to remain and the marriage broke down due to violence before the application was processed, the concession could not be relied upon because the breakdown had occurred after the probationary period, as in *R v SSHD ex p Mckenzie* [2002] Imm AR 94. The prescribed kind of evidence was also lacking in this case, although there was reliable evidence of the violence. As the terms of the policy were not fulfilled the applicant was refused indefinite leave to remain. She sought to have the policy declared unlawful, but the High Court declined to do so. Just because some meritorious cases were excluded this did not make the policy unlawful.

9.4 Abuse of the institution of marriage and civil partnerships

As discussed at the beginning of this chapter, the intervention of immigration law in personal relationships is something which raises strong emotions, bringing regulation by the state into an intimate area of human life. The basic framework of the present rules on relationships was set more than 20 years ago in a climate of suspicion, and in the last few years there has been a new era of law-making, intervening directly in the actual ceremonies which take place in the UK.

As discussed in chapter 7, the Immigration and Asylum Act 1999 s.24 placed a duty on registrars to report to the Secretary of State any marriage which they have reasonable grounds for suspecting will be a 'sham marriage'. This duty arises if the suspicion is formed before, during, or immediately after the marriage or civil partnership, or (though it is difficult to imagine how reasonable suspicion could be founded upon documentation) upon receiving notice of the intended marriage. A 'sham marriage' is defined in s 24(5) as one which is entered into by a person 'who is neither a British Citizen nor a national of an EEA state other than the UK . . . for the purpose of avoiding the effect of one or more provisions of the UK immigration law or rules'.

The section does not authorize the registrar to refuse to perform the marriage, which must in any subsequent legal action be treated as lawful and valid unless declared otherwise in proceedings under Family Law Act 1986 s 55.

The 'sham marriage' is one entered into 'for the purpose of' immigration advantage. This could indicate that immigration must be the sole purpose of the marriage for the registrar to form such a suspicion. This interpretation is to be preferred, but it is also possible to read it as meaning that immigration avoidance is one among a number of purposes, which would make this provision more wide ranging than the primary purpose rule. The same Act removed in-country rights of appeal against removal for people obtaining leave to remain by deception (s 10), leaving only a human rights appeal for an individual to argue for their marriage in the UK. In Parliamentary debate in the House of Lords the Minister for the Home Office revealed that numbers of reports by registrars had doubled after the provisions came into force, but less than 5 per cent of these reports resulted in arrests, and only about one third of arrests resulted in criminal charges being brought. The number of convictions secured is not mentioned. In addition, an unspecified number of people were removed from the UK.

In 2005 regulations were introduced under Asylum and Immigration (Treatment of Claimants etc) Act 2004 ss 19–25 which affect the marriage of all non-EEA nationals in the UK, whatever their immigration status. The Immigration (Procedure for Marriage) Regulations 2005, SI 2005/15 and the Registration of Marriages (Amendment) Regulations 2005, SI 2005/155 prescribe seventy-six registry offices at which people subject to immigration control must give notice of marriage, in person, with their partner. The marriage itself need not take place there. This element of the new provisions is potentially an inconvenience; however, more intrusive is the second provision, which is that any non EEA national who is not settled in the UK (SI 2005/15 reg 6) or does not have entry clearance specifically for marriage (2004 Act ss 19(3)(a), 21(3)(a), 23(3)(a)) must obtain the consent of the Secretary of State before marrying and pay £135 for a certificate of approval (reg 8). If both parties need consent, each must obtain (and pay for) a certificate of approval. The Parliamentary Joint Committee on Human Rights considered that this was likely to 'be incompatible with the right to marry because it introduces restrictions on that right for wide class of people which are disproportionate to the legitimate aim of preventing sham marriages and which may impair the very essence of the right' (para 68 JCHR Fourteenth Report session 2003–4). The provisions engage not only Article 12 but also Article 14. Because the provisions apply only to marriages performed by registrars, there is in effect an exemption for Church of England marriages; the provisions therefore discriminate unjustifiably on grounds of religion or belief, and on grounds of nationality.

These provisions apply to non-visa nationals who marry in the UK but do not intend to make their home here. So for instance a New Zealander, who decides to celebrate their marriage in the UK perhaps for family reasons must make that decision before they enter the UK, so that they can obtain a marriage visit visa. Otherwise the registrar must decline to accept notice of their marriage.

As set out by the IDIs, the guidance on granting a certificate of approval creates a system of even more draconian controls than the statute. The guidance requires that the applicant has extant leave of at least three months. This does not cater for the plans of, for instance, a student who plans to marry at the end of their student leave, and it may invalidate plans that were within the law when made. This and other aspects of the scheme make immigration status a determinant of whether a person may exercise the civil and personal right to marry. Clearly, asylum seekers fall outside this provision as the majority have no leave. They are catered for as 'exceptional', requiring 'compassionate circumstances' to be shown as to why they should not return to their home country and marry there or apply for entry clearance as a married partner. The reasons for this in the case of asylum seekers do not need spelling out and are not, of course, exceptional. The Home Office guidance is that 'where possible' the asylum claim should be decided before a certificate of approval is given for marriage. Where the asylum claim is refused, the certificate of approval should be refused, *even if an appeal is lodged*. Contrariwise, if the decision or appeal has been outstanding for more than 18 months, then consideration may be given to granting a certificate of approval. Of course, if the wait is now for an appeal the certificate may have been turned down long ago. There is no right of appeal against refusal of a certificate.

The drop in notices of marriage was reported as evidence that those who have not applied would have been entering sham marriages (BBC news, 25 April 2005). However, it is clear that under these provisions asylum seekers have no right to marry, as the burden is on them to show *exceptional* reasons why they should not return to their home country to do so. They may therefore think £135 too much to pay for an application which at worst may prevent them marrying *and* expedite a refusal of their asylum claim. The Churches Commission for Racial Justice found that people had entered into non-Christian religious marriages, then been denied a certificate of approval of their registry office marriage, but not been notified of this. They were detained by an immigration officer waiting at the registry office for that marriage ceremony (Response by the Churches' Commission for Racial Justice to the UK Government's document: *Controlling Our Borders: Making Migration Work for Britain. Five-year strategy for asylum and immigration*).

From 5 December 2005 all the above provisions applied, *mutatis mutandis*, to civil partners registering under the Civil Partnership Act 2004.

On 10 April 2006 the High Court held that the interference with the right to marry was disproportionate, and there was unjustified discrimination on grounds of religion and nationality (*R (Baiai, Bigoku & Tilki) v SSHD* [2006] EWHC 823 (Admin).

9.5 Unmarried partners

The law on admission of unmarried partners has had a turbulent history. It is contentious as it raises moral and social issues, which, in the context of immigration, readily become political. Setting aside polygamy, some couples are not able to marry in UK law. This may be because they are related too closely, or too young, or married to someone else and unable to get a divorce, or, prior to 5 December 2005, because they are the same sex. Sound health and social reasons are thought by UK Governments to justify prohibiting marriage between those regarded as too young or too closely related, and no concessions are made in immigration law to accommodating such relationships. Attitudes are more variable in relation to those who are married or of the same sex, and in addition to those who have no choice there are a high number of heterosexual couples who choose not to marry. While the law may refuse to ratify a relationship, there are also human rights issues involved in denying family life to couples who, for whatever reason, are not married. The admission of unmarried partners did not obtain a stable place in the immigration rules until 2 October 2000. The previous rule was abolished in 1985, and unmarried partners since then had been considered only under concessions. These are more vulnerable to withdrawal and indeed in February 1996 the then concession which only allowed entry for heterosexual couples, was withdrawn in response to pressure from Stonewall and other civil libertarian groups to extend the concession to gay and lesbian couples. A new concession was granted with effect from 13 October 1997, as part of the programme of the new Labour Government. This one included same sex couples, but also contained a new and onerous requirement, that the couple show four years' cohabitation in a relationship prior to marriage before the application. Where by definition one partner is settled in the UK and the other not this presented obvious obstacles. The concession was amended on 17 June 1999 to reduce the period of cohabitation to two years. It also required that the couple should be able to show a legal obstacle to marriage and granted a two-year probationary period. It was the terms of this concession which became the new rule on 2 October 2000 (HC 395 para 295A). There was further consideration of the discrimination between married and unmarried partners and the White Paper *Secure Borders Safe Haven* para 7.8 announced an intention to remove the distinction. This was carried out in the April 2003 rule changes which abolished the requirement for a legal obstacle to marriage. By changing the probationary period for married partners to two years the Government achieved greater parity between the married and the unmarried. The only differences now are that an unmarried couple, whether same or different sexes, must show that any previous marriage or comparable relationship has broken down, they must have lived together for two years before applying for entry, and that they are not so closely related that the law would prevent their marriage. Where they have lived together for four years the applicant partner will be able to gain immediate settlement as married partners do.

The IDI May 2003 Ch 8 s 7 Annex Z para 2 concedes 'short breaks apart would be acceptable for good reason, such as work commitments or looking after a relative'. They suggest that up to six months spent in this fashion would be acceptable providing it was clear that the relationship continued throughout the period. Visiting often will not amount to cohabitation, but the cohabitation does not have to have been in one country, and there does not need to be an established joint home if they have, for instance, been living alternately at each other's separate homes.

Other requirements for unmarried partners such as the present and settled sponsor, accommodation and maintenance, are as for married couples and are interpreted in the same way.

The relationship is protected by Article 8 ECHR. In *Marckxx v Belgium* (1979) 2 EHRR 330 the ECtHR held that there should be no discrimination between the married and unmarried in relation to the status of their children, though, as discussed in chapter 3, some underlying discrimination may well continue between heterosexual and same sex couples in that the latter are regarded as enjoying private rather than family life. Since *Fitzpatrick v Sterling Housing Association Ltd* [1999] UKHL 42, *Mendoza v Ghaidan* [2003] 2 WLR 478 and the Civil Partnership Act 2004 this distinction is not supportable in UK law.

9.6 **Fiancé(e)s**

Finally, it is possible for an individual who is not yet married but engaged to be married to a settled person to apply for entry clearance as a fiancé(e). The requirements are set out in para 290 of the rules. They are as for a married partner except that they refer to the situation after the marriage, and in place of an existing valid marriage is the requirement that the fiancé(e) is seeking leave to enter *for* marriage to a settled person. The rules for fiancé(e)s have also been amended throughout to include civil partners.

Partly because of the waiting time involved between application and decision, it may happen that the marriage takes place after the application but before the decision has been made. In this case, if the entry clearance officer is informed that the marriage has taken place, the application will proceed as a married partner application. If the marriage takes place after a fiancé(e)'s application has been refused but before an appeal has been heard, how it is treated may depend on how far the appeal has proceeded. When an appeal is lodged the entry clearance officer would normally review the case when they receive the grounds of appeal. If they have received notice of the marriage by then, they may choose to treat this as a fresh application for entry clearance for a married partner. The case can then be reconsidered on this basis. Otherwise, the fact of the marriage will be relevant at the appeal hearing to the intention of the parties.

If a fiancé(e) application succeeds, leave is granted to enter the UK for a period of six-months, during which time the marriage must take place, and there is a prohibition on working (para 291). Leave is also conditional on not having recourse to public funds. If the marriage does not take place during the six-month period a further extension 'for an appropriate period' (para 294) may be granted to enable the marriage to take place, provided the Home Office is satisfied that there is good cause for the delay, there is satisfactory evidence that the marriage will take place at an early date, and all the other conditions for leave to enter continue to be met (para 293).

9.7 **Other adult relatives**

9.7.1 **Admissible relatives**

Other adult relatives may be admitted for settlement if they qualify under para 317 of the rules. The relationship by which their admissibility is determined is their relationship to the sponsor. Those relatives admissible are limited to:

(i)   widowed parents or grandparents aged 65 or over;
(ii) parents or grandparents travelling together at least one of who is 65 or over;
(iii) a parent or grandparent aged 65 or over who has remarried or entered into a second civil partnership but cannot look to the married partner or children of the second relationship for financial support; and
(iv) a parent or grandparent under the age of 65, or son, daughter, sister, brother, uncle, or aunt over the age of 18 if living alone in the most exceptional compassionate circumstances and mainly dependent financially on relatives settled in the UK.

Other relatives may be considered outside the rules, but only where there is a close emotional bond and very strong compassionate circumstances.

9.7.2 **Financial dependency**

Parents and grandparents over 65 must be 'financially wholly or mainly dependent' on the sponsor. Those applying on the basis of the most compassionate circumstances need only show that they are financially wholly or mainly dependent on relatives settled in the UK, not necessarily the sponsor. This gives some scope for responsibility for financial support to be shared and still come within the rules.

Case law has established that the dependency must be a necessary one. The requirement has survived despite a challenge to this judge-made law in *Chavda v ECO Bombay* [1978] Imm AR 40 that the rules should be given their ordinary everyday meaning (following *Brutus v Cozens* [1972] 1 WLR 484) and should not be open to having further provisos inserted into them. In declining to accept this argument the court referred to the purposive construction, a fairly recently adopted principle at that time in relation to the rules. The court's reasoning is revealing: 'the question of dependency has to be construed in the context of immigration control. The question of genuineness runs through all the immigration regulations . . . dependants have to show their genuine need.' The difficulty of importing a test of necessary dependence is that it then depends on a judgment as to what is necessary, and this brings decision-makers once again into the arena of making judgments about matters which may vary between cultures.

This was illustrated in the case which established the test of 'necessary dependence', *Zaman v ECO Lahore* [1973] Imm AR 71. Here, an elderly farmer and his wife were refused entry clearance to join their son in the UK. They were financially dependent upon him because Mr Zaman gave the modest income from the farms to his sons who were still resident in Pakistan, in accordance with custom. The tribunal held that their dependence was not necessary. This case contrasts with *ECO New Delhi v Malhan* [1978] Imm AR 209. In this case the familial duty described perhaps came nearer to the tribunal's idea of family responsibilities. The appellant's eldest son had voluntarily taken over her main support. He had done this out of a desire to fulfil his moral obligations. The tribunal held that she was entitled to look to him for support. She should not be compelled to look to 'more distant' relatives (her brother and father).

The question also arises: what steps to maximize income is it reasonable to expect the applicant to take? In *Chavda* itself the appeals of the widow and her daughter were allowed. It was accepted that she was not in a position to compel her three sons who lived with her to work, so from her point of view the dependency on her eldest son in the UK was a necessary and not a contrived one. Where the sons could clearly get work this might have been different, as in *Hasan v ECO Bombay* [1976] Imm AR 28. In *Piara Singh* (19579) INLP vol. 13 (3) (1999), p. 107 elderly parents had a spare room which they kept for visits by family members. It was held by the majority of the tribunal that they should not be expected to let this out in order to reduce their financial dependency on the sponsor.

In *Bibi v ECO Dhaka* [2000] Imm AR 385 the Court of Appeal confirmed that financial dependency may be in the form of money or money's worth. If someone had their need for accommodation, clothing, food, and other necessities provided in kind, they were financially dependent on the person who made this provision for them. In this case the appellant lived with her son and daughter-in-law and their children, and was applying to join another son in the UK who sent money regularly to the family. The money was used mainly for the children's education. The Court of Appeal found that the true situation was that the family had some dependency on the proposed sponsor, but the appellant was dependent on the family she lived with, not on her son in the UK. The principle therefore is that the applicant must be directly financially dependent on the sponsor.

9.7.3 No close relatives to turn to

A further requirement of the rules is that the applicant must be without close relatives in their own country to whom they can turn for financial support. A leading judgment on the meaning of 'close relatives to turn to' was given by Dillon LJ in the Court of Appeal in the case of *R v IAT ex p Swaran Singh* [1987] 1 WLR 1394. He read the phrase 'as importing "to turn to in case of need" — any sort of need which may afflict elderly parents'. He gave examples of illness or accident and said that the rule was one of 'broad humanity'. It should be so regarded in the future even though in some cases it had not been in the past. Family relationships should be borne in mind, and where relatives are hostile or unwilling to help they are clearly not relatives to turn to. However, while *Swaran Singh* continues to be an authority that the rule is one of broad humanity, the need referred to in this part of the rule is no longer 'any sort of need which may afflict elderly parents'. HC 395 changed the rule so that it is financial support which is in issue, here as in the previous part of the rule.

In a more recent case the tribunal has found that the issue of dependency and no close relative to turn to are 'two sides of the same coin'. Where a person was found to be dependent as of necessity on the sponsor, this would normally mean that there was no other close relative to whom they could turn (*Parekh* (14016) INLP vol. 11 (2) (1997), p. 73).

The case of *ECO Islamabad v Rehmat Bi* (16074) March 1998 Legal Action provides useful guidance on identifying financial dependency and whether there is a another close relative the applicant can turn to. It suggests that both requirements should be assessed by starting with the needs of the applicant. In *Rehmat Bi* the applicant's needs were for repairs to her house, frequent contact with her son, medical treatment, and assistance with her mobility. Her son funded the repairs, the cost of telephone calls between them and his own air fares and arranged the medical treatment. When he was there he gave her the practical assistance which she needed to get around. He had also paid for his father's funeral. She was emotionally dependent on him. In *R v IAT ex p Bastiampillai* [1983] 2 All ER 844 the court had held that where there was emotional dependency, this might tip the balance to show that dependency existed. In *Rehmat Bi*, the tribunal took the approach that where meeting needs could be done by financial outlay, as here, the applicant was probably dependent as of necessity on the person who met the expense, and this could include meeting emotional needs such as for contact with her son.

The IDI Chapter 8 s 6 para 3.2 says that where applicants are over 65, detailed inquiries are not usually necessary, though sponsorship must be assured. Annex V advises that applications should not be refused from married couples solely on the grounds that they have each other to turn to. 'Account should be taken of the age and health of the applicants as well as the ability of other relatives to visit them regularly.'

9.7.4 Living alone in the most exceptional compassionate circumstances

This part of the rule provides the only possibility for entry for adult relatives who are under 65. 'Living alone in the most exceptional compassionate circumstances' is a further condition which must be met in addition to the others. Being financially dependent on a relative in the UK and having no other close relatives to turn to are not regarded as exceptional compassionate circumstances in themselves (*Nessa* (16391) INLP vol. 13(2) (1999), p. 75). This means that families may be kept apart because there is nothing exceptional that would unite them. Indeed the whole of paragraph 317 to a lesser degree creates an obstacle to the enjoyment of family life. However, the Court of Appeal has held that it is not a breach of Article 8 for the government 'to confine the circumstances in which dependent relatives of persons living in the United Kingdom are permitted indefinite leave to enter in the way that they have done in paragraph 317' (*Husna Begum* para 12).

Living alone does not always require that there is literally no other person in the home, but that anyone who is there is not able to meet the needs of the applicant. Severe mental or physical disabilities without the necessary care being available will normally be regarded as the most exceptional compassionate circumstances (e.g., *Visa Officer Islamabad v Sindhu* [1978] Imm AR 147). The circumstances may have arisen since the applicant's arrival in the UK, if they have been here for instance on a visit. This was found to be the case in *Alyha Begum* (17162) INLP vol. 13 (3) (1999), p. 107 where in the applicant's absence her brothers in law had been taking away her possessions, and she would be isolated if she returned.

A former version of the rule made specific provision for widowed mothers. This one does not. In the case of *Akhtar Bi v ECO Islamabad* 01/BH/0002 the appellant was in this position, her sons and daughter having moved to the UK. The chair of the tribunal did not consider that she met the requirements of the rule because her situation was like that of any widowed mother whose children have left, and therefore while her sadness was very understandable her situation was not exceptional. The other two members of the tribunal found that her situation was exceptional because owing to a combination of circumstances she had had at least one of her children with her for most of her life until a few months before this application. She therefore faced living alone for the first time at the age of 57.

There are broadly two approaches taken to this rule. One is following *Swaran Singh* referred to above, construing the rule as one of 'broad humanity' and which therefore should not be interpreted in a strict and literal way. The other, referred to in a later Court of Appeal case, *Zohra Begum* [1994] Imm AR 381, requires that each word should be given its full value. The chairman in *Akhtar Bi* could be regarded as following the latter approach, and the other two members the former. The two are of equal authority. It was argued unsuccessfully in *Sayania v IAT and SSHD* CO/3136/2000 that Article 8 required the broad approach.

There are difficulties about how the effect of the financial support of the sponsor is considered to affect the applicant's situation. The Court of Appeal in *Zohra Begum* held that the rule should not be interpreted as if the sponsor's contribution was not there. On the other hand, the tribunal in *Nessa Bibi v ECO Dhaka* (21162A) may have gone too far in regarding the applicant's sound financial circumstances provided by the sponsor as an indication that she was not living in exceptional compassionate circumstances.

Like widowed mothers, unmarried daughters under 21 also were specifically included in a former version of the rule, and like widowed mothers, their applications must now show that they are living alone in the most exceptional compassionate circumstances. In *Husna Begum* the Court of Appeal found in favour of a woman of 22, all of whose immediate family were now in the UK apart from her brother who had entry clearance to travel. Evidence suggested that as a young single woman in rural Bangladesh she would be isolated and at risk. This could not be generalized to all women in this position, as each case must be decided on its facts. In *Sayania* a young woman left alone in India did not succeed in the High Court in quashing the refusal of leave to appeal to the tribunal. Burnton J did not think that Article 8 assisted or that her lonely position could bring her within the rule. The IDI Chapter 8 s 6 is to a similar effect, saying that the situation of such a woman may be taken into account, but does not of itself bring her within the rule.

9.7.5 Terms of stay for a successful relative

Entry clearance for dependent relatives will function as leave to enter and remain indefinitely providing the entry clearance is endorsed that it is to have that effect (Immigration (Leave to Enter and Remain) Order 2000, SI 2000/1161). There is no probationary period.

Maintenance and accommodation requirements have already been discussed above and must be met in order for the application to succeed. Despite the apparent scope in the rules for sharing responsibility, in practice the sponsor will be placed in a position of liability for the relative's support, and the IDI goes further by saying that joint sponsorship is not allowed (Ch 8 s 6). Paragraph 35 of the rules gives power to immigration authorities to require the sponsor to sign an undertaking that they will be responsible to their relative's maintenance. The effect of this is to disbar the sponsored relative from any claim to key means-tested benefits for five years from the date of admission to the UK. The benefits affected are income support, income-based jobseeker's allowance, housing benefit, and council tax benefit (Social Security (Persons from Abroad) Miscellaneous Amendment Regulations 1996). If the relative does make a claim, the Social Security Administration Act 1992 and the Social Security Administration (Northern Ireland) Act 1992 empower the paying authorities to recover any income support from the person who gave the undertaking. Refusal by the sponsor to give an undertaking is a discretionary ground for refusal of entry clearance under para 320.

An undertaking is a formal document. In *Ahmed v Secretary of State for Work and Pensions* [2005] EWCA Civ 535 the Court of Appeal held that a statement by the sponsor that he was 'able and willing' to maintain and accommodate his uncle was a statement of his then circumstances designed to show to the entry clearance officer that the requirements for granting entry clearance were met. These words did not amount to an undertaking, which was a solemn promise for the future. Formal undertakings often also stated liabilities which could be incurred for breach, though this was not essential. The sponsor's uncle therefore was not debarred from a claim for backdated benefit on the grounds of being a person who had leave to enter the UK 'as a result of a maintenance undertaking' (Immigration and Asylum Act 1999 s 115).

9.8 Children

9.8.1 Introduction

The immigration rules on entry of children to the UK are only one aspect of law which affects children in an immigration context. The rights of parents to enter to visit a child in the UK, private international law provisions concerning abduction, custody, and adoption all have a bearing on children's lives as well as complex nationality rules. For instance, a child born in the US to American and Canadian parents enters the UK as a baby with her mother after a separation, but no divorce. Ten years later, she wants to go abroad with her school. On what kind of passport can she travel? Children are also affected by rules on legitimacy, on entitlement to education and may go into care so that public child care law is involved. This leaves out of account all the special problems faced by child asylum seekers.

It may be seen from this that the law relating to children and immigration cannot be considered fully in isolation. This is an area of increasing complexity now warranting special texts (see, for instance, Coker, Finch, and Stanley 2002). This section is therefore limited in its aim and scope. It aims to explain some of the particular immigration rules relating to children in a way that illustrates the relationship between what might be broadly categorized as a 'family law approach' and an 'immigration law approach'. The focus is on rules relating to entry of children.

What is meant by a 'family law approach' here is one which pays attention to the quality of relationships and in particular the welfare of the child. Those versed in family law will be familiar with the welfare principle found in Children Act 1989 s 1, which says that when the court is making any decision about the upbringing of a child, 'the child's welfare shall be the court's paramount consideration'. A similar principle is found in Adoption and Children Act 2001 s 1. What is meant here by an 'immigration law approach' is one which focuses on control of entry to the UK. The Court of Appeal in *In re S (Children) (Abduction: Asylum Appeal)* [2003] Imm AR 52 drew attention to the need for co-ordination between the family courts and the immigration authorities including tribunals. Such co-ordination may be difficult to achieve when the underlying purposes are not always consistent with each other. Neither are they always in direct conflict.

Clearly, whether a child is permitted to move to a different country, which may entail living with different relatives, or being adopted, a decision is being made about the upbringing of the child. The welfare principle does not appear in the immigration rules, and the judgment of the Court of Appeal is that the welfare of the child is not paramount in immigration matters (*R v SSHD ex p Gangadeen* [1998] Imm AR 106). Although not to overstate the case, it is a primary consideration which must inform decisions, and must be balanced against other interests (*R v SSHD ex p Ahmed and Patel* [1999] Imm AR 22).

The High Court decision in *R v SSHD ex p Mobin Jagot* [2000] INLR 501 reveals that different outcomes may be indicated by these two approaches. Mobin had spent most of his childhood in the UK with his grandparents, and had never had an easy relationship with his parents in Malawi. When his other grandmother was terminally ill he was sent to Malawi to visit her and, at the age of 12, was refused entry on his return. He appealed the refusal and as this appeal took place in the UK, it was in practice not only in order to obtain leave but also against removal. The policy guidance DP069/99 required 'strong reasons' to justify removal of a child who had spent a substantial and formative part of his life in the UK. The Home Office advanced the possibility of family life with his parents as such a strong reason. It pointed out that his parents were wealthy enough to look after him. Moses J ordered the Secretary of State to reconsider.

The Secretary of State's refusal letter is quoted extensively in the judgment of Moses J. The quoted extract begins: 'the change in policy relates specifically to deportation and illegal entry cases, and not to on-entry, port cases, such as your client's' (para 13).

From the point of view of the child's welfare there can be little difference between whether the child is to be prevented from resuming life where he has lived it for more than seven years, or sent away from where he has lived for seven years. However, in terms of the immediate experience, for a 12 year old to be told unexpectedly by strangers that he cannot return home is, one might guess, more traumatic than leaving home with his whole family. The refusal letter places importance on the fact that Mobin had just spent four months with his parents. The fact that this was not his own choice but was a family duty and that he had run up a £1,000 phone bill to his grandparents reveals how he felt about being there. However, what we are loosely calling the immigration approach is more concerned with financial viability. There is a pervasive concern with financial support and non-reliance on public funds. Evidence that a person has done something is evidence that they can do it. It is therefore a viable alternative to entry to the UK, eligibility for which has to be proved. The quality of relevant relationships does not feature highly in the rules or policies.

In a family law context it is unthinkable that the wishes and experiences of a competent 12 year old would not be given a significant place in the decision. Also, in terms of his care arrangements there would be a bias in favour of the status quo, particularly if the status quo was working well.

The rules relating to entry of children will not be considered in detail here. Principles of accommodation and maintenance are already familiar, and when children enter to join both parents, whether or not travelling with a parent, the only additional requirement is that the child is 'not leading an independent life, is unmarried and has not formed an independent family unit' (para 297(iii)). The reason for such a rule is to avoid entry of more than one household. The rule change of October 2000 preventing third party accommodation for children did not prevent the arrangement in *ECO Lagos v Sokoya* 00/TH002272 where teenage sisters were to be accommodated in their father's flat. He had retained the tenancy when he moved to live with his new wife precisely for the purpose of accommodating his daughters.

Adequate accommodation was given an unusually extended meaning by the Court of Appeal in *M & A v ECO* [2003] EWCA Civ 263. Other children of the parents the children were applying to join had been taken into care, and one had died as a result of serious abuse. The court had no remit to consider welfare within the rules where children apply to join their own parents. They came to the decision that the accommodation was not adequate because the children would not be safe there. The applicants were 16 and 17 years old, which makes this decision all the more remarkable.

The rules which give rise to more contention and case law are those which apply when the child is only joining one parent or relative.

9.8.2 Sole responsibility

When the other parent of the child is still living, it must be shown that the parent the child seeks to join has 'sole responsibility' for them (HC 396 para 297(i)(c)). In many cases it is, of course, highly unlikely that in practical terms the parent in question will have had sole responsibility, and they will certainly not have done where the child has been living with someone else and is now joining the parent in the UK. Why have such a rule? The rationale for it is only to grant entry to a child if they can be regarded as the responsibility of a person in the UK. This immigration rule underscores a parental obligation, but does not support admission of a child if someone else could be considered responsible for them. The focus is on the role and obligation of the parent as a determinant of where a child should live. This is not an emphasis which would be familiar in family law, although sole responsibility may be identified by an order made by a family court. If there is a residence order in favour of the UK parent, this is regarded as a strong indicator that they have sole responsibility in immigration terms. Some custody orders obtained overseas are similarly regarded (IDI Dec 2000 Ch 8 Annex M para 4.4).

The sole responsibility rule does not give separated parents and children the power of choice over where the child should live. An example given in the IDI makes this apparent:

Two foreign nationals living abroad have a child, then separate. One parent comes to the United Kingdom and obtains settlement. The child remains with the parent abroad for several years, then at the age of 13+ wishes to join the parent in the United Kingdom to take advantage of the educational system. There is no reason why the child should not remain with the parent who lives abroad. In this case the parent who lives in the United Kingdom would not be considered to have sole responsibility. (Annex M para 4.1)

The suggested motivation here creates an imputation of abuse of the rule, however, it appears that in terms of the sole responsibility rule the outcome would be no different if the child and custodial parent had started to argue and the family thought it was time for a change in the interests of the child.

The Court of Appeal in the case of *Nmaju v IAT* [2001] INLR 26 held that there were two points of principle which arise in determining sole responsibility. One is the quality of control which will amount to sole responsibility, the other is for what period of time that control must be exercised. In the IDI's example given above, the child was left in the care of a parent. Where the child is left in the care of other relatives, then there may still be a conclusion that the UK resident parent does not have sole responsibility even though this may mean that no one does. The quality of control which will give rise to a finding of sole responsibility requires a retention of ultimate responsibility for the child. The Court of Appeal acknowledged that when someone else is in fact looking after them, they will have day-to-day care. This does not affect the question of responsibility. Financial support and decision-making and having ultimate responsibility for ensuring that the child's needs are met are indicators of responsibility. A parent may have delegated these to another relative, but retain the ultimate responsibility. In such a case the implication in *Nmaju* is that action taken by the caring relatives would be taken 'under the direction' of the responsible parent. A decision for instance as to which school the child should attend would involve a parent who had sole responsibility. The parent would be expected to show a continuous interest in the child's welfare and upbringing.

Where there are two parents actually involved, the tribunal in the case of *Zahir* 00/TH/02262 held that sole responsibility is still capable of arising, for instance, if one parent's role was clearly subsidiary, though it was not so on the facts in that case. *Dawson v ECO Accra* 01/TH/1358 demonstrates the difference between an affectionate parental relationship and sole responsibility. Here the sponsor had made six visits to see his son; there were frequent telephone calls between them and occasional letters. However, it did not appear that the sponsor had played a significant part in important decisions affecting his son's welfare and upbringing. This shows a difference between an absent but involved parent, and one who retains responsibility. In this case it was also significant that the appellant's mother had continued to play an active part in his upbringing.

The other issue in *Nmaju* is that of the period of time for which sole responsibility must be assumed. In that case three children sought to join their mother in the UK. She had left them in the care of their father in 1988 when she came to the UK. In September 1996 he said that he was too old to look after them any longer and left them in the care of a maid. In November of that year their application to join their mother was refused on the basis that if she had had sole responsibility it was only for two months and that was too short a period of time. No period of time is mentioned in the rule, but the tribunal had relied on former Court of Appeal decisions where the parent had had sole responsibility for a 'not insubstantial part' of the child's life (*R v IAT ex p Uddin* [1986] Imm AR 203 and *R v IAT ex p Sajid Mahmood* [1988] Imm AR 121). In those cases however that parent had initially lost the argument because they had not had care of the child for the whole of the child's life. The phrase 'a not insubstantial period' therefore was what had occurred in those cases and was coined to show that the period for which the parent had in fact had responsibility was sufficient. The cases did not lay down any requirement that the period had to be not insubstantial. In *Nmaju* the reality of the situation at the time of the entry clearance decision was that the mother had sole responsibility. This was sufficient to meet the requirements of the rule, even though it had only been for two months.

According to para 6 of the rules a parent includes a step-parent, an adoptive parent, and an unmarried father, if paternity is accepted or proved. If the child turns out, as in *ECO Accra v Attafuah* [2002] UKIAT 05922, after DNA testing not to be the father's natural child, it seems there is no provision parallel to that in nationality law to treat the child as the child of that person.

9.8.3 Exclusion undesirable

The welfare of the child takes greater priority under the next sub-paragraph of the rule, 'that there are serious and compelling family or other considerations which make exclusion of the child undesirable.' This is not a question of whether it would on balance be better for the child to move to the UK. For instance in *Dawson* the tribunal in refusing the appeal on this ground noted that there was no evidence of mistreatment of the appellant or of his mother or stepfather according him a lack of respect. It is possible using this part of the rule to enter to join a relative other than a parent. The IDI Ch 8 Annex M para 1 Dec 2000 emphasizes that this basis for entry is only to be used when parents or relatives in the child's own country are *unable* to care for him or her. The IDI states that the family circumstances which make exclusion undesirable may relate to the sponsor, but only if the sponsor is a parent. This appears to be an attempt to avoid children being brought in as carers for other relatives in need.

Case law on the 'exclusion undesirable' rules has suggested that it is only if the living conditions in the child's country of origin are intolerable that the situation in the UK should be considered. However, this is now thought to be too harsh. It is not a question of comparing the two to find out which is better, but if for instance as in *Rudolph* [1984] Imm AR 84 a father is incapable of caring for a child, that of itself could make exclusion undesirable.

The same case noted that the rule is intended to unite families not divide them. Some overall view must be taken therefore, including such factors as the willingness and availability of the overseas adult to look after the child; the living conditions available for them; the greater vulnerability of small children, and the need for family unity (*Hardward* 00/TH/01522). In *Hardward* itself there is still an emphasis on conditions abroad as a starting point, even in that case where the appellant was already in the UK and applying to vary leave. The appellant lost because although there were compelling family reasons why she should stay in the UK, it was not convincingly shown that her father in Jamaica was unable to care for her.

The case of *Hardward* predated the implementation of the Human Rights Act by a few months. The application under the 'exclusion undesirable' rule was turned down, but the tribunal considered whether, given the imminence of the Human Rights Act, it should make a recommendation using Article 8. The tribunal suggested that para 298(i) of the rules was incompatible with the Human Rights Act:

> . . . the onus of justifying that interference under Art 8(2) shifts to the immigration authorities. That is in clear contrast with the wording of the rule set out at paragraph 298(i) which places the burden throughout on the appellant to justify why her exclusion would be undesirable. (para 19)

This argument seems to have much force.

9.8.4 Adoption

Inter-country adoption is a growing and complex subject, combining immigration and family law.

This brief coverage just raises some of the issues associated with it. It is necessary to distinguish between adoption which takes place of a non-British child in the UK, and adoption which takes place overseas with the intention or consequence that the child moves to the UK.

9.8.4.1 *Adoption in the UK*

The adoption of a non-British child in the UK by a British citizen confers British nationality immediately upon the making of the adoption order (British Nationality Act 1981 s 1(5)). In the case of *In re B (a minor (AP)* [1999] 2 AC 136 the House of Lords established new principles for immigration considerations in the adoption of children in the UK. B had visited the UK with her mother. She attended school in Leeds while they stayed with her grandparents, and appeared to be thriving, so her mother left her there when she returned to Jamaica. B and her grandparents applied for exceptional leave for B to stay in the UK as it appeared to be in her best interests, all the more as her father in Jamaica had now died, and her mother and sister were living in very reduced circumstances. Her application was turned down. They were advised that the only way that B could stay in the UK would be for her grandparents to adopt her. Her mother gave consent to this arrangement, but the Home Secretary intervened to oppose the adoption. He also made it clear that if just a residence order were made in favour of the grandparents, he would still seek to deport B. As Lord Hoffmann says in his judgment at 140,

Ms B had only two years of minority left. And although the benefits to her from being able to spend those two important years living with her grandparents and going to school in Leeds were plain and obvious, it would not ordinarily be necessary for her to be adopted. Were it not for her precarious immigration status, she could simply have stayed with her grandparents or, if the situation needed to be formally regulated, the court could have made a residence order under the Children Act 1989. But the Home Office made it clear that if the court merely made a residence order, it would nevertheless order her deportation. Thus the acquisition of British citizenship by adoption was an essential element in securing her the advantages of living with her grandparents and continuing at her school.

The Court of Appeal had accepted the Home Office's proposition that 'the court should ignore benefits which would result solely from [a] change in immigration status when determining whether the child's welfare calls for adoption' (at 141). As the acquisition of right of abode was the main benefit, it discharged the adoption order. The House of Lords considered that this interpretation flouted the terms of the Adoption Act, which required the judge to 'have regard to "all the circumstances" and to treat the welfare of the child "throughout his childhood" as the first consideration'. It was impossible to ignore the immigration benefits of the adoption. Lord Hoffmann continues with a passage (at 141) which has great significance for adoptions, and arguably for other cases concerning children:

No doubt the views of the Home Office on immigration policy were also a circumstance which the court was entitled to take into account, although it is not easy to see what weight they could be given. Parliament has not provided, as I suppose it might have done, that the adoption of a non-British child should require the consent of the Home Secretary. On the contrary, it has provided that the making of an adoption order automatically takes the child out of the reach of the Home Secretary's powers of immigration control. The decision whether to make such an order is entirely one for the judge in accordance with the provisions of section 6. In cases in which it appears to the judge that adoption would confer real benefits upon the child during its childhood, it is very unlikely that general considerations of 'maintaining an effective and consistent immigration policy' could justify the refusal of an order. The two kinds of consideration are hardly commensurable so as to be capable of being weighed in the balance against each other.

The House of Lords laid down a new principle in allowing immigration benefits to be considered along with all others which would accrue to the child from the adoption.

The difference between this case and cases involving for instance sole responsibility, is that the House of Lords is here interpreting and applying the Adoption Act, in an application to which as they point out, the Home Office is not a party. In the case of the entry of a child to join a parent with sole responsibility, the provision being applied and interpreted is an immigration provision. Immigration decisions are not specifically brought within the Children Act 1989 so as to benefit from the welfare principle. They are not even brought within the welfare principle by the UN Convention on the Rights of the Child. This Convention provides that the best interests of the child shall be a primary consideration in any decision of a public body touching on the welfare of a child (Article 3). However, as stated earlier, the UK has entered a reservation to the Convention insofar as it would apply to immigration and asylum matters. The legality of this reservation has been doubted (see, for instance, the opinion of Nick Blake and Sandhya Drew prepared for Save the Children UK); nevertheless it remains in force.

9.8.4.2 *Adoption outside the UK*

A child adopted outside the UK may enter the UK for settlement if the requirements of HC 395 para 310 are met. Note that in this case the adoption does not automatically confer British citizenship. Here it is a question of whether the adoption has taken place in circumstances which mean that it will be recognized. Policy considerations have been to prevent adoption being used as a means of circumventing immigration control and to protect children from abuse. Before March 2003 in order to meet the requirements of the rules the adoption had to be 'in accordance with a decision taken by the competent administrative authority or court' in his country of origin or residence. This rule still exists, and applies where the adoption was by legal order, however the rules now also make provision for *de facto* adoptions.

'Administrative' does not mean necessarily part of the civil administration, it just means an authority other than a court and therefore a properly licensed religious body is included (*Tarinder Kaur* 01/BH/0048). However, following a rule change on 18 September 2001 (Cmnd 5253) the adoption will only be recognized if it has taken place in one of the countries recognized by the Adoption (Designation of Overseas Adoption) Order 1973, SI 1973/19. The adoption of Tarinder Kaur would therefore not now be recognized as India is not included in the 1973 order. Many countries have developed their adoption proceedings since 1973, and it is surprising that such an outdated provision should become mandatory in 2001. Furthermore, the Hague Convention on the Protection of Children and Co-operation in Respect of Inter-Country Adoptions 1993 is moving towards a different system of international recognition of adoption orders, and adoptions under the Hague Convention are also provided for under the immigration rules paras 316 D–F.

Recognition of the country's adoption process is not enough to bring the child within the requirements of the rule. Paragraph 310 requires that at the time of the adoption both of the adoptive parents were resident together abroad or that either or both were settled in the UK. In addition it lays down other requirements of the adoption, namely that the adopted child has the same rights and obligations as any other child of the marriage; that the child was adopted due to the inability of others to care for them; that there is a genuine transfer of parental responsibility to the adoptive parents; that the child has lost or broken ties with their family of origin, and that the adoption is not one of convenience to facilitate admission to the UK. These requirements are more stringent than those for an adoption order in the UK which would not necessarily require that the child was adopted 'due to the inability of others to care for them' nor that the child has lost or broken ties with their family of origin. Indeed it is no longer thought good practice in family law to insist upon a child severing contact with their family of origin. In *Boadi v ECO Ghana* [2002] UKIAT 01323 the tribunal took account of this in its interpretation of the rule, holding that severing ties with a family of origin did not mean severing emotional ties, but just that the adoption was not an arrangement which could be seen as reversable. A different view of the rules had been taken in the case of *Kamande v ECO Nairobi* [2002] UKIAT 06129 a few months earlier in which the tribunal refused to recognize the adoption for the purposes of the rules because although responsibility had been transferred, the appellant still retained a strong emotional relationship with his grandparents who had brought him up. It was their aging which had prompted his adoption by his aunt in Britain, and the approach here carries echoes of the 'sole responsibility' rules, in not giving recognition to the family's choices.

When an adoption is arranged within the family, for instance the adoption of a niece or nephew where a couple is infertile, it does not fulfil the latter two requirements of the rules. *In H (A Minor) (Adoption: Non-Patrial), Re* [1997] 1 WLR 791 the Secretary of State, as in *Re B*, intervened in an adoption case, applying to overturn the adoption of a child who entered the UK for a family wedding and was adopted by the relatives he came to join. It was a genuine adoption, and the Court of Appeal declined to overturn it simply because the motivation arose from their infertility. In *J (A Minor) (Adoption: Non-Patrial), Re*, [1998] 1 FLR 225 the Court of Appeal in a comparable case again refused the Secretary of State's application to overturn the adoption order. Although there might be an element of deception in the child's entry, as it seemed that the intention to enter for adoption was present at the beginning, this did not mean the adoption itself was a sham. The Court of Appeal distinguished between deception used to gain entry to achieve a genuine adoption and deception as to the nature of the adoption itself. The Court expressed a view that while the adoption rules were so restrictive the Secretary of State was not well placed to argue that they should not be circumvented by genuine applicants (see Macdonald 2001:455).

These cases would not have been helped by the rule change concerning de facto adoptions, as the adoption must have taken place prior to entry. The adoptive parents and child must have been living together for a year before the application. If the child cannot gain entry or stay under the adoption rules an alternative is to apply using the rule that exclusion is undesirable. In effect in these two cases, the Court of Appeal declined to apply the immigration rules although their wording was plain, as to do so would conflict with the best interests of the child, which is the prime consideration in adoption proceedings.

These two cases preceded the Human Rights Act. Two Court of Appeal cases since commencement of the Human Rights Act reveal two very different approaches. In *Radhika S v ECO New Delhi* [2005] EWCA Civ 89 the Court of Appeal adopted a strict interpretation of the requirement of HC 395 para 310(ix) that the adoption was due to the inability of the original parents to care for the child. They held that inability did not include unwillingness, as in the present case where the appellant's parents did not want a girl, were not willing to care for her and arranged for her adoption by her aunt and uncle who were eager to have a girl. The Court considered Human Rights Act 1998 s 3 which requires that the rule be interpreted so as to uphold Convention rights as far as possible, but it was not possible, they thought, to construe 'unable' so as to include 'unwilling', and rejected the appellant's invitation to take the more proactive approach to statutory interpretation suggested by the House of Lords in *Ghaidan v Godin-Mendoza* [2004] 3 WLR 113. The entry of the girl under 'exclusion undesirable' rule was also rejected.

The decision in *Radhika* does not refer to the earlier Court of Appeal case of *Singh v ECO New Delhi* [2004] EWCA Civ 1075 in which the court had to consider an application for entry clearance following an intra-family adoption which did not and never could meet the requirements of the immigration rules because the child had not severed ties with his family of origin. Indeed, he was being cared for well by his parents pending being able to join his adopted parents, his aunt and uncle, with whom he had a strong relationship and who cared for him deeply. His birth parents had three children, but his aunt and uncle had one daughter and were not able to have more children. The adoption was carried out according to a Sikh ceremony. The case had had a very protracted history, including a decision by the ECtHR that an application was admissible because the refusal to recognize adoptions carried out in India was *prima facie* discriminatory. The Court of Appeal heard and decided an application purely upon Article 8 grounds (see chapter 3). It had no doubt that the substantial relationship between the child and adoptive parents amounted to family life. The fact that it did not meet the UK's stringent requirements in the immigration rules should not be allowed to impede the reality of genuine family life and entry clearance should be granted. Munby LJ's judgment powerfully demonstrates how the concept of family life must be understood in the UK's multicultural society.

Regulations made under Adoption and Children Act 2002 s 83 appear only to provide for adoptions under the Hague Convention, and outside the Convention, for adoptions of a foreign child in the UK, or adoptions abroad effected less than six months before the child enters the UK. The Adoptions with a Foreign Element Regulations 2005, SI 2005/392, in force from 30 December 2005, lay down an extensive system of regulation and approval for adoptive parents. However, they may not have an impact on de facto adoptions under the immigration rules because of the requirement for the parents to have lived with the child for a year prior to the application for entry. For adoptions recognised in law, the impact will still depend on when the adoption took place.

9.8.5 **Evidence**

The issue of credibility which we have encountered so often has been raised particularly in relation to two issues concerning children — their age, and whether they are 'related as claimed'. The extensive questioning and interviewing, village visits, excessive reliance on the discrepancy approach, and distressing refusals of genuine applicants have to a large extent been swept away by the advent of DNA testing. This is not infallible and is limited in what it can prove. Nevertheless, DNA evidence can rarely be effectively disputed and the scope for all the other evidence about relationships is much reduced. Disputes about age occur particularly in the case of unaccompanied asylum seeking children (UASCs) who should be treated differently from adults and not detained. See chapter 15.

9.9 **Refugees and those with forms of concessionary leave**

Once a person has obtained refugee status they have a right to be joined by their immediate family. This right has had some conditions added to it in the immigration rules, para 352A, which require that the couple intend to live permanently together, that the marriage is subsisting, and that the marriage did not take place after the person who has been granted refugee status left their country of habitual residence in order to seek asylum. This need not be their country of nationality or where they feared persecution *(A (Somalia)* [2004] UKIAT 00031).

The right to family reunion is one of the benefits of refugee status over and above the other kinds of protective and temporary leave granted to those whose refugee claims fail but who are nevertheless permitted to stay in the UK. It only applies to married partners and minor children (HC 395 paras A to F). Those with exceptional leave to remain under the pre-April 2003 provisions could apply for their family to join them after being in the UK for four years. After April 2003, family members will be granted entry once the principal applicant has been granted indefinite leave to remain. This would normally be after three years of humanitarian protection or six years' discretionary leave. However, unlike exceptional leave to remain, the granting of ILR after these periods of leave will be subject to a review of the continuing need for protection, and so it seems that the arrival of family members will be delayed pending the outcome of this review. As with ELR, if family members are already in the UK they will be granted leave in line, and there is provision for exceptional entry before the time set where there are compelling compassionate circumstances. It is evident from the provision itself that separation of a family is not by itself expected to amount to such a circumstance. In all cases apart from those granted refugee status there is a maintenance and accommodation requirement.

All the above provisions are found in the API on family reunion. The right of refugees arises from the Refugee Convention; the remaining provisions are all concessionary. The questions therefore arises, what if family reunion is denied to someone under the concession, say because maintenance is not thought to be adequate? This is one of the few areas where the principles still come into play concerning an appeal against denial of a concession, as discussed in chapter 8. The tribunal in *Soleiman* [2002] UKIAT 07140 held that this question is now subsumed within the consideration of Article 8. Where entry clearance for family has been refused, an appeal is bound to raise the question of lack of respect for family life, and will proceed on that footing.

9.10 **Conclusion**

It may seem incredible that 20 years ago family settlement in the UK was as controversial a topic in Parliamentary debates as asylum is now. Family settlement is no longer the charged political issue that it used to be, but the rules on family settlement still carry the real burden of policy on integration and diversity. That they continue to be changed, and the reasons for these changes given in the 2002 White Paper illustrate that the immigration rules on family settlement are still instruments of social policy.

In comparison with the 1960s and 1970s, the law relating to family settlement is now relatively transparent. The IDIs and guidance to ECOs are published, concessions are increasingly integrated into the rules; even the initial entry clearance interview is more controlled, as the reports of the Entry Clearance Monitor, while not referring to family applications, cast some public light into initial decision-making (see chapter 6).

This greater transparency combined with the albeit limited effect of Article 8, is no more than is necessary and appropriate, given that in matters of family settlement the decisions which are made have a fundamental effect on the welfare and happiness of the individuals concerned.

QUESTIONS

1   What is the immigration purpose which is sought to be achieved by the probationary period for partners? Is this something which should be regulated by immigration control or by families and family law?

2   Why is there no probationary period for other adult relatives?

3   Draft your own immigration rule for the admission of children, taking into account the policy priorities you would consider most important. How does this compare with the existing rules?

FURTHER READING

Bevan V. (1986) *The Development of British Immigration Law* (Beckenham: Croom Helm).

Blake, N., and Husain, R. (2003) *Immigration, Asylum and Human Rights* (Oxford: Oxford University Press), Chapter 4.

Coker, J., Finch, N., and Stanley, A. (2002) *Putting Children First* (London Action Group).

Jones, A. (2002) 'A Family Life and the Pursuit of Immigration Controls', in Cohen, S., Humphries, B., and Mynott, E. (eds) *From Immigration Controls to Welfare Controls* (London: Routledge).

Juss, S. (1997) *Discretion and Deviation in the Administration of Immigration Control* (London: Sweet & Maxwell).

McKee, R. (1999) 'Primary purpose by the back door? A critical look at 'intention to live together' *Immigration and Nationality Law and Practice* (1999) vol. 13(1), pp. 3–5.

Mole, N. (1987) *Immigration: Family Entry and Settlement* (Bristol: Jordan & Sons).

Pearl, D. (1986) *Family Law and the Immigrant Communities* (Bristol: Jordan & Sons).

Pearl, D & Menski, W. (1998) Muslim Family Law 3rd edn. (London: Sweet & Maxwell).

Rogers, N. (2003) 'Immigration and the ECHR: are new principles emerging?' EHRLR 1, pp. 53–64.

Sachdeva, S. (1993) *The Primary Purpose Rule in British Immigration Law* (Stoke on Trent: Trentham).

Shah, P. (2002) Children of Polygamous Marriage: an Inappropriate Response *Immigration and Nationality Law and Practice* (2002) vol. 16, no. 2, pp. 110–112.

Sondhi, R. (1987) *Divided Families British Immigration Control in the Indian Subcontinent* (London: Runnymede Trust).

10

Entry for temporary purposes

SUMMARY

Most entry to the UK is for a temporary purpose. This chapter considers the law relating to temporary purposes aside from employment. The law concerning visitors is discussed and the application of the rules and importance of appeal rights is noted in the context of respect for family life as required by Article 8 Human Rights Act. The rules concerning students are discussed and their connection with the employment market. The theme of credibility is seen to run through the application of the rules in both these categories. Finally, there is a brief outline of the rules relating to au pairs and working holidaymakers.

10.1 Introduction

This chapter reviews the law concerning entry to the UK for temporary purposes. The majority of passengers arriving in the UK do so not for settlement but for temporary purposes. The emphasis of the chapter is on the most commonly encountered reasons for temporary entry, namely as a visitor or a student.

10.2 Visitors

More than 90 million people each year travel to or through the UK. The vast majority of these are visitors, i.e., people who are coming for a brief period for reasons such as business, tourism, or visiting family, and who do not intend to stay for settled purposes. Despite the steady increase in the numbers of visa national countries, it is still the case that the great majority of visitors to the UK do not require entry clearance. Many come from the European Economic Area, and EEA nationals do not even require leave to enter for a visit. They also come from countries such as the USA, Canada, Japan, New Zealand, and Australia, whose nationals require leave to enter but not visas. In 2004 there were 97.2 million arrivals from outside the Common Travel Area, 85 million of whom were EEA nationals (Control of Immigration: Statistics UK 2004, 14/05).

The law relating to visitors is not much concerned with this majority. Non-visa nationals, for instance Japanese tourists, may obtain leave to enter on arrival, and only in a very rare case will there be refusal or any legal issue arising. The law relating to visitors is concerned with essentially the same issues as much of the rest of immigration law. It is concerned with deterring illegal entry, overstaying and asylum claims; it operates on the basis of discretionary judgments challengeable by limited appeal rights. It affects the family lives particularly of settled people from the Asian subcontinent, and in operation lays emphasis on the credibility of the applicant. Of course there are more matters involved in visitor applications than these. However, these familiar themes are clearly present.

The visa regime itself, as we have already seen (chapter 6) is designed to prevent illegal entry and deter asylum claims. No more will be said about this here. The right of appeal against refusal of entry clearance for visitors was removed by the Asylum and Immigration Appeals Act 1993. This meant that the only possibility of challenging refusal of entry clearance was by judicial review. As we have already noted, judicial review is concerned not with the merits of the decision but with the decision-making process. Usually in the case of refusal of a visa, this is the question of whether the entry clearance officer's decision was unreasonable, and it is rarely possible to show that this was the case (see, for instance, *R v SSHD ex p Kurumoorthy* [1998] Imm AR 401 or *R v ECO Accra ex p Aidoo* [1999] Imm AR 221). One effect of a lack of appeal right is that much of what happens is, as it were, off the record. There are few recent tribunal cases, and given the limitations of judicial review, there is a relatively small body of law on the application of the rules.

The Immigration and Asylum Act 1999 ss 59 and 60 reinstated a right of appeal for family visitors after protests at its abolition, in particular in relation to the effect on settled families from the Asian subcontinent. The Report of the Independent Entry Clearance Monitor gives global statistics on entry clearance. These statistics reveal that the refusal rate for South Asia is consistently higher than the average refusal rate. In 2002–3 and 2003–4 the refusal rate for the West Indies and Atlantic leapt up to also well over the average. Because of Commonwealth links, giving rise to a greater number of settled people in the UK with family in South Asia and the West Indies than in many other regions of the world, the impact on these settled families of a high entry clearance refusal rate from these parts of the world is significant. It is where refusal can affect attendance for instance at weddings and funerals and other aspects of family life that human rights issues are most likely to arise in relation to visitor applications. Policies on refusal may also give rise to race discrimination issues.

To summarize, visitors form by far the greatest number of UK arrivals. Most do not require prior entry clearance, but of those that do, the highest number of refusals takes place in South Asia, thus affecting settled communities in the UK. The right of appeal against these refusals was however withdrawn from 1993 to 1999, leaving only the unsatisfactory remedy of judicial review. The law in this area is much concerned with credibility. The effect on settled communities raises human rights issues.

10.2.1 **Requirements of the rules**

10.2.1.1 *Purpose of visit*

A person who wants to enter the UK as a visitor must meet the requirements laid down in the immigration rules, HC 395 para 41, and in other specialized rules if they are coming for private medical treatment (para 51–54) to visit their child at school (56A–C) or as a child visitor (46A–F). Certain activities are prohibited for visitors, but none are prescribed. Paragraph 41 requires that the visit must not be for the purpose of

(a) taking employment in the UK;

(b) producing goods or providing services in the UK, including selling goods or services direct to members of the public; or

(c) studying at a maintained school.

The visit may therefore be for any purpose which does not contravene these requirements, provided the individual is not excluded for a general reason under para 320 (see chapter 6). Common purposes for a short stay are holidays, family visits, or to transact business. The reason must also not be one which is covered by other immigration rules. In *Gusakov* (11672) the applicant was planning to stay with a family to improve her English and help look after their children. The ECO refused the application on the basis that in substance she was coming as an *au pair*, but as a Russian citizen she fell outside the *au pair* scheme and therefore she was neither a visitor nor an *au pair* and could not be granted entry. The IAT held that as a matter of law there are few restrictions on what a visitor can do. The authorities could not prevent her spending her time as a visitor in looking after children or improving her English. What the visitor intends to do with their time is not crucial in the case of a family visit (*W(Ghana)* [2004] UKIAT 00005) ILU vol. 7 no. 3).

10.2.1.2 *Duration of visit*

The visitor must state the period of time that they intend to stay and this must not exceed six months. There is no automatic entitlement to six months' leave if a lesser period would be sufficient to fulfil the purposes of the journey (para 42), for instance a business meeting on a fixed date would only need a short period of leave. In practice six months' leave should usually be given even when less would satisfy the purpose (July 2005 IDI Ch 2 s 1 para 2.3). Two exceptions are stated by way of example: where the passenger already has entry clearance for a shorter period, and permitting entry for three months or less for holders of Refugee Convention travel documents issued by a signatory to the Council of Europe agreement of 1959 on the Abolition of Visas for Refugees. In 2003 the UK suspended its recognition of these travel documents, which means a refugee visitor now needs a visa, but there seems to be no reason not to grant them six months like other travellers.

A visitor who has been given less than six months and continues to satisfy the requirements of para 41 may apply before the expiry of their leave for a further period up to the maximum, although the IDI Annex A advises that the original reasons for granting short leave should be obtained from the immigration service, and consideration given to whether these still apply.

Where an application for an extension is made which would take the visitor beyond the six months, the Home Office should not refuse the application outright but consider granting leave up to the maximum as mentioned above. For instance in *Wong* (11979) the appellant stayed for five months as a visitor, then the full two years available as a working holidaymaker (see below), then applied for a further three months as a visitor. The Home Office responded that 'any further extension' would lead to a stay of more than six months as a visitor. The IAT held that the Home Office could have considered granting a shorter period, i.e., something up to a month, which would have meant that the appellant would not exceed six months' leave as a visitor.

The IDI advises in para 4 of Annex A that 'there is no restriction on the number of visits a person may make to the UK, nor any requirement that a specified time must elapse between successive visits.' The frequency of visits however is something that will be considered in the light of the purpose of the visits, and may affect the view taken of the visitor's credibility. The IDI gives guidance that a visitor should not normally spend more than six out of any twelve months in the UK, although there will be legitimate exceptions such as for private medical treatment.

10.2.1.3 *Maintenance and accommodation*

Evidence of the visitor's financial status is required to assess their capacity to maintain themselves during their stay, as another requirement under para 41 is that there must be no recourse to public funds.

While some assurance about the applicant's financial circumstances is necessary, the purpose is only to show that the applicant has the capacity to maintain themselves and return. This does not require their finances to be a model of clarity according to the tribunal case of *Osibamowo* (12116). The assessment of this requirement involves an examination not only of the means of the visitor but also, particularly where a family visit is proposed, of the means of those who will support them. It therefore also involves some difficult questions about means and standard of living.

One of the contentious issues in visitor applications arises from the application of this part of the rule. The problem is illustrated by the case of *Hussain* (10037) in which the ECO refused entry clearance on the basis that the trip expenditure was out of all proportion to the applicant's income. The ECO doubted whether a proportionate benefit would be obtained from the visit. The IAT found that the satisfaction of seeing family was quite sufficient reason for the trip and the expenditure involved. The visit did not need to be a demonstrably wise financial move. However the appellant still lost in this case because he could not show that he could afford the airfare home. There was a similar approach in *Kaur v ECO New Delhi* [2002] UKIAT 05692 in which the tribunal said that the emotional value of the trip might well mean that the visitor would pay more than strict economics might dictate. However, in *Iskola* (11334) it was held relevant that one year's income from the applicant's business was equivalent to the price of the air tickets. The IAT held that the refusal of entry clearance was justified. The difficulty here is that the difference in standard of living and income between the applicant's home country and the UK may make it very difficult for the applicant to show that the trip is financially viable. This is not really because of this part of the rule taken alone, but because of the way it interacts with the requirement to show intention to leave.

10.2.1.4 *Intention to leave*

As with other temporary purposes, a key requirement of the visitor rules is proof of the intention to leave at the end of the period permitted. Like the other requirements this is something which the applicant is required to prove, but only on a civil standard of the balance of probabilities. In order to meet this standard of proof the applicant will need to adduce circumstantial evidence from which the immigration officer will make a judgment. Evidence from the sponsor may help to build a picture of the applicant's intention (*DM* [2005] UKIAT 130 ILU vol. 8 no. 19). They will consider matters such as what incentive the applicant has to return, e.g., whether they have family and work commitments in their home country. In *Aye* (10100) the tribunal said that an apparent lack of incentive to return should not of itself be treated as a reason to refuse. This is clearly right in principle, otherwise the less engaged and committed a person's life, the less chance they would have to expand their horizons by travel. However, lack of incentive could, the tribunal said, be taken into account as part of all the circumstances which would be used to develop a full picture of the applicant's intentions. The IDI Ch 2 s 1 Annex A para 1 Nov 2000 illustrates the difficulty of proving this intention:

the fact that a passenger . . . may be able to produce a return ticket (and other supporting evidence) does not guarantee that he intends to abide by his conditions of stay of that his intention to leave at the end of his visit is genuine.

The immigration officer or ECO in considering incentive to return may take into account the economic circumstances in the applicant's home country by comparison with those in the UK. There are many cases in which this reasoning is demonstrated, (see *Ashfaq Ahmad v ECO Islamabad* [2002] UKIAT 03891 below in the context of intention to work). Such considerations are fraught with the potential for stereo-typing and discrimination. In *R v ECO ex p Abu-Gidary* CO 965 1999 the argument was advanced for the applicant that the ECO's reasoning in this respect, if taken too far, could result in no young single women from developing or poor countries being able to obtain entry clearance as visitors. The applicant for entry clearance, who was the daughter of the applicant for this judicial review, had made numerous unsuccessful applications before. The case was heard before the commencement of the Human Rights Act 1998 and Race Relations (Amendment) Act 2000, so arguments could not be relied upon from those statutes. However, it was argued in the context of irrationality that the application of the requirement of strong financial circumstances amounted to indirect discrimination as fewer people of the applicant's racial group would be able to comply with it. The potential visitor was a recent university graduate who on her earlier applications had not had a job, but at the time of her most recent application did have a job to return to. In a country riven by conflict and offering very limited opportunities for independence for women, this was a considerable achievement, but the ECO did not regard it as an incentive to return, describing her income from the job as 'modest'. The view of the High Court was more sympathetic. That approach is also found in tribunal decisions such as *Ogunkola v ECO Lagos* [2002] UKIAT 02238 in which the tribunal endorsed the view that 'if lack of economic incentive to return to the country of origin were sufficient to found a refusal of a visit application, then no person living overseas whose standard of living was lower than that prevailing in the UK could ever come on holiday here, or visit relatives settled here. That is not the law' (para 7).

Government scepticism about the intention of visitors to return home is illustrated by the proposal in the 2002 White Paper *Secure Borders, Safe Haven* (Cm 5387) to prevent switching from visitor to spouse status. The White Paper says:

In 1999, 76% of those granted leave to remain on the basis of marriage had been admitted to the UK for another purpose and 50% of those who switched into the marriage category did so within 6 months of entry. As it seems unlikely that such a large percentage of this number would develop permanent relationships within such a short period of time, the indication is that many of these persons had intended to marry all along but had not obtained leave to enter on this basis and had therefore lied about their intentions to the entry clearance officer. Alternatively, they may have entered a bogus marriage to obtain leave to remain after arrival. (para 7.11)

This leaves out of account that the entrant may have lied about their reason for entry, not because they did not intend to marry their partner, but because they did, and would prefer to be in the country with them than to wait abroad. They may also have more confidence in their capacity to deal with the Home Office and any problems in the application while in the UK. This points up a central issue concerning credibility to which we shall return, that deception or mistakes about one matter do not necessarily demonstrate bad faith about the substance of the application. This reasoning by the Home Office also leaves out of account, in the case of visitors, the effect of six-months limited leave on a new relationship. A person who has entered as a *bona fide* visitor and formed a relationship in that time has a difficult choice to make.

As an additional requirement to the intention to leave, the visitor must also show that they can meet the cost of the return or onward journey, the basis of the refusal in *Hussain*. This may be simply proved by the purchase of a return ticket. The cost of return, duration of the visit, and adequate maintenance and accommodation are more easily proved than intention to leave. The other question of intention under the visitor rules requires proof of a negative, that the visitor does not intend to work.

10.2.1.5 *Intention to work*

Paragraph 41 requires that the visitor does not intend to take employment in the UK. This is not necessarily proved by evidence that they can be maintained and accommodated. In *Ashfaq Ahmad v ECO Islamabad* the tribunal found that the sponsor could maintain and accommodate the visitor, and in fact this had never been in dispute. However, the sponsor could not control the actions of the visitor. While the sponsor may genuinely intend only a family visit, the visitor, as a free adult, may make other choices, such as working during their stay. The sponsor cannot prevent this and so the application for entry clearance could be refused on the basis of the incentive which the visitor would have to work, based on a view of his financial circumstances.

The tribunal in *Mistry v ECO Bombay* [2002] UKIAT 07500 put the matter rather starkly as follows: 'It comes down to the question of whether someone making a modest living in India must inevitably be regarded as too much prey to the temptations of doing much better here, at least in cash terms, to be regarded as a genuine short-term visitor' (para 7). The implied answer here is 'no', but the discriminatory potential of such a blanket judgment would be very clear.

10.2.2 **Credibility**

The immigration rules do not contain a further heading, 'credibility,' but this issue lies behind all the requirements we have discussed above. Annex A to the IDI Ch 2 s 1 July 2005 does begin with a section headed 'Credibility' which advises officers to investigate the background to applications if they have doubts. The Annex says that the proposed purpose of the visit 'must bear some reasonable relationship to [the visitor's] financial means and his family, social, and economic background. Previous immigration history and evidence of a pattern of family migration, both here and abroad, are also matters to be taken into account'.

The issue of credibility therefore also brings in other factors which are not included in the rules. The practice of taking family migration history into account was approved in the two judicial review cases cited earlier, *Aidoo* and *Kurumoorthy*. Both held that family members' migration histories were a relevant matter to the exercise of discretion. In the case of *Aidoo*, the sponsor and applicant's half-brother had overstayed and there was suspicion that the applicant might do the same. In *Kurumoorthy* the ECO thought that the applicants, who were a couple, might consider following the wife's sister's example. She, however, had done nothing unlawful. She had come on a visit to her children and had applied while in the UK for indefinite leave to remain, which was granted. However, in *Gurgur v ECO Istanbul* [2002] UKIAT 024626 the tribunal found that a history of lawful migration in a family should not be used to prevent the appellant from visiting her children and grandchildren in the UK.

In relation to the maintenance and accommodation requirement, as the above cases show, there can be a difference of opinion about the use and adequacy of funds. The effect is that all too easily the examination can become a trial of credibility. In a close examination of a subjective state such as intention, credibility is clearly relevant. However, it is easy for credibility to become elevated out of its rightful place and be treated as the overriding factor. At worst, the process then resembles a criminal trial where if a witness's credibility can be attacked, the whole of their evidence can be undermined. Time and time again, the tribunal has stated that the issue of credibility in the immigration context should not be so used. Where there are discrepancies in evidence which do not go to the question in issue, these should not be held against the applicant. A clear case of the misuse of the discrepancy approach in the context of visitor applications is that of *Singh* (10139). The applicant was a 40-year-old married man in India who had applied to visit his brother in the UK. There was a discrepancy between him and his brother on the ages of the brother's children and on whether the brother paid maintenance to his former wife. The tribunal held that these were not matters of which he would necessarily have an accurate knowledge, and a negative assessment of his credibility based on such discrepancies was unreasonable. There were other more relevant factors which supported his credibility, for instance that he had visited before and had left before his allotted time. These should have been given more weight.

10.2.3 Entry clearance

The requirements set out in paragraph 41 apply to all visitors. Where they are met the applicant may be granted leave to enter at the port. Where entry clearance has been obtained beforehand the enquiry into these matters will have been completed before arrival and the entry clearance will function as leave to enter (Immigration (Leave to Enter and Remain) Order 2000, SI 2000/1161: see chapter 6). The rules concerning visitors do not require that a visitor obtains entry clearance. However, a person who comes from a visa national country must obtain entry clearance for any purpose, including a visit. Visa national countries include a number of Commonwealth countries, so the belief which is sometimes held, that Commonwealth citizens may visit their UK relatives without prior entry clearance, is a false one. It depends on the Commonwealth country from which they come. For instance, Australian nationals have no such restriction; Indian nationals do.

The rate of refusal of leave to enter at the port to visitors from some non-visa national countries (notably in the Caribbean) is higher than for visitors from other countries. It can therefore be advisable for nationals of those countries to obtain entry clearance, and the rules permit though they do not strictly require it (para 23A). Even before the Immigration (Leave to Enter and Remain) Order 2000, SI 2000/1161: entry clearance would ease the traveller's passage through immigration control and help to avoid wasted airfares and the distress of refusal at the port. There is a further advantage of applying for entry clearance where the visit is to a close family member, which is that refusal may attract a right of appeal. There is no appeal against refusal of leave to enter without entry clearance (Nationality, Immigration and Asylum Act 2002 s 89(2)).

10.2.4 Family visit appeals

As mentioned above, the Immigration and Asylum Act 1999 reinstated a right of appeal against refusal of entry clearance for family visits. A 'family visitor' is defined in the Immigration Appeals (Family Visitor) (No. 2) Regulations 2000, SI 2000/2446 reg 2(2) as a person who applies for entry clearance in order to visit

(a) their own son, daughter, grandparent, grandchild, uncle, aunt, nephew, niece or first cousin;

(b) their own or their spouse's parent, brother or sister,;

(c) their own or their son or daughter's spouse;

(d) their step-parent, step-child or step-brother or sister;

(e) any person with whom they have lived as a member of an unmarried couple for at least two of the three years before the application for entry clearance was made.

The relationships that will qualify may be redefined by regulations to be made under Nationality, Immigration and Asylum Act 2002 s 88A, inserted by Immigration, Asylum and Nationality Act 2006 s 4.

There appears to have been concern in government at reintroducing a right of appeal outright, and the reintroduction was accompanied by a review, to examine aspects of the working of the system, and a fee charged to appellants. The fee was the subject of a good deal of public outcry. It was to be refunded if the appellant won their case. The fees were seen to be a disincentive to use the system, a right of appeal being as it were given with one hand and taken away with the other. The charge for appeals (in addition to visa fees) had not been made before in the immigration system, and was seen disproportionately to affect black and Asian people. The fee was reduced, and finally abolished, with effect from 15 May 2002 (SI 1147/2002), however, the reason given was the inconvenience of administering it, and research was inconclusive as to whether it deterred people from appealing (see Gelsthorpe, Thomas, Howard, and Crawley 2004).

This research showed that oral appeals were far more successful than those which were decided on the papers only, having a success rate of 73 per cent compared with 38 per cent. Appellants were often unaware what the choice of these two kinds of appeal meant. In the Government's five-year strategy published in February 2005 there is a proposal to end oral appeals.

10.2.5 Family visits and Article 8

It may be recalled from chapter 3 that what respect for family life requires, or what constitutes an interference with family life, depends to some extent on the particular relationship. Also, as we have seen, Article 8 cannot be used to *establish* family life if it does not already exist. We noted this in the case of *ECO Lagos v Imoh* [2002] UKIAT 01967 in which an application was made for a four-year-old girl to join her aunt in the UK as a dependant. The application was doomed to fail because the aunt was not settled. However, the Tribunal found that there was no family life in this case but rather an attempt to create one. It said: 'Article 8 requires that there is as a matter of fact family life in existence and the mere payment of money for the care of a child and one visit to see that child, is not capable of creating a family life' (para 5 of the judgment).

One might ask, though, whether Winsome Imoh would have been refused entry clearance just to visit her aunt rather than to join her as a dependant, and if so, whether she could have challenged this successfully using Article 8. The case of *Praengsamrit v ECO Bangkok* [2002] UKIAT 02791 may be considered by way of comparison. In this case an aunt applied to visit her niece, and was turned down on the basis that there had been insufficient contact between the two of them. Article 8 was not argued, but the Vice President of the Tribunal held that:

There is no need to prove contact as an expression of devotion which one might expect between husband and wife. They are relations whose family life goes back over the period of the niece's life. That sort of relationship does not to my mind require to be demonstrated by evidence of frequent contact. It is of the essence of family life that the bond is there to be renewed as and when the occasion arises when members of a family are separated by considerable distances as in this case.

This must be a familiar idea to anyone with relatives who live at a distance from them. It suggests that the better way for the courts to approach Article 8 cases is not to consider whether family life exists, but rather what respect for family life requires in this instance. As discussed in chapter 3, this will vary from one situation to another. It may not require a Government to respect the choice of residence of a married couple who could live elsewhere, but it is difficult to see how it would not require at least the possibility of contact. In *Ramsew v ECO Georgetown* 01/TH/2505 the Tribunal confirmed that family visit cases do normally engage family life. On the other hand, in *Hussain and Noor v ECO Islamabad* (01/TH/2746) the Tribunal held that family life was not interfered with by refusing a visit. It could be carried on by other means, for instance letters and phone calls. Even though this might be the case, the lack of personal contact affects the *quality* of family life (see comment in ILU vol. 6, no. 19, p. 16). The approach in *Ramsew* is implicitly endorsed in *Ashrif v ECO Islamabad* 01/TH/3465 in which the tribunal held that there did not have to be a particular reason for the visit at a particular time. 'The whole point of family visits is that the existence of the family ties of themselves will normally furnish the reason for the visit' (para 14).

The list of family members in the regulations has been criticized as being insufficiently comprehensive. However it has proved difficult to find an agreed extension as concepts of the family differ so widely (see Review of Family Visitor Appeals, June 2003).

10.2.6 Change of circumstances

As we have seen in chapter 6, where there is a fundamental change of circumstances after the grant of entry clearance, this may justify cancellation of leave to enter (HC 295 para 321A). In the context of visitor cases the question may arise whether a change in the purpose of the visit is fundamental enough to justify such cancellation or refusal. In *Waqar* (12569) a visitor's visa was granted without interview to Mr Waqar who was planning to travel as part of an official party. The visit, although by an official, was to be a short, private visit. In the event the official did not make the trip, but Mr Waqar did, and was refused entry on the basis of the change of circumstances. The adjudicator and the IAT agreed that this change of circumstances did not remove the basis of his claim to admission.

In *Dapaah* (11823) the principle established in *Eusebio* (4739) was reiterated, namely that the question of the effect of a change of circumstances is a question of fact and degree, particularly when the applicant is seeking entry under the same rule as the one under which they obtained entry clearance. In a visitor case a change of sponsor does not warrant cancellation of leave to enter. However, the change of circumstances may not have to take the journey outside the visitor rules altogether in order for leave to enter to be refused or cancelled. In *Hiemo v Immigration Officer Heathrow* (10892) the appellant's original application had been to visit his sister. On arrival at Heathrow he sought instead 20 days to attend a training course at the Church of Scientology in East Grinstead. His sister had gone to Germany. The tribunal held that the change of circumstances was fundamental and the refusal was justified. While his current proposed purpose would fall within the visitor category, the change did not have to take the application out of the category to warrant refusal of leave to enter.

10.2.7 Particular purposes

10.2.7.1 *Carers*

Applications from people wanting leave to enter to care for a sick friend or relative in the UK may be refused on the basis that this is outside the rules; however IDI Jun/01 Chapter 17 s 2 para 2 advises that where the care will be for a short time, entry for this purpose may be considered under the normal visitor rules. This was illustrated by *Mahid v ECO Dhaka* [2002] UKIAT 00935 where the applicant sought to enter to care for his severely disabled cousin. The cousin, I, had previously been cared for by his father, mother and brother. However, his father had become ill, his brother had started a university course and his mother was unable to lift I alone. The Social Services Department had offered a system of carers, but the family preferred to have I cared for by the family. It was clear that the need was long term, although the application was made for six months leave as a visitor, it was said on a respite basis. The case is one of those referred to in chapter 3 in which the tribunal misidentified the legitimate aim, citing 'the prevention of disorder or crime' (para 10). On the issue of proportionality the tribunal said: 'it is not proportionate to expect those duties to be taken over by one young man travelling all the way from Bangladesh' (para 12). Unfortunately for Mr Mahid and his cousin, this is an example of a misuse of the concept of proportionality. The tribunal seems to have lost sight of the fact that it is harm done by the interference, i.e., the refusal of entry clearance, which must be proportionate to the legitimate aim pursued by the ECO. Whether the family decision is proportionate to their circumstances and resources is not an Article 8 question.

Family visitors caring for children have sometimes been challenged on the basis that this is acting as a childminder and so contravenes the requirement not to take employment. As a result of a combination of case law and the IDIs the position on this is now relatively clear. Visitors may not be paid for childcare. Beyond this, the tribunal in *Jumawan* (9385) states the principle as follows. If the essence of the application is to take over domestic responsibilities to enable another family member to obtain gainful employment then it may be justified to refuse entry clearance. This is a task which could be undertaken by a third party employed for the purpose. However, merely because a person intends to occupy some or all of their visit in the care of their grandchildren, which could be done by an employee, it does not follow that domestic employment is the applicant's object. Leave to enter as a visitor may still be granted.

The IDI July 2005 Ch 2 s 1 Annex B para 7 says that it is acceptable for visitors to act as temporary childminders where, in addition to the points made above, the visitor is a close relative of the parent (e.g., parent, sibling, in-law), neither parent is able to supervise daytime care of the child, and neither parent has an immigration status leading to settlement.

10.2.7.2 *Business activities*

The requirement not to sell goods or services must be distinguished from permissible business activities. Paragraph 40 includes in the visitor rule someone who comes to 'transact business'. Examples of what this might mean are also given in the paragraph: attending meetings and briefings, fact-finding, negotiating, or making contracts with UK businesses. The July 2005 IDI Ch 2 s 1 Annex A para 4 acknowledges that business reasons may entail staying in the UK for weeks or months, and the distinction which should be made is between such business visits and a person who is 'basing himself here and holding down a specific post which constitutes employment requiring a work permit'.

Annex B gives more detailed guidance, listing typical business visitors and then a number of activities which strictly fall outside the visitor rules but which lead to admission as a matter of administrative policy. These include lorry drivers and coach drivers who are genuinely working an international route; tour group couriers; conference speakers; advisers; consultants; trainers; troubleshooters, etc., provided they are employed abroad by the company to which the client firm belongs and that training does not go beyond classroom instruction; representatives of foreign manufacturers coming to repair, service, or install machinery or equipment under certain conditions, and so on. People coming for these activities and fulfilling all the criteria in the IDI should therefore expect to be admitted as visitors. However, as this is a policy and not a rule, providing the policy is rationally applied, immigration officers may make an exception and refuse admission if the circumstances genuinely warrant this.

Amateur entertainers, sportspeople and professionals coming for incidental purposes such as book launches or auditions are also covered in Annex B and should be admitted as visitors, but not those who are coming to take depositions for foreign court proceedings (July 2005 IDI Ch 2 Annex B para 7).

10.2.7.3 *Academic visitors*

The IDIs provide for other more detailed concessions for further special classes. Academic visitors are one such case. Sponsored or privately financed researchers including those on exchange visits or sabbatical or coming to give a single lecture may be given leave for up to 12 months outside the rules but by virtue of an established concession discussed in Annex B. As in other cases, the requirements attaching to this concession are all directed towards avoiding its being used to create a situation where the person is in reality in employment in the UK or filling a genuine vacancy.

10.2.7.4 *Private medical treatment*

It is not permissible to come to the UK for the purpose of receiving National Health Service treatment. A person who is here as a visitor also may not take advantage of the National Health Service unless there is an emergency and they belong to one of a limited list of countries set out in Annex F to IDI Dec/01 Ch 2. However, entry for private medical treatment is a special category in the rules, and entry is permitted for this purpose if the requirements of para 51 are met. Most of the usual visitor requirements in para 41 must also be met. However, a visitor for private medical treatment does not automatically need to show that their visit is for a fixed period of less than six months and that they will leave at the end of that period. Instead, the duration of the visit is linked to the duration of proposed treatment.

A medical visitor must therefore show that they do not intend to take employment, produce goods or services, or study, that they can maintain and accommodate themselves without recourse to public funds, and meet the cost of their return or onward journey, all as per para 41. The maintenance and accommodation requirement in this case will entail showing that all the costs of treatment can be met. Further, in para 51, they must show they intend to leave the UK at the end of their treatment, and if they have a communicable disease they must satisfy the medical inspector that there is no danger to public health from their entry to the UK.

The other requirements of para 51 depend on requests being made for information by the immigration service. In particular, they may require evidence of the nature of the illness and treatment, of the arrangements for treatment including frequency duration and cost, and availability of funds to meet those costs (para 51 and IDI Dec/01 Ch 2 Annex F). Evidence should come from a registered medical practitioner who holds a consultant post. The treatment must be shown to be finite, but the decision-maker should take a reasonable view of this, relating it to the condition which is being treated.

While six months leave will initially be given, there should be no obstacle to extending this if the appropriate evidence can be shown of the necessity for such extension and that all requirements continue to be met. Extensions will not be given however for treatment from a GP or alternative health practitioner, although initial leave to enter may be granted for this purpose.

10.2.7.5 *Parents of a child at school*

Parents of a child at school in the UK are also subject to a set of special visitor rules, found in paras 56A, B and C. They must meet the requirements of para 41. Additionally, the child must be attending an independent fee paying day school and must meet all the applicable requirements of the student rule in para 57 (see below). The child must be under 12 years of age and the parent must be able to provide satisfactory evidence of adequate and reliable funds for maintaining a second home in the UK and that they are not seeking to make the UK their main home (para 56A).

Under para 56B a parent who meets these requirements may be given twelve months leave, subject to a condition not to take employment. This may be renewed for further periods of 12 months, providing all the conditions continue to be met. Once the child is 12, the parent will no longer be able to obtain leave to remain.

10.2.7.6 *Marriage visits*

New immigration rules (HC 346) have been introduced to provide specifically for visitors who do not intend to settle in the UK to enter the UK in order to marry (paras 56D–F).

10.2.8 **Switching immigration categories**

In general, a visitor must leave at the end of their visit, and opportunities to stay under a different immigration rule have now almost vanished. A non-visa national may become a student at degree level or above, but needs entry clearance if they wish to stay for studies below that level (HC 395 para 60 (i)(b) and (c), inserted into the rules on 1 October 2004). Note that there is no objection to a person admitted as a visitor undertaking a short course of studies which will be completed within their period of leave (IDI Dec. 2004 13.10.2).

10.3 **Students**

There is a centuries-old tradition of travel to other countries in pursuit of learning and education. As a former imperial power, Britain has played a significant role as host to students seeking opportunities which could not be provided in their country of origin, and entry as a student is the commonest short-term immigration reason after visitors. In the year 2002, a peak year, some 369,000 people obtained entry as students. In 2004 the figure was 294,000, but part of this apparent fall is accounted for by the fact that for over half the year nationals of the EU accession states are no longer counted in these figures. Students are not only from the Commonwealth but also from many other nations as well. In fact a British education has been a significant way in which British influence has been maintained and extended in the world, as well as providing developmental and economic benefits for those who obtain their education in the UK.

Therefore in terms of government policy the entry of foreign students involves not only the practices of the immigration service but also the education system, cultural exchange, foreign relations, finance, and, potentially, employment and industrial or vocational training. The purpose of the student's entry is learning, and, probably, obtaining a qualification. The course of attendance at the educational institution is the bare minimum which the student desires and the government must grant to make the entry meaningful. Around this other variables, such as how much the student is charged for their course, whether they or their spouse are allowed to work, whether they are allowed to stay after their course, for how long and for what purposes, may be changed from time to time in accordance with policy objectives. These may not have to do only with education but also with economic conditions, with needs in the UK employment market, and political debates about race or the welfare system.

Very broadly, over the 40 years or so since the Commonwealth Immigrants Act 1962, the rules relating to students have changed from being brief and welcoming, through increasing complexity and restriction, to a recent selective relaxation. This last development is addressed particularly to those who intend to train for occupations in which the UK Government perceives a need to recruit and retain workers. The removal of the requirement to show intention to leave for graduates and medical students, with effect from 17 October 2001, was a significant step in this direction. The limited information available on how students will be affected by the Government's proposed five-tier system of managed migration suggests there will be a polarization between different kinds of students, with more control and bureaucracy overall, and the application of a points system. All these developments are discussed in the course of considering the rules below.

The current rules governing the entry of students are extensive and detailed. They are found in paragraphs 57–87F of the Immigration Rules, para 57 setting out the basic requirements for entry. In addition to general rules applying to most student applicants they cater expressly for particular categories of student such as student nurses as well as particular purposes such as resitting examinations, writing up theses, or being a student union sabbatical officer.

The rules are designed to address four areas of government concern: genuineness or bona fides of the student's intention, genuineness of the educational institution, financial independence of the student, and control of access to employment.

10.3.1 **Type of educational institution**

Vetting of the educational institution has become simpler since the introduction of the Department for Education and Skills' Register of Education and Training Providers. Now a student will only obtain leave to enter if the institution at which they intend to study is listed on this register.

Such institutions are either:

(a) a publicly funded institution of further or higher education; or

(b) a *bona fide* private education institution which maintains satisfactory records of enrolment and attendance; or

(c) an independent fee paying school outside the maintained sector.

The case of *Syed Tareq Ali v ECO Dacca* [2002] UKIAT 02541 suggested that the adjudicator had power to go behind the decision of the Secretary of State that the college was not *bona fide*. Although the requirement that the college is bona fide remains in the rules, since the introduction of compulsory DfES registration, presumably registration will be regarded as conclusive and this criterion not applied on an individual basis. The only challenge then would be the college's challenge by judicial review of a refusal to register them.

There is no general age requirement in the student rules, and they include entry to the UK to attend an independent school. Paragraph 57(iii) of the rules says that children under 16 can qualify as students, but only 'if they are enrolled at an independent fee-paying school on a full-time course of studies which meets the requirements of the Education Act' and is registered with the Department of Education and Employment.

The first part of the requirement, that of acceptance for the course, is simply established by objective evidence such as an acceptance letter from the educational establishment.

10.3.2 **Full-time course**

Paragraph 57(ii) of the rules prescribes the kind of course for which a student may obtain leave. It must be either:

(a) a recognized full-time degree course; or

(b) a weekday full-time course involving attendance at a single institution for a minimum of 15 hours' organized daytime study per week of a single subject or directly related subjects; or

(c) a full-time course of study at an independent fee-paying school.

Where the course is a full-time degree course, nothing further needs to be shown about the number of hours attendance required. It is recognized that very little organized study may be involved. For instance, in the case of a research degree there may be no organized class time, and in the case of some universities very few hours' attendance are required at undergraduate level (as in the traditional Oxbridge pattern of tutorials and individual study).

In the case of other full-time courses at private institutions, 15 hours of organized daytime study is required. Guidance defines 'daytime' study more specifically by excluding weekend study and evening classes which start after 6 p.m. Study at the Open University will qualify for entry for certain postgraduate work only (DSP 12.16, IDI).

The requirement that the course is full-time is intended to exclude people whose main occupation in the UK is not study but paid work. This not only relates to the question of genuineness but also arises from a time when the protection of the domestic labour market was a major preoccupation in immigration policy. The rules on students working during their studies (considered below) have now been considerably relaxed, as have the 'no-switching' rules, also considered below. However, there is no evidence that the requirement of full-time study is breaking down.

10.3.3 **Ability to follow the course**

The question of whether the student is able to follow the course will have already been assessed by the educational institution, and it is unlikely that immigration officers will be equipped to improve on that judgement. As a requirement of the rules, it is not a primary assessment of the student's ability. It is in the immigration rules as being relevant to genuineness, and immigration officers should not attempt to go behind the academic judgement of the educational institution. In particular a superficial assessment of English language ability may be misleading and unwise. The DSP advises that adequate English needs to be demonstrated 'in general terms' and where the educational institution offers prior teaching in English or has set an entry standard that the applicant has met, this should be enough. However, in *ECO Islamabad v Asif* [2002] UKIAT 07454, the Tribunal held that the ECO was entitled to differ from the University. The applicant's English at the time of arrival was not strong, but he had a place on a ten-week language course preceding his degree course. The ECO was not convinced that he would be able to start a degree course in English even after the language course, and the Tribunal held that he was entitled to come to that view. In *DC* [2005] UKIAT 00011 ILU vol. 8, no. 6 the tribunal held that the applicant's choice to be interviewed by the ECO in her native language should not be regarded as evidence of lack of capacity to pursue a course in English unless she had been warned that that inference could be drawn.

The immigration officer or entry clearance officer may, in order to satisfy themselves that the student is able to follow the course, consider the student's existing educational record and qualifications. The High Court in *R v SSHD ex p Mohotty* [1996] Imm AR 256 confirmed that the immigration officer was entitled to take account of the applicant's academic record in assessing the likelihood of his leaving the UK at the end of his studies. The applicant in that case had initially been admitted to take a one-year course leading to a management diploma. He had initially failed his assessments and received extensions of his stay enabling him to complete the course over three years. He then proceeded to a course leading to an Accountancy Part 2 examination. After failing this three times he went home to Sri Lanka to get married. At the time of the High Court application, which was for leave to move for judicial review of a refusal of leave to enter to retake the examination, the results were awaited of his fourth re-sit. It was argued on his behalf that his academic record was not a matter which the immigration officer was entitled to take into account. However, Popplewell J decided that in considering whether he was likely to leave at the end of his studies, the immigration officer was entitled to take account of 'the whole background' which included his academic progress. He accordingly refused leave.

The student's academic record is more obviously relevant when a student applies not for initial entry to the UK, but for an extension of stay. *R v IAT ex p Gerami* [1981] Imm AR 187 illustrates how this requirement developed. At the time of that case the rule governing extensions was para 12 of HC 82 which did not expressly require proof of progress in studies. Paragraph 12 was to be read with para 4 which said that 'account is to be taken of all the relevant facts'. Mr Gerami, who had retaken his A levels and then failed his university first-year examinations twice, had been refused an extension in these terms, 'the Secretary of State, taking into account your prolonged lack of success in your examinations, is not satisfied that you are a genuine student'. It was argued for Mr Gerami that assessment of his academic ability was a matter for the education authorities such the Polytechnic at which he was enrolled, and not for the Home Office. If he had been seeking to 'use his studies so as to obtain perpetual leave to remain in this country as a perpetual student' then this would have been a different matter. However, Woolf J held that the discretion to take into account academic record was not confined to abuse of the rules. A poor academic record would not preclude an extension being granted, but was 'a matter which the Secretary of State must inevitably have regard to in deciding whether to enlarge leave'. Evidence of progress in studies became an express requirement for extensions in HC 394 and has remained so in subsequent rules.

The inclusion of this provision in the rules for extension of stay makes the demonstration of progress an independent requirement which puts beyond doubt that an extension may be refused even if the student is doing their best. In *Joseph* (17615) it was submitted on behalf of the appellant that her achievements were not far out of the normal range of student progression. The Secretary of State, adjudicator and tribunal disagreed. It was accepted that she might be trying, but 'a view has to be taken on ability' and the tribunal took the view that she did not have the ability to complete the course of study. The consultation on the proposed five-tier system proposes that educational establishments will engage in more regular reporting and monitoring of overseas students.

The applicant, in order to succeed, needs to demonstrate their ability and the appropriateness of the course for them by explaining how it fits in with their own life plans. General statements about their country's aspirations or development will not suffice. This is also relevant in applying the rule on intention to study and leave at the end of studies.

10.3.4 Intention to study and to leave at end of studies

The intention to study is in a sense, although central, absorbed by the proof of all the other requirements. If the student has been accepted on a qualifying course at a *bona fide* institution, can support themselves and intends to leave at the end of their studies, it would be perverse to make an issue of whether they intended in fact to be a student unless there is clear evidence which raises doubt about this.

The intention to leave at the end has been in the past a more litigated issue because it relates directly to perceived abuse of the rule in order to stay in the UK. Doubt about a student's intention to leave at the end has been a major factor underlying decisions on student leave. Enquiries may cover the cost of studies, the availability of suitable courses in the passenger's country of residence and whether the proposed study is reasonable for a person of his family, social and economic background. This can be assessed by weighing the material benefit to the applicant, including enhanced job opportunities, against the cost of the course.

The UK Government is now keen to attract graduates as workers in the UK. In a substantial change of policy in October 2001, the requirement to show intention to leave was removed for students applying to undertake a recognized degree course or equivalent at a UK-funded public further or higher education institution or a *bona fide* private education institution which maintains satisfactory records of enrolment and attendance. The change applies to students applying for degree courses that are conditional on their first successfully completing foundation or English language courses, and to student nurses, doctors, and dentists. The indications are that the new system will include a similar provision. This policy change removes this requirement from a large number of student applicants. The paragraphs that follow therefore refer only to non-medical students applying for non-degree courses.

In deciding whether there is cause for doubting that the student intends to leave at the end of their studies, decision-makers should avoid relying on evidence which is purely circumstantial. For instance in the case of *Bourchak* (17209) the adjudicator had concluded that the applicant was unlikely to leave the UK at the conclusion of his studies because soon after his entry clearance interview he started a course at a university in Algeria and because he was nearing the age for military service. The tribunal accepted that the clearest evidence of his intentions, which are after all a state of mind, was to be found in the answers of the appellant at interview. His stated intention had not been challenged by the interviewer and so there was no evidence for doubting it. This decision and the terms of the IDI follow older reported Tribunal decisions such as *ECO New Delhi v Bhambra* [1973] Imm AR 14 where it was held that '[g]rounds for doubting the genuineness of an applicant's intentions must be based on some evidence (as opposed to suspicion)'.

The factors referred to in the IDI have been endorsed by case law as relevant to the question of intention to return, and cases have turned on points such as the cost of the course in relation to the family budget, the job opportunities which would be opened to the applicant by the course, etc. The consideration of such factors is a highly value-laden matter. The reported adjudicator's decision in *Islam v ECO Dacca* [1974] Imm AR 83 famously refused to confine anticipated benefit from the course to economic benefit. He said, 'There is still some truth, though hard to discern in these material times, in the Victorian belief that to be a crossing sweeper with a BA degree is better than to be a crossing sweeper without a BA degree. Knowledge for the sake of knowledge is a benefit, whatever way one looks at it.' Furthermore, there was no basis in the rules for confining the applicant's future expectations to his home country. Although at that time the rules were not intended to lead to settlement in the UK, there might be many other countries in which he could flourish.

The question of the benefit to the applicant of the course of study is however often seen in economic terms. In *Goffar and Dey v ECO Dacca* [1975] Imm AR 142, the appeals failed partly because the applicants could not show that they had made enquiries about computing opportunities in Bangladesh. This does not mean that the adjudicator was wrong in *Islam*. It is not necessary that job opportunities be available to the student in their home country, but rather that failing to enquire about such opportunities may cast doubt on the student's genuineness. This will particularly be the case where the cost of the course is great in terms of the applicant's family income.

Entry clearance officers may ask about whether the applicant has a family or job to go back to. However these factors are not now listed in the IDI as relevant factors. Cases such as *Seinn Mya Aye* (10100) have established that an incentive to return is not required, and enquiries of this sort may easily turn into looking for such an incentive.

The question of the availability of similar courses in the applicant's home country is material, but is a difficult one to assess as it goes to the heart of the reasons to travel for study. In *DC* [2005] UKIAT 00011 the applicant wished to study for a diploma in health and social care. There might, as a matter of fact, be a course of this kind in the Philippines, but the tribunal accepted that there was need for investigation of the applicant's contention that a British course would carry more weight. This in turn would be relevant to her future job opportunities in the Philippines, a crucial matter in assessing her intention to return at the end of studies.

10.3.4.1 *End of studies*

The intention which must be shown is to leave at the end of the student's studies. This is not necessarily the end of the course for which they now apply. It may be that there will be a natural progression to further studies, and it is only at the end of such further studies that the student is expected to leave. Paragraph 57 (iv) says 'intends to leave the UK at the end of his studies', and case law has consistently interpreted this to mean at the end of all proposed studies, not the present course. For instance, in *X v ECO Karachi* (18688) the appellant intended initially to undertake a course at the City Business College, London, which would last for six to eight months. There would then be a succession of follow-up courses available to him, and he might stay for up to two years before returning to be part of the sponsor's business operations in Pakistan. The tribunal held that the adjudicator had been wrong to require evidence of intention to leave at the end of the first course.

The Government's proposal in the consultation on the five tier system would cut across this established interpretation of the rules, as students would be expected to have a certification of sponsorship entitling them to study a particular course at a particular institution. Arrangements for extending or changing this have not been published at the time of writing.

10.3.4.2 *Wish or intention*

In the guidance concerning applications after entry the IDI says that a 'student who expresses the wish to remain in the UK beyond his studies should not be refused without the opportunity to clarify his intentions'. This conforms with the earlier trend of case law in which a distinction has been made between a wish and an intention. This question arose because sometimes applicants seem to have been penalized for their own honesty. In the context of a visitor appeal the tribunal in *ECO Hong Kong v Lai* [1974] Imm AR 98 found that the respondent and his family members whom he wanted to visit in the UK would like him to be able to settle there some day, but appreciated that at the present time he did not have a basis for such a settlement. Therefore there was no intention other than to leave at the end of the allotted period, even though the idea of staying was desirable. This raises particular problems for students who would like to work in the UK but at the time of making an application for leave to enter as a student are not in a position to formulate any such intention. The IDI encourages immigration officers not to find an intention to stay when there is in reality only a wish. Now, of course, in the case of degree or medical students, such a wish would be unproblematic as there is no need to prove an intention to leave.

An uncertain or conditional intention to leave the country at the end of studies should not necessarily be detrimental to an application. So held the tribunal in

Sivasubramaniam (13174) where the appellant stated that he intended to leave the country when his studies were completed 'provided it was safe to do so given the uncertain situation in Sri Lanka and particularly in view of an incident of shooting of certain members of his family and the destruction of his home'. His recognition that he might not be able to return to Sri Lanka immediately on the completion of his studies was simply a recognition of the reality of the situation. The tribunal said that he was if anything 'too honest in merely expressing recognition of his inability to forecast the future'. How and whether this policy will survive the five-tier system is also unknown.

10.3.5 Meeting costs

The rule which directly addresses the requirement of financial independence is para 57(vi), that the student:

is able to meet the costs of his course and accommodation and the maintenance of himself and any dependants without taking employment or engaging in business or having recourse to public funds.

Despite this explicit wording, para 58 provides that leave may be given 'with a condition *restricting* his freedom of employment' (emphasis added) not *prohibiting* employment. This is all that the rules permit in respect of an actual student (for a prospective student a prohibition on working may be given: see later).

The difference between a prohibition and a restriction is significant. A prohibition means that any work done will amount to a breach of condition with the resulting possible penalty of removal (Immigration and Asylum Act 1999 s 10) or criminal prosecution (Immigration Act 1971 s 24). A restriction permits work within limitations.

The nature of the standard restriction on work has changed significantly since a government initiative in 1999 to attract overseas students. It is no longer necessary to obtain the permission of the Department of Employment before obtaining work. Students may now take up to 20 hours' work per week in term-time, and are free to work as many hours as they wish during vacations. Students are also now entitled to use Job Centres to look for jobs and apply for them, which they were previously not permitted to do. They may also take internships of three months or less with an employer or prospective employer and carry out work placements in limited circumstances.

There are still some restrictions on the type of work that may be done. They may not engage in business, self-employment, or provide services as a professional sportsperson or entertainer, nor 'pursue a career' by filling a full-time permanent vacancy (IDI Dec 2004 3.16.1). In relation to business or self-employment, the case of *Strasburger v SSHD* [1978] Imm AR 165 still has force. The appellant was in something of a cleft stick. She was an art student who wanted to stay in the UK as a self-employed artist. She had sold some paintings during her time as a student. In order to remain in self-employment she had to show that she could maintain herself. Unfortunately from that point of view, her earnings were considered insufficient. If they had been sufficient, there would have been a risk of her breaching her conditions as a student. As it was, the tribunal held that sale by an art student of their artwork was not a breach of conditions. Although this was decided under HC 82, it is applicable to the present as a guide to permitted self-employment as a student.

The relaxation of the restrictions on students working during their studies is a reflection not only of reduced anxiety about protecting jobs but also of government desire to attract overseas students who pay higher fees than home students, and who may contribute ultimately to the skilled labour force. Of course the option of working makes study more economically viable, although for the most part students are not allowed to refer to prospective earnings in proving that they will be able to support themselves. This rather contradictory position is alleviated in just two situations. It is now possible for an immigration officer or entry clearance officer to take into account earnings from part-time work if the student will be studying at a further education college or university and has guaranteed work at the same institution (IDI Dec 2004 3.15.4) or if the earnings are similarly guaranteed and come from a sandwich placement.

Paragraph 77 allows the spouses and children of students to work providing the student they are accompanying has been granted leave for twelve months or more. Prior to October 2000 the rule said that 'Employment is to be prohibited except where the period of leave being granted is 12 months or more'. It now reads 'Employment may be permitted where the period of leave being granted is or was 12 months or more'. This more positive wording suggests that this permission is the norm which spouses and children of students could expect. Again, such earnings may not be shown prospectively as a source of maintenance for the family, but if the spouse is already in employment then their earnings may be taken into account (3.15.4). In reality the spouse's earnings may be used to support the student and their family once they have arrived.

To obtain entry, aside from the allowable earnings, common sources of income upon which students may rely are: sponsorship from a private individual such as a relative, sponsorship from a government department or employer, savings and grants (including from UK sources). The IDI also points out that students may be charged low fees or reduced fees or even have their fees waived altogether, and all of these arrangements are acceptable for the immigration purpose of showing that the cost of tuition can be met.

These financial questions are likely to be subsumed within the new points system.

10.3.6 Extensions of stay

Students may be given leave for the duration of their course, or for a shorter period. Paragraph 58 says 'an appropriate period depending on the length of his course of study and his means'. The IDI suggests that students should be given leave for the period of the course 'unless there is doubt about them which makes a shorter landing preferable'.

A student may therefore need to extend their stay as a student, either because the leave originally granted was not as long as their course, or because they want to continue with further studies. Applications for extensions will be considered under para 60 of the rules which contains the following requirements.

First, if the applicant is a visa national, they must have been admitted to the UK with a valid entry clearance as a student. The case of *Okello v SSHD* [1995]

Imm AR 269, CA confirms that the rules are mandatory in this respect. Mr Okello was a Ugandan and so a visa national. He had entered the UK as a visitor and applied for variation of leave as a student. However, despite some relaxation in the 'no-switching' rules (see below), the prohibition on switching for visa nationals remains absolute.

This applies also to the dependants of students who may have engaged in studies themselves while in the UK with leave as the dependant of a student. The end of their partner or parent's leave will interrupt their studies if they are a visa national as they will have to leave the UK and obtain entry clearance to return as a student. The exceptions to this are if a visa national was admitted as a prospective student (see below) they may change to student status, and a switch is permitted to post-graduate medical or dental training. A letter of the Home Office IND to an International Student Adviser at Sheffield University stated on 14 December 2000 that this was not a suitable case for a concession. The visa national, who was writing up her PhD, would need to leave the country to obtain entry clearance to return and complete it as her husband's student leave would expire before she had finished her writing up. Rules introduced on 20 September 2000 to enable extensions of stay for writing up a thesis (Cm 4851, inserting para 69J) would not avail her as she did not originally have student leave in her own right.

Second, the applicant must meet all the requirements for student leave and be enrolled on a full-time course of study which meets the requirements for admission as a student.

Third, the applicant must show satisfactory evidence of regular attendance and progress on the current or a previous course. Some of the issues in assessing progress have been discussed above in the context of assessing initial ability to follow the course and reference should be made back to the cases discussed there. The IDI here gives some further guidance on how effort with limited success will be regarded:

Where there are doubts as to progress but attendance is satisfactory and all other requirements are met, leave may be granted but with a warning that failure to produce evidence of satisfactory progress could result in a refusal to grant a further extension of stay in that capacity. (IDI Dec 2004 3.14.3)

In *Juma v SSHD* [1974] Imm AR 96 the tribunal held that improved attendance after the application had been refused would not be a ground for reversing that refusal by allowing the appeal.

Fourthly, the applicant must not, as a result of extension of stay, spend more than two years on short courses at lower than degree level (i.e., courses of less than one year's duration, or longer courses broken off before completion). The intention of this rule is made clear in the sub-heading relating to it in IDI para 3.17: 'Short Courses — Perpetual Students'. The paragraph says that the rule is not intended to affect those 'with a clear study plan showing a logical progression from one course to another'. However, it advises that enquiries should be made where a student has 'enrolled on a new course which bears no relation to previous studies' or is re-enrolling on the same or a similar course 'without apparently making progress', or breaks off mid-course for 'no good reason and then seeks to commence another course', or 'there is any reason to suspect that a student is making his studies an excuse for remaining in the UK for some other purpose'.

Finally, official sponsorship must not have come to an end, or, if an official sponsor is for some reason unable to continue the sponsorship then they must have given written consent for studies to continue supported by other sponsorship which the student must demonstrate is adequate.

The burden of proof that these requirements are met is on the applicant. There is therefore no legitimate expectation that an extension will be granted simply because circumstances have not changed. Each application for leave to remain in the UK was a free-standing and independent application to be considered afresh. So held the Court of Appeal in *Adegoke v SSHD*, 97/1720/4 22 July 1998.

Where student leave has expired but there is sufficient evidence of the student's place on the next course, the Home Office may give an extension of leave to tide the student over between courses.

There are special provisions in the rules for extensions of stay for resitting examinations (paras 69A–F), writing up a thesis (69G–L) and serving as a student union sabbatical officer (87A–F). All these provisions were introduced in the rule changes of October 2000 and they follow the principles of the main student rules, e.g., the time allowed for each purpose is limited, restrictions on working continue, and so on.

Present law is that poor attendance on a course does not deprive a student of student leave. In *R (on the application of Zhou) v SSHD* [2003] EWCA Civ 51 the Court of Appeal held that the attempt to remove the applicant as in breach of his conditions of stay was misconceived. He had stopped attending college, and had been working, but only within the limits allowed by his student leave. The Home Office contended that he was no longer a student, but this was wrong. If they believed his studies had come to an end they should have curtailed his leave under the immigration rules, which would then have given him the right of appeal. As it was he had been detained pending removal, for which there was no lawful authority. In line with *Zhou*, if a student who has lapsed in their studies leaves the country, their student leave may be cancelled if they attempt to return (*B (Nigeria)* [2004] UKIAT 00055 ILU vol. 7, no. 11).

10.3.7 Student nurses

There are special provisions in the rules for student nurses, found in para 64 of the rules. Some of the requirements are equivalent to those for other students, namely having been accepted on the course, the accommodation and maintenance requirement, the ability and intention to study, the intention to leave at the end of studies, the requirement not to engage in business or employment except in connection with the course.

The kind of course for which they must be accepted and the nature of the educational institution are naturally different, and rather intriguingly, the rules include a requirement that acceptance on the course must not have been obtained by misrepresentation. Most notably, following the October 2001 policy change, student nurses no longer need to show that they intend to leave at the end of their studies.

10.3.8 Postgraduate doctors and dentists

Paragraphs 70–75 of the rules set out specific provisions for these two groups. Graduates of medical schools may take limited periods of employment prior to registration with the General Medical Council, i.e., the usual period that intending doctors must work as a house officer before they are eligible to be fully qualified. There is also a provision for post-registration (qualified) doctors and dentists to carry out further, though limited, post-graduate training. These two groups are also exempt from the requirement to show intention to leave at the end of studies. The rules were amended on 19 July 2005 to reflect the changes in the training structure for the professions of medicine and dentistry, and now reflect three levels of training.

Clearly, these activities are more in the nature of employment or training on the job than study. Nevertheless they are dealt with in the student rules. As further schemes are devised in order to develop and attract the skilled work force which the UK needs, the boundary between leave as a student and permitted employment is beginning to blur.

10.3.9 **Prospective students**

Paragraphs 82–87 of the rules deal with applications to enter as a prospective student. This kind of entry gives the opportunity for someone who wants to study in the UK but does not yet have arrangements finalized to come to the UK before those arrangements are completed. This is the only immigration category from which a visa national can change to ordinary student or student nurse status, and the rules concerning extension of stay as a student or student nurse (paras 60 and 67) were amended on 18 September 2002 by Cm 5597 to make this clear.

In order to obtain leave to enter for this purpose an applicant must show:

(i) that they have a genuine and realistic intention of undertaking, within six months of their date of entry, a course of study which would meet the requirements for extension of stay as a student or student nurse; and

(ii) that they intend to leave the UK at the end of their studies or on the expiry of leave as a prospective student if the arrangements do not come to fruition to the satisfaction of the Home Office; and

(iii) that they are able without working or recourse to public funds to meet the costs of study, accommodation and maintenance of themselves and their dependants both during the initial period of leave and during their studies.

Note that this group is given a prohibition on working, not a restriction. This can and should be lifted once student leave is given, and the usual restriction imposed. However, during the initial period of leave, which will be a maximum of six months, the student must support themselves from their own resources without taking paid work.

The rules relating to prospective students are the only ones in the student rules which retains the words 'genuine and realistic', a key phrase in earlier case law. There is no indication in the consultation on the five tier scheme of whether this category will survive.

10.3.10 **Students' families**

Paragraphs 76–78 of the rules deal with the entry of spouses of students, and paras 79–81 with their children. The spouses and children of students and prospective students should be given leave to enter and remain for the same period as the student who is their spouse or parent. These rules are like an amalgam of the student rules and the family rules. The usual capacity must be shown to accommodate and maintain without recourse to public funds, spouses must have a subsisting marriage and intend to live with each other as spouses during their stay, children must be under 18 and must not be married or have formed an independent life. As mentioned earlier, where at least 12 months' leave is granted to the student, the family members will be permitted to work. As the leave of a prospective student will only be six months, it follows that their spouse and children will not be able to work during this period. The spouse must intend to leave the UK at the end of the leave granted, and the children not to stay in the UK beyond any period of leave granted to their parents. The family of students who do not need to show intention to leave at the end of studies will also not need to show this. Where a child passes 18 during their parent's stay as a student, their leave will not be curtailed.

10.3.11 **Entry clearance**

Since all nationalities now require entry clearance for leave of more than six months (see chapter 6), in effect most student leave now requires entry clearance. The exceptions are non-visa national prospective students, who obtain leave for less than six months, and non-visa nationals already in the UK in another capacity who apply to switch to study above degree level (rule change 1 October 2004).

Following implementation of the Immigration, Asylum and Nationality Act 2006 there will be no appeal against refusal of entry clearance, despite opposition to this proposal from University Vice-Chancellors. It may seem to conflict with the Government's policy statements issuing a warm welcome to overseas students. The Immigration Advisory Service report (press release 23 February 2005) that they win a high proportion of student appeals, reaching 75 per cent.

10.3.12 **Switching status**

The temporary nature of student leave has previously been fiercely guarded by successive governments to prevent student leave from being used as a path to settlement. In addition to the focus on proving intention to leave at the end of studies, this has also been done by limiting the immigration categories to which a person can switch at the end of their studies.

The rules prevent switching to other temporary categories such as *au pair* (para 92)or working holidaymaker (para 98 which permitted extension as a working holidaymaker was deleted on 7 February 2005), although students who can continue to support themselves and want to sightsee may stay as a visitor for a maximum of six months. Students may stay as Commonwealth citizens with UK-born grandparents seeking employment (para 189), or as a child, dependent relative or partner of a settled person (Part 8 of the rules generally).

The area of most contention and change is that of students staying for work. In accordance with the policy changes reflecting the government's recognition of the need for skilled workers, and the removal of the requirement for degree level and medical students to show intention to leave at the end of studies, an option has been introduced for graduates, student nurses and post-graduate doctors and dentists, to stay for work-permit employment.

The work permit scheme is discussed in chapter 11. Transferring from student to work permit status has in the past been very difficult, in part because it was necessary to leave the UK to make the application for a work permit. This requirement has now been relaxed for graduates. A practice endorsed by the IDIs became a rule on 18 September 2002 by the insertion of a new para 131A in the rules. This allows an extension of stay for employment where the applicant has had leave as a student, has completed the degree course, meets the conditions for work permit employment, holds a work permit and has the written consent of their official sponsor if any. Similar arrangements are indicated for the five-tier system. Equivalent provisions for nurses, doctors and dentists are contained in para 131B.

The Training and Work Experience Scheme was introduced to allow people to do work based training for a professional or specialist qualification, a graduate training programme or to undertake work experience, and switching into this scheme is possible for students (para 119). As with work permits, the employer must make the application to Work Permits (UK) for permission to employ the person in that capacity.

The other side of the coin is the capacity to switch *into* student status. The most common previous leave is as prospective student, which has been discussed earlier, and visitor. A visa national visitor may not switch into student status, but a non-visa national visitor may switch to a degree course or higher.

Note that an application to switch status is an application for a variation of leave which may be refused if the general grounds of refusal apply in para 322 HC 395. There have been a number of cases of refusal of variation of leave to become a student on the basis of para 322(7), namely, a failure to honour a declaration or undertaking as to the intended duration or purpose of the previous leave. In relation to that paragraph the Tribunal in *Tekere* 01TH00174 said that an undertaking or declaration was a formal matter, not just a statement of present intentions. It implies a promise, or something more than a mere statement. *Ahmed v Secretary of State for Work and Pensions* [2005] EWCA Civ 535 was to a similar effect. A visitor stating their intention to leave is not making a declaration or giving an undertaking. This was followed by the Tribunal in *Rwabeta* 01TH01960. It must be so, otherwise para 322(7) could be used to prevent any switch from a temporary category.

10.4 *Au pairs*

There follows a brief treatment of another temporary category of entry, that of *au pairs*. This is given for the sake of completeness, and for more detail reference should be made to practitioner works such as Macdonald or the *JCWI Hand book*.

The relevant immigration rules are paras 88–94. *Au pairs* come to the UK to live for a time with an English speaking family for the purpose of learning English, and to help in the home for a maximum of five hours per day (para 88). They are to receive appropriate time for study, a reasonable allowance, and two free days per week. This is not regarded as an employment relationship, and the description of the *au pair* scheme as given in para 88 is an immigration requirement for entry to the UK; it is not a contract which the *au pair* can enforce once they have entered the UK.

The *au pair* scheme only applies to people between 17 and 27, unmarried, without dependants, who are nationals of the 11 countries listed in para 89. This list is, very roughly, of some countries bordering the European Union (though it includes Greenland but not Morocco). The *au pair* scheme has traditionally applied to Europeans but is unnecessary for those with EC free movement rights. As nationals of more countries obtain freedom of movement through the creation and gradual expansion of the European Union, the scope of the *au pair* scheme has diminished. The *au pair* must not intend to stay in the UK as an *au pair* for more than two years, must intend to leave the UK at the end of their stay as an *au pair*, and be able to maintain and accommodate themselves without recourse to public funds. All these requirements are found in para 89.

In *The Queen on the application of Ezgi Payir* [2005] EWHC 1426 (Admin) Stanley Burnton J confirmed that *au pairs* come within the definition of 'workers' for EC law purposes (see chapter 5). Therefore a Turkish *au pair* may take advantage of rights given by Article 6 of Decision 1/80 of the Council of the Association between the EU and Turkey whereby after a year's legal employment she could apply for further leave to remain to work for the same employer. The two-year limitation was unlawful in relation to Turkish workers.

10.5 Working holidaymakers

Finally, this chapter takes a brief look at entry as a 'working holidaymaker'. A number of countries have schemes like this which enable young people to travel and work. The standard visitor visa allowing a maximum stay of six months does not enable an extended experience of another country and its life, but the working holidaymaker scheme gives a greater opportunity by allowing a stay of two years, which can be funded at least in part by paid work.

The details of the scheme are found in HC 395 paras 95–103 (but without 98–100, which have been deleted) and are expanded upon in the IDI Ch 4 s 2, particularly Annex C.

In order to qualify as a working holidaymaker the applicant must be a 'national or citizen of a country listed in Appendix 3, or a British Overseas Citizen; a British Overseas Territories Citizen; or a British National (Overseas)' (para 95). Appendix 3 lists Commonwealth countries with the exception of Lesotho. They must be within a specified age bracket, unmarried (unless their spouse qualifies under the same rule and applies to come too), have no child who would be more than five years old at the end of their stay, intend to leave at the end of the working holiday, and be able to maintain and accommodate themselves without recourse to public funds (para 95). All this builds up the picture of a young person who has not settled down, and in fact earlier versions of the immigration rules provided explicitly that the scheme was for an extended holiday before settling down.

In 2002 the Home Office carried out a consultation to consider reform of the scheme. Figures it had produced showed that in 2000, 96 per cent of applicants were from New Zealand, Australia, Canada, and South Africa. In *Pancholi v ECO Bombay* [2002] UKIAT 04170 the greater ease of applicants from wealthier countries in fulfilling the rules was noted by the adjudicator. Equally important, in the particular case the tribunal was careful to point out that the Indian applicant did fit the requirements of the rules. The rules could be applied in a non-discriminatory way providing the decision-maker did not look for the stereotypical Australian traveller. Clearly there were problems in new Commonwealth nationals getting access to the scheme, but whether, noting the advice of the tribunal in *Pancholi*, the problem lay in the rules or their application was another question.

Following the consultation, rule changes took effect on 25 August 2003. Before the changes, in addition to the requirements above, applicants had to be between 17 and 27 when given leave to enter (not at the date of any appeal: *M(India)* [2004] UKIAT 00057 ILU vol. 7, no. 11). They should have sufficient ties in their home country that they had an incentive to return, but not financial commitments which would give them an incentive to engage more fully in the UK economy. This was illustrated in *Shahzad v ECO Karachi* [2002] UKIAT 03380 in which the adjudicator, in assessing the applicant's incentive to return, went too far by requiring him to be 'well settled' in his home country. The tribunal pointed out that this was not required, in fact rather the opposite. The same point arose, with the same result, in *K(India)* [2004] UKIAT 00020 ILU vol. 7, no. 5. This was a refusal under the amended rules on the ground that the applicant was unlikely to return at the end of his leave — probably an inappropriate confusion with the visitor rules, given the new possibility of switching to work permit employment.

The original requirement was that work must be 'incidental' to the holiday. The holiday might be sightseeing, but equally it might be resting and visiting family. This was normally interpreted by ECOs and the Home Office to mean that the holidaymaker should only work for about 50 per cent of their time in the UK. In the consultation the Home Office suggested that there was abuse of the scheme by people working full-time during their stay. The applicant need not have work arranged already, although plans as to the sort of thing they might do would be expected. They were not permitted to engage in business, provide services as a professional sportsman or entertainer or pursue a career.

This restriction on the kind of work a holidaymaker could do was removed by the rule changes on 25 August 2003. Also in these rule changes the age limit was raised to 30, the reference to work being 'incidental' was removed, and replaced by a requirement that the entrant intends to 'take employment as an integral part of a working holiday' (para 95(vi)). The intention appeared to be to address the discriminatory effect of the scheme by allowing more freedom to work, at the same time tackling abuse by legalizing what working holidaymakers were said to be actually doing.

The requirement to have no commitments which would require a regular income was also removed, (Cm 5949) and changes made to enable a working holidaymaker to stay in the UK for work permit employment in certain circumstances (HC 395 para 131D).

In the course of the consultation the Government considered but rejected the idea of extending the nationalities involved, considering that the other changes would be sufficient to widen the scheme's availability. These should be seen in the context of endeavouring to control entry to the UK and prevent illegal working while at the same time widening legal entry for work. Both before and after the changes, it is not necessary for the applicant to have a sponsor in the UK, although a sponsor is one way of proving that there will be no reliance on public funds. Alternatively such proof can come from savings, realistic work plans and so on.

After the 2003 changes, some posts experienced a significant increase in applications. Comparing regional figures for 2002–3 and 2003–4, applications in Equatorial Africa and South East Asia rose by around 400 per cent and in South Asia by more than three times this figure. Refusal rates fell in all these regions, perhaps reflecting that the rules were easier to comply with. However, they were still high, particularly in South Asia (62.6 per cent) and Equatorial Africa (33 per cent). Quayum and Chatwin (2004) report that after these rule changes, ECOs in some posts were still applying (a) the old rules and/or (b) the old attitudes. There was not the rate of successful applications from poorer Commonwealth countries that might have been expected if the rule changes had really removed the discrimination in the system. Compare the refusal rates for Australia and the South Pacific, fairly steady between these two years at 0.2 and 0.3 per cent. Interesting too, in comparing rich and poor countries of origin are the refusal rates with the Southern Africa region: Pretoria 7.7 per cent, Harare 37.4 per cent (2003–4).

On 8 April 2005 the Government suspended applications in Malaysia, Sri Lanka, Botswana, Namibia, and Nigeria (The Times 9 April 2005). On 8 February 2005 the rules changed again to limit work to one year of the applicant's two-year stay and partially restore the restrictions on the kinds of work a holidaymaker might do by once again prohibiting engagement in business or professional sport. The capacity to change to work permit employment was limited to shortage occupations. These changes apparently reinstated those parts of the rules one might imagine would most affect applicants from poorer countries. On 15 June 2005 the specification was reinstated that entry clearance is for two years, as it has been since 1994. This appeared to have been omitted in error in the earlier changes (letter IND to Camden Community Law Centre 14 July 2005).

The restoration of the limits on work was explained by the Home Office in the same letter by concerns that 'the scheme might have come to be regarded as an avenue for entry for the purposes of economic migration, and that its cultural exchange ethos might be undermined'. At the same time the scheme is becoming subject to bilateral agreements which include provision for the UK to suspend its operation at any particular diplomatic post where the rise in applications exceeds the average rise in applications overall and affects the working capacity of the post.

The net result of the consultation, the finding of discrimination against poorer applicants and abuse of the system by successful applicants, the subsequent changes and their reversal, seems to be to slightly tighten the system against abuse by specifying 50 per cent working time in the rules (though this is still unenforceable unless a condition is attached to leave), to support the UK's need for workers by gearing work permits to shortage occupations (see chapter 11), but to leave the discriminatory aspects unaffected.

10.6 **Conclusion**

The temporary purposes reviewed in this chapter facilitate travel, and cultural exchange and learning especially for young people. By and large, they do not fit the image of what is considered to be 'immigration' and, indeed, the *Black's Law Dictionary* definition regards immigration as entry to a country 'for the purpose of permanent residence'. Nevertheless, as we have seen, immigration law and immigration control are concerned with regulating these movements, which are the very essence of what travel (as opposed to immigration) is all about for many people. The earlier dominant concerns with avoiding people gaining settlement and access to the UK labour market is breaking down now that the UK is going through another period of need for workers. It is entry specifically for work, therefore, that we shall move on to consider in the next chapter.

QUESTIONS

1   Is the existence of family life for the purposes of Article 8 dependent on the legal context in which it arises?

2   The Department for Education and Skills encourages universities to recruit overseas students. The Court of Appeal in *Asif* said that the ECO could refuse leave to a student on the basis of his English language ability. Who should decide whether a student is able to follow a course of study?

3   How would you have redrafted the working holidaymaker scheme?

FURTHER READING

Dunstan, R. (2003) 'Family visitor visa applications: an analysis of entry clearance officer decision-making in 2002' *Immigration and Nationality Law and Practice* vol. 17, no. 3, 170–178.

Dunstan, R. (2004) 'Family visitor visas: ECO decision-making 2000–2003', *Immigration, Asylum and Nationality Law* vol. 18, no. 2, pp. 100–105.

Gelsthorpe, V., Thomas, R., Howard, D., Crawley, H. (2004) 'Family visitor appeals: an examination of the decision to appeal and differential success rates by appeal type' *Immigration, Asylum and Nationality Law* vol. 18, no. 3, pp. 167–185.

Gillespie, J. (1994) 'The new immigration rules: visitors and students' INLP vol. 8, no. 4, pp. 126–128.

Macdonald, I., and Webber, F. (2001) *Macdonald's Immigration Law and Practice*, 5th edn

Quayum, M. and Chatwin, M. (2004) 'For Whites only? Does the working holidaymaker scheme still discriminate?' *Immigration, Asylum and Nationality Law* vol. 18, no. 2, pp. 94–99.

UKCOSA Manual (2005) Part 1 (London: Butterworths).

11

....

Entry for work and business

SUMMARY

This chapter deals with the law relating to entry for work. It gives a brief history of the development of this branch of immigration law, then considers the operation of the work permit system, the rules for non-work permit employment, and the new schemes to attract talented people to the UK. The exclusion of asylum seekers from work is also touched upon, and the forthcoming system of managed migration.

11.1 Introduction

In the previous two chapters we have seen that the immigration rules restrict or prohibit paid work for people who enter the UK for other temporary reasons. The policy underlying rules such as these is to protect paid work for the benefit of UK residents. Entry for the purpose of work is only permitted in accordance with the particular schemes and rules governing work. Applications to enter for work are considered as a contribution to the economic welfare of the country, and conditions for granting them will depend more on those perceived needs than on the plans and life circumstances of the person seeking entry. Following on from this, leave to enter for work is always for a limited period initially, although such leave may lead eventually to settlement. From 2002, asylum seekers have been prohibited from working though they may apply for permission to do so if their claim has been outstanding for more than a year. Working in the UK is a right for European nationals; often a necessity for those who seek settlement; permitted for some categories of entrant; prohibited for others, and for those whose skills the UK seeks to attract, it is a lawful and positively encouraged means of entry. In modern day conditions the distinctions between these groups are breaking down. Castles regards the merging of work and settlement as an inevitable process. The natural pattern of migration which he describes is that as spouses arrive and children are born, foreign workers lose their mobility (Cohen, R. (ed.) 1995). However, the trend of present UK policy may be to try to reverse this process and keep categories more separate.

This chapter concerns the entry of workers as workers. First we shall look at the history and development of the law, then at the current legal provisions in the light of our current stage in history. We shall see that the law on entry of workers still bears the features of a scheme designed to meet economic objectives.

11.2 **A brief history of entry to the UK to work and the development of the work permit scheme**

Work permits began in 1916 as a form of permission to work which was issued only to foreign nationals, i.e., non-Commonwealth citizens including Europeans. Work permits were issued for certain kinds of skilled work, but Dummett and Nicol comment that the purpose of the scheme in these early times was 'not very clear' (*Subjects, Citizens, Aliens and Others*, 1990:111). Only a relatively small number of foreign nationals came to work in the UK and the scheme was in part a carryover from the wartime practice of monitoring the presence of 'aliens'. It may be recalled that at this time Commonwealth citizens were British subjects and had, in theory, an unfettered right to enter the UK, though few actually did so.

After the Second World War there was active recruitment to fill Britain's labour needs. Thousands of work permits were issued following very specific recruitment drives, e.g., of Italian men for coalmining. In 1945 the Government instituted the European Voluntary Workers' Scheme (EVWS) which for six years recruited Europeans from the refugee camps for three-year contracts in jobs assigned by the Ministry of Labour. They were to be single people without dependants; they initially obtained no settlement rights and were not treated as full citizens. Alien workers could be directed towards specific occupations as a condition of entry whereas British subjects could not. Paul's work reveals a mixed and changing agenda in relation to these European workers. Crudely summarized, this consisted initially of explicit short-term recruitment to fill labour shortages, then, after initial successes, government began to think in terms of 'the benefits that come from the assimilation of virile, active and industrious people into our stock' (Paul 1997:84). The expectation shifted towards selected European migrants learning English, marrying British citizens, integrating, and solving the labour problem. The Ministry of Labour maintained the right to deport those who ' "through ineptitude or general low mental capacity" or "undesirable character" proved useless' and to refuse entry to disabled refugees or married women with children (Paul 1997:79). The welcome was conditional, and strongly controlling, but national resources were devoted to making it work. In its crudest form the recruitment of foreign workers may be seen as like the operation of a valve, opened when the nation needs certain kinds of workers, and closed when it does not. Bevan, writing in 1986, paints this kind of picture (e.g., p. 278). While it may be seen that even today the form of the work permit scheme is based on national need, allowing recruitment for the skills and jobs which the resident work force cannot supply, there are also rights for the worker to be joined by their family and to apply for settlement in due course. The EVWS and other work permit schemes for Europeans after the Second World War illustrate the valve model with a double agenda. The new workers were selected initially for their usefulness to the labour market and their returnability, being aliens, and therefore entirely subject to immigration control. Quickly, however, they were selected for their assimilability, being white and European.

Low pay and local resentment often accompany the employment of foreign workers, and this may have been a factor contributing towards the shortness of the life of the EVWS scheme. Dummett and Nicol (1990:176) refer to trade union opposition, for instance that of the National Union of Mineworkers, to Poles and Italians being employed in the mines. Another factor may have been that European workers were no longer needed as Commonwealth citizens were filling the vacancies. As described in chapter one, Commonwealth servicepeople, who had fought or otherwise served Britain during the Second World War, returned to make a living and a future in the UK. During the 1950s, Commonwealth citizens were actively recruited by major employers such as London Transport, and the British Hotels and Restaurants Association, with inducements such as the payment of fares to the UK. Much of this work was low paid. As with the EVWS, public opinion ranged between regarding the new workers as saviours of the nation or as taking the jobs of British workers. Paul suggests that in government the welcome was not even ambivalent towards the 492 British subjects who arrived from the West Indies on the *Empire Windrush*, in 1948: 'The colonials were met and housed to avoid "disorder" and with the determination that this was to be a once-only affair' (Paul p. 118). The linkage made between labour market issues and race is covered in chapter one, and the reader is referred to that chapter for fuller discussion.

During this period, then, there were two systems of entry for work operating alongside one another. For foreign nationals the work permit system continued. Public attention, however, was focused not on the entry of foreign nationals but of Commonwealth citizens, who entered by virtue of their right as British subjects, but did so at this time because of the labour shortage and accompanying recruitment campaigns.

In 1962 vouchers were introduced for Commonwealth citizens. Category A vouchers were for Commonwealth citizens with specific jobs to go to; Category B were issued by British High Commissions overseas to Commonwealth citizens with recognized skills or qualifications considered to be in short supply; Category C was open, but issued on a 'first come first served' basis, with a priority for war service. Work vouchers, unlike work permits, carried a right to immediate settlement. However, prior to the scheme, Commonwealth citizens would have been able to settle anyway, and the voucher scheme limited their right to do so. Commentators note that even from its beginning it was a process which subjected Commonwealth citizens to the UK's market needs, and for which their settlement was a necessary concession (see, for instance, *Worlds Apart: women under immigration and nationality law* (ed. Bhabha, Klug and Shutter) WING (1985) and Holmes, *John Bull's Island: Immigration and British Society* (1988)).

The 1965 White Paper restricted entry further by abolishing Category C vouchers and limiting the rest to 8,500. The Immigration Act 1971 completed the process by bringing foreign nationals and Commonwealth citizens within the same work permit scheme. Work vouchers were abolished altogether. The remaining work-related advantages of being a Commonwealth citizen were lost, with the exception of the non-permit basis for entry mentioned below for Commonwealth citizens with a UK born grandparent. On the same date as the 1971 Act came into force, the UK became a member of the European Communities, giving European nationals the right to travel to the UK for work.

In 1979 the work permit scheme was reviewed. This was a time of high unemployment, and the result of the review was to tighten the conditions for obtaining a work permit, so that these only became available for workers with a high degree of professional skill, qualifications, or experience. In 1989 economic circumstances were different, and a further review had a rather different outcome. Devine and Barrett-Brown note that 'there was sustained economic growth with an increasing demand for highly skilled labour, an increase in internationalization in the way business was operating and substantial inward investment by foreign companies' (2001). The Department of Employment was then responsible for the work permit scheme. In the light of these economic conditions its traditional policy of protecting the resident labour force needed some modification to support the development of an enterprise economy. For instance, this required certain applications to be processed more quickly and with fewer demands on employers where they were clearly furthering business growth and investment. The 1989 review therefore resulted in the development of a two-tier system within the work permit scheme. Tier 1 was for applications which would be processed with less investigation. This two-tier system remains in place today and its current criteria will be examined shortly.

In the twenty-first century the conditions of the labour market are different again and the terms of the debate also different. A research report for the Home Office, International migration and the UK: Recent Patterns and Trends, summarized the current issues as being 'the contribution labour migration can make to alleviating the possible impacts of demographic change; a need to compete in a global skills market to remain economically competitive; and a need to recruit overseas workers to meet specific labour shortages' (Dobson, Koser, Mclaughlan and Salt 2001). The first of these three issues, that of Europe's ageing population, was also discussed in the United Nations report of 2000, Replacement Migration. Projections of the numbers of migrant workers that would be needed to sustain European economies briefly became headline news. There was an announcement of change of policy by Minister for Immigration, Barbara Roche, who declared that there would be a new route of primary immigration for people with the skills Britain needed (The Independent 21 July 2000). The labour migration survey casts doubt on these projections, and additionally points out that migrant workers also age, so migration is not a complete answer to the problems of an ageing population. Nevertheless, it has a part to play, and all three factors obtained a place in forming government policy as evidenced in the 2002 White Paper Secure Borders, Safe Haven (Cm 5387). This White Paper was significant in indicating, for the first time since the 1960s, that there might be a positive role for new primary immigration, 'managed migration' to meet the need for workers: 'if we are able to harness the vitality, energy and skills of migrants, we can stimulate economic growth and job creation' (para 3.5).

Globalization and the dominance of information technology are also changing the picture very rapidly. Transnational companies need to place their own skilled workers in countries where they choose to site their operations, increased industrialization in developing countries creates needs for training and travel, ease of travel and transport opens opportunities for workers and for education which in turn changes expectations. For instance, in 1992 the European Union sponsored schemes which allowed approximately 86,000 students to study in other European countries. A decade earlier there was almost no exchange of this kind (Findlay in Cohen, R. (ed.) 1995).

The work permit scheme was opened up to a significant degree by a review carried out in 2000 and 2001. Qualifications of eligible workers were reduced, occupations in which there were shortages were included in the faster procedure of Tier 1 and switching employers within the UK became easier. From its inception, the work permit system had been administered by the government department concerned with employment, by a unit now called Work Permits (UK), formerly the Overseas Labour Service. In June 2001 Work Permits (UK) was transferred from the Department of Education and Employment to the Home Office. A Statement of Changes to the Immigration Rules changed the name of the Department in the rules but no other changes were made to the rules or the legal basis for the issue of work permits. In conjunction with this change the powers of Work Permits (UK) were expanded by enabling them to grant work permit extensions and in-country applications, without the applicant needing to correspond separately with the Home Office. This was also in the interests of speed and streamlining for employers who already have someone available to do the work they need. IND are therefore only involved when the application is made (as most are) from outside the UK. This attempt to make the system more responsive to the needs of business seems, simply from the figures, to have worked. The number of extensions almost doubled in 2004 as compared with 2000.

The 2002 White Paper Cm 5387 recognized shortages of workers in the UK in the most and least skilled sectors of work, and proposed moves in the direction of reinstating economic migration as a lawful option. A general intention to move to the UK to improve one's standard of living by working has not been and still is not a lawful basis for entry unless the application comes within allowable categories. The White Paper concept of 'managed migration' was implemented not in the Nationality, Immigration and Asylum Act 2002 but in schemes and rules outside statute. For instance, like other industrialized nations (see Mclaughlan and Salt 2002), the UK introduced a new Highly Skilled Migrants Programme (HSMP), aimed at the most skilled, which may lead to settlement. Significantly for later developments, both the HSMP and the new innovator scheme were based on a points system, common in other Commonwealth countries but not previously used in the UK. Expansion of the working holidaymakers scheme was also proposed as discussed in the previous chapter, and of the Seasonal Agricultural Workers Scheme (SAWS) considered below. In May 2003 a new sectors-based scheme was introduced which extended the work permit scheme from its traditional base in professional work to fill needs in the food-processing and hotel and catering industries (Cm 5829).

The fact that many asylum seekers are highly skilled and professional people have led some commentators to make the link between the UK's labour shortage and skilled asylum seekers present here but unable to work. See, for instance, the *Immigration, Nationality and Refugee Handbook* (JCWI 2002:421). The Home Secretary in 2003, David Blunkett, however, demonstrated a great determination that entrants to the UK should come by prescribed means only. On 24 October 2003 he announced that 15,000 families whose asylum claims had been outstanding for more than three years would be considered for settlement and work in the UK. This was to 'clear the decks' before tougher measures were proposed (press release 295/2003). On 13 November 2003 entry clearance was made compulsory for all work permit holders who were coming to the UK for more than six months. The effect of these measures was to seal off the possibility of asylum seekers obtaining work permits. The transition from asylum claimant to worker, which had been briefly tried in few cases, would no longer be possible.

On 1 May 2004 ten new Member States acceded to the European Union. As described in chapter 4, the UK, unlike most of its European partners, granted nationals of the new Member States an immediate right to work, provided that they register under the Workers Registration Scheme. The Government's fifth Accession Monitoring Report detailed that there were 293,000 applicants to the scheme between 1 May 2004 and 30 September 2005. A significant number of these were already in the UK at 1 May 2004 (32 per cent in the first quarter). Applicants were working particularly in administration, business and management, hospitality and catering, agriculture, manufacturing and food, fish and meat processing. 'Between July 2004 and September 2005, over 4,000 Accession country nationals registered as bus, lorry and coach drivers and almost 7,500 as care workers. There were 700 teachers, researchers and classroom assistants; almost 400 dental practitioners (including hygienists and dental nurses); and over 500 GPs, hospital doctors, nurses and specialists' (2005:1). The main impact on the UK's labour market was felt in agriculture and fishing, in which employment grew sharply (Portes and French 2005).

Correspondingly, quotas were established in the Seasonal Agricultural Workers Scheme, and then reduced, and quotas were reduced also in the newly created Sectors Based Scheme. As already described in the last chapter, criteria for the working holidaymaker scheme were tightened again very soon after having been relaxed. The positive tone towards economic migration which emerged in the 2002 White Paper did not seem to be sustained. In April 2004 the government announced a ' "top to bottom review" of managed migration routes to assess the extent to which they were subject to abuse or otherwise open to improvement' (Selective Admission para 4.8). The results were a number of measures tightening immigration control, not limited to the economic categories which were the broadly understood scope of the term 'managed migration'.

In February 2005 the publication of the White Paper *Controlling our Borders: Making migration work for Britain* (Cm 6472) announced the introduction of a points system in four tiers encompassing all immigration for work or study, privileging the most skilled both in terms of entry and settlement. In July a consultation document was published, entitled 'Selective Admission'. The tiers had expanded to five, and the criteria were uncompromisingly economic. Tier 1 is described as 'the most highly skilled individuals and people with large sums of money to invest' (para 6.6). Consultees are invited to suggest what attributes should be important for this category. Youth, English language ability, and recognized qualifications are mentioned as a start. It is likely to draw on the Highly Skilled Migrant Programme, combined with features found in points schemes in other countries. Tier 2 is for 'skilled individuals with a job offer where there is a labour market demand'. The document suggests that a Skills Advisory Body should be set up to advise on skill shortages and the state of the labour market, though it is unclear how this would differ from existing bodies. Other occupations where there is a specific overseas requirement may come into Tier 2. Tiers 1 and 2 could lead to settlement. Tier 3 is entitled 'low skilled workers' but confusingly the consultation document includes a heading in this section 'Accession Workers'. It stresses the need for guarantees that a low-skilled worker would return to their home country. Tier 4 is for students, and Tier 5 for a disparate group of people including those on 'youth mobility' schemes and 'visiting workers'.

It is envisaged that all except Tier 1 will need a sponsor, and that sponsors will be drawn further into the system of immigration control, being required to report on whether the migrant is engaged in the occupation for which they came. Sponsors too would be rated; the implication in the consultation document is that they would be rewarded for approved levels of compliance and monitoring. Sponsors would include universities, most of which do not have any system for distinguishing between absence from classes as a result of sickness, boredom or simple default. It would include the largest corporation, as well as the smallest local business.

People in some (lower) tiers may need to pay a bond, returnable when they leave the country. This is likely to act as a significant disincentive. However, disincentive to enter low-paid occupations for which fewer qualifications are required seems a major thrust behind the scheme. The government's position is that there are enough EEA workers now to fill those posts, so others are not needed. Restaurant owners apparently disagree: 'most east Europeans wouldn't know a thing about the spices we use or the way we prepare dishes'. Language would be a barrier too (Enam Ali, Guild of Bangladeshi Restaurateurs, The Guardian 30 January 3006).

From a legal point of view, perhaps the most disturbing and radical aspect of the proposed scheme is that applications would be made at entry clearance posts abroad. The Immigration Law Practitioners Association says that the current work permit scheme: 'is probably the most efficient and effective employment related scheme in the world. It is employer-led and accessible. Work permit applications are processed by teams of highly trained caseworkers' (response to consultation, November 2005). Decision-making in the entry clearance scheme on the other hand, as we have seen, is still of questionable quality (chapter 6). 'Selective Admission' was published at the same time as the Government proposed in the Immigration, Asylum and Nationality Bill 2005 to remove the right of appeal from entry clearance decisions. The minister's justification in Parliament was that decision-making in the new system would be robust and on the basis of objective, accessible criteria (HC Debs July 5 2005).

The proposed scheme does not appear to include self-employed business people, and it is not clear how many of the existing categories of entry will be included. There is a profound contradiction between the avowed intention to serve the economic needs of Britain, and the transformation of entry for work into a non-responsive, routinised immigration decision. The proposals pay scant regard to factors such as the capacity of a worker to have their family with them, change into different employment or settle. They seem to be based on a view that economic advantage is to be calculated in terms of money and labour during working hours, turning the clock back to the early days of the European Volunteer Worker scheme. Indeed an interesting parallel emerges from BBC news coverage of working conditions for eastern Europeans working for one major agricultural employer in the east of England:

The workers sleep in bunk dorms but also have entertainment facilities, free English lessons twice a week and barbecues and a sports pitch for summer nights. On days off, there are coaches to tourist attractions such as Oxford or Alton Towers. ('A foreign corner of an English field' 11 October 2004)

Compare this list of requests from the Ukrainian representatives of European Volunteer Workers in 1948: observance of more national holidays, more organized sports within the hostels, more native-language books in the library, more English lessons and a Ukrainian edition of the BBC show 'Workers' Playtime' (Paul p. 88). The phrasing clearly indicates that these facilities (apart from 'Workers' Playtime' in Ukrainian) were already being provided.

As discussed earlier, Paul compared this with the more grudging reaction to black British subjects who entered to work in the 1940s and 1950s. In 2005 government reaction to new Commonwealth take-up in the working holidaymaker scheme was to tighten the conditions again (see previous chapter) and when Bangladeshi restaurateurs moved swiftly to take up the opportunity to recruit workers in the new sectors-based scheme was to close the catering and hospitality sector. Simplistic comparisons may be unwise. Nevertheless the overall impression of the policy underlying the current proposals is that it is based on a vision of an open door for people who are already highly skilled, highly paid, and fluent in English; a monitored scheme for people from eastern Europe to fit in with labour demands, overlapping with a highly controlled scheme for people to do low-paid work, probably also from eastern Europe; cultural exchange including study for people who are financially independent, and immigration control for the rest.

The consultation closed in November 2005, and at the time of writing the results of this and the full proposals for the scheme are awaited.

Given the current state of uncertainty in relation to immigration for work, the present schemes are described here more in principle than in detail so that the reader may appreciate the position under the current law, and also the nature of the changes as they occur.

There are a number of specific ways in which a person may lawfully work in the UK. First, they may be someone who does not need permission or further permission to work. Second, they may be eligible for a work permit. Third, they may come to the UK to do work which is expressly provided for by the immigration rules and Immigration Directorate Instructions, so called non-work permit employment. Fourth, they may qualify as self-employed business people under the immigration rules. Finally, they may come within one of the special schemes for people with certain qualities, characteristics, or assets. We shall deal with each of these possibilities in turn.

11.3 Needing no permission to work

There are various people who may enter the UK to work without needing any kind of permission from the immigration authorities. These are:

(a) British citizens, including those from the Overseas Territories, as they have right of abode (British Overseas Territories Act 2002 and Immigration Act 1971 s 1);

(b) Irish citizens, who are exempted from immigration control in the Common Travel Area (Immigration Act 1971 s 1(3) and see chapter 6);

(c) EEA nationals, as they have a right to freedom of movement for the purpose of work under the EC Treaties (see chapter 5);

(d) Commonwealth citizens with a right of abode in the UK (see chapter 2);

(e) People who have indefinite leave to remain in the UK (see chapter 6), in other words, are settled;

(f) People with entry clearance in the form of a certificate of entitlement (see chapter 6); and

(g) People who are on their 'probationary period' as a married or unmarried partner (HC 395 paragraphs 282 and 295B).

In addition to those who need no permission to work there are three groups of people who may be granted permission to work, after which the Home Office exercises no further control over the kind of work that they do. These are, first, people who have been granted refugee status; second, those students who are covered by the general consent discussed in chapter 10, which permits them to work without restriction in the vacation and up to 20 hours per week in term-time, and their dependants; third, Commonwealth citizens with UK ancestry. This last is a special category in the immigration rules, HC 395 paras 186–193, which provide that a Commonwealth citizen aged 17 or over who can prove that one of their grandparents was born in the UK, that they intend to seek work in the UK, and can maintain and accommodate themselves and any dependants without recourse to public funds may be granted entry clearance and subsequently leave to enter for four years in this capacity. The capacity and intention to work is all that the applicant needs to prove, they do not have to have a particular job to come to. This kind of leave may lead to settlement, though numbers of people seeking and obtaining such settlement are low, at about 4,000 each year. Providing that the general terms of entry have been kept, so that the person has in fact been working, it is not necessary to show that employment has been continuous. Using its power to discriminate on the basis of information (see chapter 8), the Home Office suspended applications from Zimbabweans in 2004, having formed a view that they were abusing the scheme. In November 2005 applications were resumed (Home Office press release 21 November 2005). 'Selective Admission' gives no indication of the future of this scheme under the five tier system.

11.4 Work permit employment

11.4.1 Nature of work permit scheme

The work permit scheme is unique in immigration law in that work permit decisions, although vital to obtaining leave to enter, are taken outside the IND, in fact until 2001 the work permit scheme was governed by two separate government departments. The operation of the scheme is discretionary and decisions are based on policy rather than legal rules.

Leave to enter for work permit employment is needed, and this is granted under the immigration rules (paras 128–130) by immigration officers or entry clearance officers. However, the role of the Immigration and Nationality Directorate in reality has been secondary to the role of Work Permits (UK) as the influential decision is the one to grant the work permit. This is the sole province of Work Permits (UK).

The maintenance of this separate aspect of decision-making has certain repercussions. Bevan wrote that decisions as to whether work permits should be issued, in what numbers and for what occupations were taken by a government department whose decisions were 'unsupervised and surrounded by secrecy' (1986:280). The fluctuating nature of the labour market and of policies as to how it should be served means that the policy on dealing with certain kinds of work permit applications changes frequently. The conditions of eligibility for work permits are not found in the immigration rules but in guidance notes issued with work permit application forms and other notes and statements, which are accessible on the website of Work Permits (UK) (workingintheUK.gov.uk). Bevan's assessment would therefore be only partly true today as the criteria are more publicly available than 20 years ago. However, their discretionary and non-statutory basis means that they are open both to change without formalities and to variations to suit economic policy. The way that criteria will be applied is therefore largely unregulated and is accessible mainly to specialists who maintain contact with decision-makers. This flexible and policy-based nature of the work permit scheme has been able to grow up easily outside the IND structure, but bringing Work Permits (UK) within the Home Office has not changed these characteristics as they derive not only from the involvement of a separate government department but also from the scheme's economic role and purpose.

The legal basis for the scheme is unique. Neither the immigration rules nor the immigration statutes refer to the making of work permit decisions, but only to the existence of work permits. The decision to issue a work permit, although now made within the Home Office, is not a Secretary of State decision within the Immigration Acts. McLaughlan and Salt make the intriguing suggestion that the power to issue work permits comes from 'the Crown Prerogative within the context of the Immigration Act 1971' (2002:136). However, this may be doubted, as even before the House of Lords decision *Council of Civil Service Unions v Minister for the Civil Service* [1985] AC 374 HL which established that an exercise of the prerogative was subject to judicial review, work permit decisions were treated as judicially reviewable (see, for instance, *Pearson v IAT* [1978] Imm AR 212, CA). Furthermore, the issue of work permits does not find a place in established accounts of the prerogative, and the Court of Appeal in *R v SSHD ex p Northumbria Police Authority* [1988] 1 All ER 556 cautions against using the prerogative as a legal basis for government action in the absence of any specific authority. In *R v Secretary of State for Education and Employment and SSHD ex p Shu Sang Li* [1999] Imm AR 367 Dyson J describes the scheme as 'operated on behalf of the Secretary of State for Education and Employment' and 'not a statutory scheme' but one which 'sets out the policy adopted by the Secretary of State in relation to work permits.' *Macdonald's Immigration Law and Practice* describes the work permit scheme as 'a manifestation of policy similar to Home Office concessions outside the Immigration Rules' (2001:370). The conclusion seems to be that the issue of work permits is indeed a manifestation of policy, just that, without any further legal basis. Scarcely anyone would want to challenge the existence of the power, which is of benefit to all concerned. The question of its nature is relevant to challenging decisions, as discussed below. The new five-tier system envisages integration between work permit and immigration processes, in one decision, apparently to be made at the entry clearance post in the case of applications from abroad. However, co-ordination with labour policy and communication with employers will still be necessary. Not only is there a risk that poor decisions will be made at entry clearance posts, there is also the risk of a lack of transparency about where decisions are coming from. These questions of the source of power and accountability may become more acute if the now well-known procedures of Work Permits (UK) disappear.

11.4.2 Challenging work permit decisions

As decisions to issue or refuse work permits are not, as yet, subject to the immigration rules nor are they an exercise of the Secretary of State's discretion outside the rules, they are not appealable within the immigration appeals system. All that may be appealed to the immigration appellate authorities is the immigration decision to refuse leave to enter or remain when a work permit or extension of a work permit has been refused. However, such an appeal is unlikely to succeed as lack of a work permit is a valid reason for refusal of leave (by Nationality, Immigration and Asylum Act 2002 s 88 a work permit is an 'immigration document', the lack of which may found an unappealable refusal of leave). The effect of this is that the 'real' decision, the one which actually determines whether the prospective worker will gain entry, is the work permit decision and this is subject only to a limited right of internal appeal within Work Permits (UK). The lack of appeal to any judicial body is a further illustration of the nature of the work permit scheme as an expression of economic policy which is not, like other immigration decisions, treated as a matter affecting the exercise of fundamental rights. From this point of view, the removal of appeal rights from entry clearance applications in the 2006 Act is not as much of a change in law as for other entry clearance applicants. However, the impact of removing entry for work decisions to entry clearance posts could be at least as damaging.

A failure to issue a work permit may be challenged by judicial review, but the highly discretionary nature of the scheme means that a challenge is unlikely to succeed (see, for instance, *ex p Li*).

As the effective decision is the work permit decision, and leave will not be given under para 129 without a work permit, the Secretary of State or immigration service could be argued, in administrative law terms, to be unlawfully delegating or fettering their discretion. Variations on this argument were made in a number of early cases, but did not succeed. In the case of *Munasinghe v SSHD* [1975] Imm AR 79 the Tribunal held that it was within the power of the Home Secretary to provide, in rules made under Immigration Act 1971 s 3(2), for consultation with the Department of Employment, and this is so even though the Department of Employment is not assigned any responsibility directly by the Act itself. In *Lim Chow Tom v SSHD* [1975] Imm AR 137 the argument of unlawful delegation was made, relying on the case of *H. Lavender & Sons Ltd v Minister of Housing and Local Government* [1970] 3 All ER 871 in which the minister was found to have unlawfully delegated planning powers because he held himself bound by the decision of another minister (Agriculture, Fisheries and Food) in relation to a planning application. However, the Tribunal did not accept this argument as they considered *Lavender* distinguishable on the basis that under the immigration rules the Home Secretary was required in certain cases to refer applications to the Department of Employment. This distinction is not entirely clear, and is even less clear when the tribunal expand on their reasoning, saying: 'if the Department of Employment (against whose decision there is no appeal within the Immigration Rules) is not prepared to approve the proposed employment the respondent [i.e., the Home Secretary] has no discretion in the matter.' It is indeed difficult to see the difference between this formulation of the position and a minister fettering their own discretion. A similar conclusion was reached in *Chulvi v SSHD* [1976] Imm AR 133 in which the Tribunal found that the Home Secretary had discretion in relation to leave to enter but that that discretion 'should not be exercised contrary to the principle . . . that the granting of permission to take a particular employment is essentially a matter for the Department of Employment'. The case law was reviewed by the Court of Appeal in *Pearson* which came to the same conclusion. The immigration rule then in force was held to be a guideline which indicated how the Home Secretary would 'as a matter of general policy, exercise his discretion' but there would still be room for making an exception. The Secretary of State retained the final decision on entry, as reinforced by the High Court decision in *R (on the application of Thapa) v SSHD* [2004] EWHC 3083 (Admin) in which Bennett J held that the issue of a work permit did not give rise to a legitimate expectation that the claimant would be given leave to remain in the UK.

It follows from what has been said above that there is a limited number of appeal cases in this area of immigration law. Judicial review of refusal of a work permit is available, but success is unlikely, and Macdonald suggests that employers may be reluctant to pursue refusals in the courts (2001:372). Indeed it is evidently more cost-efficient for them to employ someone else rather than hold a post open and fight for a work permit for a particular individual. The prospective worker of course is the real loser, and they may well be outside the country with little prospect of launching successful litigation, especially if the employer is not keeping the post open for them. The new five-tier system seems to envisage that all applications will be made by the entrant rather than the employer. This will not bring them much closer to a remedy, though a system of internal review is proposed, as at present within Work Permits (UK).

Not being governed to a significant extent by accessible and binding rules of law, work permits are an area of practice in which the publication of Immigration Directorate Instructions (IDIs) and guidance notes is of crucial importance. In this chapter we shall rely on those of the IDIs which have been published and on the guidance notes available on the Work Permits (UK) web site. Paragraph numbers are not given for the guidance notes, because although the substance does not change greatly, minor changes are introduced every few months and the paragraph numbers change accordingly. However, a very full contents list makes it easy to find particular subjects.

11.4.3 Structure of work permit scheme

The work permit scheme may be divided into three categories, firstly business and commercial, secondly sportspeople and entertainers, these two groups forming together the main work permit scheme, and thirdly the training and work experience scheme (TWES). It is the business and commercial scheme which is divided into the current Tier 1 and Tier 2. The application for a work permit is made by the prospective employer and must be an application for a named person to do a specific job. The application for entry to the UK under the immigration rules is then made by the employee, under HC 395 para 128, as a holder of a valid work permit.

11.4.3.1 *Business and commercial*

Qualification level
The work permit scheme has become geared to facilitating the entry of skilled and qualified people. For an employer to obtain a work permit, the post for which they are recruiting must require certain minimum qualifications. Additionally, for a work permit to be issued the particular applicant who has been appointed must show that they meet these qualifications and are thus a suitable person for the job. The minimum qualifications are:

(a) a UK equivalent degree level qualification; or
(b) a Higher National Diploma level qualification which is relevant to the post on offer; or
(c) a Higher National Diploma (HND) level qualification which is not relevant to the post, plus one year of relevant work experience; or
(d) three years of experience using specialist skills acquired through doing the type of job for which the permit is sought. This should be at National or Scottish Vocational Qualification (N/SVQ) level 3 or above.

These qualification requirements are easier to fulfil than those which applied before the 2000–1 review when experience was required in addition to a degree and HNDs were not regarded as relevant qualifications. N/SVQ level 3 experience would be for instance as a suitably qualified paramedic, dental nurse or veterinary nurses. Experience gained through working illegally in the UK will not be taken into account.

No suitably qualified resident worker
The idea that the job cannot be filled by the resident work force has historically been fundamental to the work permit scheme. 'Resident' means someone who is an EEA national or has settled status in the UK within the meaning given by s 33 Immigration Act 1971. As an EEA national has a right under the EC Treaty Article 39 (ex 48) to enter the UK for work, there is no necessity for a work permit in their case, and a settled person by definition (s 33) has no restrictions on their stay in the UK which includes no restriction on their working. The inclusion of EEA national in the definition illustrates that policy on the protection of the workforce is now a Europe-wide matter, not just a national one. This requirement is proposed for Tier 2 of the five-tier programme.

It is for the employer to show that they have attempted to recruit a resident worker but that no suitable person is available. Extensive evidence is required of recruitment methods and the reasons why a suitably qualified resident worker was not employed, nor one who with training could do the job. Copies of advertisements must be sent to Work Permits (UK) and these must give all details of the post including salary and experience required. They must also show that the post was advertised in the most suitable media, Europe-wide, for that job.

Since the 1989 review which divided the work permit scheme into two tiers, the requirement to show there is no suitably experienced and qualified resident worker does not need to be met in relation to posts coming within Tier 1, and since the 2000 review, increasing numbers of posts have been brought into that exempt category.

Where the advertising requirements do apply, the relaxation of qualification criteria discussed above does not necessarily help the employer to obtain a worker through the work permit scheme. The intention of relaxing qualification criteria was to help recruitment to meet the labour shortage. However, there is a para-doxical effect in that if the requirements for the post are easier to fulfil, it may be harder for an employer to show that they cannot fill the vacancy from the resident labour force.

Tier 1

The recognition of a skills shortage in the UK and the increasing demand of global-ized business for mobility and flexibility have led to greater numbers of work per-mit applications being designated as falling into Tier 1, which is speedier and less onerous for the employer. Applications for business and commercial permits falling into this tier are not required to give such extensive detail of the proposed employee's qualifications and experience, and do not have to demonstrate that it has not been possible to recruit from the resident labour market by sending details of recruitment methods and advertising. Applications falling into Tier 1 include intra company transfers and board level posts. Applications for work permits to effect intra company transfers enable transnational companies to transfer skilled employees within the company to work in the UK. For the company to qualify the British and overseas companies must be part of a group of companies controlled by the same parent or holding company or one company must own the other. The post must need an established employee who has essential company knowledge and experience. For the individual to qualify, they must have at least six months experience working for the overseas company. Board level posts are at senior board level where the individual has a personal daily input into directing the company at strategic level and substantial board level experience.

The growing transnational quality of the business world creates a different need for mobile workers from the traditional purpose of the work permit scheme. It is not simply the case that the national economy lacks particular skills or workers and looks elsewhere to recruit them, but for large companies national boundaries have less meaning. The work permit system has adapted to this working environment. Findlay identifies a new group of migrant workers which he calls 'skilled transients', that is, 'highly skilled persons moving internationally on relatively short-term assignments before returning to their place of origin or transferring to another international location' (Cohen:1995).

Tier 1 also includes new posts that are essential to an inward investment project which brings jobs and money to the UK. This is for investment by overseas com-panies, not individuals. Individual investors and people intending to set up their own businesses may obtain entry clearance in their own right under special cat-egories of the immigration rules (HC 395 paras 201 and 224) and do not come within the work permit scheme. The rules for individuals setting up in business however are far more onerous. In order for posts to qualify under Tier 1 the invest-ment in this category must be a minimum of £250,000.

The remaining category of Tier 1 applications is that of occupations in which there is deemed to be a shortage of workers. A large number of Tier 1 work permit applications are made in this category. As the name implies, it is for occupations for which Work Permits (UK) acknowledges that there is a very short supply of suitably skilled and qualified people. Shortages are identified by meetings with governing bodies of the industries concerned. Occupations are divided into general categories, including engineering, health care and information technology, and within each category the shortage occupations are set out in detailed and specific lists (specifying, e.g., 'Design and Development of Electronic Systems with Embedded Software'). The lists are available at workingintheUK.gov.uk. By their nature, the lists change regularly. The kinds of occupations included in the shortage category were considerably expanded in the 2000–1 review. This seems to be an unambiguous extension of the reach of the work permit scheme and this is where the expansion of the minimum qualifications has a significant effect. Here there is both no advertising requirement and unlike the categories which are for the benefit of transnational companies, the individual recruited does not need to have an existing relationship with the employer. The intention is clearly to help recruit non-residents to obtain skilled jobs which are not sufficiently filled by resident workers. Occupations are not included in this category just because the skills, knowledge, or experience that they require are rare. If, although unusual, there are enough people to fill the need, then there is no shortage and the occupation will not be listed.

Other criteria

Apart from the establishment of qualifications, and either fulfilling the advertising requirements or showing that the application comes within Tier 1 as described above, there are a number of other criteria applying to both Tier 1 and Tier 2 applications. These are set out in the guidance notes. In summary, the employer must be British-based, and the employee must be employed by that British-based employer. This may sound too obvious to be worth mentioning, but the distinction is between employment by a British employer and a temporary transfer from an overseas subsidiary or a secondment from overseas. Where the situation is really one of temporary transfer or secondment then it is more appropriate to retain the overseas contract of employment. The vacancy must also be a genuine one which existed before the work permit application as the work permit scheme is geared to meeting existing economic need, not to creating jobs for particular individuals.

In general an employee would work at the employer's place of business. However, it may also be that an employee works at the address not of the business but of its clients. In this case the employer must be providing a service at the client's address, not just sending personnel, otherwise there is no true distinction between an employer and an agency.

As we have seen, employing foreign workers on lower pay and worse conditions than resident workers has, in addition to the simple injustice, has caused a great deal of opposition to those foreign workers. It is a condition of the grant of a work permit that the pay and conditions of employment must be at least equal to those normally given to a resident worker doing similar work. In particular they must meet all relevant UK legislation including by payment of the national minimum wage, compliance with the Working Time Regulations (1998), SI 1833/1998 as amended, payment of Class 1 National Insurance contributions and PAYE income tax and the employer must also comply with any relevant licensing requirements.

This is welcome, but historically the worst practices probably occurred outside the work permit scheme, and this is still the case. Whereas the scandals of the 1960s were seen in the long hours and low pay of for instance the Pakistani workers in northern towns and cities, the most acute problem of exploited foreign workers identified now by the Government is to be found in illegal working. The issue of illegal working is discussed later in this chapter.

Finally, the potential employee must not have a controlling or significant interest in the British-based company. This is identified as a shareholding of more than 10 per cent. This was raised in the 2000–1 review from the previous rough figure of 5 per cent, but seems inconsistent with the 49 per cent shareholding allowed to a sole representative (see below). As in that case, the intention here is to ensure that the prospective entrant is an employee, not self-employed or an owner of the company.

11.4.3.2 *Sportspeople and entertainers*

Work permits for sportspeople and entertainers are part of the main work permit scheme. The basic principles relating to sportspeople and entertainers are not very different from those in the business and commercial section. The principle of not employing a person where a resident worker could have done the work is the same, as are the requirements for illustrating that all efforts have been made to employ a resident worker. However, the emphasis on the qualities of the person for whom the permit is obtained is rather different. Instead of showing that there is a need which is not being met, the emphasis is more on showing the unique contribution that can be made by the person or group in question, though this is a question of emphasis rather than absolute difference.

A separate set of guidance notes is available at workingintheUK.gov.uk. Sportspeople will be those who are 'internationally established at the highest level in their sport, and whose employment will make a significant contribution to the development of that particular sport in this country at the highest level.' Entertainers are 'people who have performed at the highest level and have established a reputation in their profession; and people/groups who are engaged to perform or do work which only they can do'. Entertainers may apply as individuals; they may also apply as groups if they are a unit company, which is 'a large group of entertainers who have performed together in their own country and have toured overseas as part of an established production before entering the UK'. For instance, an orchestra will be a unit company, a pop group will not. Members of a pop group would thus have to apply individually. Cultural artists are defined as 'people who are skilled in foreign arts that are rare or unavailable in this country and can make a contribution to the arts, cultural relations and cultural awareness'. Finally, technical or support people may enter in this category if they have proven technical or other specialist skills, and their 'work is directly related to the employment of an entertainer, cultural artist, sportsperson or a dramatic production'.

Where someone makes a unique contribution because of their particular skill or creativity the question of available resident workers becomes irrelevant. Work Permits UK has agreed with the governing bodies of various sports that individuals with a certain level of international standing will be granted work permits without the need to show that no resident worker is available. In the case of football, for example, work permit criteria may be agreed which entail that a player must have played for his country for a percentage of its competitive 'A' team matches and the player's country must be at an agreed place in the official FIFA world rankings for that period. The competitive 'A' team matches are defined as a World Cup Finals or Qualifying group game or a Football Association confederation tournament game. For established entertainers or cultural artists there is no need to consider whether a resident worker could do the job. If Madonna is touring, fans do not want to see someone else instead. There is also a list of festivals to which artists may travel to appear without a permit. The list for 1 May 2003 to 30 April 2004 was of nearly fifty festivals including, for instance, the Edinburgh International Festival and Glastonbury.

11.4.3.3 *Duration of work permits*

As part of the 2000–1 review, from 1 November 2000 the duration of work permits is longer and more flexible. They may be issued for any period up to 60 months, depending on the job. For entertainers and sportspeople who come for an event, the duration of the permit is limited to the time that is needed for the engagement to be completed. For both business and sports or entertainment purposes it is possible to apply for a multiple entry permit which allows workers based overseas to enter for short periods on a regular basis rather than applying for a new work permit every time they want to come to the UK. Multiple entry permits are issued for a minimum of six months and a maximum of two years (HC 395 paras 199A and B, inserted by Cm 5597). After four years of work and residence the work permit holder may apply for settlement (HC 395 para 134). As is usual for settlement applications, the grant of settlement is a discretionary matter (*Parviz Saddati* (11564)), though of course the discretion must be exercised fairly and rationally. The Home Office's Immigration Statistics show a rapid increase of those who obtained settlement after four years on a work permit, from 4,445 in 2000 to 16,210 in 2004. The spouses and dependants of work permit holders accounted for a further 17,050 settlers in 2004, and the total number of people who settled for employment related reasons was 42,265, an increase of 43 per cent on the previous year.

It may be that the upward trend accounts for the change of policy direction in 2005.

11.4.3.4 *Switching into and out of work permit employment*

The work permits scheme is designed for a British employer to bring in a specific employee from abroad. This raises the question, what if they want to employ someone who is already in the UK but who cannot legally work without a work permit?

If the worker is already in other work permit employment in the UK, since 2000 the prospective new employer does not have to show that no resident worker is available, providing the new role is of the same kind as their original work permit employment. Where the worker changes the kind of job they do, whether within the same employer or for a new employer, a recruitment search will have to be carried out to satisfy Work Permits (UK) that no resident worker is available.

The immigration rules used not to make any provision for switching into work permit employment for a person who was already in the UK in another immigration capacity. As the rules were silent on the point there was a discretion to allow an extension of stay for this purpose, and the use of this discretion developed in accordance with the policy of retaining graduates in the UK. IDI Chapter 5 Annex C Aug/01 para 3 explained that the discretion was primarily to facilitate the employment of graduates in shortage occupations, 'to minimise disruption to UK businesses that have urgent need of a particular person with specific knowledge and skills' and 'to support inward investment'. The concession was used in respect of student nurses, postgraduate doctors and dentists as well as other graduates, and Commonwealth holidaymakers. In accordance with the 2002 White Paper proposal (Cm 5387 para 3.14), the rules now make explicit provision for these groups to stay for work permit employment (HC 395 paras 131A, B and D).

The requirement for entry clearance (see below) now effectively seals off the possibility of a skilled asylum seeker obtaining a work permit.

11.4.3.5 *Entry as a work permit holder*

So far in this part of this chapter we have been looking at the policy and guidance issued by Work Permits (UK) which indicate when a work permit will be granted. Currently the decision to give leave to enter for work permit employment is a separate one taken by immigration officers and is governed by the immigration rules paragraphs 128–130. The first three requirements set out in para 128 will almost invariably be met if a work permit has been issued. These are that the applicant:

(i)   holds a valid work permit;

(ii)   is not of an age which puts him outside the limits for employment; and

(iii)   is capable of undertaking the employment specified in the work permit.

Additionally the rule requires that the applicant does not intend to take employment except as specified in the work permit, is able to maintain and accommodate themselves and dependants adequately without recourse to public funds, and in the case of a work permit which is valid for 12 months or less, intends to leave the UK at the end of the approved employment. On 13th November 2003, rule change HC 1224 introduced a requirement for all work permit holders to have entry clearance unless their permit is for less than six months or they are a British national. Until this rule change it seemed that immigration requirements did not in practice add much in the way of hurdles to overcome for most work permit applicants. A number of factors seemed to herald a more perfunctory role for immigration officers in work permit cases.

The five-tier proposal seems to reverse that trend.

11.4.3.6 *Family members*

The spouse, unmarried partner, and dependent children of work permit holders may enter for a period not exceeding that granted to the worker (HC 395 paras 194–199 and 295J). The requirements for entry as a spouse, unmarried partner, or child are similar to those for family settlement (see chapter 9) with the relevant differences which follow from the different status of the primary migrant. These are that family members intend to leave at the end of their stay and, in the case of spouses and unmarried partners, that they must intend to live together during the stay (not necessarily permanently). The requirement which is in the settlement rules for spouses to have met does not appear, and adjustments are made in the rule relating to children such that they enter either with both parents or the sole surviving or responsible parent. As in the case of children coming for settlement there is also a provision that allows leave to enter outside these criteria if there are serious and compelling family reasons which make exclusion undesirable. All family members of work permit holders require entry clearance in that capacity, whether or not they are from visa national countries. There is no restriction on family members working, though they may not rely on public funds.

These requirements for entry apply also to family members of those coming for employment in one of the non-work permit bases for entry discussed later in this chapter. There is no indication how family members will be treated in the five tier system.

11.4.4 Training and Work Experience Scheme (TWES)

The significance of TWES is reduced since the 2000 amendments to the work permit scheme as many of the people who would formerly have been admitted under TWES will now come within the main scheme. As in the main scheme, since 13 November 2003 entry clearance is required for all TWES trainees unless their permit is for less than six months or they are a British national (HC 395 para 116 (vii) inserted by HC 1224).

As the name implies, the purpose is to enable individuals to gain skills and experience through work-based learning, which builds on their previous education and training and which they intend to use on their return overseas. TWES permits are issued either for work-based training leading to a professional or specialist qualification or for a period of work experience. TWES trainees must be employed by the employer who made the application in accordance with the full standards of pay and conditions which would apply to a resident on training or work experience. However, unlike the main work permit scheme the role of a TWES entrant, either for training or work experience, must be supernumerary, i.e., extra to the employer's normal staffing. This is to avoid the TWES scheme being used to take the place of permanent jobs.

Training must be completed in the shortest possible time, so Work Permits (UK) will expect a TWES trainee normally to take examinations at the first possible sitting. Permits for training will be issued for the expected period of the training to obtain the desired qualification (HC 395 para 117) and former time limits have been abolished.

The minimum entry level qualification for TWES is N/SVQ or equivalent, but the person may also need to have relevant work experience to enable them to benefit from the programme. The qualification to which the training leads should be a professional or specialist qualification which requires an NVQ level 3 for entry to training. Work experience must be managerial or at least NVQ level 3 or equivalent.

TWES permits are not issued for sports and entertainment or multiple entry.

11.4.4.1 *Switching into and out of TWES*

The only immigration status which enables the holder to switch into TWES is that of student (HC 395 para 119(i)). A student may obtain a TWES work permit to stay in the UK as a TWES trainee after the end of their studies if all the other requirements of the rule are met. A person in the UK in any other immigration capacity must leave the country in order to apply for TWES. It is possible for a TWES permit holder, with consent of the Home Office, to transfer between employers to do the same kind of training or experience, but only for the balance of time left on their original leave to enter or remain.

A TWES permit holder may not switch directly into work permit employment. In order to obtain a permit on the main work permit scheme they must have been out of the country for 12 months if they had a TWES permit for up to 12 months, or 24 months if they had a TWES permit for longer than 12 months. This buttresses the purpose of TWES, which is that the trainee will return to their home country to use their experience or qualifications, and this should be borne in mind at the application stage as TWES is not a route to settlement.

The consultation document does not indicate how this scheme would fare under the five-tier system.

11.4.5 Sectors-based scheme

This new scheme was introduced in 2003 to meet shortages of workers in the hotel and catering and food processing businesses (mainly meat and fish). The shortages were in occupations which would not meet the usual requirements of the work permit scheme. The occupations for which permits were issued included for instance kitchen assistants, bar staff, fish packers, meat cutters, and trimmers. A quota of permits was issued; the first tranche on 30 May 2003 included 7,500 set aside for workers from EU accession countries. This was made possible by a ministerial authorization of discrimination under the Race Relations Act 1976 (see chapter 8). Workers must be between 18 and 30, and must be employed on the same conditions as resident workers would be. In key respects the scheme is like the rest of the work permit scheme, the employer must show that there is no resident worker available to fill the job and so on. Immigration rules were introduced also on 30 May 2003, HC 395 paras 131I–K (Cm 5829).

The distinction between immigration and work permit decisions became painfully apparent. In Bangladesh in particular, there was a rush to apply for permits. On 15 June 2004, the Government announced, as an interim measure prior to the introduction of country-specific quotas, a limit on the number of SBS permits that may be issued to a single nationality (per Keith Best, IAS Chief Executive, 11 October 2004, Curry Life Round Table Conference). The limit was 20 per cent of each sector's quota. The quota for Bangladeshi applications had already been reached in the hospitality sector so this sector was soon afterwards suspended for Bangladeshi nationals. However, 89 per cent of the prospective workers were refused entry clearance. The employers had paid £153 for the work permit, but the application of immigration criteria, particularly the requirement to show intention to leave at the end of 12 months, demolished most of the applications. Bangladeshi restaurant owners ended feeling aggrieved that their expectations had been unfairly raised (per Keith Best as above). The entire quota for the hospitality sector was suspended in June 2005.

The quota for accession state nationals was not filled, although other applicants from those states were turned away (see Annual Report of Independent Race Monitor 2003–4).

11.5 Specified occupations — non-work permit employment

Non-work permit employment is the third basis upon which a person may lawfully work in the UK. This applies to groups and occupations specified in the immigration rules, providing the requirements attaching to each occupation are met. All groups in the rules need entry clearance, with the exception of seasonal agricultural workers who need a Home Office work card issued by an approved scheme operator. Importantly at the present time, until the implementation of the 2006 Act, these groups have all had a relevant and substantive right of appeal, unlike work permit applicants. The rules in each case require that the person will be able to maintain and accommodate themselves without recourse to public funds, and that the person does not intend to take employment except within the terms of that particular rule. In the case of all except teaching exchanges and seasonal agricultural workers the applicant must intend to work full-time. In chapter 10 we considered the rules for *au pairs* and working holidaymakers. These are also special categories of entry for work purposes under the rules, and were separated out because they have historically more in common with students and visitors.

For details of the particular categories and requirements to be met under these sets of rules, reference should be made to the rules themselves and a practitioner work such as *Macdonald's Immigration Law and Practice*. Here we are concerned to pick out common threads, issues of principle, and to identify the part played in immigration control by these specific categories. For the most part the occupations listed entail certain ties to the country from which the worker comes, which cannot be replicated by a resident of the UK. There is no competition with the resident work force for permanent jobs as the posts are, nor the most part, essentially international. For instance, employees of overseas governments (paras 160–168) or broadcasters (paras 136–143) cannot effectively be replaced by UK residents. The category of ministers of religion does not neatly fit this description, and that of seasonal agricultural workers does not fit it at all. However, these groups have different roles to play in the development of immigration policy, as discussed below.

11.5.1 Ministers of religion

While most religious groups may be satisfactorily served by resident ministers, for faith communities who are in a minority in the UK it may be more difficult to find fully trained ministers. These immigration rules enable minority faiths to recruit fully trained ministers from abroad. The category also recognizes the international character of most religious organizations and enables exchanges between religious communities. In order to apply as either a minister, a missionary, or a member of a religious order, an individual must have relevant training and/or experience (para 170(i)). A sponsoring organization is required, and it is necessary to show an intention to work full-time in the proposed role (HC 395 para 170(ii)). The criteria for dealing with applications are elaborated in considerable detail in the Immigration Directorate Instructions. Notes are given in Chapter 5 Annexes Q, R, T, and U on recognized religious organizations and both core and ancillary duties to be expected of a minister. By way of contrast with this present elaborate system of rules and guidance, at the beginning of the era of control of workers entering the UK, ministers of religion, missionaries, and members of religious orders were one of the few categories of employee who were exempt from the work voucher scheme (Commonwealth Immigrants Act 1962, Instructions to Immigration Officers, Cmnd 1716 para 21).

Following the 2002 White Paper *Secure Borders, Safe Haven* agenda of 'integration with diversity in modern Britain', it is now possible to switch into the category of minister so that a theological student who has been studying in the UK is able to continue as a minister after their studies. The same rule change in 2004 introduced an English language requirement for ministers. The need for this requirement was located in the disturbances in northern towns in summer 2001 in relation to which the White Paper put forward the view that religious leaders needed to be able to communicate effectively with leaders of other faiths (para 3.31). There is a parallel here with the language and citizenship provisions on nationality in the subsequent statute (Nationality, Immigration and Asylum Act 2002: see chapter 2).

11.5.2 Seasonal agricultural workers

The SAWS is an unusually clear cut modern example of recruitment which is highly controlled to meet the economic need of the country. It is essentially a short-term programme. Workers are only given leave to stay for six months in the year, and leave in this category cannot lead to settlement.

The scheme is aimed at full-time students (para 104(i)) who work for authorized operators (para 104(ii)). These workers fill a need for agricultural work which fluctuates over different times of the year, and which is not filled by the resident work force. The 2002 Review of the Seasonal Agricultural Workers Scheme noted 'a decline in the supply of other traditional sources of seasonal and casual labour, such as students from the UK and other European Union countries' (para 3.3.3). This was attributed to the greater availability of less hard and more remunerative temporary work, and to difficulties in moving on and off benefits, particularly when such work was not only temporary but might also be intermittent because of weather conditions. European students and working holidaymakers would rather work in cities, and while the June 2001 census showed that 34 per cent of the agricultural work force was temporary, recruiting these vital workers was becoming more difficult. The majority of seasonal agricultural workers are from Eastern Europe and attending agricultural college in their home country. The Home Office, to meet the need for such workers, and following the 2002 consultation, decided to increase the annual quota of SAWS workers from 20,000 to 25,000, remove the upper age limit of 25, extend the period of the year for which people could be recruited, and extend the kind of work permitted, provided it remains agricultural and seasonal. After a further review the quota was cut to 16,250 for 2005 as much of the necessary agricultural work was being done by the new East European workers.

Both SAWS and SBS are destined for absorption into Tier 3 in the proposed system.

11.5.3 Sole representatives

Because of the wide potential of the category of sole representative a short account will be given here of its requirements. This category, rather than being directed towards a specialized employment market allows an overseas firm to set up branches or subsidiaries in the UK. The purpose of the sole representative's entry must be to set up such a branch or subsidiary. They must have been recruited and taken on outside the UK by a firm which has its headquarters and principal place of business outside the UK and which has no branch, subsidiary, or other representative in the UK (HC 395 para 144). The parent company must be a genuine commercial enterprise and the decision on this will take into account the length of time that the company has been established, its turnover, profitability, number of employees etc. The sole representative also must be a senior employee with full authority to take operational decisions by establishing and operating a registered branch or wholly owned subsidiary of the overseas firm (HC 395 para 144). It is expected that the applicant will be someone who has been employed by the parent company for some time and holds a senior position with them.

In order to show that the business is not transferring its operations to the UK, the sole representative must not be a majority (i.e., more than 49 per cent) shareholder in the firm which employs them (HC 395 para 144(iv)). The IDI suggests that any shareholding above 30 per cent 'should attract detailed scrutiny' (Annex J para 2.2).

If two representatives of the same firm come to the UK they cannot both be admitted in this non-work permit category. One may be treated as a sole representative, and after that person has entered they may make an application for a work permit for the other.

If a branch or subsidiary is established within the 12 months' leave initially allowed to the sole representative (HC 395 para 145) then a further maximum of three years stay may be granted in that capacity (para 148). The case of *Trivedi* 00/TH/1059 INLP vol. 14, no. 3, p. 176 confirms that if a sole representative then applies for settlement after four years in their capacity as sole representative, it is not necessary for the branch or subsidiary to have been established for four years. In other words, they could establish the branch in the eleventh month of their first year and still qualify to apply for indefinite leave to remain at the end of four years in the UK.

11.5.4 Resident domestic workers

The entry of domestic workers in private households has been included in the immigration rules since 18 September 2002 by Cm 5597, replacing the former concession. This concession was introduced in 1980 when the Department of Employment stopped issuing work permits for unskilled workers. It operated in an anomalous way, as it was based on a fiction, the fiction apparently being derived from the dependence of the domestic worker on their employer, and their lack of a separate legal basis for entry. The concession enabled domestic workers already employed by those entering the UK for instance as visitors or business entrants to come to the UK with their employer. The fiction was that the domestic worker (i.e., a cook, a nanny, a chauffeur, etc.) obtained entry clearance as a visitor, which of course prohibited paid work. The reality was they were entering for paid work, but domestic work with a named employer. The arrangement was described as a concession because this was work for which a work permit would normally be required, but was unavailable. Entry clearance was therefore granted on a basis which meant that the employee was unable to change their employer after arriving in the UK as their entry clearance prohibited paid work. The worker was in a catch-22, because if they argued that this restriction should not apply because they were not really a visitor but a worker, their terms of work were held to be restricted to the one employer. The appellant in *Mendoza v SSHD* [1992] Imm AR 122 attempted to argue that she had obtained entry as one of a category, namely, that of domestic servants employed by wealthy non-UK residents. This argument failed, the Tribunal relying on the argument that without the concession a work permit would be required, and this would prevent a change of employer.

This feudal situation was changed in 1998 when the terms of the concession were altered to permit employees who had suffered abuse or exploitation to change employer. The new term applied to those already in the UK at the date of change (23 October 1998) but others could be considered on a case-by-case basis. In the new rules in force from 18 September 2002 the requirement to stay with the same employer has gone, as has the limitation of entry to those whose duties exceeded standards laid down in the International Standard Classification of Occupations. The employer was previously obliged to set out the terms of employment and undertake to maintain and accommodate the employee and this is still the case under the immigration rules (para 159A).

The IDI contains other protection against abuse, requiring that the employee should initially be interviewed separately, and both parties given written information on the legal obligations contained in the employer/employee relationship. However, the IDI also states that entry may not be refused on the basis that the employer refuses to provide an assurance that they will pay the national minimum wage (para 3.3).

11.6 **Establishing a business**

Part 6 of the immigration rules is devoted to leave to enter or remain for people seeking to set up in business. It includes also provision to enter or remain as an investor, and incorporates relevant provisions of the EC Association Agreements with Bulgaria, the Czech Republic, Estonia, Hungary, Latvia, Lithuania, Poland, Romania, and Slovakia. For new EU member countries these still operate as a minimum standard for self-employment as the free movement rights granted so far only relate to employment.

No particular kind of business is contemplated, and the form of the business may be as a sole trader ('trading' here does not imply buying and selling, it refers to anyone who is in business on their own), a partnership or a company (para 200).

In relation to setting up a business as in many other areas, the early immigration rules were rather open and flexible. For instance, Cmnd 1716, the instructions to immigration officers which accompanied the Commonwealth Immigrants Act 1962, stated that

[s]elf-employed people and persons seeking to set up business on their own account should be admitted freely unless it seems unlikely that they will make a sufficient living and may therefore need to seek employment for which a voucher would ordinarily be necessary or to have recourse to public funds. (para 23)

This broad approach to assessing self-employed or business applications has now been replaced with very detailed rules requiring minimum investment, creation of employment and so on. The pre-1973 rules, however, are preserved in the case of Turkish nationals because of the ruling of the European Court of Justice in the case of *R v SSHD ex p Savas* [2000] 1 WLR 1828. The court applied the standstill clause in Article 41 of the Additional Protocol to the EC–Turkey Association Agreement, which provided that EU countries should not, after the date of the agreement, introduce new obstacles to Turkish nationals setting up in business in EU countries. HC 510, in force on 1 January 1973, therefore provides the relevant rules for Turkish nationals, and these give more favourable conditions, for instance allowing switching into self-employment from visitor status.

All business applicants require entry clearance. It is therefore (with the exception of Turkish nationals as mentioned above) not possible to switch to the business category from another one such as visitor, except for the Highly Skilled Migrants Programme discussed below. The applicant must leave the country in order to make their application, but occasionally the Home Office may waive this requirement if for instance there is no safe or functioning British post to which the applicant can return to make their application.

A distinguishing feature of business applications is that this category is intended for owners of businesses and may not be used for an employee as this would be to subvert the work permit system. The business need not be a new business, however, as the applicant may take over or join an existing business. It is essential, whether the business is a new or existing one, that the applicant has a minimum of £200,000 of their own money to invest in the business, and that the business needs this investment (para 201). This must be money held in their own name over which they have control and which they will invest in the UK business. It must be new money, not already in the business, and fully available for that purpose, so not tied up for instance in a house. The minimum investment requirement does not apply to nationals of countries which are party to EC agreements (paras 212–214).

The requirement to show the investment is needed seems to be intended to ensure that the application is a genuine one. As Macdonald points out, the question is not whether the applicant can demonstrate that the UK economy needs their services. The question of market forces and feasibility is not irrelevant as it has a bearing on profitability (2005:556), but the main question is whether this business can be demonstrated to need £200,000 worth of investment. If very little investment is needed then the application will not succeed. Despite the very open wording of para 200, this requirement influences the kind of business that can be set up or joined by nationals of countries outside the EEA or with EC agreements. For instance, starting or joining a business as a window cleaner or street trader would be unlikely to require an investment of £200,000.

The remaining requirements of the rule, though onerous, are generally addressed to the same issues namely, ensuring that the person will be financially self-sufficient and ensuring that the application is not a disguised application for employment. Additionally, to demonstrate the economic benefit of the business the applicant will be required to show that two new jobs will be created (para 201).

11.6.1 Writers, composers, and artists

Writers, composers, and artists are a special category of business applicant for whom the requirements of the immigration rules are not nearly so extensive. There is no minimum investment, job creation requirement, etc. It is simply necessary that they are established in their work, both in the sense of having had their work published, performed, or exhibited and in the sense of being able to support themselves and any dependants from their own resources without working except as a writer, composer, or artist. This opens up the possibility of using other resources than just the current proceeds of their work, providing they do no other work (see paras 232–239).

There are some rather bizarre distinctions between those who may apply under these rules and those who must apply for a work permit as an entertainer. Annex J to the IDI Ch 6 makes this plain. For instance, television and radio scriptwriters need a work permit but playwrights may apply as writers under para 232 of the rules. The creators of some artistic installations using the human body would need to decide whether to define themselves as sculptors or dancers, as sculptors may apply under para 232 whereas dancers are treated as entertainers and so must apply for work permits. Finally, composers come within the rules, but musicians do not, which puts a singer/songwriter in an interesting position. In Macdonald's discussion of this he suggests that such a person entering under para 232 as a composer would face difficulties if they sing as they are working outside their self-employment, singing being regarded as employment. However, only a well-known singer may obtain a work permit, thus making it difficult for new entertainers to enter the UK. He suggests that composers may conduct their work, but not perform otherwise without the permission of Work Permits (UK) (2005:561).

11.6.2 **Investors**

Since 1994 there have been provisions in the immigration rules to enter the UK as an investor. An investor must have at least £1 million of their own money, of which they intend to invest not less than £750,000 in the UK 'by way of UK Government bonds, share capital or loan capital in active and trading UK registered companies' (HC 395 para 224(ii)). The investor must also intend to make the UK their main home and be able to support themselves and dependants without recourse to public funds — a rather extraordinary requirement as of course the possessor of such wealth would not qualify for any means-tested benefit. They must also be able to support themselves without taking employment, as again this would circumvent the work permit scheme. Leave may be granted for 12 months in the first instance, extendable to four years, and entry in this capacity may lead to settlement.

11.7 **Special schemes**

The rules governing entry for business are geared to the creation of jobs and investment in the UK and to attracting business people with significant financial assets. Skilled and creative people may not of course be wealthy, and the new twenty-first century objective to attract skilled people to the UK required some flexibility so that talent as well as wealth would be a basis for admission. Four new schemes have been devised since 2000, the innovators scheme, the Highly Skilled Migrants Programme, The Science and Engineering Graduates Scheme and the

Fresh Talent:Working in Scotland Scheme. The first two schemes are still highly selective, but they at least reduce the standard of wealth required for entry. Maclaughlan and Salt (2002) concluded that the UK had moved 'faster and further' than any other developed country except Australia and Canada in terms of the range of specific schemes to attract the highly skilled.

11.7.1 Innovators

The innovator scheme is for people with new and creative business ideas, and is aimed at science and technology generally, and e-commerce in particular. The objective is to facilitate the setting up of such businesses, but without the requirement for minimum capital laid down by the rules for other business entrants. There must be enough money available to finance the business for the first six months after arrival in the UK, but this may be provided by a third party and need not be the innovator's own money. Like other business applications, the proposal must be one which will create two full-time jobs in the UK. The innovator must own at least 5 per cent of the shares in their company, which must be registered in the UK, and they must be able to support and accommodate themselves and any dependants without working outside the business until it is able to provide an income. If these criteria are met, the application will be assessed on a points system in which there are scores for work and business experience, proven entrepreneurial ability, educational qualifications (again there is an emphasis on science and technology), a realistic business plan, job creation potential, the new and creative aspects of the proposal, how much will be spent on research and development, and personal references. It will be apparent that this is not a scheme to help start inexperienced people in business. The Home Office said that the aim was to attract people who would bring 'exceptional economic benefit' to the UK.

11.7.2 Highly Skilled Migrants Programme

Similarly, the Highly Skilled Migrants Programme is looking for more than just talent. As for the innovators' scheme, the HSMP seeks proven ability and a track record, not only in terms of qualities and qualifications, but also in terms of earnings. The 2002 White Paper says that the aim of the scheme is to attract 'high human capital individuals, who have the qualifications and skills required by UK businesses to compete in the global marketplace' (para 3.18). The HSMP is also run on a points system. In this scheme points are allocated for educational qualifications, work experience, past earnings and achievement in chosen field. Like the work permit scheme and SAWS, entry to the HSMP is by means of another document which verifies the applicant's eligibility. Fitness for the programme is separately assessed by Work Permits (UK), and is not a matter for the entry clearance officer. In their use of points, both this and the innovator scheme may be seen as prototypes of the five tier system, but the consultation document does not indicate how comparable decisions (presumably in the first tier) will be made. The IDI and the scheme guidance set out the number of points that will be allocated: for instance, 30 for a PhD, 25 for a masters degree and so on. The earnings requirement is also explicitly set out. Some factors are a matter of judgement, for instance the difference between 'significant achievement' (15 points) and 'exceptional achievement' (25 points). Exceptional achievement is intended to be a rarity. April/ 05 Ch 5 Annex Z4 para 2 gives the examples of winning a Nobel Prize or Oscar.

Changes in 2003 made the scheme more accessible. The points required were reduced, a different system was set up for those under 28, and some account may also be taken of a skilled partner. The applicant must have earned a minimum figure and will be awarded more points if they have earned a higher figure. The earnings figures are set in different groups to reflect different earnings levels around the world, but this is a very rough measure, putting for instance all European countries in one group.

Both the innovator scheme and the HSMP can lead to settlement. Leave on the innovator scheme is for 18 months in the first instance, extendable to four years. Leave for the HSMP is 12 months initially, again extendable to a total of four years. An applicant on the HSMP must sign a declaration to say that they intend to make the UK their main home. The UK, like other developed countries, is competing not only to attract but also to retain highly skilled people.

11.7.3 **New graduates**

The SEGS and Fresh Talent schemes are both directed to new graduates. The Fresh Talent: Working in Scotland scheme enables graduates of Scottish higher education to receive 24 months' leave within which to obtain work permit employment, set up a business which would qualify for leave under the immigration rules, or obtain a place as a highly skilled migrant or innovator. The SEGS gives 12 months' leave to those who have graduated in a listed discipline within the last 12 months, within which to obtain further leave as for the Fresh Talent scheme. Graduates on both schemes must be able to maintain and accommodate themselves without recourse to public funds.

11.8 **Illegal working**

In the 2002 White Paper the Government also signalled its intention to tackle illegal working. In the immigration context 'illegal working' means the employment of people who are subject to immigration control and do not have one of the lawful bases for work which have been discussed in this chapter. This aspect of unlawfulness however often goes hand in hand with other unlawful practices by the employer such as low pay, breach of health and safety regulations, failure to pay income tax and national insurance contributions, and so on. The last mentioned are almost inevitable as the worker needs to be left out of official records or they may be traced. In effect they also have no remedy against unfair dismissal.

Sanctions against employers for employing those not entitled to work have already been discussed in chapter 7. It was also noted that to date these sanctions appear to have been ineffective to prevent the abuses just described. However, Portes and French report that early indications are that the Accession Workers' Registration Scheme appears to have reduced illegal working (2005:15). Trafficking is briefly discussed in chapter 14, in the context of criminalizing activities connected with immigration.

11.9 **Conclusion and the future**

The broad welcome to economic migration combined with greater specificity in terms of the UK's needs, which appeared to be heralded by the 2002 White Paper, is vanishing already. Policy is repeating old patterns rather than breaking the mould. Comparison between government response to take-up of opportunities by east Europeans on the one hand, and Bangladeshis and new Commonwealth working holiday makers on the other, is reminiscent of the years after the Second World War. At that time too Britain had a labour shortage, though at that time it was the Commonwealth citizens who had a right to come and the Europeans did not.

On the other hand, the system of entry for work may be on the threshold of the greatest change since its beginnings. Although the form and content of this is still unknown in detail, the broad outlines suggest a scheme which lacks the sophistication of the present work permit scheme. ILPA and others suggest that the result will be to surrender the current responsive, speedy and employer-led process and to submit decisions on entry for work to officials whose training and working environment is geared to a culture of gate-keeping. The work-related schemes currently operated by entry clearance officers have been the subject of the first race discrimination claims under the rights of appeal instituted on that basis, but the new scheme makes no proposal for guarding against this bias.

The tiered system itself has not been disclosed in detail, but on the limited information available it appears to give a clear message that the most qualified and wealthy are welcome to come and stay, but others will be strictly limited in their aspirations. The proposed new system, allied to the loss of appeal rights against refusal of entry clearance, does nothing to redress the current lack of remedy for an aggrieved applicant. On the other hand, it is not clear that it will continue to be responsive to the needs of employers in the way that the current work permit scheme is. We may end up with the worst of both worlds.

Entry for work does not attract a great deal of public comment, by comparison with the entry of asylum seekers although the numbers involved are far greater. For instance, in the year 2004, work permit approvals, excluding TWES, for people applying out of the UK, (which excludes extensions and changes of employment) numbered 82,715. In the same year, there were 33,960 asylum applications in the UK (Home Office Statistics 2004). It may be that the ban on asylum seekers working is one factor which creates the disparity in public perception.

In some ways, immigration law concerning workers operates separately from other areas of immigration law. The rules are self-contained, the work permit system unique, the policy objectives are more overtly intertwined with economic policy. Government policy is to maintain a distinction between the highly skilled and financially independent, who are sought for settlement, and low paid low skilled workers, who may come for limited periods as needed. Asylum seekers are outside the pale altogether. It would be an interesting policy objective to seek for connections between the needs of the UK and the needs of those who desire to enter it.

QUESTIONS

1 What are the objections to allowing asylum seekers to obtain work permit employment in the UK? Do these arguments apply to allowing them to work while their claim is being decided?

2 Describe what you see as the advantages of the new tiered system.

3 What is the justification for special categories of non-work permit employment?

FURTHER READING

Andonian, B. (2002) 'Desirable Aliens' *Solicitors Journal* vol. 146, no. 9, pp. 218–219.

Bevan, V. (1986) *The Development of British Immigration Control* (Beckenham: Croom Hill), Chapter 7.

Castles, S. (2000) *Ethnicity and Globalisation: from migrant worker to transnational citizen* (London: Sage).

Cohen, S. (2000) 'Never mind the racism . . . feel the quality' *Immigration and Nationality Law and Practice* vol. 14, no. 4, pp. 223–226.

Devine, L. and Barrett-Brown, S. (2001) 'The Work Permit Scheme — an analysis of its origin and scope' *Immigration, Asylum and Nationality Law* vol. 15, no. 2, pp. 92–101.

Dobson, J., Koser, K., Maclaughlan, G. Salt, J. (2001) *International Migration and the United Kingdom: Recent patterns and trends* RDS Occasional Paper no. 75.

Gillespie, J. (2000) 'Review of work permits' *Immigration, Asylum and Nationality Law* vol. 14, no. 2, pp. 75–76.

Home Office (2006), A Points-Based System: Making Migration Work for Britain.

JCWI (2003) *The Politics of Managed Migration* JCWI Bulletin. Autumn Issue.

Joshi, S. (2002) 'Immigration Controls and Class', in Cohen, S., Humphries, B., and Mynott, E. (eds) *From Immigration Controls to Welfare Controls* (London: Routledge).

Macdonald, I, and Webber, F. (2005) *Macdonald's Immigration Law and Practice*, 6th edn. (London: Butterworths), Chapter 10.

McLaughlan, G. and Salt, J. (2002) *Migration Policies Towards Highly Skilled Foreign Workers* (London: Migration Research Unit, University College London).

Momsen, J. H. (ed.) (1999) *Gender, Migration and Domestic Service* (London: Routledge).

Naidoo, U. (2000) 'Playing conditions: the new work permit scheme for footballers' *Immigration and Nationality Law and Practice* vol. 14, no. 1, pp. 14–18.

Paul, K. (1997) *Whitewashing Britain: Race and Citizenship in the Postwar era* (New York: Cornell), Chapters 3, 4 and 5.

Portes J. and French S. (2005) *The impact of free movement of workers from central and eastern Europe on the UK labour market: early evidence* DWP Working paper no. 18.

Stalker, P. (2000) *Workers without frontiers; the impact of globalization on international migration* (Geneva: Lynne Reiner/ILO).

SECTION 5
The asylum claim

12

The asylum process and appeals

SUMMARY

This chapter describes the asylum process from application through to cessation of refugee status. It discusses the problems of fairness and evidence that have arisen in the asylum process including the concept of credibility and the safe third country and country of origin provisions which may prevent a claim or appeal from being heard at all.

12.1 The nature of an asylum claim

12.1.1 Asylum and migration

The distinction between seeking asylum and other reasons for migration is a modern one. It is a distinction which present-day governments in Europe impose in the way that systems of law and administration deal with potential entrants to a country. In reality however the distinction is not necessarily clear-cut, and in earlier times, no such distinction was made even in law. Stevens (in Nicholson and Twomey 1998) says:

There is evidence to suggest that England was acting as a country of refuge from as early as the 13th century. Until the late 18th century, however, the word 'refugee' had not become a generic term; rather, individuals fleeing from persecution or oppression were viewed, alongside other foreigners, as 'aliens' with nothing to distinguish the normal migrant from those with cause to escape their countries of origin.

In Shah's discussion of the consequences of the Africanization polices pursued by Kenya, Tanzania, and Uganda in the 1960s he makes the point that those Asian citizens of the UK and Colonies who were forced to leave East Africa were in a practical sense refugees (2000:77). The focus at the time was on Britain's obligations to its nationals, but the phenomenon of flight from serious discrimination is in reality a search for asylum. As we have seen in chapters 1 and 2, the situation was dealt with by way of immigration restrictions. However, the Africanization policies which forced them out may be compared with the Serbianization policies which forced those of Albanian descent to leave Kosovo in search of asylum in the 1990s and who were treated as asylum seekers in the UK. The policies were characterized by favouring Africans (or Serbs) over Asians (or Albanians) in matters such as employment, business, and public office.

The House of Commons Home Affairs Committee identified the issue:

The difficulty of distinguishing between economic and non-economic causes of migration is compounded by the fact that the two categories may frequently overlap. Some refugees are undoubtedly motivated solely by the impossibility of continuing to live without persecution in their own countries. Some may be fleeing persecution in their homeland and be seeking a better job and income than is available there. Some may be primarily seeking to improve their economic position which is limited by the political or economic instability in their country of origin. Yet others will have identified the asylum system as a means of gaining access to the economic prosperity and welfare systems of Western Europe. (Second report of Session 2003–4 Asylum Applications HC 218 para 42)

Refugee status is a matter of legal definition as much as personal circumstance. The UK legal system is moving towards greater procedural integration of immigration and asylum claims (the 'Integrated Casework Directorate') but not greater substantive harmonization of rights. The intention and effect of the organizational integration is not to recognize the real continuum between asylum and migration but to facilitate removal of failed asylum seekers who may often be in breach of immigration law, for instance as illegal entrants.

12.1.2 The legal concept of asylum

The legal concept of asylum is nowhere near as old as the practice of seeking it. Dummett and Nicol (1990:143) say that 'the granting of asylum to refugees is as old as the concept of sovereign states'. The legal idea was originally conceived as a matter between states, not, as we tend to see it now, as a matter of an individual's claim for protection from a particular country. This original idea still has importance in the development of asylum law.

A national has the right to expect protection from their government. One way of looking at refugee status would be to say that it arises when that relationship has broken down to the extent that the state is not giving protection. Traditionally, the right involved in asylum is said to be the right of the state to grant asylum, not the right of the asylum seeker to receive it (see, for instance, Grahl-Madsen, *The Status of Refugees in International Law* (1972). This refers to the international nature of asylum and is an assertion that the state cannot demand the return of its nationals (except in legally controlled extradition proceedings). The state owes its nationals a duty of protection, and nationals owe a duty of allegiance, but the state cannot insist on its nationals being returned to its territory; another state can assert the right to give them asylum. Asylum thus arises from the relationship between states. Although the Universal Declaration of Human Rights 1948 Article 14 recognizes the right to 'seek and enjoy' asylum this may be seen on close reading not to be a right to *be granted* asylum. Indeed, Shah (2000:61) recounts how at the stage of negotiating the terms of the Declaration a British amendment removed the words 'to be granted', substituting 'enjoy'. This means to be able to benefit from the status once it is granted, but not to be granted it. Interestingly, moving rather in the opposite direction, the new European Charter of Fundamental Rights recognizes a 'right to asylum' (Article 18). The legal status of this charter was discussed in chapter 4.

The corollary of asylum as a right of the state and not of the individual is that the state has no obligation to grant asylum. This legal doctrine should not be overemphasized, however. The Geneva Convention Relating to the Status of Refugees 1951, (the Refugee Convention) which is the primary source of refugee law, contains in Article 33(1) the obligation which is central to the whole scheme of refugee protection, the obligation of *non-refoulement*, which is in these terms:

No Contracting State shall expel or return (*refouler*) a refugee in any manner whatsoever to the frontiers of territories where his life or freedom would be threatened on account of his race, religion, nationality, membership of a particular social group or political opinion.

It may therefore be said that while a state does not have an obligation to grant asylum, it does have an obligation not to return someone on its soil to persecution. *Refoulement* can happen directly, by putting someone on a plane to their home country, or more controversially it is said that it may be done indirectly, by making their life so miserable and impossible that the better choice is to return and risk persecution. In this latter respect some of the UK's legal provisions denying welfare support to asylum seekers have attracted adverse comment (see, for instance, Harvey in Twomey and Nicolson 1998). The obligation of *non-refoulement* applies to people seeking refugee status as well as those who are granted it, as the status is declaratory, in other words, to be granted refugee status means to have it recognized that one *is* a refugee, rather than to be made a refugee (Goodwin-Gill 1996:141).

Arguably, Article 33 is limited to those already on the territory of the contracting state. The combination of the lack of duty on the part of the state to grant asylum and this limitation on Article 33 has meant that states have been free to develop policies which prevent asylum seekers from ever reaching their territory in the first place. We have seen in chapter 7 how visa rules, airline liaison schemes, juxtaposed controls, and carrier sanctions operate with this effect (see also, for instance, Blake in Twomey and Nicholson 1998), and the development of criminal sanctions is discussed in chapter 14. This territorial view of Article 33 is not universally shared. Goodwin-Gill, for instance, espouses the view that the Convention has extra-territorial effect (1996:141 *et seq*). He describes the actions of the US in intercepting refugees on board ships from Haiti and returning them to Haiti as a breach of the obligation, despite the Supreme Court ruling permitting the practice in *Sale, Acting Commissioner, INS v Haitian Centers Council* 113 S Ct 2549 (1993).

It is clear that the Refugee Convention does not apply to people who are still in their country of origin (*R v Immigration Officer at Prague Airport ex p European Roma Rights Centre* [2004] UKHL 55) and does apply once the asylum seeker reaches the territory of a destination state. These points however do not address the situation in the *Sale* case, i.e., when the asylum seekers are in transit. This question has had life and death importance in relation to allowing boats to land. The most well-known example in recent times was the refusal of the Australian Government to allow landing to the Norwegian ship the *Tampa*, which had rescued hundreds of asylum seekers from drowning. Despite international criticism and partially successful constitutional challenges in the Australian courts, the Refugee Convention did not avail the travellers. Head cites the lack of extra-territorial reach as a failure of the Convention (2004:22), and see Willhelm for an account of Australia's legal response.

12.1.3 Refugee Convention

The 1951 Refugee Convention sets out the internationally agreed definition of who is a refugee and standards for treatment of refugees and is the legal basis for refugee claims. Refugee law is thus still fundamentally a part of international law. Different jurisdictions develop the law of the Convention in somewhat different ways. This and the following chapter have the limited objective of providing an introduction to refugee law in the UK. The emphasis is therefore on the interpretation of the Convention in the UK, but reference is made to the case law of other jurisdictions. The House of Lords in *Adan v SSHD* [2001] 1 All ER 593 affirmed the view that the Convention should be given a consistent interpretation among the contracting states in order to provide an effective system of refugee protection. The greater accessibility of the case law of other jurisdictions now makes the objective of consistency more attainable and knowledge of the case law of other jurisdictions is essential to a full understanding. The procedure for recognizing refugee status is left to individual states, although procedures should be devised within the standards of fairness set out by the Executive Committee of the United Nations High Commissioner for Refugees (UNHCR).

The Refugee Convention was originally drafted to deal with the displacement of people as a result of the Second World War. It restricted the definition of refugees to those whose fear of persecution arose from events occurring in Europe before 1 January 1951. The Protocol of 1967 removed the time restriction and promoted a gradual removal of the geographical restriction but the refugee definition was not changed. The definition is derived from the needs and negotiations of the time, and its central requirement for a fear of persecution arises from the treatment of political dissidents in what were then the Communist countries of Eastern Europe and the Soviet Union. The main present day causes of refugee movements are not the escape of political dissidents from persecution, but armed conflict, large scale human rights abuses and natural disaster. Thus, the legal concept of asylum and its manifestation in the 1951 Refugee Convention are only a small part of the international phenomenon of people seeking refuge. Flight from war and natural disaster was not in the mind of the drafters of the Refugee Convention. Its terms do not lend themselves easily to these situations, and the vast majority of uprooted people in the world do not apply for legal status through the Refugee Convention. Most people who are forced to leave their homes are internally displaced which means that they remain in their country of origin. The number of people in this position remained constant from 2001 to 2004 at about 25 million (Global IDP Project, *Global Survey 2004*). Those who left their home country in search of safety and would be termed refugees amounted to over 9 million in 2004 (2004 Global Refugee Trends UNHCR 2005). The UNHCR is the body given the task, worldwide, of protecting all refugees and addressing the issues which give rise to refugee movements. People who have fled intolerable conditions but not used the Convention are referred to as *de facto* refugees, a much larger group than Convention, called *de jure*, refugees. In 2004 around half of the refugee population under UNHCR care was granted protection under the Convention, some were granted protection under other international instruments, and the majority were granted refugee status on a group basis. In Europe however the majority (76 per cent) were granted status on the basis of an individual determination process, and it is this process and the law governing it that we are studying. This legal processing, case by case, of individual refugee claims is a tiny part of the global picture in relation to refugees.

There are calls from a number of quarters for the Convention to be amended, but these come from opposing viewpoints. Some would like to see the Convention widened to include more contemporary forms of refugee movement, and situations that are at present difficult to bring within the Convention, such as the oppression of women and the abuse of children. Others would prefer to narrow the definition and so reduce the numbers of refugees that states can be obliged to take. Therefore while the Convention definition is a product of its time, a redraft would be the product of the present time, in which refugee movements are a more contentious issue internationally than they were at the time of the original Convention.

The UNHCR Handbook is a major aid to interpretation of the Refugee Convention. Its use was endorsed by the House of Lords in *T v SSHD* [1996] 2All ER 865 and it will be referred to frequently throughout this chapter.

12.1.4 Political nature of asylum

The grant of asylum might seem to imply criticism of the state of origin, as recognized by the Court of Appeal in *Krotov v SSHD* [2004] EWCA Civ 69: 'it is in the very nature of adjudication upon asylum issues that the tribunals or courts concerned with them are, for the purposes of surrogate protection underlying the 1957 Convention, obliged to examine and adjudicate upon events internal to another state' (para 42). This is a humanitarian act, and thus should not be construed as a hostile action. As Dummett and Nicol say, quoting Lauterpacht: 'An enemy of his government is not an enemy of mankind' (1990:144). Unfortunately, sometimes an asylum claim which fails *may* be treated as a hostile act, not one committed by the government in the state where the claim was made, but by the asylum seeker themselves. There is therefore sometimes a risk that people whose asylum claim has failed may face persecution on returning to their country of origin for having made a claim. The question then is whether the failed asylum claim can give rise to a claim for asylum in itself (see, e.g., *Senga* (12842) discussed in the next chapter).

It follows from Lauterpacht's principle not only that a home state must allow an asylum claim to be made and to be successful without taking revenge, but also that governments should not band together against the asylum seeker. Lauterpacht also says that the international community is not one of mutual insurance for the maintenance of established governments and that treason is not an international crime. The definition of 'national security' used in the House of Lords judgment in *Rehman v SSHD* [2001] 3 WLR 877 asserts the principle that a threat to the security of one nation is a threat to all, and casts doubt on whether Lauterpacht's view is still regarded as valid. The picture developing in relation to 'international terrorism' does have elements of mutual insurance for the maintenance of established governments. This theme is explored more in chapter 14 in the context of exclusion from asylum.

Despite the humanitarian principles, there is no doubt that the grant of asylum is intimately connected with politics at all levels. Macdonald makes no bones about this:

The recognition rate for refugees has less to do with merits than with politics. Thus between 1989 and 1998 Canada granted refugee status to over 80% of applicants from Sri Lanka, France to 74%, and the UK to 1%: Refugee Council response to the Home Secretary's Lisbon Proposals, January 2001. (2001:468 n 2)

Not only the outcome but also the conduct of refugee cases is subject to political considerations. For example, at the outbreak of war with Iraq at the beginning of 2003, the hearing of Iraqi asylum appeals was suspended by the Immigration Appellate Authority, initially for six weeks. At a legal level, it is possible to see reasons for this as it could be difficult to assess the risk of persecution to an individual when the country to which they would be returned is in chaos. At a political level, to grant asylum to those individuals at that stage could be seen to undermine confidence in the outcome of the war. The Home Office often announces suspension of removals to a country at a time of civil disturbance. This was done for instance in the case of Sierra Leone. However, in the Iraqi cases the suspension was not only of the Home Office's own executive action but was of the judicial process, and at the request of the Home Office.

12.1.5 Legal nature of the refugee claim in the UK

The Refugee Convention contemplates an individual application process, and the way that many states parties to the Convention have chosen to do this is by creating systems for establishing legal entitlements. The system for claiming asylum has thus become integrated into the legal systems of signatory states and has become a branch of law in its own right. In the UK the choice was made at an early stage to give this responsibility to the Home Office, the same government department that deals with immigration, rather than an independent body. Although the same government department is often involved in immigration and asylum, in some countries such as Canada and New Zealand, there is a separate status determination process with an appeal against refusal of refugee status. This is not the case in the UK, where the trend is rather for asylum decisions to become increasingly intertwined with the immigration system. As noted earlier, this closer relationship is not with the aim of creating flexibility in the system to accommodate to real life circumstances of the claimant, but rather to facilitate removal. The refugee claim in law is quite unlike other claims to migration as it is a claim for international protection rather than to be admitted to a particular territory pursuant to the immigration policies of a particular country. As such, there is a strong case for an independent refugee claim determination system, quite separate from the Immigration and Nationality Department. In the UK, the increasing incorporation of asylum into the immigration system has tended to bring the border control mentality into the grant of asylum, so that it appears less controversial to make extensive use of detention and other draconian control measures, such as the removal of welfare support, because dealing with asylum claims is seen as part of managing migration and policing a frontier (see, for instance, Kostakopoulou and Thomas 2004 and Cornelisse 2004).

The Aliens Act 1905 gave the courts jurisdiction over the question of whether a person's circumstances would give grounds for exemption from deportation where political asylum could be claimed. However, when the 1905 Act was repealed and replaced by the Aliens Restriction Act 1914 and 1919, the exemption for refugees disappeared. Refugee status was a matter for the Secretary of State (*Bugdaycay* [1987] AC 514), not an independent body and not the appeals authority.

Immigration statutes continued to omit any provision for refugees until the Asylum and Immigration Appeals Act 1993 provided that a claim for asylum was a claim that it would be contrary t[...] Convention for the claimant to be remo[...] *refoulement* obligation under Article 33, and ga[...] claim. However, although there is a process to [...] when it is refused there is no appeal against refusal o[...] against the associated immigration decision. So for instan[...] against refusal of leave to enter the UK or a decision that the[...] from the UK (Nationality, Immigration and Asylum Act 2002 s 82)[...] 'the removal of the appellant in consequence of the immigration de[...] breach the UK's obligations under the Refugee Convention' (2002 Act s [...] means that the tribunal hearing an appeal in reality determine whether the a[...] lant qualifies for refugee status, even though they are not, on a successful outcome for the appellant, entitled to grant refugee status, because that is a matter for the Secretary of State. The appellate body can only say that leave to enter should be granted, or that the appellant should not be removed, as the case may be. This was so even in a case where failure to apply policy in an asylum decision amounted to unfairness and an abuse of power. The court made a declaration that the claimant should be granted indefinite leave to remain, and declined to make a declaration of refugee status as 'that is a status conferred on the basis of criteria prescribed in an international treaty and should not be conferred if those criteria are not at the time of the decision satisfied' (para 37). This matter had not been determined at the hearing (*SSHD v R (Bakhtear Rashid*) [2005] EWCA Civ 744).

The Court of Appeal in *Saad, Diriye and Osorio* [2002] Imm AR 471 reiterated the traditional view that the refugee decision is one for the Secretary of State, but added 'We are not however to be taken as deciding that the question whether a person is a refugee can never be decided by the courts' (para 20).

There is an exception to this which is the so-called 'upgrade appeal', where a person has, instead of refugee status, been granted more than one year of humani-tarian protection or discretionary leave (see later). A person in this situation may appeal against rejection of their asylum claim (2002 Act s 83, confirmed in *Saad, Diriye and Osorio*). In terms of this task, however, in looking at all the evidence for and against the claim, Simon Brown LJ said in *Ravichandran v SSHD* [1996] Imm AR 97 at p. 112 that 'in asylum cases the appellate structure . . . is to be regarded as an extension of the decision-making process'. There is no escaping that in reality the judicial body determines the substance of the asylum claim.

The relationship between the courts and the Secretary of State in relation to the asylum decision is the institutional aspect of the legal nature of an asylum claim. The substantive aspect is the relationship between the Refugee Convention and domestic law. The presumption is that Parliament intends to legislate compa-tibly with Treaty provisions, subject to displacement by express contrary indication. However, in the case of the Refugee Convention the situation is more complex. The whole refugee determination process is an application of the standards and principles of the Refugee Convention, so even without statutory incorporation, the provisions of the refugee definition in the Convention are applied every day by Home Office decision-makers and, in effect, by courts and tribunals. Section 2 Asylum and Immigration Appeals Act 1993 provides:

Nothing in the Immigration Rules (within the meaning of the 1971 Act) shall lay down any practice which would be contrary to the Convention [i.e. the Refugee Convention].

irport and another ex p
erred to this section as a
gee Convention (para 7).

f State in accordance with the
nvention and Protocol relating

ims are decided are set out in
lum Policy Instructions (APIs),
e reference to incorporation, it
ase that applying for asylum was
graph 327 provides:

o claims that it would be contrary to the
ons Convention and Protocol relating to
r required to leave the United Kingdom

e source of the definition of an asylum
on should be dealt with, but the actual
Convention, not the rules.

Clai..
purpose of se..

Thus far, we can see ... tween the Convention and the rules, but what of statute? Current authori..., resented by *R (on the application of Pepushi) v Crown Prosecution Service* [2004] EWHC 798 (Admin) is that where a statute clearly conflicts with the Refugee Convention, the statute prevails, even though this defeats part of the protection of the Convention. This is the approach taken by the Asylum Policy Instructions to a conflict between Immigration and Asylum Act 1999 s 31 and Article 31 of the Convention (see chapter 14). The disturbing implication of this is that Parliament can legislate its way out of international obligations, though, interestingly, not in contravention of Directive 2004/83. In relation to delegated legislation the position is different. Although not yet challenged in the courts, the conclusion of the Parliamentary Joint Committee on Human Rights was that delegated legislation which conflicted with the Convention and made under a statutory power that purported to give effect to the Convention was ultra vires (see chapter 14 re Specification of Particularly Serious Crimes Order 2004, SI 2004/1910).

12.1.6 Asylum and human rights

Claims for asylum under the Refugee Convention may raise questions of human rights. Often the experiences feared or fled by refugees are violations of human rights, and human rights law has a bearing on the establishment of a refugee claim. At the same time, many violations of human rights are without redress either nationally or internationally, and an asylum claim is not a claim that human rights have been or will be violated, but a claim that the refugee has a well-founded fear of persecution. International human rights norms are used to help to determine what amounts to persecution, as this is not defined in the Refugee Convention itself, but their place in this definition is a matter of debate. Human rights claims within a domestic system may also be used as a safety net where refugee claims fail, and in

many countries including the UK a successful human rights claim may give rise
to a lesser status of protection than refugee status, described near the end of this
chapter.

12.2 **Process of making an asylum application**

The outline of the process of making an asylum application will be described in
this section in order to give the context for the legal issues that arise. Making an
asylum claim is, in practice, a difficult thing to do within the law. Even before
deterrent provisions were as fully developed as they are now, the predicament was
described by Schiemann J in the case of *Yassine v SSHD* [1990] Imm AR 354 at 359:

The effect of the Carriers' Liability Act 1987 coupled with the Secretary of State's action in the
present case is to pose substantial obstacles in the path of refugees wishing to come to this
country. This is because:
1. Visa nationals require a passport before coming here;
2. You [sic] cannot get a visa on the basis of being a refugee in a country where you are being
    persecuted because at that stage you [sic] are usually not outside the country of national-
    ity and thus do not fall within the definition of refugee and there is no provision for such
    situation in the immigration rules;
3. By reason of the 1987 Act carriers are disinclined to carry those without visas.

The Asylum and Immigration (Treatment of Claimants etc) Act 2004 has
introduced further obstacles which will be discussed later in this chapter and in
chapter 14.

Asylum applications may be made at the port of entry or at a later stage after legal
or illegal entry. The latter are known as 'in-country' applications. The first stage in
either route is usually an 'asylum screening interview'. In its five-year plan in February 2005 the Government announced a 'new asylum model', elements of which
are gradually coming into effect. In this model, the first interview will determine
which route the claim is to follow. The full model envisages some nine routes or
'segments', including 'detained fast track', minors, and 'late and opportunistic
claims'.

The screening interview does not deal with the substance of the claim, but in
current practice is to establish the identity and nationality of the applicant, to take
fingerprints and photographs and decide whether their route of travel suggests that
they could be returned to a safe third country. If this is the case, details of their
journey will be noted and any periods of time spent in countries en route. Safe third
country provisions and their development are described at the end of this chapter,
as the remainder of the material here follows the process of a claim which is
considered in the UK.

After the screening interview the applicant is given an asylum registration card
(ARC) which holds biometric details, a prototype of the current UK Government's
identity cards for all. A decision is taken on whether to detain the applicant or
admit them on temporary admission (see chapter 15). Applicants from countries
deemed safe or whose claims can be decided quickly may be detained immediately
in Harmondsworth Removal Centre or Oakington Reception Centre and subjected

to the 'fast-track' procedure (see below). There are also two induction centres, the first of a planned comprehensive system for asylum clams, to which an applicant may be sent at this stage. Someone who is temporarily admitted rather than detained will be given a Statement of Evidence Form (SEF) to complete and return within ten working days. The form must be completed in English and accompanied by translations of any written evidence relied on.

Shortly after return of the SEF, the applicant will be interviewed. After the interview, the decision will be communicated to the applicant by letter. Where, as in the majority of cases, the application is refused, the applicant receives what is known as a 'reasons for refusal' letter. These are discussed below in relation to the quality of decision-making. Asylum interviews require specific discussion.

12.2.1 Asylum interviews

The asylum interview is the applicant's opportunity to put their case in person. The SEF is structured around the refugee definition, and may not have given the scope for personal explanation. Also, at the interview there must be an interpreter when the applicant requires it, so while they may have had to cope with the SEF without translation facilities, this is not the case in the interview. Combined with the SEF the interview gives the body of information upon which the claim will be decided, and is very important to its success or failure.

The UNHCR Handbook says,

While the burden of proof in principle rests on the applicant, the duty to ascertain and evaluate all the relevant facts is shared between the applicant and the examiner'. (para 196)

The API on interviewing says that

The purpose of the asylum interview is to establish the facts of an asylum claim. Whilst an asylum claimant might have submitted information to the Home Office previously, the asylum interview will be the principal opportunity for a claimant to set out their claim and for the caseworker to examine any details they consider necessary. (para 2.2)

Thus, the interview should not be an adversarial process, but rather a collaborative investigation. Numerous inquiries into the asylum process have nevertheless commented on the poor and combative quality of asylum interviewing. For instance, Amnesty International records a perception by Home Office caseworkers of the interview as an opportunity to obtain material to attack the applicant's credibility by noting inconsistencies between the interview and the SEF and storing them up for a later refusal letter rather than putting the inconsistency to the applicant then and there (2004:20). The current APIs are a model of good practice in this respect, advising that any such discrepancies 'are thoroughly probed at interview', but it is clear from repeated studies of decision-making that the high standard of the APIs is not necessarily maintained in practice. Interviewers have also been criticized for chaotic questioning, not dealing with the relevant issues, appearing adversarial and intimidating, and not dealing sympathetically or appropriately with those who have suffered trauma such as rape or torture (e.g., Asylum Aid 1999, Amnesty International 2004).

From 1 April 2004 it is no longer possible in most cases for an applicant for asylum to have public funding for a representative to be present at their asylum interview. The Court of Appeal in *R (Dirshe) v SSHD* [2005] EWCA Civ 421 held that in these circumstances, where the applicant had no public funding either for a representative or for their own interpreter, the overall fairness of the process required that the applicant be able to tape record the asylum interview, so that there is some record of it independently of that kept by the Home Office. The earlier case of *Mapah v SSHD* [2003] EWHC 306 (Admin) went in the opposite direction, but this was when legal aid was available for a representative to attend.

Dirshe has been interpreted in the API as an obligation to record the interview 'on request by the claimant'. Applicants may request an interpreter or interviewer of their gender, but this is of little use if they do not have advice about this before interview. Not only is publicly funded legal advice rarely available for asylum interviews but, as discussed in chapter 8, is now generally in very short supply. Immigration Law Update reports that the Home Office acted rapidly upon the requirement to tape interviews, but the Legal Services Commission has been less willing to fund the time for lawyers to listen to the tapes (vol. 8, no. 11, p. 28).

12.2.2 Quality of initial decision-making

The initial decision on an asylum claim is crucial for a number of reasons:

- Most obviously, it concerns matters of fundamental human rights, and affects the physical safety, the material and psychological well-being of the applicant
- As a public law decision of a governmental body it is an exercise of power and uniquely disposes of the matter in question (unlike say a private commercial transaction in which if a greengrocer puts up their prices the customer can decide not to buy or go somewhere else)
- The applicant has little chance of obtaining legal representation to appeal a wrong decision as sources of advice are few and far between
- Asylum law and procedure is demanding and complex, and an unrepresented appellant has little chance of succeeding
- If the applicant can obtain legal advice, the work and public expense of undoing a wrong decision can be considerable, causing a burden on the legal system
- The asylum decision is an implementation of an international protection treaty. The decision-maker has a responsibility to implement this so as to maintain the standards and principles of that international scheme.

The actual quality of asylum decision-making has by no means matched its importance. Criticism of the process has been sustained from a variety of sources. Since 1995 eleven major reports from governmental and non-governmental organisations have been published which are highly critical of the asylum decision-making process. They are listed in the reading at the end of this chapter. The reports on quality focused broadly on three areas: the interview, the reasons for refusal letter, and information about asylum seekers' country of origin. This last subject is treated separately below at 12.8.3.

Asylum Aid drew attention to 'unfair and arbitrary methods' as 'the norm' and found that 'many people with valid reasons for seeking the UK's protection were refused asylum on the basis of cursory and careless examination and fundamental misunderstandings of the situations of refugees' (1999:1). Across all the reports, concerns are found in common, including:

- medical evidence corroborating horrific abuse was dismissed or misunderstood;
- proof was required to an excessively high standard (see below and chapter 13 for the asylum standard of proof);
- minor ambiguities or discrepancies were used to discredit the applicants, even when these had no bearing on the basis of the asylum claim;
- insensitivity in interviewing about serious trauma, particularly torture and rape;
- ignoring evidence relating to an individual;
- but also turning down claims on the basis that country-wide human rights reports documented abuses but did not refer to the applicant personally;
- unreasonable assertions about individual credibility;
- inappropriate use of standard paragraphs in reasons for refusal letters;
- making findings at odds with the evidence.

The reports contain dozens of examples. Just one which illustrates some of the points above is that of an asylum seeker who had over a hundred burn marks on his back, and bruises where he had been held down. The reasons for refusal letter opined: 'Taking into account your appalling lack of credibility the Secretary of State considers that in fact these wounds were inflicted at your request in an attempt to strengthen your claim' (Asylum Aid 1999:19).

Asylum Aid (1999), the Medical Foundation and the Constitutional Affairs Committee considered that there had been an improvement in the quality of interviewing and decision-making over the time upon which they were able to comment. However, serious concerns remained. The Home Office's written guidance had improved greatly, so that the Medical Foundation in 2004 was able to say that the APIs were on the whole good. Crucially, though, the APIs were not necessarily followed, and it was clear that monitoring and research had to continue along with a programme of measures to generate better quality decisions.

One, albeit contested, indicator of the quality of initial decision-making is the number and outcome of appeals. The Home Affairs Committee noted:

Over the past ten years there has been a steep rise in initial-level appeals ... from 2,440 determined in 1994 to 64,405 determined in 2002. This has been accompanied by a significant rise in the proportion of appeals which are successful, from 4% in 1994 to 22% in 2002. (Second Report 2003–4 HC 218 para 122)

The Committee took this as an indication that 'there are still grounds for concern about the poor quality of much initial decision-making by immigration officers and caseworkers' (para 143). The Government took the view that the way to deal with an increase in the number of appeals was to cut down the right of appeal. Thus, in the Asylum and Immigration (Treatment of Claimants etc) Bill which became the 2004 Act they proposed reducing the appeals system to one tier. When asked to report on the Bill the Home Affairs Committee took this view of the problem and the solution:

The real flaws in the system appear to be at the stage of initial decision-making, not that of appeal. We recommend that the implementation of the new asylum appeals system should be *contingent* on a significant improvement in initial decision-making having been demonstrated. In particular, the relevant sections of the Act should not be brought into force until the statistics show a clear reduction in the number of successful appeals at the first tie, adjudication level. (First Report 2003–4 HC 109, para 43)

The Committee repeated this view in its report on asylum applications (HC 218 para 143) and the Constitutional Affairs committee supported the recommendation (HC 211 recommendation 5). The remit of the Constitutional Affairs Committee's second report was to consider the effects of the 2002 Act and whether it had improved efficiency savings and improved the quality of the appeal process. Ostensibly, neither this nor the Home Affairs Committee in its first report was concerned with the asylum application process. However, the conclusion of both was that the problem did not lie in the arena of appeals and the matters addressed by the legislation. The real problem lay in the quality of initial decisions. The Home Affairs Committee recommended that there should be 'greater "front-loading" of the applications system, that is, putting greater resources into achieving fair and sustainable decisions at an early stage' (HC 218 para 144). It recommended more good-quality legal advice and interpretation at an early stage, recruitment of more caseworkers with specialist knowledge of asylum seekers' countries of origin and review of the 'overall calibre and training' of those who take initial decisions (para 144).

The most recent report referring to asylum decisions is the 2005 report of the Independent Race Monitor, in which she says:

I reviewed samples of initial decisions and concluded that there was evidence of inappropriate decision-making. In some instances, caseworkers disbelieved claimants who told 'similar stories' about events, assuming they must have learned the details from others. Several refusal decisions were based on caseworkers' assumptions about what should have occurred, or on small discrepancies and inconsistencies in accounts of events, giving the impression that there was a tendency to disbelieve, and whatever the applicant's experience, some grounds for refusal would be found. (para 18)

It appears that although there have been improvements, much still needs to be done. The House of Commons Committee of Public Accounts recommended that IND find out why appeals are upheld, particularly among nationalities for which the highest rates of appeals are allowed (recommendation 7).

The Government responded to the Constitutional Affairs Committee that they did not accept that the quality of initial decision-making was poor (Cm paper 6236) and the single tier proposal was not only retained but swiftly implemented.

Sometimes case law reveals a lack of training or information within the decision-making process. For example, from October 2000 there was a policy in force that asylum seekers should not be refused asylum on the ground that they could relocate in the Kurdish Autonomous Area, having travelled through government-controlled Iraq. This was on the ground that travel through this route would not be safe for a failed asylum seeker. Mr Rashid was refused asylum during the currency of this policy, on the ground that he could relocate to the KAA. He did not know of the policy. Nor apparently did any caseworker or lawyer for the Home Office at any of the six decision-making points in his claim and appeal, though it was well known to some others. The Court of Appeal held that this was unfairness amounting to an abuse of power (*SSHD v R (Bakhtear Rashid)* [2005] EWCA Civ 744).

12.2.3 **Non-compliance refusals**

Paragraph 340 of the immigration rules allows the Secretary of State to refuse an asylum or human rights claim where there is 'failure, without reasonable explanation, to make a prompt and full disclosure of material facts, either orally or in writing, or otherwise to assist the Secretary of State in establishing the facts of the case'. This includes failure to report for fingerprinting, or to complete an asylum questionnaire (the SEF), comply with a request to attend an interview or report to an Immigration Officer for examination.

In *Haddad* (00HX00926) the Tribunal held that refusal must not be for non-compliance alone. The rules require, as we have seen, that applications must be determined in accordance with the Refugee Convention. Therefore even in a case of non-compliance, whatever evidence is available about the claim, even if it is in the form of brief notes taken by the immigration officer on arrival, must be considered (API on non-compliance 2.2). See Macdonald (2005:784–5) for further discussion of the law surrounding these refusals.

Although the position following *Haddad* is that a refusal may not be issued on the grounds of non-compliance alone, it is clearly unsatisfactory that a matter of perhaps life and death should be determined without an interview, or even on the basis of just a few notes. There is room for speculation as to what difference, if any, it would make if Article 6 ECHR were applied to refugee claims. Article 6 requires a fair and public hearing in the determination of civil rights and obligations. As there is no civil right to asylum, Article 6 could only apply, if at all, to the right to have a claim assessed. The determination of whether this has happened in a sense only occurs at an appeal hearing. Perhaps the application of Article 6 would open the decision-making process to greater scrutiny at the tribunal. See also the Court of Appeal's discussion of fairness in *R(on the application of the Refugee Legal Centre) v SSHD* [2004] EWCA Civ 1481, discussed below.

12.3 **Fast-track procedures**

There are two main procedures and legal routes into fast track asylum decision-making. One procedure is based at Harmondsworth Removal Centre, the other at Oakington Reception Centre. On 20 July 2004 rules came into force enabling the Harmondsworth fast-track procedure also to operate at Campsfield House Removal Centre (Immigration and Asylum Appeal (Fast Track Procedure) (Amendment) Rules 2004, SI 2004/1891).

The route associated with Oakington is used for those asylum seekers who come from countries that are designated safe by statute or statutory instrument, based on the Secretary of State's belief that there is 'in general' or relating to a particular part or a particular group, no risk of persecution in that country. These provisions are known colloquially as a 'White list'. Applicants from these countries may expect to have their case certified as unfounded, and so to have no right of appeal in the UK. This certification is discussed below, and detention at Oakington is discussed in chapter 15.

Selection for Harmondsworth is not based on a statutory presumption of an unfounded claim, but on a departmental list which may change frequently, compiled under the authority of a ministerial authorisation to discriminate on the basis of nationality, Race Relations Act 1976 s 19D, as explained in chapter 8. This list is of countries from which applications may be deemed suitable for quick decision. This usually means refusal as shown by the Asylum Statistics; for instance in the third quarter of 2005 there were 325 initial decisions at Harmondsworth of which one or two were grants of asylum. Claims at Harmondsworth are to be decided in three days. Time limits for appeal then allow two days for notice of appeal, two days for a respondent's notice, and the hearing must be fixed within two days after that. (Immigration and Asylum Appeal (Fast Track Procedure) Rules 2005, SI 2005/560). The UNHCR has commented that the two day time limit for appealing is too short, and runs the risk of returning someone to persecution and thus contravening the Refugee Convention (Asylum and Immigration Tribunal — Fast Track Procedure Rules, Response to Consultation CP(R) 05/05 Department for Constitutional Affairs).

The lawfulness of the fast track was challenged by the Refugee Legal Centre, but the Court of Appeal held that although the system was not operating with sufficient flexibility, and improvements should be made, it was not *inherently* unfair and therefore could not be said to be unlawful (*R (on the application of the Refugee Legal Centre) v SSHD* [2004] EWCA Civ 1481 at para 25). The Refugee Legal Centre obtained an unusual costs order before the Court of Appeal hearing, protecting them, in view of the public interest nature of the case, from liability for the Secretary of State's costs in the event that they lost — as they did.

IND's operational instructions were revised to respond to the Court of Appeal's comments on the need for guidance about when to be flexible in the operation of the fast track procedure. The April 2005 version make provision for such contingencies as for example the illness of the applicant, non-attendance or lateness of representative and the need for more evidence to be gathered. The emphasis is on retaining the speed of decision-makings, to the extent of allowing IND caseworkers to decide the probative value of evidence before they have actually seen it. The instructions may be seen at ind.homeoffice.gov.uk (Detained Fast Track Processes — Operational Instructions).

Harmondsworth is intended only for single men, interpreted by the Minister for Citizenship and Immigration as 'men who have no dependants on their claim' (HC Debs 16 Sept 2004 col 158WS). The claimant argued in *Kpandang v SSHD* [2004] EWHC 2130 Admin that his detention in Harmondsworth was unlawful partly because he had a partner and child. McCombe J was persuaded that 'single' meant that there were only detention facilities for men on their own, not that it referred to their marital status. He also held that short detention in reasonable circumstances would not in general be a breach of Article 8 and was not in this situation given other justifications for detaining the claimant (see *R (on the application of Saadi) v SSHD* [2002] UKHL 41, discussed in chapter 15).

The 2003 report into conditions of detention at Harmondsworth by the Chief Inspector of prisons found that the centre was 'unsafe'. There was a hunger strike in May 2004 in protest at the length of detention, poor legal advice and assaults by staff. Although the legal process is fast, once the claim has been denied and the appeal lost, the claimant may then face a considerable period in detention before being removed. BID found that two months' detention following failure of the claim was common, and reported an instance of ten months of such detention (BID to Des Browne, Minister for Citizenship and Immigration 15 March 2005).

There were disturbances at the centre on 19 and 20 July 2004 when a detainee, Sergey Baranuyck, was found hanged in a shower room. A report into the disturbances by Sue McAllister, Head of Security Group, H M Prison Service found, ironically, that the open and unstructured nature of the detention for 501 young men, without the usual system of earning privileges associated with prisons, was in part to blame for the tensions in the centre (HC 1265, November 2004). A further report by the Chief Inspector of Prisons in July 2005 found that there had been some improvements but that shortcomings remained, including in reception procedures and access to competent legal advice. There was another suicide at Harmondsworth on 19 January 2006, the thirteenth in immigration detention in the UK since 2000.

Under the new asylum model, 'detained fast track' will be a 'segment' of asylum cases. Some commentators welcome this development as a genuine step towards more effective decision-making, crucially if it is accompanied, as the Home Office says it will be, by an improvement in interviewing and decision-making. There is a danger, however, that Home Office administrative procedures become too closely associated or confused with legal status or rights. As Farbey says, 'there is no difference between asylum claimants in Harmondsworth and elsewhere, save that the Home Office has decided that Harmondsworth cases can be speedily processed' (2004:199). These claimants are subjected to a different set of appeal procedure rules, with shorter time limits for action to be taken. The judicial process has therefore been changed according to the view taken by one party of the merits of the proceedings.

12.4 'Safe' countries of origin

In a sense, the Harmondsworth/Campsfield fast track is the latest in a history of developments in which generalized presumptions are made about the merits of a class of asylum claim. The idea that a claim can be 'manifestly' or 'clearly' unfounded is a part of this (see below), as is the practice of identifying certain states within which there is 'in general no serious risk of persecution' (Nationality Immigration and Asylum Act 2002 s 94(5)), known as 'safe countries of origin' or a 'White List'. People from these countries are detained at Oakington Reception Centre.

In *Asylum Statistics 2004* a list headed 'Key changes to reduce the number of asylum applications' begins with 'Non-suspensive appeals', referring to the safe country of origin provisions of the 2002 Act (p. 9). It is therefore clear, if there were any doubt, that safe country of origin provisions are designed to have a deterrent effect on asylum claims. Blanket statements of safety sit rather uneasily with the requirement to investigate whether the particular applicant is at risk. They raise questions, as we shall see below, about the use and provision of 'country information', that is, reports on the state of human rights in the country generally, which are often important sources of evidence as to risk.

The doctrine that certain countries are generally safe has been used in the UK to restrict the appeal rights of asylum claimants from those countries, either by limiting their appeal to one tier, or expediting the claim or both, and eventually to remove the in-country appeal altogether.

The first official 'White List' in the UK was created under powers in the Asylum and Immigration Appeals Act 1993. There was an expedited process and restricted right of appeal where the applicant could be returned to a country in which it appeared to the Secretary of State that there was 'in general no serious risk of persecution'. The countries were listed in Asylum (Designated Countries of Destination and Designated Safe Third Countries) Order 1996, SI 1996/2671 as Bulgaria, Cyprus, Ghana, India, Pakistan, Poland, and Romania. At the second Parliamentary reading of the Bill which preceded the 1996 Act the Secretary of State announced the criteria that he used to designate a country or territory as follows:

(a) The country or territory was one in which there was in general no serious risk of persecution;

(b) It was one from which a significant number of asylum claims to the UK were made; and

(c) A very high proportion of those claims were refused.

The claimants in *R v SSHD ex p Javed and Ali* [2001] Imm AR 529 challenged the designation of Pakistan as a country in which there was in general no serious risk of persecution. They relied in particular on the House of Lords judgment concerning women in that country in *Shah and Islam* (see chapter 13) and the recorded position of Ahmadis there. The challenge raised interesting constitutional questions. The Order had been made by affirmative resolution in Parliament, and for the Secretary of State it was argued that the affirmative resolution was a proceeding in Parliament. To interfere with it would therefore be a breach of Article 9 Bill of Rights 1689 which prohibits proceedings in Parliament from being questioned in the courts. The Court of Appeal did not accept that argument. By approving the Order, Parliament had not debated its justification in detail or examined the evidence for it. Even though the Order was made by affirmative resolution it was still delegated legislation and as such open to judicial review in the usual way. Having disposed of the constitutional point the Court of Appeal found that on the evidence concerning women and Ahmadis the Secretary of State's decision to include Pakistan in the White List was irrational.

A later challenge to the inclusion of India failed (*R (Balwinder Singh) v SSHD and Special Adjudicator* [2001] EWHC Admin 925) on the basis that 'in general' did not mean 'recurring', 'ongoing' or 'predictable'. It referred to the spread of persecution over the population, and the persecution of Sikhs was considered to affect too small a percentage of the population to amount to persecution 'in general'. Burton J also found that there was nothing illegal in the Secretary of State having a policy of this kind, and that this did not interfere with each case being decided on its merits.

However, the White List had proved very controversial. It was, after a time, abandoned and in the Bill preceding the 1999 Act, the Government confirmed that there would be no new White List (Cm 4018 para 9.9).

The concept of claims 'without foundation' had its first statutory expression in the 1993 Act. This included claims which were considered as 'manifestly unfounded' and 'manifestly fraudulent'. The fundamental requirement of such a designation is that the claim is considered to raise no issue as to the UK's obligations under the Convention. Similar provisions were repeated in Sch 4 of the 1999 Act. Some of the grounds that were considered to make a claim 'manifestly unfounded' have undergone transformations in various versions of the immigration rules (para 341) in relation to credibility, and reappeared in criminal offences created by the 2004 Act, for instance, failing to present a passport or identity document (see chapter 14).

In the Nationality, Immigration and Asylum Act 2002 the concept of a 'clearly unfounded' claim and a new White List were brought together. Section 94 provides that there will be no in-country appeal if the Secretary of State certifies that the human rights or asylum claim (or both) are clearly unfounded. This is of enormous importance to the applicant, as if the certificate is not defeated they face removal from the country without any appeal (non-suspensive appeal — i.e. the appeal does not suspend the removal). Subsection (3) says:

If the Secretary of State is satisfied that an asylum claimant or human rights claimant is entitled to reside in a State listed in subsection (4) he shall certify the claim . . . unless satisfied that it is not clearly unfounded.

Three points may be made about this subsection. It contains a duty as it uses the word 'shall'. This limits the scope for judicial review of the exercise of a discretion. Secondly, there is a presumption that this duty will be exercised unless the Secretary of State is satisfied that there are reasons to the contrary. The burden of proof is therefore on the claimant to show that the claim is not clearly unfounded. There is room for judicial review of the Secretary of State's failure to be so satisfied, but as the burden is on the claimant, more will be required to show that no reasonable Secretary of State could have failed to be satisfied that the claim is not clearly unfounded. The double negative here is clumsy but required for accuracy. The meaning of 'clearly unfounded' may be discovered by looking at recent case law on the meaning of 'manifestly unfounded'. The change seems to be attributable only to a drive towards the use of shorter words detectable in the 2002 Act. Finally, the listing of states does not relieve the Secretary of State of the obligation to make the decision to certify in a particular case. Although the presumption is that the claim will be certified clearly unfounded, that decision must still be made. In *ZL and VL v SSHD and Lord Chancellor's Department* [2003] 1 All ER 1062 the Court of Appeal set out the decision-maker's process of reasoning to certify a claim clearly unfounded:

   (i) consider the factual substance and detail of the claim

   (ii) consider how it stands with the known background data

   (iii) consider whether in the round it is capable of belief

   (iv) if not, consider whether some part of it is capable of belief

   (v) consider whether, if eventually believed in whole or in part, it is capable of coming within the Convention. (para 57)

It concluded that there was 'no intelligible way' of certifying a claim from a listed country except by this same process (para 58). *Koceku* clearly demonstrates that in every case a view must be taken of the merits of the case, even when the applicant comes from a White List country.

In *R (on the application of Razgar) v Secretary of State for the Home Department* [2003] EWCA Civ 840 the Court of Appeal held that whether a claim was manifestly unfounded (here, a human rights claim) was a question of whether it was arguable, and this is the accepted test. The House of Lords decision in this case did not overturn this point. Where there is a factual dispute the Secretary of State must leave this to be argued. This was demonstrated in the *Ahmadi* case which absorbed news coverage for a short while (*R (Ahmadi) v SSHD* [2003] ACD 14). There were disputed points under Article 8, in particular the needs of some family members for psychological and medical care and thus their human rights claim could not be certified as manifestly unfounded. They were entitled to have these points considered.

There is a power in s 94 to add to or remove from the list by Order made by the Secretary of State. The grounds for addition are very similar to those in the White List of 1996, namely that the Secretary of State is satisfied that

(a) there is in general in that State or part no serious risk of persecution of persons entitled to reside in that State or part, and
(b) removal to that State or part of persons entitled to reside there will not in general contravene UK's obligations under the Human Rights Convention (s 94(5)). Initially the statute listed the ten states which were due to accede to the European Union on 1 May 2004.The 2004 Act s 27(4) deleted these states as a tidying-up exercise after accession.

Under the predecessor of s 94 (s 115, which was a short-lived transitional provision) an Order was made, adding Albania, Bulgaria, Serbia and Montenegro, Jamaica, Macedonia, Moldova, and Romania. Under s 94 orders have been made, adding Bangladesh, Bolivia, Brazil, Ecuador, Sri Lanka, South Africa, and Ukraine (Asylum (Designated States) (No. 2) Order 2003, SI 2003/1919) and India (Asylum (Designated States) Order 2005, SI 2005/330).

Criticisms could be and have been made of the inclusion of a number of these countries. For instance, it is difficult to reconcile the inclusion of Albania with the UK Government's commitment to improve its policy and practice in relation to the protection of women trafficked for sex, Albania being one of the major centres of organized crime of this kind. Certification of an Albanian case was successfully challenged in *R (Koceku) v SSHD* [2003] EWHC 2063 in which Newman J said that the evidence of a sufficiency of protection in blood feud cases fell short of a standard which would make Mr Koceku's case unarguable. There had been conflicting findings in relation to protection in similar Albanian cases in the very recent past.

In *A v Secretary of State for the Home Department* [2003] EWCA Civ 175 the Court of Appeal found the Jamaican appellant at risk of her life and of degrading treatment, giving rise to breaches of Articles 2 and 3 if she were to be returned. The speed with which a claim may be refused and the person returned without an appeal hearing may give rise to real risks in individual serious cases such as that of A. In *Atkinson v SSHD* [2004] EWCA Civ 846 (see chapter 13) the Court of Appeal held that there was at least an arguable case that the criminal justice system offered insufficient protection for the applicant in Jamaica. The claim should not have been certified.

It may be apparent that there are two levels of decision which may be challenged. One is the more specific decision to certify the particular claim, as in Atkinson's case, as clearly unfounded. The more fundamental challenge is to the designation of a country within s 94. The designation of Bangladesh was successfully challenged in *R on the application of (Zakir Husan) v SSHD* [2005] EWHC 189 (Admin). Wilson J held the inclusion of Bangladesh to be irrational and therefore unlawful in the light of a volume of evidence about widespread human rights violations in the country. The more or less unanimous picture painted by CIPU reports at the time of the designation of Bangladesh was that violence in politics was pervasive, the use of torture was widespread, abuse of children and violence against women and religious minorities was common and widespread and corruption endemic (*Hasan* para 55). Bangladesh was removed from the list of safe countries on 22 April 2005 (Asylum (Designated States) (Amendment) Order 2005, SI 2005/1016).

The arguments in *Hasan* raised some important and interesting questions about the basis for designating a country as 'in general' one in which there is no serious risk of persecution. The Secretary of State relies in part on the low number of successful asylum claims from a country in determining whether it can be designated. Wilson J exposed the fallacy in this reasoning. Drawing on some of the more trenchant language used in some of the tribunal decisions refusing Bangladeshi claims, he pointed out that poor economic conditions might well drive some people to make asylum claims which would be refused, but that this did not indicate a low risk of persecution in the country. It was disclosed that in Parliament a minister had replied that concerns about human rights in Bangladesh, did not mean that 'the vast majority' of Bangladeshi nationals were at risk of having their human rights abused, apparently confusing the question of whether there was in general a serious risk of persecution with a risk of general serious persecution. The Minister advanced the reason for designation that 'it gives people the message that it is not worth coming unless they believe that they have a genuine claim'(para 21). The certification process does not, of course, test the genuineness of the applicants' beliefs.

In 2002 4,980 asylum seekers came from the countries added by the second order, 820 obtained permission to remain in the UK. 3,180 were from Sri Lanka, and a further 170 people from Sri Lanka won their appeals in the first three months of 2003 (The Guardian 18 June 2003). The inclusion of Sri Lanka followed a peace accord in that country, but conflict broke out again very shortly after the order was made. In 2004 the UN Human Rights Committee made an important ruling, calling on the Sri Lankan government to cease using confessions which have been extracted by torture (Advocacy.net news bulletin no.23 2 November 2004).

In *ZL and VL v SSHD and Lord Chancellor's Department* [2003] 1 All ER 1062 the Master of the Rolls held that the inclusion of a country in the White List did not mean that there was no risk of any breach of Convention rights. Decisions are still made in tribunals which suggest a risk of persecution in listed countries. For example there was a risk to the appellant in *V (Ukraine)* [2003] UKIAT 00005 in a rural area in Ukraine because of attitudes to his sexuality. Indeed it seems to be easier to identify what inclusion in the White List does not mean rather than what it does mean. Persecution is only in the most extreme cases a phenomenon encountered 'in general' in a country. This is inherent in the concept of discrimination. In *Hasan* the evidence was that Bangladesh ranked worst in the world on a Corruption Perceptions index (UK Foreign and Commonwealth Office 2004) and was either second or fourth worst in the world for violence against women

(Immigration and Refugee Board of Canada). The widespread nature of torture and police brutality and corruption meant that any individual could be at risk. So whatever a country is in which there is 'in general' no serious risk of persecution, it is not this, following *Hasan*.

The 2004 Act contains a further power for the Secretary of State to certify a state or part of a state safe in relation to a group of people (s 27(5), inserting s 94(5A) in the 2002 Act). The power was used for the first time in December 2005 to desig- nate Ghana and Nigeria safe for men, along with the full designation of Mongolia (Asylum (Designated States) (No. 2) Order 2005, SI 2005/3306).

The designation of safe countries of origin has been a contentious issue in the European Union. There were negotiations to incorporate a list of safe countries of origin as part of the Council Directive 2005/85/EC of 1 December 2005 on minimum standards on procedures in Member States for granting and withdrawing refugee status. The criteria are more demanding than the UK's current provisions, requiring that there is 'generally and consistently' (i.e., over time) no persecution, torture, inhuman or degrading treatment or punishment, or threat of indiscrimin- ate violence in international or internal armed conflict (Annex II of the Directive). EU countries have been unable to agree on whether candidate countries meet these criteria, and so the Presidency decided to set aside the attempt to agree in order to allow the procedures directive to meet its timetable for implementation (14383/04 ASILE 65). Within Europe there is still strenuous opposition to the concept of safe countries of origin and accelerated or suspensive procedures. See ECRE March 2005 and Statewatch 2004.

Again, conditions of detention are a cause for concern. Detention in Oakington was found lawful by the House of Lords in *Saadi* in part because conditions were relaxed and the period of time was short. Oakington has a reputation as 'the most benign of all immigration detention centres' (Prisons and Probation Ombudsman 2005). It was all the more disturbing then when a BBC programme 'Detention Undercover: The Real Story' revealed 'a sub-culture of abusive comment, casual racism, and contempt for decent values'. A report followed by the Prisons and Probation Ombudsman which made recommendations for 'establishing a more just and proper system'. While the report notes the many good qualities of Oakington and its staff, it draws an interesting conclusion:

the very purpose of immigration detention is to exercise coercive power over foreigners prior to their removal from the country. It is perhaps not a surprise that this function, combined with the attitude towards asylum-seekers and other would-be immigrants of some sections of the media, can become a breeding ground for racist and abusive word and deed.

12.5 'Clearly unfounded' claim

The first certifications under s 94 were purely on the basis of country of origin. From June 2003 the power has been used in individual cases, preventing an appeal on the merits of that case. Certification under s 94 has serious consequences, and 2002 Act s 111 provided that a monitor of certification be appointed to oversee the operation of this system which would deprive human rights and asylum claimants of an in-country appeal. There was a delay in appointing the monitor, whose first report was published on 21 July 2005. The sub-text of the report is the difficulty of drawing conclusions on quality from quantity. The figures do not give a full picture. Among the most telling aspects of the report are the finding that 25–50 per cent of certification cases are dealt with through Oakington Reception Centre, and thus receive competent representation because of on-site legal services (paras 37 and 46). Even these representatives were not always able to take on judicial review; finding competent legal representatives who were able to carry out judicial review was extremely difficult (paras 108 and 109); 147 decisions to certify were withdrawn after judicial review proceedings had been commenced (para 124). All files from that group inspected by the monitor showed that the certification decision should not, in her view, have been taken in the first place (para 129).

There is a further power in s 94(7) to certify the human rights claim with the result that the country to which the person is to be removed is to be deemed safe for Refugee Convention purposes. It applies the same deeming provision to *any* country where the Secretary of State certifies human rights will not be violated as s 11 of the 1999 Act applied to European countries being regarded as safe third countries (see below). Following the litigation on the effect of s 11, such a certificate is challengeable on human rights grounds by judicial review (though not in-country appeal) but not on asylum grounds. Doughty Street Chambers noted that this power had not been used (2004:98).

12.6 Credibility

Arguably, the subject of credibility could fill a chapter on its own, or be dealt with in the next chapter, or chapter 14, or this one, or not at all. In determining refugee claims the question of credibility is both everything and nothing. It is not an aspect of the refugee definition to be satisfied, like the matters covered in the next chapter, and yet the majority of asylum claims which are lost are lost precisely because of adverse findings on credibility — in other words the decision-maker does not believe the applicant's story.

The case of *Chiver* (10758) is an authority on the proper approach to credibility. The adjudicator in that case pointed to the discrepancies in the respondent's story in order to, in the words of the Tribunal:

list the matters which were adverse to the respondent's case and to reflect his belief that they did not affect the kernel of his story. He adopted the approach which is urged upon adjudicators i.e. to weigh up the evidence and to indicate that which is believed and that which is not.

From this it may be gleaned that some inconsistencies are not fatal to the claim. The question is whether the immigration judge believes the core of what is claimed. In the same case the Tribunal pointed out that there may be perfectly valid and understandable reasons for exaggeration or not telling the truth, which do not mean the asylum claim is not valid. For instance, a claimant may embroider their story if they fear it is not strong enough or change facts which they fear will be thought implausible. Gorlick (2002) quotes Hathaway as making the same point, that dishonesty, though not to be encouraged, is explicable for instance 'when bad advice is received from traffickers or others viewed by an asylum seeker as an expert'.

Immigration judges are warned about judging facts to be implausible. Hathaway (1991:81) points out that it is not in the nature of repressive societies to behave reasonably. Decision-makers should not place weight on their own subjective and culturally bound views about a claimant's demeanour or way of giving a statement or evidence.

In *R v IAT ex p Chunu Miah* (CO/2318/1994), an immigration case concerning the former 'primary purpose' rule, Collins J held that the adjudicator should look at the reasons for the lies that were told, rather than simply debarring the applicant because lies were told. If the untruths did not affect whether he came within the immigration rules, they should not have a determinative effect upon the claim.

In *Slimani* 01/TH/00092 in a starred determination the tribunal restated the principle that decision-makers should give reasons for finding evidence, in this case expert evidence, to be implausible. The issue of credibility is not only concerned with the view the decision-maker takes of the appellant, but is also bound up with the conduct of hearings and the whole question of fairness in the decision-making process.

Assessing credibility, of course, happens at initial interviews with asylum seekers as well as in hearings. The Medical Foundation and other organizations which support torture victims say that insufficient attention is given to the effects of trauma on memory when assessing inconsistencies. The UN Committee Against Torture also advise that these effects should be taken into account.

The immigration rules in HC 395 para 341 say that the Secretary of State will have regard to matters which may damage a claimant's credibility. These are

(i)   that the claimant has adduced manifestly false evidence in support of his claim, or has otherwise made false representations, either orally or in writing;

(ii) that the applicant has lodged concurrent claims for asylum in the United Kingdom or in another country.

This version of the rules came into force on 1 January 2005, but as at January 2006 the published API had not been updated, the available guidance relating only to the quite different former rule. In either case it is doubtful whether a policy of erecting hurdles for establishing credibility is within the spirit of paras 195–202 of the UNHCR Handbook, which deal with the examination and interview process. The applicant should be given the benefit of the doubt in establishing their claim (UNHCR Handbook para 196) where supporting evidence is not available.

Despite the arguments against codification of issues affecting credibility, the Asylum and Immigration (Treatment of Claimants etc) Act 2004 s 8 creates a new obligation for a 'deciding authority' to take into account as damaging the claimant's credibility factors which that authority 'thinks' are deliberately misleading. It further sets out a list of behaviours which *shall* be treated as designed to conceal information or mislead. These include failure to produce a passport, destruction of documents and failure to answer a question, in each case without reasonable explanation. Other matters are listed without provision for a reasonable explanation: production of a document which is not a valid passport as if it were and failure to claim in a safe third country or make a claim before an immigration decision or arrest under an immigration provision.

This extraordinarily draconian provision (so says Macdonald 2005:818) contradicts the core principle that an evaluation of all the facts is necessary, and deception about one matter does not necessarily mean that the claim itself is false. In the whole immigration and asylum field, this provision is a rare and possibly unique instance of Parliament interfering with the discretion of the Home Office civil servant as executive decision-maker, and it does so in a manner adverse to the asylum seeker. The Secretary of State, however, having proposed the measure, is unlikely to object.

The judiciary are not so quiescent. In *SM Iran* [2005] UKAIT 00116, an early case on the use of s 8, the tribunal made it clear that it was not going to be overly bound by this Parliamentary attempt at inroads into the decision-making process. The Adjudicator stated that he had taken account of all relevant matters under s 8 'including all matters pertaining to her account of travelling from Iran to the UK'. The Secretary of State submitted that s 8 should be taken as the starting point for credibility, but the tribunal disagreed. It said that s 8

has the incidental effect of interfering with the well-established rule that the finder of fact (in this case, the Adjudicator, or immigration judge) should look at the evidence as a whole, giving each item of it such weight as he or she considers appropriate. That is unfortunate, and may in some circumstances be difficult to manage . . . it is inevitable that the general fact-finding process is somewhat distorted, but that distortion must be kept to a minimum. There is no warrant at all for the claim . . . that the matters identified by section 8 should be treated as the starting point of a decision on credibility. The matters mentioned in s.8 may or may not be part of any particular claim; and their importance will vary with the nature of the claim that is being made, and the other evidence that supports or undermines it. (paras 7 and 9)

The tribunal treats the factors listed in s 8 as just part of the overall assessment of evidence, and refuses to allow the section to create a blanket presumption against the asylum seeker.

Sometimes errors are seen in an adjudicator or immigration judge's approach to credibility similar to some of the problems we have noted in relation to initial decision-making. For instance, a negative view may be taken of the claimant's credibility based on the decision-maker's response to the claimant, and then other evidence discounted in the light of that view. This practice was noted in the Amnesty International report on initial decision-making, and appeared in the decision of an adjudicator in *Mibanga v SSHD* [2005] EWCA Civ 367. The Court of Appeal found that the adjudicator should have looked at all the evidence, including that from the Medical Foundation and a professor with extensive knowledge of the Democratic Republic of Congo, before forming a view of the claimant's credibility. It was not appropriate to treat the claimant as not credible and then discount other evidence on the basis of that. The same issue arose, with the same result, in *Diaby v SSHD* [2005] EWCA Civ 651. In a similar vein, in *Koca v SSHD* [2005] CSIH 41, the Adjudicator should have put to the appellant the discrepancies upon which she based her adverse credibility findings. The tribunal in *MM Democratic Republic of Congo* AIT [2005] 00019 gave further guidance on the treatment of the claimant's evidence. A decision-maker should be wary of relying on the demeanour of a witness. Conclusions drawn from this are too likely to be subjective and rely on interpretation of behaviour. It is the *content* of evidence rather than the way it is given that should inform credibility. Still it is legally permissible to find the claimant's account inherently implausible. Here, the appellant claimed to have escaped leaving his clothes in the hands of a solider who was restraining him, and then have vaulted a six-foot wall while six other soldiers were outside the house in which he and his family had been seized. His advocate at the tribunal advanced possible explanations, but the tribunal held that where there were possible explanations, these should be advanced by the claimant, not speculated upon by his representative. In the absence of such alternative explanations the adjudicator had not been wrong to find this account inherently implausible, and to do so it did not need to be outside the realm of human experience, thus declining to follow an Australian decision, *W148/00 A v Ministry for Immigration and Multicultural Affairs* [2002] FCA 679.

The question of inherent improbability is a fraught one as it is at best a condensation of objective factors into one word without explicit analysis, and at worst simply an expression of subjective assumptions. The Court of Appeal in *Gheisari v SSHD* [2004] EWCA Civ 1854 repeated the advice that just because something is inherently improbable does not mean it is not true.

The issue of credibility is entangled with that of subjective fear. This issue is discussed further in the next chapter, where it is contended that decision-makers should not be looking to establish that the refugee has a subjective state of trepidation about what they might face if returned to their home country. One of the difficulties of trying to prove that they have, is that it requires the decision-maker, perhaps versed in law but not in psychology, to assess the inner state of a person whose culture and circumstances may be very far from their own. Hathaway and Hicks (2005, see Further reading for chapter 13) describe how this impossible quest leads decision-makers to attempt to 'objectify' the asylum seeker's state of mind with questions such as 'did you claim asylum at the first opportunity?'. The implication is that if not, the asylum seeker was not genuinely afraid. Thus the assessment of credibility may be bound up with a search for subjective fear, a search which arguably should not be undertaken.

12.7 Asylum appeals

As explained at the beginning of this chapter, an appeal against the refusal of an asylum claim is made by appealing the underlying immigration decision on asylum grounds. The appeal system and grounds in outline have been discussed in chapter 8.

There are differences of principle, however, between appeals on asylum grounds and other appeals. The appeal process, as mentioned at the beginning of this chapter, is in a sense an extension of the asylum decision process. The tribunal also carries the obligation of non-refoulement, and there is some obligation in the direction of a more inquisitorial process, rather than being simply an arbiter between two arguments. This should not be taken to the point of excessive intervention in cross-examination, taking hostile points against the appellant which the Home Office had not thought fit to raise (*XS Serbia and Montenegro* [2005] UKIAT 00093).

As the House of Lords said in the case of *Bugdaycay v SSHD* [1987] AC 514, an asylum claim involves matters of such great importance that judicial bodies should subject each case to 'the most anxious scrutiny'. Evidence should be admitted of 'any matter which the tribunal thinks relevant to the substance of the decision, including evidence which relates to a matter after the date of the decision' (2002 Act s 85(4)). This is particularly important and relevant in asylum claims where the question to be determined is what may happen to the asylum seeker in the future.

12.8 Evidence

We have already considered the question of credibility, which is an aspect of the assessment of evidence. This section will consider the admission of late evidence, the treatment of expert evidence, and the evaluation of evidence about the claimant's country of origin.

12.8.1 Late evidence

Although matters up to the date of the hearing may in theory be relevant in an asylum claim, as in other litigation the parties are still required to comply with procedure rules (here, the Asylum and Immigration Tribunal (Procedure) Rules 2005, SI 2005/230) and serve evidence on the other side within a specified time before the hearing. This time is set by the tribunal giving directions. Of course sometimes evidence is late, and the procedure rules say that the tribunal 'must not consider any written evidence which is not filed or served in accordance with those directions unless satisfied that there are good reasons to do so' (r 51(4)). The 'anxious scrutiny' which should be applied to asylum appeals is relevant in determining whether such good reasons exist. So said the tribunal in *MD Pakistan* [2004] UKIAT 00197 in which the appellant was present and ready and willing to give oral evidence. Although his statement had been filed late, there was no prejudice to the Home Office in admitting the statement. In *SA Sri Lanka* [2005] UKIAT 00028 the tribunal held again that the anxious scrutiny required in an asylum claim meant that the adjudicator should have admitted a medical report which had a bearing on the appellant's credibility. The Home Office had not sent a representative to the hearing but the tribunal held that by this omission they had deprived themselves of the opportunity to comment on it, and the appellant should not be penalized on that account.

12.8.2 Fresh evidence or fresh claim

The points above raise the question of finality in legal proceedings. When does the asylum claim cease? If it is focused on future risk, and there is a substantial change in the asylum seeker's country of origin the day after she has lost her appeal in the tribunal, what then? What if new evidence comes to light before she is removed which substantiates the risk she feared? Although the tribunal is concerned with the risk to the appellant of persecution on return, the state of affairs which is under consideration is that at the date of the hearing. If this were not so, the matter could go on being re-opened indefinitely. However, the decision must be made on the best evidence as to the facts, and new facts may come to light. As discussed in chapter 8 in relation to *E and R v SSHD* EWCA Civ 49 CA, a mistake as to fact may, in certain circumstances, amount to an error of law and thus be appealable particularly in asylum cases. In that case the Court of Appeal said that the sort of mistake of fact that would give rise to this conclusion would occur when there was

- a mistake as to existing fact;
- of which evidence was uncontentious and objectively verifiable;
- when the appellant or their advisers were not responsible for the mistake;
- and the mistake played a material though not necessarily decisive part in the tribunal's reasoning.

Evidence of such a mistake could be admitted, usually on the principles derived from the case of *Ladd v Marshall* [1954] 1 WLR 1489. These are: that the fresh evidence could not have been obtained with reasonable diligence for use at the trial (here, the tribunal hearing); if given, it would probably have an important influence on the result; it is apparently credible thought not necessarily incontrovertible (*E and R* para 23). These principles may be departed from in asylum cases in exceptional circumstances when the interests of justice so require (*E and R* para 91). In these cases the human rights reports produced after the date of the hearing added to the tribunal's understanding of the position as it was at the date of the hearing. They did not concern matters arising later.

Sometimes it will be appropriate, after an asylum claim has been refused and an appeal lost, to make a fresh claim for asylum. This will only be considered when new submissions are significantly different from the material which has been previously been considered, as prescribed in para 353 of the immigration rules:

The submissions will only be significantly different if the content
1) Had not already been considered;
2) Taken together with the previously considered material created a realistic prospect of success, notwithstanding its rejection.

Collins J added in the case of *R (Rahimi) v SSHD* [2005] EWHC 2838 (Admin) that 'the realistic prospect of success test is a low one. It really amounts to little more than there is a reasonable chance that the claim might succeed' (para 12). In this case a newspaper article carrying a request for disclosure of the whereabouts of the claimant had been published after the adjudicator had refused the claim. Collins J thought that given the grey area between prosecution and persecution in Afghanistan, the claim should be investigated again.

For a full account of the law relating to evidence in asylum appeals, reference should be made to a practitioner work such as Macdonald.

12.8.3 Country of origin information

The availability, reliability, relevance, and scope of information about an asylum seeker's country of origin are enormously important in asylum decisions and appeals. The claim is that the asylum seeker fears persecution in their country of origin. To substantiate or refute this there must be evidence of relevant state practices, and this may be gleaned from governmental reports and non-governmental organizations, particularly those that monitor human rights. Common sources relied on are the Home Office's own country reports, the human rights reports from the US Department of State, Amnesty International, Human Rights Watch. It is rare for such a report to mention the asylum seeker personally, although this may happen, and there may be references to others with whom she is associated. The main value of country information from the asylum seeker's point of view is to establish the likelihood of what will face them on return, given what can be shown of how their country treats others like them. It is rare that an asylum seeker will have resources to compile substantial country information on their own behalf, and although independent experts may be instructed, the asylum seeker will often be reliant on information produced by organizations who do not have them or their case in mind.

The Home Office has its own country information unit which produces reports about countries of origin of asylum seekers. Since the revival of the White List, the collection of country information has a further importance in that it may inform a decision to designate a country under s 94 of the 2002 Act. In recognition of this, the 2002 Act provided for a new Advisory Panel on Country Information, but in the case of *Hasan* it was disclosed that the panel did not consider themselves sufficiently resourced to engage in the question of designation, and declined to do it.

Unfortunately, Home Office country reports have often not been suitable to bear the weight placed upon them, and this has been compounded by their being inappropriately used. In 2003 the Immigration Advisory Service carried out an analysis of 15 Home Office country reports and found that the majority were unreliable. There were multiple inaccuracies, mis-quoting and omission of relevant information. The Home Office relies mainly upon other source material rather than its own researchers in the field, and the IAS research found that the tendency was to be selective in a way that put a positive slant on the material from other sources. There was also a tendency to use Home Office opinion in the reports, which claim to be factual (Carver 2003). A second IAS research project in 2004 examined the text of twenty-three country reports and compared them with their source material. There was an improvement from the previous year, but still over-reliance on one source and poor sourcing generally (Carver 2004). For a robust approach by ECtHR to assessment of background material see *Said v Netherlands* App. No 2345/02.

A further development in the search for consistency in relation to conditions in a country is the designation of 'country guideline cases'. The authoritative beginning of this idea is with the Court of Appeal in *S v SSHD* [2002] EWCA Civ 539. As Laws LJ pointed out in that case, the notion of a precedent which is binding as to fact is 'foreign to the common law' (para 26). For this reason alone, the proposition should be treated with caution that findings of fact made in one case about say, Zimbabwe, should be binding in another case. However, one can readily see that asylum cases present the law with a new phenomenon. It is not common in other areas of law that litigants make comparable assertions about the same background situation. Asylum law may be an appropriate field for the development of a new principle. Laws LJ continued, that in the context of asylum claims, the unusual idea of a factual precedent 'may be benign and practical' (para 28). He advanced two reasons for adopting the practice: the waste of judicial and other resources in hearing evidence about similar factual issues repeatedly, and the need for consistency in decision-making, which is an aspect of justice as is the right of the individual to be heard on the particulars of their claim. The latter principle gave rise to a number of provisos, which should be strictly applied if factual precedents were to be allowed as a possibility:

- In making a decision which is intended to give guidelines on conditions in a country, the tribunal must apply the duty to give reasons 'with particular rigour'.
- Such a decision must be 'effectively comprehensive. It should address all the issues capable of having a real as opposed to a fanciful bearing on the result, and explain what it makes of the substantial evidence going to each such issue'.
- The facts of an individual case must still be examined.
- Country guideline cases may provide a backdrop against which that individual examination takes place, recognising that 'the impact of the political reality may vary as between one claimant and another'.

The practice of promulgating and following Country Guideline cases (designated CG in the case name) grew up quickly after *S*. The Immigration Advisory Service carried out research and consultation on the use and nature of country guideline cases. Their work reveals many concerns including the following:

- Country guideline cases may be out of date for the case in hand, or worse, based on obsolete material.
- Factual findings specific to a particular claimant may be elevated into country guidance.
- Country guideline decisions may not be referenced properly, so that a future claimant is unable to distinguish their case from the CG because they cannot identify the evidence.
- 'the judiciary operate under severe time constraints and a reference to a Country Guideline case is sometimes used as an alternative to giving reasons rather than an aide to decision-making' (p. 20).
- Some country guideline cases have been designated where the dismissal of the claim was based on a *lack* of evidence.
- Even in a CG case, evidence was sometimes used and dismissed selectively without objective reasons being given, particularly by preference being given to government reports over other sources. (IAS 2005)

The IAS challenged the concept of country guideline cases as importing an artificial degree of certainty 'on an uncertain and often rapidly changing country situation'. Even if one accepts the concept, the IAS research suggests that the reality does not match up to the cautious standards set by the Court of Appeal in *S*.

The tribunal has embraced the notion of country guideline cases. There are now hundreds in relation to particular issues such as 'risk on return — Ivory Coast' which are listed on the AIT website. The tribunal's practice direction goes much further than *S* in relation to their weight as precedents. It says that the most recent CG case 'shall be treated as an authoritative finding on the country guidance issue identified in the determination . . . so far as that appeal:

(a) relates to the country guidance issue in question; and
(b) depends upon the same or similar evidence'. (4 April 2005, para 18.2)

Even more unequivocally: 'any failure to follow a clear, apparently applicable country guidance case or to show why it does not apply to the case in question is likely to be regarded as grounds for review or appeal on a point of law' (para 18.4 endorsed in *R & others v SSHD* [2005] EWCA Civ 982). The exception is when there is other, inconsistent authority that is binding on the Tribunal.

This approach is moving the CG system into something like a more specific form of 'White-listing'.

12.9 Refugee status

In the rare case where refugee status is granted (3 per cent of initial decisions in 2004 and 19 per cent of appealed cases) the Refugee Convention sets out the legal consequences of recognition. Refugees have a right to the issue of a travel document, an important right bearing in mind that they may well not have a passport of their country of origin or be able to travel using it. They are entitled to social rights on favourable terms and the intention of the Convention is that they should be integrated into the host society. The rights listed in the Convention include freedom of religion and religious education (Art 4), the protection of industrial property such as inventions and of rights in artistic work (Art 14), the most favourable rights of non-political association, housing, and of wage-earning employment or self-employment that are accorded to foreign nationals in that country (Arts 15, 17, 18, and 21), full access to courts and to elementary education (Arts 16 and 22). For a really comprehensive account, see Hathaway 2005.

12.10 Cessation

The Refugee Convention Article 1C makes provision for refugee status to end in certain circumstances. Most refer to the voluntary actions of the refugee. The exception is Article 1C(5), that 'because the circumstances in connection with which he has been recognized as a refugee have ceased to exist' he can no longer 'refuse to avail himself of the protection of the country of his nationality' or, if stateless, his former residence. The host state bears the burden of proving this, and refugees should not be subject to continual examination of their status as this undermines the very security the Convention aims to give (see the UNCHR Handbook para 135). It has not been common that a person would be required to leave for this reason, and the cessation of refugee status has not been a major issue in the UK, particularly as its practice was to grant indefinite leave to remain to those granted refugee status.

This may well change in the next few years. The European directive on qualification as a refugee provides that only a three year residence permit need be given to refugees and their families (Council Directive 2004/83/EC Art 24). The directive must be transposed into UK law by 10 October 2006 and provides a minimum standard. On 30 August 2005 UK policy changed to giving five years' leave to refugees, instead of indefinite leave. The Asylum Policy Instructions on refugee leave explain that asylum cases may be reviewed, and set out the triggers for review.

These include that there has been a 'significant and non-temporary change' in the conditions in the refugee's country of origin. The instructions explain that a review will not take place using this provision without consultation with UNHCR and announcement in Parliament, and set out the substance of Article 1C(5) as a guide for a decision-maker to 'take into account'. It will be important in the implementation of this new provision that focus is retained on the circumstances of the individual.

12.11 Humanitarian protection/discretionary leave

Many signatory states to the Refugee Convention make provision for a safety net status where a person is held not to qualify for asylum, but there are compelling reasons why they should not be returned to their home state. The Refugee Qualification Directive 2004/83 provides for a form of 'subsidiary protection' (Art 18). In the UK, as noted in chapter 1, the Secretary of State has the capacity to act outside the immigration rules to the benefit of the applicant. This power has been used to grant leave called 'exceptional leave to remain (ELR)', and no distinction was made in that status between asylum seekers and others. The implication was that the person did not fit into the legal categories but nevertheless their circumstances were such that they should not be forced to leave. ELR could be granted because of treatment the person would face in their home country or because of their ties and circumstances in the UK. The grant of ELR could be used very flexibly, for instance as part of the policy to clear the backlog of asylum claims which built up in the 1990s (see Macdonald 2001:578).

Following the commencement of the Human Rights Act on 2 October 2000, ELR was the status granted to those whose removal from the UK would breach their human rights. The new human rights claim under Immigration and Asylum Act 1999 s 65 made the human rights and protective uses of ELR explicit and enforceable by the claimant.

From 1 April 2003, ELR was abolished and two new statuses were made available for people whose asylum claim failed: humanitarian protection or discretionary leave. For non-asylum applications there is another status called leave outside the rules. For the first time this creates a distinction between asylum and non-asylum claims and a distinction between the need for international humanitarian protection and other compassionate reasons for not removing a person.

Humanitarian protection is tied to a prospective violation of human rights which would be recognized in UK and international law, and restricted to preventing violations of Articles 2 and 3 ECHR except where 'a person's removal would be in breach of Article 3 of the ECHR because of their medical condition'. In this case, says the API, 'the person is not in need of international protection and so would not qualify for Humanitarian Protection' (para 2.4). A sharp dividing line is drawn between circumstances of the individual which excite compassion, and danger to them from their home state, even to the extent of distinguishing between different breaches of Article 3.

Humanitarian Protection was at first granted for three years initially, but in August 2005, to coincide with the change to refugee leave, the initial period of humanitarian protection was changed to five years. HP may lead to settlement if the 'circumstances which gave rise to the need for protection' still exist at the end of that period. This is a reduction in security compared with ELR, which was normally granted for four years after which a settlement application could be considered without the need to show a continuing need for protection. The API on humanitarian protection however says: 'It will not normally be necessary to conduct an in-depth review to determine whether the individual is still entitled to Humanitarian Protection, as long as the application is made before the existing leave expires. Background character and conduct checks will usually suffice.' Principles of internal flight and sufficiency of protection (see next chapter) will be applied in considering whether to grant humanitarian protection (API).

Exclusions also apply, but are more severely drawn than for refugee status (see chapter 14). People who would be excluded by Article 1F are excluded, but so is a person who has committed a 'serious crime' whether political or not. 'Serious' is defined as a crime for which the person has been sentenced to more than one year's imprisonment in the UK or a crime specified by the order made under s 72 of the 2002 Act. They may also be excluded for any of a number of listed reasons including glorifying or fomenting terrorist violence or 'fostering hatred which may lead to inter-community violence in the UK'. Persons excluded from humanitarian protection may be considered for a six-month period of discretionary leave.

In general discretionary leave may be given to avoid breaching the person's Article 8 rights in the UK, in case of medical or severe humanitarian risks which would breach Article 3 and in very limited circumstances where other human rights violations are feared on return. Other exceptional cases should, according to the API, be considered for leave outside the rules rather than discretionary leave. The initial grant of DL is normally three years but may be less in specified cases. It is less secure than humanitarian protection, as it will not lead to settlement until six years have elapsed, and there will be a review after three years which may result in the end of the leave.

There is a potential contradiction in that Article 8 claims are generally based on strength of family ties in the UK, which would generally become stronger with the passage of time. This was addressed in *R (on the application of Shahid) v SSHD* QBD Admin 13 October 2004. Gibbs J held that it was reasonable to grant three years discretionary leave instead of indefinite leave to remain. If there was no significant change in circumstances the leave would be extended at the end of three years and the claimant could eventually expect to obtain ILR. Its grant would enhance his enjoyment of his Article 8 right, but the lack of it did not interfere with it beyond the allowable interference under Article 8.2.

Both these new categories are more circumscribed than ELR, particularly in the criteria which may be used to grant them. Both forms of leave will be open to regular review in accordance with the Refugee Qualification Directive 2004/83. The direction of change reduces security of status.

12.11.1 The October exercise

We saw in chapter 3 how sometimes delay by the Home Office in processing an asylum claim can have consequences which need to be considered as part of the question of whether denial of leave or removal is proportionate as required by

Article 8. We have also seen that the backlog of asylum claims became a major political issue. Accordingly, the government announced on 24 October 2003 a one-off policy to help clear the backlog. The criteria for consideration for indefinite leave to remain were:

- The applicant applied for asylum before 2 October 2000; and
- The applicant had at least one dependant aged under 18 (other than a spouse) in the UK on 2 October 2000 or 24 October 2003.

There were specified exclusions for those who had criminal convictions or whose presence was otherwise not conducive to the public good etc.

Litigation has ensued about the terms of the policy and its reach. For instance, what if another member of the family has a form of leave (*K (Russia)*) UKIAT [2004] 00082, or a child is born after 24 October 2003? The Home Affairs Committee was not entirely happy that the amnesty had been declared, fearing it would set a precedent.

12.12 Safe third country

Finally, we consider the application and development of safe third country provisions. Where these apply, an asylum claim need not be heard in the UK at all. The basic contention is that the claimant may be safely sent somewhere other than their country of origin or where they fear persecution. Where an asylum seeker has travelled through another country which might have heard their claim then the safe third country provisions may mean that they are removed without going through any of the processes described above, except the initial screening interview, which identifies safe third country cases. The notion of 'burden-sharing', now a key element in the development of policy in Europe, has always been a function of international refugee law. Indeed one of the preambles to the Refugee Convention is to this effect:

the grant of asylum may place unduly heavy burdens on certain countries, and that a satisfactory solution of a problem of which the United Nations has recognized the international scope and nature cannot therefore be achieved without international co-operation.

In addition to 'burden-sharing' the safe third country provisions also enact the idea that 'refugees who come directly from their country of origin are entitled to greater rights than those who may be forced by circumstances, or may elect, to adopt a more circuitous route to safety' (Tuitt 1996:111). The use of safe third country provisions is widespread. For instance, on 29 December 2004 Canada implemented a safe third country agreement with the USA, thereby closing its land border to most asylum claims and effecting a significant reduction in asylum claims overall. The Canadian Council for Refugees refers to this as 'the government's unstated purpose' (2005:26).

12.12.1 Development of safe third country provisions

Prior to any statutory provisions the decision to remove an asylum claimant was a matter of administrative discretion, subject only to the obligation of non-refoulement under Article 33 Refugee Convention. The case of *Musisi v SSHD* [1987] AC 514 established that the doctrine of non-refoulement applies to indirect as well as direct refoulement. In that case the appellant sought asylum from Uganda, but had travelled to the UK from Kenya and applied to enter as a visitor. The immigration service proposed to remove him to Kenya, but there was evidence from that country that they would not accept him and would in fact send him back to Uganda where he feared persecution. The House of Lords found that although the decision on this point was within the discretion of the Secretary of State, he had failed to consider the question adequately, having not addressed the question of danger. *Yassine v SSHD* [1990] Imm AR 354 was the first reported case of the UK refusing to deal with an asylum application on the basis that the applicant was in transit to another country which would admit him. In the 16 years since then, safe third country provisions have become a key element in refugee law and practice, though from official figures their effect is difficult to quantify. Refusals on safe third country grounds are assimilated with other refusals giving rise to non-suspensive appeals (see later) and cases in which no appeal was received (Asylum Statistics UK 2004 para 43). No indication is given as to the number or outcome of judicial reviews.

Protection against indirect refoulement as it arose in *Musisi* found its way into the immigration rules, but together with an obligation to return the asylum seeker to a country through which they had travelled, if it was safe to do so. HC 395 para 345 provided the elements of safe third country principles:

- the applicant has not travelled directly from the country of persecution;
- there is another country to which they could be sent as they could have made their asylum claim there; and
- this would be considered safe in the sense that the life or freedom of the asylum applicant would not be threatened (within the meaning of Article 33 of the Convention) and the government of which would not send the applicant elsewhere in a manner contrary to the principles of the Convention and Protocol.

If these elements are present, the applicant will be sent to that country for their asylum application to be considered.

It may be apparent that using this rule requires a lot of fact-finding on the part of the Secretary of State. Information is needed about the third country, not only about its systems of refugee protection, but also about the asylum claimant's travel route and their experiences. The Secretary of State had a discretion under this rule but one which it is difficult to exercise properly.

There was a risk that asylum claimants would simply be returned by the third country to the UK, especially in view of the fact that where he was satisfied that a case met these criteria, the Secretary of State was under no obligation to consult the authorities of the third country before the removal of an asylum applicant (para 345).

This is what happened, and for some years there was a phenomenon known as 'refugees in orbit' whereby asylum claimants were shunted from one unwilling country to the next and back again. Both Tuitt (1996:119) and Macdonald (2001:547) suggest that this might constitute inhuman or degrading treatment contrary to Article 3 ECHR.

The first statutory provision to endorse removals to a safe third country was the Asylum and Immigration Appeals Act 1993, which allowed the Secretary of State to certify that a country was one which respected the Refugee Convention and was therefore safe for the applicant. This would trigger an accelerated process for the claim, which would be certified as 'without foundation'. The certificate could be challenged on appeal to a special adjudicator, and Macdonald comments in the preface to his fourth edition that as result of these new appeal rights 'special adjudicators have been able to analyse in greater depth the laws and practices of many countries in Europe and elsewhere and the sweeping assumptions of the Home Office about the safety of asylum seekers have failed to bear scrutiny in many cases' (1995:v).

This seems not to have been what the Home Office had in mind, and a further Bill was introduced in Parliament which provided that asylum seekers could be removed *before* their appeal took place. While the Bill was going through Parliament, the House of Lords held in *R v SSHD ex p Abdi and Gawe* [1996] 1 WLR 298 that the Secretary of State was not obliged to disclose all evidence upon which he had reached his view of Spain as a safe country to which the applicants could be sent.

The Bill became the Asylum and Immigration Act 1996, in which s 2 provided that if the Secretary of State certified that the safe third country conditions were met the claimant could be removed to European or designated countries before the appeal took place. The conditions were:

(1) the asylum seeker is not a national or citizen of the country to which s/he is to be sent;
(2) his/her life and liberty would not be threatened there by reason of his/her race, religion, nationality, membership of a particular social group or political opinion;
(3) the government of that country would not send him or her to another country otherwise than in accordance with the Refugee Convention.

The successful appeal procedure was abolished, though certificates could still be challenged by judicial review.

In one such judicial review, (*Adan and Aitseguer* [2001] 2WLR 143) the House of Lords held that France and Germany were not safe third countries because they used the accountability theory in relation to non-state actors instead of the protection theory (see next chapter). In coming to this decision the House of Lords held that only one true interpretation could be ascribed to Article 1(A)(2) of the Refugee Convention. This overruled the previous Court of Appeal decisions in *Kerrouche v SSHD* [1997] Imm AR 610 and *Iyadurai v SSHD* [1998] Imm AR 470, both of which had decided, in a similar context, that there was a range of permissible meanings. The meaning of the Convention is, they decided, an autonomous meaning, in accordance with the purposes of the Convention, and cannot differ as between states. This view was later endorsed by the House of Lords in *Sepet and Bulbul* [2003] UKHL 15. In *Adan and Aitseguer* the House of Lords held that the Secretary of State had to satisfy himself of the safety of the destination for the two asylum seekers. Accepting the assurances of the receiving state did not fulfil the requirement of the 1996 Act that the Secretary of State was *satisfied* that the safe third country conditions were met. He could not be satisfied if he did not have the evidence. In *Bouheraoua and*

Kerkeb [2001] Imm AR 614 CA a certificate in relation to Greece was set aside on similar basis.

However, with the repeal of Asylum and Immigration Act 1996 s 2, safe third country provisions changed again in a very significant way. Section 11 Immigration and Asylum Act 1999, as amended by Nationality, Immigration and Asylum Act 2002 s 80 contained a deeming provision which entailed that Member States of the European Union are '*to be regarded as*' places in which the safe third country provisions were met. If the Secretary of State certified that the claimant was not a national or citizen of the member state to which they were to be sent (s 11(2)(a)), and the member state accepted responsibility under standing arrangements (then the Dublin Convention; see later), the claimant could be removed to the third country without a substantive hearing of their claim. The crucial question following the commencement of 1999 Act s 11 was whether anything of *Adan and Aitseguer* could survive this deeming provision. Cases in the lower courts decided that s 11 was conclusive, and left no room for challenging the certificate. This was confirmed obiter by Simon Brown LJ in *Ibrahim* [2001] Imm AR 430 CA and followed in *Hatim* [2001] Imm AR 688 and *Samer and Richi* [2002] Imm AR 190 in both of which it formed the ratio.

In *R (Yogathas) and R (Thangarasa) v SSHD* [2002] 3 WLR 176 certifications were challenged in the House of Lords, for Yogathas under the 1996 Act and Thangarasa under the 1999 Act. Both were to be returned to Germany. In relation to Yogathas, for whom the issues could be examined, the House of Lords acknowledged that there were some differences between the UK and Germany on the interpretation of the internal protection alternative, but that these were not substantial and the certificate should stand. In relation to Thangasara, Lord Bingham acknowledged that in relation to the certification of a European country 'the argument which succeeded in *Adan and Aitseguer* [2001] 2 AC 477 is effectively blocked'. The case proceeded on the basis that this was the case, and Simon Brown LJ's words in *Ibrahim* had to be regarded as conclusive:

Parliament has ... in unambiguous terms, dictated that henceforth France, amongst other member states, is to be regarded as a safe third country. Of course the Secretary of State is not bound to certify in every case, but where he chooses to do so, in my judgment that certificate cannot be impugned on the grounds that France after all is not properly to be regarded as a safe third country.

Thangarasa could still mount a human rights challenge to removal but the human rights argument was lost, following *TI v United Kingdom* [2000] INLR 211. Although *Thangarasa* left open the possibility of a human rights challenge to avoid removal even where there could be no challenge to a safe third country certificate, the 1999 Act also introduced a power for the Secretary of State to certify the human rights claim as manifestly unfounded, against which there was no in-country right of appeal.

Safe third country provisions have hardened further in the Asylum and Immigration (Treatment of Claimants, etc) Act 2004. Schedule 3 contains three lists of safe third countries and a fourth provision enabling certification in relation to an individual. The first list consists of twenty-six other countries of the European Economic Area, the exception being Liechtenstein. These countries are deemed to be safe places to return an asylum claimant whom the Secretary of State certifies is not a national of that country. They are deemed to be safe in three respects:

- the applicant will not face persecution contrary to the Refugee Convention in that country
- that country will not send the applicant to another country where there was a risk of such persecution
- that country will not send the applicant to another country where there is a risk of human rights violations.

Furthermore, the Secretary of State is also obliged to certify that a human rights appeal concerning the immediate consequences of removal to that country would be unfounded, unless s/he is satisfied that it would not be. This refers to any other human rights implications of removal aside from the possibility of onward removal from the destination state, for instance a claim that family or private life in the UK will be infringed by the removal (Art 8), or that the applicant faces a risk of degrading treatment in the receiving state (Art 3). The effect is that anyone who may be returned to a European country will be returned without an appeal unless the Secretary of State is persuaded that there would arguably be a breach of human rights in doing so.

There can be no judicial review of the safety of the First List country for refugee or human rights Convention purposes as the statutory presumptions put these matters beyond challenge. The Parliamentary Joint Committee on Human Rights doubted the compatibility of these provisions with the UK's obligations under the Human Rights Act and ECHR in 'precluding any individual consideration of the facts of a particular claimant's case and conclusively ousting the jurisdiction of the courts to hear a claim that removal to a third country on the First List would breach the claimant's rights because of the risk of onward removal' (Thirteenth Report on Session 2003–4 (HL paper 102, HC paper 640)). It would prevent, for instance a challenge to the return of a Libyan to Italy on the basis that she might be returned to Libya from there (see chapter 4). The government's rationale is that the first list is intended to apply to countries which are signatories to the ECHR, so they may be assumed to comply with the requirement not to refoule in breach of human rights (HC Standing Committee B col. 355 22 January 2004).

The second list is of countries designated by order by the Secretary of State (none yet at the time of writing). It deems the destination country safe for Refugee Convention purposes, and also contains an obligation for the Secretary of State to certify human rights claims, but does not deem the third country safe in terms of refoulement contrary to human rights. The Third List allows the Secretary of State to designate countries for the purposes of the Refugee Convention only. A return to a country in this category may still be individually certified as safe for human rights purposes. All these three provisions also debar appeal on the safety issues from abroad, and any immigration appeal in the UK. Part 5 of Schedule 3 provides for individual certification of refugee and human rights claims where the person may be returned to another third country.

The 2004 Act repeals the safe third country provisions in the 1999 and 2002 Acts, though not s 94 of the 2002 Act regarding certification of human rights claims and its consequences. Notwithstanding the repeal, the Asylum and Immigration (Treatment of Claimants, etc.) Act 2004 (Commencement No. 1) Order 2004, SI 2004/2523 para 3 states expressly that certificates under the 2002 and 1999 Acts continue to be valid

12.12.2 **Dublin Convention and Dublin II**

This increasingly unchallengeable system of certification and removal without appeal is a manifestation of the Common European Asylum System. The European Union is particularly interested in preventing the phenomenon of 'refugees in orbit' by ensuring that at least one Member State accepts an application for asylum, stopping asylum seekers moving around the European Union in search of the country which seems to them to offer the best prospects and precluding multiple claims by one person in different Member States. The first mechanism adopted across the whole Union to do this was the Dublin Convention (OJ C 254 19.8.1997), which came into force in 1997. The Dublin Convention had no direct effect in the UK as it was a Treaty entered into under the Third Pillar of the European Union. In *R v SSHD ex p Behluli* [1998] Imm AR 407 the Court of Appeal confirmed that the Convention could not give rise to any direct rights or obligations in national law. It was a mechanism that could be used to implement a removal, for instance in the UK when the Secretary of State certified under the 1996 Act.

Council Regulation (EC) No 343/2003 OJ 2003 L 50/1 has replaced the Dublin Convention and is a regulation which is directly effective and directly applicable in national law without implementing measures (EC Treaty Art 249(2)). The Regulation, known as 'Dublin II', came into effect on 1 September 2003. Its purpose, like that of the Dublin Convention, is to establish the criteria and mechanisms for determining the Member State responsible for examining an asylum application lodged in one of the Member States by a third country national. Dublin II, in its Recitals, confirms 'the principles underlying' the Dublin Convention, and its provisions are very similar to those of the Convention. The criteria for deciding which state takes responsibility for the asylum claim include for instance where a claimant has a family member who has been recognized as a refugee or is an asylum seeker and is legally resident in a Member State, that state will be responsible for the claim, providing the persons concerned agree (Arts 7 and 8). Unaccompanied minors should be dealt with in the country where they make their application (Art 6). Also a Member State which issues a residence permit or visa will be responsible normally for a claim from the holder of that permit or visa (Art 9). Where there is evidence of illegal entry into a Member State, the state so entered remains responsible for processing the asylum seeker's claim for 12 months. After that, or in the event of there being no evidence of illegal entry, the member state in which the asylum seeker was living for the last five months is responsible (Art 10). The underlying principle is that except where these and other provisions apply to determine a responsible state, the claim should be processed in the first Member State at which the asylum seeker lodges an application (Art 13).

In *R (on the application of Mosari) v SSHD* [2005] EWHC 1343 Lightman J held that where the claimant had entered Hungary as a minor with his adult cousin, and made an asylum application there, Hungary remained the country which had responsibility under Dublin II to determine which state should hear the asylum claim. The fact that the claimant was now living with his uncle in the UK since his clandestine entry here did not mean that the UK had to take responsibility under Article 6. His original entry to the EU and first claim was made in Hungary, and family life here would not disturb that unless to proceed with the return to Hungary was disproportionate. Lightman J held that it was not.

Article 15 provides that 'Any Member State ... may bring together family members, as well as other dependent relatives, on humanitarian grounds based in particular on family or cultural considerations'. This at first sight appears to be a powerful route for an asylum seeker to argue for family unity, not necessarily in the country which would otherwise be responsible for deciding their claim. However, in *R (on the application of G) v SSHD* [2005] EWCA Civ 546 the Court of Appeal held that Article 15 did not create a right for asylum seekers, but was only intended 'to regulate the relationship between two or more Member States' (para 25).

There are some procedural changes in the regulation by comparison with the Convention, the most significant of which is perhaps the reduction of time limits for states to reply to another state and to take back an asylum seeker. In *Omar v SSHD* [2005] EWCA Civ 285 the dates of decision for Mr Omar fell after Dublin II came into force, but in the transitional period, during which applications were to be decided in accordance with the Convention. As the Dublin Convention was not incorporated into UK law it did not give rise to any directly enforceable rights for the asylum seeker (*Zequiri v SSHD* [2002] Imm AR 42). Where time periods for transfer of responsibility were not kept, the asylum seeker could not therefore say that the transfer lapsed for non-compliance. The Court held that the procedural provisions in Dublin II did not have direct effect as there were no clear words to create the rights which would then flow for the asylum seeker. Mr Omar could not insist that the UK take responsibility for his claim when there was a delay in transferring responsibility back to Italy.

12.12.3 Effect of current safe third country provisions

Macdonald refers to 'a lava flow of presumptions of safety and relentless removal of in-country appeal rights' (2005:795). The combination of European developments and UK legislation has created a system which leaves very little opportunity for an asylum seeker to have their claim heard in the UK if they have travelled through Europe.

Schedule 3 to the 2004 Act completes the process begun by the 1996 Act. Where an asylum seeker may be removed to a First List country, their asylum claim will not be determined in the UK. They will be removed to Europe for their claim to be heard, and they cannot appeal that removal at any stage. Any other human rights claim they have will almost certainly be certified as clearly unfounded so they will be unable to pursue it in the UK. That certificate may be challenged by judicial review, but the burden will be on the asylum seeker to show that there is an arguable case.

The 2004 Act gives the Secretary of State power to amend the Second and Third Lists but not the First. This means that any evidence that a European country was not complying with ECHR obligations concerning onward removal would have to go to Parliament. An application for a declaration of incompatibility under Human Rights Act 1998 s 4 would be possible, but even if successful would not automatically suspend operation of the incompatible statutory provision.

Certification also raises constitutional questions about the institutions involved in the asylum claim process. It is difficult to assess the real merits of safe third country decisions in the absence of an independent body to determine refugee claims.

QUESTIONS

1   Is it appropriate to see the Home Office as the opponent in asylum appeals, or is this unnecessarily confrontational?

2   How would you explain to an asylum seeker detained in Harmondsworth the meaning of their detention?

3   What would be your priorities for change in the asylum system?

FURTHER READING

Amnesty International (2004) *Get it right: how Home Office decision-making fails refugees,* Amnesty International UK.

Asylum Aid (1995) No Reason at all.

Asylum Aid (1999) Still no Reason at all.

Barnes, J. (2004) 'Expert Evidence – The Judicial Perception in Asylum and Human Rights Appeals'. (2004) International Journal of Refugee Law, vol. 16, no. 3, pp. 349–357.

Canadian Council for Refugees (2005) Closing the Door on Refugees: report on safe third country agreement 6 months after implementation, CCR August.

Carver, N. (2003) *Home Office Country Assessments: An Analysis* IAS September.

Carver, N. (2004) *Home Office Country Reports: An Analysis* IAS September.

Cohen, J. (2001) 'Questions of Credibility: Omissions, Discrepancies and Errors of Recall in the Testimony of Asylum Seekers' *International Journal of Refugee Law* vol. 13, no. 3.

Constitutional Affairs Committee Second Report 2003–04, *Asylum and Immigration Appeals* HC 211.

Cornelisse, G. (2004) *Human Rights for Immigration Detainees in Strasbourg: Limited Sovereignty or Limited Discourse?* European Journal of Migration and Law 6: 93–110.

ECRE March 2005, Comments on Amended proposal for a Council Directive on minimum standards on procedures in Member States for granting and withdrawing refugee status, as agreed by the Council on 19 November 2004.

Costello, C. (2005) The Asylum Procedures Directive and the Proliferation of Safe Country Practices: Deterrence, Deflection and the Dismantling of International Protection? *European Journal of Migration and Law*, vol. 7, no. 1, March 2005, pp. 35–70(36).

Doughty Street Chambers, *Blackstone's Guide to the Asylum and Immigration Act 2004* (Oxford: OUP chapters 8 & 9)

Good, A. (2004) 'Expert Evidence in Asylum and Human Rights Appeals: An Expert's View'. (2004) International Journal of Refugee Law, vol. 16, no. 3, pp. 358–380.

Gorlick, B. (2002) *Common Burdens and Standards: legal elements in assessing claims to refugee status* UNHCR Working paper no. 68.

Hathaway, J.C. (2005) *The Right of Refugees under International Law* (Cambridge: Cambridge University Press).

Head, M. (2004) 'The Global "War on Terrorism": Democractic Rights under Attack' in *Global Governance and the Quest for Justice* (ed. Brownsword, R.) (Oxford:Hart).

Home Affairs Committee report on asylum applications (*Asylum Applications,* Second report of 2003–04, HC 218, 26 January 2004).

House of Commons Public Accounts Committee (*Improving the speed and quality of asylum decisions* Fourth Report 2004–05 HC 238).

Kostakopoulou, D. and Thomas, R. (2004) *Unweaving the Threads: Territoriality, National Ownership of Land and Asylum Policy* European Journal of Migration and Law 6:5–26.

Medical Foundation (2004) *Right first time,* (Smith, E.).

National Audit Office (2004) *Improving the Speed and Quality of Asylum Decisions*, report by the Comptroller and Auditor General HC 535 Session 2003–04 23 June 2004.

Pretzell, A., and Hruschka, C. (2001) 'Non-State Agents of Persecution: A Protection Gap in German Asylum Law?' IANL vol. 15, no. 4, pp. 221–227.

Rhys-Jones, D., and Verity-Smith, S. (2004) 'Medical Evidence in Asylum and Human Rights Appeals'. (2004) International Journal of Refugee Law, vol. 16, no. 3, pp. 381–410.

Statewatch (2004) EU divided over list of 'safe countries of origin' — Statewatch calls for the list to be scrapped.

Stevens, D. (2001) 'The Immigration and Asylum Act 1999; A Missed Opportunity?' *Modern Law Review* vol. 64, 3, pp. 413–438.

Thomas. R. (2005) *Asylum Appeals: The Challenge of Asylum to the British legal System* in The challenge of asylum to legal systems Shah P. (ed.) (London:Cavendish).

UNHCR (2005) Provisional observations of UNHCR on Amended proposal for a Council Directive on minimum standards on procedures in Member States for granting and withdrawing refugee status.

Woodhouse, S. (2004) *The Annual Report of the Certification Monitor*.

Willhelm. E. (2005) 'Don't bother Knocking': Australia's response to Asylum Seekers' in *The challenge of asylum to legal systems* (Shah P. (ed.)) (London:Cavendish).

Yeo, C. ed. (2005) *Country Guideline cases: benign and practical?* (London: IAS).

13

The refugee definition

SUMMARY

This chapter examines the definition of a 'refugee' found in Article 1A of the UN Convention Relating to the Status of Refugees. Although at the time of drafting the Convention this may not have been the main preoccupation of contracting states, it is now a paragraph every phrase of which has been extensively examined in courts and tribunals worldwide. The case law relating to the main aspects of the Article is discussed, and some of the controversies which surround refugee definition.

13.1 Definition of 'refugee'

Refugee status is determined by applying the definition found in Article 1A(2) of the Refugee Convention, which says that a 'refugee' is a person who:

Owing to a well-founded fear of being persecuted for reasons of race, religion, nationality, membership of a particular social group, or political opinion, is outside his country of nationality and is unable or, owing to such fear, is unwilling to avail himself of the protection of that country; or who, not having a nationality and being outside the country of his former habitual residence . . . is unable or, owing to such fear, is unwilling to return to it.

The rest of this chapter consists of an exploration of this definition as it has been interpreted by courts and tribunals.

13.2 The fear

The centrality of the requirement of fear places a greater emphasis on the experience and circumstances of the individual than the refugee protection measures which preceded the 1951 Convention. Arugably, the fear has both a subjective and objective aspect. The *UNHCR Handbook* paras 37–50 suggests that both are necessary.

13.2.1 Subjective fear

The subjective aspect is the refugee's own experience of fear. Paragraphs 40 and 41 of the UNHCR Handbook discuss the way in which the subjective element may be evaluated, and what it may contribute to the possibility of attaining refugee status. These paragraphs suggest that the requirement of subjective fear gives scope for taking account of the effect of circumstances on an individual. For instance, 'one person may have strong political or religious convictions, the disregard of which would make his life intolerable; another may have no such strong convictions' (para 40). Therefore similar circumstances may bear differently on different people. The assessment of the subjective state of fear, according to para 40, involves engaging in 'an assessment of the personality of the applicant . . . since the psychological reactions of different individuals may not be the same in identical conditions'. However, tribunals tend to steer away from too intense a psychological scrutiny of the subjective fear. The proper and usual approach was expressed as follows by the Tribunal in *Asuming v SSHD* (11530):

> we understand 'fear' in an asylum claim to be nothing more nor less than a belief in that which the appellant states is likely to happen if he returns to his country of origin . . . one should not approach the issue on the basis of a need to assess whether a person is 'afraid' in the sense of being fearful rather than courageous.

In law and practice subjective fear is secondary to objective fear. The objective aspect of the fear is the question of whether or not it is well-founded, i.e., whether or not the events that the claimant fears are indeed likely to come about.

Hathaway says that 'the use of the term "fear" was intended to emphasize the forward-looking nature of the refugee claim, not to ground refugee status in an assessment of the claimant's state of mind' (1991:75). This approach supports the purpose of the Convention which is to protect people from actual persecution and was used and approved in the leading Tribunal case of *Gashi and Nikshiqi* [1997] INLR 96. The same standard of proof applies to the subjective and objective aspects of fear (*Asuming*). The third colloquium on challenges in international refugee law produced the Michigan Guidelines on Well-Founded Fear (adopted March 28 2004). These took a further step in this same direction by suggesting that the different psychological effects of the same circumstances should be considered not in relation to establishing the 'fear' but only in relation to persecution. The Guidelines in effect endorse *Gashi and Nikshiqi* and Hathaway's earlier work, but more strongly, saying not only that there is no need to look for a state of trepidation, but that doing so is harmful, discriminatory and wrong (see Hathaway and Hicks 2005). For a contrary view, see Tuitt (1996:96–97) who argues that the central importance accorded to the test of objectively well-founded fear may be seen as part of a legal trend which enables the state to make generalized statements about safety which defeat an asylum claim.

We can summarize by saying that the subjective aspect of the fear is an anticipation that persecution would result if the asylum seeker returned to their home country. In general it will not come into question where there is evidence that the fear is well founded.

13.2.2 Objective fear

The applicant has the burden of proving that their fear is well founded, i.e., that there are objective grounds for believing that the fear will materialize. In proving that they face a risk of persecution in their country of origin the refugee faces substantial difficulties. Not only are they outside their country of origin, in an unfamiliar environment, without access to common reference points, witnesses or documents, but also, communication with their country of origin may be difficult or impossible. The very nature of their claim means that governmental sources in their own country will not be willing to provide supporting evidence. The refugee is not likely to have substantial documentary evidence proving their claim, they may not even have documents proving their identity. On the other hand, the consequences of refusing a valid claim could be extremely serious. As the Tribunal said in *Asuming*, 'Asylum cases differ from most other cases in the seriousness of the consequences of an erroneous decision, in the focus of the decision on the future, and the inherent difficulties of obtaining objective evidence'. In such a situation, the question of what standard of proof must be reached by the asylum claimant is all important. Are they required to prove beyond reasonable doubt that they will be persecuted on return (the criminal standard) or on balance of probabilities (the civil standard) or on the lower standard that there is a risk of persecution or a reasonable likelihood (the standard formerly used in the 1993 Act in relation to whether torture may have occurred)?

13.2.2.1 *Standard of proof*

It is settled law since the House of Lords' judgment in *R v SSHD ex p Sivakumaran* [1988] AC 958 that the asylum seeker should be required to establish a reasonable degree of likelihood that their fear will materialize i.e. that persecution will take place. The standard of proof to be applied was variously described in that case as 'a reasonable chance', 'substantial grounds for thinking', 'a serious possibility', and 'a one in ten chance'. Lord Keith's formulation 'reasonable degree of likelihood' is generally taken to express this standard.

The question was further explained by the Court of Appeal in the case of *Karana-karan* [2000] Imm AR 271. Sedley LJ said that a refugee claim is not like a civil claim in which there are two competing sets of evidence, one of which the judge must prefer. A refugee claim is not an adversarial process at all. It is a public law investigation of a claim to international law protection. In a civil claim, for the purpose of deciding between parties, facts are taken to be proved if the court is satisfied that they are more likely than not to have happened. Once a matter of evidence has reached this threshold it is treated as a certain event. In a refugee claim the primary question is not what happened in the past, though this may be important evidence. The primary question in a refugee claim is what may happen in the future. The claim turns on fear of a future event, namely, persecution. Whether this fear would materialize if the refugee returned is something no one can know for sure. An assessment of what may happen in the future must take into account all the available evidence. To discount the possibility of events having happened in the past on the basis that in the decision-maker's view it was 'more likely than not' that they did not occur, would be to approach an asylum claim like civil litigation, and would limit the decision-maker's proper assessment of the situation. The decision-maker in an asylum claim must take account of the possibility that their own judgment of what may have happened may be wrong, and the consequences of relying on this as evidence of what may happen in the future. To summarize, an asylum claim should not be assessed by treating facts as established or not on the civil standard, but should be approached as a whole, taking into account all the evidence, attributing weight according to the quality of that evidence, and excluding only matters which the decision-maker can be sure are not as claimed. This approach follows that of Simon Brown LJ in *Ravichandran*, who said that the question of a well-founded fear of persecution for a Convention reason is a single, composite question.

In the case of *Kaja* (11038) an experienced Tribunal convened for the purpose of resolving the question held that the *Sivakumaran* standard of proof should be applied to the question of whether past events had taken place as well as to whether persecution would take place in the future. So, if the applicant claimed that they had been beaten in custody and that this would recur, both matters need to be proved to be a reasonable likelihood. In fact, the tribunal said, past events and future risks were all part of the same question which should be approached as a question of reasonable likelihood. To divide past events from assessment of future risks is artificial as assessment of future risk will depend in many cases to a great extent on an evaluation of what has happened in the past. *Kaja* has been relied upon since as authority for the proposition simply as stated above, that the lower standard of proof should be applied to past events as well as the chance of future occurrences. Brooke LJ in *Karanakaran* suggested that this is an oversimplification of the tribunal's judgement which amounts to mis-stating it, and that the decision should be applied using its full reasoning. This was that a decision-maker in an asylum claim will be faced with four kinds of evidence:

1. evidence whose validity they are certain about;
2. evidence they think is probably true;
3. evidence to which they are willing to attach some credence, but would not go so far as to say that it is probably true; and
4. evidence to which they are not willing to attach any credence at all.

The contentious area is the third category of evidence, as this falls below the standard of proof which would warrant reliance upon it in a civil claim. The Tribunal's view in *Kaja* was that the asylum decision-maker should not exclude such evidence from their mind.

Karanakaran steers decision-makers away from a mechanistic approach to the standard of proof in *Sivakumaran* and *Kaja*. It is not that the asylum seeker must prove the matters alleged to the standard of reasonable likelihood. In itself this can become a rather meaningless word game, as though the phrase had the precision of a percentage and as though events and risks could be proved to a quantifiable degree. Rather, although *Sivakumaran* and *Kaja* represent appropriate standards if standards are required, and for this purpose the Court of Appeal follows *Sivakumaran* and approves *Kaja*, the inherent uncertainty of future possibilities and of the evaluation of evidence must be understood. Assessing an asylum claim is not a matter simply of fact-finding but, crucially, of evaluation. It must be approached as a whole, as a public law enquiry into the need for protection rather than as an exercise in proving facts to a standard.

The application of this approach is a question of assessing the evidence in every case. Evidence of a likelihood involves evidence of context and surrounding factors which may suggest for instance trends of behaviour by police or security forces. Asylum cases therefore rely not only on evidence concerning the particular applicant, but also on evidence of what has happened to people who are in a comparable situation to the applicant and of trends for instance, in political repression as may be relevant in the country concerned. As discussed in the previous chapter, these kinds of evidence are procured by using expert evidence and regularly produced reports on the overall situation in particular countries by organizations such as Human Rights Watch, Amnesty International, the US State Department, and the Home Office's Country Information and Policy Unit (CIPU).

In chapter 3 we mentioned that the same standard of proof is used in asylum and Article 3 ECHR cases. This is the prevailing view, though there are arguments to the contrary. Two cases in the Court of Appeal which dealt with a failed asylum claims show that whatever the general situation, the ultimate question is whether there is a real risk (as the test is phrased in the Article 3 context) to this applicant. In *Hariri v SSHD* [2003] EWCA Civ 807 the Court of Appeal said that the appellant's case depended entirely on whether he would suffer ill-treatment as a member of a class, either of draft evaders or of those who had left Syria without authority. Therefore the question of whether there was generally a pattern of ill-treatment of such people was crucial to establishing whether there was a real risk to the appellant. The Tribunal was therefore not wrong to look for 'a consistent pattern of gross and systematic violation of fundamental human rights' in order to establish whether there was a real risk. However, there are clear risks of over-applying such a formulation, identified by Sedley LJ in *Batayav v SSHD* [2003] EWCA Civ 1489: 'Great care needs to be taken with such epithets. They are intended to elucidate the jurisprudential concept of real risk, not to replace it' (para 38). He then used the example of a car with faulty brakes, quoted in chapter 3. Even if the brakes only fail one time in ten, most people would think there was a real risk of travelling in such a car. There do not have to be frequent or routine brake failures for this to be the case. In *AA v SSHD* [2005] UKAIT CG, which concerned the risk to failed asylum seekers on return to Zimbabwe, the Tribunal followed *Batayav* and reiterated the warning against over-formulation. It noted that in *Batayav v SSHD (No. 2)* [2005] EWCA Civ 366 the Court of Appeal had taken *Hariri* too far in looking for 'conditions in that system that are universal' (para 5) in order to establish risk. The Tribunal gives a helpful explanation of how the approach has to be different in different cases in order to answer the crucial question of whether there is 'real risk' to the appellant. The courts are moving in the direction of preferring the concept of 'real risk' to 'reasonable degree of likelihood'. This is not with any intention to change the standard of proof, but in order, as explained by Macdonald (2005:688) to avoid straying into calculations of probability rather than staying with the question of danger to the applicant.

13.2.3 Timing of fear

The well-founded fear must, at the time of the claim, be an operative cause of the asylum seeker's being away from their country of origin. In the case of *Adan* [1998] Imm AR 338, the House of Lords considered whether historic fear, i.e., fear in the past, would be sufficient to found refugee status, and concluded that it would not. Article 1(A)(2) says that it is 'owing to a well-founded fear' that the refugee 'is' outside their country of nationality. In Mr Adan's case, he could not, at the time of his claim, avail himself of the protection of his country (Somalia) as there was no effective government to offer that protection. However, the initial fear which had caused him to flee had subsided as President Barre had fallen and the risk to him of persecution was accordingly lessened. The House of Lords said that there were two parts to a refugee claim, the 'fear test' and the 'protection test', and held that Mr Adan could not obtain refugee status because the fear did not still exist, even though no governmental protection was available and there were risks to him consequent on the continuing civil war.

In *In re B; R v Special Adjudicator ex p Hoxha (UNHCR intervening)* [2005] UKHL 19 the House of Lords considered an argument centred on the cessation clause in Article 1C of the Refugee Convention. As discussed in the last chapter, this clause provides for the ending of refugee status when there has been such a radical change in the circumstances in the refugee's country of origin that they can no longer fail to avail themselves of their country's protection. There is an exception in Article 1C where a refugee is able to 'invoke compelling reasons arising out of past persecution'. In this case the refugee status is not ended. The appellants in *Hoxha* had not obtained refugee status because of the changed circumstances in Kosovo. They argued that the persecution they had suffered in the past was nevertheless so severe that they should not be obliged to return. The House of Lords rejected this argument. An exception to the cessation clause could not be used to achieve refugee status for someone who had not achieved it on their asylum application. Their fear was not current, as was required in order to obtain protection.

13.2.4 Refugee *sur place*

The opposite situation also arises, where a refugee has left their country of origin without fear for some other purpose, e.g., a holiday or study, but during their absence an event such as a change of government takes place which causes them to fear persecution should they return. In this case the fear is the operative cause of their remaining outside their country of nationality, even though it was not the cause of their leaving it. They are thus entitled to claim refugee status and are referred to, following the French, as a refugee *'sur place'*.

It follows that if events since the applicant's arrival in the UK may give rise to a well-founded fear, these events may take place not only in the applicant's home country but equally in the UK, in fact they may be the actions of the applicant themselves. This was established by the Court of Appeal in *Danian* [2000] Imm AR 96, in which it was confirmed that refugee status could be granted after the applicant was at risk of persecution in his country of nationality because of his activities in the UK. This was followed by the tribunal in *Siddeig* (20082) who found that the applicant should be granted refugee status on account of his activities in the UK with the Communist Party of Sudan. Communist Party activity would be likely to result in persecution in Sudan, even if no such activity had taken place in that country.

This decision does not necessarily mean that a person may create their own refugee status cynically by undertaking political activities in the UK when they have no genuine political motive. This question has been considered in a number of cases since *Danian*. The Court of Appeal in *Iftikhar Ahmed v SSHD* [2000] INLR 1 explained that *Danian* simply brings the decision back to the essential question, 'is there a serious risk that on return the applicant would be persecuted for a

Convention reason?' That risk may be created by the applicant's own cynical or unreasonable conduct but may still be real. The evaluation of how real it is would of course be affected by some doubt as to the applicant's own credibility.

In *Danian* itself the Court endorsed the view of the UNHCR:

it should be borne in mind that opportunistic post-flight activities will not necessarily create a real risk of persecution in the claimant's home country either because they will not come to the attention of the authorities of that country or because the opportunistic nature of such activities will be apparent to all including to those authorities.

It follows that it is a mistake to dismiss the claim without considering the effect of activities in the UK on the applicant's prospects on return (*R v IAT ex p Mafuta* [2001] EWCA Civ 745).

Mr Danian himself ultimately lost his appeal when the case came back to the Tribunal, after the Court of Appeal decision. The Tribunal considered that lack of good faith undermined the credibility of a well-founded fear of persecution. It took the view that if Mr Danian's motives were cynical, then he did not have a fear, and on the facts of his political involvement in the UK, the Nigerian authorities would not impute to him a political opinion.

13.2.4.1 *Rejected asylum claims*

A related issue is the effect of the asylum claim itself on what treatment the individual might face on return. The Home Office occasionally accepts as a matter of policy that returning people to particular countries may not be possible because the fact of having made an asylum claim may bring reprisals from their home government. In the case of Libya the Home Office adopted a policy of this kind in 2001 (see *Hassan* [2002] UKIAT 00062). More recently, the only country to which as a matter of policy removals have not been taking place has been Zimbabwe (letter Des Browne to Keith Best IAS published 12 July 2004). However, amid protest, in November 2004 the Home Office lifted this moratorium. In Zimbabwe some politicians welcomed the move, but Information Minister, Jonathan Moyo, considered that returnees should be treated with suspicion as they could be 'trained and bribed malcontents', sent to disrupt the election (newsvote.bbc.co.uk 17 December 2004). The resumption of returns caused not only a political storm, but also scores of asylum seekers to go on hunger strike in detention. Numerous applications were lodged for judicial review of removal directions. Eventually the Home Office was forced to concede that removals to Zimbabwe could not continue at least until the hearing of a test case. Interestingly, on the same day that the Home Secretary was compelled to this position, the European Parliament issued a far-reaching resolution on Zimbabwe, calling for the strengthening of sanctions and condemning the regime but making no reference to the return of failed asylum seekers (7 July 2005).

All pending judicial reviews were stayed, and the Tribunal gave a special judgment on the issue in October 2005 (*AA v SSHD* [2005] UKAIT CG). Although the decision can only bind the individual case, the Tribunal deliberately set out lengthy summaries of evidence about the situation in Zimbabwe, with the intention that this would guide all the outstanding cases.

Evidence was accepted that the documents of those forcibly returned to Zimbabwe were routinely retained by airline staff and handed to the authorities in Harare. On days when returned asylum seekers were aboard a plane, there was an increased presence of the Central Intelligence Organisation at Harare airport, and these officials instead of the usual immigration officers would interview the returnees. The Home Office was unable to offer evidence of the fate of individuals after that. The appellant was able to produce some evidence of cases of ill-treatment.

The asylum case of *AA* was not strong. The Tribunal took the view that it was a worthless claim. Nevertheless it was bound by *Danian* that even where a claim was made in bad faith, the applicant must be protected from a real risk of ill-treatment on return. It suggested that *Danian* was due for reconsideration as it was decided before the Human Rights Act, and returnees would be protected under Article 3 if there was a real risk to them. This attitude may also be detected in the EU Directive on qualification as a refugee, which permits Member States to deny refugee status where the risk of persecution 'is based on circumstances which the applicant has created by his own decision since leaving the country of origin', providing this does not conflict in the particular case with Refugee Convention obligations (Article 5). The tribunal considered that there was an unpalatable effect of this case, that it appeared that the system could be misused and still result in protection. However, it laid this to an extent at the door of the Home Office who had implemented procedures whereby returnees were actually *put* at risk by distinguishing them from other passengers and handing them over to the authorities, and had failed to monitor or attempt to trace whether any individuals were in fact safe. The Tribunal's decision was overturned on appeal ([2006] EWCA Civ 401).

In addition to general country policies, it may be necessary to argue that the return of a particular failed asylum seeker is not safe. This often arises in relation to the return of Kurds to Turkey as there are concerns about the authorities' treatment of them on arrival. In *Degirmenci v SSHD* [2004] EWCA Civ 1553 the Court of Appeal held that there needed to be a full assessment of the evidence relating to the treatment on return of a failed asylum seeker such as the appellant. Where, for instance, as in *Yapici* (below) the appellant had left the country in breach of reporting conditions, this would increase the risk of their coming to the notice of the authorities.

13.3 Persecution

The concept of persecution is central to the recognition of refugee status. It is not conclusively defined, and in fact the UNCHR Handbook expressly avoids attempting to lay down any such definition, saying that whether threats or actions will amount to persecution 'will depend on the circumstances of each case' (para 52) and 'it is not possible to lay down a general rule as to what cumulative reasons can give rise to a valid claim to refugee status' (para 53). One approach, in a line of cases of which *Jonah* [1985] Imm AR 7 is the oft-quoted authority, has been reliance on the dictionary definition: 'to pursue with malignancy or injurious action.' However, this requires a focus on the motive and actions of the persecutor. It might be said that a person tortured once in a police station and then released has not been 'pursued' and that a person who would be prosecuted for any expression of their sexuality is not the target of malignancy but of government policy. Whereas the dictionary definition would work for some cases, it does not for others. This approach is falling into disuse in favour of retaining the flexibility indicated by the Handbook.

Both academic commentators and tribunals have commented that this lack of precise definition is appropriate to the nature of the Convention as a living instrument. The tribunal in *Gashi* adopted the submission of the UNHCR that: 'for the Convention to be a living instrument of protection, the term "persecution" must be interpreted in a manner that best achieves its humanitarian object and purpose.' The Tribunal itself went on to say that 'it would be a mistake to attempt a definition of persecution which could in any way restrict its power to meet the changing circumstances in which the Convention has to operate'. A simple formulation is that persecution = serious harm + failure of state protection (set out in this way by the Refugee Women's Legal Group (*Women as Asylum Seekers* 1997:9)). This is a workable formulation which underscores the crucial aspect of state responsibility and has been used by the courts, for instance by Lord Hoffmann in *R v IAT & SSHD ex p Shah and Islam v IAT* [1999] 2 AC 629.

Clearly, there must be an analysis of whether what is feared in a particular case is persecution. However, it would be closer to the current direction of case law to say that the decision-maker should not be seeking to *define* persecution but to *identify* it. The difference is that a definition is an attempt to provide in the abstract a statement that will apply in a wide range (preferably all) circumstances, whereas identification starts with a set of circumstances and asks whether these amount to persecution. This might be similar to a doctor who considers the patient's symptoms in the light of all available knowledge and then decides whether they have the disease, rather than trying to list an exhaustive set of symptoms and then asking whether the patient fits into them.

A commonly used starting point for identifying persecution is that proffered by Hathaway:

The sustained or systemic violation of basic human rights demonstrative of a failure of state protection in relation to one of the core entitlements which has been recognized by the international community. The types of harm to be protected against include the breach of any rights within the first category, a discriminatory or non-emergency abnegation of a right within the second category or the failure to implement a right in the third category which is either discriminatory or not grounded in the absolute lack of resources. (1991:112)

The three categories to which he refers he sets out in the following way:

Category one:
Freedom from arbitrary deprivation of life, from torture, cruel, inhuman or, degrading treatment or punishment, from slavery, imprisonment for breach of a contractual obligation, retroactive criminal prosecution, freedom of thought, conscience and religion, and the right to be recognized as a person in law.

Category two:
Freedom from arbitrary arrest and detention, right to a fair trial, equal treatment including in access to public employment, freedom of expression, assembly and association, of movement inside a country, to leave and return to one's country of origin, to form and join trade unions, to take part in public affairs and vote, and protection for privacy and the family.

Category three:

The right to work, including just and favourable conditions of employment, to an adequate standard of living including food, clothing and housing, to the highest attainable standard of health, to education, and to engage in cultural, scientific, literary, and artistic expression.

This approach, the human rights approach to persecution, was broadly adopted by the UNHCR and from them by the Tribunal in *Gashi and Nikshiqi*. It has been used and endorsed by the higher courts for instance the House of Lords in *Horvath v SSHD* [2000] 3 All ER 577 and *Sepet and Bulbul v SSHD* [2003] UKHL 15. It will be adopted as a useful basis here for classifying kinds of persecution for the purposes of discussion. However, while an extremely useful framework it is not final or definitive, and as we shall see has some limitations (and see for instance Wilsher 2003).

We shall return to the consideration of these categories shortly when we consider what kind of treatment might amount to persecution, the 'serious harm' element of the RWLG formula. For the moment we shall turn attention to the second part: the failure of state protection.

13.3.1 **Failure of state protection**

In the leading case of *Horvath* Lord Clyde explains the requirement for state involvement as follows: 'It is no part of the international scheme that people should qualify as refugees merely because private persons in their home state seek to interfere with their rights and freedoms.' Taking the idea a little further, Lord Hope said: 'The general purpose of the Convention is to enable the person who no longer has the benefit of state protection against persecution for a Convention reason in his own country to turn for protection to the international community.' This is known as the principle of surrogacy. The underlying idea is the fundamental breakdown in the relationship between citizen and State, so that the citizen can no longer rely on the State for the protection which is their due, and must look instead to the international community. This may entail that the state is actively the persecutor, as when the police routinely torture people in their custody. Alternatively, it may entail that others perpetrate the serious harm, as when skinheads attack Roma people, but the state fails to protect them. When persecution is carried out in this way by non-State actors, further legal problems arise, and these are discussed below.

Professor Hathaway's reference to the 'systemic violation' of rights suggests that the violation is part of the functioning of the State system, the State endorses the violations, implicitly by not providing redress or explicitly by for instance oppressive legislation, or covertly, by promoting brutal interrogation by security services.

This may be distinguished from, although it is connected to, the question of whether ill-treatment must be *systematic* to amount to persecution. This is sometimes used in the same way as 'systemic', i.e., meaning 'part of the State system' in which case, taking into account non-State actors, it is an appropriate description of persecution. However, it may also be used to mean 'repeated' or 'persistent', which will often be appropriate but not always.

13.3.2 **Must persecution be persistent?**

The EU Directive (Council Directive 2004/83/EC of 29 April 2004 on minimum standards for the qualification and status of third country nationals or stateless persons as refugees or as persons who otherwise need international protection and the content of protection granted) follows the earlier EU Joint Position of 4 March 1996, in saying that acts feared will be persecution if sufficiently serious by reason of 'their nature or their repetition.' These are phrased as alternatives which suggests that an act which is sufficiently serious need not be repeated to amount to persecution.

The question of whether a single instance of ill-treatment may amount to persecution was briefly considered by the Court of Appeal in *Demirkaya* [1999] Imm AR 498. In that case the Tribunal had failed to have regard to earlier very serious ill-treatment as an indication of what could happen to the appellant on his return, and for this reason the Tribunal's decision could not stand. The Court did not need to explore in detail the question of a single instance. However, the authorities were comprehensively reviewed in the case of *Doymus* 00/TH/01748 which both follows and expands upon the judgment of the Court of Appeal in *Demirkaya*. The Tribunal quoted the words of Stuart-Smith LJ in that case:

At one end of the scale there may be arbitrary deprivation of life, torture and cruel, inhuman and degrading treatment or punishment. In such a case the conduct may be so extreme that one instance is sufficient, but less serious conduct may not amount to persecution unless it is persistent. (para 15)

The dictionary definition approach did not, the Tribunal thought, necessarily imply persistent ill-treatment, but it had often been used that way. If there were any conflict between that and the purposive approach, i.e., an approach governed by the purpose of the Convention then the purposive approach should prevail.

This must mean that a single violation of a first category right would constitute persecution. This is so not only in common sense (a single threat to life is enough) but also by reference to the human rights instruments from which these standards are derived. For instance 'no one shall be subjected to torture or to cruel, inhuman or degrading treatment or punishment' (Art 9 ICCPR as well as Art 3 ECHR). This does not allow an exception if the torture happens only once, and case law under these Articles treats single acts of torture or cruel, inhuman or degrading treatment, or punishment as violations. The Tribunal cited other academic writers and the UNHCR also as authorities that while persistency is a usual characteristic of persecution, it is not an inevitable one. A review of case law of other jurisdictions revealed that persistency was generally though not always a characteristic of persecution. The conclusion drawn by the Tribunal was that 'persistency is a usual but not a universal criterion of persecution.' The treatment which Mr Doymus had suffered on a previous return to Turkey was sufficiently serious to amount to a violation of Article 3 ECHR or Article 9 ICCPR and therefore would amount to persecution.

The Tribunal stressed that this case could not readily be applied to others as it turned on its own facts which were unusual in that Mr Doymus had suffered on a previous return to Turkey as a failed asylum seeker; therefore there was strong evidence of specifically what might await him on another return. However, the review of authorities and the reasoning in *Doymus* is useful in providing guidance on the issue of whether a single instance of ill-treatment could amount to persecution.

There is no requirement to be 'singled out' for persecution (*R v SSHD ex p Jeyakumaran* [1994] Imm AR 45). If the persecutory treatment is for a reason included in the Convention (see below), the fact that others who share the same characteristic are treated similarly may be evidence that supports the asylum claim but it does not detract from it. As Lord Lloyd said in *Adan* at 348: 'It is not necessary for a claimant to show that he is more at risk than anyone else in his group, if the group as a whole is subject to oppression'. Conversely, there is no need for all those sharing the characteristic to be persecuted (*Shah and Islam*).

The final form of the EU Directive does not contain an earlier proposed clause which would have made it irrelevant that the applicant comes from a country where there is large scale oppression.

13.3.3 Severe ill-treatment

The conclusion that a single instance of sufficiently severe ill-treatment may amount to persecution is a consequence of taking a human right approach to the question of what amounts to persecution. A single instance of loss of life is a severe violation of human rights, and whether that falls within a dictionary definition of 'persecution' is immaterial. A single instance of torture is persecution as the right to be free from torture is an absolute right. It admits of no justification or derogation. This was made very clear by the House of Lords in *R v SSHD ex p Sivakumar* [2003] 1 WLR 840 where even the applicant's suspected involvement in terrorism could not justify the appalling torture he had experienced. The question in relation to a fear of torture is not whether a single instance would amount to persecution but rather what constitutes torture.

There is guidance in Criminal Justice Act 1988 s 134 which brings into UK law the UN Convention against Torture and Other Cruel Inhuman or Degrading Treatment. Article 1(1) defines torture as:

An act by which pain or suffering, whether physical or mental, is intentionally inflicted on a person for such purposes as obtaining from him or a third person a confession, punishing him for an act which he or a third party has committed or is suspected of having committed, or intimidating him or a third person, or for any reason based on discrimination of any kind, when such pain or suffering is inflicted by or at the instigation of or with the consent of public officials or other person acting in an official capacity.

This Article has not been widely referred to in refugee cases, but was used as guidance by the High Court in the case of *R v SSHD ex p Javed and Ali* [2001] EWCA Admin 7. It suggests that not only the conduct but also who carried it out and the reason are significant in determining whether it amounts to torture. In *Javed and Ali*, Turner J found 'the clearest evidence that both had been tortured in the past'. In the case of Zulfiqar Ali this was the actions of the authorities in threatening him, keeping him awake for two and three days at a time, and breaking his nose. However, the Secretary of State and Special Adjudicator had not considered that this treatment amounted to torture.

In *Demirkaya* the Court of Appeal found that it would be open to a tribunal to find that beating in detention would not amount to cruel, inhuman or degrading treatment, or punishment. However, if particularly cruel or vicious it could. In *Doymus* the applicant had described being stripped naked, sprayed with cold water from a hose, and beaten with a stick while his hands were tied behind his back. The Tribunal recognized that this was degrading treatment, and was likely to 'give rise to feelings of fear, anguish, and inferiority capable of humiliating and debasing him and possibly breaking his physical and moral resistance'. It is not just the level of ill-treatment which is relevant but also these psychological effects. As mentioned earlier, this would be a breach of Article 3 ECHR or Article 9 ICCPR and it was unnecessary to determine whether it amounted to torture. The judgment in *Doymus* is helpful in linking an act of persecution so explicitly to human rights norms. In *Demirkaya* the Court of Appeal expressly disapproved trying to categorize behaviour such that a particular level of ill-treatment would amount to persecution. The question should be looked at in the round. 'Is this person at risk of persecution for a Convention reason?' The Court said that this was a question of fact.

The definition of 'torture' given above refers to the motive of the torturer, however, in a case such as *Doymus* there is no examination of the motives of the police. It was an essential and undisputed element of Mr Doymus' claim that he was at risk because of his political affiliations, and the precise anticipated motives of the police on any particular occasion do not require inquiry. All the more so is this the case as torture cannot be justified and so even if their motive was to preserve law and order this would not prevent the feared action being persecution. In the light of this, the fear of rape and other serious sexual assault receives anomalous treatment in refugee law.

13.3.3.1 *Rape and other sexual assault*

The API repeats the approach we have discussed above, and includes 'rape and other serious sexual violence' as an example of treatment which 'will amount to persecution for the purposes of the Convention if committed for a Convention reason and the authorities are unable or unwilling to provide effective protection'. It is listed alongside torture. The Immigration Appellate Authority's Asylum Gender Guidelines contain a section establishing the severity of sexual violence and suggesting that it is a violation of the right not to be subjected to torture or cruel inhuman or degrading treatment or punishment. Cited in support of this argument are the Statutes of the International Tribunals for Former Yugoslavia and Rwanda, which list rape as a crime against humanity, and the ECHR Article 3 case of *Aydin v Turkey* (1997) 25 EHRR 251 para 83 in which the Court said:

> Rape of a detainee by an official of the State must be considered to be an especially grave and abhorrent form of ill-treatment given the ease with which the offender can exploit the vulnerability and weakened resistance of his victim.

In refugee claims, however, past rape or fear of rape in the future is not always treated as persecution. The case of *R v Special Adjudicator ex p Okonkwo* [1998] Imm AR 502 demonstrates the reasoning which has been used to deny a refugee claim based on rape. The question arose in the context not of considering rape as persecution but of considering whether rape could constitute torture and so, under the legislation then in force, guarantee the applicant a full right of appeal. Collins J supported the distinction made by the adjudicator between rape committed 'merely to seek sexual gratification' and rape committed for some other motive. If it was 'merely to seek sexual gratification' then it was a common crime on a par with assault, and would not amount to torture unless repeated. It was argued for the applicant that rape constituted torture in part because the psychological effects can be similar to those referred to in *Doymus*, namely of fear, anguish, humiliation, and inferiority, and also because of the severity of the physical ill-treatment. The Asylum Gender Guidelines para 2A.18 quote Assistant Commissioner Wyn Jones of the Metropolitan Police: 'We want to kill the myth that rape is sexually motivated — it is usually intended to inflict violence and humiliation.' A fundamental disagreement about the nature of rape and other sexual violence affects whether it will be regarded as persecution. Of course the necessary element of state involvement must exist, but even this is not simple to identify. A crime which is investigated and punished is not persecution, a rape by a police officer of a person in detention which is part of a state-endorsed routine method of humiliating prisoners would surely be persecution. In *Okonkwo* the situation was between these two extremes as the assailant was an army officer who had threatened the applicant. She had suffered violence on other occasions from the authorities. She was not in detention at the time of the rape, but was attacked by the roadside and left there. The location and the lack of formal relationship between the assailant and applicant influenced Collins J in his agreement with the adjudicator. However, this leaves out of account the exercise of power by a member of the military forces and the lack of redress which the applicant experienced.

The reasoning in *Okonkwo* has been followed in later cases, for instance in *Farhat Saeed Chaudhary* 00/TH/00304 in which the adjudicator found and the Tribunal accepted that rape by police could have been for sexual gratification and was therefore not persecution. Again in *R v IAT ex p Arafa Shaban* [2000] Imm AR 408 the motive of the rapist who was a member of the ruling political party, the applicant being associated with the opposition, was regarded as relevant. The question of whether a police officer who rapes is abusing power was considered more fully in *Muriu* 00/TH/02139 but no conclusion was reached as evidence of the rape was not considered strong enough. In *Bajraktari* [2001] EWHC Admin 1192 Harrison J found that rape did not constitute torture because it was not used to extract information.

The case law in this area in the UK has been slow to recognize the political nature of much sexual violence. At the level of adjudicator decisions there is a wide variation in how and whether the Asylum Gender Guidelines are implemented. This unsatisfactory situation is partly because the Convention makes no provision for gender-specific forms of persecution. The EU Refugee Qualification Directive 2004/83 EC permits but does not prescribe recognition of 'acts of a gender-specific . . . nature' as persecution, and specifically includes 'acts of sexual violence' (Art 9.2). The UNCHR Global Consultations Summary Conclusions on gender-related persecution say that one of the main problems facing women asylum seekers is 'failure to recognize the political nature of seemingly private acts of harm to women' (para 4). The kind of harm may be relevant: in *P and M v SSHD* [2004] EWCA Civ 1640 forcible subjection to female genital mutilation was accepted as severe ill-treatment which, combined with the absence of state intervention to prevent or punish it, amounted to persecution.

Perhaps the most significant development in the law in relation to gender-related persecution, and specifically the use and effects of sexual violence, is in the judgment of Lady Hale in *In re B(FC) (Appellant) (2002) R v Special Adjudicator ex p Hoxha (FC) (Appellant)* [2005] UKHL 19. She describes with simple clarity the use of sexual violence upon women as a weapon of war and the effect which may be compounded by a society which

adds to the earlier suffering she has endured the pain, hardship and indignity of rejection and ostracism from her own people. There are many cultures in which a woman suffers almost as much from the attitudes of those around her to the degradation she has suffered as she did from the original assault. (para 32)

In the particular circumstances of this case, no asylum claim depended on this point, and so the whole judgment is obiter. It is nevertheless an influential development in the law of asylum from fear of sexual violence and its social consequences.
We shall return to this issue in discussing Convention reason below.

13.3.4 Second category rights

If the feared treatment is not of the most severe kind then the identification of persecution becomes more complex. In relation to violations of rights in Hathaway's second category, for instance detention, ill-treatment in detention short of torture, or denial of a fair trial, international human rights' instruments give states some limited power to derogate or to justify infringements. For example, detention may be justified for one of a number of listed reasons in Article 5 ECHR. This is reflected in refugee law. The leading case which demonstrates this is *Sandralingham and Ravichandran* [1996] Imm AR 97, CA. This case arose from periodic round-ups by the Sri Lankan police of young Tamil men and their detention for questioning, sometimes for periods of days. The appellants had been so detained, and had also been ill-treated in custody. They alleged that ill-treatment in custody and arbitrary arrest and detentions each separately constituted persecution. It was accepted that the situation had improved since the time when they were detained. There was therefore no reasonable likelihood of repetition of ill-treatment in detention and so this part of the claim fell out of the picture. In considering detention as possible persecution, the Court of Appeal held following factors were relevant:

(i)   the frequency of round-ups and the length of the detentions resulting;
(ii)   the situation prevailing in Colombo at the material time and the Sri Lankan government's undoubted need to combat Tamil terrorism;
(iii) the true purpose of the round-ups and the efforts made to arrest and detain only those realistically suspected of involvement in the disturbances.

The Court of Appeal endorsed the respondent's argument that

young male Tamils are not arrested and detained because they are Tamils but rather because they may have been involved in some outrage. The round-ups are not arbitrary. The very fact that the particular sub-groups identified by the Amnesty Report are especially vulnerable to arrest shows that the true objective of the round-ups is to combat terrorism rather than discriminate against Tamils as such. (at 108)

It accepted that the authorities' attempts to control disorder had affected Tamils the most because more of the disorder had occurred in areas where Tamils lived. Detention of excessive length could amount to persecution, repeated detention of the same person could amount to persecution if it was not justified by an appropriate level of suspicion of that individual's having committed a criminal offence, and ill-treatment in detention would normally amount to persecution. However, if innocent people were accidentally caught up in a legitimate policing exercise, this was not persecution even if they were likely to be of a particular minority. This last point shows that it is difficult to consider persecution separately from the reason for the persecution. The separation is indeed artificial though necessary for the purposes of analysis and discussion. The reason for persecution is discussed below under the heading of 'Convention reason'.

In *Ravichandran* Staughton LJ said that 'Persecution must at least be persistent and serious ill-treatment without just cause'. It is apparent how this arises from the facts of *Ravichandran* in which a single instance of detention was not held to be persecution, but persistent or repeated detention might be, but the statement should not be taken out of context to require that persecution must *always* be persistent. It is an example which shows that it is more appropriate to think of identifying persecution than defining it. Staughton LJ's words helped in that case to identify that the arrests in question should not be regarded as persecution, but should not be taken as a definition which can then be applied to unrelated situations. Repetition and severity are both elements which must be considered.

13.3.4.1 *Prosecution or persecution?*

Continuing the consideration of second category rights, it is undeniable that the state has a right to prosecute its citizens, even a duty to do so in order to maintain law and order for the benefit of others. The UNHCR Handbook puts it in this way:

Persecution must be distinguished from punishment for a common law offence. Persons fleeing from prosecution or punishment for such an offence are not normally refugees. It should be recalled that a refugee is a victim — or potential victim — of injustice, not a fugitive from justice. (para 56)

However, prosecution may amount to persecution in certain circumstances. If a punishment is excessive, this may turn prosecution into persecution. For instance, it may be within lawful bounds of State action for there to be some penalty for adultery, but stoning to death goes beyond that (*Shah and Islam*).

The discriminatory application of the law may also turn prosecution into persecution, as suggested in the quotation above from *Ravichandran*. If people had been detained *because* they were Tamils, then this could have amounted to persecution. The Handbook gives the example of prosecution for an offence of public order for the distribution of pamphlets, which could be 'a vehicle for the persecution of the individual on the grounds of the political content of the publication' (para 59). In *Sivakumar* in the Court of Appeal [2002] INLR 310 Dyson LJ used the following words which were quoted with approval by the House of Lords:

Where a person to whom a political opinion is imputed or who is a member of a race or social group is the subject of sanctions that do not apply generally in the state, then it is more likely than not that the application of the sanctions is discriminatory and persecutory for a Convention reason. (para 30)

The House of Lords added the caveat that this should not be used to suggest a rebuttable inference in the legal sense. In *Asante* [1991] Imm AR 78 the Tribunal found that the reason for prosecution was the political opinion imputed to the applicant, and this rendered the prosecution persecutory for Convention purposes.

The issue is less clear when an individual is not targeted for enforcement for a discriminatory reason, but enforcement of the law has a discriminatory impact. On the face of it the claims of Turkish Kurds for refugee status on account of conscription into the military raise this issue as a significant proportion of the work of the military may be engaged in action against their own minority. However these claims have on the whole not been successful. This is dealt with further below in relation to the Convention reason for persecution and the implications of objection to military service.

Prosecution may also amount to persecution where there is a lack of due process or fairness in the criminal process. Hathaway says that where 'the decision to prosecute, the process under which the charge is heard, or the nature of the sentence imposed is politically manipulated' (1991:172) then the prosecution may found a refugee claim. The allegations were of this kind in *Khan v SSHD* [2003] EWCA Civ 530 where the appellant fled Bangladesh after a violent demonstration, as a result of which he had been charged and a warrant issued for his arrest. He believed that he would not be granted bail, would be detained in inhuman and degrading conditions for a long period of time, and would not receive a fair trial. The adjudicator had held that what he feared was prosecution rather than persecution, but the Court of Appeal agreed that the case must be reconsidered by the IAT when Mr Khan was able to prove that he had been sentenced to ten years' imprisonment in his absence. Where an individual is prosecuted for exercising fundamental human rights, then the prosecution may well be persecutory, but this will depend additionally on whether, in the circumstances, some curtailment of freedom is justified in the public interest, and if so, whether the curtailment imposed by the criminal law has exceeded what is justified. In Mr Khan's case there may have been grounds for charging a public order offence, but this could not justify an unfair trial.

As mentioned earlier in relation to failed asylum seekers, many cases have concerned the question of whether a Kurdish dissident will attract the attention of the authorities on return to Turkey and so be at risk. In *Yapici v SSHD* [2005] EWCA Civ 826 the Court of Appeal held that a proper decision must have regard to the effect of the appellant's leaving the country in breach of reporting conditions. Although the appellant was in breach of an administrative requirement, his reason for being in breach and the fact that it could bring him to the notice of the authorities were relevant to whether he would be at risk on return.

13.3.5 Discrimination as persecution

The violation and threatened violation of rights in Hathaway's third category gives rise to difficult questions in refugee claims. The Refugee Convention protects against persecution, but not against discrimination. In an age which has coined the term 'ethnic cleansing', when does one become the other? This is one of the challenges to the international framework of human rights and refugee protection which was probably not contemplated in this form when the Convention was first drafted.

A formative case on this issue is *Gashi and Nikshiqi*. The appellants in this case were ethnic Albanians from Kosovo in Serbia. They had evaded military service, and their claim was based in part on the consequences for them of this evasion if they were to return and in part on the level of discrimination they would face as ethnic Albanians in Kosovo. In considering whether this would amount to persecution the Tribunal drew on the internationally accepted view of the Convention as a living instrument. It said 'it would be a mistake to attempt a definition of "persecution" which could in any way restrict its growth to meet the changing circumstances in which the Convention has to operate'. There was an abundance of evidence before it about the situation of ethnic Albanians in land, such as Kosovo, under Serb control. The government policy was referred to as 'Serbianization', implemented by, for instance (quoting from the Tribunal's summary of evidence):

the removal of senior Albanians in the courts and public sector generally and restrictions in even the most menial of employment, e.g. street vendors. 80% of Albanians lost their posts . . . There is no control or evidence of any intended control by the central authority of the police in Kosovo and the police are all Serbians. There is a systematic state policy which, it is said, permits this police misbehaviour. In day to day life Albanians are harassed, subjected to house searches, beating, torture at police stations, constant checks carried out at random without any recourse to courts with an effective system to provide adequate remedies and protection to ethnic Albanians.

As a consequence the Tribunal found that Mr Gashi and Mr Nikshiqi, in addition to prosecution for draft evasion, faced physical abuse, inability to obtain employment, and constant and persistent harassment by police uncontrolled by government. This amounted to persecution. The Tribunal's decision adopts the reasoning of the UNHCR on the question of discrimination without alteration. *Gashi and Nikshiqi* was by no means the first case to recognize denial of third category rights as a basis for refugee status, but the extensive judgment made it an authoritative and important turning point in this respect.

Where discrimination in social rights is feared, the decision as to whether this amounts to persecution necessarily involves an assessment of the action taken by the government to protect its citizens. This can be particularly difficult where bitter inter-ethnic wars have been fought and a new government attempts to bring the situation back to normal. The case of *Mrvaljevic* 00/TH/02863 was one of many in which the tribunal had to consider the risk to a Serb of returning to Croatia. Mr Mrvaljevic, like some other asylum claimants, had fought against the Croats in the Serbian forces (the army of the Republika Srpska Krajina, RSK). At the time of his appeal before the tribunal the new Croatian Government was showing commitment to promoting a peaceful co-existence between Serbs and Croats and preparing legislation to that end. The Serb National Council had welcomed the announced reforms and was intending co-operation. The Tribunal accepted that Mr Mrvaljevic was at risk having fought against the Croats, and his house had been firebombed shortly after he had been warned to leave Croatia. There was clear evidence that returning members of the Serb forces were being arrested for war crimes without necessarily any evidence against the particular individual. The Tribunal accepted expert evidence that until the effects of the changes in government in Croatia had had time to work through, there remained a risk of persecution of Serbs who served in the OS RSK during the war.

Some six weeks later, a differently constituted Tribunal (in the case of *Protic* 01/TH/00098) dismissed the appeal of another ex-member of the Serbian forces on the basis that the situation was improving, and that although there was risk of prosecution for war crimes, a number of people had been released for lack of evidence, showing that due process was being re-asserted and that arbitrary punishment was not likely to occur. Mr Protic had also received threats, and had been attacked by Croats in the past. The Tribunal's decision recognized that Serbs were suffering discrimination in Croatia, but placed emphasis on the improving situation and the reduced risk to the appellant.

Although each case can only be decided on the risk to the particular applicant, it will be apparent that these are highly political decisions. The recognition of an asylum claim is an acknowledgement that this individual is not being protected by their own government, and particularly when discrimination is the basis of the claim, this involves, in effect, judgments about the functioning of that society. Before conflicts in the former Yugoslavia, there was a short period when the British media was full of reports of Roma people fleeing severe discrimination in eastern European countries (see, for instance, report in Patrin Web Journal, October 22 1997). The British Home Office Minister, Mike O'Brien, appeared on television to say that the majority of these claims would not be entertained as it was the job of the asylum seekers' own governments to resolve issues of discrimination, and they would not interfere in the internal matters of another state.

On the whole, applications from European Roma continued to be turned down, though it has been questioned by academic commentators (see, for instance, O'Nions 1999) whether claims have been genuinely considered on an individual basis as required by the Refugee Convention. Since 1 May 2004 most such claims are no longer possible as countries of origin of most Roma claimants are now members of the EU. On the face of it, this is a beneficial development for those wishing to escape conditions of economic deprivation amounting to discrimination, as they have a right to enter the UK for work. The rare case where international protection within Europe is what is needed rather than work is prevented by the Refugee Directive 2004/83, which provides for refugee claims only from third country nationals and those who are stateless. As a minimum standard this could of course be exceeded, but the political consequences of giving refuge to a European national are unlikely to be countenanced by any Member State.

The UNHCR Handbook suggests that discrimination may amount to persecution in certain circumstances:

This would be so if measures of discrimination lead to consequences of a substantially prejudicial nature for the person concerned, e.g. serious restrictions on his right to earn a livelihood, his right to practise his religion, or his access to normally available educational facilities. (para 54)

The emphasis in the Refugee Directive is on non-derogable rights, but there is scope for persecution to arise from 'an accumulation of various measures, including violation of human rights, which is sufficiently severe as to affect an individual in a similar manner to' severe violation of basic human rights. The Directive allows for claims based on discrimination, but only with reference to 'legal, administrative, police or judicial measures'. This seems to indicate a retreat at European level from countenancing claims with an economic basis, though some have succeeded in the past.

The question according to the Tribunal in *Gujda* (18231) was whether the denial of social rights, to education, housing, and so forth, is such that it interferes 'with a basic human right to live a decent life'. It must also be grounded in discrimination, not an absolute lack of resources in the state; citizens of countries where the majority live in extreme poverty cannot claim asylum on this basis. In *Harakal (also known as Harakel) v SSHD* [2001] EWCA Civ 884 the Court of Appeal found that a lifetime of serious discrimination should be taken into account in allowing the asylum claim of a Roma from the Czech Republic. The Court of Appeal described it as 'significant discrimination in all facets of his life throughout his life'. In *Chiver* (10758) the asylum application succeeded before the adjudicator where the claimant was a miner from Romania who had refused to take government orders to take part in breaking up anti-government demonstrations. He was dismissed from his job as a result, and refused a work card. Without this he was unable to obtain a job or any state benefits. He went on hunger strike, and was arrested and beaten by a policeman. His claim was based substantially on the denial of the right to a livelihood, and succeeded on this. It is noteworthy that although discrimination amounting to persecution is on the whole a more recent use of the Refugee Convention, a claim like this is a classic refugee claim such as might have been envisaged by the drafters of the Convention. It is one in which the State makes normal life impossible for a political opponent.

13.3.6 Non-State actors

We have already stated that persecution requires some level of State involvement, but this does not mean that it is always the state which actually carries out or threatens the persecution. The UNHCR Handbook at para 65 says: 'where serious discriminatory or other offensive acts are committed by the local populace, they can be considered as persecution if they are knowingly tolerated by the authorities, or the authorities refuse, or prove unable, to offer effective protection.' Thus, persecution may be accepted as such when carried out by, for instance, members of a different ethnic group from the asylum claimants, if the State is not able to protect them. This was the situation in *R v SSHD ex p Jeyakumaran*, in which Tamils resident in Colombo were the victims of reprisals by local Sinhalese (majority ethnic) residents, and were not protected by the State. Although the victims were not 'singled out' for persecution by the Government, the High Court held that they were nevertheless persecuted, as the State failed to protect them.

This is by way of example only. A person may be persecuted by a member of the same group as themselves as the Sri Lankan cases of Tamils fearing Tamils clearly demonstrate.

An agent of the State remains an agent of the State for Convention purposes even though their actions do not necessarily reflect official government policy. For instance, the Turkish police who tortured Mr Doymus were not necessarily implementing a policy which the Turkish Government would acknowledge; in fact, rather the reverse, as Turkey is anxious to improve its human rights record. However, if such actions are not controlled and prevented then they amount to persecution by the State. Where there is proper redress for such incidents then there would be no fear of repetition and thus no reasonable likelihood of persecution in the future. In this sense persecution by State and non-State agents is quite similar. If the individual can be protected then ill-treatment may have occurred, but it is not persecution. If there is no effective protection then there may well be persecution whether the actions are those of State agents or not. There may be, as in the rape cases such as *Okonkwo* discussed earlier, a question of whether the persecutor is acting in an official capacity. If they are not, the question becomes one of whether the State protects against the action, although in cases of sexual assault there is an anomalous tendency to regard the absence of official relationship as fatal to the claim of persecution even before deciding the protection question.

The leading case on the question of persecution by non-State actors is the House of Lords case of *Horvath v SSHD*. The appellant was a Roma from the Slovak Republic who based his asylum claim on fear of violence by skinheads and on discrimination in employment, the right to marry, and education. The Tribunal concluded that any failure of these social rights in his case did not amount to persecution. The Court of Appeal agreed, and the appeal went to the House of Lords only on the question of the failure of state protection against the skinhead violence. Three questions were considered by the House of Lords.

First, it considered whether the concept of 'persecution' could refer simply to serious harm, or whether it necessarily incorporated a failure of State protection. The House of Lords held that it did include a failure of State protection. This differs from the UNHCR (1995), which interprets the ordinary meaning of the term 'persecution', in the light of the Convention's purposes, as 'that it embraces all persecutory acts irrespective of whether or not the complicity of the state is involved'.

Second, the refugee definition requires that a person is 'unwilling' to avail himself of State protection. This could mean that the person is unwilling to do so because of their fear of persecution despite whatever State protection is available; in other words, they have no confidence in it. Alternatively it could mean that they fear being persecuted precisely because they have gone to the police. The House of Lords held that it was the second of these.

Third, if persecution implies a lack of State protection, what is the test for determining whether there is sufficient protection against a person's persecution in the country of origin? Is it sufficient that there is in that country a system of criminal law which makes violent attacks by the persecutors punishable and a reasonable willingness to enforce that law on the part of the law enforcement agencies? Or must the protection be such that it cannot be said that the applicant has a well-founded fear? The first alternative focuses on whether the State is doing its best, the second on whether risk is actually minimized or eliminated for the applicant.

Lord Hope said that the proper approach to this task was not 'to construe its language with the same precision as one would if it had been an Act of Parliament' but rather to give the words 'a broad meaning in the light of the purposes which the Convention was designed to serve'. He identified the key relevant Convention purpose as

> to be found in the principle of surrogacy. The general purpose of the Convention is to enable the person who no longer has the benefit of protection against persecution for a Convention reason in his own country to turn for protection to the international community. (at 383)

This approach is known as the protection theory. It is to be contrasted with the attribution theory which has been followed in some other European countries according to which persecution is not recognized as such unless it can be attributed to the State. This way of setting out the issue by Lord Hope at an early stage in the judgment seems to be a classic endorsement of the protection theory. However, there is a curious contradiction. The House of Lords found that persecution included by definition a failure of State protection, that the applicant needed to be unable or unwilling to avail themselves of the protection of the State because they feared persecution for doing so and that a system with a reasonable willingness to enforce it was sufficient for protection. The net result of this is much closer than Lord Hope's statement suggests to the attribution theory. Given his identification of the surrogacy principle, it does not seem appropriate to regard the judgment as authority that the UK has abandoned the protection approach for the attribution approach. However, it must be said that the effect is not actually to focus on the failure of state protection for the asylum seeker, but rather on whether the State should be regarded as culpable, which, judging by the preamble to the Convention, is not its purpose. As Lord Hope stated in the beginning, the purpose is to protect where State protection has failed. The focus in *Horvath* has turned from the refugee to the State.

Despite the contrast Lord Hope draws with interpretation of statute, the case of *Horvath* does seem to illustrate the risk of overdefining. It is a complex decision, in which it is not easy to ascertain a majority view on any particular point. Schiemann LJ in *Noune v SSHD* The Times 20 December, 2000, CA made these points in relation to *Horvath*:

As a study of the many judgments and speeches in that case shows, the law in relation to persecution by non-state actors was unsettled and difficult to understand . . . [if it was inter-preted to mean] . . . that where the law enforcement agencies are doing their best and are not being either generally inefficient and incompetent (as that word is generally understood implying a lack of skill rather than a lack of effectiveness) this was enough to disqualify a potential victim from being a refugee [this would be] an error of law. (para 28)

Schiemann LJ goes on to say that the crucial question is whether there was a reasonable likelihood of the appellant being persecuted for a Convention reason. This case too concerned the sufficiency of State protection, but the Court of Appeal, while bound by *Horvath*, came back to that central question of the risk to the appellant. *Horvath* has been more explicitly followed in other cases, for instance *Banomova v SSHD* [2001] EWCA Civ 807 CA in which on comparable facts the Court of Appeal held that the police were willing to protect the appellant who had withdrawn her complaint after death threats and so, following *Horvath*, there was sufficient protection.

On the other hand in the case of *R (Bodzek) v Special Adjudicator* [2002] EWHC 1525 Admin an adjudicator's decision that there was no evidence that the Polish State was unwilling to protect a Jewish family who had been the target of anti Semitic attacks was held to be Wednesbury unreasonable. They had suffered from acts of personal violence, vandalism, and graffiti of their property for ten years, and had been forced to move house. They complained that the police response was inadequate as no attempt was made to identify the perpetrators. The adjudicator had accepted that the State was not unwilling as it was difficult to pursue a prosecution when the identity of the assailants was not known. The applicants' case was that it was a policing job to investigate and identify the assailants, and they had given what information they could. *Horvath* was followed by the Administrative Court, which on the evidence of years of police inaction, held it could not be rational to say that the State was not unwilling to act.

Horvath has been somewhat refined by the Court of Appeal in *Bagdanavicius v SSHD* [2003] EWCA Civ 1605 in that the Court in that case emphasized that punishment after the event was not sufficient protection. Also the Court incorporated the principle from the ECHR case of *Osman v UK* (1998) 29 EHRR 245 that where the authorities were or should have been aware of the applicant's particular protection needs but failed to do anything about it, then there was a failure of state protection. These points bring the questions back in the direction of the situation of the particular applicant, though without changing the main findings in *Horvath*. Furthermore, the House of Lords in *Bagdanavicius* gave such an unqualified endorsement of the application of the *Horvath* approach to an Article 3 case that it is clear there is no retreat from it ([2005] UKHL 38).

A number of cases before and after *Horvath* elaborate the requirement for both willingness and effectiveness. The Federal Court of Canada in *Annan v Canada (Minister for Citizenship and Immigration)* IMM 215–95 said that 'pious statements of intent' about outlawing genital mutilation had not resulted in any action to do so and so not in protection for the asylum claimant. The Court of Appeal in *R (on the application of Atkinson) v SSHD* [2004] EWCA Civ 849 held that a lack of effectiveness would entail a systematic failure applying to individuals in the same group as the applicant, here, people who were or were seen to be informers for the People's National Party. It was not just a failure in relation to some individuals.

In *P and M v SSHD* the IAT held that evidence, that the police prosecuted due to public pressure after a woman had been killed by her husband and another had been seriously burned with acid, suggested there was State protection against domestic violence. The Court of Appeal said this was to 'miss the point'. Where the police had to be compelled by such extreme circumstances to act (para 26), this did not amount to protection.

The requirement for an effective legal system has been taken as a starting point by some decision-makers: if there is an effective system then this applicant would not be at risk. This has some resonance with the s 94 provisions discussed in the last chapter by which the Secretary of State may determine that in a particular country 'there is in general no serious risk of persecution'. The Court of Appeal in *Mishto v SSHD* [2003] EWCA Civ 1978 advised against taking this approach. In this case the adjudicator had considered the protection system for women in Albania and concluded it was sufficiently effective, therefore whatever the strength or weakness of the appellant's case, there was no real risk to her so he did not need to investigate the facts in order to find against her. The Court of Appeal held that in this particular case there was no injustice done to the applicant, but as a rule this approach would be unwise. General conditions in a country must be evaluated in the light of the circumstances of the particular applicant. The Tribunal in *Hussein v SSHD* [2005 CSIH 45] had taken a similar approach. The Court of Session's decision illustrated how the general meshes with the particular and cannot be considered aside from it. The appellant stated that he had not proceeded with a complaint to the police about shooting at his house because a bribe had been required. The Tribunal found that Pakistan had a sufficiently protective legal system, but made no findings on whether the bribe had been requested by a single corrupt officer or whether the appellant could not expect protection without a bribe because of the system. In the latter case there would be no effective protection. The Court on appeal held that it was essential to go back and investigate this question.

The question of non-State actors has been one of the major questions dividing European countries in the course of the negotiations over the refugee qualification Directive. France and Germany have not in the past recognized persecution by non-State actors, which, as we have seen, was one of the reasons for challenges to France and Germany as safe third countries. Belgium and Greece have also been found to differ from the UK in this respect. This 'protection gap' has been a significant source of concern in Germany, where there have been moves for reform to recognize persecution by non-State actors. However, the Refugee Qualification Directive 2004/83 recognizes persecution by non-State actors where the state is unable or unwilling to protect (Art 6), though differences may remain over the meaning of this. Article 7 states that there will be protection when reasonable steps are taken to prevent the suffering or persecution by, *inter alia*, the operation of an effective legal system, in effect following *Horvath* and leaving open the questions considered above.

13.3.6.1 *Sources of protection*

It follows from the principle of surrogacy that protection need not be offered by the State itself, providing it is offered by a State-like entity which is capable of providing protection. *R (on the application of Vallaj) v Special Adjudicator and Canaj v Secretary of State for the Home Department* [2001] INLR 342 CA concerned the proposed return of the appellants, who were Kosovar Albanians, to Kosovo. The court held that UNMIK (the United Nations Interim Administration Mission in Kosovo) supported by KFOR (the internal security force in Kosovo) had an international law obligation to protect Kosovans, which it was in fact discharging with the host country's consent, and this was enough to satisfy the Convention requirement for protection.

There have been a number of cases considering whether the administration of the Kurdish Autonomous Area in the north of Iraq constituted a State-like entity capable of affording protection. The decision in *Maghdeed v SSHD* [2002] UKIAT 03631 was that it did not. It was accordingly not safe to return the appellant there.

The Refugee Qualification Directive 2004/83 states that protection can be provided by 'parties or organisations, including international organisations, controlling the State or a substantial part of the territory of the State' (Art 7.1b). The European Council on Refugees and Exiles (ECRE) is disturbed by this inclusion on the grounds that 'state-like authorities are not and cannot be parties to international human rights instruments and therefore cannot be held accountable for non-compliance with international refugee and human rights obligations' (ECRE information note October 2004).

In situations of civil war, there will not be a refugee claim where all sections of society are similarly in fear (*SSHD v Adan* [1999] 1 AC 293). However, this principle should not be stretched too far. It applies where law and order have broken down, there is no effective government and it is not possible to say that a clan or faction or political party control an area in which they might be able to persecute members of another clan or faction or political party. Macdonald points out that there are a number of countries which have been in a state of armed conflict for many years, but a functioning government continues to exist (2001:507). Examples are Sri Lanka, Algeria, or Angola. Refugee claims from these countries are assessed in the normal way. Claims however from Somalia, as Adan was, give rise to questions of whether there is persecution for a Convention reason. The House of Lords required, for a successful claim, that where society had broken down into continual conflict, 'the individual or group has to show a well-founded fear of persecution over and above the risk to life and liberty inherent in civil war' (349).

13.3.6.2 *Agents of the State*

There remains the question of how to assess the level of protection which should be available when the State is the persecutor. In one sense, this is a nonsense. If the State is the persecutor there is no source of protection and the question of sufficiency of protection does not arise. It was devised in *Horvath* specifically to deal with a case of non-State actors. However, the question was opened in the case of *Svazas v SSHD* [2002] 1 WLR 1891, a case of maltreatment by the police of a person in custody. Sedley LJ held to the view that there is no role for a protection test in the case of mistreatment by agents of the State, e.g., police officers. However, the rest of the court considered that there was a spectrum of state responsibility, involving questions which would involve difficult matters of proof for asylum seekers, such as the seniority of the person involved. The crucial question remained, it said, whether the individual can obtain protection.

No doubt this question will be considered further in case law.

13.4 **Internal relocation**

The concept of internal flight or internal relocation has a connection with persecution and State protection. Simply put, the internal flight or relocation doctrine, also called the internal protection alternative, is an assertion that the asylum seeker, instead of going abroad, could have found and could still find, safety in their own country. If established, then the asylum claim will be lost as there is no well-founded fear of persecution. Although consideration of internal flight will raise the question of what options were available to the asylum seeker, by the time the argument is being made in the UK it must, more importantly, address whether the asylum seeker could now safely return. The Michigan Guidelines on the Internal Protection Alternative (the product of an international consultation and colloquium in 1999) say that internal protection analysis must be 'directed to the identification of a present possibility of meaningful protection within the boundaries of the home state' (para 8).

The foundational case in relation to internal relocation is that of *Robinson* [1997] 3 WLR 1162. The appellant was a Tamil from northern Sri Lanka and had connections with the LTTE (Tamil Tigers). He claimed asylum in the UK following the assassination of the President of Sri Lanka by Tamil militants in May 1993, but his claim was refused. The Special Adjudicator held that while he could not reasonably be expected to return to an area controlled by the Tamil Tigers as he might be recruited against his will to support them, he could safely return to Colombo as it was controlled by the Sri Lankan authorities. He was in Colombo at the time of the President's assassination and had been briefly detained there. The Special Adjudicator, however, did not expressly consider whether it was reasonable to expect the appellant to relocate in Colombo on the basis that this was an unreviewable matter of the Secretary of State's discretion. He did however consider whether Mr Robinson had a well-founded fear of persecution in Colombo.

The Court of Appeal decided that appellate authorities do have jurisdiction to consider the reasonableness of the internal flight alternative. As for the question of what is reasonable, that must be decided by looking at all the circumstances. The

Court of Appeal took guidance from the Australian case of *Randhawa* 124 ALR 265, suggesting that factors to be taken into account in determining whether it was reasonable to expect the appellant to relocate would include, for instance, the accessibility of the 'safe' part of the country, any danger or hardship of travelling there, the quality of internal protection in the country, i.e. does it meet 'basic norms of civil, political and socio–economic human rights'? To this one might add that safety of re-entering the country at all is relevant for internal flight as for any return (*Degirmenci v SSHD* [2004] EWCA Civ 1553).

The question to be answered was, it suggested, that posed in the Canadian case, *Thirunavukkarasu* (1993) 109 DLR (4th) 682, namely: 'would it be unduly harsh to expect this person, who is being persecuted in one part of his country, to move to another less hostile part of the country before seeking refugee status abroad?' The Canadian court had given the following examples:

While claimants should not be expected to cross battle lines or hide out in an isolated region of their country, like a cave in the mountains, a desert or a jungle, it will not be enough for them to say that they do not like the weather in a safe area, or that they have no friends or relatives there, or that they may not be able to find suitable work there.

These are extremes to illustrate the principle, which has been expanded upon in English case law referred to by the Court of Appeal. Nolan J in *R v IAT ex p Jonah* [1985] Imm AR 7 considered that it was unreasonable to expect a senior Ghanaian trade union official to go back to what was in effect a hideaway, a very remote village accessible only by a 15-mile walk through the jungle. On the other hand, in both *R v SSHD ex p Yurekli* [1991] Imm AR 153 (CA) and *R v SSHD ex p Gunes* [1991] Imm AR 278 the courts held that it was not unreasonable to expect Turkish Kurds to relocate in a part of Turkey away from the villages where they faced persecution. In *El-Tanoukhi v SSHD* [1993] Imm AR 71 the Court of Appeal held that it was not unreasonable to expect a claimant who lived in a part of Lebanon under Israeli control to relocate in a different part of Lebanon.

The Court of Appeal in *Robinson* reiterated, putting the matter beyond doubt, that this question goes directly to whether a person may be regarded as a refugee in the terms of the Convention. If the internal flight alternative is available, then they have no well-founded fear of persecution in their home country.

Since *Robinson*, case law has explored the factors to be taken into account, but has not changed the basic question of whether it would be unduly harsh to expect the claimant to relocate. For instance, *R v IAT ex p Singh* CO/488/2000 showed a similar approach to *Thirunavukkarasu*. Here, the claimant, who was involved in the Sikh separatist movement, had been arrested four times and seriously mistreated. However, after he moved to Uttar Pradesh he was able to live safely. He had problems retaining employment there, but the Court did not place great weight on that, focusing almost entirely on the question of whether he could still be safe in Uttar Pradesh, and concluding that he could.

Clearly the question of whether internal relocation is unduly harsh must take into account persecution which may arise for a Convention reason in another part of the country simply from the claimant's living normally and exercising basic human rights. The case of *Iftikhar Ahmed* has already been discussed in the context of religious persecution. The Court of Appeal held that no internal protection alternative was viable. Mr Ahmed would continue to proclaim his Ahmadi faith wherever he went. There would therefore be a reasonable likelihood of persecution in any part of Pakistan. The Court of Appeal in *Hysi v SSHD* [2005] EWCA Civ 711 held that the tribunal had given insufficient consideration to whether it would be unduly harsh to expect a young man to return to Kosovo and hide his mixed ethnicity. The Court thought that the Australian case of *Appellant S 395 v Minister for Immigration and Multicultural Affairs* [2004] INLR 233 cited the correct principle:

It would undermine the object of the Convention if a signatory country required [refugees] to modify their beliefs or opinions or to hide their race, nationality or membership of particular social groups before those countries would give them protection.

In *HC v SSHD* [2005] EWCA Civ 893 the Court of Appeal held that the decision regarding the appellant's refugee and human rights claims had to be made again because the adjudicator, in considering that the appellant could return to a different part of Lebanon, had failed to take sufficient account of the cumulative effect of being homosexual and a Palestinian refugee. She had also not taken into account significant evidence of conditions in that country for homosexuals when holding that he would be safe in a place other than the refugee camp where he grew up.

These cases illustrate that the internal protection alternative must not be used so as to require the refugee to live in a way that replicates the persecution they flee. However, where the internal protection alternative could be seen as condoning persecution but this does not affect the refugee personally, the result may be different. This is illustrated in the case of *AE Sudan* [2005] UKAIT 00101 ILU vol. 8 no. 12. The appellant was internally displaced because of the activities of government backed militias, who were carrying out so-called ethnic cleansing, i.e. killing, raping and destroying the homes of whole populations of a particular ethnicity. The AIT held that even though to live in a part of the country where he would not be persecuted by the militia was doing what the militia wanted, as he could be safe there he would not be able to claim refugee status outside Sudan. This was so even though he could not be said to be obtaining the protection of his government, as the government allowed the militia action and it was not through their protection that he could live elsewhere, but simply because the militia did not operate there. This decision is in conflict with the UNHCR Guidelines on Internal Protection 23 July 2003:

Where internal displacement is a result of 'ethnic cleansing' policies, denying refugee status on the basis of the internal flight or relocation concept could be interpreted as condoning the resulting situation on the ground, and therefore raises additional concerns.

13.4.1 Standard and burden of proof in relation to internal flight

As the internal flight alternative would be raised by the Secretary of State, it could seem appropriate that the Secretary of State would have the burden of proving that it would *not* be unduly harsh to return the claimant. This is strongly suggested by the Michigan Guidelines (para 14). Alternatively, if the Secretary of State raises the point, does the burden then shift to the claimant to show that it would be unduly harsh, and if so, to what standard of proof? In *Ali v SSHD* [2002] UKIAT 05231 the history of this question is briefly given. Previous tribunals, for instance in *Manoharan* [1998] Imm AR 460, held that the claimant had the burden of proof on the balance of probabilities, and in *Sachithananthan* 01/TH/00596 that the claimant had to show that there was a serious possibility that relocation would be unduly harsh. The API suggests that the burden of proof is on the applicant to show that relocation would be unduly harsh (API Internal Relocation, para 1.).

The Court of Appeal in *Karanakaran v SSHD* [2003] 3 All ER 449 rejected these approaches and held that there was no standard of proof in the civil sense. Its reasoning has been discussed above in relation to the standard of proof for establishing a well-founded fear of persecution and all that was said there applies here. It held that measurements of probability were out of place in an asylum claim. The claimant did not have to prove to a certain standard that particular events were likely to occur, but the decision-maker should take into account all the evidence and decide whether it was unduly harsh for the claimant to return to a different area. The API also cites *Karanakaran*, so there is a lack of clarity in the instructions as to who must show what, although the assessment is summarised as a matter of 'common sense' (para 2).

The application of this approach in subsequent cases shows a move away from the legalism which cases about the burden and standard of proof threatened to introduce, and allows for a fuller appreciation of the factors bearing upon the claimant.

The risks of persecution in the claimant's home area must be considered first, because it is against these that the proposed location must provide protection. Symes and Jorro point out that this means a claim should not be certified as unfounded (see chapter 12) on the basis of internal protection (p. 221).

13.4.2 Assessment of internal protection

There area number of recurring questions in relation to internal protection:

- Is internal protection feasible or an unduly harsh solution when past persecution was by the State?
- What standard of living or protection of rights must there be in the alternative site of protection?
- What if risks are at an end in the claimant's home area but may persist elsewhere?

13.4.2.1 *Past persecution by the State*

Elias J, in *R v IAT ex p Sellasamy* CO/3238/99, said:

In my view the fact that on his return he is protected by a state which has, albeit through a different agency and in a different area, inflicted great pain and humiliation on him, is potentially highly material to the question of whether it would be unduly harsh to expect him to return. (para 33)

The Michigan Guidelines on the Internal Protection Alternative (para 16) say that there should be 'a strong presumption against finding an "internal protection alternative" where the agent or author of the original risk of persecution is, or is sponsored by, the national government'. UNHCR Guidelines 2003 take a similar position. However, Elias J declined to find such a presumption. He found that past persecution by the State was material to the question of whether return would be unduly harsh, but if the evidence was that there was a safe part of the country, then the asylum seeker could still be returned there.

The authority now is *Januzi, Hamid, Gaafar and Mohammed v SSHD* [2006] UKHL 5 in which Lord Bingham said 'there is no absolute rule' or presumption (para 21). He referred to the spectrum of State responsibility we noted earlier in the case of *Svazas*, and said that the relationship between the State and the act(s) of persecution must be assessed: 'The more closely the persecution in question is lined to the state, and the greater the control of the state over those acting or purporting to act on its behalf, the more likely (other things being equal) that a victim of persecution in one place will be similarly vulnerable in another place within the state' (para 21). He does not refer, though Elias J did in *Sellasamy*, to whether the severity of the persecution has any bearing on this question. Amnesty International evidence to the New Zealand Refugee Status Appeals Authority suggested it should (see Symes and Jorro p. 219).

13.4.2.2 *Risks in site of internal protection and basis of comparison*

These questions have been very important in relocation cases. A case can be made that the Refugee Convention sets the standard of protection that is appropriate for a refugee. This standard should therefore be available in the site of alternative protection. The Michigan Guidelines and a number of New Zealand authorities support this view (see Symes and Jorro p. 218). However, in *E v SSHD* [2003] EWCA Civ 1032 the Court of Appeal held that what is required in the site of relocation is protection from persecution, not delivery of other human rights. The House of Lords agreed. The Refugee Convention was not intended to define rights in the claimant's home country. It endorsed the UNHCR Guidelines in saying that relocation

requires, from a practical perspective, an assessment of whether the rights that will not be respected or protected are fundamental to the individual, such that the deprivation of those rights would be sufficiently harmful to render the area an unreasonable alternative. (para 28, in para 20 [2006] UKHL 5)

In relation to socio–economic rights, the question would be whether what is lacking is the 'the real possibility to survive economically'.

In reaching its conclusion the Court was supported by the European Refugee Qualification Directive which, as it said, imposed a 'standard significantly lower' than the Michigan Guidelines and New Zealand cases would require (para 17).

This case disposes of a question which has hovered over internal protection cases: the basis of comparison in assessing internal protection is between the proposed location and the refugee's home area, not with the country of asylum. The latter question is relevant to a human rights claim, and humanitarian leave may be granted where return to another area is considered to breach human rights.

13.4.2.3 *Safety of home area*

Finally, if persecution has ceased in the home area, that is not a basis for refugee status, even if conditions remain risky elsewhere in the country (*Canaj and Vallaj v SSHD and Special Adjudicator* [2001] INLR 342). However, risks elsewhere in the country may make the home area inaccessible and thus invoke the doctrine of non-refoulement. This issue arose in numerous cases of planned return to the Kurdish Autonomous Area of Iraq (KAA) as there were no direct flights to the KAA and an asylum seeker would need to travel through Baghdad. In *Osman Mohammed v SSHD*

[2002] UKIAT 05816 the appellant feared persecution by Iraqi security forces. His appeal was dismissed mainly because the KAA was found to be a State-like entity capable of providing protection.

This issue is also wrapped up with the viability of return to a home area. In *Maghdeed v SSHD* [2002] UKIAT 03631 the appellant came from the Northern Iraqi city of Mosul, inside the part of Iraq controlled by Saddam Hussein, though close to the border with the KAA. On the failure of his asylum claim the Secretary of State gave the undertaking which was usual in such Iraqi cases, namely not to return him to that part of Iraq controlled by Saddam Hussein, but only to the KAA when this became physically possible. The KAA was thus regarded as a safe area. However, it was successfully argued on his behalf that the KAA was not a State-like entity capable of providing protection and so it could not provide a viable internal protection alternative. The Michigan Guidelines underscore settled law in this respect; that 'the denial of refugee status is predicated not simply on the absence of a risk of persecution in some part of the state of origin, but on a finding that the asylum-seeker can access internal protection there' (para 20). In deciding that the KAA could not provide protection, the tribunal followed *obiter* comments in the Court of Appeal case of *Gardi* [2002] 1WLR 2755 CA. However, the judgment in *Gardi* was declared a nullity by a differently constituted Court of Appeal ([2002] EWCA Civ 1560) because the appeal was from a Scottish adjudicator and should have gone to the Court of Session, not the Court of Appeal. Amazingly, none of the judges or advocates in the earlier hearing had noticed this fatal flaw. There was therefore no authoritative judicial decision on the protection capacities of the KAA before the arrival of US and British forces. However, in relation to many internal relocation cases, such as *Maghdeed*, the safety of the KAA should never have been in issue. As discussed in chapter 12, in a refusal letter dated 16 January 2004 the Secretary of State disclosed that

from October 2000, there was in existence within the Home Office a general policy that internal relocation to the former KAZ [Kurdish Autonomous Zone, sometimes described as 'area'] from government controlled Iraq would not be advanced as a reason to refuse a claim for refugee status. This was based on the stance of the Kurdish authorities of not admitting to their territory those who were not previously resident in that area because of a lack of infrastructure and resources. *(Rashid v SSHD)*

13.4.3 Summary

Reading case law on internal flight can be confusing. Who is arguing or proving what? It may be seen like this:

Step 1: Asylum claim is assessed and risk is found of persecution in home area.

Step 2: Secretary of State asserts that the claimant would not face persecution in another area of their home country.

Step 3: Secretary of State, looking at all relevant factors, determines that it would not be unduly harsh for the claimant to return to a different area.

Step 4: In reply the claimant *may* argue that there is a risk of persecution elsewhere

Step 5: Whether or not there is a risk of persecution elsewhere, the claimant may argue that it would be unduly harsh to return them to that area.

Step 6: Undue harshness is assessed, bearing in mind whether the risks in the alternative site would amount to indirect refoulement.

Step 7: If they would, the claimant is a refugee

Step 8: Even if it is found that this would not be the case, it is open to the asylum country to grant the claimant humanitarian leave.

In the event of the asylum claim failing for lack of a Convention reason, the Secretary of State may argue that although the claimant faces a risk of inhuman treatment in their home area (in breach of Art 3) they would not do so in another area, and so should return there. The disputed question is whether the claimant may then argue, and whether the secretary of State has to consider, whether return to that area would be unduly harsh for reasons falling short of breaches of Article 3. If so, must these involve discrimination or other human rights breaches?

13.5 **Causal link**

Returning to the Article 1A definition, we see that a refugee is one who is 'outside his country of nationality, and owing to a well-founded fear of being persecuted *for reasons of . . .*', and then the list of Convention reasons appears.

This apparently simple connecting phrase has significance in the case law of the Convention and in the determination of who is a refugee. The persecution must be carried out for one of the Convention reasons, but as the UNHCR Handbook points out 'Often the applicant himself may not be aware of the reasons for the persecution feared. It is not, however, his duty to analyse his case to such an extent as to identify the reasons in detail' (para 66). The reasons in detail in fact may not all be important as there is no requirement that the persecution is carried out solely for Convention reasons. Reasons may in reality be very mixed and the personal motivation of the persecutor is not generally regarded as the key to this (see Goodwin-Gill 1996:50). For instance, in the case of *Sivakumar* referred to above, the House of Lords were aware that the persecutors might have the suppression of terrorism among their motives for torturing the appellant. However, the reason that he was tortured was a mixture of his ethnicity and supposed political stance. Thus it may be seen that the law of the Convention is not concerned with the personal motivations of the persecutor. These are an aspect of individual criminality but are not connected with the failure of the state to protect which is the phenomenon that Convention decision-makers are concerned to identify. The relevant reason for the persecution is the structural reason in that society, not the personal reason of the persecutor. Again we can see that the case of sexual attacks is treated quite differently as in *Okonkwo* and the cases following discussed above, the supposed personal motive of the persecutor was regarded as overriding. Musalo (2003) proposes that some of this inconsistency in relation to gender-based claims would be resolved by a more widespread adoption of what she calls a 'bifurcated approach' to causation — namely, that there will be persecution for a Convention reason if either the ill-treatment or the failure of protection is for a Convention reason.

The question of the causal link, or *nexus*, was considered at length by the House of Lords in *Shah and Islam*. It considered the Canadian approach which is to use the 'but for' test, as in UK discrimination law. This is by asking the question: 'but for their gender, would these people be persecuted?' It is tempting to say that this is sufficient, and that in *Shah and Islam* (see below) the two women would not have been persecuted but for their gender. However, this approach is not favoured as, following its use in tort law, it brings with it the question of how much of the cause the Convention reason needs to be i.e., 60 per cent, 40 per cent, etc. (see discussion in Hathaway and Foster 2003). This is a fruitless path which, it is suggested, it is better not to tread.

Lord Hoffmann suggested that drawbacks in the 'but for' test were revealed by the example of women raped in a situation of general lawlessness. The women would not be raped but for their gender but the reason for this treatment would also be the breakdown in law and order, and not their gender. This analysis is open to question in that men are subject to rape, but the power imbalance between men and women suggests that women are more likely to be raped, therefore one might argue that women would not be raped but for this imbalance which is left uncontrolled by the breakdown of law and order. They would not be raped but for their gender not because they are women but because they are women in a society where lawlessness exposes them to the underlying power imbalance. Nevertheless, one can disagree with the example and still see the point Lord Hoffmann is making, which is that causation should be sought at the structural level, in the lack of protection. He demonstrates this with the example of a Jew in Germany punished for failing to obey the racial laws, who is thereby persecuted for their race. The reason for this is that there is no State protection against such punishment and the state's lack of protection is also grounded in race. Whether the individual who initiates the prosecution hates Jews or not is irrelevant. Whether there are additional reasons, such as conducting a census, for identifying Jews is irrelevant. The reason in that society that that person is suffering that treatment is that they are a Jew.

The effects of taking a subjective approach to causation are illustrated in the case of *Omoruyi v SSHD* [2001] Imm AR 175 in which the appellant sought asylum following death threats from the Ogboni cult as he refused to comply with their demands in relation to his father's burial. The Court of Appeal found against the appellant on the grounds that the Ogboni were not motivated by the appellant's religion (Christianity) to persecute him but by his non-compliance with their requirements. Anyone else who had similarly failed to comply would be treated in the same way. Simon Brown LJ said: 'The Nigerian State Authorities in the present case were not unable or unwilling to protect the appellant because of his being a Christian but rather because he was at risk for having crossed this particular cult.' Simon Brown LJ thus looked for motivation first in the non-State persecutors and secondly in the state, and finding none, concluded that there was no causal link to the appellant's religion. Hathaway and Foster (2003) provide a different analysis of this decision. The question, they suggest, should be 'why is the applicant in the predicament he is in?' rather than 'why does the persecutor wish to harm the applicant or the state refrain from protecting him?'. The answer then would be 'because he was a Christian'. Hathaway and Foster contrast *Omoruyi* with the similar Australian case of *Okere v MIMA* 157 ALR 678 (Aust Fed C Sept 21 1998). In this case the court held that the causal nexus was satisfied. It noted that religious persecution often takes indirect forms, and if this form of causation were not accepted:

Persons who have a well-founded fear of persecution for reasons of their refusal to work on the Sabbath could be found not to have a well-founded fear of persecution for reasons of their religion; the persecution feared by them would be related to their refusal to work and not to their religion.

Lord Hoffmann in *Shah and Islam* also identified a fallacy which had confused the Court of Appeal, namely the idea that all members of a group have to be persecuted in order for the reason for persecution to be membership of that group. The reason these two women were persecuted was because they were women in society which discriminates against women. Not all women in the society need to be discriminated against for this to be the case.

The question of causal nexus was briefly considered by the House of Lords in *Sepet and Bulbul*. The result is not entirely clear. Lord Bingham reiterated the generally accepted view that the motive of the perpetrator is not the reason. The question is what is the real reason. It is not clear how the real reason is ascertained, though the question may be approached consistently with *Okere*. In *Gaoua v SSHD* [2004] EWCA Civ 1528 the Court of Appeal held that the question of what was the real reason for the risk of detention and persecution upon return could be answered in the following way. If it was because he was perceived to hold radical opinions, this would found an asylum claim. If it was 'just' to obtain information about Algerian terrorists in the UK, then 'arguably' it would not. This case should be compared with *Sivakumar* (above).

The question of causal nexus may become merged with the identification of the Convention reason for the persecution. In *K v SSHD* [2004] EWCA Civ the Court of Appeal held that the appellant was a member of a family and thus of a particular social group, but that this was not the reason for the persecution. The 'persecutor's purpose' was to add to the distress of the first person persecuted by persecuting his wife. This appears to apply a subjective test of motivation to the question of causation, and with respect, it appears that the question of causation is central to the case but without being the subject of judicial consideration. It may be that confusion is generated by the jurisprudence on families as a particular social group (see 13.5.4.5) in which the reasons for the persecution of an individual are relevant to whether their family members receive the protection of the Refugee Convention. The Court thus focused on this question.

13.6 Convention reason

Persecution only gives rise to refugee status if it is 'for reasons of race, religion, nationality, particular social group or political opinion'. The first three reasons can be briefly dealt with, the other two require closer examination.

13.6.1 Race

Convention law does not require a technical definition of race. The Handbook says that race 'is to be understood in its widest sense to include all kinds of ethnic groups that are referred to as "races" in common usage' (para 68). It is not impossible for there to be persecution of members of the same race for reasons of race. The

Federal Court of Australia in the case of *Perampalam v Minister for Immigration and Multicultural Affairs* (1999) 55 ALD 431 notes that the LTTE (Tamil Tigers) would approach Tamils for financial support. The implication is that pressure could be brought to bear.

The Handbook also emphasizes the seriousness of racial discrimination, and that where such discrimination interferes with the exercise of fundamental rights, or has serious consequences, this is likely to amount to persecution. It may be recalled that the European Commission on Human Rights found the state's action in passing racially discriminatory legislation capable in itself of amounting to a violation of Article 3 ECHR (*East African Asians v UK* (1973) 3 EHRR 76). Claims of persecution of Roma have been accepted as being for reasons of race (e.g., *Horvath, Harakal*).

It is difficult to reconcile the European Commission on Human Rights' decision and the strong statements of the Handbook with the repeated failure of Roma claims. These two sources seem to regard discrimination for reasons of race as something like an aggravating feature, affecting fundamental human dignity. In the reported Roma cases however there is little evidence that this played a part in the reasoning. The emphasis was rather on questioning or establishing the seriousness of the violations of other human rights (to physical security, housing, etc.) and it is as if, basing their claim on discrimination in relation often to social rights, the Roma have had an uphill struggle. The racial dimension, rather than being seen as an aggravating factor, seems invisible.

13.6.2 Religion

While there is scope for arguing about what is religion, in fact this has not been a major issue in asylum case law. More common issues have been what degree of self-restraint might be expected of the asylum seeker, what level of constraint is acceptable by a government, and therefore what kinds of religious activities should be absolutely free from state interference.

Although Hathaway places freedom of religion in his first category of rights, both the International Covenant on Civil and Political Rights (Art 18) and the ECHR (Art 9) allow some limitations by the state on that freedom where these are prescribed by law and 'necessary to protect public safety, order, health, or morals or the fundamental rights and freedoms of others' (ICCPR Art 18(3).

The ICCPR Article 18 also provides: 'No one shall be subject to coercion which would impair his freedom to have or to adopt a religion or belief of his choice'. The freedom therefore includes the freedom to change faith, or to hold a different faith from the official state religion, and this has arisen in numerous cases, for instance *Beshara* (19443) concerned a Christian under pressure to convert to Islam. Mr Beshara lost his claim because the tribunal were satisfied that the Egyptian Government took steps to protect its citizens from undue pressure by religious groups.

There are a number of cases regarding those of the Ahmadi faith, regarded variously as a sect of Islam or as a separate faith, since they follow a man they believe to be a later prophet. These cases cover many of the issues which arise in claims of refugee status for reasons of religion. In *Ahmad v SSHD* [1991] Imm AR 61 the Court of Appeal had held that the state of the law was not in itself persecution. Proclaiming the Ahmadi faith was illegal under the terms of a Presidential Ordinance no XX of 1984, however, Slade LJ accepted the Secretary of State's evidence that 'most

Ahmadis live ordinary lives, untroubled by government, despite the existence of the Ordinance'. Mr Ahmad failed in his claim. This had been based partly on the assertion that if he did proselytize he would be subject to persecution. However, the Court of Appeal held that there was insufficient evidence to show that he would do in future what he had not done before. This raises the question, considered but not decided in the earlier case of *Mendis v SSHD & IAT* [1989] Imm AR 6, as to whether a claimant could be expected not to speak out, which could mean not exercising a fundamental human right. The problem from the State's point of view, as Balcombe LJ pointed out in that case, is the asylum claimant could create their own asylum claim by insisting on their right to voice unwelome views if they return home.

The case of *Ahmed (Iftikhar) v Secretary of State for the Home Department* [2000] INLR 1, was somewhat different in that Mr Ahmed had suffered intense harassment personally before leaving Pakistan and regarded proselytizing as an essential element of his religion. The Court of Appeal accepted that he would not be likely to desist. It referred to *Ahmad* and to *Mendis* but distinguished this case because Mr Ahmed had already demonstrated what he would do and it was not a question of speculation, nor of the state of the law in itself being regarded as persecution. He did not fear prosecution under the Ordinance, but rather a continuation of the harassment he had already experienced. The State was unlikely to protect him from this. If the state did intervene at all it would be to prosecute him rather than protect him. The case of *Danian* should be used to decide that even if Mr Ahmed's behaviour was thought unreasonable, the real question was whether he was likely face persecution on return. It is, of course, highly relevant that in the behaviour which some may think unreasonable he was exercising a fundamental right. He was therefore accorded refugee status.

The ICCPR and ECHR refer to freedom to *manifest* one's religion or beliefs. The case of *Ahmed* shows that how the belief is manifested may to an extent be determined by the requirements of the particular belief. This will still not prevent state authorities from curbing religious expression where the permissible reasons in the ICCPR and ECHR apply.

13.6.3 Nationality

This Convention reason also is given a straightforward and inclusive interpretation, not restricted to citizenship, and so overlaps with race. The UNHCR Handbook notes that in conflict within a state where there are 'two or more national (ethnic, linguistic) groups . . . It may not always be easy to distinguish between persecution for reasons of nationality and persecution for reasons of political opinion'. As both are Convention reasons, there is no real need to do so.

Persecution on grounds of nationality could include where citizenship is denied to a minority. Though Czech and Slovak Roma have been in this position (see O'Nions 1999) once again there was little evidence of this being used to their advantage in asylum claims.

13.6.4 Particular social group

This Convention reason has given rise to more litigation than any other and it is more open to interpretation than the preceding ones. It has the capacity to some extent to enable the Convention to meet needs not originally envisaged, but is not a cure-all or catch-all category. As the Tribunal said in *Montoya* [2002] INLR 399 para 24:

> The convention is not intended to protect all suffering individuals, only those who can show that the risk of persecution in their case is for an enumerated Convention ground. If ignoring this principle the PSG grounds were read too widely, the enumeration of grounds would be superfluous; the definition of 'refugee' could have been limited to individuals who have a well-founded fear of persecution without more.

As a general starting point for determining whether a claimant comes within a social group which could be protected by the Convention, it is useful though not essential to consider the principle of *ejusdem generis*. In other words, to construe particular social group as being of the same kind as the other Convention reasons. This does not mean that social group repeats the other reasons, but that by having regard to the defining characteristics of the other reasons it may be possible to identify a social group for Convention purposes.

To use the *ejusdem generis* rule it is therefore necessary to identify the key characteristics of the other Convention reasons. The US Board of Immigration Appeals in the case of *Acosta* (1985) 19 I and N 211 did this as follows:

> Each ... describes persecution aimed at an immutable characteristic: a characteristic that either is beyond the power of the individual to change or is so fundamental to individual identity or conscience that it ought not to be required to be changed . . . The shared characteristic might be an innate one such as sex, colour, or kinship ties, or in some circumstances it might be a shared experience such as former military leadership or land ownership.

Very similar qualities were identified in *Attorney General for Canada v Ward* (1993) 2 SCR 689, an application by a member of the Irish National Liberation Army for asylum in Canada. The Supreme Court built on what was said in *Acosta*, and suggested the following 'working rules' for identifying a particular social group:

(1) groups defined by an innate or unchangeable characteristic;
(2) groups whose members voluntarily associate for reasons so fundamental to their human dignity that they should not be forced to forsake the association;
(3) groups associated by a former voluntary status, unalterable due to historical permanence.

None of this should be regarded as cast in stone, and exceptionally cases may well find social groups outside these descriptions. However, what we shall refer to as the Ward criteria have been extensively relied on by the courts.

The leading case in the UK on identifying particular social group is *Shah and Islam*, to which reference has already been made in the context of causal nexus. The case resolved a number of disputed points in relation to the identification of social group. The facts were, in the case of Mrs Shah, that her husband was violent and turned her out of their home in Pakistan. She arrived in the UK and gave birth to a child shortly afterwards. She was afraid that her husband might accuse her of adultery and denounce her under Sharia law for the offence of sexual immorality. The court accepted evidence from an Amnesty International report on the position of women in Pakistan that the legal system discriminated against women in particular in its rules of evidence. For instance for the most severe charges of sexual immorality, the evidence of women would not be heard. Arrests on such a charge could be made without preliminary investigation and could result in prolonged detention. For those convicted 'there is the spectre of 100 lashes or stoning to death in public' (549e). Mrs Shah was therefore afraid of such a result in her case.

Mrs Islam also had a violent marriage, but she had remained in it for 20 years. She was a schoolteacher. One day, a fight broke out at the school between two young supporters of rival political factions. She intervened and one faction became hostile and accused her of infidelity. These accusations were repeated to her husband who was a member of the same political faction. Mrs Islam's husband assaulted her and she was admitted to hospital twice. She left her husband and stayed briefly with her brother, but unknown men then threatened him and she could not stay.

It was clear in practical terms that these women faced persecution for reasons of their gender. However, gender is not a Convention reason. The Court of Appeal held that they were not members of a particular social group. One reason for this was a doctrine propounded that the members of the group must associate with each other, there must be some cohesiveness, interdependence or co-operation, this was what made them a *social* group. None of the possible ways of defining a group of which Mrs Shah and Mrs Islam were members produced groups with this characteristic. The House of Lords dealt with this unambiguously. Contact among group members was not required. The examples given in *Ward* of characteristics which might form a social group (e.g., language, sexuality) do not suggest such contact. The groups are social groups in the sense of being recognizable in the context of the society in which they arise (per Lords Hoffmann, Hope and Millett at 571a and 569e).

The second reason that the Court of Appeal held that the women were not part of a social group was the difficulty of defining the group without reference to the persecution. It is settled law, e.g., in *Savchenkov* [1996] Imm AR 28, that the group must exist independently of the persecution, and groups such as 'women subject to death by stoning for adultery' or 'women subject to domestic violence without redress' incorporate the persecution into the definition.

The problem was resolved by asking what was the reason for the persecution. It was because they were women, but not only this. They were still women after fleeing to the UK but did not still anticipate persecution. The reason was that they were women in a society which discriminates against women. This was not to use the persecution as a way of defining the group, but to use discrimination, and to acknowledge that women may be perceived as a group in a society which discriminates against them. This may be further explained by taking another example which was used, that of left-handed people in a society which discriminates seriously against left-handedness. It may readily be seen that in such a society left-handed people would be regarded as a group in a way that they are not in a society which does not so discriminate.

To summarize, the group is a social group in the sense of being a group in the context of a society. It is necessary first of all then to ascertain the society within which the group appears. The group may (but need not) be identified by discrimination against them in relation to a characteristic identified in the Ward criteria. There is no need for social cohesiveness in the group. The upshot in *Shah and Islam* was that the social group was found to be 'women in Pakistan', or 'women in a society that discriminates against women'.

13.6.4.1 *Other women in comparable situations*

Lord Hoffmann noted in *Shah and Islam* that it is odd that gender is not a Convention reason. Its absence lies behind the discussion earlier of the recognition of rape as persecution. However, in the absence of gender from the Convention itself, case law has developed ways of including gender-specific persecution. Indeed, the UNHCR guidelines on the meaning of 'particular social group' point out that case law in some jurisdictions has recognized 'women' as a social group. The applicant must still show a risk of persecution for reasons of her membership of that group (2002 para 10).

Shah and Islam has been applied in a number of claims by women in comparable situations in Pakistan. For instance, *Altaf* 00/TH/01370 concerned a woman from Pakistan who had given birth to children outside marriage. Given the evidence in *Shah and Islam* the tribunal clearly felt bound to find in her favour. In the case of *Liaquat* [2002] UKIAT 04408, the appellant feared violence from her husband however there was no allegation of sexual infidelity so she was not facing prosecution in a discriminatory system. The Tribunal accepted evidence that discrimination against women in Pakistan might be less than at the time of *Shah and Islam* but still took the view that it was serious enough to warrant the designation of women in that society as a social group. However, although she would suffer on her return as a woman on her own, particularly as she had mental health problems, they were not convinced that her husband would track her down, and so she could return to a different part of Pakistan. The implications are twofold. It suggests that if she were faced with the violence of her husband this would amount to persecution given the lack of protection in that system, even without facing prosecution. On her own the discrimination she would face would not amount to persecution. A woman without male protection in Pakistan was found to be a member of a social group in *Begum* (21357). However, it seemed that ethnicity played a part in that finding as she and her young niece were Mohajirs, namely descendants of Indian refugees who came to Pakistan at the time of the partition.

In relation to other countries, courts and tribunals have required substantial evidence that a parallel ought to be drawn. This succeeded in *Kaur* [2002] UKIAT 03387 in which the tribunal considered the case of a woman from rural India who had had an adulterous relationship in the UK which resulted in the birth of a child. The tribunal quoted Lord Hoffmann's guidance that the group must be identified in the context of the society from which the appellant came. They noted evidence that honour killings were still common in rural India and concluded, 'looking at the Appellant's background in rural India in the light of the social, cultural and religious mores, women in the Appellant's circumstances are identifiable as a particular social group', in part because she would not be able to expect protection from the Indian authorities. This unfortunately does not specify the characteristics of the group, which makes it a difficult case to apply in other situations.

In *R v Special Adjudicator Ex P Ivanauskiene* [2001] EWCA Civ 1271 the Court of Appeal granted leave to appeal on the basis that it was arguable that the Lithuanian State failed to protect women from violence.

The claimant in *Castro* [2002] UKIAT 00199 sought to follow *Shah and Islam* in arguing that as a woman suffering domestic violence in a country which discriminated against women she was a member of a particular social group. The Tribunal accepted all these facts, but considered that there were significant moves to improve the position of women in Ecuador and so she would be able to obtain State protection.

In *P and M v SSHD* the Secretary of State conceded shortly before the hearing that the appellants were part of a particular social group. P had been subject to serious violence by her husband including death threats and received no state protection. Her husband was a police officer who had friendships with high ranking police officers. The evidence was that violence against women was taken as normal in Kenya, and that death or life-threatening injuries would have to occur before police would take action. The particular social group was 'women, who are disadvantaged in Kenya because of their position in society' (para 21, quoting the adjudicator).

13.6.4.2 *Women in other situations*

Shah and Islam has been used with varying degrees of success in other situations by women. In *R (N) v SSHD* [2002] EWCA Civ 1082, the claimant sought to argue that as a woman who had suffered double rape by armed forces who took away her son (and had probably killed him) she was a member of a particular social group. This was because rape by soldiers was common and uncontrolled in that locality. The adjudicator had found that the rape was for sexual gratification, and once again this argument prevailed even before the Court of Appeal, who saw no merit in the argument that women in that locality were a social group. They saw the situation as one of uncontrolled lawlessness by soldiers and did not construe this in the light of discrimination. This was in part because there was not the extensive evidence of women's position that had been before the House of Lords in *Shah and Islam*, so one can speculate that in a comparable situation further evidence of discrimination could make a difference to the outcome.

Claims based on the fear of forced female genital mutilation (FGM) have often, but not always, failed because the court has considered that the group cannot be defined apart from the persecution. In *Hashim* [2002] UKIAT 02691 the tribunal declined on this basis to find that young girls in Sudan were a particular social group. For the same reason the Court of Appeal in *Fornah v SSHD* [2005] EWCA Civ 680 declined to find that young women in Sierra Leone were a social group, and neither were young women in Sierra Leone who had not undergone female genital mutilation. The Court identified a number of distinctions from *Shah and Islam*. They found, for instance, that women in Pakistan would continue to suffer the persecutory consequences; but by construing the harm in *Fornah* as limited to the act of circumcision itself, once it had happened, the Court thought that there was no continuing persecution.

Claims based on FGM may succeed where societal discrimination and lack of protection is proved. In *P and M* the Court defined the particular social group of which M was a part as women in Kenya, particularly Kikuyu women under 65. They had immutable characteristics of age and sex which existed independently of persecution and could be identified by reference to their being compelled to undergo FGM (para 41). The appellant's father had joined the Mungiki sect which enforces FGM, and his behaviour had become more aggressive following this. He and about twenty other members of the sect had performed a forced FGM on the appellant's mother, who died as a result. He then married another member of the sect who insisted that the appellant and her sister should be circumcized. Both refused. Five members of the sect were involved in raping M and violently assaulting her. Her sister was forcibly circumcized and M was told she would be next. The demonstrated level of social violence towards certain women and the lack of protection made it difficult in this case to deny that such women have immutable characteristics which make them vulnerable to ill-treatment.

The Court of Appeal in *Liu v SSHD* [2005] EWCA Civ 249 said that 'the need to establish a particular social group should not become an obstacle course in which the postulated group undergoes constant redefinition' (para 12). The Court remitted the case to the Tribunal for reconsideration with guidance as to the treatment of Chinese women giving birth or becoming pregnant in breach of China's one-child policy. Relying on cases in Canada and Australia, the court was of the view that the current direction of development was in favour of finding a particular social group in such cases. They also said that persecution may form part of the means of identifying the group (as was done in *P and M*), though not the sole means. This judgment was promulgated after the hearing in *Fornah*, though before the judgment was given in that case, and there seem to be some conflicts between the two approaches.

Lone women in threatening environments have also sought to establish membership of a particular social group. In *NS (Afghanistan CG)* [2004] UKIAT 00328 the Tribunal found that lone women in Afghanistan are at risk of abuse, without adequate judicial redress and protection, and that the appellant could establish a fear of persecution as a member of the particular social group of women in Afghanistan (see Women's Asylum News issue no. 49 February 2005). There was a striking finding in *HM (Somalia)* [2005] UKIAT 00040. The Tribunal said:

What then is the cumulative picture? Women in Somalia form a PSG not just because they are women, but because they are extensively discriminated against. Second the measures of discrimination to which women in Somalia are exposed include legislative, judicial and police or militia discrimination in the way in which women can obtain and suffer from seeking protection from the (regionalised or local) clan-based authorities. Thirdly, the serious harms they face from male sources arise in the context of very limited ability by these authorities to protect them. Finally, the measures of discrimination they face are extensive, intense and sustained. (para 35)

As a young, single woman the appellant faced real risk of persecution 'by reason of her membership of a particular social group, namely women'.

Shah and Islam has been explained at some length as it is the foundation for all that follows. It has been expanded upon and further explained in the case of *Montoya*. Before moving on to the application of these principles to other potential social groups, there is a further principle which merits discussion.

13.6.4.3 *Social perception*

The UNHCR Guidelines identify two approaches to the recognition of a particular social group. One is the 'protected characteristics' approach, which we have used and referred to as the application of the *Ward* criteria. The other is based on social perception. They recommend the adoption of a single standard that incorporates both approaches (2002 para 10). Social perception adds an important element in that there may be persecution of a particular social group that does not meet the *Ward* criteria. Common employment is sometimes suggested as an example. However, even without the connection to fundamental characteristics required by the *Ward* criteria, the identity of the group might be well-known and acknowledged in society; hence the introduction of the concept of social perception. This approach was used in the blood feud case of *Skenderaj* [2002] Imm AR 519, as follows.

A blood feud arose following the distribution of land to private owners after the fall of the Communist Government in Albania. There was a dispute between neighbours about entitlement to a particular plot, which escalated into violence which was in turn perpetuated by each family upon the other. Mr Skenderaj applied for asylum as a member of the social group of male family members of a family subject to a blood feud. The reason for turning down Mr Skenderaj's claim was the finding that his family was not a group identified by Albanian society. *Skenderaj* followed *Shah and Islam* in saying that the group must be identified in the context of the society in which it arises. However, the Court of Appeal went much further than this by saying that the group must be identified *by* that society. As Mr Skenderaj's family was, the court thought, only identified as a group by the other family in the feud, this would not make them a social group.

Unfortunately, the reasoning in *Skenderaj* does not clearly support the need for a social perception principle as it is based on what seems to be a mistaken critique of *Shah and Islam*. It is possible to see the role for social perception which the Court indicates, but the reasoning of the judgment does not support it. The attempt to present social perception as a necessary requirement is surely mistaken. A requirement for recognition by the society in which the persecution arises would present serious pitfalls. For instance, it is unthinkable that Pakistani society, whether government or otherwise, should be required to identify women in that country as discriminated against and thus a social group. Opinion on the matter would obviously be divided.

The particular social group is a legal construct in the hands of the decision-maker in the refugee claim, not a naturally arising phenomenon. Its identification is a matter for those decision-makers *in the context* of the society in which it is said to arise. Clearly, as the Court of Appeal found, in non-state actor cases it cannot be acceptable to identify a social group simply on the attribution of some members of society. It does seem right, and in accordance with *Shah and Islam*, to say that the group should be identifiable within that society, and of course that will often mean that members of that society would be able to identify the group. However, to say that they must be identified *by* that society is open to the (perhaps mis) interpretation that if the society is unaware of what it is doing to a group of people then they cannot be a social group. It introduces an unnecessary element of subjectivity and risks replicating the very discrimination from which the asylum claimant seeks redress. It is suggested here that this risk is apparent in the case of *Fornah*, where Auld LJ thought that social perception by the allegedly persecuting society was essential to finding a particular social group (para 43). Comparison of this view with that taken of M in *P and M* may reveal that the requirement for perception *by* the society is complex and value-laden — as of course is the earlier assertion here that this is a matter for the decision-maker. The Refugee Qualification Directive 2004/83 takes the following approach on this matter:

Article 10.1 Member States shall take the following elements into account when assessing the reasons for the persecution:
    . . . (d) a group shall be considered to form a particular social group where in particular:
    . . . that group has a distinct identity in the relevant country, because it is perceived as being different by the surrounding society.

Contrary to the points made above, one might say that a benefit of the social perception approach is that it does account for irrational prejudice as a basis for persecution, taking the matter out of the hands and choice of the victim as does the *Ward* approach.

Skenderaj also raises the question of whether a particular social group is necessarily discriminated against. Again, the reasoning does not really advance the question, although it is an important one. For the present it is safe to say that discrimination is fundamental to the purposes of the Convention, and will often identify a social group, but is not absolutely required.

Having considered some of the follow-on from *Shah and Islam* and the construction of social group we shall now consider some other particular social groups, and other issues in relation to defining social groups will arise in these contexts.

13.6.4.4 *Sexuality*

Shah and Islam expressly laid the foundation for resolving some of the inconsistencies that had bedevilled claims of asylum based on sexuality. Claims from homosexuals had been denied and granted on the basis of particular social group, but there had been no authoritative judgement on the matter. The issue was and is seriously in need of clarification as, according to Outrage!, fourteen gay asylum seekers committed suicide between 2001 and 2004 rather than return after the failure of their claim (uk.gay.comUK 17 December 2004). Although the comments of their Lordships in *Shah and Islam* must be regarded as obiter they said, and it is the inescapable conclusion of their reasoning in the case, that homosexuals may constitute a social group if, as a group defined by their sexuality, they suffer discrimination. Sexuality is clearly within the *Ward* criteria, either as an innate or unchangeable characteristic or else as something fundamental to human dignity which a person should not be required to forsake, depending on the view one takes of sexuality. It was mentioned in *Ward* as a possible basis for a claim based on social group.

Discrimination needs to be established in the context of the particular society in which the claim arises. In the case of *Jain v SSHD* [2000] INLR 71 the Secretary of State accepted that following *Shah and Islam* practising homosexuals in India formed a particular social group. Homosexual intercourse was a criminal offence, and although the social climate was changing, and prosecution was less likely, that atmosphere of discrimination would have other consequences such as the appellant not being able to engage in a sexual relationship with a normal degree of openness.

However, in *R v Special Adjudicator ex p T* [2001] Imm AR 187 the applicant was accepted to be a member of a social group, but there was no likelihood of persecution unless he 'flaunted' his sexuality. Homosexuality was a criminal offence in Pakistan but prosecution was not common. It was argued for T that criminalizing his private life was a breach of Article 8 ECHR. This has been held to be so in the case law of the ECHR, (e.g., *Dudgeon v UK* (1981) 4 EHRR 149 and *Modinos v Cyprus* (1993) 16 EHRR 485) but the High Court held that this did not constitute persecution. In this case it seems, although it would be rash to draw extensive conclusions from it, that membership of a particular social group defined by discrimination + arguable breach of a qualified right does not = persecution. As we discussed at the beginning of this chapter, the use of human rights to identify persecution does not mean that refugee law is interchangeable with a system of human rights protection. In *The Queen on the application of M v IAT (SSHD interested party)* [2005] EWHC 251 (Admin) the appeal was limited to the question of violation of Article 8, the asylum claim having failed. The appellant's argument was that he would have unacceptably to curb his homosexual behaviour (thus violating Art 8) if he were to return. Henriques J found that he could return to Kenya because in his particular situation the persecutory acts had only been suffered at or near his home, and he could live elsewhere without fear.

Shah and Islam has meant that homosexual claimants will be identified as members of a particular social group where there is a significant element of discrimination against them in their country of origin. However, this does not mean that claims will succeed as the question of severity of treatment still has to be established to show persecution. The cases above show rather different attitudes on the part of the court towards the importance of sexual freedom and expression. *In SSHD v Z, A v SSHD, M v SSHD* [2002] Imm AR 560 Schiemann LJ emphasized that such cases are very 'fact sensitive' and that general pronouncements about particular countries should be avoided. In *MN Kenya* [2005] UKIAT 00021 the Tribunal held that in order to make a proper determination on whether there was a real risk that the appellant would be persecuted on return, it was necessary to find out what a natural expression of his sexuality would be. Some people wish to keep their sexuality private; for others, it is a central aspect of the identity they want to be known. Once this is ascertained, it is necessary to find out how a person living in the way that would be natural to them would be treated in that country.

In *R (Dawkins) v SSHD* [2003] EWHC 373 Admin, again a human rights claim after an asylum claim had failed, Wall J held that the existence of law criminalizing homosexuality in Jamaica could not found a human rights claim where there was no likelihood of substantial discrimination or violence and abuse. See also *R (on the application of Bazdoaca) v SSHD* [2004] EWHC 2054 (Admin) for a similar assessment of Moldova. These cases suggest that a certain level of interference with the right to a private life will not be enough warrant a claim for protection in another state. Similarly in *V (Ukraine)* [2003] UKIAT 00005 the tribunal considered that in the cities of Ukraine the applicant would have no problem unless he deliberately advertised his sexuality.

There is some parallel here with claims based on religious practice, although it seems that more latitude is allowed to the state in relation to restricting sexual expression. In *T* an argument was made for the claimant similar to that in *Iftikhar Ahmed*, namely that if he would in fact express himself in a way that would draw opprobrium upon him, then there was a reasonable likelihood of persecution. It may be recalled that in Mr Ahmed's case this argument succeeded, as he could not be expected to moderate his religious expression more than he was accustomed to doing. However, the court held that T could not expect the same level of tolerance of his sexual behaviour in Pakistan as he had experienced in the UK, and could be expected to act accordingly. The Court of Appeal in *Z v SSHD* [2004] EWCA Civ 1578 accepted that the implication of *Danian v SSHD* [1999] INLR 533 and *Ahmed v SSHD* [2000] INLR 1 was that an asylum claim could be established where to live in their own country a person would be required to modify their behaviour to a level that constituted persecution. It seemed that they were willing to apply the logic of Ahmed to the situation of a homosexual compelled to hide their sexuality or relationship. However, they found this was not the case here as the court did not consider there was any evidence as to why Mr Z had kept his sexuality hidden when he lived in Zimbabwe or that he would want to live more openly in the future. The remarks about the application of *Danian* and *Ahmed* are therefore *obiter*.

The 'fact specific' nature of these cases is illustrated by the case of *Penagus* 00/TH/ 00670 which concerned a homosexual from Colombia. In that case it could be said that the violence indicated in *Dawkins* had happened, in that the appellant's part ner had been the victim of a brutal murder. While the Tribunal expressly avoided making sweeping statements about the whole of Colombia, it did accept that in the appellant's locality the malevolence against him as a homosexual was such as to amount to persecution. On the facts, it was not reasonable to expect him to live in another part of Colombia. However, in *Ramirez-Rojas* 00/TH/00714 the claim of a Colombian lesbian was refused despite evidence of 'widespread homophobia in Colombia' on the ground that there was no reasonable likelihood of persecution.

The question of risk of persecution for homosexuals in Iran has been hotly con tested in the Tribunal, cases going each way, including finding against the appli cant on the basis that discretion in behaviour could be exercised. The question has now been settled at this judicial level by *RM and BB (Iran)* [2005] UKIAT 00117 and *HS (Iran)* [2005] UKAIT 00120. The tribunal in *RM and BB* found that there was a real risk that homosexual activity, which is a crime according to the Islamic Punishment Act, would be punished by lashings and/or imprisonment. This was confirmed in *HS (Iran)* where the Tribunal made unequivocal findings that the appellant, who had already been ill-treated in prison and subjected to assaults because of his sexu ality, would face prosecution and severe penalties including imprisonment and lashings and would be likely also to experience further serious ill-treatment in custody. The Tribunal noted that recent executions of homosexual young men could not with certainty be attributed to their sexuality, but the appellant did not have to prove that he would be killed in order to succeed, as he did, in his refugee claim.

Prior to *Shah and Islam*, cases on homosexuality differed widely. Case law after *Shah and Islam* suggests that this may continue to be the case, not on the identifica tion of social group, which is greatly simplified, but on the question of the likeli hood of persecution and the threshold of treatment which will warrant such a finding.

13.6.4.5 *Families*

Cases which seek to identify a family as a particular social group raise some difficult issues in relation to the construction of social group. Clearly, the first element in the *Ward* criteria is satisfied. There is an innate characteristic which is the blood tie, or there is a characteristic so fundamental that the person should not be required to change it in marriage or a comparable relationship. There is an argument, not yet concluded, that a particular social group must have a civil or political status, and the family does have civil status in that its ties are recognized and even created by law. Article 23 International Covenant on Civil and Political Rights says: 'The fam ily is the natural and fundamental group unit of society and is entitled to protec tion by society and the State.' However, although cases on family as a social group often repeat the assertion that a family can be deemed a particular social group for Convention purposes, in fact they rarely are.

One of the crucial issues is whether the original persecution of a family member must be for another Convention reason. For instance, if, as in *Quijano v SSHD* [1997] Imm AR 227 the first person in the family was targeted because he had refused to co-operate with a drugs cartel, this was not a Convention reason. When other members of his family were then persecuted by the drugs cartel, they were persecuted for being members of a family rather than for refusing to take part in drug-dealing, but the Court of Appeal held that as the original reason was not a Convention reason, although a family could in theory be a particular social group, here they would not be so for Convention purposes. This case contradicts on the same point the earlier case of *R v IAT ex p De Melo* [1997] Imm AR 43 in which on judicial review Laws J found two sisters to be members of a particular social group as the family members of a Brazilian farmer who had refused to grow drugs. As Laws J's comments were, as he acknowledged, obiter, as on the facts he found against the appellants, and as the later decision is by the Court of Appeal, to the extent that general rules can apply the approach in *Quijano* is currently more authoritative, although difficult to reconcile with the wording of the Convention.

K v SSHD [2004] EWCA Civ followed *Quijano* with the same result. The appellant feared persecution because her husband had been detained and ill-treated. She and her family were royalists associated with the late Shah of Iran. The adjudicator had not found evidence that the husband's persecution was for a Convention reason. The Court of Appeal held that this made the case like *Quijano*, in that if the original persecution was not for a Convention reason then persecution of family members was not a basis for refugee protection. The Court accepted that the family was a particular social group, but membership of it was not the reason for the persecution. The reason for the persecution was to add to the distress of the first person persecuted. As noted above, this reasoning applies a subjective test of causation.

A significant authority in relation to families as a particular social group is *Skenderaj* which was discussed earlier in relation to the idea of social perception in identifying a social group. *Quijano* precedes and agrees with *Skenderaj* on the need for an original other Convention reason, and the requirement that the family be recognized by that society as a particular social group. In *Quijano* on that point Roche L.J. said this:

For the family to become 'a particular social group' within the meaning of the Convention, it must, in my judgment, be a family which is being persecuted or likely to be persecuted because it is that family. In that situation membership of the family will entitle a claimant for refugee status to political asylum. The use of the word 'particular' before the phrase 'social group' is of great importance, in my opinion. A good example of such a family in times past would have been the Bourbon family in France during the time of the French Revolution.

A case which succeeded on this ground was *Jaramillo-Aponte and Ayala 00/TH/00428* in which it was found that the appellants were being persecuted as members of the Escobar family. It was not possible to identify a reason for the start of the feud, which had claimed many lives, and the Tribunal said:

It may be that the very uncertainty as to the root of the persecution aids in establishing a case under the Convention, for the only established reason for persecution is the family membership. In our view, therefore, the appellants are likely to be persecuted as family members and, as such, to be persecuted for a Convention reason. (para 34)

It was not evident in that case that the Escobar family were in any way marked out in society as would be required by *Skenderaj* and *Quijano*.

It is difficult to reconcile *Jaramillo-Aponte and Ayala* with other blood feud cases. For instance in *Hurtado* [2002] UKIAT 03158 there were ninety-two members of each family who had been killed in a feud that had gone on since 1983, for obscure reasons, possibly connected with an argument over a bunch of bananas. The tribunal commented: 'The Hurtado family were simply an ordinary family which had got involved in a feud.' Then less surprisingly: 'It would be artificial to regard it as a particular social group.' Then somewhat confusingly: 'Even if the family was a group, the fear of persecution was not because of membership of the group but because of fear of reprisals.' This latter seems to say that fear of persecution is because of fear of persecution, unless it is meant to imply a degree of responsibility for the consequences of continuing the feud. In a number of cases, for instance *Correa* 00/TH/1177, approved by *Skenderaj* a 'straightforward blood feud' is said not to give rise to a particular social group. This means where no other Convention reason can be identified behind the feud.

In determining whether a family is a 'particular' one in the sense suggested by Roche LJ, it would be a mistake to require as much as did the tribunal in *Hurtado*, which opined: 'it is said that the Hurtado name itself marks someone out for adverse attention, although I cannot see how this can be the case as clearly, by Lilia's own admission, her mother has remained in Santuario and never had any problem.' *Shah and Islam* made it clear that not all members of the group need to be persecuted in order for the group to be a particular social group.

13.6.4.6 *Other status*

There is a wealth of case law relating to a wide range of possible social groups. Here we seek to give an understanding of some further categories which demonstrate general principles.

The quotation given earlier from *Acosta* is a principle accepted in the UK's interpretation of the Convention, namely that those people protected from persecution are those who cannot, if they remain in their homeland, make a choice which would prevent the treatment they fear. This issue has been discussed in relation to persecution for reasons of religion or as a member of a particular social group defined by sexual orientation. It was addressed directly in *Ouanes v SSHD* [1998] Imm AR 76, a Court of Appeal case concerning an Algerian midwife who, as she was required to do, gave contraceptive advice as part of her practice. As a result of doing so she received threats from religious fundamentalist groups opposed to this advice. The question was whether her employment was something so fundamental to her conscience that she should not be required to change it. The leading judgment was given by Pill LJ who said at 82:

A common employment does not ordinarily have that impact upon individual identities or conscience necessary to constitute employees a particular social group within the meaning of the Convention. I accept the possibility that fellow employees may constitute a particular social group if, by reason by the nature of their employment or the addition of other links to those of employment, the above principle applies. Employment as a member of a religious order could be an example.

Examples of others who have applied on the basis of particular social group are a Colombian landowner (*Montoya*), a wealthy educated Sierra Leonean mine owner

(*Diallo* 00/TH/01231), a rich Lithuanian entrepreneur (*R v Special Adjudicator ex p Roznys* [2000] Imm AR 57). The words of Burton J in the last-named case probably sum up the courts' and tribunals' approach: 'I do not consider that it is arguable that possession of money puts you into a particular social group, namely a particular social group with money as opposed to those who do not have money.' *Montoya* 'seeks to clarify post-Shah and Islam criteria for establishing whether there exists a particular social group'. In that case the adjudicator had accepted the existence of a particular social group of private landowners, but the Tribunal accepted the Secretary of State's view that Mr Montoya was targeted because he had money, and this, as expressed by Burton J, is not a social group.

13.6.4.7 *Overlap with political opinion*

Particular social groups may overlap with political opinion, for instance in a significant number of cases attempting to establish social group or imputed political opinion on the basis of either refusal to participate in criminal activity or of being a hunted witness to a criminal act. These are discussed below. Both grounds were argued in *Montoya* in which the Tribunal laid down the principle: 'it is not necessary in order to qualify as a [member of a] particular social group that a person actually has the characteristics of the group in question. It is enough that he will be perceived to be a member of the group.' This has a similarity to the approach to political opinion which we now turn our attention.

13.6.5 **Political opinion**

A political dissident was the typical figure of a refugee who was the focus of the Refugee Convention when it was first drafted and political dissent continues to play a significant part in establishing refugee claims. Political opinion as a Convention reason however goes much wider than this.

Political expression is valued as an essential requirement of democracy as without debate and freedom of political speech democracy cannot thrive. In the case law of the ECHR political speech is protected more fully than other forms of expression as the court allows a narrower margin of appreciation to states which seek to restrict it (see, e.g., *Lingens v Austria* (1986) 8 EHRR 407). In refugee claims the question arises as to whether an opinion is political. Sometimes this is obvious, such as support for a political party. Sometimes it is less obvious, for instance a woman in Iran who refused to conform to a strict dress code and wore make-up was regarded by the tribunal in *Fathi and Ahmady* (14264) as expressing a political opinion.

Guidance was given in the Tribunal case of *Gomez* 00/TH/02257 on the characteristics of a political opinion: 'To qualify as political the opinion in question must relate to the major power transactions taking place in that particular society.' This makes it clear that not only party politics is intended, so for instance attending an anti-globalization protest would be an expression of political opinion. Current Asylum Policy Instructions say that 'if a woman resists gender oppression, her resistance is political' (API Assessing the claim part II para 9.5).

A political opinion may be expressed or it may be imputed by the persecutor. Hence it is not the holding of the opinion which is the important point to establish, but how the claimant is perceived by the persecutor. This is not to reverse all that was said earlier about the motivation of the persecutor. A detailed enquiry into their motives is not required. What is required is to ascertain what is the reason for the persecution.

A number of relevant principles are cited in the case of *Noune v SSHD* [2000] All ER (D) 2163 CA. The appellant was an Algerian worker with a responsible position in the national Post Office. She was approached on numerous occasions by masked men asking her to send messages to Japan and the Soviet Union, offering her 'protection' in return. She was threatened with violence or other serious consequences if she did not comply and the suggestion made to her was that it was her duty to help. Those who approached her wore religious dress, whereas her appearance and demeanour were of a Westernized woman. There was plentiful evidence of killings by religious extremists in Algeria, and there was evidence of 'Westernized' women being targeted, but no evidence that she had been threatened for this reason, rather for her non-co-operation.

The Court of Appeal held *inter alia* that:

1. The motives of the persecutor may be mixed, and they can include non-Convention reasons: it is not necessary to show that they are purely political.
2. Political opinion may be express or imputed.
3. It follows that in order to show persecution on account of political opinion it is not necessary to show political action or activity by the victim: in some circumstances mere inactivity and unwillingness to co-operate can be taken as an expression of political opinion. (UNCHR Handbook para 80)
4. If it is shown that there is a reasonable likelihood that the persecutor will attribute a political opinion to the victim and persecute him because of it, the fact, if it be a fact, that the persecutor would be in error in making that attribution does not disqualify the victim from refugee status. (para 8)

The Court of Appeal held that the facts were capable of giving rise to a claim on the basis of political opinion and remitted the case to a tribunal for decision.

As referred to above, cases concerning witnesses of crimes and people refusing to co-operate with criminal activity have been argued under both social group and political opinion. For such claims to be seen as relating to the 'major power transactions in a society' the criminal activity in question must have a relationship to those power transactions. Like social group, political opinion must be construed in the context of the society in which it arises. In the UK for example, it would not constitute political opinion to refuse the request of a common criminal to kill for him. However, to refuse to do the same at the request of say, Special Branch, could be a political action and might suggest a political opinion. Goodwin-Gill suggests a wider definition of political opinion as one 'on any matter in which the machinery of the state, government and policy may be engaged' (1996:49).

In *Acero-Garces* (21514) the appellant had witnessed the murder of a policeman and since then had been subject to serious threats and harassment. This had to be seen against the background in Colombia of the drugs cartels, in the words of the Tribunal 'a power unto themselves. The links between the narcotic industry, crime and the government is very thoroughly documented'. The Tribunal found that she risked persecution for reasons of political opinion, 'that the appellant is seen to be on the side of law, order and justice and against disorder, chaos and injustice; and it is these dark forces that control government.'

There was a different result in *Storozhenko v SSHD* [2002] Imm AR 329, CA. Here the appellant had witnessed drunken police officers driving a speeding car which knocked down and injured a young girl. When he remonstrated with them one of them hit in the face with a baton, breaking his jaw. He made a formal complaint at the police station but there was no action taken, and after this he began to receive serious threats and was attacked. The US State department report was critical of police corruption in Ukraine. The Court of Appeal accepted that he was being persecuted for attempting to bring a police officer to justice, but said it was 'manifestly artificial to talk in terms of imputed political opinion' (para 44).

The case of *Gomez v SSHD* is a starred appeal which sets out a number of points intended to clarify issues in these cases where some attitude may be imputed to the victim by a non-state perpetrator but it is arguable as to whether this is a political opinion. *Gomez* was heard before *Storozhenko* but would support the conclusion in that case.

The Tribunal confirmed established case law that the fundamental rights of the victim must be protected. So a person should not be in fear because they have exercised the rights to freedom of thought, conscience, opinion, expression, association, and assembly. To qualify as political an opinion must relate to the major power transactions taking place in that particular society. Where a non-State actor is not itself a political entity the Tribunal thought it would be difficult to regard an opinion imputed by them as political. This must be open to question as a group of thugs might target a person whose views they dislike, even though they themselves had no political affiliation or purpose. Conversely, where persecutors had political views about those they targeted, it might not always be the political opinion that motivated their actions. A generalized political motive did not lead to the conclusion that the persecutor perceived what the claimant has said or done as political. So, a group of party political thugs might attack an individual because of their vulnerability.

In *Gomez* itself, features of the Colombian context made it more possible than otherwise that criminal elements or guerrilla organizations would view the words or actions of those they persecuted as representing a political opinion. This was certainly true of FARC, the guerrilla organization being considered in this case.

Gomez disapproved of the attempt in *Acero-Garces* to create a fixed category of persons on the side of law order and justice. The Tribunal said 'reference, Star Wars-style, to "dark forces" does not serve the interests of objective decision-making'. This should not have been regarded as a political position.

Where social group has been used in these kinds of situations it has tended not to be a successful argument, as for instance in *Savchenkov* [1996] Imm AR 28 CA the appellant argued unsuccessfully that he was a member of the group of individuals whom 'the mafia seeks to recruit and who refuse'.

In *Gaviria* [2002] Imm AR 163 it was held that there could be a claim based on imputed political opinion where the appellant witnessed the murder of a member of the Hurtado family and later agreed to have their 15-year-old daughter to stay with her. She was raped by one of the men she saw involved in the murder and received threatening phone calls. It was accepted that the liberal political opinions of the Hurtado family would be imputed to her by the Correas family, a conservative family, well connected with the police, who had vowed to wipe them out. These are the same two families each of whom made claims that were discussed in the previous section on social group. The Correas claim was dismissed on the grounds that it was just a 'straightforward blood feud', the Hurtado claim was dismissed on a similar basis and that there was not persecution because some of the family were not persecuted. The ground of political opinion seems to have been available in *Gaviria* because the political affiliations of the families were brought into the argument before the court.

13.6.5.1 *Conscientious objection*

Conscientious objection as a form of political opinion has generated a volume of case law from which certain principles may be distilled. Guidance is found in paras 167–174 of the UNHCR Handbook, though in places this is tentative and does not conclude that there will be a right to refugee status in all the circumstances raised.

There is a tension between the right of the state to demand military service from its citizens, and the right of the individual not to be forced to do something which goes against their conscience. All states have the right to demand military service from their nationals; some have a system of compulsory military service for all, some employ conscription only in times of war. In each case it is usually a criminal offence either to refuse to join up or to desert the armed forces. An exemption from prosecution and an alternative to military service is given in some countries to those who can establish a genuine conscientious objection to military action. However, by no means all states provide this, although the trend is moving towards doing so (see, for instance, Schnöring 2001). In a 1998 survey by War Resisters International, referred to in the UK's leading case on conscientious objection, *Sepet and Bulbul*, the following figures were given. 'Of 180 states surveyed, some form of conscription was found to exist in 95. In 52 of those 95 states the right of conscientious objection was found not to be recognized at all. In a further 7 of those 95 states there was no known provision governing a right of conscientious objection. In the remaining 36 states the right of conscientious objection appeared to be recognized to some extent' (para 18).

Prosecution for avoidance of military service is not regarded as persecution unless the punishment is disproportionate or is inflicted or impacts in a discriminatory way. For instance, some countries, including the USA, still maintain the possibility of the death penalty for refusal to serve.

Refusal to undertake military action which is against international law can found refugee status. Lord Bingham in *Sepet and Bulbul* states established law in this way:

There is compelling support for the view that refugee status should be accorded to one who has refused to undertake compulsory military service on the grounds that such service would or might require him to commit atrocities or gross human rights abuses or participate in a conflict condemned by the international community, or where refusal to serve would earn grossly excessive or disproportionate punishment. (para 8)

This is partly endorsed in the Refugee Qualification Directive 2004/83 where persecution includes prosecution or punishment for refusing to perform military service which would entail committing war crimes, crimes against peace, crimes against humanity or against the purposes and principles of the UN or serious non-political crimes. Earlier drafts of the Directive allowed for broader grounds of conscience to found a refugee claim, but these were lost in the negotation process.

The cases of *Radivojevic and Lazarevic* [1997] 2 All ER 723 were heard with *Adan and Nooh*, and concerned objection to military service. Here the appellants objected to service in the former Yugoslavia in an action that was internationally condemned. However, it was held in the Court of Appeal (and this point not pursued to the House of Lords) that even in such a conflict the individuals themselves must object to the condemned action on principle, not just be 'opportunistic draft evaders' in order to obtain asylum. So at one end of the spectrum, refusing military service in violation of international law may found refugee status, and at the other, refusing military service because of a wish not to fight will not. In between are the contested areas.

In the case of *Sepet and Bulbul* the two appellants were Turkish Kurds who objected to military service for the Turkish Government. They did so because they opposed the Turkish Government's policy towards the Kurds, and feared that they might be sent to a Kurdish area and required to commit atrocities against their own people. Turkey provided no alternative to military service. Draft evaders were liable to a prison sentence of between six months and three years, which was not thought disproportionate.

Their claim was framed as conscientious objection, but it was clear that they did not have a conscientious objection to military service as such, but only in the present circumstances. Nevertheless, their objection was evidently a political opinion and could not unreasonably be regarded as a reason of conscience. The Convention reason was therefore established, but the question was whether imprisonment because of this political opinion could amount to persecution, when imprisonment for refusal not based on such an opinion would not.

The decision of the House of Lords illustrates one of the limitations of framing asylum law in human rights terms. Their Lordships considered the submission for the appellants that there was a recognized human right of conscientious objection, for instance implied in the Universal Declaration of Human Rights Article 18, which provides for a right to manifest belief. If there was such a right, then it could be argued that a discriminatory denial of the right could amount to persecution. However, their Lordships concluded that the weight of the evidence was that to date there is no such human right although there are developments in that direction.

The House of Lords and Court of Appeal each made the distinction between 'absolute' and 'partial' conscientious objectors. Absolute objectors would object to all military action for reasons of conscience. This would include people who were pacifists without a religious belief, and people whose pacifism arose from a belief system which normally entailed it, such as Quakers or Buddhists. There was authority to suggest that in the case of absolute objectors at least that prosecution could amount to persecution. This was accepted without question by the special adjudicator in the case of *Zaitz v SSHD* [2000] INLR 346. In the Court of Appeal, Buxton LJ distinguishes between conscientious objectors and others who desert or evade the draft. Only in the second case does he find the proportionality of the punishment to be relevant. In the case of conscientious objection, the implication is that any punishment at all could amount to persecution.

In its Resolution on the Annual Report on International Human Rights and European Union Human Rights Policy, released on 16 March 2000, the European Parliament called on 'the Council of Ministers and on European Union Member States to grant asylum rights or refugee status to conscientious objectors and deserters from countries where the right to conscientious objection is not recognized . . .' (resolution A5–006/2000 para 68). Schnöring says that 'few governments have responded positively to this call' (2001:157), and as we have seen, the Refugee Qualification Directive does not go this far.

The House of Lords judgment in *Sepet and Bulbul* was not different in that respect. In the light of their finding that there was no human right of conscientious objection their Lordships considered that punishment for refusal of military service would *not* amount to persecution per se, reversing *Zaitz* to the extent that that case could be regarded as deciding otherwise.

Partial objection referred to people such as the appellants in these cases whose objection was a political one based on the practices and policy of the Turkish military, not on military action as such. In this case, the greater includes the less, because if there is no right of conscientious objection then even less will punishment of 'partial objectors' amount to persecution.

Not only *Zaitz* but a long line of tribunal cases had gone in opposite directions on the question of whether absolute conscientious objection can found a claim to refugee status. It is important, given that this is the first House of Lords authority on the issue, to note in what respects the case is binding. The appellants were partial objectors. The case must therefore be taken to decide that partial objection per se will not found a claim to refugee status. Comments that absolute objection does not give rise to a refugee claim must be regarded as obiter. While such a claim will be difficult to establish as it cannot be asserted that conscientious objection per se is a human right, there may be cases where for instance the right to freedom of religion is violated with sufficient severity to amount to persecution. Laws LJ dissented in the Court of Appeal on this issue.

The starred Tribunal case of *Foughali* 00/TH/01513 thoroughly explores the situations in which military service may give rise to a Convention claim. Although it though it must now be read in the light of *Sepet and Bulbul*, some issues are untouched, such as the finding that refusal to perform military service due to the repugnant nature of that service could found refugee status. This followed para 171 of the UNHCR handbook which suggests that where military action has drawn the condemnation of the international community, punishment for refusal may amount to persecution. In *Krotov v SSHD* [2004] EWCA Civ 69 the Court of Appeal considered a Russian soldier's refusal to participate in the Chechen war. The Secretary of State argued that the British asylum decision-making and appeal process could not be drawn into the kind of international judgments that would be required in order to grant refugee status on this basis. The Court of Appeal disagreed. They held that there were plenty of norms of international law to which reference could be made, and refugee status could be founded on objection to military service where that service would involve participation in acts which were contrary to basic rules of conduct as defined by international law. It was not necessary to wait for formal condemnation of the conflict by the international community. The claim could succeed if combatants could be punished for refusing to act in breach of basic rules of human conduct or if the genuine fear of such punishment was a reason for refusing to serve.

Not all cases of Turkish Kurds refusing military service will necessarily fail, even following *Sepet and Bulbul*. The case of *Aydogdu* [2002] UKIAT 06709 succeeded because the appellant left Turkey at a time when the military action he would have been called upon to undertake would have been condemned by the international community. This was in 1997–98 when, in the Tribunal's words, 'The policy of the Turkish army, albeit against a determined and vicious enemy, did result in international condemnation as it involved a programme of compulsory village clearances and the large scale displacement of the Kurdish civilian population' (para 18).

It is of course the case, as the Court of Appeal recognized in *Krotov*, that the question of international opinion on a war is a highly political matter. A number of American conscientious objectors to the war in Iraq have sought refugee status in Canada, the first one of which has been refused. Other soldiers who objected to the war but did not flee have been sentenced in the USA to imprisonment or hard labour (Amnesty International press release 13 May 2005).

A soldier cannot claim refugee status on account of risks from terrorists (*Fadli v SSHD* [2001] Imm AR 392). Being a soldier entails taking the risk of losing one's life in the service of one's country, and this is no different if the enemy is an internal one (here, the GIA, a fundamentalist group in Algeria). However, conditions of military service may be such as to amount to persecution if they are inhuman, as was acknowledged in *Foughali*.

13.7 **Conclusion**

This chapter has given an introduction to refugee law in the UK, but no more. This field is now so vast that a glance at some key issues and an examination of some of the key cases is all that is really possible in a small part of a larger book. The next chapter examines some of the legal restrictions upon refugee claims.

QUESTIONS

1   What are the benefits and the problems of operating with an international definition of who is a refugee?

2   Should gender be a Convention reason?

3   Is discrimination in relation to social rights a suitable basis for an asylum claim?

FURTHER READING

Berkowitz, N. and Jarvis, C. (2000) *Asylum Gender Guidelines* (London: Immigration Appellate Authority).

Crawley, H. (2001) *Refugees and Gender* (Bristol: Jordan & Sons).

Endicott, T. (2001) 'International Meaning: Comity in Fundamental Rights Adjudication' *International Journal of Refugee Law*, vol. 13, no. 3, 293–309.

Goodwin-Gill, G. (1996) *The Refugee in International Law* (Oxford: Clarendon Press).

Goulbourne, S. (2000) 'Refugees, state sovereignty, and the Geneva Convention' INLP vol. 14, no. 4, pp. 213–222.

Harvey, C. (2000) *Seeking Asylum in the UK: Problems and Prospects* (London: Butterworths).

Hathaway, J. (1991) *The Law of Refugee Status* (Ontario: Butterworths Canada Ltd).

—— (2002) 'The Causal Nexus in International Refugee Law' *Michigan Journal of International Law*, 2002 Winter vol. 23, pp. 207–221.

—— and Foster, M. (2003) 'Membership of a Particular Social Group' *International Journal of Refugee Law* [2003] IJRL 15(3), 477–491.

—— (2003) 'The Causal Connection (Nexus) to a Convention Ground' *International Journal of Refugee Law* [2003] IJRL 15(3), 461–476.

—— and Hicks, W.S. (2005) 'Is there a subjective element in the refugee convention's requirement of 'well-founded fear?' *Michigan Journal of International Law* Winter vol. 26, pp. 505–525.

Kelly, N. (2001) 'The Convention Refugee Definition and Gender-Based Persecution: A Decade's Progress' *International Journal of Refugee Law* vol. 13, no. 4, 559–568.

Kelly, N. (2002) 'Internal Flight/Relocation/Protection Alternative: Is it reasonable?' *International Journal of Refugee Law* vol. 14, no. 1, pp. 4–44.

Lambert, H. (2001) 'The Conceptualisation of "Persecution" by the House of Lords: *Horvath v SSHD*' *International Journal of Refugee Law* vol. 13, no. 1/2, pp. 16–31.

Majid, H. (2005) 'Appeals based on female genital mutilation: An examination of recent trends in decision-making by the Immigration Appeal Tribunal' *IANL* vol. 19, no. 1, pp. 7–19.

Millbank, J. (2004) 'The Role of Rights in Asylum Claims based on Sexual Orientation' *HRLR* vol.4, no. 2, pp. 193–228.

Moore, J. (2001) 'Whither the Accountability Theory: Second-class status for Third-Party Refugees as a Threat to International Refugee Protection' *International Journal of Refugee Law* vol. 13, nos 1/2, pp. 32–50.

Musalo, K. (2003) 'Revisiting social group and nexus in gender asylum claims: a unifying rationale for evolving jurisprudence', Spring, 52 *DePaul L. Rev.*, p. 777.

—— (2006) 'Claims for Protection Based on Religion or Belief'. International Journal of Refugee Law (2004), vol. 16, no. 2, pp. 165–226.

Nicholson, F. and Twomey, P. (1998) *Current Issues of UK Asylum Law and Policy* (Aldershot: Ashgate).

O'Nions, H. (1999) 'Bona fide or Bogus? Roma Asylum Seekers from the Czech Republic' *Web Journal of Current Legal Issues* 3.

Pearce, H. (2002) 'An Examination of the International Understanding of Political Rape and the Significance of Labelling it Torture' *International Journal of Refugee Law* vol. 14, no. 4, pp. 534–560.

Schnöring, K. (2001) 'Deserters in the Federal Republic of Yugoslavia' *International Journal of Refugee Law* [2001] IJRL 13, 153–173.

Shah, P. (2000) *Refugees, Race and the Legal Concept of Asylum in Britain* (London: Cavendish).

Stevens, D. (2004). *UK Asylum Law and Policy* (London: Sweet & Maxwell), Chapters 1 and 2.

Symes, M. and Jorro P. (2003) *Asylum Law and Practice* (London: Lexis Nexis Butterworths).

UNHCR (2002) UNHCR Guidelines on International Protection, 7 May 2002, Membership of Particular Social Group and Gender-related Persecution.

—— (2003) Guidelines on Internal Protection

—— Handbook on Procedures and Criteria for Determining Refugee Status.

Wilsher, D. (2003) 'Non-State Actors and the Definition of a Refugee in the UK: Protection, Accountability or Culpability?' *International Journal of Refugee Law* (2003) vol.15, no. 1, pp. 68–112.

Yeo, C. (2002) 'Agents of the State: When is an Official of the State an Agent of the State?' *International Journal of Refugee Law* (2002) vol. 14, no. 4, pp. 509–533.

14

Criminalization and excluding an asylum claim

SUMMARY

This chapter is concerned with the process of increasing criminalization of migration and of making an asylum claim, and with the provisions whereby an individual can be excluded from refugee status because of their conduct. It shows how these powers have increased rapidly in recent years in the light of the objectives of deterring asylum claimants and combating terrorism.

14.1 Criminalizing asylum claims

There is a right in international law to seek asylum (UDHR 1948 Art 14, echoed in the European Charter of Human Rights) but, as we have seen, it is difficult to exercise within the law. In *R v Naillie* [1993] AC 674 HL the House of Lords held that arriving in the UK and requesting asylum without attempting to deceive did not make the defendants illegal entrants. However, in *Saadi v SSHD* [2002] UKHL 42 the House of Lords held that detention of asylum claimants was lawful 'to prevent unauthorized entry' (HRA Art 5(1)(f)). It did not go so far as to say that unlawfulness was contemplated. Indeed there was clear evidence that it was not. As Collins J said at first instance, the claimants were doing all they could to enter lawfully. The asylum seekers were detained pending determination of their claim, simply in order to facilitate immigration control (see chapter 15 for full discussion of the law on detention).

Scheimann J in 1989 described the difficulties faced by asylum claimants in the face of visa regimes, carrier sanctions and now we would add border control measures such as the placement of airline liaison officers. As a consequence, he said, an asylum seeker has the option of:

1. lying to the UK authorities in his country in order to obtain a tourist visa or some other sort of visa;
2. obtaining a credible forgery of a visa;
3. obtaining an airline ticket to a third country with a stopover in the UK.
   (*Yassine v SSHD* [1990] Imm AR 354 at 359)

We might add a fourth option: clandestine entry.

We shall shortly examine some of the specific criminal measures which are in place, and shall see that these sanctions, the lack of lawful option as described in *Yassine*, and the acceptance that asylum seekers may be treated in a punitive manner even without any wrongdoing (*Saadi*), combine to create a murky zone between legality and illegality within which asylum claims are made. Among the results of this are that an asylum seeker may be convicted and punished for acting in a way they could not avoid, and that others who might help them gain entry are deterred from doing so through fear of the law. Equally troubling, the boundary between asylum seeker and criminal is blurred in the minds of officials who deal with them and of the public.

Though these risks have become heightened, they have always been present for refugees because of the secrecy in which some have been forced to leave their countries, and the difficulty of obtaining documents. The Refugee Convention therefore made provision for this.

14.2 **Article 31**

Article 31 of the Refugee Convention says that refugees coming directly from the country of persecution should not be punished on account of their illegal entry or presence, provided they present themselves without delay and show good cause for this. In the case of *R v Uxbridge Magistrates Court ex p Adimi, R v Crown Prosecution Service ex p Sorani, R v SSHD ex p Kaziu* [2000] 3 WLR 434 three people who travelled on false documents were prosecuted. The purpose of Article 31 was to provide immunity for genuine refugees whose quest for asylum reasonably involved a breach of the law. The court recognized that this could be a matter of necessity for a genuine refugee, and therefore the Secretary of State rather than the Crown Prosecution Service should decide when asylum seekers should be prosecuted for travelling on false documents. It was a matter relating to conduct of immigration and asylum, not to the need to punish criminal activity generally. They could use Article 31 to stay the criminal proceedings.

This means that where there are grounds to believe that Article 31 will apply, a prosecution should not be brought. A joint Memorandum of Good Practice for liaison between the police, IND, CPS and the Law Society concerning the prosecution of refugee claimants for offences concerning the use of false documents advises that if an immigration officer thinks that Article 31 might apply, a suspect should be granted police bail pending resolution of the asylum claim (Macdonald 2001:681).

Following the judgment in *Adimi*, a statutory defence to forgery, deception and falsification of documents was enacted in Immigration and Asylum Act 1999 s 31. It inserts the key provisions of Article 31 into the statute, with the effect that its provisions may now be relied upon as a defence. However, s 31 is more restricted than Article 31 and the *Adimi* judgment. For instance, the defence is available only to someone whose refugee claim succeeds, whereas *Adimi* applied Article 31 to asylum seekers. This is crucial to the effectiveness of Article 31 as otherwise any asylum seeker could be penalized before their claim is determined. It also has the effect that there is no defence for someone whose claim is made on what they themselves consider to be proper grounds, but who does not succeed in law. This elides the genuine but unsuccessful claimant with the dishonest one, and confuses deception in the means of obtaining entry with deception as to the substance of the claim. The Court of Appeal in *R v Kishientine* [2004] EWCA Crim 3352 made it clear that the criminal court could have no part in assessing the merits of the asylum claim so as to deal with any of these objections.

Article 31 refers to people 'coming directly' from the country of persecution, but the court in *Adimi* did not take this too literally. They held that there could be some element of choice by refugees as to their destination, and a short-term stopover on the journey could not be used to say that the refugee had not come to the UK directly. Section 31 limits the defence to situations where the defendant can show that in any third country at which they have stopped on the way to the UK they could not reasonably have expected to obtain refugee protection.

Section 31 as interpreted by the API takes a more restrictive approach than *Adimi* to the question of whether someone has presented themselves as soon as possible. UNHCR says that 'delay caused by an asylum seeker's wish to approach a lawyer or a voluntary organization first to seek advice is not unreasonable and should not preclude the protection of s 31.' They were concerned that account was taken of proper reasons for delay, such as the effects of trauma, language differences, lack of information, previous experiences which have resulted in a suspicion of authority, and a feeling of insecurity. UNHCR issued detailed advice on the API, but this has not been implemented, and the Home Office relies on the primacy of s 31 as statute over and above the provisions of the Refugee Convention. This view was confirmed in *R (on the application of Pepushi) v Crown Prosecution Service* [2004] EWHC 798 (Admin) where the court held that there is no scope to claim the protection of Article 31 Refugee Convention, even though the protection offered by Immigration and Asylum Act 1999 s 31 is explicitly narrower. Mr Pepushi had stopped in France and Italy long enough to claim asylum. Section 31 gave no scope to extend the defence. The court had an obligation to read the words of the statute which was intended to give effect to the Convention compatibly with the Convention; where this was not possible, parliamentary sovereignty entailed that the statute prevailed. Unlike the Human Rights Act, there is no provision for a declaration of incompatibility.

The joint memorandum of good practice was never published (Macdonald 2005:979). It advises close cooperation between police, prosecutors and the immigration service, reliance on both Article 31 and s 31, and that prosecution should proceed only in the clearest of cases. The use of the Article as well as the section means that prosecutions should not necessarily proceed even where the strict terms of s 31 are not met. It is a question of whether prosecution is in the public interest. The Joint Parliamentary Committee on Human Rights was concerned that 'a significant number of people have been wrongfully imprisoned' for offences to which s 31 should have provided a defence. Estimated figures ranged between 1,000 and 5,000 (Fifth Report of session 2003–04, HL paper 35 HC 304, para 10). People who were wrongly convicted and imprisoned have received average compensation of £40,000 (Macdonald 2005:979).

14.3 **Offences**

Using deception may result in a number of criminal charges. The use of deception to seek or obtain leave to enter or remain in the UK or to seek the avoidance of enforcement or removal action is an offence contrary to Immigration Act 1971 s 24A (as inserted and amended by the 1996 and 1999 Acts). The use of false or altered documents is an offence contrary to s 26(1)(d), and the Forgery and Counterfeiting Act 1981 is also quite often used in cases of alleged false documents. The two Immigration Act offences carry a maximum sentence of six months imprisonment, but for an offence under Forgery and Counterfeiting Act s 3 in *R v Kolawole* [2004] EWCA Crim 3047 the court gave guidance that 'The appropriate sentence for using or holding with the intention of use one false passport, even on a guilty plea by a person of good character, should usually be within the range of 12 to 18 months' imprisonment'. This was because of the increase of public concern on these matters.

14.3.1 s 2 Asylum and Immigration (Treatment of Claimants etc) Act 2004

A practice which has troubled the Home Office has been that of asylum seekers who destroy their documents while on their journey to the UK. This may be on the advice of agents who have organized their travel. While in broad terms the possible motivations for this can be guessed at, this does not give any indication in an individual case of why a person was so determined to conceal their identity, prevent the possibility of return, or otherwise conceal their means of travel, as the case may be. The desire to start a new life anonymously, or conceal a deception, or fear of persecution are clearly all possible motives.

In order to prevent this practice, the Asylum and Immigration (Treatment of Claimants etc) Act 2004 introduced a new offence of attending an asylum interview without a passport or similar document (s 2), unless it is produced within a three day grace period after the interview (s 2(3)(b)). Statutory defences include:

- To produce a false immigration document and to prove that this was used for all purposes in connection with the journey to the UK.
- To prove that he travelled to the UK without, at any stage since he set out on the journey, having possession of an immigration document.
- Reasonable excuse, which does not include destruction of the document unless that was for a reasonable cause or beyond the claimant's control.
- Reasonable cause in this context does not include delaying an asylum decision, increasing one's chances of success, or complying with the instructions of a facilitator (smuggler) unless it would be unreasonable to expect non-compliance in the circumstances (s 2(7)(b)(iii)). It is hard to imagine when it would be more reasonable to rely on a speculation about the needs of a system the asylum seeker has not yet personally encountered than on the advice of the person who has got them this far. The instructions to immigration officers implementing the section suggest that it would be unreasonable to expect non-compliance with advice where the asylum seeker has been threatened or intimidated so that this amounted to force.

In *R v Bei Bei Wang* [2005] EWCA Crim 293 the defendant had travelled for six months through several countries with an agent who had retained her passport at all points except for the moment of going through passport control. The Court of Appeal commented that her situation was not very different from that of someone who had not had possession of a travel document at all, or someone who travelled on forged documents. In the latter case, there would be a defence under Immigration and Asylum Act 1999 ss 2, and 31 would provide a defence to a different criminal charge in the event of a successful asylum claim. A lighter sentence was therefore appropriate. The sentence was also reduced in *Lu Zhu Ai* [2005] EWCA Crim 936 in which the court reiterated the very specific purpose of this offence, the distinction between s 2 and offences of fraud etc, and, as in *Bei Bei Wang*, the significant deterrent element in the sentencing. The court also noted that it was difficult in these cases to take full account of individual circumstances. The components of the alleged offence could be considered, i.e. the journey and to what extent the defendant had control of their travel document, but the merits of their asylum claim could not be considered at all by the criminal court.

This separation of the criminal issues from an assessment of the circumstances in the defendant's home country occurs also when criminal courts recommend deportation as part of a sentence (see chapter 16). There are advantages and disadvantages to this separation. On the one hand, it may be more appropriate for the criminal courts not to investigate and assess questions which require evidence about matters unconnected with the criminal case, and which may benefit from experience of that country or expertise in relevant matters. On the other hand, the defences in s 2 and the existence of s 31 demonstrate recognition that the means of travel and entry to the UK are connected with the circumstances of leaving and the reasons for it, and thus relevant to their asylum claim. Destruction of a passport makes it more difficult to return a person to their country of origin against their will. The s 2 offence is based on the proposition that it is not legitimate to obstruct one's return, an asylum claim having failed, even if that was based on fear of return rather than a cynical desire to obstruct the legal system. In other words, no relevant *mens rea* is required for the s 2 offence. The defendant is in an invidious position. If they have destroyed their passport in an attempt to ensure their own safety this fear is very relevant to the success of their asylum claim, but admitting its destruction will make them guilty of an offence and liable to imprisonment.

As Macdonald points out (2005:975), where the facts are in dispute, in the light of tightening controls by carriers the court may disbelieve a passenger's assertion that they never had a travel document. Although the offence is designed to curb destruction of documents before arrival, this is based on the assumption that the passenger did have such a document. If they actually did not, s 2 operates as a new criminal sanction against travelling without a travel document, even though this is a defence to the charge. Arriving without a travel document does not in itself amount to the offence of illegal entry, as there is in law no entry, nor is it an attempt to commit the offence of illegal entry as by definition it only arises at an interview. It does not target a person who attempts to remain hidden, but rather one who may have arrived by clandestine means but makes an application to regularize their stay. The underlying mischief is the destruction of travel documents but there is no requirement on the prosecution to prove this as the *actus reus* is simply presentation at interview without the document. The burden of proof is on the defendant to show they never had one. The Parliamentary Joint Committee on Human Rights considered whether this reverse burden meets the requirements of Article 6(2) ECHR. They did not reach a concluded view on that matter, but accepted that in principle it could be justifiable to place the burden on the defendant of showing an excuse for the destruction of a passport. This was with the caveat that immigrants should have access to information on the effect of destroying travel documents, even on the advice of facilitators (para 23).

In addition to problems with the offence itself, there is the problem of its being wrongly used. We have already noted that many people, probably thousands, have been wrongly prosecuted for offences to which s 31 would have provided a defence. The Joint Parliamentary Committee on Human Rights, reporting on the Bill voiced their concern (Fifth Report of session 2003–04, HL paper 35 HC 304, para 10) that like the offences of forgery and falsification of documents, s 2 might be wrongly used, thus penalizing even more asylum seekers and breaching Article 31. The defence of never having had a travel document was introduced to go some way towards alleviating the Committee's concerns. The press reported 230 asylum seekers arrested and 134 convicted in the first six months of s 2 being in force ('Asylum seekers jailed for having no passports' The Guardian 18 March 2005).

14.3.2 Those who assist or arrange entry

The whole problem is contained in the rather bland heading to this section. Should it read 'those who assist unlawful immigration' or 'those who assist asylum seekers'? Section 25 Immigration Act 1971 would suggest both. As indicated by its high maximum sentence, this has been treated as one of the most serious immigration offences. In the Immigration Act 1971 it was originally titled 'Assisting illegal entry and harbouring'. It consisted then of knowingly being concerned in 'making or carrying out arrangements for securing or facilitating the entry into the United Kingdom of anyone whom he knows or has reasonable cause for believing to be an illegal entrant' and of harbouring such a person. The maximum sentence increased from seven to ten years in 2000 (1999 Act s 29) and to 14 years in 2003 (2002 Act s 143). These sentences, and the powers in ss 25C and D to seize vehicles owned by a person convicted, are aimed at those who profit from arranging illegal entry, and show the prominent place that this offence plays in the government's campaign to prevent people smuggling and organized deception. It can be committed however simply by allowing an illegal entrant to stay in one's home. By its nature this offence may be committed abroad. Section 25(5) therefore provides for British nationals to be liable for the offence whether committed inside or outside the UK.

The Nationality, Immigration and Asylum Act 2002 greatly extended this offence and split it into three parts. The offence in s 25 is to do an act 'which facilitates the commission of a breach of immigration law by an individual who is not a citizen of the European Union'. The definition of immigration law is wide, covering any provision which controls entitlement to enter or be in a member state. This gives enforcement in the UK's criminal law to the control of immigration law in relation to any country in Europe, and reflects the development of immigration control into an aspect of international policing activity (as discussed in chapter 7). A British citizen in Albania organizing a marriage of convenience in Italy could be charged under this section. It would also catch an accountant in London preparing accounts for a Czech business to give a false impression that its main centre of operations was in Germany. The new offence in s 25B is assisting entry in breach of deportation or exclusion orders by European citizens. This closes the loophole which would otherwise have opened up after the creation of the specific offence in s 25 directed at facilitating entry by non-Europeans.

Section 25A has the extraordinary heading of 'helping asylum seeker to enter UK'. The offence is 'knowingly and for gain' to facilitate the arrival of someone the defendant knows or has reasonable cause to believe is an asylum seeker. There is a defence for someone acting on behalf of an organization which aims to help asylum seekers and does not charge for its services. Setting aside the rather jarring presentation of this offence, here it should be noted that the quality of the asylum claim is irrelevant. This offence is not aimed at asylum seekers but at those who profit from their need to find a way into the UK. Controlling such commercial arrangements for illegal entry is a matter of some priority in the emerging immigration law of the EU (see generally chapter 4). Relevant European provisions here are Directive 2002/90 and Framework Decision 2002/946, and the UK has opted in, but the offences under the expanded s 25 go beyond what is required by European measures. Notably, the s 25A offence of 'helping an asylum seeker to enter the UK' does not entail that the entry be illegal, simply that the entrant is an asylum seeker, whereas the Directive and Framework Decision require criminal sanctions for the facilitation of entry or transit 'in breach of the laws of the state concerned', not penalties on the travel arrangements of asylum seekers per se. Directive 2002/90 Article 1.2 allows any Member State not to apply sanctions where the 'aim of the behaviour is to provide humanitarian assistance to the person concerned'. The British defence is limited to organizations who do not charge for their services.

The facilitation offence in s 25 relates to assisting an illegal entrant. There is no requirement that the entrant themselves be guilty of or charged with a criminal offence. Illegal entry may be treated as a criminal offence, but usually immigration enforcement would be used, i.e. removal (see chapter 17). The criminal offence of illegal entry is more tightly drawn (s 24(1)(a)). To be guilty, the person must know that they are entering in breach of the law so this must be proved, and they must actually enter, although an attempt may be charged as such. Entry involves passing through immigration control, not just physically arriving. Section 28 extends the time limit for prosecution from the usual six months to three years if the evidence of the alleged offence has come to light in the previous two months. If the prosecution is brought within six months, the burden of proof is changed from the normal criminal one; it lies on the defendant to show that they had leave to enter (s 24(4)(b)). Once a criminal conviction has been obtained, the illegal entrant is still present and the immigration situation still has to be dealt with, so there is no obvious benefit in incurring the expense of a criminal prosecution.

The offences under s 25 are committed by people who can claim in some way to be serving the interests of the person whose entry is arranged. Once this has happened, the entrant is free of the smuggler or agent if they have paid for their services. This is not so in the case of trafficking. Section 145 Nationality, Immigration and Asylum Act 2002 created a new offence of trafficking in prostitution. This marked the UK's first statutory attempt to control this growing trade, which involves the forcible transport of people to work for the trafficker, often in the sex industry but also in other forced labour. Section 145 was swiftly repealed and replaced by offences in the Sexual Offences Act 2003. Characterizing the offence as primarily an immigration matter tended to take the focus away from the trafficker and place it on the unlawful immigration status of the victim. Moving it to the Sexual Offences Act more clearly addresses international crime. After the deaths of twenty-three Chinese cockle pickers who drowned in Morecambe Bay in February 2004, it was no longer possible to ignore other labour exploitation by traffickers and gangmasters. The Asylum and Immigration (Treatment of Claimants etc) Act 2004 introduced a new offence of trafficking for exploitation. Exploitation includes slavery and forced labour, using threats or deception or someone's youth or vulnerability to force them to provide benefits or services, and encouraging the sale of human organs (s 4).

Trafficking has been the subject of much international activity. The UK is required to participate in EU actions which develop the Schengen *acquis*, and these included the Council Framework Decision 2002/629 on trafficking in human beings which requires the Member States to have criminal penalties for trafficking offences. Under UK Presidency at the end of 2005 the EU adopted an Action Plan on trafficking in Human Beings. However, the UK has not opted into the directive on residence permits for trafficking victims (Directive 2004/81); neither has it signed the Council of Europe's Convention on Action against trafficking Human Beings (Treaty series 17). On 5 January 2006 the Home Office launched its own consultation on tackling trafficking (*Tackling Human Trafficking — Consultation on Proposals for a UK Action Plan*). It includes the question as to whether the UK should institute automatic reflection periods, i.e. a period during which immigration enforcement will be held in abeyance while the victim considers their situation. This is required by the Council of Europe Convention. There is also a reference in the consultation document to the idea of residence permits for trafficking victims. Currently both these are possible but only on a case by case basis. Reflection periods of three months and residence permits where the victim faces danger in their home country have previously been lobbied for by international human rights organizations such as Amnesty International, Anti-Slavery International and UNICEF UK.

14.3.3 **Immigration and criminal law**

Immigration offences are not covered in detail in this book. Their prosecution is an aspect of criminal law rather than immigration law. Nevertheless immigration offences are created in immigration statutes rather than in criminal justice statutes, and immigration officers now have powers almost identical to those of the police in relation to immigration offences, illustrating that this kind of law enforcement is seen as an aspect of immigration control. We have briefly discussed a few of the offences that have direct relationship with other human rights issues, particularly asylum claims. However, the whole area of interaction between immigration law and criminal law raises human rights issues of various kinds. For instance, a person subject to immigration control is subject to double jeopardy in the criminal courts as they may be deported in addition to any other sentence. This issue is considered in chapter 16. There are numerous minor and regulatory immigration offences. A new offence of failing to co-operate with removal action is considered in chapter 17. Offences which may be committed by employers and advisers and powers in relation to these are dealt with in chapters 7 and 8. A chart of the comparative rights on criminal arrest and arrest for an immigration reason appears on this book's companion website, together with an account of the enforcement powers of immigration officers.

We now move on to a quite different area of penalties relating to actual or alleged criminal activity — exclusion from an asylum claim.

14.4 Exclusion, expulsion, and anti-terrorism

The Refugee Convention provides both for the exclusion of individuals from initially obtaining refugee status (Art 1F), and the expulsion of recognized refugees and asylum seekers from the host state as a result of their actions there (Arts 32 and 33(2)). The significance of this area of law has increased rapidly in recent times as powers are interpreted and strengthened in the context of the escalation in international action and domestic legislation against terrorism. This began before 11 September 2001, but has accelerated since then.

Questions of exclusion from refugee protection are not only questions of refugee law. In *Gurung v SSHD* [2003] Imm AR 115 the Tribunal adopted the summary conclusions from the Lisbon expert roundtable, held as part of the 2001 UNHCR Global Consultations on International Protection, to say that 'there is a need, in the interpretation and application of Art 1F, to draw on "developments in other areas of international law since 1951, in particular international criminal law and extradition law as well as international human rights law and international humanitarian law" ' (para 34). In the domestic context, these refugee law provisions must also be read in conjunction with recent legislation on terrorism, the Terrorism Act 2000, the Anti-terrorism, Crime and Security Act 2001 and the Terrorism Act 2006.

Article 1F Refugee Convention makes exclusion from refugee status mandatory for: A person with respect to whom there are serious reasons for considering that he has committed:

(a) A crime against peace, a war crime, or crime against humanity as defined in international instruments.

(b) A serious non-political crime outside country of refuge prior to admission to that country as a refugee.

(c) Acts contrary to purpose and principles of UN.

The Tribunal decision in *Gurung* encouraged adjudicators to take the initiative in promoting a greater use of exclusion under this provision (paras 38 and 144). It referred to Lord Mustill's comment in the case of *T v SSHD* [1996] 2 All ER 865, that while the wording of Article 1F had not changed, the world around it had. It continued:

In the aftermath of the events of 11 September these thoughtful words remind us that, whilst there is nothing new about criminality, the precise forms and methods used by those who perpetrate violent acts or crimes continue to undergo change. (para 33)

The Tribunal considered that the 'well-settled principle that the Refugee Convention is a living instrument' applied to the interpretation of exclusions as much as of the requirements to establish refugee status. In this respect too it must be interpreted 'so as to give a contemporary response to contemporary realities' (para 35). Immigration judges should be more ready to use the exclusion clauses, and it was not only allowable but actually their duty to raise Article 1F even where the parties had not, if its application to the facts of the case was 'obvious' (para 47). The Tribunal accordingly laid down guidance for immigration judges in dealing with Article 1F. We shall return to this case in relation to Article 1F(b) below. Another reason to think that the use of Article 1F may be increasing is the Home Office policy referred to in *Gurung* (para 17) of considering exclusion where the asylum applicant is a member of an organization proscribed under the Terrorism Act 2000. The relationship between these provisions is discussed below. Article 1F only a short while ago was a relatively unused provision. Now its use is growing with significant implications for human rights.

This section on exclusions will begin by considering each of the Article 1F grounds in turn.

14.4.1 **Article 1F(a): Crime against peace, war crime, crime against humanity**

There are several international instruments which elaborate on the meaning of these crimes, and some are listed in Annex VI of the UNHCR Handbook. Examples are the 1948 Convention on the Protection and Punishment of Genocide and the four 1949 Geneva Conventions for the Protection of Victims of War. There has been very little UK case law concerning crimes against peace, war crimes, and crimes against humanity.

Article 6 of the Charter of the International Military Tribunal includes in the definition of a crime against peace 'planning, preparation, initiating or waging a war of aggression, or a war in violation of international treaties, agreements or assurances'. The Tribunal in *Amberber* 00/TH/01570 made it clear that just participating in such a war would not amount to a crime against peace. The Tribunal emphasized that an act of aggression was an act by a state against the territorial sovereignty or political independence of another state (UN General Assembly Resolution 3314). Mr Amberber as an active member of an armed group (AAPO) in Ethiopia had not committed a crime against peace, even though he procured and supplied arms to other members of the group. His appeal against exclusion was allowed. The UNHCR Guidelines 1996 on the application of exclusion clauses say 'there are few precedents if any for exclusion of individuals under this category' (para 27). *Amberber* was followed in *PK (Sri Lanka — risk on return — exclusion clause) Sri Lanka* [2004] UKIAT 00089 where the parties and the Tribunal agreed that the Adjudicator was wrong to apply Article 1F(a) where the claimant had been an active fighter in the LTTE. Although he had been responsible for the deaths of soldiers, there was no evidence that these killings were unlawful acts of war.

War crimes are crimes committed within the context of war, in violation of the law of war 'including the mistreatment of civilians and prisoners of war, or the infliction of unjustified property damage during wartime' (Hathaway 1991:216). Originally, they were conceived of as occurring only in wars between nations, but the International Criminal Tribunal for Former Yugoslavia established that they may also occur in internal conflicts (UNHCR Guidelines para 30 and n 20, referring to *Dusko Tadic* case no IT 94 I T).

Crimes against humanity are defined in Article 6(c) of the Charter of the International Military Tribunal as:

Murder, extermination, enslavement, deportation and other inhumane acts committed against any civilian population, before or during war; or persecutions on political, racial or religious grounds in execution of or in connection with any crime within the jurisdiction of the Tribunal, whether or not in violation of the domestic law of the country where perpetrated.

Symes' *Case Law on the Refugee Convention* (2000) quotes an example from the Canadian case of *Sivakumar v Canada (MEI)* [1994] 1 FC 433 to show that private individuals may commit such a crime. Linden JA in *Sivakumar* refers to the *Flick Trial, US Military Tribunal at Nuremberg, Law Reports of Trials of War Criminals*, vol. IX, p. 1 when several industrialists were convicted of crimes against humanity for using slave labour in their factories. In their document Addressing Security Concerns without Undermining refugee protection the UNHCR concurred 'with the view that the 11 September attacks constituted a crime against humanity' (para 13). An individual will only be responsible however if they engaged in a positive act with a conscious intention (UNHCR Guidelines para 39).

The incidental killing of civilians during military action is neither a war crime nor a crime against humanity but the deliberate massacre of the people of a whole village could be both.

14.4.2 Article 1F(b): Serious non-political crimes

This is the more commonly used ground of exclusion in the UK and some case law has grown up around it.

14.4.2.1 *Meaning of 'serious non-political crime'*

The leading case on the definition of serious non-political crimes is the case of *T v SSHD* [1996] 2 All ER 865, which concerned a member of an organization in Algeria that intended to secure power, was prepared to use violence to achieve its ends, and had been declared illegal in 1992. The special adjudicator found that the appellant was involved in and had had prior knowledge of a bomb attack on the airport in Algiers in which ten civilians had been killed, although there was a dispute about the level of intended damage and of the appellant's knowledge of that. He had also been engaged in planning a raid on an army barracks to seize arms in which one person had died. The question for the House of Lords was whether these offences were serious non-political crimes. This involved a consideration of what was meant by 'serious', what made a crime political and what degree of involvement in an offence was required to exclude the person concerned from refugee protection. The House of Lords endorsed the UNHCR Handbook's extended section on Article 1F exclusions (paras 151–161), which suggests that a 'serious' crime in this context 'must be a capital crime or a very serious punishable act' (para 155).

The question of the seriousness of the crime and its political or non-political character to an extent run together. The common law character of the crime must be weighed against its political nature. Some crimes are so serious that their common law nature outweighs any political motivation. So in this case, the killing of ten civilians was too great a crime to warrant being called 'political'. There also had to be a sufficient link between the political purpose to be served and the act carried out. Lord Lloyd suggested a test. First of all, for a crime to be political it must be committed for a political purpose, 'that is to say, with the object of overthrowing or subverting or changing the government of a state or inducing it to change its policy'. Second, there must be 'sufficiently close and direct link between the crime and the alleged political purpose. In determining whether such a link exists, the court will bear in mind the means used to achieve the political end, and will have particular regard to whether the crime was aimed at a military or governmental target, on the one hand, or a civilian target on the other, and in either event whether it was likely to involve the indiscriminate killing or injuring of members of the public' (at 787).

T's degree of involvement was held sufficient to exclude him from refugee status. He had not planted the bomb or carried out the raid, but he had planned the raid and was a political organizer for the group which planted the bomb. He had sufficient knowledge of the plan, even if it did not extend to details.

The approach of the tribunal to implementing these principles has not always been consistent. In *Hane* [2002] UKIAT 03945 the appellant was a Maoist Party member in Nepal who had been involved in an armed raid on a police station in which two policemen were injured. This was in the context, described by the Tribunal, of a high level of violence between Maoists and State authorities. For a period of time reported by Amnesty International the official figures were 548 Maoists, three soldiers, and one policeman killed. The appellant was a wanted man, but the Adjudicator had concluded that this was for prosecution not persecution. He did not consider Article 1F, but on appeal to the IAT it was accepted for the appellant that he would be excluded from refugee protection by Article 1F.

By comparison in *Gnanasegaran* [2002] UKIAT 00583 the appellant was an active member of the LTTE (Tamil Tigers) in Sri Lanka. He and two other members were wanted for the murder of one or two policemen. The Tribunal concluded, following *T*, that this was a political crime. It concluded:

Disturbing though we find it in the circumstances of this case that 'the perpetrator of a repellent crime should insist on the hospitality and protection of any nation whose borders he can manage to penetrate' (from the judgment of Lord Mustill in T . . .) we consider that this appeal must be allowed.

In *Mete* (17980) the appellant's account was disbelieved by the Tribunal, but if he had stored arms for Dev Sol as claimed (grenades and a handgun), that would, in the view of the Tribunal, have excluded him under Article 1F.

Lord Mustill was assisted in *T* by the concept of 'terrorism', however, there is no internationally accepted definition of terrorism and the definition in the Terrorism Act 2000 is extremely wide. It is probably more useful and accurate in the application of Article 1F to apply the wording of the Article and to use the test propounded by Lord Lloyd. The Tribunal in *Gurung* also advised a cautious approach to the notion of 'terrorism', and identifies particular differences between serious non-political crimes and terrorism. For instance, a serious common law robbery or a murder are not terrorism but are serious non-political crimes. In *Jesuthasan* 01/TH/ 01444 the loose use of the word 'terrorist' to describe the appellant without considering the elements of Article 1F meant that the adjudicator's decision was overturned. There is also a fundamental contradiction in that definitions of terrorism make reference to its political purpose, and it is generally understood to have one.

Terrorism Act 2000 s 1 refers to a 'political, religious or ideological' purpose. However, the excluded crimes in Article 1F(b) are by definition non-political, and so suggesting that the excluded person is a 'terrorist' muddies the water considerably. The phrase 'non-political' is certainly not meant to refer to crimes which have a religious or ideological purpose, though no doubt it will be so used if a case is presented in which the common law element outweighs the religious or ideological element.

14.4.2.2 *Restrictive interpretation*

There are a number of general principles of importance in the application of Article 1F. It has generally been accepted that the Article should be construed restrictively because it deprives a person of protection who would otherwise qualify for refugee status. A decision to exclude them may expose them to persecution (UNHCR Handbook para 180). This principle of construing the Article restrictively was reconsidered by the tribunal in *Gurung*. It was still accepted, but with this qualification:

37. If the underlying purpose of the Refugee Convention is protection of human rights, then it is surely relevant, when applying the Exclusion Clauses, to take account of the extent to which those guilty of Art 1F crimes have violated the human rights of others. As set out in the Preamble, the objects of the Refugee Convention are not confined to protection of the rights of refugees; they begin by referring to the principle that 'human beings shall enjoy fundamental rights and freedoms without discrimination'. In our view, the greater the scale of the violation of the human rights of others by those who perpetrate acts or crimes proscribed by Art 1F, the less rationale there is for a restrictive approach. To take the example of an individual terrorist who exploded a nuclear device in a large city, in such a case we doubt that a restrictive approach should have any place at all.

This said, when the Tribunal summarized its conclusions it started with the principle that exclusion clauses should be applied restrictively (para 151).

The Tribunal in *AA* (see below) suggested a gloss on this principle in *Gurung*, namely that although the exclusion clauses should be interpreted restrictively, they should not be applied restrictively. This enabled an extension of the use of Article 1F(c) discussed below.

14.4.2.3 *Inclusion before exclusion*

Another established principle, though shaken somewhat by *Gurung*, was that inclusion should be considered before exclusion. In other words, that the question of eligibility for refugee status should be considered before the question of whether the person should be excluded from it. The Lisbon expert roundtable conclusions give a number of reasons for this:

- Exclusion before inclusion risks criminalizing refugees.
- Exclusion is exceptional and it is not appropriate to consider an exception first.
- Non-inclusion, without having to address the question of exclusion, is possible in a number of cases, thereby avoiding having to deal with complex issues (though one might also put this point the other way round).
- Inclusion first enables consideration to be given to protection obligations to family members.

- Inclusion before exclusion allows proper distinctions to be drawn between prosecution and persecution.
- Textually, the 1951 Convention would appear to provide more clearly for inclusion before exclusion. . . .
- Interviews which look at the whole refugee definition allow for information to be collected more broadly and accurately.

We might add another reason, which is that the UNHCR Handbook advises striking a balance between 'the nature of the offence presumed to have been committed by the applicant and the degree of persecution feared' (para 156). This balance cannot be struck if the feared persecution has not been fully considered. However, the same roundtable discussion notes that this practice is declining in states, and in *T* Lord Mustill said that that the political or non-political character of the offence could not depend upon the consequences that the offender might suffer on return. In the UK the requirement for balance was excluded by the Anti-terrorism, Crime and Security Act 2001 s 34, which says that exclusions from refugee status 'shall not be taken to require consideration of the gravity of events or fear' which might give rise to refugee status. This section is tucked away in a statute, rushed through Parliament in three months following the events of 11 September 2001, and apparently addressed to international security issues.

The Anti-terrorism, Crime and Security Act 2001(ATCSA) introduced a power for the Secretary of State to certify that an asylum claim which was to be heard before the Special Immigration Appeals Commission is excluded under Article 1F or 33(2) (see below), which prevented the claim for inclusion in the Convention from being heard at all. The Immigration, Nationality and Asylum Act 2006 extends this to appeals before the Immigration and Asylum Tribunal, and thus to all asylum appeals. The statutes make no concession to the principle of 'inclusion before exclusion' as once the Secretary of State has certified, the tribunal must begin considering the statements in the Secretary of State's certificate. If the tribunal agrees with those statements it must dismiss the claim for asylum (before considering any other aspect of the case) (s 33 of the 2001 Act, replaced by s 55 of the 2006 Act).

This is both an extraordinary provision and extraordinary terminology. The phrase 'agrees with' suggests that the certificate contains an opinion rather than facts. Indeed the certificate is 'that the appellant is not entitled to the protection of Article 33 of the Convention' (s 55(1)) because the exclusions apply, which is a legal opinion. There is no scope for challenging the factual basis of the certificate as the only appeal is on a point of law. Under the 2001 Act judicial review was excluded but this is not the case under the 2006 Act. The only limitation is that where the Secretary of State certifies that Article 33.2 applies in the AIT, as opposed to SIAC, this must be on national security grounds.

14.4.2.4 *Standard of proof*

The standard of proof of allegations which would lead to exclusion is a matter of some importance, even more so following the statutory provisions just discussed, as its establishment will prevent the asylum claim from being heard. The decision in *Gurung* on this point gives grounds for concern that the paramountcy of refugee protection may be lost. The Article says that a person will be excluded if 'there are serious reasons for considering' that they have committed one of the acts discussed. The Lisbon Expert Roundtable says this should be interpreted as a minimum to mean 'clear evidence sufficient to indict', and that in view of the seriousness of the issues and the consequences 'appropriate procedural safeguards derived from human rights law' should be in place (para 17). The UNHCR also suggests that the standard of proof should be higher than 'reasonable suspicion' (Addressing Security Concerns without Undermining Refugee Protection para 17). The Tribunal in *Gurung*, invoking the holistic approach in *Karanakaran*, declined to find that the Secretary of State has any legal burden of proof, i.e., that the matters must be proved to a certain standard. It concluded, 'there is no need to go beyond the words of article 1F, i.e., ". . . serious reasons for considering . . ." ' (para 95).

In so deciding, the Tribunal in *Gurung* endorsed the tribunal's decision in *Thayabaran* (18737) that the Secretary of State bears an evidential burden, i.e., has the obligation to introduce evidence of the alleged actions. However, after that passage, the decision in *Thayabaran* goes on to refer to the distinction drawn by Lord Mustill in *T* between extradition and exclusion. The importance of this, it said, lay in the burden of proof. It continued:

> In asylum matters, as Lord Mustill said, there is a general duty not to expel unless the exclusion clause applies. In an asylum case (as distinct from an extradition case) it is the Secretary of State who is relying on the exclusion clause. We think that the usual principle 'he who asserts must prove' applies to this issue. The matter was not, however, the subject of argument before us, because Mrs Elam conceded on behalf of the Secretary of State that the respondent bore the burden of proof on this issue.

A similar position was taken in the earlier case of *Kathiripillai* (12250): 'One starts from the position that the burden of proving that the appellant loses the protection of the Convention under this article lies on the respondent.'

Gurung makes an explicit distinction between an evidential and a legal burden, which is not addressed in these cases although the straightforward wording of *Kathiripillai* seems to capture the reality. Nevertheless, the decision in *Gurung* has precedent value whereas the other two do not. It is a starred determination 'for the purpose of giving guidance to adjudicators on the proper approach to the Refugee Convention's exclusion clauses at Article 1F' (para 1). It is also a decision of the President of the Tribunal and two Vice Presidents. It must be regarded as authoritative on this point, although with respect it is suggested that the reasons for the approach in *Karanakaran* do not apply to Article 1F. This Article is not, like the refugee determination itself, concerned with speculation about future possibilities, it is concerned with events that have already occurred. The uncertain quality of evidence should not be allowed to dictate the standard of proof when the consequences of a wrong decision could be so serious. It is precisely these consequences which also guided the Court of Appeal in *Karanakaran* to take a holistic view of the assessment of the claim. It is suggested that, contrary to the view stated in *Gurung*, the principles in *Khawaja* [1984] AC 74 could apply here to warrant a standard of proof at the higher end of the civil standard, for similar reasons (see chapter 17). Failing to exclude when exclusion could have been warranted does not preclude other actions to deal with the matters alleged, for instance there is no objection to the refugee standing trial for criminal acts where this is a possibility. UNHCR's view is that where an asylum seeker is not excluded and extradition would entail a return to persecution, 'prosecution in the country of asylum is . . . the appropriate response' (Addressing Security Concerns para 24).

The words of the Article, 'serious reasons for considering', are deceptively simple, and clearly do not require a criminal standard of proof, but their interpretation could become increasingly important for asylum seekers.

14.4.2.5 *Complicity*

The question of complicity is the question of how implicated the claimant is in the wrongful acts. In the case of *T*, although the appellant had not planted the bomb or carried out the raid, he had taken part in the planning and preparation of the latter and as a political organizer had at minimum an incriminating level of knowledge of the former. The degree of complicity which will result in exclusion is related to the nature and seriousness of the offence. Knowledge in advance that a demonstration may well erupt into stone-throwing and damage to property is a very different matter from knowledge in advance that a bomb will be planted in a densely popu-lated area. Level of control in the organization may be taken into account. As mentioned above complicity normally entails 'a positive act and conscious inten-tion' (UNHCR Guidelines para 39). This may be affected by duress. In the words of the Nuremberg Tribunal, 'The criterion for criminal responsibility . . . lies in moral freedom, in the perpetrator's ability to choose with respect to the act of which he is accused' (quoted in UNHCR Guidelines, para 38).

In *Gurung* the question of complicity arose directly as the main evidence against the appellant was his membership of a Maoist organization which used violent means. In the current climate in the UK this starting point raises very significant issues. Subsequent to *T*, the question in case law has generally been 'what was the claimant's relationship to the offence(s)?' Determination of the character of the offence(s) as political or not and of the claimant's relationship to the offence(s) has taken into account their membership of an organization. In fact it would rarely be the case that an offence would be considered political without the appellant being a member of a political organization.

The Tribunal in *Gurung* poses a different question: 'is mere membership at the time of the commission of acts or crimes proscribed by Article 1F enough to entitle an adjudicator to conclude that an appellant is excluded . . .?' (para 103).

It notes that the consistent approach of previous case law is that mere member-ship is not enough. However, it seems to depart from that previous approach, sug-gesting that in certain circumstances membership might be enough. In so doing it endorses the following passage from the UNHCR's *Addressing Security Concerns*:

Where, however, there is sufficient proof that an asylum-seeker belongs to an extremist inter-national terrorist group, such as those involved in the 11 September attacks, voluntary mem-bership could be presumed to amount to personal and knowing participation, or at least acquiescence amounting to complicity in the crimes in question. In asylum procedures, a rebuttable presumption of individual liability could be introduced to handle such cases. Draw-ing up lists of international terrorist organisations at the international level would facilitate the application of this procedural device since such certification at the international level would carry considerable weight in contrast to lists established by one country alone. The position of the individual in the organisation concerned, including the voluntariness of his or her membership, as well as the fragmentation of certain groups would, however, need to be taken into account. (para 18)

The Tribunal says that adopting this approach is necessary 'to reflect the realities of modern day terrorism' (para 106).

The UNHCR calls for an internationally agreed list of relevant organizations. There are indeed a number of initiatives at the international level which are aiming to produce international standards which will effectively combat international terrorism and prevent the refugee system from being used to assist its growth. The European Union has adopted a Proposal for a Council Framework Decision on Combating Terrorism (COM 2001 521), but there are still not effective international lists of organizations membership of which might warrant exclusion from the Refugee Convention.

14.4.2.6 *Effect of UK legislation*

In common with many other countries, the UK uses a national list in the form of organizations which are proscribed under the Terrorism Act 2000. The grounds for proscription are that the organization is concerned in terrorism (s 3) and this is defined as committing, participating in, promoting or encouraging or otherwise engaging in terrorism. The Terrorism Act 2006 proposes to add that an organization promotes or encourages terrorism if it glorifies it. This means to praise or celebrate it in such a way as to give people to understand that such conduct should be emulated and presumably it is something which falls short of 'encouragement'. The commitment to this provision was part of the Prime Minister's statement on what action the government would take after the 7 July bombings in London.

In Sch 2 to the 2000 Act as it received Royal Assent was a list of Irish organizations including the Ulster Defence Association (UDA) and the Irish Republican Army (IRA). These have been supplemented by Amendment Orders. The first one came into force on 29 March 2001 proscribing a long list of organizations including Al-Qa'ida, the LTTE and the PKK (Terrorism Act 2000 (Proscribed Organizations) (Amendment) Order 2001, SI 2001/1261). The second one, adding four more organizations, came into force on 1 November 2002, and includes by way of explanation:

The entry for Jemaah Islamiyah refers to the organisation using that name that is based in south-east Asia, members of which were arrested by the Singapore authorities in December 2001 in connection with a plot to attack US and other Western targets in Singapore. (Terrorism Act 2000 (Proscribed Organisations) (Amendment) Order 2002, SI 2002/2724)

These orders are an aspect of the UK's contribution to 'the war on terrorism'. As organizations, in the government's view, become implicated in such incidents, they will be proscribed in the UK. A statement made by the Prime Minister on 5 August 2005 on measures the Government proposed following the bombings in London in July 2005 expressed an intention to proscribe more organisations, specifically Hizb-ut-Tahrir and the successor organization of Al Muhajiroun. These proposals were highly controversial, and in the event, a further fifteen Islamic organizations were proscribed, though not the two mentioned (Terrorism Act (Proscribed Organisations) (Amendment) Order 2005, SI 2005/2892). What, however, is the meaning of 'proscription'? By Terrorism Act 2000 ss 11, 12, and 13 it is an offence to belong to a proscribed organization or to profess to do so, to invite support for a proscribed organization which is not restricted to money or other property, to arrange or support or address a meeting in order to support a proscribed organization, or to wear an item of clothing or display an article suggesting support for a proscribed organization.

Judging by the Home Office policy referred to in *Gurung*, in the context of Article 1F, the proscription of an organization is being used to provide *prima facie* evidence that the organization falls into the group membership of which, following *Gurung*, raises a presumption against the asylum claimant. There is a defence under Terrorism Act 2000 s 11(2) that the organization was not proscribed when the person charged became a member and that the person has not taken part in the activities of the organization since it was proscribed. The presumption of exclusion under Article 1F should be displaced by establishing the same facts.

There are dangers in making this link between membership of a proscribed organization and exclusion from refugee status, particularly on the basis of a national rather than an international list. The first is that the UNHCR refers to membership of an 'extremist terrorist group'. Although it quoted an obvious example of mass murder of civilians, in general it is not so easy to identify 'an extremist terrorist group'. Kirby J in the Australian case of *Applicant A v MIMA* 190 CLR 225 (Aust. High Ct, Feb 24 1997) famously said of particular social groups under the Convention that judges 'will recognize persecuted groups of particularity when they see them'. This approach has not been followed, and it is suggested that the 'I know one when I see one' approach to extremist terrorist groups also will not satisfy the rule of law. However, this is what is risked in the absence of any international definition, even of terrorism, let alone of 'extremist groups'.

There is an all too obvious danger that a national list will include groups for political reasons. The old adage 'one man's terrorist is another man's freedom fighter' is particularly pertinent in this context. Without some scope for this still to be the case, the Refugee Convention would be undermined, as persecution for reasons of political opinion is an archetypal qualification for refugee status. It is easy to recognize the events of 11 September 2001 as an atrocity, but it is not easy to derive a principle from this.

Already the proscribed list in the UK has the capacity to make a significant impact on refugee claims. As mentioned, the LTTE and PKK are included. Very many asylum claims from Sri Lanka are brought by LTTE members. Similarly, a large number of Turkish claims are brought by members of the PKK or indeed other proscribed groups. However, in cases such as *Gnanasegaran* referred to above, the applicant member of the LTTE was awarded refugee status even when he had committed very serious crimes because he faced ill-treatment for reasons of political opinion and his crimes were political ones. The connection of the events of 11 September 2001 with this aspect of refugee status is potentially very damaging to the whole refugee framework of protection. Taking UNHCR's whole document, rather than individual paragraphs, the implication is that membership of an 'extremist terrorist group' could be taken as *prima facie* evidence of a crime against humanity, i.e., using paragraph (a) rather than paragraph (b) of Article 1F. If the matter were approached like this, there would be less concern that people would be wrongly excluded from refugee status. Complicity in a crime against humanity is a very serious charge which could only be approached with great care and requiring significant proof. However, there is a danger that the approach in the UK as exemplified by the Home Office policy referred to in *Gurung*, will result in membership of a nationally proscribed organization (proscription being achieved simply by Order of the Secretary of State) being regarded as *prima facie* evidence of involvement in a serious non-political crime. The contradiction here is apparent, that membership of a political organization is *prima facie* evidence of non-political criminal activity. There is a plausible confusion in the UK because membership of the proscribed organization is a crime, that this will be regarded as grounds for exclusion under Article 1F, even though the crime is clearly political.

14.4.3 Article 1F: Acts contrary to purpose and principles of UN

The purpose of this paragraph, was summarized in the Canadian case of *Pushpanathan* [1998] 1 SCR by Bastarache J: 'The rationale is that those who are responsible for the persecution which creates refugees should not enjoy the benefits of a Convention designed to protect refugees' (para 63). There is no explicit restriction in this paragraph, or paragraph (a), to acts carried out before arriving in the country of refuge, although there is in paragraph (b). A likely reason for this is that the drafters of the Convention had in mind those people to whom this paragraph has traditionally been applied, namely 'only to those operating on a state level and perpetrating crimes of national or international significance' (Pretzell *et al* 2002:149 and UNHCR Guidelines 2003). Article 33.2 provides for exclusion of individuals on account of their actions after arrival in the country of refuge. It was probably not in the minds of the drafters that provision would be needed to exclude people who committed political crimes after arrival in the country of refuge. However, *Pushpanathan* countenanced some extension:

The category of persons covered by Art 1F(c) was not, however, restricted to persons in positions of power. Although it may be more difficult for a non-state actor to perpetrate human rights violations on a scale amounting to persecution without the State thereby implicitly adopting those acts, the possibility should not be excluded.

In *Singh and Singh v SSHD* (SIAC 31 July 2000) the Special Immigration Appeals Commission held that Sikh activists who were supporting armed struggle in India from the UK could be excluded from refugee status under Article 1F(c). They had conspired to commit acts of violence in India and had been involved in transporting explosives. The fact that these actions were in pursuance of a fight for self-determination did not provide a defence against exclusion. They could not have been excluded under Article 1F(b) because these acts were committed after arrival in the country of refuge. The SIAC found that as there was no express limitation of Article 1F(c) to individuals carrying governmental authority, none should be implied. The crucial finding was that the UN unequivocally condemns terrorism. The actions of Singh and Singh could be brought within the definition of terrorism in the UK (Terrorism Act 2000 s 1). Therefore terrorist acts such as these were contrary to the purpose and principles of the UN.

Singh was followed in the Immigration and Asylum Tribunal in *KK (Article 1F(c)), Turkey)* [2004] UKIAT 00101, a decision which bears close examination. The claimant had been active in Kurdish politics while living in Turkey, had been arrested, detained and interrogated on seven occasions, and had fled after being implicated in a serious bombing incident. He had been active in the PKK (Kurdistan Workers Party) and Dev Sol, which became DHKP-C. Both are proscribed organisations in the UK (see below). The Secretary of State accepted that he had a well-founded fear of persecution in Turkey because of his political opinions. Before his asylum claim was determined, KK was found guilty of arson and conspiracy to commit arson in relation to attacks in London on a Turkish travel agent and Turkish bank. No-one was injured in the attacks.

The Secretary of State sought to exclude him from refugee status under Article 1F(c). UNHCR argued that the crimes referred to in this paragraph are those with an international or global dimension, capable of affecting relations between states. The use should be exceptional and usually confined to those in positions of power or influence. Although it could be appropriate to broaden it to include individuals who committed acts of terrorism with international consequences, this should only be done in the most extreme cases. This follows *Pushpanathan*.

The Tribunal held that the act was political, as it was continuing the fight against the Turkish government which the claimant had been involved in in Turkey. In the country of refuge no distinction should be drawn between common crime and political crime. The refugee would be subject to that legal system. The Tribunal concludes:

> there are some acts which, despite being political or politically-inspired, do not depend for their criminality on the individual matrix of power within a particular state. These acts, in our view, are those which are intended to be covered by Article 1F(c). That subparagraph does not apply to every crime, nor to every political crime. It applies to acts which are the subject of intense disapproval by the governing body of the entire international community. (para 85)

This is the crux of the Tribunal's decision. The act that KK had committed came within the UK's controversial and wide definition of terrorism under Terrorism Act 2000 s 1. The UN condemned terrorism and so his action brought him within Article 1F(c).

KK was followed in *AA (Palestine)* [2005] UKIAT 00104 ILU Vol.8 no.12 in which the appellant had been arrested while on a suicide bombing mission. The Tribunal criticized the adjudicator for not raising the question of Article 1F. Whether paragraph b or c would be applied would be left to the adjudicator, but the advantage to the Secretary of State in using paragraph c was evident here as the tribunal held that paragraph c contains no requirement that the crime in question be non-political in order to attract exclusion, therefore if an act is accepted to come within this paragraph there does not need to be any enquiry into whether the common law criminal element outweighs any political motivation. The UNHCR Handbook and guidance was rejected even more emphatically than in *KK* as an authority on the interpretation of the Convention, and UN material condemning terrorism relied on instead.

The matter is put beyond doubt by the following provision in the Immigration, Asylum and Nationality Act 2006:

> In the construction and application of Article 1(F)(c) of the Refugee Convention the reference to acts contrary to the purposes and principles of the United Nations shall be taken as including, in particular —
> (a) acts of committing, preparing or instigating terrorism (whether or not the acts amount to an actual or inchoate offence), and
> (b) acts of encouraging or inducing others to commit, prepare or instigate terrorism (whether or not the acts amount to an actual or inchoate offence).

Parliament has taken over the function of the judiciary in interpreting an international Convention. The effect is surely coming closer to the vision that Lauterpacht warned against, the international community becomes 'one of mutual insurance for the maintenance of established governments' (see previous chapter).

The Tribunal in *KK* and *AA* rejected the argument that sentences served for offences committed served to expiate the crime so that the person would no longer be excluded from international protection. They also rejected the argument that there should be a balance between the persecution the appellants would face and the harm caused by the actions which resulted in their exclusion. Once the 2006 Act provisions are in effect, this question will not even arise.

14.4.4 Article 33(2)

Much of the above in relation to proscription and Article 1F may, however, be academic in the worst sense. Article 33(2) of the Refugee Convention provides an exception to the non-refoulement obligation. This is where there are 'reasonable grounds' for regarding the refugee as 'a danger to the security of the country in which he is' or in relation to a person 'who, having been convicted by a final judgment of a particularly serious crime constitutes a danger to that country'. This paragraph has also not been often used, but by way of example was held to go against the appellant in *A v SSHD* CA 16/2/2004. He had been convicted in the UK of a serious sexual assault on his daughter, and of the rape of a woman.

The effect of the exclusion is to allow *refoulement*, rather than, as with Article 1F, exclusion from refugee status. This provision is intended for use where a refugee engages in serious criminal activity in the host country. The emphasis is on danger to the country, i.e., conviction of a particularly serious crime should not of itself warrant exclusion if the person would not constitute a danger to the country. Goodwin-Gill says:

Application of Article 33(2) ought always to involve the question of proportionality, with account taken of the nature of the consequences likely to befall the refugee on return. The offence in question and the perceived threat to the community would need to be extremely grave if danger to the life of the refugee were to be disregarded, although a less serious offence and a lesser threat might justify the return of an individual likely to face only some harassment or discrimination. (1996:140)

14.4.5 UK legislation affecting Article 33.2

UK statute now contradicts these principles in two ways. First, as mentioned earlier, ATCSA s 34 prevents precisely this question of proportionality from being taken into account in refoulement under Article 33(2) as well as exclusion under Article 1F. The Tribunal in *A v SSHD* held that there was no reason to restrict the application of s 34 to terrorist cases. It is generally worded, and despite its inclusion in an anti-terrorism statute, there is no other evidence that it should be restricted to that context. The question under Article 33(2) was whether the appellant was a danger to the public.

Second, the Nationality Immigration and Asylum Act 2002 s 72(2) resiles entirely from the obligation to make the necessary judgement under Article 33(2) as to danger to the community. It says:

A person shall be *presumed* to have been convicted by a final judgment of a particularly serious crime and to constitute a danger to the community of the United Kingdom if he is —
(a) convicted in the United Kingdom of an offence, and
(b) sentenced to a period of imprisonment of at least two years. (emphasis added)

By s 72(11) this does not include a suspended sentence but does include a hospital order. The offence of belonging to a proscribed organization under Terrorism Act 2000 s 11 carries a maximum sentence of ten years. This comes close to making membership of the LTTE, PKK, and so on grounds for *refoulement* without the commission of any serious non-political crime, although the presumption in s 72(2) is rebuttable.

The impact of s 72 took a further leap on 12 August 2004 with the coming into force of the Nationality, Immigration and Asylum Act 2002 (Specification of Particularly Serious Crimes) Order 2004, SI 2004/1910. This is made under the power in s 72(4) to specify further crimes, having the same effect as a conviction under s 72(2). The order specified 183 offences including not only rape, murder and stockpiling biological weapons, but also theft, entering a building as a trespasser intending to steal and aggravated taking of a vehicle. Section 72 is stated to be 'for the purpose and construction of article 33.2 of the Refugee Convention. The Parliamentary Joint Committee on Human Rights advised the government that the Order was incompatible with Article 33(2) of the Refugee Convention 'because it includes within its scope a number of offences which do not amount to "particularly serious crimes" within the meaning of Article 33(2)' (Joint Committee on Human Rights Twenty-second Report Session 2003–04). As the Human Rights Committee pointed out, legislation which is designed to give effect to international obligations must be interpreted compatibly with those obligations. If the order is incompatible with the Convention then it follows that it is *ultra vires* the 2002 Act. The Committee made this finding, and went on to express doubts about the compatibility of s 72 itself with the Refugee Convention on the grounds that a presumption undermined the case by case basis of refugee determination, reversed the burden or proof as stated in Article 33.2, and precluded the application of a proper proportionality test to each case (paras 32–36). The provisions also drew strong criticism from the UNHCR (see press release 7 November 2004), but the Government was undeterred.

SB Haiti [2005] UKIAT 00036 was decided after the implementation of s 72 but on pre-2002 Act law, as the decision under appeal had been taken prior to the 2002 Act. Here, a history of repeated offending including burglary, theft, possession of an imitation firearm was held not in itself to constitute a danger to the community such as to deprive the appellant of the protection of Article 33, unless he had, following the words of 33.2, been convicted of a 'particularly serious crime'. This had to be taken literally, the Tribunal thought, and none of the above offences would qualify. He lost his refugee status however because he had also committed an offence of wounding, which the Tribunal thought was 'particularly serious'. Interestingly, this had been committed after receiving indefinite leave to remain as a refugee, and the Tribunal did not think that should affect its view of the matter.

Section 72 seems to make it easier to remove a refugee than another person convicted of a criminal offence. As discussed in chapter 16, deportation must be conducive to the public good, and a serious criminal record would normally be required to show this. A presumption of deportation after a two-year prison sentence would be disproportionate and out of keeping with authority in the law of deportation as normally applied. Treating refugees less favourably conflicts with the obligation to facilitate the assimilation of refugees under Article 34 Refugee Convention.

This section sets a disturbing precedent in legislating in contravention of the Convention, not only of its spirit, but also of its express terms in Article 33(2). As there is no international body charged with the enforcement of refugee law, there is no mechanism for striking down such a legislative provision. The combination of s 72 and the new re-interpretation of Article 1F(c) discussed above means that the potential sanctions against refugees and asylum seekers for criminal acts, even against property, are extremely serious.

14.4.6 Article 32

This Article, in contrast to Article 1F and 33(2), gives a refugee protection against expulsion and in that respect complements Article 33(1), but its terms are surprisingly weak. It applies to recognized refugees, and says that they shall not be expelled save on grounds of national security or public order. Proper legal process for appeal must be allowed. In effect this makes a refugee in the UK liable to deportation like any other foreign national, but with a higher threshold to be reached by the state to justify expulsion. Also, this is not a *refoulement* provision. The state must allow the refugee a reasonable period within which to seek admission to another country.

14.5 Conclusion

The direction of change in Europe is towards curtailing asylum rights. European developments promise a less secure status for refugees and a greater willingness to exclude by reason of the threat posed by individuals. The UK, however, has already expanded the use of exclusion and even the defining conditions which enable it to take place. The linkage made between asylum and terrorism, has been demonstrated in this chapter not just to be political talk but something that is rapidly becoming a matter of law.

QUESTIONS

1 Why does the Refugee Convention exclude from protection those who have committed a serious non-political crime? Is there still a justification for limiting this exclusion to non-political crimes? What would be the effect of excluding people from protection for *any* serious crime?

2 Why might an asylum seeker travel on a false document?

3 The offence under s 2 of the 2004 Act is committed in transit to or on arrival in the UK. How is its deterrent effect achieved?

FURTHER READING

Blake, N., and Hussain, R. (2003) *Immigration, Asylum and Human Rights* (Oxford: Oxford University Press), Chapter 7.

Bowring, B. and Korff, D. (2004) *Terrorist Designation with regard to European and International Law: the case of the PMOI* Paper for International Conference of Jurists, 10 November 2004.

Brennan, R. (2006) Immigration Advice at the Police Station, 3 edn (Law Society Publishing).

Bruin, R., and Wouters, K. (2003) 'Terrorism and the Non-derogability of Non-refoulement' *International Journal of Refugee Law* vol. 15, no. 1, pp. 30–67.

Finch, N. (2002) 'Refugee or terrorist?' *Immigration Asylum and Nationality Law* vol. 16, no. 3, pp. 144–147.

Gilbert. G, (2001) Current issues in the application of the Exclusion Clauses UNHCR Global Consultations on International Protection.

Gilbert, G. (2003). 'Protection after September 11th' *International Journal of Refugee Law* vol. 15, no. 1, pp. 1–4.

Lindsley, F. (2003) 'Compensation and Prosecution — asylum seekers travelling on false documents after *ex p Adimi' Immigration Asylum and Nationality Law* vol. 17, no. 2, pp. 144–147.

Pretzell, A., Krushnder, D., and Hruschka, C. (2002) 'Terrorism and the 1951 Refugee Convention' *Immigration, Asylum, and Nationality Law* vol. 16, no. 3, pp. 148–165.

UNHCR (2002). UNHCR *Addressing Security Concerns without Undermining Refugee Protection* 2002.

—— (2003) Guidelines on International Protection: Application of Exclusion clauses: Article 1F of the Convention Relating to the Status of Refugees.

Yeo, C. (2001). 'The Internal Flight Alternative: Counter-Arguments' IANL vol. 15, no. 1, pp. 9–16.

SECTION 6

Enforcement

15

Detention

SUMMARY

The deprivation of liberty is one of the most serious infringements of fundamental human rights. In immigration law individuals may lose their liberty through the exercise of a statutory discretion by the Home Office or immigration officers and so guidelines and safeguards for the exercise of this discretion are crucial. The statutory powers and executive guidelines are examined here, together with the human rights and common law rules which apply. Legal provisions are set in the context of empirical research into detention decisions. The use of detention is seen as an increasingly frequent phenomenon in the asylum process, and the former use of indefinite detention for foreign terrorist suspects is also considered.

15.1 Introduction

'In English law every imprisonment is *prima facie* unlawful, and . . . it is for a person directing imprisonment to justify his act'. These well-known words of Lord Atkin in the wartime internment case of *Liversidge v Anderson* [1942] AC 206 at 245 are still a proper statement of legal principle. Detention is not lawful unless authorized by law. This is the reverse of the usual rule in English law, whereby anything is lawful providing it is not specifically prohibited. Detention however interferes with one of the most basic human rights, that of physical liberty, and the advent of the Human Rights Act 1998 strengthens the common law by providing in Article 5 a statutory right which may only be infringed in prescribed circumstances. In this chapter we shall consider, first, human rights standards having a bearing on immigration detention; second, lawfulness under the Human Rights Act 1998; and third, lawfulness in other domestic law, as immigration detention is an action of a public body which must be carried out within administrative law principles. Before these legal provisions we shall consider the present use and context of immigration detention.

15.1.1 Present context

Outside the sphere of immigration and asylum, the deprivation of physical liberty is regarded as the most serious punishment available in the criminal justice system in the UK. Within the immigration and asylum system detention may be imposed upon people who are not charged with any crime and nor even suspected of committing one.

The statutory basis for detention has barely changed since the implementation of the Immigration Act 1971 on 1 January 1973. In broad terms, detention may take place pending completion of examination, pending a decision to remove or the execution of removal directions, or pending deportation. In the first decade after the Act came into force, the power to detain was used mainly as a way of enforcing a refusal of leave to enter. For instance, a visitor or student who had been refused at the port might be detained overnight (see for example Weber and Gelsthorp 2000). Lengthy detention beyond this was rare.

From the mid-1980s the number of asylum applications began to rise, and the Home Office was not able to process asylum applications quickly enough to prevent a backlog arising. A survey by the Joint Council for the Welfare of Immigrants revealed that in the case of certain asylum claims there was an increasing resort to detention as a matter of course (Ashford 1993). From detention of a few hours to resolve some outstanding point, or to effect removal, immigration detention became quite commonly detention of weeks and months duration. Kurdish detainees went on hunger strike in protest at their mass detention on arrival. One detainee who was released and subsequently detained again after his asylum claim was refused was suffering from a profound depression at the prospect of return to Turkey and set fire to himself with fatal consequences (see *Shah* 2000). These and other protests have occasionally persuaded the Home Office to some temporary change of policy, however the trend since the mid–1980s in relation to detention has been a steady increase in its use. At the end of June 2005 there were approximately 2,153 people in immigration detention. This had dropped to 1,695 at the end of September (Asylum Statistics 2nd and 3rd quarters 2005). The number of detention places had increased to 2,984.

While numbers are increasing, it is not possible to say with any certainty whether people are being detained pending examination or following refusal or pending removal or deportation because no statistics are published on the legal stage reached by detainees. Following a fire at Yarl's Wood detention centre in February 2002 Lord Rooker answered a question in the House of Lords about the stage reached by the 385 people who were held there. While the majority were 'removable' only 46 had actually had removal directions set against them (HL Deb 25 Feb 2002 cited in BID Submission to UN Working Group on Arbitrary Detention 2002).

Nevertheless, it is possible to say that the vast majority of those in immigration detention are asylum seekers; as a typical proportion, 78 per cent, of the detainees recorded in June 2005, and 76 per cent in September.

The Immigration and Asylum Act 1999 made extensive provision for 'detention centres'. However in the Nationality, Immigration and Asylum Act 2002 s 66 these were renamed 'removal centres'. This was despite fierce opposition in Parliament concerning the message given to newly arrived asylum seekers about the way that their claim was regarded, and the injury to democracy protested by peers when it was revealed that the name change had already taken place before the clause had even been debated in Parliament.

The power to detain a person for immigration reasons is an administrative power rather than a judicial one. It is a power to detain pending the next decision or action to be taken, not a sentence passed for a wrong committed. However in the now lapsed Anti-terrorism, Crime and Security Act 2001 immigration detention became blurred with criminal detention. At the other end of the spectrum of reasons for detention, in the Nationality, Immigration and Asylum Act 2002 there is a blurring of the distinction between compulsory detention and the provision of accommodation for welfare. The expansion of detention is not only in numbers but also in concept, and as we have seen in chapter 12, some asylum seekers are now detained from arrival to removal. This chapter will explore the existing legal authorities for immigration detention, and the extent to which this expansion is supported by law.

15.2 Human rights standards

International human rights instruments show unanimity on the issue of detention. United Nations Declaration of Human Rights Article 9: 'No-one shall be subjected to arbitrary arrest, detention and exile;' International Covenant on Civil and Political Rights Article 9(1): 'Everyone has the right to liberty and security of person. No one shall be subjected to arbitrary arrest or detention'; European Convention on Human Rights Article 5: 'Everyone has the right to liberty and security of person. No one shall be deprived of his liberty save in the following cases and in accordance with a procedure prescribed by law . . .'.

All these three international human rights documents demonstrate a concern with arbitrariness, a key principle in assessing the lawfulness of detention, and this is a matter of both the content and process of decision-making. The United Nations Human Rights Commission's Working Group on Arbitrary Detention visited the UK in 1998 to examine the situation of migrants and asylum seekers in detention. In its report it identified a number of concerns relating to the reasons for detention, the duration of detention, the availability of independent review of detention, and limited consideration of other options before resorting to detention. The organization Bail for Immigration Detainees (BID) has identified governmental failure to address the recommendations of the Working Group, and made a submission (Immigration Detention in the United Kingdom September 2002) to the Working Group, inviting it to return to the UK for a further inspection. Some of these specific concerns will be referred to in the sections that follow.

15.2.1 Detention of asylum seekers

Article 14 of the Universal Declaration of Human Rights provides that the 'right to seek and enjoy asylum' is a basic human right. For this and humanitarian reasons UNHCR's Guidelines on applicable Criteria and Standards Relating to the Detention of Asylum Seekers (February 1999) say that as a starting point or general principle asylum seekers should not be detained (Guideline 2). They point out that asylum seekers are often detained because they have entered the country illegally. However, as UNHCR acknowledges, 'they may not be in a position to comply with the legal formalities for entry' and may be 'forced to arrive at, or enter, a territory illegally'. Detention of asylum seekers as illegal entrants, though widely accepted in Europe looks like a *prima facie* breach of Article 31 of the Refugee Convention (see chapter 14).

The Guidelines allow that in exceptional circumstances asylum seekers may be detained. Such detention must comply with applicable national and international law; it must be exercised in a non-discriminatory manner and subject to judicial or administrative review with the possibility of release where no grounds for its continuation exist (Guidelines para 5). A further set of procedural safeguards advises minimum guarantees such as 'prompt and full communication of any order of detention, together with reasons for the order, and their rights in connection with the order, in a language and in terms which they understand,' legal assistance, and so on (Guideline 5). The 15th meeting of the Standing Committee in June 1999 suggested that for detention to be lawful there should be a legal regime governing it, and the exceptional reasons which UNHCR acknowledge may warrant detention should be 'clearly prescribed in national law'.

The exceptional reasons are as follows:

(a) to verify identity;

(b) to determine the elements on which the claim for refugee status or asylum is based, but not 'for the entire status determination procedure, or for an unlimited period of time';

(c) in cases where asylum-seekers, acting in bad faith, have destroyed their travel and/or identity documents or have used fraudulent documents intentionally to mislead the authorities of the State in which they have claimed asylum;

(d) to protect national security and public safety.

Unaccompanied minors, pregnant and nursing mothers should not be detained, and alternatives to detention should be actively sought in the case of unaccompanied elderly people, those who have suffered torture or trauma, or who have a mental or physical disability. People in these groups should only be detained after medical advice that detention would not adversely affect their health or well-being.

The Guidelines advise that asylum seekers should not be detained in prisons, and that where this is unavoidable they should not be detained with those who are detained for criminal justice reasons, i.e., convicted or remand prisoners. Basic hygiene, medical, exercise, and legal facilities should be provided. There should be segregation of women and men and the opportunity for religious activity and contact with friends and relatives. While the guidelines do not have any binding effect, Simon Brown LJ in *R v Uxbridge Magistrates Court ex p Adimi, R v Crown Prosecution Service ex p Sorani, R v SSHD ex p Kaziu* [2000] 3 WLR 434 at 444 said that they should be given 'considerable weight'.

15.2.2 **European Convention on Human Rights**

Article 5 ECHR begins with a presumption of liberty:

Everyone has the right to liberty and security of person. No-one shall be deprived of his liberty save in the following cases and in accordance with a procedure prescribed by law . . .

Unlike the qualified rights in the Convention where the legitimate purpose of interfering with the right is couched in terms of broad public policy objectives, the legitimate purposes in Article 5 are for specified purposes only. There will be a breach of Article 5 whenever detention is not for one of the reasons specified in the Article. There are two specific purposes which are related to immigration, 'to prevent unauthorized entry' into the country and 'detention of a person against whom action is being taken with a view to deportation or extradition' (Art 5(1)(f)).

In every case the detention, in addition to serving the purpose which is expressly allowed, must also be lawful. The meaning of lawfulness here has two limbs. Firstly, lawfulness entails that a 'procedure prescribed by law' has been followed. This has a similar meaning to that employed in other Convention Articles which require that a measure infringing a right must be 'prescribed by law'. This means that the detention is in accordance with substantive and procedural rules of national law (*Conka v Belgium* (2002) 34 EHRR 54), and that the quality of that law is compatible with the rule of law (*Amuur v France* (1996) 22 EHRR 533 para 50). It requires that the legal provision in question be accessible and precise.

The second limb of lawfulness in the context of Article 5 is that the detention 'should be in keeping with the purpose of Article 5, namely to protect the individual from arbitrariness' (*Chahal v UK* (1996) 23 EHRR 413, *Amuur v France, Conka v Belgium*). The case law of the ECHR on the question of arbitrariness shares some of the principles identified by that the UN Working Group on Arbitrary Detention, for instance, procedural fairness, limits on the duration of detention, the legitimacy of reasons for detention, and the availability of review.

15.2.2.1 *Procedural fairness*

In *Conka v Belgium* the Court found a breach of Article 5.1 in that the reasons given for detention were misleading. Notices were sent to about seventy asylum seekers, requiring them to attend police stations to enable the files concerning their asylum applications to be completed. At the police station they were served with an order to leave Belgium, a decision for their removal to their country of origin and notice of their detention for that purpose. They were detained and removed.

The ECtHR found that this was a breach of Article 5.1 in that the wording of the notice which brought them to the police station was a deliberate ploy by the authorities to mislead the applicants in order to ensure the compliance of the largest possible number. The Court said that the action of the police in misleading asylum seekers about the purpose for which they were requested to attend the police station and thereby detaining them by deception could be found to contravene the principle against arbitrariness.

The mass nature of the deception practised by the police in this case attracted particular criticism by the Court. In addition to Article 5.1, the Court by a narrow majority found a violation of Protocol 4 Article 4, which prohibits collective expulsion of aliens.

Conka v Belgium has an uncomfortable echo in Weber and Gelsthorpe's research on UK detention decisions (2000). They discuss individuals called for interview to hear the final result of their asylum claim. No deception is alleged, but the statements of some immigration officers interviewed reveal a discomfort with lack of information. For instance:

What I remembered about the interviews and feeling uncomfortable about it was that often the asylum seeker would come to those interviews not realising what they amounted to, and then they would be detained. It sort of felt wrong to me. But you see if they were told they probably wouldn't have shown up. (p. 92)

15.2.2.2 *Limit on duration of detention*

In *Chahal* the European Court of Human Rights held that where a person was detained with a view to deportation, the principle of lawfulness required that the deportation proceedings should be 'prosecuted with due diligence' (para 113). If they were not, the detention would cease to be lawful. Mr Chahal had been in detention for four years by the time of his application to the ECtHR. Two further years were spent waiting for his case to reach the Court, bringing his total detention to six years, though the Court could only consider the legality of the first four. The domestic proceedings were complex, involving deportation proceedings, two refusals of asylum, two applications for judicial review, the second of which was also refused on appeal by the Court of Appeal, and then refusals of leave to appeal to the House of Lords by both its Judicial Committee and the Court of Appeal. The ECtHR commented that the case involved 'considerations of an extremely serious and weighty nature'. It went on to say, 'It is neither in the interests of the individual applicant nor in the general public interest in the administration of justice that such decisions be taken hastily' (para 117). While a lack of due diligence could give rise to a breach of Article 5.1(f) as a violation of the principle of lawfulness, the Court here held that there had not been undue delay on the part of the Government.

In *Amuur v France* four asylum seekers were detained at an airport in the international zone. Their conditions were fairly comfortable, and they were free physically to board another flight out of France, although their safety in the event of this could not be assured. The government argued that this did not amount to detention. The Court said that such conditions were a restriction on liberty. This might be necessary to prevent unauthorized entry, but should not be unduly prolonged. In this case they were restricted for 20 days. This length of time turned a restriction into a deprivation of liberty, which is detention.

15.2.2.3 *Quality of legal reasons*

The quality of legal reasons for detention also has a bearing on the question of arbitrariness.

In *Dougoz v Greece* (2002) 34 EHRR 61 the ECtHR considered the quality of the domestic law which authorized Mr Dougoz's detention, in the light of the Court's principles on arbitrariness and the rule of law. His detention was not properly authorized by domestic law in that the authority relied on, Section 27.6 of Law no 1975/1991, referred to the detention of aliens subject to a ministerial order for expulsion. However in this case the expulsion of Mr Dougoz had been ordered by a court and not a ministerial decision. Second, Section 27.6 only permitted detention if the person subject to the expulsion order was considered to be a danger to public order or might abscond. Mr Dougoz had been released from detention after a criminal sentence on the explicit view of the indictments chamber that he was not a danger, would be unlikely to commit further offences, and need not be detained. This being the case, his detention was not actually authorized by domestic law, and so would have fallen at the first hurdle. However, there was a purported authorization in domestic law, in that the Deputy Public Prosecutor offered the opinion that Decision no. 4803/13/7A/18.6.92 of the Minister of Foreign Affairs, Justice and Public Order, which also made provision for the detention of aliens subject to expulsion by administrative order, could be applied by analogy to those who were recommended for expulsion by a court. The ECtHR did not consider that the opinion of a senior public prosecutor 'constituted a "law" of sufficient "quality" within the meaning of the Court's case law' (para 57). Indeed it may be seen that this purported legal decision carries a classic hallmark of arbitrariness in that one party is deciding which laws should be applicable for the punishment of the other.

The quality of legal reasons may initially be accepted, but may become unlawful if the reasons cease to apply. In the case of *Chahal* the alleged threat to national security posed by Mr Chahal was accepted by the Court to be a sufficient reason, but to avoid arbitrariness there needed to be a check on the continuing application of this reason. This check was provided by the former advisory panel (see chapters 8 and 16).

15.2.2.4 *Review of detention*

The availability of review is a separate heading of challenge under the ECHR, as Article 5.4 provides:

Everyone who is deprived of his liberty by arrest or detention shall be entitled to take proceedings by which the lawfulness of his detention shall be decided speedily by a court and his release order if the detention is not lawful.

In the case of *Chahal v UK* the former advisory panel procedure was held to be a sufficient guarantee against arbitrary reasons, in that the panel could review the grounds for detention and check that it was still warranted in the interests of national security. There was therefore no breach of Article 5.1. However, it did not satisfy the requirements of Article 5.4 as the panel did not have the qualities of a 'court'. It lacked the normal qualities of judicial procedure, the right to representation, to notice of the case against the appellant, and so on. Even allowing for the need of the state for secrecy in national security matters, some fairer procedure could be devised. This decision led to the demise of the advisory panel and the creation of the Special Immigration Appeals Commission (see chapter 8).

15.3 **Immigration detention under the Human Rights Act**

Article 5(1)(f) has been applied in the UK by the House of Lords in the case of *R v SSHD ex p Saadi, Maged, Osman and Mohammed* [2002] 1 WLR 3131. The implications of this case are considerable, and it will be given extended treatment here.

The case was a challenge to the regime at the Oakington Reception Centre which represented a significant plank of government policy. It was built upon the power in s 4 Immigration and Asylum Act 1999 for the Secretary of State to 'provide for, or arrange for the provision of, facilities for the accommodation of persons (a) temporarily admitted . . . (b) released from detention . . . or (c) released on bail . . . under any provision of the Immigration Acts.' These are all people whom there is a statutory power to detain, but in relation to whom a decision has been made either not to detain or to release from detention. The Oakington regime was specifically for new arrivals in the UK, and was for group (a), those temporarily admitted. In the case of those accommodated at Oakington, they would by definition be people who did not come within the existing criteria for detention, the decision having been made that they were suitable for temporary admission. The regime at Oakington was described in the Home Office Operational Enforcement Manual as 'relaxed' (para 38.1). It was a kind of 'soft' detention. However, residence there was compulsory (by an amendment to Immigration Act 1971 Sch 2 para 21), and there could be no doubt that in the terms of the ECHR it amounted to a deprivation of liberty.

How, then, was it possible, in law, to justify the detention of those deemed by previous criteria to be suitable for release? The announcement of the regime by Immigration Minister Barbara Roche set out the new criterion:

In addition to the existing detention criteria, applicants will be detained at Oakington where it appears that their application can be decided quickly . . . Detention will initially be for a period of about seven days to enable applicants to be interviewed and an initial decision to be made'. (HC written answers 16 March 2000 col 263)

On its face, this criterion is quite opaque. Does it mean people whose claims to refugee status are so obvious that they should be processed quickly and enabled to establish their new life without delay? An example might be someone of a known persecuted minority who has obviously been tortured. The Home Office guidance for immigration officers on selection for Oakington included the 'Oakington Countries List', with columns of 'suitable' and 'unsuitable' cases by country. It is apparent from the entry of known persecuted groups in the '*un*suitable' list that the expectation of dealing with a claim quickly arose chiefly from judging it ill-founded. The Asylum Statistics 2001 show that of 8,330 Oakington cases decided in that year, 99 per cent were refused, 1 per cent were granted asylum and less than 1 per cent were granted exceptional leave to remain (the less substantial but still protective status abolished in December 2002). Further evidence quoted in the House of Lords showed that over 40 per cent of Oakington cases refused were certified as manifestly unfounded (para 18). The current use of Oakington for certified unfounded cases was discussed in chapter 12. 98 per cent of cases were refused in 2004 (Asylum Statistics).

In the case which ended up in the House of Lords, the four appellants were all detained in Oakington. All were Iraqi Kurds claiming asylum. Dr Saadi arrived openly at Heathrow and immediately claimed asylum. The other three arrived concealed in the back of a lorry and claimed asylum on arrival. The House of Lords proceeded on the footing that all were detained under Immigration Act 1971 Sch 2 para 16(1), i.e., the power to detain 'pending examination'. There was little doubt that the detention was lawful in domestic law without consideration of the Human Rights Act. The question in the House of Lords was whether detention for the purpose of enabling a speedy decision could come within the language of Article 5(1)(f).

The detention was clearly not 'with a view to deportation' as the claims of the four had not yet been determined. It could therefore only fall within Article 5(1)(f) if it was 'to prevent unauthorised entry'. It was accepted that there was not thought to be any risk of the appellants absconding. Indeed it was on this basis that they were detained at Oakington and not somewhere more secure. In what sense, then could the detention be said to be preventative?

The appellants argued that detention could only be said to be 'to prevent unauthorised entry' if it was necessary for that purpose. The House of Lords rejected this contention. They did this by relying on the case of *Chahal* which concerned the second part of Article 5(1)(f), in which it is permitted to detain a person 'in respect of whom action is being taken with a view to deportation.' The detention need not be necessary 'to prevent his committing an offence or fleeing' (*Chahal* para 112). Therefore, the House of Lords reasoned, it also need not be necessary to prevent unauthorized entry, so long as the process of authorization was proceeding with due diligence, as indeed a deportation needed to do in order for detention to remain lawful.

A crucial question if Article 5(1)(f) is to authorize the detention, is what constitutes unauthorized entry? 'Unauthorized entry' is not a term found in UK immigration law. At first sight we are therefore inclined to equate it with 'illegal entry' which is our nearest equivalent. However, in this context it cannot be the original arrival, clandestine though that was in three cases. That is already in the past and cannot be prevented. Also, the same reasoning was applied to all four applicants and Dr Saadi had not entered clandestinely but quite openly. Another possibility is that the unauthorized entry would be the making of a fraudulent asylum claim. However, firstly there was no evidence that this was intended, secondly any leave to enter obtained as a result of an asylum claim must be assumed to be properly granted, and a fraudulent claim detected and refused, thus not achieving any 'unauthorized entry', thirdly, detention has no rational connection to this since it in no way affects the validity of the claim made. The fraud would be defeated by the decision-making process, not by detention. Another possibility is that the unauthorized entry is the asylum seeker going to ground, but this will not apply here as the risk of absconding had already been ruled out. It cannot of course be the making of an asylum claim, which, as we have seen, is an international law right. As Collins J said in the High Court in *Saadi*:

Once it is accepted that an applicant has made a proper application for asylum and there is no risk that he will abscond or otherwise misbehave, it is impossible to see how it could reasonably be said that he needs to be detained to prevent his effecting an unauthorised entry. He is doing all that he should to ensure that he can make an authorised entry. (para 29)

The House of Lords, surprisingly in view of the statutory and human rights authority available, resorted to the principle of sovereignty, which statute and human rights law are to a degree designed to mitigate, and quoted *Oppenheim's International Law*:

The reception of aliens is a matter of discretion, and every state is by reason of its territorial supremacy competent to exclude aliens from the whole, or any part, of its territory. (para 31)

This, for the House of Lords, was the starting point. If this is the starting point then, so reasoned Lord Slynn, every entry is unauthorized until it is authorized. The entry of the appellants was therefore, quite simply, unauthorized because it had not been authorized.

The House of Lords' reasoning resulted in a judgment that the Secretary of State has the power to detain a person while the decision is made to authorize their entry, even if it is not necessary to do so. Lord Slynn, giving the only reasoned judgment, went on to say that the methods of selection of Oakington cases '(are they suitable for speedy decision?)', the objective of speedy decision-making and 'the way in which people are held for a short period . . . and in reasonable conditions' were not arbitrary or disproportionate and therefore did not fall outside the Article 5 requirements of lawfulness (para 45). He accepted the 'need for highly structured and tightly managed arrangements' in the interests of speed (para 46). It is perhaps unfortunate in this context that the House of Lords did not take account of the high number of appeals against Oakington decisions and the slightly higher than usual success rate of such appeals (Asylum Statistics 2001).

Close scrutiny of the *Saadi* judgment suggests no greater justification for detention than administrative need. This is an extremely worrying principle. The judgment does not identify when the alleged unauthorized entry takes place, but it may suggest that this is on arrival, as every entry is unauthorized until it is authorized. If this is the case Article 5(1)(f) appears redundant as such an occurrence cannot be prevented by anything which happens after disembarkation. On another viewing, more consistent with existing UK law, the entry is the passage through immigration control and obtaining leave. The effect of this then is that detention is authorized simply in order to carry out the business of immigration control. The governing principle is then nothing more than proportionality.

A surprising feature of this case is that although it was the first case after the Human Rights Act in the House of Lords to consider the issue of detention, the case was not decided using the principles of the Act, but rather the principle of sovereignty. As every detention, as we have noted, is a *prima facie* breach of human rights, this does seem something of a missed opportunity. It is perhaps unfortunate that the first case of this kind involved a short period in 'soft' detention, as this may have clouded the issue.

15.3.1 Reconsidering *Saadi*

It may be useful to consider what it would mean to approach the decision in *Saadi* using the Human Rights Act. As we saw in chapter 3, it is appropriate to use not only the Act itself but also the principles implied in the ECHR. A principle commonly referred to is that in Article 31(1) Vienna Convention on the Law of Treaties:

A treaty shall be interpreted in good faith in accordance with the ordinary meaning to be given to the terms of the treaty in their context and in the light of its object and purpose.

Article 5 must therefore be interpreted in accordance with its ordinary meaning in the light of the object of protecting the individual from the arbitrary action of the state. The House of Lords said that detention did not have to be necessary in order to be preventative. However if no unauthorized entry was contemplated after arrival by any of these appellants, there is at the very least a question here about the ordinary meaning of the words 'to prevent'. Ovey and White say that 'any general presumption that treaty obligations should be interpreted restrictively since they derogate from the sovereignty of States is not applicable to the Convention'. These points seem to lead in the direction of giving the words of the Convention a meaning which is the more protective of rights. The meaning given by the House of Lords to the words 'to prevent unauthorised entry' seems closer to 'while a process is going on which may turn an unauthorised entry into an authorised one'.

While the interpretation of the ECHR is relevant, it is not determinative, as here the case is brought under the Human Rights Act. Section 3 states that 'so far as it is possible' to do so, legislation must be interpreted so as to uphold Convention rights. This obligation applies to interpreting the Human Rights Act itself, and so here to Article 5 (Sedley LJ in *Douglas v Hello Ltd* [2001] 2 WLR 992 para 135). This interpretive duty has been discussed in chapter 3, but it is beyond dispute that an effort must be made to interpret statutory words so as to uphold Convention rights. If language is to be strained this may only be done to *uphold* a Convention right, not to defeat it. It may be suggested that the House of Lords decision strains the meaning of the words 'to prevent', but in so doing defeats a Convention right.

The approach of the House of Lords equating the first and second parts of Article 5(1)(f) does not attach any significance to the difference in wording between the two parts of the paragraph. The second part states in terms that enforcement action is already pending against the detained person, and it is worded as a wide power. The first part, saying 'to prevent' suggests a more narrow purpose. On the other hand, it is not appropriate to use too legalistic a means of interpreting Convention rights. There is a tension in the decision between the principle of proportionality, which seems to have inclined the House of Lords in favour of the Secretary of State, and the fundamental nature of the right to liberty which, the whole thrust of Article 5 suggests, should only be taken away in defined circumstances.

15.3.2 Other UK case law on Article 5

As detention is normally challenged by bail applications which are unreported, there have been few reported decisions on the question of detention. However, the growth in the use of detention and the possibility of asserting human rights has generated some judicial review. A judgment in the High Court illustrates the way that beginning with the obligation in s 3 Human Rights Act and fundamental nature of the right to liberty can influence the outcome (*R (on the application of Amirthanathan)* [2003] EWHC 1107 Admin). The principle of proportionality inclined the judge in this case to find the detention unlawful. It is Home Office policy not to detain a person pending an appeal (and see Immigration Act 1971 Sch 2 para 29). The claimant's solicitor had indicated an intention to appeal, and had ten days within which to lodge the appeal. Before the appeal could be lodged the claimant was detained. He was released three days after the appeal was lodged. Singh J held that this was disproportionate.

On reaching the Court of Appeal, *Amirthanathan* was joined with the case of *Nadarajah* (see below). The question of proportionality in relation to Article 5(1)(f) was taken further. Counsel for the appellants argued that the application of proportionality in *Saadi* meant that detention needed to be proportionate to the reasons for it, that is, in these cases, where detention in Article 5(1)(f) terms was 'with a view to deportation', proportionate to the assistance with removal that it afforded (*Nadarajah & Amirthanathan v SSHD* [2003] EWCA Civ 1768 para 46). The Court of Appeal disagreed, holding that the ECtHR in *Chahal*, in holding that detention did not need to be reasonably necessary for the purposes of deportation, disposed of this argument.

In both *Amirthanathan* and *Nadarajah* the Court of Appeal found that the detentions fell foul of Article 5 because acting on a policy that was undisclosed did not comply with the requirement that the detention be prescribed by law; the policy was not accessible (paras 67,69 & 72).

In *SSHD v Hindawi & Headley* [2004] EWCA Civ 1309 the majority of the Court of Appeal found that the right of prisoners who were subject to a deportation order to have their case referred to the Parole Board did not come within the ambit of Article 5. This did not mean that there would be no parole decision in their case, but that this would be the responsibility of the Secretary of State, following recommendations by the Carlisle Committee, rather than necessarily the responsibility of the Parole Board.

Detention under the Anti-terrorism, Crime and Security Act was challenged, not under Article 5, as the UK had derogated from this Article, but under Articles 14 and 15. This challenge is discussed later.

15.4 **National law basis of powers to detain**

The power to detain is a statutory power, found in Immigration Act 1971 Schs 2 and 3 and in Nationality, Immigration and Asylum Act 2002 s 62. As discussed earlier, it is a power ancillary to immigration control and it is therefore exercisable by reference to stages of the immigration process. In terms of the statutory provisions giving power to detain, no distinction is made between asylum seekers and others, although as we have already seen, the great majority of immigration detainees are in fact asylum seekers. Powers to detain are possessed both by immigration officers and by officials in the Home Office, though as a matter of policy, the immigration officer's power to detain is normally exercised by a Chief Immigration Officer. Immigration officers have powers to detain which follow from their border control functions. They may detain pending examination, pending a decision whether to remove and pending removal (Sch 2 of the 1971 Act). These powers of detention may be exercised whenever the decision or examination takes place. In other words they may apply for instance to a clandestine entrant at a port, a person who has been examined at the port, or someone who has been waiting months for a decision and comes back to the port for further interview.

Until the 2002 Act the Secretary of State only had power to detain pending deportation (Sch 3 of the 1971 Act). This went hand in hand with the original division of powers in the 1971 Act (see chapter 6) which made the Secretary of State responsible for 'in-country' decisions to grant or vary leave to remain and to deport, and immigration officers responsible for decisions on entry. That division of function has, as we have seen, broken down in relation to asylum seekers and human rights claimants, following the extension of the Secretary of State's powers to be able to grant leave to enter in such cases (Immigration (Leave to Enter) Order 2001, SI 2001/2590). The 2002 Act contains provisions which are intended to make the powers of the Secretary of State and immigration service interchangeable in relation to asylum seekers (ss 62(3) and (4)). The Secretary of State therefore now also has power to detain pending examination, a decision whether to remove and removal, in relation to asylum and human rights applicants (ss 62(1) and (2)).

Part 4 of the 2002 Act contains these new powers of detention. The sections contain some quite obscure drafting; for instance, that the power to detain is exercisable when the Secretary of State has reasonable grounds to suspect that he may make a decision to give or refuse leave to enter or a decision whether to give directions for removal. This is strange indeed, raising the Kafkaesque spectre of detention ending at the point where the Secretary of State decides not to make a decision, or of a person being detained when the Secretary of State reasonably suspects that he is about to grant leave to enter (s 62(7), read with 62(1) and 62(2)). The use of the word 'suspect' is also peculiar, suggesting a kind of introspective self-policing by the Secretary of State. However, the intention of the drafting seems to have been to make the power to detain as wide as possible without necessarily invoking these bizarre extremes. They were explained by the Parliamentary Secretary to the Lord Chancellor's department during the Standing Committee stage of the 2002 Bill as an attempt to simplify the process (House of Commons Standing Committee E 14 May 2002 cols 233–234).

The combined changes of the Immigration and Asylum Act 1999 and the Nationality Immigration and Asylum Act 2002 have certainly widened the scope of the power to detain. In the 1971 Act as originally enacted the power to detain pending removal was a power to detain someone 'in respect of whom directions may be given' (Sch 2 para 16(2)). In other words, someone who had already been deemed subject to removal, and before the 1999 Act this meant someone upon whom notice had been served that they were deemed an illegal entrant. The 1999 Act, as well as widening the grounds for removal (see chapter 17), also amended para 16(2) to permit detention where there were 'reasonable grounds to suspect' that a person might be subject to removal. This means that even where the removal decision has not been taken, for instance because the claim is not decided, or it is not clear to which country the claimant may be removed, they may still be detained. There are limits to this power, discussed below. Section 62, in mirroring this provision, gives the Secretary of State the widest possible power to detain.

Finally there may be detention by the Secretary of State after the recommendation of a criminal court that the person be deported, providing the person is not on bail or in prison already by virtue of the judgment of the court (1971 Act Sch 3 para 2(1)). The paragraph says that the person shall be detained unless the Secretary of State directs release. This might be thought to create a presumption in favour of detention. If this were the case the Secretary of State might be able to argue that when someone had served their sentence no decision would need to be taken about their liberty, they would just stay in detention until they were deported. However, this was found not to be the case in *The Queen on the Application of Sedrati, Buitrago-Lopez and Anaghatu* [2001] EWHC Admin 418, in which Moses J granted a declaration that Sch 3 para 2 created no presumption in favour of detention upon completion of a sentence of imprisonment. Such a presumption would breach Article 5, and Moses J interpreted the statute so as to uphold Convention rights. Therefore the Secretary of State must actively decide in each case whether the prospective deportee should be detained.

15.4.1 Criteria or reasons for detention

The statutory power to detain is a discretion, which should only be exercised upon specified criteria otherwise it risks breaching the principle against arbitrariness. The statutory provisions give a power to detain a person at a particular immigration stage. The categories may be regarded as statutory preconditions for detention, in that if a person were detained who did not come within these their detention would be unlawful. The statutes however do not indicate whether a *particular individual* should be detained. In each case the decision to detain is a discretionary one, and the immigration statutes are silent on the question of what criteria should lead to detention. The BID Submission to the UN Working Group on Arbitrary Detention criticises the absence of statutory criteria. The arguments for laying down criteria in statute are they would be more publicly accessible, so providing a greater degree of compliance with the rule of law and thus the requirement of lawfulness in Article 5. Statutory criteria would be subject to parliamentary debate and thus democratic control over change. They would also be more readily enforceable.

15.4.1.1 *Status and nature of guidance*

As it is, the statutory discretion is exercised on the basis of guidance and policy. Although guidance does not have statutory force, failure to have regard to established guidelines gives grounds for challenge in administrative law (*R v SSHD ex p Khan* [1985] 1 All ER 40). Non-compliance with the detention criteria has been held to be a reason to grant a declaration that continued refusal of bail was unlawful. *R v SSHD ex p Glowacka and Brezinski* CO/4237/95, CO/4251/95 was an application for leave to move for judicial review of decisions to detain. Owen J granted leave saying 'when there has been, on the face of affairs presented by the Applicant, clear breach, perhaps even an ignorance of the policy which has been declared by the Secretary of State, there is a public reason for granting leave'.

The challenge in *Saadi* was not to non-compliance with criteria, but to the application of a new criterion. The emphasis in the House of Lords' judgment is on the Home Office's entitlement to have a policy rather than the detainee's capacity to challenge failure to comply with that policy. In this context it says, *obiter*, 'the Home Office is entitled to adopt a policy in relation to procedures to be followed, a policy which may be changed from time to time as long as it does not conflict with relevant principles of law' ([2002] UKHL 41 para 11). Their Lordships did not elaborate on what these relevant principles are, but the principle against arbitrariness is undoubtedly one.

The Government is entitled to adopt a policy to deal with asylum claims, and so the existence of a criterion referring solely to asylum seekers is not unlawful or objectionable. The application of a more punitive criterion to asylum seekers is of much more doubtful legality (see, for instance, Art 31 Refugee Convention) but the House of Lords' judgment in *Saadi* does not suggest that they regarded the Oakington criteria as punitive.

Guidance to immigration officers on detention decisions is issued in the form of Immigration Directorate Instructions, formerly Immigration Service Instructions. Disclosure of these IDIs came rather later than in other areas. They now form part of the IND Operational Enforcement Manual, Chapter 38, and the heart of the instructions is a list of factors to take into account in making a detention decision (38.3). In recent revisions of Chapter 38, the discretionary nature of the decision to detain is far less prominent, the implications of Articles 5 and 8 are set out more fully and precisely (38.1.1.1 and 2). The advice

There are no statutory criteria for detention and each case must be considered on its individual merits. The following factors must be taken into account when considering the need for initial or continued detention. The list is not exhaustive neither is it in any order of priority has been replaced with:

In order to be lawful, immigration detention must be for one of the statutory purposes for which the power is given and must accord with the limitations implied by domestic and ECHR case law.

This represents a significant change in the formal presentation of the power to detain. An assessment of the effect on actual decision-making might require a repetition of a research project carried out by Weber and Gelsthorpe on decisions made in 1998 and 1999 (Cambridge Institute of Criminology 2000). Much depends on the immigration officer's perception of the width of their discretion. Weber and Gelsthorpe found that 38 per cent of officers thought they did not have a wide discretion, 28 per cent thought that they did have a wide discretion, 17 per cent thought it wide enough and 17 per cent thought there was scope within limits. As the researchers comment, within an organization decision-making rapidly becomes routinized so that decision-makers easily lose sight of the amount of discretion they actually (or theoretically) hold. Despite the width of the earlier instruction quoted above, local practices develop, and this may account in part for the very different detention figures between different ports of entry. For instance, 32 per cent of all arrivals were detained overnight at Manchester's Terminal 2 as compared with 1.5 per cent at London Heathrow's Terminal 1(Weber and Gelsthorpe 2000). This disparity is noted by Macdonald as grounds for concern about the arbitrariness of the UK's detention practice (2001:790).

15.4.1.2 *Content of guidance*

The current version of Chapter 38 begins with the three main approved policy reasons for detention, as set out in the 1998 White Paper, *Fairer, Faster and Firmer —
A Modern Approach to Immigration and Asylum*, (Cm 4018): to confirm identity or the basis of the claim, prevent absconding, or effect removal. It then adds the Oakington criteria, and the fast track at Harmondsworth effective from March 2003, discussed below. The introductory general points conclude with:

To be lawful, detention must not only be based on one of the statutory powers and accord with the limitations implied by domestic and Strasbourg case law but must also accord with this policy.

This sets out a framework for lawfulness that was lacking in previous forms of the guidance, and in a more detailed section headed 'Factors influencing a decision to detain' principles are set out embodying the presumption of liberty and the need for individual consideration of individual cases. Unfortunately, the revised set of particular factors which follows is very confusing. It says;

For detention:
- what is the likelihood of the person being removed and, if so, after what timescale?
- Is there any evidence of previous absconding from detention?
- Is there any evidence of previous failure to comply with conditions of temporary admission or bail?
- has the subject taken part in a 'determined attempt' to breach the immigration laws (examples given here include attempted or actual clandestine entry);
- is there a history of complying with requirements of immigration control (e.g. by applying for a visa, further leave etc);
- what are the person's ties with the UK? Are there close relatives (including dependants)

here? Does anyone rely on the person for support? Does the person have a settled address or employment?

- What are the individual's expectations about the outcome of the case? Are there factors such as an outstanding appeal, an application for judicial review or representations which afford incentive to keep in touch?

Against detention:
- 'is the subject under 18?';
- 'has the subject a history of torture?'
- 'has the subject a history of physical or mental ill health?'.

It seems strange to label an inquiry into family circumstances or the state of the case as being points *'for* detention'. The coherence of the guidelines at this point is lost. Earlier instructions also advised consideration of compassionate factors such as a medical condition of a dependent relative, and the duration of detention to date, particularly if it was as a result of a failure on the part of the Home Office to resolve the case. These considerations were removed in the 1997 instructions which seemed to represent a move towards a tougher policy on detention. Ultimately, the above enquiries must, if the person is to be detained, crystallise into one or more of six listed reasons for detention which are ticked on a standard form (OEM 38.6.3). These reasons, and the thirteen listed factors which are used to determine whether the reason exists, were referred to in *Amirthanathan* and *Nadarajah* as 'an important part of the published policy' (para 55).

In addition to the factors 'against detention' above, there are others also who are said (OEM 38.10) to be unsuitable for immigration detention:

- the elderly, particularly where supervision is required;
- pregnant women, unless there is the clear prospect of early removal and medical advice suggests that there is no question of the baby arriving before this;
- people with serious disabilities.

The revised guidelines require independent evidence of torture in order to deem a person unsuitable for detention (38.10). This presents enormous difficulties for someone who is detained on arrival, who has no opportunity to provide such evidence.

Those with a violent or serious criminal background are, according to 38.10.1, among the very few immigration detainees who may or should be held in prison. Others include 'where there is specific (verified) information that a person is a member of a terrorist group or has been engaged in terrorist activities'. There is no guidance on recognising a terrorist group, but imprisonment of a person on account of membership of a group not proscribed would be questionable. Conversely, use of the criterion of simple membership of a proscribed group in a person's country of origin, for instance the PKK or LTTE, would increase the risk to asylum seekers of detention in prison without necessarily implying any risk they might pose in the UK warranting more secure conditions.

The instructions include a policy statement that detention should be authorized only when there is no alternative. This accords with the presumption of liberty protected by Article 5 ECHR and with the position of the UN Working Group on Arbitrary Detention.

In the Cambridge research, which took place before the Oakington regime began, 4.4 per cent of immigration officers interviewed said that they detained someone to 'expedite a claim'. Although this did not appear as an allowable reason in the IDI, the process of taking into account the likelihood of early removal can easily spill over into detaining *in order to* effect an early removal. The Oakington and Harmondsworth regimes seem to have become just this. A boundary was set by the case of *Conka v Belgium* in which administrative convenience had been taken to an extreme and this was a breach of Article 5.1. The UNHCR Guidelines specifically exclude administrative convenience from being a legitimate basis for a detention decision.

The policy and guidance found in the Operational Enforcement Manual do not represent the total policy in relation to detention. Where statements and usual practices communicated to practitioners they are entitled to rely upon these. In the case of *R (on the application of Nadarajah)* [2002] EWHC 2595 Admin, Stanley Burnton J found that detention was unlawful because the claimant had been detained although the Home Office knew that his solicitor was about to apply for judicial review, and they had made it known that in these circumstances five days would be allowed for the application to be lodged. It had not communicated a further aspect of the policy, which was that it acts more quickly in the case of second or third applications, as this was. The Court of Appeal agreed with the High Court. The case was joined with *Amirthanathan* in the Court of Appeal because both concerned unlawfulness through a departure from published policy. The policy in issue in *Amirthanathan* was not to suspend detention where an intention was expressed to apply for appeal or review, but only when the application was actually made. The Court of Appeal thought that a policy not to regard notice of intention to appeal as reason for not detaining would not necessarily be arbitrary and irrational if published (para 63). The effect of such a policy is to detain someone for a few days until their solicitor commences proceedings, and then be obliged to release them because removal is not imminent. *Macdonald* says that 'the distress, disruption and cost of such a practice hardly seems sensible'. The current OEM contains this: 'An intimation that an appeal or proceedings may or will be brought would not, of itself, call into question the appropriateness of continued detention' (38.14). There is an echo of *Conka v Belgium* in the standard of fairness to be expected of the Home Office in these situations.

15.4.1.3 *Application of criteria*
The research carried out by Weber and Gelsthorpe into decisions to detain compared actual reasons given for detaining asylum seekers with the Home Office criteria. The research found that 'arriving clandestinely or without proper documentation have come to be considered as the norm' and do not necessarily incline the immigration officer to decide to detain, even though at the time these factors appeared in the standard reasons for detention. This 'normalization', they found, was due primarily to the large and increasing numbers of people immigration officers were dealing with, but also to their growing understanding that asylum seekers face sometimes insuperable barriers to travelling by legitimate means. On the other hand, the evidence of Amnesty International and the Medical Foundation (for the care of victims of torture) is that those who have suffered torture are still being detained (see, for instance, Dell and Salinsky 2000).

There is also evidence that other groups who should very rarely be detained, according to the instructions, are being detained in circumstances which are not justified as being exceptional. These detainees include pregnant women and the mentally ill. (See, for the effect of such detention on mothers and babies, 'A Crying Shame: Pregnant asylum-seekers and their babies in detention' (2002) and, for the impact on mental health, 'A Second Exile: the Mental Health Implications of Detention of Asylum Seekers in the United Kingdom' (1996) and 'Fit to be Detained? Challenging the detention of asylum seekers and migrants with health needs' (2005).)

Weber and Gelsthorpe's research uncovers a contradiction at the heart of detention policy. The instructions emphasize the likely length of detention and the prospects of removal as major factors in deciding whether to detain a person. In other words, if immigration officers think that it will be possible within a fairly short timescale to disprove a claim, this would weigh in favour of detention. Therefore immigration officers faced with a new asylum applicant need to form a judgment about whether and how soon that person is likely to be removed from the UK. However, immigration officers do not make decisions on asylum applications as these are made by the Home Office. In fact they are encouraged, in the interests of fair process, to distance themselves from making a judgment about the substance of claims. Immigration officers interviewed acknowledged that they had limited knowledge about the basis of a grant of refugee status, and that it could be difficult to predict the outcome of a case.

15.5 Detention of families

Established policy in relation to the detention of families was that it should generally be avoided, and should, if at all, take place 'only to be as close as possible to removal so as to ensure that it lasted no longer than a few days' (Cm 4018 para 12.5). There is evidently far less risk of a whole family absconding, even prior to removal. In October 2001, a policy change was announced that would allow detention of more families. A letter from the Home Office to various representatives organizations, on 25 October 2001 announced an increase of family detention provision. The detention criteria for families were to be brought more closely into line with the criteria for detention of people without children, although the Home Office also stressed that this would only be where it was considered necessary, particularly in view of the possible breach of Article 8 (see Cole 2003).

The reason for the policy change was obscure:

The decision to change the detention criteria in terms of families was indeed a Ministerial one. It was not derived from statistical evidence but rather was based on a recognition that in some cases families would give rise to similar concerns that might be encountered in relation to single adults and that accordingly there would be occasions when it would be appropriate to detain families for longer periods and at other points in the process than simply a few days immediately prior to removal. (Letter to BID, Immigration Services Detention Policy Unit 18th June 2002 quoted in Cole (2003:96))

There seems to have been a strong policy imperative to increase power to detain families. An opposition amendment to the Nationality, Immigration and Asylum Bill 2002 would have prohibited the detention of those under 18, but this was strongly and successfully resisted by the government, as was a further amendment which would have prohibited their detention for more than seven to ten days. The revised OEM maintains the position that families 'can be detained on the same footing as all other persons liable to detention' (38.9.4). There must be due regard for Article 8 rights. The increase in detention of children, with and without their families, has been provided for by an increase in the provision of family units, so that family places in 2005 reached 456. 286 family beds have been opened at Yarl's Wood, the detention centre previously destroyed by fire, and this has become the main centre for detention of families.

In December 2003 the Government began to publish statistics on children in detention in the quarterly figures. The figures show that at any one time there are scores of children in detention. Inevitably, figures only show those children who are detained with their families, as those whose age was disputed would be shown as adults. For families who contacted Bail for Immigration Detainees (BID), the average length of detention was 49 days (BID press release 9 November 2004).

15.5.1 Detention of unaccompanied children

The UNHCR Guidelines and the UN Working Group on Arbitrary Detention both state that children should not be detained.

The UN Convention on the Rights of the Child (CRC) Article 22 says:

States Parties shall take appropriate measures to ensure that a child who is seeking refugee status or who is considered a refugee in accordance with applicable international or domestic law procedures shall, whether unaccompanied or accompanied by his or her parents or by any other person, receive appropriate protection and humanitarian assistance in the enjoyment of applicable rights set forth in the present Convention and in other international human rights or humanitarian instrument to which the said States are Parties.

The UK has entered a reservation to the Convention in relation to immigration and asylum matters, and this has implications for a number of aspects of the UK's treatment of asylum-seeking children, including detention. These implications are fully discussed in an opinion given in November 2001 by Nicholas Blake and Sandhya Drew for Save the Children. They identify the effect of this reservation as, firstly, to exclude the principle that decisions concerning children should be taken in the best interests of the child as required by the Children Act 1989 and international human rights conventions including the CRC. Secondly, the reservation asserts 'the primacy of executive discretion in the implementation of a system of immigration control' (Blake and Drew para 6). These two effects combine, and the evidence seen by Blake and Drew brought them to the conclusion that the primary consideration in the treatment of unaccompanied asylum-seeking children was immigration status (para 34).

Blake and Drew also draw attention to the effect of the decision in *Saadi* on children (although the case had only reached the Court of Appeal, the outcome was the same). They say 'it is inconceivable that the best interests principle could contemplate even a short-term detention of child asylum seekers for administrative convenience whilst their protection claims are processed'. This supports their general argument that the reservation to the CRC should be withdrawn because Article 5 has not sufficiently protected children and further support from international human rights principles is necessary.

In *R v Secretary Of State For The Home Department ex p Howard League For Penal Reform & Department Of Health (Interested Party) (2002)* [2002] EWHC 2497 (Admin), Munby J found that Home Office guidance was wrong in law in so far as it stated that the Children Act 1989 did not apply to people under 18 in prison service establishments. The duties owed by a local authority to children under the Act continued to be owed while children were in Young Offenders institutions. This may have an application to children in immigration detention.

15.5.2 Age disputes

An unaccompanied person under 18:

(i) will not generally be detained or subject to fast track procedures;

(ii) if their asylum claim is refused will only be removed from the UK if adequate care and reception arrangements are in place in their country of return;

(iii) may benefit from being looked after by local authorities under the Children Act

(R (on the application of I and O) v SSHD [2005] EWHC 1025 (Admin) para 32)

Therefore procedures for resolving whether someone is over 18 are crucial. Furthermore, the age assessment process itself can compound the suffering of a traumatised young person; see *R (on the application of T) v London Borough of Enfield* [2004] EWHC 2297 (Admin) for a disturbing account of this. It should be borne in mind that the fact of dispute does not necessarily reflect on the asylum seeker's good faith, as the measuring, recording and concept of age may be treated differently in their country of origin from the UK. It is the UK's measure which is determinative.

The chief Home Office guidance on the measurement of age and conduct of age disputes is found in the Asylum Process Manual. Important features of the guidance are:

- A claimant *must* be given the benefit of the doubt with regards to their age unless their physical appearance *strongly* suggests that they are aged eighteen or over. (para 2)

- Social Services age assessments should be regarded as authoritative. (3.4)

- Paediatricians' reports *must* be considered. (3.3)

The Operational Enforcement Manual, on the other hand, gives contradictory guidance where age is disputed:

- Unaccompanied minors must only be detained in very exceptional circumstances and then only overnight, with appropriate care, whilst alternative arrangements for their care and safety are made. (38.9.3)

- 'where an applicant claims to be a minor but their appearance strongly suggests that they are over 18, the applicant should be treated as an adult'. (38.9.3)

- But 38.9.3.1 advises giving the applicant the benefit of the doubt,

no doubt leaving immigration officers in something of a quandary.

Binding judicial authority on a local authority's conduct of age disputes is to be found in *R (on the application of B) v Merton LBC* [2003] 4 All ER 280:

- A local authority must make its own decision and not simply adopt the stance of the Home Office.
- There must be adequate information to make this assessment.
- This will include asking the child about their education, family, activities and history.
- The assessment cannot normally be made on the basis of physical appearance alone except in an 'obvious' case.

By way of example, A arrived at Heathrow from Afghanistan. He did not know his precise age, but his mother had informed him he was 14 years old. The social services department assessed his age in a cursory fashion, without giving reasons, as adult. A was detained as an adult but eventually determined to be 16. In a consent order signed on 8 October 2004 the Secretary of State accepted that he had unlawfully detained A for 12 days, and accepted that he was liable in damages for that unlawful detention (*In the Matter of an application for judicial review between R (on the application of A) and SSHD* CO/2858/2004).

In *R(on the application of I and O) v SSHD* [2005] EWHC 1025 (Admin) the immigration officer relied on guidance in the APM in preference to the view of an experienced and senior paediatrician, who assessed the claimants as more likely than not to be 17 years old, and with a margin of error of plus or minus two years. Later assessments by social services departments confirmed that the claimants were likely to be 17. Owen J held that it was irrational for the Home Office to rely on the immigration officer's view in preference to that of Dr Michie, and irrational to place a greater weight on the view of social services assessments as a matter of policy (see above).

Despite the general agreement that detention is inappropriate for children, it appears to be happening on a significant scale. A report for Save the Children, based on thirty-two case studies of children detained either with their parents or on their own where age was disputed, found that the length of detention varied from 7 to 268 days, with half detained for more than 28 days (Crawley and Lester 2005). The Chief Inspector of Prisons was critical of the detention of children in Tinsley House and Dungavel removal centres (HMIP 2005).

15.5.3 Detention of children and families and Article 8

The detention of children is clearly an interference with private and/or family life. In *R (Konan) v SSHD* [2004] EWHC 22 Admin the six-month detention of a mother and her two-year-old daughter was unlawful. The detention was in breach of policy and of common law rules as the removal could not be effected because judicial review of it was pending. Detention was also a *prima facie* breach of Article 8. The court held that if and to the extent that proportionality applied, the Secretary of State's policy should be taken as representing his view of what is proportionate.

The Ay family, who were much in the news in the UK because the mother and four children were detained in one room in Dungavel removal centre for over a year, were granted temporary humanitarian leave in Germany, because of the trauma experienced by the children in British detention (The Observer 7 November 2004).

15.6 **Alternative to detention — temporary admission**

The law on detention cannot be fully understood without appreciating that wher-ever there is a power to detain there is also power to grant temporary admission (Immigration Act 1971 Sch 2 para 21 and Nationality, Immigration and Asylum Act 2002 s 62(3)). This is the usual status for people whose applications for entry or asylum claims have not been determined, and for anyone else who may be subject to detention as an illegal entrant, recalling that detention should only be used as a last resort.

Temporary admission is granted for a fixed period which may be renewed. The person admitted must report back to the Home Office or immigration service at the expiry of the period. At this point there may be a risk of detention, and there is no right of appeal against a refusal to extend temporary admission.

Temporary admission may be subject to residence or employment restrictions and requirements to report to the police or an immigration officer (1971 Act Sch 2 para 21(2)). Residence restrictions may include the requirement to reside in accommodation provided under Immigration and Asylum Act 1999 s 4 or National-ity, Immigration and Asylum Act 2002 s 26. Employment restrictions are now routinely imposed on asylum seekers. The practice whereby this restriction was lifted after six months has been discontinued. The restrictions may be varied, and the power to detain continues throughout the period of temporary admission. However if a person is re-detained, although a breach of conditions is not specific-ally required by the schedule, the lack of such reasons would give rise to a finding of arbitrariness (see Macdonald 2001:780) unless, as is common, it is to carry out removal.

This is a curious kind of limbo status. As we have seen, in the context of European law the ECJ were not prepared to regard someone on temporary admission as not having entered (C–357/98 *R v SSHD ex p Yiadom* [2003] ECR I–9265). She had been present in the UK for months and this was regarded as unreal. We have also seen that time spent on temporary admission may count towards a period of residence for nationality (see chapter 2). However, there are welfare support implications and a person temporarily admitted has no appeal rights.

References to a person who is liable to be detained always include a person on temporary admission. Some implications of this are discussed below.

15.7 **Jurisdiction to detain pending removal or deportation**

This jurisdiction raises some crucial questions; in particular whether detention is lawful when there are obstacles in the way of removal. 1971 Act Sch 2 para 16 permits detention when there are reasonable grounds for suspecting that a person may be removed. However, what if the person may be removable at some point, but at present is not?

The nature of an asylum claim is that it would be contrary to the UK's obligations under the Refugee Convention to return the person to a country where their life or freedom would be threatened (Immigration and Asylum Appeals Act 1993 s 1 and

Refugee Convention Article 33). It is in breach of the principle of non-refoulement to remove an asylum seeker from the UK until their claim has been determined, and this is confirmed in Nationality, Immigration and Asylum Act 2002 s 77, which prevent removal while an asylum claim is pending. As we have seen in chapter 12, an exception is made to this in safe third country cases, where asylum seekers are removed before their claim is determined.

Where an asylum seeker who was not detained initially is detained following a decision to remove them but before their claim is finally determined, it could be argued that as the removal cannot be implemented, detention on this basis is unlawful. An argument to this effect was made in the case of *Samateh* [1996] Imm AR 1 in the context of deportation. However, the Court of Appeal found that the power to deport subsists even when it cannot be implemented, and so detention on this basis was still lawful. The 2002 Act makes it clear that it is only the removal itself which cannot happen while the claim is pending. Removal directions can be issued, a deportation order can be made, and other preparatory steps taken (s 77).

In a Privy Council case, *Tan Te Lam and others v Superintendent of Tai A Chau Detention Centre and others* [1996] 4 All ER 256), the applicants were among those who fled from Vietnam to Hong Kong in the late 1970s, the 1980s and early 1990s. They were of Chinese ethnic origin, and under the agreed repatriation arrangements it was the policy of the Vietnam Government not to accept repatriation of non-Vietnam nationals. Therefore, although they were detained pending removal under the Immigration Ordinance of Hong Kong, as non-Vietnamese nationals they would not be removable. The Privy Council said that this was not an aspect of the discretion to detain, it went to the question of jurisdiction to detain in the first place (at 266j). There was no jurisdiction to detain 'pending removal' people whom there was no power to remove. This must be distinguished from the position in *Samateh*, where there was jurisdiction to remove, even though it could not at present be exercised.

Where there is jurisdiction to remove, but not the physical ability to do, questions arise about how long this detention can go on, and whether a person may remain on temporary admission, if they cannot be removed. Section 67(2) 2002 Act provides that where a provision refers to a person who is liable to detention, it shall be taken to refer to a person who for purely practical reasons or because of international legal obligations cannot currently be removed from the UK. Most unusually, the section is retrospective (s 67(3)).

This rather obscure section has important effects which were considered in *R v SSHD ex p Khadir (Appellant)* [2005] UKHL 39 and [2003] EWCA Civ 475. Mr Khadir's asylum application had been refused but he could not be returned to the Kurdish Autonomous Area of Iraq as there were no direct flights and any travel via Baghdad would not be safe. The British Government had been in negotiation with Turkey over the return of Iraqi Kurds, but they were not enthusiastic to permit travel of Kurdish people through their territory, and discussions had stalled. Usual practice at that time would have been to grant exceptional leave to remain on the basis that return was not safe or possible. The Home Office's initial refusal to do so was quashed in the High Court. Mr Khadir was not in reality subject to removal and therefore it was not lawful to detain him. If there was no basis for detention there was no basis for temporary admission. His status should change to ELR.

The government was in the process of drafting the 2002 Bill and took the opportunity of inserting s 67(2) and (3) in order to remove the obligation to grant ELR to Mr Khadir and people in a similar situation (*R (on the application of Khadir) v SSHD* [2003] EWCA Civ 475 para 90). The unambiguous retrospectivity meant that although the Court of Appeal held that Crane J's decision in the High Court was correct when it was taken, it must be overturned. Mr Khadir must be treated as liable to detention even though he could not be removed, and thus only eligible for temporary admission, not ELR. The Court of Appeal acknowledged that there was an argument as to whether this retrospective application to Mr Khadir might breach Article 6 ECHR, but this could not be considered as, following *Maaouia v France* (2001) 33 EHRR 42 immigration matters were outside Article 6 (see chapter 3). The House of Lords upheld the effect of the Court of Appeal's judgment, though for different reasons. Lord Brown of Eaton-under-Heywood, giving the only reasoned judgment, found that the '*Hardial Singh* line of cases' (see below) referred to the exercise of the power to detain and not to its existence. In other words, length of detention affects the exercise of the discretion to detain, which becomes unreasonable if it goes on too long. It does not affect the power to detain. He regards *Tan Te Lam* as an exception in this respect 'because there was simply no possibility of the Vietnamese government accepting the applicants' repatriation' (para 33). The result was that their Lordships found that Crane J at first instance had been wrong to hold that Mr Khadir was not liable to detention, and thus not only the application of s.67 but also its existence was unnecessary. Lord Brown's rather stark conclusion was that ' "pending" in paragraph 16 means no more than "until" '(para 32).

Lord Brown raised a question, 'how the fact that someone has been temporarily admitted rather than detained can be said to lengthen the period properly to be regarded as "pending . . . his removal" ' (para 31). Ironically, this is in a sense one effect of this judgment, as it will be possible for people to be maintained for even longer periods in the limbo state of temporary admission, yet without the Home Office being required to concede that removal is unrealistic, and grant a more beneficial status. The periods spent in this way on temporary admission can be far longer than any reasonable (and thus lawful) length of actual detention. On release from such excessive detention, however, removal would still be possible in law, and this appears to be Lord Brown's point. Length of time was not intended to displace the removal. The result dovetails with the new status of discretionary leave, the conditions for which are more restrictive than ELR, and do not include 'likely difficulty in enforcing departure from the UK' (*Khadir* CA para 48). Compatibility with Article 5 was not considered by the court, as physical liberty was not in issue.

15.8 **Length of detention**

As mentioned at the start of this chapter, one of the concerns of the UN Working Group on Arbitrary Detention is that in the UK there is no fixed statutory limit on the length of time a person can be detained. In July 1997 a research report considered treatment of asylum seekers in twelve countries including the UK. It found 'the UK detains more people, for longer periods, with less judicial supervision than any other country we considered.' Also 'in almost all other countries detention is time limited and subject to judicial control' (1997:63).

Clearly, the combination of no time limit and limited judicial control is a disturbing one from a human rights point of view. However, this does not mean there is no control at all of how long a person is detained.

If the purpose for which detention is authorized ceases to apply, then the detention is no longer authorized. This was the case in *R v Special Adjudicator and SSHD ex p B* [1998] INLR 315 in which the Secretary of State was initially in doubt as to the applicant's true identity, and this was one of the reasons for detention. However, after he had provided convincing proof of this his detention became unlawful.

There is also an implied limitation of a reasonable time to achieve the purpose sought by the detention, as was held in *R v Governor of Durham Prison ex p Hardial Singh* [1983] Imm AR 198, although as mentioned in relation to *Chahal v UK*, a substantial period of time may still be lawful if this is necessary to complete legal proceedings.

The courts are willing to judge whether detention continues to be necessary and regard the prospective length of detention as a factor in the lawfulness of the original detention decision. In *Hardial Singh* Woolf J said 'if there is a situation where it is apparent to the Secretary of State that he is not going to be able to operate the machinery provided in the Act for removing persons who are intended to be deported within a reasonable period, it seems to me that it would be wrong for the Secretary of State to exercise his power of detention' (at 200). In that case Woolf J directed the applicant's release, finding that 'the Home Office have not taken the action they should have taken and nor have they taken that action sufficiently promptly' (at 202). Mr Singh had been in detention for five months and had attempted to take his own life. The Court similarly intervened in the case of *Wafsi Suleman Mahmod* [1995] Imm AR 311 in which Laws J held that ten months was too long to try to persuade Germany to take back a man granted asylum in Germany who had been convicted of a criminal offence whilst on a visit to the UK. The Home Office activity during the ten months was described as 'nothing but fruitless negotiations.'

In *Tan Te Lam*, in which the applicants had been in detention for 44 months, Lord Browne-Wilkinson summarized the law as follows:

First, the power can only be exercised during the period necessary, in all the circumstances of the particular case, to effect removal. Secondly, if it becomes clear that removal is not going to be possible within a reasonable time, further detention is not authorised. Thirdly, the person seeking to exercise the power of detention must take all reasonable steps within his power to ensure the removal within a reasonable time.

The Court of Appeal applied these principles in *R (on the application of I) v SSHD* [2002] EWCA Civ 888. Although lengthy detention of itself is not a reason for release, the length of time a person has already been in detention was a factor referred to in earlier internal instructions as being relevant to whether detention should be continued, and this was found to be so by the Court of Appeal. The appellant was an Afghani asylum seeker who had been found guilty of a criminal offence. Like the applicants in *Sedrati, Buitrago-Lopez and Anaghatu*, Mr I was detained under Sch 3 para 2 of the 1971 Act after the end of his criminal sentence and pending deportation. However, in his case removal was not practically possible as there were no flights from the UK to Afghanistan. Bearing some similarity to *Mahmod*, the Home Office was engaged in activity which might still have resulted in his removal in that they were engaged in negotiations with countries neighbouring Afghanistan for the return of Afghani asylum seekers whose claims had failed. The *Hardial Singh* point, the second in Lord Browne-Wilkinsons's formulation in *Tan Te Lam*, was the crucial one for Simon Brown LJ in the Court of Appeal. Was it going to be possible to remove Mr I within a reasonable period of time, bearing in mind the time he had already spent in detention? Simon Brown LJ held that the Home Office's 'hope' that negotiations with neighbouring countries would bear fruit was not sufficient, given the time that Mr I had already spent in detention. By the time the case came before the Court of Appeal he had been in administrative detention (i.e., after the end of his criminal sentence) for sixteen months. He should therefore be released. Dyson LJ thought that the time had already spent in detention was enough to justify release.

Section 67(2) of the Nationality, Immigration and Asylum Act 2002 does not affect these decisions. Section 67(2) does not *give* jurisdiction to detain, but where such jurisdiction exists it entails that practical difficulties in the way of removal will not prevent a person from being regarded as subject to detention. In a case where detention has gone on too long, detention must cease. The question arises though whether the condition of being *subject to* detention but not actually detained (like Mr Khadir) can also go on too long, and whether, if detention ceases because it has gone on too long, liability to detention also ceases. The House of Lords' judgment in *Khadir* would suggest not. Their Lordships' interpretation of the 'the *Hardial Singh* line of cases', contrary to the understanding of Macdonald (2005:1139) is that they do not affect jurisdiction to detain but only its exercise. The effect of this seems to be that temporary admission can go on for as long as it takes to arrange a removal, as long as there is 'some prospect of achieving this'. This represents a fairly low test for the Secretary of State. Moreover, if someone is actually detained for an unreasonable period, they can expect to be released from detention, but not from liability for detention. In October 2005 the Minister for Immigration, Asylum and Nationality indicated that twenty-one Iraqis would be released from detention, as it was not currently possible to arrange their return to the Kurdish Autonomous Area. Their release however is on bail, confirming the effect of *Khadir* and s 67(2).

The UK is a party to the International Covenant on Civil and Political Rights, Article 9.1 of which provides that 'no one shall be subjected to arbitrary arrest or detention'. The UK has not accepted the right of individual petition for breaches of the Covenant. However, Australia has done so, and in the case of *A v Australia* (1997) 4 BHRC 210 was found to be in breach because of a lengthy detention. The UN Human Rights Committee said, 'detention should not continue beyond the period for which the State can provide justification'.

15.9 **Judicial supervision**

The question of judicial safeguards is central to issues about the lawfulness of detention. There must a possibility of bringing such arguments before the court. As mentioned earlier, the UN Working Party on Arbitrary Detention regarded the lack of judicial oversight as a matter of concern. There are some mechanisms for review of detention, however the major criticism is that none is automatic.

15.9.1 **Right to reasons for detention**

Notice of reasons for detention may help the detainee to challenge the decision. Outside the Human Rights Act there is no right in primary legislation to reasons for detention. Article 5.2 provides that a detained person 'shall be informed promptly, in a language which he understands, of the reasons for his arrest'. As mentioned above, the UNHCR Guidelines on Applicable Criteria and Standards relating to the Detention of Asylum Seekers carries similar advice. The Home Office produces a checklist of reasons, reflecting the criteria in the OEM. This is given by immigration officers to detainees, with boxes ticked to show which standard reasons for detention apply in their case.

These standard forms were first introduced during the period of the Cambridge research project referred to above, and were discussed with immigration officers during the research. There were doubts about whether they reflected all the reasons that were actually used. As the research had already shown that reasons outside the criteria were being employed, this may suggest that the form was an attempt to ensure that only sanctioned reasons were actually used. However, there was also confusion about whether the form was additional to oral reasons or replaced them, and some thought it more appropriate to write a paragraph on the actual case. There is scope then for doubting whether the real reasons are actually disclosed by the checklist even though in most cases these standard reasons are now routinely given. The practice of using other reasons was disclosed in *Saadi* in the High Court in which it was revealed that the applicants had not been given the actual reason for detention, namely that the claim could be processed quickly (now on the standard form). In the House of Lords Lord Slynn observed that this failure of reasons did not invalidate the detention or make it unlawful (para 48). On the other hand, in *R (on the application of Faulkner) v SSHD* 1/11/2005 the High Court granted a declaration that detention was unlawful when the claimant had not been informed of the reasons for it namely, that he posed a risk of absconding or a risk to the public.

At least in secondary legislation there is an obligation to give reasons on initial detention, and monthly thereafter (Detention Centre Rules 2001, SI 2001/238 r 9).

15.9.2 **Bail**

A crucial safeguard for anyone in detention is the possibility of applying for bail. A bail application may, but need not, address the question of the lawfulness of detention. There may be jurisdiction to detain but in a bail application the argument is principally that the discretion to detain should not continue to be exercised in the particular case; the applicant should therefore be released. The question of the lawfulness of detention may be closely intertwined with such an argument, but it is not necessary to attack the jurisdiction in order to make a bail application.

Immigration and asylum detainees have a right to apply for bail, but unlike the position in criminal cases there is no automatic bail hearing. The Immigration and Asylum Act 1999 contained a scheme for a system of automatic bail hearings, but this was never implemented and was repealed by s 68(6) of the 2002 Act. The reason given for this repeal was that the appellate authorities (i.e., tribunals and adjudicators) would be unable to cope with the volume of work (Standing Committee E col 256). However, this is puzzling as the bail hearings were to have taken place before magistrates (s 44 of the 1999 Act 'to the court'). There is no statutory presumption of a right to bail, but the Chief Adjudicator's Guidance notes to adjudicators confirm that there is a common law presumption. This means that the burden of proof to show that bail should not be granted rests on the Secretary of State. The standard of proof is the balance of probabilities.

15.9.2.1 *Eligibility to apply for bail*

The right to apply for bail is found in Immigration Act 1971 Sch 2 paras 22 and 29 and Immigration and Asylum Act 1999 s 54.

The exception is that those detained pending examination under 16(1) do not have a right to apply for bail until they have been in the UK for seven days (paragraph 22 (1B)).

15.9.2.2 *Power to grant bail*

An immigration officer of ordinary rank does not have power to grant bail. Under paras 22, 29, and 34 bail may be granted by a chief immigration officer or an immigration judge. However, the Nationality, Immigration and Asylum Act 2002 s 68 takes away the power of the chief immigration officer to grant bail to anyone who has been detained for more than eight days, and gives it to the Secretary of State. This changes the previous position in which anyone who could detain could also release on bail. Immigration judges retain the power to grant bail, however there may be difficulties in obtaining legal aid to be represented before them.

15.9.2.3 *Conditions for the grant of bail*

Bail may be granted on condition that the person bailed reports at a specified time and place, usually a police station or the immigration officer. Bail will be made subject to recognizances. These are pledges of money which will be forfeited if the person does not report to bail. Under Immigration Act 1971 Sch 2 para 22(1A) the applicant for bail must provide their own recognizance. This may be for a nominal sum such as £10 where a person has no assets, as may often be the case particularly if they are an asylum seeker. In addition, if it appears necessary to ensure that the person will answer to bail, further recognizances may be taken from people who are willing to stand as surety for a fixed sum proportionate to their means. The Chief Adjudicator's guidelines for adjudicators make it clear that sureties are not essential, and should not be routinely required. Adjudicators are reminded that 'asylum seekers rarely have relatives or friends in the UK who can act as sureties'. Sureties may be required 'if that will have the consequence that a person who might not otherwise be granted his liberty will be granted it' (*R v SSHD ex p Brezinski and Glowacka* CO 4251/1995 & CO 4237/1995, unreported, 19 July 1996). Conditions may be fixed such as that the bailee resides in a certain place, and other conditions may be imposed, but only if they are strictly necessary. The Secretary of State may pay for travelling expenses incurred in meeting reporting restrictions or bail conditions (2002 Act s 69).

15.9.3 *Habeas corpus*

The lawfulness of detention may be challenged by the prerogative writ of *habeas corpus*. This is an ancient remedy which has been regarded as constitutionally important as it is a means whereby a court can inquire into the reasons for any detention and order immediate release. The basis of the jurisdiction is 'a detention or imprisonment which is incapable of legal justification' (*Halsbury's Laws* vol. 1(1), para 208). Although an alien has as much right as a subject to apply for *habeas corpus* (see *Khawaja v SSHD* [1984] AC 74 at 111: 'He who is subject to English law is entitled to its protection') it is of little use in challenging immigration detention. The reason for this is there is nearly always a jurisdiction to detain, i.e., the basic statutory precondition is in existence. The question is usually how that juris- diction has been exercised. This is a matter for judicial review, not *habeas corpus*. The amendment brought in by Immigration and Asylum Act 1999 s 140(1), permit- ting detention where there is a reasonable suspicion that directions for removal may be given means that it is even more unlikely that jurisdiction can be questioned.

Where there is a question of the jurisdiction to detain this can be argued in both judicial review and *habeas corpus* proceedings and where appropriate both sets of proceedings can be pursued simultaneously. The relationship between the two was considered by the Court of Appeal in *R v SSHD ex p Sheikh* [2001] Imm AR 219 who pointed out that *habeas corpus* proceedings may be brought at any time that an applicant is detained, and are not subject to the strict time limits applicable in judicial review. Furthermore, *habeas corpus* is a writ of right, whereas permission must be sought for judicial review. Where the challenge is really to the underlying immigration decision, e.g., the refusal of leave to enter, then judicial review is the appropriate procedure, not habeas corpus (*R v SSHD ex p Muboyayi* [1991] 4 All ER 72). Finally, Macdonald's view on the 1999 Act amendment was that 'this change sounds the death-knell for habeas corpus in removal cases, save where there is no reasonable suspicion (i.e., *mala fides* is alleged) or where detention is excessively lengthy (the *Hardial Singh* situation)' (2001:762).

15.9.4 **Other legal routes to challenge detention**

A decision to detain is not a decision relating to entitlement to enter or remain the UK, and is not appealable under Nationality, Immigration and Asylum Act 2002 s 82. The most common route to challenge the legality of detention has been judicial review. However, now both the benefits and limitations of the Human Rights Act and the increased use of administrative detention have given impetus for the use of private actions. In these damages can be claimed on a broader basis and there is greater scope for disclosure of evidence and cross-examination. Two important cases in this developing area will be discussed here.

Youssef v Home Office [2004] EWHC 1884 QB was an action for false imprisonment by reason of the length of the detention and the unrealistic prospects of removal. Reading the judgment gives a rare insight into negotiations conducted between the UK and a foreign government. The claimant was a leading member of Egyptian Islamic Jihad, which mounted high profile terrorist attacks. He claimed asylum and was excluded under Article 1F, but faced likely torture on return. For comment on the political process see, e.g., The Guardian 16 November 2004.

Three months before the refusal decision in December 1998, Mr Youssef had been detained under Special Immigration Appeals Commission Act 1997 s 3(2)(a), for reasons of national security. Even though the case predated the Human Rights Act, his removal to Egypt would have been a breach of Article 3, following *Chahal v UK* (1997) 23 EHRR 413, as there was a reasonable likelihood of torture or other inhuman or degrading treatment on his return. The UK Government sought assurances from the Egyptian Government of fair treatment for Mr Youssef but these were not forthcoming. A key issue in the case was whether there was any realistic prospect of obtaining such assurances, so as to justify Mr Youssef's continuing detention until 9 July 1999, when negotiations were accepted to have failed and Mr Youssef was released.

Mr Youssef was initially detained pursuant to statutory authority. Detention remained lawful while it was reasonable for the UK to be negotiating with the Egyptian Government, but would cease to be so, following *R v Governor of Durham Prison ex p Hardial Singh* [1984] 1WLR 704, when there was no realistic prospect of his being removed. The decision on this was for the Secretary of State. He argued that the standard by which the reasonableness of his view should be judged was the *Wednesbury* standard, but the court disagreed. 'Where the liberty of the subject is concerned the court ought to be the primary decision-maker as to the reasonableness of the executive's actions, unless there are compelling reasons to the contrary . . .' although '[T]he court . . . should make allowances for the way that government functions and be slow to second guess the executive's assessment of diplomatic negotiations' (paras 62–63). The relationship between this case and *Khadir* is a field ripe for exploration.

In *ID and others v Home Office, BID & ILPA intervening* [2005] EWCA Civ 38 the Court of Appeal reinstated particulars of claim which had been struck out in the lower court, allowing the appellants to proceed with an application for false imprisonment. A family on arrival in the UK had been detained in Oakington for a week. Following *Saadi* they could not succeed in any action challenging that detention. However, their claim was then refused, and they were moved to Yarl's Wood detention centre. The fire there started the night that they arrived. They lost their possessions, and were lucky to escape with their lives as they had been locked in and the guards forgot to let them out. In a state of shock, they were then transferred to Harmondsworth. The Court of Appeal held that their action in tort concerning the latter two periods of detention should be heard by the courts. The Home Office had argued that immigration officers were immune from suit in making decisions pursuant to statute. The Court of Appeal (Brooke LJ giving the only reasoned judgment) considered the limited immunities from suit still available in the case of decisions to detain, and concluded that there was no such immunity for immigration officers.

The Home Office relied also on an argument that 'the power of a state to control immigration ... extends beyond the simple control of entry to encompass the treatment of aliens and the control of their activities while they are present or resident in the State (para 71). This amounted to an attempt to argue that foreign nationals are not subject to the same law as nationals and do not have full redress in the courts. This argument was dealt with in *Khawaja* [1984] AC 74 and so the Court of Appeal held in *ID*. The Court also rejected an argument that the claim was an abuse of process: 'there is nothing in the slightest bit peculiar about an individual bringing a private law claim for damages against an executive official who has abused his private rights' (para 57).

ID is an important decision. Although for the particular claimants it is only the beginning of the road as they have yet to have their action heard, the Court's approach on the principles re-opens the way to redress for unlawfully detained claimants, which seemed to be closing down.

15.10 Detention and accommodation

The Government's early plans to provide large accommodation centres for asylum seekers pursuant to their power in Immigration and Asylum Act 1999 s 4 have run aground on planning objections and local opposition.

A fall in asylum claims is also cited as a reason for not pressing ahead (HC 9 June 2005 WA col 653).

The conceptual and practical blurring between detention and accommodation is likely to manifest in new and smaller centres designed to house asylum seekers from claim to removal. For an understanding of accommodation as a form of support for asylum seekers, reference should be made to reading listed below.

15.11 Indefinite detention

Detention of foreign nationals outside the rule of law has become a feature of Western governments' conduct of the 'war against terrorism'. Whether this practice, being now subject to challenge, is transient or spreading is at present unknown. Two well-known examples are the US' maintenance of detention at Guantanamo Bay in Cuba, and the UK's detention of suspected international terrorists without trial in Belmarsh. As has already been discussed in chapter 1, Anti-terrorism Crime and Security Act 2001 Part IV was a misuse of immigration powers.

The Anti-terrorism, Crime and Security Act 2001 was the UK Parliament's legislative response to the attack on the World Trade Centre on 11 September of that year. The Government claimed that intelligence information suggested that there were people operating within the UK who had international terrorist connections, but against whom there was insufficient evidence to bring a prosecution. Against British nationals operating in such a way there would be no sanction. However, foreign nationals could be deported on the grounds that their deportation was conducive to the public good (see *Rehman v SSHD* [2001] 3 WLR 877 for a case in point). Deportation, however, would not be possible if a person faced torture or inhuman or degrading treatment or punishment contrary to Article 3 EHCR (*Chahal v UK* (1996) 23 EHRR 413). The Government's proposal, enacted in the 2001 Act, was indefinite detention, i.e., detention under Sch 2 or 3 pending a removal or deportation that could not take place.

A person could be detained under s 23 if the Secretary of State reasonably believed their presence in the UK to be a risk to national security and reasonably suspected that person of international terrorist activities or connections.

The provision clearly breached Article 5.1 as detention was not pending deportation or extradition or a criminal trial. Accordingly, the UK Government derogated from Article 5 to the extent that it would be breached by this Act (Human Rights Act 1998 (Designated Derogation) Order 2001). This meant that Article 5 was ineffective to the extent that it conflicted with 2001 Act provisions, both for the purposes of action in Strasbourg (Art 15 ECHR) and under the Human Rights Act (HRA s 1(2)). The validity of the derogation was challenged by the first twelve people to be detained under s 23. The challenge initially came before the Special Immigration Appeals Commission (SIAC) who granted a declaration under Human Rights Act 1998 s 4 that the detention power was incompatible with Article 14 ECHR.

Article 15 only allows a government to derogate from a Convention right in times of war or 'other public emergency threatening the life of the nation'. This must be 'to the extent strictly required by the exigencies of the situation' (Art 15). SIAC found that a derogation in relation only to foreign nationals could not be strictly required. There was evidence that the threat came from British nationals as well as foreign nationals. If the derogation was required to protect the public, then what was strictly required was a derogation to permit the detention of all those who presented a threat, not just those who did not have British nationality. The derogation therefore was not only not strictly required, it was discriminatory and a breach of Article 14.

The Court of Appeal disagreed and overturned SIAC's declaration (*A, X, Y, and others v SSHD* [2002] EWCA Civ 1502). Its approach follows in the footsteps of the House of Lords in the national security case of *Rehman* as it they considered that in measures concerning 'a public emergency threatening the life of the nation' . . . 'the same general approach' was appropriate, namely one of deference to the Home Secretary who is in a special position to be able to assess the evidence and take the decision. It was therefore prepared to accept the Home Secretary's assertion that only the detention of non-nationals was necessary.

The UK's continued detention of eleven men under these powers attracted criticism from the committee of Privy Counsellors (the Newton Committee) convened to review the legislation, the Parliamentary Joint Committee on Human Rights (in its Fifth, Sixth and Eighth Reports of 2003–04), The UN Human Rights Committee, the European Commissioner on Human Rights (Opinion 1/2002, August 2002), and many NGOs and other commentators.

The House of Lords overturned the Court of Appeal's decision in a momentous judgment (*A v SSHD* [2004] UKHL 56). Nine judges sat in the Lords, demonstrating the constitutional importance of the issue. They reiterated the fundamental constitutional importance of the right to liberty, and that the law applies equally to all.

They noted that SIAC had found as fact that 'there are many British nationals already identified — mostly in detention abroad — who fall within the definition of suspected international terrorists, and . . . there are others at liberty in the UK who could similarly be defined' (para 32). Also, 'allowing a suspected international terrorist to leave our shores and depart to another country, perhaps a country as close as France, there to pursue his criminal designs, is hard to reconcile with a belief in his capacity to inflict serious injury to the people and interests of this country' (para 33). These points had been made by the European Commissioner for Human Rights and by the Newton Committee, who recommended the repeal of these powers and their replacement with measures 'to deal with all terrorism, whatever its origin or the nationality of its suspected perpetrators'. The lack of rational connection to the aim to be achieved made the measures both disproportionate and discriminatory.

The derogation was not, they thought, limited to what was strictly required by the exigencies of the situation. Lord Bingham of Cornhill referred to the very strict bail conditions upon which one detainee had been released. These were less draconian than detention, but presumably considered sufficient. As the derogation was discriminatory and so in breach of Article 14, it was also in breach of Article 26 ICCPR and thus not consistent with the UK's other international obligations, as required by Article 15.

Although doubts were expressed by others of their Lordships, Lord Hoffmann alone found that there was no threat to the life of the nation warranting derogation under Article 15. The life of the nation should not be equated with individual human lives, but rather with the values and practices that constitute the collective life. 'Terrorist violence, serious as it is, does not threaten our institutions of government or our existence as a civil community', he said, and most memorably: 'The real threat to the life of the nation, in the sense of a people living in accordance with its traditional laws and political values, comes not from terrorism but from laws such as these' (paras 96 and 97).

The majority found that s 23 was disproportionate and thus in breach of Article 15, and discriminatory and thus in breach of Article 14. They issued a quashing order in relation to the derogation order and a declaration of incompatibility in relation to s 23. Only Lord Walker of Gestingthorpe dissented.

Baroness Hale of Richmond referred in her judgment to the use of torture abroad in obtaining evidence against the appellants which founded these detentions. This was not for consideration in these appeals as that related to the challenge of the detention of the individuals rather than the legality of the derogation and the statute. She rightly predicted, however, that this issue might come before their Lordships in time (*A v SSHD* [2005] UKHL 71).

The Government's response to the House of Lords' judgment has already been discussed in chapter 1. The detainees' bail conditions were swiftly transposed into control orders under the 2005 Act. A special provision exempted them from judicial oversight (PTA 2005 s 3(1)(c)).

This section would not be complete without a reference to *The Queen on the application of Abbassi v Secretary of State for Foreign and Commonwealth Affairs* [2003] UKHRR 76, a challenge to the Foreign Secretary's exercise of prerogative in interceding for the British prisoners held in the American military base in Guantanamo Bay, Cuba. The case in essence concerns the impotence of the British Government to intervene in the affairs of another nation and of the citizen to challenge that. However it proceeded on the accepted basis that the detainees had access to no legal review of their detention, that detention was indefinite and that they had no access to legal advice or representation. Within the confines of the legal principles available to it, the Court of Appeal could only reiterate the primacy of liberty, and that every detention is a *prima facie* breach of law (para 60). They were powerless to intervene as the matter was in the political, not the legal sphere. As discussed in chapter 1, the impasse resulted in a break with constitutional convention when Lord Steyn spoke in a non-judicial setting to criticize the detentions (The Independent 26 November 2003).

15.12 Conclusion

We end this chapter as we began, *Liversidge v Anderson* dealing with wartime internment, and *A v SSHD* dealing with internment in a different kind of public emergency. In *Liversidge v Anderson*, although the House of Lords found for executive, the case is remembered more for Lord Atkin's dissent than it is for its ratio. As *A v SSHD* takes its place in legal history it will be interesting to see whether the majority or the dissent leaves a stronger print on history. The 8:1 decision that the detentions were unlawful has given the case a claim to be 'one of the most constitutionally significant ever decided by the House of Lords' (MLR Belmarsh special issue p. 654). Lord Bingham's leading judgment carefully marshalls international law to reach the majority conclusion, and this is important not only for the outcome but also because it shows that the UK is subject to international restraints upon government. The minority view which has had impact though is not Lord Walker's dissent on the outcome but Lord Hoffmann's on the emergency threatening the life of the nation. To reach this view he invokes the common law, not human rights, and his ringing statement 'the real threat to the life of the nation . . .' has been more quoted than the pages of closely reasoned judgment which subject to the UK to international human rights law. The subject matter is not accidental. Reviewing *Saadi, Khadir* and judgments of the lower courts we may detect the persistence, appearing in many forms, of resort to a power which is resistant to restraint. This chapter has shown that although *prima facie* unlawful, detention is on the increase, and even statutorily enshrined human rights can be defeated by a judicial assertion of the State's power to control aliens. The administrative power to detain pending determination of a claim has grown far beyond its original use for visitors overnight, and become the foundation for a whole new system of detention. Perhaps what this chapter really illustrates, although indirectly, is that the political context of the law is sometimes the most influential factor.

QUESTIONS

1 Does the House of Lord judgment in the case of *Saadi* recognize the right in Article 14 UDHR to claim asylum?

2 Is it appropriate that the decision to detain should be a discretionary one without statutory criteria to guide its exercise?

3 Should asylum seekers have an automatic bail hearings as criminal suspects do?

FURTHER READING

Amnesty International (1996) *Cell Culture: The Detention and Imprisonment of Asylum Seekers in the United Kingdom* (London: Amnesty International).

Bail for Immigration Detainees (2002) *Immigration Detention in the United Kingdom, Submission to the United Nations Working Group on Arbitrary Detention* (London: BID).

Bail for Immigration Detainees (2005) *Fit to be Detained? Challenging the detention of asylum seekers and migrants with health needs* (London: BID)

Blake, N., Buchan, S., Kawani, F., Owers, A. (1997) *Providing Protection: Towards fair and effective asylum procedures* (Justice, ILPA and ARC).

Burnham, U. (1998) 'Negligent False Imprisonment: Scope for re-emergence?' *Modern Law Review* vol. 61, no. 4, p. 573.

Cohen, R. (1994) *The Frontiers of Identity* (London and New York: Longman), Chapter 4.

Cole, E. (2003) 'The Detention of Asylum-seeking families in the UK' IANL vol. 17, no. 2, pp. 96–113.

Dell, S., and Salinsky, M. (2001) 'Protection not Prison: Torture Survivors Detained in the UK' Medical Foundation for the Care of Victims of Torture, September 2001.

Fenwick, H. (2002) 'The Anti-terrorism, Crime and Security Act 2001: A proportionate response to September 11th?' *Modern Law Review* vol. 65, no. 5, 724–762.

Macdonald, I., and Webber, F. (2005) *Macdonald's Immigration Law and Practice*, 6th edn. (London: Butterworths, Chapter 17).

McLeish, J., Culter, S., Stancer, C. (2002) *A Crying Shame: Pregnant Asylum Seekers and their Babies in Detention* (Maternity Alliance, BID, LDSG).

Modern Law Review (2005) 68(4) Cases Section: Special Issue on Belmarsh.

Poole, T. 'Harnessing the Power of the Past? Lord Hoffmann and the *Belmarsh Detainees* Case' *Journal of Law and Society* vol. 32, no. 4, pp. 534–561.

Pourgourides, C. K., Sashidharan, S. P., Bracken, P. J. (1996) *A Second Exile: The Mental Health Implications of Detention of Asylum Seekers in the United Kingdom*, (Birmingham: Northern Birmingham Mental Health Trust).

Sawyer, C., and Turpin, P. (2005) 'Neither Here Nor There: Temporary Admission to the UK'. International Journal of Refugee Law, vol. 17, no. 4, December 2005, pp. 688–728.

Shah, P. (2002) *Refugees, Race and the Concept of Asylum* (London: Cavendish), Chapter 8.

Sharpe, R. J. (1989) *The Law of Habeas Corpus*, (Oxford: Clarendon), pp. 117–123.

Smith, K. (1999) 'The reality of detention: a reaction to the Immigration and Asylum Bill' *Immigration and Nationality Asylum Law and Practice* vol. 13, no. 3, pp. 96–99.

Tomkins, A. (2002) 'Legislating against Terror: the Anti-terrorism, Crime and Security Act 2001' *Public Law* Summer, pp. 205–220.

UNHCR (1999) *Revised Guidelines on Applicable Criteria and Standards Relating to the Detention of Asylum Seekers*.

Wadham, J. (2002) 'Why Lawyers should be ashamed of the latest ruling on internment' *New Law Journal* vol. 152, no. 7054, p. 1633.

Warbrick, C. (2002) 'The Principles of the European Convention on Human Rights and the Response of States to Terrorism' *European Human Rights Law Review* 3, pp. 287–314.

Weber, L., and Gelsthorpe, L. (2000) *Deciding to Detain: How Decisions to Detain Asylum Seekers are Made at Ports of Entry* (Cambridge: Cambridge Institute of Criminology).

Wilman, S., Knafler, S., Pierce, S. (2004) 2nd edn *Support for Asylum Seekers* (London: Legal Action Group).

16

Deportation

SUMMARY

This chapter gives a brief history of the power of deportation, then discusses in some detail the application of the main ground which remains after recent legislative changes: that the deportation is conducive to the public good. There is discussion of the various ways in which tribunals assess the effect upon the public of criminal behaviour and whether this should warrant deportation. There is an extended discussion of the case of *Rehman*, the first national security deportation case heard by the Special Immigration Appeals Commission. The chapter concludes with some points on particular issues which arise in considering the effect of deportation on family and private life.

16.1 Introduction

Deportation has a long history. The word conjures up images of forced removals, divided families, and poor conditions on board crowded ships. Deportations still take place, though they are now not the most common legal means of removing someone from the UK; the more common route now is administrative removal, which is dealt with in the next chapter. In the year 2004, 56,920 people were forced by law to leave the UK. Of these, only 705 were removed after deportation action. Deportation offers more rights to the person removed than does the process of removal. It is the older power, and more developed in legal terms; even though the numbers deported are now relatively small, the issues involved are significant ones.

The process of extradition, which may have an interaction with asylum claims but which arises in relation to non-immigration criminal issues, will not be considered in this book. Supervised and voluntary departures are considered later in this chapter.

16.2 What is deportation?

Deportation is a process of enforced departure from the UK, pursuant to an order signed by the Home Secretary, which also prevents the deportee from returning to the UK unless and until the order is revoked. In this respect it may be distinguished from the other forms of enforced departure. Although removal, supervised and voluntary departure will affect the ability of the individual to return to the UK, unlike a deportation order they do not have any continuing legal force beyond the departure date. Paragraph 362 of the immigration rules sets out the effects of a deportation order:

(1) it requires the person who is the subject of the order to leave the UK

(2) it authorizes that person's detention until they leave the UK (subject to a common law restraint on the length of detention, as discussed in the previous chapter)

(3) it prohibits that person's re-entry for as long as the order is in force

(4) it invalidates any leave to enter or remain given to the person before the order was made or while it was in force.

The first formal step in the deportation process is the notice of decision to deport, which gives the reasons for the decision, the country to which it is proposed to deport the person, and notice of appeal rights. Appeal is against the notice of decision to deport. Once the deportation order is signed it becomes valid and there is no further appeal, though it may be possible to appeal a refusal to revoke the order (Nationality, Immigration and Asylum Act 2002 s 82(2)(k)).

Entry while the deportation order is still in force makes that person an illegal entrant (Immigration Act 1971 s 33A).

16.3 History of the power to deport

The origin of the power to deport was arguably in the prerogative of the Crown to regulate the entry and stay of aliens. As a prerogative power can only be used in relation to aliens (*R v IAT ex p SSHD* [1990] 3 All ER 652: see chapter 1), in this early stage Commonwealth citizens could not be deported. The law regulating deportation began to develop when the exercise of the power was first controlled by statute in the Aliens Act 1905. Under the statute deportation could only take place after conviction of an imprisonable offence, or if a magistrates' court certified that the person had been sentenced elsewhere for an extradition offence, or had:

Been found in receipt of any such parochial relief as disqualifies a person for the parliamentary franchise, or found wandering without ostensible means of subsistence, or been living in insanitary conditions due to overcrowding.

Criminality, poverty, and the spread of disease have often been mixed in with immigration policy, as discussed in chapter 1. The operation of appeal boards was suspended in 1914, and although for a short time there was a review panel, its decisions were unpopular with the Home Office and it was abolished again. Effectively, from 1914 to 1955 people who were to be deported had no access to appeal or independent review.

We have seen that the Commonwealth Immigrants Act 1962 marked an historic shift in the relationship between the UK and its Commonwealth citizens. Not only did it provide the first powers to refuse them entry, it also provided the first powers to deport Commonwealth citizens, though originally this too was only for criminal offences on the recommendation of a criminal court (s 6). Interestingly in the light of recent debates in the Council of Europe on protection against deportation for long term residents, the 1962 Act s 7 provided protection against deportation for anyone who could prove they had been ordinarily resident in the UK for five years prior to conviction.

The Immigration Appeals Act 1969 widened powers in relation to Commonwealth citizens by giving the power to the Secretary of State to deport Commonwealth citizens who were in breach of their conditions of admission (s 16), again with an exemption for those who had been ordinarily resident for five years. The power to impose conditions was only introduced by the 1962 Act. This was a significant step as it developed deportation as a means of enforcing immigration rules, not only a means of excluding people who were considered socially undesirable. The Immigration Act 1971 made the position of aliens and Commonwealth citizens broadly the same, in that deportation became possible for both groups for breach of condition or overstaying, when conducive to the public good and after recommendation by a criminal court (s 3). This power applied to all those who were subject to immigration control, and aliens and Commonwealth citizens were not separately treated by the Act, though there were some Commonwealth citizens who were exempt (see below). From that time onwards, apart from the exemptions, the distinction between Commonwealth citizens and aliens for deportation purposes has vanished.

The Immigration Act 1988 s 5 restricted the possible grounds for appeal against deportation for people who had been in the UK for less than seven years. After this change, people who had been in the UK less than seven years who were being deported for breach of condition or overstaying could not argue their case on the merits of whether they should be deported, but only on whether there was power in law to deport them. This restriction was interpreted strictly, as demonstrated in the case of *Harjinder Kaur Singh* TH/26/1199 where the tribunal found the appeal was limited to whether there was power in law to deport. The manner in which that power was exercised was outside their jurisdiction and if the Secretary of State had failed to have regard to his policy on domestic violence, there was nothing they could do about that.

The Asylum and Immigration Act 1996 added a further ground for deportation — obtaining leave to remain by deception. Despite the widened grounds and the restricted appeal rights, a person who was to be deported still had greater rights than one who was to be removed in that they had a right to appeal from inside the UK which the person to be removed did not. The Immigration and Asylum Act 1999 translated most of the grounds for deportation into grounds for removal, thereby further reducing appeal rights. It is an open question whether this reduction in rights was balanced in the 1999 Act by the introduction of the human rights appeal which applies to removal as well as deportation (see, for instance, *CM* below).

In summary, until the implementation of the 1999 Act, the scope of the power to deport increased, while the rights of people who were to be deported decreased. With the implementation of the 1999 Act, deportation as a legal route became less important. In the Nationality Immigration and Asylum Act 2002 a new right of appeal was introduced against a decision to deport following the recommendation of a criminal court (s 82(2)(j)). Interestingly the Bill which preceded the 1999 Act included this right of appeal, but it was removed by a late amendment sponsored by the government in the House of Lords.

16.4 **Rationale for deportation**

The power to deport is most commonly used in relation to people who have been convicted of a criminal offence. Its use is not intended to be a further punishment for the criminal offence, but should only be considered when the person's continued presence in the country impinges on the life of the public in a way that is contrary to the public interest (Immigration Act 1971 s 3(5)(a) and *R v Nazari* [1980] 3 All ER 880). Every society contains a certain level of criminal activity and so crime in itself does not warrant deportation. The Court of Appeal in *Raghbir Singh* [1996] Imm AR 507 said that the Secretary of State should consider 'whether it is bad for the country for him to remain'.

A moment's reflection will reveal that the question of whether it is conducive to the public good to remove someone from the country is one on which opinion can differ greatly. To set out the extremes, on one view of the matter, any wrongdoing is bad for the country and therefore any person who commits a criminal act should be removed. This view as well as other policy considerations was reflected in the penal policy of the eighteenth century which resulted in the transportation of those who had committed criminal offences to North America or Australia, which were then colonies of Britain. This was not an immigration law matter. Transportation was a punishment and applied to British subjects, but it was seen as a public good that people who had committed criminal offences should be taken out of the country. At the other end of the spectrum of opinion, removing the criminal from society does not address the causes of crime and to push criminality away does not deal with it constructively. Furthermore the wrongdoing of a non-citizen is no greater than the wrongdoing of a citizen. The possession of citizenship (and so exemption from deportation) is an irrelevant technicality given that one may apply for naturalization and so become a citizen after three years' residence in the UK, or on the other hand have lived here all one's life and still not have citizenship. The discrimination which results from the deportation of the non-citizen, combined with the harm to family and social networks, is a greater fracturing of the social fabric than the continued presence of someone who has committed a criminal offence. Punishment as meted out by the court is already intended to deter others and prevent re-offending and if it fails to do so that is a matter for criminal policy, not immigration control.

Whether or not one adopts the latter view, the extreme option of 'out of sight out of mind' is no longer available. For the most part neither the UK nor other countries any longer have domination over territories remote from themselves to which they can transport wrongdoers (although 'out of sight, out of mind' is perhaps now practised with a different groups of people, subject to extraordinary rendition or detention in military bases). Deportation is not to a remote place but usually to the deportee's country of nationality. However they may not have lived there for a considerable period of time, perhaps for the whole of their adult life. Which country should take responsibility? Increased international co-ordination of policing raises also the question of international co-ordination of criminal justice systems, but social attitudes to crime also differ widely. Deportation, if it is a solution at all, is only a local solution, and engages the question of how the destination state will treat the deportee. Indeed the punitive attitude of the destination state is now sometimes argued in deportation appeals as a reason why the person should not be deported (see, for instance, *M v SSHD* [2003] 1 WLR 1980 para 10 and *Oviasoghie v SSHD* [2002] UKIAT 06038 para 12).

If deportation is not a punishment, the philosophical basis for it is hard to find in an age where there is not a no-(white)man's land to which the criminal can be transported. It is sometimes viewed as a sanction for a kind of breach of hospitality, but where a person has spent all their working life in the UK and contributed as much as many citizens, this does not hold up.

16.5 Exercise of the power to deport

Section 5(1) Immigration Act 1971 expresses the power to make a deportation order as a power of the Secretary of State. However, in accordance with the *Carltona* principle (*Carltona Ltd v Commissioner of Works* [1943] 2 All ER 560 CA), properly authorized officials may carry out the function of the Secretary of State and in doing so their actions count as the actions of the Secretary of State. In the context of deportation, the *Carltona* principle authorizes deportation action to be taken by officials of the Home Office. However, this would not automatically be taken to include immigration officers, who, as we have seen, are a separate service within the Home Office, and in the case of deportations would have been involved in the investigation of the case. In 1988 the Secretary of State authorized certain nominated immigration officers of the rank of inspector also to make deportation decisions. This delegation was challenged in the case of *Oladehinde and Alexander v Secretary of State for the Home Department* [1991] 1 AC 254, but the House of Lords upheld the delegation. The court's concern about procedures being properly applied was met by the practice of making written records of the decision-making process, ensuring that immigration officers who had been involved in the investigation process were not involved in the deportation decision, and referring to the Home Office any proposed deportation where the person has compassionate circumstances or has been in the UK for a long time.

Deportation orders are usually signed by the Home Office Immigration Minister, but the Immigration Directorate Instructions (IDI Ch 13 s 1 para 5 Sept 2001) say that contentious cases may be signed by the Home Secretary. The Home Secretary has normally signed personally deportation orders which are made on what we may loosely call national security grounds. These grounds are discussed more specifically below. The Nationality, Immigration and Asylum Act 2002 s 97 brings together all immigration decisions made on these grounds, and provides that there will be no right of appeal if the Secretary of State certifies that the decision was taken by them personally wholly or partly in the interests of national security or the relationship between the UK and another country (s 97(2)). Section 99 allows the Secretary of State to issue a certificate under s 97 while an appeal is pending and thereby to prevent the appeal from continuing.

Where there is no right of appeal, there is nevertheless the possibility of an application to have the case heard by the Special Immigration Appeals Commission (see chapter 8).

16.6 **Who is liable to be deported?**

Section 3(5) Immigration Act 1971 says that 'a person who is not a British citizen' may be deported. Here the term 'British citizen' has the meaning given to it by s 2 Immigration Act, as substituted by British Nationality Act 1981 s 39. It therefore includes not only those who have British citizenship but also Commonwealth citizens who retained right of abode when the British Nationality Act 1981 came into force, as discussed in chapter 2, namely those who married a British man before 1 January 1983, or who had a UK born parent.

There are other exemptions also. By Immigration Act 1971 s 7 Commonwealth and Irish citizens who were ordinarily resident in the UK on 1 January 1973 (the date that the 1971 Act came into force) and meet a further residence condition are exempt from deportation. The case of *Lawrence Kane v SSHD* [2000] Imm AR 250 confirmed that the only further residence condition which can now be applied is that the proposed deportee had been ordinarily resident for five years before the decision to deport was taken (s 7(1)(b) and (c)). The other basis for exemption in s 7(1)(a), which was residence in the UK at all times since the 1971 Act came into force, ceased to have independent effect at the end of 1977.

Unusually in counting periods of residence, according to Immigration Act s 7(2), remaining 'in breach of immigration laws' counts towards this five-year period. Case law has established that this only applies to people who overstay their period of leave, and not to those who entered illegally in the first place. Time spent in prison however does not count (*Lawrence Kane*). Section 8(3) provides an exemption from deportation for diplomats and their families.

The point which is sometimes a difficult one to grasp is that even people who have indefinite leave to remain and are settled are liable for deportation unless they are exempt under s 7. There used to be an exemption for Commonwealth wives of Commonwealth men settled in the UK before 1973, but this was abolished by s 1 Immigration Act 1988. The abolition of this security for Commonwealth women was in breach of a guarantee which had been given by s 1(5) of the Immigration Act 1971, that Commonwealth citizens would be no less free to come and go after the 1971 Act than they were before. The 1988 Act repealed that section and caused a furore by removing the rights of Commonwealth citizens. However, without constitutional protection, given the UK's doctrine of the legislative supremacy of Parliament, such promises cannot be relied upon. Even after the passage of the Human Rights Act it is by no means certain that the right to family life of Commonwealth citizens living in the UK would be held to outweigh the government's right to control immigration.

As discussed more fully in chapter 5, EEA nationals are only liable to be deported on the grounds that their continued presence is a threat to public policy, public security, or public health. This ground for deportation is set out in Directive 2004/38, and implemented in UK law by the Immigration (European Economic Area) Regulations 2006, SI 2006/1003, as amended.

There is an important question as to the comparability of the criteria for deportation of EEA nationals and non-EEA nationals. For EEA nationals the Directive is an exception to the underlying EC right of freedom of movement and as such should be interpreted restrictively (Case 41/74 *Van Duyn v Home Office* [1974] ECR 1337). No such right can be claimed by non-EEA nationals. On the other hand, a non-EEA national to be deported from the UK will almost invariably have indefinite leave to remain. A question to bear in mind as we examine the case law is whether such leave to remain in the UK carries any protective power comparable with European freedom of movement.

While a person may be liable for deportation, they cannot be deported unless the grounds exist. The grounds for deportation are set out in s 3(5) as amended by Immigration Asylum Act 1999 Sch 14 para 44. The subsection now reads as follows:

A person who is not a British citizen shall be liable to deportation from the United Kingdom
(a) if the Secretary of State deems his deportation to be conducive to the public good; or
(b) if another person to whose family he belongs is or has been ordered to be deported.

In case law and literature prior to the 1999 Act, deportations under what is now s 3(5)(a) are referred to as 's 3(5)(b)' deportations, and what is now s 3(5)(b) was s 3(5)(c).

16.7 'Conducive to the public good'

It has been noted in the historical introduction to this chapter that this ground for deportation or exclusion has a long history. The provision in the Aliens Act 1905 for deportation on grounds of criminal convictions or destitution is in this spirit, that it is not in the public interest for such persons to remain. Even before that a view of the undesirability of the immigrant was a basis for exclusion under the prerogative. It is a broad power, not confined to any one interpretation of the meaning of the public good. In *Raghbir Singh* it was said that the subsection 'covers a whole range of circumstances limited only by conventional public law and *Wednesbury* rules and the doctrine in *Padfield v Minister of Agriculture*,' i.e., normal administrative law limitations of reasonableness and impartiality.

Since the commencement of the Human Rights Act it is arguably artificial to consider the question of what is conducive to the public good separately from the question of what is necessary in a democratic society. This arises in every case where deportation interferes with the deportee's right to private or family life, which it often will do. Cross-reference should therefore be made to the discussion of Article 8, the right to respect for private and family life (chapter 3).

In European cases there appears to be a higher threshold. The case of *R v Bouchereau* [1978] QB 732 among others held that in order to justify deportation the threat to public policy or security of the person's continued presence must not only be a genuine one but also sufficiently serious to warrant derogation from the free movement right.

The courts in reviewing deportation decisions have not engaged in depth with the question of what is conducive to the public good, or conversely, what is 'bad for the country'. On the whole, the matter has been treated as one of policy which the

Home Secretary is best placed to decide. Nevertheless, the immigration rules require certain factors to be taken into account by the courts, there are policies which govern deportation decisions, and counter-arguments may be raised under the Human Rights Act.

16.7.1 Criminal offences

The commission of criminal offences is the most common basis for deportation under what is now s 3(5)(a). The ground under s 3(5)(a) should be distinguished from deportation after recommendation by a criminal court, which will be considered later. Deportation under s 3(5)(a) is a decision of the Secretary of State when the criminal court has not recommended deportation and is independent of the criminal justice system.

16.7.1.1 *Previous convictions*

In European cases Council Directive 2004/38 and Regulation 21 of the EEA Regulations 2006 provide that 'previous convictions shall not in themselves constitute grounds' for deportation, and in non-European cases simply having committed a criminal offence would not satisfy the requirement that the deportation should be conducive to the public good. This provision has been qualified by the ECJ in the leading case of *R v Bouchereau* in which the court said that although future conduct was usually the question, in exceptional cases where the offence was serious enough past conduct alone might constitute a threat to public policy. The Court of Appeal in *Goremsandu v SSHD* [1996] Imm AR 250 (at 254) affirmed the European Court of Justice saying that 'some offences are so serious, in the sense that they are sufficiently repugnant to the generally accepted standards of morality, that the continued presence in the community is unacceptable'. The seriousness of the offence may therefore make it possible for there to be a deportation based simply on the fact of the conviction, and this is so for European and non-European cases.

16.7.1.2 *Seriousness*

A consistent view of the gravity of a class of crime probably emerges most clearly in relation to drug offences, and these are probably also the commonest source of decisions to deport based on the public good. A strong statement was made by Beldam LJ in the case of *Marchon* [1993] Imm AR 384 where the Court of Appeal reviewed the proper approach by the Secretary of State to serious drug offences. In relation to identifying the public interest which would be the Secretary of State's proper concern, he said:

It would in my judgment be difficult to imagine a more fundamental interest than the unrelenting pursuit of the fight against the deliberate debilitating and destructive influence of dealing in, and importing into society, addictive and lethal drugs such as heroin and cocaine. It seems to me that even the hint that society was prepared [to] tolerate such conduct, by accepting the presence of persons who have been prepared to import large quantities of such drugs under the cloak of legitimate business, would undermine the overwhelming public interest in defeating this subversive trade.

Marchon was a case particularly likely to attract strong comment, as the potential deportee was a consultant psychiatrist and so the Court considered his behaviour was an abuse of trust and power. However, the statement was not restricted to such circumstances and a similar approach is evident in numerous Tribunal cases where no position of special trust or particular social standing arises. For instance in *Townsend* (22078) the appellant had been out of detention for two years before the date of the hearing, and had stayed out of trouble for that time. This was strong evidence that he was unlikely to re-offend or harm the public interest in the future. Nevertheless, the Tribunal regarded his offence (supply and possession of cannabis and crack) as serious, in particular because crack quickly became addictive, and upheld the deportation.

Marchon refers to 'large quantities' of drugs, and the street value of the drugs imported in that case was £450,000. In *Luciani* [1996] Imm AR 558 which reinforced the strong message of *Marchon*, the street value was £15 million. However, the Tribunal is prepared to regard simply the fact of a drugs offence as serious and contrary to the public good, even if the amounts involved are relatively small, as is illustrated in *Roger* (17891). In this case a Belgian national of previously good character succumbed to temptation to import ecstasy and cocaine with a street value of £27,000 at a time when she was under financial pressure. The majority of the Tribunal did not believe that she would not re-offend, but said that anyway 'her criminal conduct itself justifies deportation'.

The Court of Appeal came close to a similar approach in the case of *Secretary of State for the Home Department v Dinc* [1999] Imm AR 380. Mr Dinc came to the UK in 1979 at the age of 27. In 1992 he was convicted of possession of one kilo of heroin and of supplying it over a period of six weeks to existing users. He was sentenced to five years in prison and the trial judge recommended deportation. He was then married to a woman who had been in the UK since the age of nine, he had two children, and had indefinite leave to remain in the UK. The Court of Appeal at 385 accepted the rationality of the Home Office view that 'in the light of the strength of the public interest in this case stemming from the nature and seriousness of the offence . . . the balance was in favour of proceeding with the deportation'.

Following the implementation of the Human Rights Act the Court of Appeal's view of the seriousness of drugs offences does not seem to have diminished as illustrated in *Samaroo* [2001] UKHRR 1150. Here there was undisputed evidence that Mr Samaroo, who had a very established family life in the UK, was unlikely to re-offend, but the seriousness of drugs offences was reiterated, and his deportation was upheld. Also in the Tribunal, the deportation was upheld of a mother of three following her conviction for smuggling cannabis and cocaine in to the UK (*Baah v SSHD* [2002] UKIAT 05998). These cases are considered again later in relation to the court's role in deciding human rights questions.

Marchon and *Roger* are European cases in which the UK judicial bodies may not have fully applied the higher threshold indicated by (now) Directive 2004/38. However, more recent cases in the ECJ, e.g., C–348/96 *Calfa* [1999] ECR I–11 and *Nazli v Stadt-Nüremberg* [2000] ECR I–957 suggest that commission of a drugs offence should not be sufficient to justify the expulsion of a European national.

The Courts' and Tribunals' views are perhaps more mixed when it comes to sex offences. In *Fernandez* (12016) the tribunal considered that society abhorred this kind of crime (the rape and indecent assault of the appellant's stepdaughter) but did not regard the abuse of trust involved as a morally aggravating factor in the way that the consultant's abuse of trust was held to be in *Marchon*. This conduct was not considered to affect the fabric of society such that it could not be outweighed by other factors. In *Goremsandu*, by way of contrast, the Court of Appeal found that the incest with the appellant's daughter was 'sufficiently morally repugnant to the generally accepted standards of morality' that his 'continued presence was not acceptable'. In *B v SSHD* [2000] Imm AR 478, where the offences were also of incest with the appellant's daughter, the Court of Appeal quashed the deportation, applying Article 8 ECHR, on the basis that it was a disproportionate infringement with the appellant's right to respect for his private life.

In the case of *Hamill* (18719), the appellant, previously of good character, had raped a 17-year-old girl, then after his arrest for that offence had attempted a robbery of a cashier in a building society. As an EEA national he could not be deported unless his conduct was a threat to public security, public policy, or public health. The Tribunal accepted that the appellant 'had settled down' and posed no future threat to society. His continued presence therefore could not be an issue of public security. The seriousness of the offences in themselves was not such as to warrant deportation and his appeal was allowed. By way of contrast, the appellant in *Galoo* (00/GL/0009) was a Pakistani national, also convicted of rape, also of previously good character. He had received a five-year prison sentence (one year less than Mr Hamill). The rape was carried out together with another man and was described as violent. The tribunal itself in this case commented that there are numerous cases of rape and punishment similar to that of Mr Galoo in which there is no recommendation to deport. Nevertheless, and despite the fact that Mr Galoo had children aged nine and six, born and brought up in the UK, the Tribunal took the view that a violent rape like this:

strikes at the roots of society, which includes the sanctity of the family and the need for the protection of the public, particularly of those unable to defend themselves from people like the appellant.

The deportation was upheld. The appellant in *M* referred to earlier was a Bangladeshi national who had indecently assaulted two girls whom he was teaching Arabic. Here, the breach of trust was regarded as serious and his deportation was upheld despite his having a wife and children in the UK.

The seriousness with which other crimes of violence are weighed is also highly dependent upon circumstance. Simply by way of example, in the case of *Morrison* (22099) the appellant had been convicted of eleven charges including the use and possession of firearms, robbery, and wounding, and the seriousness of his offences is barely mentioned by the tribunal. On the other hand in *Yebli* (22525) the appellant, an EEA national, was convicted of robbery, false imprisonment, and using an imitation firearm. These arose from a single, though disturbing, incident, in which the appellant attacked, tied up, and robbed a British Rail clerk. The tribunal found that his physical violence was 'evidence of conduct which proved a threat to society'. In this case he 'posed a threat to the requirements of public policy if allowed to remain in the UK.' This was held to be one of the exceptional cases referred to in *Bouchereau* and *Marchon* in which past conduct in itself justified deportation. The Tribunal does not look simply at the charge which was brought, it also considers the circumstances of the offence, and it appears from the decision in *Yebli* that they were influenced by the type and intensity of the violence involved. Mr Yebli's personal circumstances did not yield strong arguments to weigh against his deportation, though his connections with the UK were not negligible. In *Serrao* TH/02010 and *Cioffo* TH10295/01 the tribunal held that serious offences of violence and blackmail were not enough to warrant deporting the EEA appellants. In each case they had been living in the UK for most or all of their adult life, and had a wife and children and an established family life in the UK. The seriousness of the offences did not mean that deportation now was necessary for public security.

In relation to crimes of dishonesty also the Tribunal considers the offences in the context of the public impact. The offence of which the appellant in *Trindade* (17775) was convicted was regarded as particularly serious because it was social security fraud. Although the value involved (£20,000) is far less than most of the drugs offences we have considered, his theft was from the public purse, and as such was regarded as a threat to society. Although he was an EEA national, the Tribunal had no difficulty in finding his continuing presence a threat to public policy. The deportation of the appellant in *Nwachukwu* (17789) was upheld because the tribunal considered that he was involved in 'serious organized crime'. He was a man of previously good character who was sentenced to 30 months' imprisonment for obtaining property by deception. Again, the crucial factor is not the offence but its circumstances.

The sentence passed by the criminal court is often referred to by the tribunal as an indication of the seriousness of the offence, however this is by no means decisive. For instance, compare the case of *Morrison* in which the tribunal's decision was clearly influenced above all by the testimony and loyalty of his wife, with that of Mr Nwachukwu. Mr. Morrison, whose deportation was lifted, was sentenced to 12 years in prison for his offences of violence and Mr. Nwachukwu to only 30 months. Mr Cioffo had been sentenced to eleven years in prison for blackmail. The length of sentence is one factor which must be considered in the context of the appellant's life circumstances.

16.7.1.3 *Re-offending*

The most obvious way in which the existence of a criminal conviction might be thought to suggest damage to the public interest is that it could indicate a tendency to re-offend. The likelihood of re-offending is one of the factors taken into account by the Immigration Appeal Tribunal in reviewing the merits of a deportation decision, and the tribunal is prepared to come to its own view of whether the potential deportee would re-offend. This depends upon the evidence specifically addressing that matter, e.g., time since release which the potential deportee has spent without re-offending, their expressions of remorse and good intentions, what incentives the tribunal can see in the person's circumstances to support those good intentions, and the views of, e.g., probation officers or social workers as to the likelihood of re-offending.

The Tribunal must of course consider the weight that it gives to these sources of evidence. The view taken of the involvement in the crime itself is important. This includes the degree of the potential deportee's involvement, their attitude to the crime and their motivation. For example, in *Pradas-Herrojo* TH/00009, the Tribunal, chaired by Collins J the then President of the IAT, heard that the appellant's motivation for drug smuggling was 'to make money'. The Tribunal's response to this was: 'it seems to us that there is no possible excuse or mitigation involved in that approach to the importation of drugs.' It was sceptical about this self-justification and reached the conclusion that: 'he says . . . he would not re-offend, but we doubt it.' There was no reason why such a motivation should not recur, and the deportation decision was upheld. In *Batili* (17857) the appellant was convicted of conspiracy to supply heroin, an offence which the Tribunal regarded as 'repugnant'. Nevertheless, the Tribunal accepted that he had allowed himself to be drawn in 'as a look out', was full of remorse and otherwise of good character. There was little risk of his re-offending and the appeal against deportation was allowed. In *Batili* the appellant had referred to his involvement as a 'misunderstanding'. The Tribunal did not dwell on this aspect of his explanation, accepting in vague terms his contention that he had been influenced. However, in *Trindade*, the appellant described his £20,000 social security fraud as a 'mistake', and this was characterized by the Tribunal as 'a serious understatement of criminal responsibility'. The deportation stood.

16.7.1.4 *Deterrence*

Even where the appellant is personally unlikely to re-offend, the judicial authorities may be prepared to uphold a deportation on the basis that it may serve as an example and deter others. The approach of the Court of Appeal in *Samaroo* is a post-Human Rights Act example of this. The case turned on the question of whether the interference with the appellant's right to respect for his family life could be justified under para 2 of Article 8. Mr Samaroo had been convicted of drug trafficking, and it was accepted that in such a case para 2 could permit deportation in the interests of prevention of crime and disorder and the protection of the health, rights, and freedoms of others. However, the interference had to be proportionate to the aim. Presumably if deterrence was unlikely to work then the interference with Mr Samaroo's private life (which was substantial as he had a wife and child and three stepchildren) could not be proportionate. However, the Court said that it was not its job to assess the effectiveness of deterrence, which was by its nature unprovable. That was a matter for the Secretary of State who was better placed to assess the matter. He did not have to prove that the particular deportation would have a deterrent effect in order to justify it. He was entitled to have a policy for the deterrence of a particular kind of crime. This is an example of the court allowing a margin of discretion to the executive in a matter of social policy.

This was more precisely explained by the Tribunal in *Cioffo*, which held that public policy considerations could warrant deportation even when the individual did not have a propensity to re-offend. This would be the case where, for instance, there was an epidemic of a kind of crime which needed to be discouraged. This policy lies behind the decision in *Samaroo*. There was not an epidemic of blackmail, and so the deterrence of others was not a necessary consideration in *Cioffo*.

This interpretation of public policy in a European case is open to question, as the Directive and EEA Regulations say that a decision to deport 'must be based exclusively on the personal conduct of the individual in respect of whom the decision is taken' (Reg 21, and Art 27.2). It can only be a matter of time before a non-European deported in the interests of deterrence challenges this using Article 14 of the Convention rights.

16.7.1.5 *Consistency*

Paragraph 364 Immigration Rules says that in relation to any deportation:

While each case will be considered in the light of the particular circumstances, the aim is an exercise of the power of deportation which is consistent and fair as between one person and another, although one case will rarely be identical with another in all material respects.

In the case of deportations based on criminal offences, this raises the particular question of consistency between co-accused. In *Arshad* (9888) the Tribunal, which had otherwise found the case for upholding the deportation compelling, felt obliged to allow the appeal because there had been no move to deport the co-accused, whose participation in the offences was comparable with the appellant's. The co-accused had four children rather than two, and a much longer residence in the UK (22 as opposed to eight years) but the tribunal did not feel that these differences were sufficient to deport one and not the other.

However, in the case of *Yasin* [1995] Imm AR 118 CA, like *Arshad* a drugs offence, the Court of Appeal upheld the deportation of one brother and not the other. The representative for the brother in the second appeal to be heard had not mentioned the case of the first to be heard, who had not been deported. In this situation the court did not have an obligation to ensure consistency between the two brothers.

16.7.2 Deception

Other matters than criminal convictions have also been found to be a basis for deportation conducive to the public good. Deception of the Home Office resulting in the grant of leave to remain is an example (*Kesse* [2001] EWCA Civ 177), and even deception used to gain entry, though obtaining entry by deception has long been a basis for the separate process of removal (see chapter 17). In 1996 obtaining leave to remain by deception became a specific ground for deportation thus removing any need for the Secretary of State to prove that deportation was conducive to the public good in such cases, and on 2 October 2000 obtaining leave in this way became grounds for removal. The Immigration Directorate Instructions suggest that where there is 'clear evidence' of a 'high degree of probability' that a person obtained leave to remain by deception before 1 October 1996, deportation proceedings can still be taken.

16.7.3 Abuse of a social institution

In a few cases deportation on the grounds of public good has been used if the Secretary of State considers that a fundamental social institution has been abused. This is unlikely to be encountered often now, though it does illustrate the width of the provision and the scope it gives to the executive. In *ex p Cheema* [1982] Imm AR 124 CA the appellant was held to have abused the institution of marriage. The case defines marriages of convenience, confirming *ex p Ullah* [1982] Imm AR 124 in which the applicant was deported for entering into such a marriage, thereby abusing an institution which is 'one of the cornerstones of our society'. This idea entered into the case of *Galoo*, discussed above, as although the criminal offence was the reason for the deportation, the Tribunal formed its view of that offence as a proper ground for deportation partly on the basis that 'it strikes at the roots of society which includes the sanctity of the family', and referred to *Cheema* in doing so. Abuse of the institution of marriage is only a relevant consideration if the marriage is not genuine at any stage. False claims, for instance that a couple are still cohabiting when they have in fact separated, or that they are legally free to marry when they are not, may lead to the grant of leave to remain on a false basis. This would be regarded as obtaining leave to remain by deception rather than an abuse of the institution of marriage, and would now be a basis for removal under s 10 of the Immigration and Asylum Act 1999.

16.7.4 **Political reasons**

The final category of deportations under s 3(5)(a), consists of those where the ground of the decision is that deportation is conducive to the public good as being in the interests of national security or of the relations between the UK and any other country (Nationality, Immigration and Asylum Act 2002 s 97(2)). Before the 2002 Act this ground also included 'other reasons of a political nature'. The difference between these and other deportations under s 3(5)(a) is that there is no appeal in the ordinary appeal process, but only to the Special Immigration Appeal Commission (SIAC). The Secretary of State also has power to take proceedings out of the ordinary appeal process and transfer them to SIAC if he or she certifies that the decision was made wholly or partly in reliance on information which ought not to be disclosed for reasons of public interest or national security or relations with other states (s 97(3)).

As in other areas of law, where the question of national security arises the balance between the state and the individual shifts further towards the State, involving curtailment of the rights of the individual. Given the curtailment of right of access to the courts there has in the past been little case law on deportation on national security or political grounds. However, developments in the last few years have brought political and national security deportations more into the public and legal sphere. First, the judgment of the European Court of Human Rights in the case of *Chahal v UK* (1997) 23 EHRR 413 was critical of UK procedures in national security cases. As a consequence, the UK Government was obliged to set up the Special Immigration Appeals Commission (SIAC), to meet the Court's concerns. Second, the growing involvement of all three branches of government (executive, judicial, legislative) in defining and controlling terrorism has brought a spotlight onto the question of exclusion from the UK for reasons connected with national security. This is not a new phenomenon following the US President's declaration of a so-called 'war on terrorism' in September 2001, although the Anti-terrorism, Crime and Security Act 2001 was expressly a response to that declaration. As we shall see below, some developments pre-date 11 September 2001, but the pace of them has been increasing.

16.7.4.1 *Basis of political deportation*

Although so-called 'political' or 'national security' deportations are treated differently from others, the formal grounds for such a deportation are still that the deportation is conducive to the public good. It is still a deportation under s 3(5)(a) and must take into account the factors in para 364 of the Immigration Rules. The bases of national security and international relations may overlap. The Secretary of State is not obliged to settle the allegations in such a way that they fit into one or another category (*SSHD v Rehman* [2001] 3 WLR 877 discussed below). Simply stating that the deportation was 'in the interests of national security, namely the likelihood of your involvement in terrorist activity' was held to be giving sufficient reason in *Jahromi v SSHD* [1996] Imm AR 20 where the Home Office gave evidence that further disclosure would jeopardize intelligence sources.

Before the changes following on the case of *Chahal v UK* (1997) 23 EHRR 413, there was no right of appeal at all to a judicial body against a political or national security deportation. The Special Immigration Appeals Commission (SIAC) which resulted from this case has already been described in chapter 8, and the first case in the SIAC holds an important place in the development of the law on national security deportations.

16.7.4.2 *Rehman's case*

Mr Rehman was a Muslim minister of religion who had limited leave to remain under the immigration rules in that capacity. He was married and had two children born in the UK. He was refused indefinite leave to remain on the grounds that the Secretary of State was satisfied that Mr Rehman was involved with an Islamic terrorist organization, that in the light of that association it would be undesirable to permit him to remain and that his continued presence in the country represented a danger to national security.

The Secretary of State added that his deportation from the UK would be conducive to the public good in the interests of national security because of his association with Islamic terrorist groups. The organization was named, though the Secretary of State's view was formed on the basis of information received from confidential sources.

The SIAC found that the evidence did not establish the acts alleged, namely that Mr Rehman had recruited British Muslims to undergo militant training, or engaged in fund-raising for Lashkar Tayyaba (LT), or knowingly sponsored individuals for militant training camps. It was accepted that he had provided sponsorship, information, and advice to people going to Pakistan for training. Such training he had regarded as purely religious and developmental. It had not been proved that he was aware of any militant content in such training.

In addition to the question of the jurisdiction of the Commission, two questions of law were appealed to the Court of Appeal and House of Lords. The first was the standard of proof to be applied. The SIAC took the view that these were serious allegations which had important repercussions for the individual involved and which impugned his good character. For these reasons, a standard of proof such as that laid down in *Khawaja* [1984] AC 74 should be applied, that is, a high civil standard of proof. It was in using this standard that they found that the matters alleged against Mr Rehman, as above, were not proved. The Court of Appeal and House of Lords approved the standard as applied to the appellant's actual involvement in alleged terrorist activities, but found that the question of danger to national security required an all round assessment of the situation, not just a finding of, as it were, guilt or innocence in relation to past events. The Court of Appeal said: 'it is necessary not only to look at the individual allegations and ask whether they have been proved. It is also necessary to examine the case as a whole against an individual and then ask whether on a global approach that individual is a danger to national security' ([2000] 3 All ER 778 at 791). The House of Lords approved this view and said that the Secretary of State was 'entitled to have regard to precautionary and preventative principles rather than to wait until directly harmful activities have taken place' (para 22). In fact the idea of a standard of proof was, said Lords Steyn and Hoffmann, not really appropriate to a case where the central question was not, as in a civil or criminal trial, whether something had happened in the past, but rather whether something was likely to happen in the future. It was an evaluation of risk. The effect of this is that the Secretary of State is entitled to make a decision, based on evidence which s/he is not obliged to disclose, that an individual who cannot be proved to have taken part in any unlawful activities, should be deported because there is, in the words of Lord Slynn, a 'real possibility' that their presence may in the future constitute a danger.

The second issue in the appeals was the question of the definition of national security. Firstly there was the question of whether the SIAC had jurisdiction to engage in the question of defining national security. The House of Lords held that this could be within the jurisdiction of a judicial body; it was a question of construction and therefore a question of law. The area of contention between the parties was whether activities in the UK which furthered the cause of an organization abroad which could use violence which was not directed at the UK could be said to endanger the security of the UK. For the purposes of the case, SIAC adopted the position that:

A person may be said to offend against national security if he engages in, promotes or encourages violent activity which is targeted at the UK, its system of government, or its people. This includes activities directed at the overthrow or destabilisation of foreign governments if that foreign government is likely to take reprisals against the UK which affect the security of the UK or its nationals. National security extends also to situations where UK citizens are targeted wherever they may be.

SIAC accepted the appellant's argument that for an activity to endanger the national security of the UK there must be some direct link between the activity and a danger to the UK. The House of Lords and Court of Appeal rejected this view. They adopted the approach of Auld LJ in *Raghbir Singh* [1996] Imm AR 507, who said at 511, 'all sorts of consequences may flow from the existence of terrorist conspiracies or organizations here, whether or not their outcome is intended to occur abroad. Who knows what equally violent response here this sort of conduct may provoke?', and of Lord Mustill in the asylum case of *T* [1996] Imm AR 443, that 'terror as a means of gaining what might loosely be described as political ends poses a danger not only to individual states but also to the community of nations'. Lord Slynn said:

It seems to me that, in contemporary world conditions, action against a foreign state may be capable indirectly of affecting the security of the United Kingdom. The means open to terrorists both in attacking another state and attacking international or global activity by the community of nationals, whatever the objectives of the terrorist, may well be capable of reflecting on the safety and well-being of the United Kingdom or its citizens . . . To require the matters in question to be capable of resulting 'directly' in a threat to national security limits too tightly the discretion of the executive in deciding how the interests of the state . . . need to be protected.

This approach is an international one, in which the fight against terrorism is seen as something in which nations have a common interest. National security is bound up with international security, thus promotion of terrorism against any state is capable of being a threat to the security of the UK, and in the context of terrorism the Secretary of State was not necessarily wrong to justify a decision on national security by reference to damage to relations between countries.

The House of Lords made a distinction between deciding what national security is, which the courts could decide, and what is *in the interests of national security*, which they regarded as a matter for the Secretary of State to decide. In the words of Lord Hoffmann: 'the question of whether something is "in the interests" of national security is not a question of law. It is a matter of judgment and policy' (para 50). Such judgments should be made by someone who was democratically accountable, not by the courts.

The deference shown to the Secretary of State's view on what is in the interests of national security, combined with the abandonment of a standard of proof, to an extent undermines the jurisdiction of the SIAC. They can indeed review all question of law, fact, and exercise of discretion, but issues of what is in the interests of national security are to be regarded as an exercise of discretion concerning risk, not one of establishing facts, and this is a discretion which the Secretary of State is best placed to exercise.

Macdonald commented on this case at the Court of Appeal stage: 'Not since the majority decision *Liversidge and Anderson* has the executive been given such deference; one can hear the Secretary of State saying "I can make national security mean anything I want it to mean" ' (2001:724).

Macdonald was commenting in May 2001, and his comparison with *Liversidge and Anderson* [1942] AC 206 was prophetic. That decision is often explained on the basis that it was taken during wartime, when the Government needs to be given more scope to act as it sees fit, even in breach of people's ordinary civil liberties. At the time of writing we are not at war. However, the response of the UK and USA to the attack on the World Trade Centre on 11 September 2001 was to legislate in way that is reminiscent of war time. In upholding the detentions under that legislation the Court of Appeal drew on *Rehman*. Its influence can also be seen in the House of Lords' judgment, where, although the detentions were found unlawful, the majority of their Lordships held that, despite their doubts about the matter, the Home Secretary had the power to decide that there was an emergency threatening the life of the nation.

Procedural rules have developed restrictively in national security cases. In decision *N v SSHD* [2005] UKSIAC 18/2002 the SIAC held that the relevant circumstances for deciding whether a deportation order ought to be revoked were to be assessed at the date of the deportation decision, not the date of the hearing. In a non-political deportation on public good grounds, heard by the AIT, under Nationality, Immigration and Asylum Act 2002 s 82(2)(k), evidence would be assessed at the date of the hearing. The effect of this is that in a political or national security case, the judicial body does not have an opportunity to decide whether facts subsequent to the decision bear out the initial assessment that the person was a danger. The Immigration, Asylum and Nationality Act 2006 includes a provision that deportation orders may be made on the grounds of threat to national security while an appeal is pending or may be brought, in contrast with other non-conducive deportations in which no order may be made until the appeal process is exhausted (s 7, excluding application of s 79 of the 2002 Act).

The London bombings on 7 July 2005 provoked further legislative proposals, and the government published a consultation paper suggesting that the power to deport on national security grounds should include 'indirect threat' (Exclusion or Deportation from the UK on non-conducive grounds: consultation document, October 2005), apparently not taking into account that the House of Lords had already sanctioned this in *Rehman*. The Home Secretary consulted on a list of 'unacceptable behaviours' which would be taken to 'demonstrate such an indirect threat'. This included writing, producing, publishing or distributing material; public speaking including preaching; running a website; using a position of responsibility to express views which the Government considers 'foment terrorism, justify or glorify terrorism, foster hatred which may led to intra community violence in the UK' and expression of 'what the Government considers to be extreme views that are in conflict with the UK's culture of tolerance'.

As we have seen in chapter 2, these behaviours have also been linked to powers to remove British citizenship.

16.8 Family members

Apart from deportations conducive to the public good, the only other people who may be deported since the implementation of the 1999 Act are family members of people who are deported under s 3(5)(a). Note that these deportations now take place under s 3(5)(b) of the 1971 Act, whereas in case law prior to October 2000 they will be referred to as s 3(5)(c). 'Family members' are defined by the 1971 Act s 5(4), as amended by the 1996 Act, as the husband or wife and children of the person to be deported. 'Children' include adopted children. When parents are unmarried, children are regarded as children of only their mother. Although the entry of second or further wives is not permitted under the Immigration Rules, in the context of deportation polygamy is recognized, as 'wife' includes each of two or more wives.

Paragraphs 365–368 of the Immigration Rules give guidance on the deportation of family members. According to these paragraphs, the Secretary of State will not normally decide to deport the spouse of a deportee where the spouse has qualified for settlement in their own right or has been living apart from the deportee. If a child is living apart from the deportee either with their other parent or because they have established themselves on an independent basis, the Secretary of State will not normally decide to deport the child. This is also the case where the child married before the deportation 'came into prospect'. Home Office internal instructions advise that where children over 16 are liable to deportation in their own right, action should be taken on that basis (IDI Ch 13 s 1 para 2.4). This seems more appropriate to the old grounds for deportation of overstaying and breach of conditions as it is unlikely that the child of a person deported for the public good would also be deportable on account of their own personal behaviour.

There are additional factors to be taken into account in the deportation of family members, and these are set out in para 367 as follows:

(i)   the ability of the spouse to maintain himself and any children in the United Kingdom, or to be maintained by relatives or friends without charge to public funds, not merely for a short period but for the foreseeable future; and

(ii) in the case of a child of school age, the effect of removal on his education; and

(iii) the practicality of any plans for a child's care and maintenance in this country if one or both of his parents were deported; and

(iv) any representations made on behalf of the spouse or child.

In *Njuguna v SSHD* [2001] EWCA Civ 688 the Court of Appeal held that these questions were irrelevant in relation to a five-year-old child. He was not, in any event, going to be able to make a life independently of his mother in the UK. If she were deported, he would be too, and issuing a notice and order in relation to him was simply taking the legal power which inevitably followed from his mother's deportation.

According to s 5(3) of the 1971 Act, a deportation order may not be made against family members if more than eight weeks have elapsed since the principal deportee left the country. Again, this in practical terms only applies where the family member has a viable life in the UK aside from their deported relative.

16.9 Criminal court's recommendation

Section 3(6) of the 1971 Act gives the power to the Secretary of State to deport following the recommendation of a criminal court. The power to make such a recommendation is a sentencing power which may be exercised by the courts in relation to a non-British citizen over the age of 17 who has been convicted of an offence which is punishable with imprisonment. Appeals against the recommendation itself are appeals against sentence and are made through the criminal appeals process.

The decision whether to follow the recommendation is a separate step, and this is the responsibility of the Secretary of State. The recommendation of the sentencing judge does not bind the Secretary of State. He or she has a different constitutional role in the decision-making process and is better placed to take a wider policy-based view of whether deportation is the right course (*R v SSHD ex p Dinc* [1999] Imm AR 380 CA).

16.9.1 Criminal courts and deportation

The general powers of the criminal courts include sentencing for immigration offences. On the other hand, people who are liable to deportation for an offence which has nothing to do with immigration may not have a flawless immigration history. There is plenty of scope for confusion here. Macdonald used some choice words to describe an aspect of the problem.

Matters have not been assisted by the tendency of the courts to describe any non-citizen guilty of an offence under the Immigration Act as an 'illegal immigrant'. The phrase is meaningless and has pejorative connotations of status that may be misleading. A student who fails to get the Department of Employment's permission before getting a summer job, a husband who forgets to apply in time for permission to remain with a wife, an alien who fails to inform the police of a change of address, are doubtless all guilty of offences which may be described as regulatory, but it would be as inappropriate to describe them as 'illegal immigrants' as it would be to describe the company which fails to make expeditious VAT returns as an illegal business. (1995:489)

Deportation for an immigration offence is not appropriate unless it would be warranted in accordance with the proper criteria for deportation discussed below. Some immigration offences are relatively trivial and the fact that they are immigration offences does not justify deportation.

16.9.2 Guidelines

Guidelines for the criminal courts in exercising their power to recommend deportation were set out initially in *R v Caird* (1970) 54 Cr App Rep 499, CA and developed in *R v Nazari* [1980] 3 All ER 880.

The first guideline is that criminal courts are concerned with the potential detriment to the UK of the person remaining in the country. This has been regarded as nothing to do with their immigration status as the detriment is through criminal activity. However, in *R v Benabbas* [2005] EWCA Crim 2113 the Court of Appeal held that where deportation was for an immigration offence, immigration status is 'not entirely irrelevant: it is part of the defendant's personal conduct ... a matter of public interest' (para 40) and 'detriment is intimately bound up with the protection of public order afforded by confidence in a system of passports' (para 41). Here the offence was of using a stolen and forged French passport contrary to Forgery and Counterfeiting Act 1981 s 3, and the recommendation was held to be warranted. By comparison with deportations under s 3(5)(a), there is a greater emphasis on the risk of re-offending, which is a key matter to be assessed, and the court will also have regard to the nature of the offence and the defendant's past record.

Second, the court in *Nazari* thought that they should not be concerned with the political situation or regime or any political threat in the defendant's home country. The Home Office rather than the criminal court was the place to assess such matters. It will readily be seen that concerns about what the defendant may face in their home country may be asylum issues, and the Secretary of State's decision to deport can be appealed on asylum grounds under s 84 of the 2002 Act. Issues concerning the political situation in the defendant's home country would be addressed in that appeal. However, the Human Rights Act affects this stance by the courts. As public bodies under s 6, they are obliged not to act in a way which is incompatible with the defendant's Convention rights. If there is clear evidence that deportation would expose the defendant to a risk for instance of torture, inhuman or degrading treatment or punishment, contrary to Article 3, then a recommendation for deportation would be a breach of s 6 and appealable within the criminal appeal system on human rights grounds.

Third, following *Nazari* the courts were to have regard to the effect of a recommendation for deportation on innocent third parties. The emphasis here was on the harm and distress caused to others, e.g., dependent children or spouse, by the deportation. One might expect this consideration to be expanded by the application of the Convention right in Article 8, to respect for private and family life.

However, the Court of Appeal in *Carmona v R* [2006] EWCA Crim 508 held that the criminal court's recommendation was not an interference with the right. Furthermore, as the criminal court was not in a position to assess any breach of the appellant's rights abroad, they could not assess them at all, and it would accordingly be irrational to consider the less directly engaged rights of family members. In so deciding they took into account that there is now a right of appeal against the Secretary of State's decision, whereas at the time of *Nazari* there was not.

16.9.3 Relationship between the Secretary of State's decision and the court's recommendation

The Secretary of State is not bound to follow the recommendation of the court but must exercise an independent discretion. The court in *Nazari* said that when a court made a recommendation for deportation, all it was doing was giving an opinion that it would be to the detriment of the country for the accused to remain. The Secretary of State then has regard to 'a larger canvas of factors' (*M v SSHD* para 24) when making the decision whether to deport. These include the policy issues referred to earlier, perhaps in relation to deterrence, and the position in the country to which the defendant would be deported.

The Court of Appeal in *M* held that the criminal court's recommendation was a relevant matter for the Secretary of State in exercising the discretion whether to deport, and he or she must therefore come to a rational view of the recommendation and in giving a reasoned decision, explain what view has been taken of it. It is not enough simply to refer to it.

16.10 Compassionate circumstances

In any deportation the ground under s 3 is only one side of the coin. Even apart from issues which may be raised under the Human Rights Act, every potential deportee is entitled to have their personal situation considered. Paragraph 364 of the immigration rules makes it mandatory for the Secretary of State to balance the public interest in deportation against compassionate circumstances, and take into account all known relevant factors.

These must include the following:

(i)   age: the Immigration Directorate Instructions say 'Generally speaking, a person will be considered for deportation in his own right if he is aged between 16 and 65, but the younger or older he is, the more weight might be attached to age as a compassionate factor;

(ii) length of residence in the UK: the longer a person has been in the UK the stronger is their case against deportation. The long residence rules discussed in chapter 6 are a highly influential factor in assessing whether the length of stay is sufficient to weigh against the deportation;

(iii) strength of connections with the UK: this covers for instance family ties and business or employment interests;

(iv) personal history, including character, conduct, and employment record;

(v)   domestic circumstances: in addition to points covered elsewhere this, according to the IDI, covers 'physical domestic circumstances such as housing, and whether the person has anyone who relies on him for support, whether physically, financially, or emotionally';

(vi) previous criminal records and the nature of any offence of which the person has been convicted: this should only include unspent convictions under the Rehabilitation of Offenders Act 1974;

(vii) compassionate circumstances; and

(viii) any representations received on the person's behalf.

The wording of the paragraph exhorts an inclusive approach to considering the potential deportee's circumstances; the matters to be taken into account must include those listed, but are not restricted to these. The requirements of this paragraph apply to the Home Secretary's decision on whether to follow a court's recommendation, as well as to a decision to deport under s 3(5).

The paragraph also says that there is a general requirement of fairness and consistency as between one case and another, yet each case must be considered on its own merits and in the light of all the circumstances. It is in this way that a case such as *Morrison* may be explicable as against for instance *Yebli* (both referred to above). Mr Morrison had an articulate wife with a responsible job who had remained committed to him throughout his long prison sentence. She was able to convince the tribunal that the appellant had a strong relationship also with her child. It was impossible for the two of them to follow him to Jamaica because of her work and the child's warm and loving relationship with his birth father and grandparents. The offences were committed at a time of personal desperation. It was clear that the loyalties involved were strong. The quality of the testimony was clearly influential in this case and weighed against the long criminal record.

In *Hamill* the some of the circumstances advanced have as much the quality of mitigation as of making a claim on compassion. For instance, he claimed to have addressed his offending behaviour in therapy groups. This is relevant and legitimate within para 364 where the obligation is to consider all relevant circumstances. Even though the body of the paragraph requires the public interest to be balanced against compassionate circumstances, this should include all the relevant circumstances advanced.

In *CM Jamaica* [2005] UKIAT 00103 ILU vol. 8, no. 12 the Tribunal compared para 364 of the Immigration Rules with the protection offered by Article 8. This case made it clear that in some respects para 364 has greater scope, and thus offers more protection to the interests of the proposed deportee. In particular, the express inclusion of the strength of ties with the UK, domestic and compassionate circumstances is wider than the accepted requirement of Article 8. It means that the interests of other family members are to be weighed in the balance, which, as we have seen in chapter 3, is not necessarily so in Article 8 claims. This was reaffirmed in *CW Jamaica* [2005] UKIAT 00110 which includes an extended and illuminating discussion about the relationship between the rules and Article 8 in the light of *Huang*. It may be recalled from chapter 3 that *Huang* was to the effect that the rules are the primary expression of Parliament's view of the desirable balance between public and individual interests. Decision-makers should thus generally defer to the rules, and only exceptionally allow human rights considerations to persuade them to depart from them. The tribunal in *CW Jamaica* reaffirmed this principle and applied it in the context of para 364, but here the effect is quite different. As the rules make provision for wider considerations than does Article 8 in countering a deportation, it is indisputable that it is only in rare cases that Article 8's specific emphasis on family life will have anything to add (see chapter 3 for further discussion).

16.11 Home Office policies

Even after the Human Rights Act policy documents giving guidance on deportations may be relevant, though in most cases their application is superseded by arguments under Article 8. Deportation and removal decisions are regulated by Home Office policy documents DP3 and 4/96 and DP069/99, concerning the effect of marriage and children on removal and deportation.

In relation to deportation DP 3/96 says, concerning cases of criminal convictions, that the seriousness of the offence should be balanced against family ties. 'Serious crimes which are punishable with imprisonment or a series of lesser crimes which show a propensity to re-offend, would normally outweigh the family ties. A very poor immigration history may also be taken into account.' Given the wide range of offences punishable with imprisonment and the subjective nature of a judgment as to what is 'serious' this gives a lot of scope for personal circumstances to be outweighed by the character of the offence.

As the main detail of these policies is addressed to removals they will be discussed more fully in the next chapter.

The long residence policies referred to in chapter 6 may be used in cases of removal and result in the granting of indefinite leave. In the case of deportation they may not be relevant as the deportee may have indefinite leave already. Accordingly they are more relevant in cases of overstaying and are discussed in the next chapter on removal. There is one specific provision concerning deportation; IDI Ch 13 s 1 para 3.2 says that someone who has been in the UK for less than fourteen years would normally be considered for deportation, but residence for longer than this will not preclude deportation.

16.12 Regularization

Because of the change in October 2000 to removal as opposed to deportation for overstaying or breach of condition, s 9 of the 1999 Act provided for a 'regularization' period for people who had overstayed and did not want to risk removal. If they came forward during the regularization period they would have the opportunity to apply for leave to remain in the UK, and if unsuccessful would face deportation with a right of appeal rather than removal. The people who had the most to gain from this were those who had been in the UK more than seven years, who would have a full right of appeal on deportation. Those who had been here for less than seven years already had restricted rights of appeal (Immigration Act 1988 s 5, now repealed) and the restricted grounds were similar to those for challenging removal, though with the important difference that the right could be exercised from within the UK. *AC Zimbabwe* [2005] UKIAT 00128 confirmed that this could include a human rights appeal.

Section 9 of the 1999 Act did not give any guarantee that leave to remain would be granted. The application would still be considered on its merits and in line with the usually applicable policy and guidance. A person therefore had no greater chance of leave to remain if they applied during the regularization period; the advantages only arose if their application was refused. The regularization period was introduced by SI 2000/265, the Immigration (Regularisation Period for Over-stayers) Regulations 2000. It began on 8 February 2000 and ended on 1 October 2000. The scheme has proceeded very slowly and has raised expectations which took years to fulfil in many cases.

16.13 Revocation

A deportation order does not expire after a period of time. It runs until it is revoked unless the person who is the subject of the order becomes a British citizen (1971 Act s 5(2)). However it may be revoked on application in accordance with paras 390–392 of the Immigration Rules. The factors which will be taken into account are:

(i)   the grounds on which the order was made;

(ii)   any representations made in support of revocation;

(iii)   the interests of the community, including the maintenance of effective immigration control; and

(iv)   the interests of the applicant, including any compassionate circumstances.

Paragraph 391 provides that the deportation order will not normally be revoked unless the applicant has been away from the UK for at least three years, unless in the most exceptional circumstances. In *Wiafe* (17224) 17 years of prior residence and her children and other family members in the UK did not count as an exceptional circumstance. These factors would have already been taken into account in the decision to deport. In *Jain* (HX00597) the detriment to the applicant's business because of his inability to attend to it personally also did not count as an exceptional circumstance. The tribunal took the view that he had an opportunity to avoid that by leaving voluntarily at an earlier stage.

Paragraph 391 also provides that revocation will not normally be authorized unless there is a change of circumstances or fresh information coming to light, either of which might materially alter the situation. The passage of time in itself may amount to a change of circumstance, but as is clear from the above, less than three years is not normally long enough. Annex A to the Home Office's internal guidance on deportation provides guidance on the periods which could be regarded as normal before revocation. It suggests three years for people deported under the old s 3(5)(a) for overstaying or breach of condition and their families, and ten years for people convicted of serious offences. These are defined as offences of violence, persistent, or large scale burglary or theft, blackmail, forgery, drug offences, and public order offences including riot and affray.

Under s 82 of the 2002 Act there is a right of appeal against the refusal to revoke a deportation order, but under s 92 this right may only be exercised from outside the country unless it is based on asylum or human rights grounds that have not been certified as clearly unfounded. Until the deportee actually leaves, time does not start to be counted towards the time before which an application can be made to revoke. From this point of view there may be nothing to be gained by attempting to stay longer, although occasionally successful public campaigns are mounted to avoid deportation even at this late stage (see, for instance, 'Resistance from Below' in *No-one is Illegal* (Cohen 2003)).

Revocation of a deportation order does not entitle the successful applicant to enter the UK. It only means that an application may be made for leave to enter under the immigration rules and this will be considered on its merits. If for some reason the order is not enforced, IDI Ch13 s 5 provides that consideration can be given to revoking it.

16.14 Supervised and voluntary departures

Once a person is aware that they may be subject to deportation, if there are no strong grounds to challenge the deportation they may wish to leave the country as quickly as possible to avoid a deportation order being made. This may happen with a greater or lesser degree of official involvement. It is possible for a person to leave of their own accord and at their own expense at any time after they become aware that they may be subject to deportation. This may be before or after notice of intention to deport has been served. Informing the Home Office of their travel plans will avoid any further action being taken and so avoid the making of a deportation order.

If the deportation order is made and the person is not aware of it, but leaves after it was made, they are still regarded as deported, and the order will have the same validity as if the Home Office had enforced the order (IDI Ch 13 s 1 para 9.1). If they leave before the order is made, even without contact with the Home Office, any deportation order made after that date will be invalid.

Alternatively a person may sign a formal disclaimer of appeal rights and agree to leave, which gives rise to the possibility of the immigration service paying for their passage (Immigration Act 1971 s 5(6)). This is known as 'supervised departure' (IDI Ch 13 s 5 para 9.2).

There are no immigration rules concerning these procedures, although supervised departure was included in the rules until 2 October 2000. In reality of course someone cannot be prevented from leaving of their own accord, and in a sense no rules are required.

Where these procedures avoid a deportation order being made they also avoid a prohibition on re-entering the UK. However, it is possible that the person's passport may be endorsed to show that the decision to deport was made and served, and this may affect future applications to enter under para 320 of the Immigration Rules.

16.15 Deportation and human rights

There is, as we have seen, no right to reside in the country of one's choice, or at least there is no such right for non-nationals of that country. The deportation per se does not therefore infringe a protected right. The principal enforceable rights which may be infringed are the ECHR Article 8 right to private and family life or Article 3 if the deportee is to be returned to conditions in the country of destination which could amount to inhuman or degrading treatment. For a full discussion of the application of these articles, reference should be made to chapter 3. The case law discussed in chapter 17 in the context of removals affecting human rights should also be considered. The legitimate aims are different, and as different social goals are entailed then the question of the margin of discretion left to the executive may be assessed differently. Making allowances for these differences, the general principles of assessing and balancing rights, for instance questions of proportionality, may be applied also to deportations. Some points particular to deportation are made here.

16.15.1 Necessity in a democratic society

In a deportation which interferes with family or private life, the Secretary of State must justify that action by showing that the deportation meets the criteria in para 2 of Article 8. In particular, that the deportation is necessary in a democratic society, in the interests of a listed public interest. In a deportation case relating to criminal conduct the public interest (or 'legitimate aim') is generally identified as the prevention of disorder or crime. In a drugs case (e.g., *Samaroo*) the Secretary of State may also rely on the protection of health and of the rights and freedoms of others. However the question of necessity must be addressed either by showing that the individual is likely to re-offend and that this re-offending is of a kind which cannot be tolerated, or that for a pressing policy reason, such as deterrence of drugs offences generally, the deportation is necessary.

The deportation must be both conducive to the public good and necessary in a democratic society. While the Secretary of State must show that the deportation is conducive to the public good, there are no specific requirements that must be met in order to do this. The burden of proof is on the Secretary of State on the balance of probabilities, and apart from a simple balancing exercise there is no indication of the weight to be given to the factors in favour of the deportee, listed in para 364 of the rules.

By contrast in Article 8 the starting position is that the individual has a right to respect for their private and family life. The public interests listed in para 2 are exceptions to that right, and may only be used to justify interfering with it not simply when it is conducive to the public good to do so, but when it *necessary* for the public good to do so. As mentioned in chapter 3, the ECHR's definition of what is 'necessary' is that it 'corresponds to a pressing social need' (*Sunday Times v UK* (1979) 2 EHRR 245). In addition to this, the harm caused to the individual by the deportation must be proportionate to the public good which will be achieved by it.

16.15.2 **Proportionality**

The approach of the Court of Appeal in *B v Secretary of State for the Home Department* [2000] Imm AR 478 is illuminating as an example of the court addressing the questions of legitimate aim and proportionality. B was an Italian national from Sicily who had been in the UK since he was seven years old. He was convicted of sexually assaulting his daughter and assaulting his son. His wife divorced him and he had no contact with his children. His parents had other children in the UK on whom they could rely if he were no longer in the country. He had some relatives in Italy and business skills and the capacity to work. The case for deportation of B was made on the grounds of the seriousness of the offence. It was accepted that B's opportunities for re-offending were limited and that it was unlikely that he would do so, therefore although the Secretary of State argued that his deportation was 'for the prevention of crime' this was not based on likelihood of his re-offending.

The Court of Appeal accepted that there could be cases of 'sufficiently serious offending, with or without a propensity to re-offend,' which would warrant deportation, but decided that this was not such a case. The legitimate aim of prevention of crime could therefore not justify deportation as the evidence was that he was unlikely to re-offend.

On the question of proportionality the Court said that although the offence was serious, deportation in this case was 'more akin to exile'. It was therefore disproportionate. Little identifiable public good would be achieved, and the harm to the individual was great. *B* was decided before the Human Rights Act came into effect; however, as the case concerned a European national, Article 8 ECHR was directly applicable as a principle of European law.

In *Mert v SSHD* [2005] EWCA Civ 832 the deportation order had been made six years earlier, but not carried out. The Secretary of State argued that if the deportation order was once appropriate it could not become inappropriate through passage of time. The Court of Appeal held that the adjudicator had carried out a proper proportionality exercise. He had taken account of the importance of the Secretary of State's policy of deterrence, but held that 14 years' residence, children born in the UK, a strong family life, and six years since the deportation order was made, meant that to carry out a deportation would be disproportionate.

The question has arisen in the Tribunal of to what extent appeal bodies can interfere with the Secretary of State's decision that deportation is a proportionate response to a public interest under para 2. The starred Tribunal decision in *Noruwa* 00/TH/2345 was mentioned in chapter 3 in the context of the debate as to the capacity of appeals bodies to decide questions of proportionality for themselves. This was an appeal against a refusal to revoke a deportation order, which, like the making of a deportation order is a discretion. The immigration judge has jurisdiction to decide that a discretion should have been exercised differently. Additionally, the Tribunal in *Noruwa* said, a decision which was disproportionate would be unlawful. There was no discretion to make such a decision. An appeal on a question of proportionality was 'a genuine appeal — not merely a review of whether the Respondent's conclusion on proportionality was open to him' (para 54). The Tribunal seems to see proportionality setting a boundary round the possible exercise of discretion, limiting it to lawful possibilities within Article 8.

The Court of Appeal in *Mert* said that *Huang* could not be directly applied to deportation cases because deportation cases involve policy issues about the prevention of crime, and these must be weighed in the balance by the tribunal. The appeal body does not 'start with a clean sheet of paper' (para 25) on the question of proportionality. They cannot question the Secretary of State's policy, but only balance it against the appellant's interests, as the adjudicator had correctly done here. However, in *CW*, decided two weeks earlier, the Tribunal held that deportation decisions were taken under the rules, specifically para 364, which we have examined. *Huang*'s reference to *Samaroo* as a policy case was because that was a judicial review on policy, not an appeal. It appears the matter is not resolved.

16.15.3 Policy

The question of the jurisdiction to decide whether deportation was proportionate also raises the question of what margin of discretion should be left to executive decision-makers, discussed further in chapter 3 and one of the most significant constitutional questions underlying the Human Rights Act. One of the principles which determines whether a margin of discretion should be left to the decision-maker is whether the court has expertise in the matter in hand. Deterrence of the particular individual is a matter which is clearly within the jurisdiction of the court. Evidence as to the individual's propensity to offend and what might prevent that are routine considerations in the criminal courts. On the other hand a matter such as the general deterrent value of deportation is said to be one of policy, and policy is a matter for the executive. The consistent application and rationality of policy have been held to be within the domain of the judiciary (e.g., *R v SSHD ex p Amankwah* [1994] Imm AR 240 and *Wheeler v Leicester City Council* [1985] AC 1054). It is arguable that in the post Human Rights Act era the UK courts will be called upon more and more to follow the practice which has developed in some other countries, of assessing social information as evidence. For instance, they might be invited to consider the statistical evidence of the effectiveness of deportation as a deterrent. However, we are not at that point yet.

QUESTIONS

1   The immigration rules adopt the principle of consistency and say that decisions should be made on the individual merits of the case. Are these principles mutually contradictory?

2   Is it justifiable to treat European nationals more favourably in the context of deportation?

3   Is deportation for criminal offences any longer justifiable in any circumstances?

FURTHER READING

Bevan, V. (1986) *The Development of British Immigration Law* (Croom Helm), pp. 305–309.

Clery, E., Daniel, N., and Tah, C. *The Voluntary assisted return and reintegration 2003: an evaluation.* Home Office RDS 2005.

Cohen, S. (2003) 'Resistance from below', in Cohen, S. (ed.) *No-one is Illegal* (Stoke on Trent: Trentham Books).

Dembour, M.-B. (2003) 'Human Rights Laws and Nationality in Collusion: The Plight of Quasi-Nationals at Strasbourg', *Netherlands Quarterly of Human Rights*, 21 (1), pp. 63–98.

O'Nions, H. (2001) 'The Human Rights of Deportees in the English Legal System' *Journal of Civil Liberties* 691, pp. 3–17.

17

....

Removal

SUMMARY

This chapter describe the grounds in law for exercising the power to remove a person from the UK. The development of the definition of an illegal entrant is described, and the effect of including within the removal power many people who formerly could only be deported. The policies and rules are discussed which may be raised to oppose a removal, and finally the application of the Human Rights Act to removals is considered in the light of recent case law.

17.1 Introduction

The power of removal is the clearest possible demonstration of the Crown's power to control the entry of foreign nationals, though this does not mean that it is an untrammelled power. It is exercised within a statutory framework, principally that of the Immigration Act 1971, amended and supplemented by the Asylum and Immigration Act 1996, the Immigration and Asylum Act 1999, the Nationality, Immigration and Asylum Act 2002 and the Asylum and Immigration (Treatment of Claimants etc) Act 2004. The power is tempered by human rights and asylum considerations; nevertheless, in 2004, 56,920 people were removed from the UK.

Directions for removal may be given without, necessarily, any kind of judicial process. A person may be put onto an aeroplane or a ship and taken to another country without any opportunity to object in advance to this course of action. Because of the abrupt and potentially speedy nature of this process, and its lack of judicial oversight, it can be described as 'summary removal'. It is difficult to imagine a more dramatic exercise of power by the executive over the individual, but its power may be mitigated by a right of appeal. Where there is an existing entry clearance or work permit then there are in-country rights of appeal, and when human rights or asylum claims are made, but only if this claim is not certified as clearly unfounded by the Secretary of State (Nationality, Immigration and Asylum Act 2002 Parts 4 and 5). There are other limited appeal rights, but these may only be exercised after removal. As a consequence, resort has often been made to judicial review, which suspends the implementation of removal.

17.1.1 **Terminology**

There is scope for a great deal of confusion in the use of the term 'removal' and associated phrases. One use of the term 'administrative removal' is to refer to removal on the grounds which used to be grounds for deportation, discussed below. This distinguishes it from removal of illegal entrants and those refused entry. Another use of the term 'administrative removal' is to refer to all removals, using 'administrative' to distinguish it from deportation which has an enduring legal effect. Finally, all enforced departures including deportation end in removal, as this term is used to describe the actual embarkation on transport which takes the person away, and all such departures are preceded by removal directions. These are served on the captain of a ship or aircraft or on a train operator and on the person themselves, telling them when and where to report in order for their removal to take place.

The term 'removal' is used in this chapter to refer to all removals as distinct from deportations. The term 'administrative removal' is not used. In a later section removal directions are discussed specifically.

17.1.2 **Expansion in use of the power to remove**

The power of removal has existed in its present form since 1 January 1973 when the Immigration Act 1971 came into force. The Act made Commonwealth citizens and aliens subject to the same legal regime, and this included the power to remove anyone who had entered in breach of immigration laws (Sch 2 and s 33). *Azam v SSHD* [1974] AC 18 confirmed that this statutory power applied even to Commonwealth citizens who had entered before the Act came into effect, and who would have been immune from removal or deportation under the previous law.

The power to remove was implemented straight away. Evans charts the growth in the use of the power of removal from 80 people in the first year of operation to a peak of 910 in 1980, dropping again to 640 in 1981. The starting figure of 80 was, he points out, a significant increase on the steady annual figure of around 60 people removed each year from 1968 to 1972. The increased number of removals in this period reflects expansion of the law governing removal at that time. The 1971 Act extended power to Commonwealth citizens, and after the implementation of the Act the courts took hold of the concept of 'illegal entrant' and extended it, as discussed below, in a way not foreseen by Parliament. In 1983 the House of Lords put the brake on this expansion.

17.1.3 **Policy on removals**

Developments in policy and practice have had at least as significant an impact on removals as developments in law. The growth in numbers of asylum seekers has been accompanied by a rise in the numbers of removals. The number of people removed as illegal entrants doubled from 1987 to 1988 and the UK Immigration Advisory Service suggested that the increase in removals was part of an attempt to curtail asylum appeals (Dummett and Nicol 1990:255). By the time of the most recent published annual figures the number of removals had shot up to 56,920 (Control of Immigration Statistics 2004 Home Office August 2005), although this was a reduction on the previous two years.

A desire to process asylum claims quickly and to remove unsuccessful applicants are significant policy drivers behind the law and practice on removal. This is borne out by the steady reduction in appeal rights against removal, particularly the powers to certify human rights and asylum claims. It was acknowledged in the Home Affairs Select Committee Report on Asylum Removals that the integrity of the asylum process relies on the capacity to effect the removal of those whose claim has failed (e.g., para 8). The Committee's report also describes the practical and legal complexities of effecting removals, and although asylum policy may drive the law, in 2004 only 12,585 of the 56,920 people removed, had sought asylum at some stage (2004 Statistics para 31).

On 16 September 2004 the British Prime Minister promised to double the number of failed asylum seekers removed by the end of 2005, though the statistical basis for this was not clear. On the other hand, there continue to be important questions about whether removals to certain countries are safe and feasible. The UNHCR made statements advising that returns to Somalia and Iraq were unsafe (16 June and 22 October 2004: unhcr.org.uk), but the Home Office declined to undertake that removals would not take place to these countries, and continued to consider them on a case by case basis. The only country to which, as a matter of policy, removals have not been taking place in recent times has been Zimbabwe, as discussed in chapter 13.

The manner in which removals are carried out is also an issue of public concern. The Medical Foundation published a report detailing excessive force useds, sometimes resulting in injury. As a consequence, CCTV cameras are to be installed in the vans used to carry out removals (news.bbc.co.uk 5 November 2004).

17.2 Grounds for removal

There are two sets of powers of removal; Immigration Act 1971 Sch 2 paras 8 and 9 gives power to immigration officers to remove people who have been refused leave to enter (para 8) and illegal entrants (para 9). Immigration and Asylum Act 1999 s 10 gives power to remove people who have overstayed the limit of their leave, or have breached conditions of leave or obtained leave to remain by deception. It also gives power to remove the families of such people.

We shall consider each of these grounds in turn. The main legal controversies have surrounded the question of who is deemed to be an illegal entrant.

17.2.1 Illegal entrants

The way that provisions concerning illegal entrants are enacted suggests a lack of importance, and it is extraordinary that powers of such a draconian nature are almost incidental in statute. The reasons are historical, but the many legislative changes since 1971 have not addressed this. The definition of an illegal entrant is found in s 33, the definition section of the 1971 Act, and the power to remove an illegal entrant is in Sch 2. A power which forms a major plank of immigration control would be more appropriately located in the body of the statute. However, the power to remove was envisaged as an administrative matter, an action which could be taken speedily by immigration officers without judicial involvement.

An 'illegal entrant' is defined in s 33(1) of the 1971 Act, as amended by the Asylum and Immigration Act 1996, as a person:

(a) unlawfully entering or seeking to enter in breach of a deportation order or of the immigration laws; or
(b) entering or seeking to enter by means which include deception by another person.

A person may be termed an 'illegal entrant' without actually entering, as s 33 covers those who 'seek to enter' as well as those who actually do. A person may be apprehended, say, at a port, and may be subject to removal as an illegal entrant if they were seeking to enter in breach of immigration laws but had not yet done so. A clandestine entrant may come within this category. Where someone presents documentation or makes an application, the nature of that documentation or application is crucial as a lawful applicant with entry clearance has a right of appeal if refused. They are also entitled to a decision within 24 hours of the end of examination failing which they obtain six months' deemed leave with a prohibition on working (Immigration Act 1971 Sch 2 para 6, though see chapter 6 for limited effect of this provision). An illegal entrant has none of these entitlements. Secondly, a person may be deemed an illegal entrant if they do actually enter illegally. We shall consider shortly what this means. Thirdly, an illegal entrant is a person 'who has so entered'. The effect of this is that there is no cut-off date for designation as an illegal entrant. Under the Commonwealth Immigrants Act 1962 a person who remained undetected for 24 hours could not be removed; the 1968 Act extended this to 28 days but there are no such periods of grace in present law. Now, a person may live for years in insecurity, not knowing whether they will be subject to enforcement action. While a long residence in this country may affect whether enforcement action is taken or is successful (see chapter 6), the possibility of that action remains until their status is regularised.

There are a number of ways in which a person may be considered to enter illegally.

17.2.1.1 *Entering without leave*

'Entering in breach of the immigration laws' was initially interpreted as meaning simply 'entering without leave'. The immigration laws were primarily concerned with the regulation of entry, so someone who entered in breach of those laws entered without having gone through that regulatory process. Specifically, 1971 Act s 3(1)(a) states:

Except as otherwise provided by or under this Act, where a person is not a British Citizen
(a) he shall not enter the UK unless given leave to do so in accordance with this Act.

Entry without leave by someone who needs leave is therefore a breach of immigration laws in that it is a breach of s 3 of the 1971 Act. Entry without leave does not require any particular state of mind or of knowledge in order to result in a person being an illegal entrant. The Court of Appeal in *R v Governor of Ashford Remand Centre ex p Bouzagou* [1983] Imm AR 69 rejected the submission that any *mens rea* was required. The breach of immigration laws does not need to be deliberate or even known to a person in order for them to have entered without leave and thus be deemed an illegal entrant.

This kind of illegal entry includes clandestine entrants who arrive in the back of lorries or land by night in a small boat on a secluded beach. It also includes people who mistakenly enter without leave, even if the mistake is that of the immigration officer. This surprising conclusion was reached in the case of *Rehal v Secretary of State for the Home Department* [1989] Imm AR 576 CA. Mr Rehal was a British overseas citizen. The immigration officer, glancing at his British passport, thought he was a British citizen and waved him through. Without a stamp in his passport, Mr Rehal had no leave to enter. The immigration officer's invitation for him to pass through was not a grant of leave but a (barely considered) decision that he did not need leave.

The same result comes about when the mistake, though still not the fault of the passport holder, is in the passport rather than the action of the immigration officer. This was apparent in the case of *Mokuolo and Ogunbiyi v SSHD* [1989] Imm AR 51 CA in which the passports of two Nigerian sisters mistakenly stated that they were British citizens. Accordingly, they were not granted leave to enter on the assumption that they did not need it. Although, like Mr Rehal, they were not guilty of any deception or wrongdoing, they, like him, were found to be illegal entrants.

The Court of Appeal's decision in *Rehal* turned on the meaning they gave to 1971 Act Sch 2 para 6, the obligation to make a decision within 24 hours, failing which the entrant has six months' deemed leave. It applies where a person 'is to be given' limited leave. The Court of Appeal interpreted this to mean where the immigration officer intends to make a decision on the question of leave. This means that if the immigration officer has not thought about it because for instance as in Mr Rehal's case they did not realise it was necessary to do so, the deemed leave provision does not apply, so the person is considered an illegal entrant. Macdonald puts forward an alternative and surely preferable interpretation that the words 'is to be given' refer to someone who needs leave, i.e. does not have right of abode (1995:70). This objective interpretation would bring within para 6 those who are deemed illegal entrants through the immigration officer's mistake. This otherwise seems an injustice, as at the time of arrival at the port there was no difference in law between Mr Rehal and any other lawful applicant for leave to enter.

Leave to enter is normally endorsed on a passport, and since the Leave to Enter and Remain Order 2000, SI 2000/1161 will often have been granted by entry clearance in advance (see chapter 6). Therefore the question of proof that it exists is reasonably straightforward except that since the Leave to Enter and Remain Order leave to enter need not always be given in writing and need not be given to the traveller personally. It may be granted by fax or e-mail or for a visitor even by telephone (art 8) and in the case of a group travelling together it might for instance be endorsed on a passenger list rather than a document produced by an individual (art 9). In these cases the burden of proof is on the person claiming that they have leave to enter to prove that is the case (art 11). This reverses the burden of proof at precisely the point at which the entrant is most vulnerable, but it is unlikely that an oral grant of leave will often be given.

Section 11(5) of the 1971 Act provides that an air or sea crew member who seeks to remain beyond the time allowed (s 8(1)) will be treated as seeking to enter the UK. If they do so in breach of immigration laws they will be regarded as an illegal entrant.

17.2.1.2 *Entry in breach of a deportation order*

The s 33 definition of an illegal entrant includes someone who enters in breach of a deportation order. This means that any person who is the subject of a deportation order is subject to removal as an illegal entrant if they enter the UK while the deportation order is still in force against them. The order is in force unless it has been revoked. A deportation order completely prohibits re-entry, whether or not the person would normally require leave to enter, e.g., if they were an EEA national they would otherwise be able to enter without leave, but as a deportee they are an illegal entrant if they do so (*Shingara v SSHD* [1999] Imm AR 257 CA).

If the person who is the subject of the deportation order had leave when the deportation order was made the leave is invalidated by the deportation order. See, for instance, the case of *Dinc* [1999] Imm AR 380 CA, discussed in the last chapter, where the respondent had indefinite leave to remain. Any leave granted during the currency of the deportation order, whether to enter or remain, is also invalidated (1971 Act s 5). The result of this is that if someone enters while a deportation order is in force against them, they enter without leave. This is the case whether they enter clandestinely or whether, by mistake or deception, they manage to obtain an apparent leave, as any such leave will have no effect.

It might therefore be objected that these words are redundant in the definition of an illegal entrant. A person subject to a deportation order is without leave anyway. This argument was advanced for the appellants in *Khawaja v SSHD* [1984] AC 74 as evidence that 'in breach of the immigration laws' should be given a narrow interpretation, i.e., restricted only to those who entered without leave. If it was open to a wider interpretation, there would be no need to specify 'in breach of a deportation order', as that would be included. However, the House of Lords rejected that argument, and while the inclusion of entry in breach of a deportation order may, strictly speaking, be redundant, it still stands.

17.2.1.3 *Entry by deception*

As indicated earlier, the possibility of becoming an illegal entrant by deception was at first a common law development. It was not in the contemplation of Parliament at the time of the passing of the Immigration Act 1971 that illegal entrants would include anyone other than those entering in breach of a deportation order or without leave (see, for instance, discussion in Grant and Martin, *Immigration Law and Practice* (1982) and Evans, *Immigration Law* (1983)). Support for this view could be obtained from the terms of the criminal offence of illegal entry, the relevant part of which only refers to entry in breach of a deportation order and entry without leave (1971 Act s 24). The courts however began to interpret 'in breach of the immigration laws' as including people who had passed through immigration control and had obtained leave to enter, but had done so by deception. The approach of the courts in a series of cases was to treat leave obtained by deception contrary to s 26(1)(c) as invalid. Section 26(1)(c) sets out a criminal offence, committed where a person:

Makes or causes to be made . . . a return, statement or representation which he knows to be false or does not believe to be true.

The courts thereby created a relationship between the definition of an illegal entrant and the criminal provisions of the Immigration Act. The statute already provided a sanction for an offence under s 26, but the courts intertwined this offence with the administrative enforcement provisions. They decided that leave obtained in this way was obtained 'in breach of the immigration laws' and therefore not leave which would entitle a person to enter.

This judicial invention was ratified by the House of Lords in July 1980 in *Zamir* [1980] 2 All ER 768. This case represented a low point for the peace of mind and security of immigrants. Their Lordships held that leave granted through the use of deception was not leave granted in accordance with the Immigration Act and could rightly found a removal as an illegal entrant. Even more disturbingly, they considered that the duty of a potential immigrant was a 'duty of candour', analogous to the duty of utmost good faith imposed upon parties in the law of contract. This meant that the applicant must disclose all potentially relevant information, and was under a duty to volunteer information, not just to answer questions. This put the applicant in the position of being responsible for deciding what was relevant, and risking being removed as an illegal entrant if they made a wrong judgement on that matter.

This decision 'provoked widespread academic criticism and a storm of protest from the ethnic communities and bodies concerned with improving race relations' (Evans 1983:314). It was reversed in important respects by the House of Lords in *Khawaja* [1984] AC 74 which held that there was no duty of utmost good faith. There must be actual or attempted deception before illegal entry could be established, not just a failure to interpret correctly the requirements of the immigration rules. This judgment put beyond doubt that entry obtained by deception could give rise to removal as an illegal entrant, but tempered the more extreme aspects of the *Zamir* judgment. The House of Lords found that the burden of proof that the person was an illegal entrant was upon the Secretary of State, and the standard was the civil standard, but this should be interpreted as being at the high end of the balance of probabilities, bearing in mind the serious consequences for the individual and the quasi-criminal nature of the allegations. Importantly, the House of Lords in *Khawaja* reversed the 'hands-off' approach which had characterized earlier judicial decisions concerning illegal entrants. The courts had shown a tendency not to investigate the facts, and in judicial review held that such investigation was outside the court's scope of enquiry as the jurisdiction is one of review of the decision-making process, not an appeal on the merits. The House of Lords in *Khawaja* held that the fact that someone was an illegal entrant was a matter which determined whether or not there was jurisdiction to act. Such 'jurisdictional facts' *did*, they said, come within the scope of the court's inquiry. The court would therefore examine for itself the evidence as to whether the person was an illegal entrant.

Following *Khawaja*, the inclusion of a person who gained entry by deception in the definition of illegal entrant was here to stay. Obtaining entry by deception became more explicitly part of the statutory definition with the Asylum and Immigration Act 1996. The offence was created of using deception to obtain or seek to obtain leave to enter or remain in the UK (amending Immigration Act 1971 s 24, renumbered again by Immigration and Asylum Act 1999 so the offence is now found in 1971 Act s 24A). An offence under that section, like an offence under s 26(1)(c) is 'in breach of immigration laws' and so makes the perpetrator an illegal entrant as found in *Khawaja*.

However, the way was still open for dispute on a number of issues which inevitably arise in the determination of questions surrounding deception. These included the effect of deception by a third party, the use of false documents, the relationship between any deception and the leave granted, and what conduct may give rise to a finding of deception, in the absence of a duty of utmost good faith.

Third party deception and use of false documents
Section 26(1)(c) refers to a representation which the entrant 'makes or causes to be made'. There has been debate as to whether a deceptive representation by a third party is included, and as the use or possession of an 'altered' document is a separate offence under s 26(1)(d), there is also scope for debate on whether the use of a false passport is included. These two issues may merge where a false document has been prepared or is used by a third party. However, the Asylum and Immigration Act 1996 resolved the question of the effect of deception by third parties by adding to the definition of illegal entrant in s 33(1) para (b): 'entering or seeking to enter by means which include deception by another person.' This addition to s 33(1) puts beyond doubt that deception by a third party will make the entry illegal and means that earlier case law on this point no longer has any effect.

The use of invalid documents is now also covered by the statutory provisions introduced by the 1996 Act. If the entrant produces a false document knowing it to be false, this is deception contrary to s 24A(1). If they are not aware of its falsity but this is the result of the deliberate act of a third party, the deception is covered by s 33(1).

Relationship between deception and leave granted
The effect of the deception is a matter of some importance. At one extreme, some acts of deception might be about a quite peripheral fact, which had very little bearing on the decision to grant entry. It would be inappropriate then to regard entry as illegal. At the other extreme, misrepresentation about a central fact such as whether the sponsor and applicant did in fact intend to marry could easily be a deception which would render the entry illegal. The question to be addressed is whether, to make an entry illegal, the deception has to be the effective cause of leave being granted, or just a factor which contributed to the decision.

The question of the effect of the deception was addressed authoritatively in *Khawaja* in which the court held that the deception should be the effective means of obtaining leave in order for the entry to be regarded as illegal. It relied on the earlier case of *R v SSHD ex p Jayakody* [1982] 1 All ER 461 in which the Court of Appeal had held that in order to render the entry illegal the fraud should be the decisive factor in the application. In other words, if there had been no deception then the application would probably have been refused. In *Bugdaycay v SSHD* [1987] 1 AC 514 the House of Lords said that the question was, if the true facts were known, whether the decision-maker would have been 'bound to refuse' the application. However, in *Bugdaycay*, the House of Lords also held that an applicant could not legitimize their entry by arguing that if they had put forward the true facts leave would still have been granted. In that case a person who applied as a visitor had not disclosed that he intended to apply for asylum. If he had applied for asylum he would not have been able to be removed. However, the House of Lords held that his argument could only be seen in the light of the application which he did in fact make, and that was deceptive, and so he was treated as an illegal entrant. The judgment seems to proceed on the basis that an applicant should not be allowed to get away with deception, but if the deception did not make any difference it is hard to see how it is effective in the *Khawaja* sense. Although *Bugdaycay* did not expressly overturn *Khawaja*, it did depart from that reasoning, and an approach more consistent with *Bugdaycay* is the one that has been followed since then as the courts have developed an approach requiring deception to be material rather than decisive. For instance, in *Sukhjinder Kaur v Secretary of State for the Home Department* [1998] Imm AR 1 (see below) the appellant argued that alternative financial sponsorship was available and so she would still have qualified for entry as her husband's wife, but the Court of Appeal did not accept this argument.

In *Durojaiye v Secretary of State for the Home Department* [1991] Imm AR 307 the Court of Appeal considered that giving false answers to questions about a student's attendance at college was 'material in the sense that it was likely to influence their decision'. This is not the same as saying that they were a matter without which a different decision would necessarily have been made. In *R v Secretary of State for the Home Department ex p Castro* [1996] Imm AR 540 at 544, the High Court considered that 'it may be sufficient for the Secretary of State to show that the deception was material in the sense that it was likely to influence the decision whether to grant leave to enter'. However, although this point has been summarized in the headnote of the case it does not seem to form part of the *ratio* as the judge found that the more stringent test of effective cause was satisfied. This judgment should therefore be treated with caution in this respect. *Sukhjinder Kaur* was not a case about illegal entry but about refusal of entry to a person who held entry clearance. The applicant had not disclosed that her husband was in prison at the time of the application, but had said he was living at his home address. The Court of Appeal held that this non-disclosure was material because it was 'likely to influence' the outcome of the application in that it affected whether her husband would be able to support her financially. The Court of Appeal accepted that *Khawaja* did not apply as this was not an illegal entry case. The duty for the appellant to disclose that her husband had been arrested arose, they pointed out, from the immigration rules, which impose a duty to disclose material facts (then para 17, the equivalent of present-day para 321). The case therefore turned on the question of what was material as this is what should have been disclosed. Here the Court of Appeal did not make any distinction between illegal entry and refusal of leave to enter. Ward LJ said: 'I agree that the time has come when we should put that [the *Jayakody*] test to rest', without referring to the context of refusing leave to enter, but also without stating that the Court regarded the two legal strands as interchangeable on this point. He followed *Bugdaycay* and *Durojaiye*, using the line of authority concerning materiality in illegal entry.

Since *Khawaja* the different statutory formulation goes some way to resolving the question. At the time of *Khawaja* a person was an illegal entrant by deception if they made representations which they knew to be false (1971 Act s 26(1)(c)). The causal relationship with the leave then granted was matter for the courts to consider. Since the 1996 Act, however, the relevant sections (24A and 33(1)) both refer to entry obtained or sought 'by means which include' deception. The use of the word 'include' suggests that there might be other factors also at work in the grant of leave. In other words that this is not a case where, apart from the deception, the decision-maker would have been 'bound to refuse'. On the other hand 'by means' implies that the deception is operative. It takes effect to bring about the grant of leave and has a bearing on the decision. The net result of this is that in order for the deception to give rise to a finding of illegal entry, it must have played a part in the decision to grant entry, but need not necessarily have been the only factor. Macdonald considers that the current statutory formulation of 'by means which include' is a decisive shift in the direction of materiality and away from the *Jayakody* test (2001:749).

Conduct — deception by silence

Before the 1996 Act, in order to show that silence was a deception giving rise to illegal entry it would have to be shown that there was a representation by silence, for instance presentation of a passport (e.g., *R v Secretary of State for the Home Department ex p Kuteesa* [1997] Imm AR 194) in order to bring the case within s 26(1)(c). However the current sections do not require that. The issue is only whether entry was gained or sought by means which include deception.

If the applicant says nothing about a relevant matter it may be because they are deliberately concealing it, or it may be because they are not aware that it is relevant and have not been asked about it. In the latter case there is no deception. Which of these is the case is matter of inference for the tribunal from available evidence. To establish illegal entry from a failure to mention something it needs to be established how much the applicant should have been expected to say. As there is not a duty of candour, what can the applicant be expected to know is relevant?

In *Cendiz Doldur v SSHD* [1998] Imm AR 352 the Court of Appeal held there was no duty on the applicant to disclose his marriage on arrival when he was not asked about it or about any change of circumstances. He was still dependent in fact on his father and could not be expected to know that this did not mean that he was still dependent in law after he had married. Although the Court of Appeal heard this case in 1998, Mr. Doldur's entry was before the 1996 Act came into force, and so the case was decided on the old law, i.e., the question of whether by his silence he made a representation which was false, contrary to s 26(1)(c). After the 1996 Act to gain a different result on the same facts the Secretary of State would need to show that the failure to mention his marriage was a deception. In the case of *Kuteesa* the applicant obtained leave to enter for two years as a student, subject to the condition that he was not to take employment. He decided not to enrol on the course for which he had been given leave, but enrolled on a later course and worked in the meantime. Shortly before he was due to start the new course his father died, and he went home to Uganda for the funeral. On his re-entry to the UK, he produced his passport and a letter from the college saying:

This student is going home as a result of a bereavement in the family and will be returning to college to continue his studies. I confirm that [there is] a place reserved for him.

The High Court held that by his silent presentation of his passport he had made a representation that he had previously fulfilled his conditions of entry. As this was false, contrary to s 26(1)(c), he was an illegal entrant. He argued that if he had revealed the true facts he would still have been granted leave to enter as to refuse would have been unreasonable. However, Harrison J disagreed. He found that the immigration officer would have refused leave to enter if he had known the full history. This was at least in part because the applicant had had leave to enter as a student on a previous occasion and worked in breach of conditions. The argument in this case illustrates how engagement with the question outlawed by *Bugdaycay* (whether leave would have been granted had the true facts been known) merges into the question of materiality (what was relevant) and even, in this case, what would have been a proper exercise of discretion.

Unlike Mr Doldur, Mr Kuteesa had done something (presented his passport) which was a positive action and could thus amount to a representation. However the case turned more on what the entrant in each case could be expected to have known was relevant, i.e., an investigation of their state of mind. This kind of reasoning survives the amendments made by the 1996 Act as the question of whether there has been deception must involve the question of the entrant's state of mind. In *Durojaiye* the passport holder obtained leave to remain, then left the country and returned again. The Court of Appeal held that the presentation of the passport on re-entry amounted to deception as the passport holder was aware that the leave stamped in it had been obtained falsely.

Standard of proof

The burden of proof that a person is an illegal entrant is on the Home Office. The standard of proof, first laid down in *Khawaja*, has been developed but not substantially altered by subsequent cases. It was said to be the civil standard, i.e., on the balance of probabilities, but at the higher end of that scale in view of the gravity of the matters in question. If the person is found to be an illegal entrant they are liable to detention and removal from the country; as liberty is at stake the burden of proof should be strictly applied.

This standard was reiterated and applied in *Doldur*. No one apart from Mr. Doldur himself knew exactly what was in his mind when he entered the UK. The Secretary of State could not prove that it was 'an irresistible inference' that he knew that his marriage was relevant to his entry to the UK, and so the allegation could not be proved to the required standard. In his judgment in *Doldur* Evans LJ relied on *R v SSHD ex p Rahman* [1997] 3 WLR 990 in which the standard of proof was that 'the degree of probability was so great as closely to approximate the criminal standard'.

However, an inference against the applicant may be drawn from the evidence if it meets the standard. For instance, in *Kesse* TH/00419, the appellant had obtained entry on the basis of marriage to a person who was subsequently found to have never been married. The tribunal upheld the finding of deception, using the standard of proof laid down in *Khawaja* and endorsed in *Doldur*, and which they described as being 'a high degree of probability'.

R (on the Application of Ullah) v SSHD [2003] EWCA Civ 1366 provided a more recent example of the application of this standard of proof. The case had proceeded without the benefit of a witness statement from the person who would have been the appellant's first wife had that marriage been valid. The Court of Appeal held that the Secretary of State could in theory proceed without such a statement, but in this case there was insufficient evidence to meet the high standard of proof that the appellant must have known of the invalidity of his marriage.

In the context of standard of proof, reference should also be made back to the section on entry without leave, as in the case of visitors who claim to have been granted oral leave to enter, or passengers who claim that their leave was granted as part of a group or for some other reason to a person other than themselves, the burden of proof is in effect cast on the traveller.

17.2.2 **Refused leave to enter**

As we have seen, a greater number of people are removed after being refused leave to enter than as illegal entrants. The Immigration Act 1971 Sch 2 para 8(1) says that where a person arriving in the United Kingdom is refused leave to enter then they may be removed on the direction of an immigration officer. This rather stark provision, read in isolation, could give an impression that anyone refused leave could just be returned forthwith to the country from which they came. This is a possibility, but not in every case, as some people refused leave to enter have a right of appeal which they may exercise in the UK. The Nationality, Immigration and Asylum Act 2002 s 92 repeats earlier provisions in giving a right of appeal in the UK to a person who holds an entry clearance or work permit. It also gives a right of appeal in the UK against refusal of leave to enter to an EEA national or their family member who claims that the refusal would breach their rights of entry or residence under European Community law and to someone who has made a human rights or asylum claim while in the UK. Section 78 provides that people who by s 92 have a right of appeal exercisable in the UK may not be removed while their appeal is pending. There is a further caveat to this, however, which is that s 94 gives power to the Secretary of State to certify asylum and human rights claims as 'clearly unfounded' in which case the appellant will lose their right of appeal in the UK, and be removable. Certificates of this kind will be issued automatically in the case of the listed states (see chapter 12). The 2002 Act therefore creates a kind of 'to and fro' motion, as in the following example:

X applies for leave to enter as student — refused — no right of appeal (s 89) — X is removable

X claims removal breaches Refugee Convention — appeal s 92(4) — X is not removable (s 78)

Secretary of State is satisfied that X is entitled to live in Mongolia, certifies claim clearly unfounded s 94 — X is removable

An asylum seeker who may be returned to a safe third country may be removed without their asylum claim being considered (see chapter 12). If an asylum seeker is wrongly removed pending appeal, the court may be prepared to grant an injunction to compel the Secretary of State to return the claimant to the UK so that his rights could be preserved pending the outcome of his appeal (e.g., *R (on the application of T) v SSHD* [2004] EWHC 869 Admin).

Removal under Immigration Act 1971 Sch 2 para 8 is therefore not necessarily permitted straight away, and whether it is permitted is not necessarily apparent immediately. A swift removal might take place for instance in the case of a non-visa national applying unsuccessfully to enter as a visitor or student, and who has no asylum or human rights claim. On the other hand there may be a lengthy process, perhaps an asylum claim with an unsuccessful appeal, and a person who is given temporary admission while their application is being processed and who has been in the UK for months or years without leave ever having been granted, is still subject to removal at the end of that process. In this case the directions for removal would be made by the Secretary of State under Sch 2 para 10, and the Secretary of State will have responsibility in any case where more than two months have passed since the refusal of leave (paras 8 and 10). Under the 1999 Act removal directions could not be given (Sch 4 para 10) while an appeal was pending, however the 2002

Act has reversed this and permits removal directions to be given even while they cannot be carried out (s 78). This is an example of the policy of the 2002 Act to streamline and speed up removals as far as possible.

17.2.3 Expansion in grounds for removal

The courts had expanded the definition of 'illegal entrants', but from 1 January 1973 until 2 October 2000 those subject to removal were restricted to illegal entrants and people refused entry at the port. On 2 October 2000 Immigration and Asylum Act 1999 s 10 came into effect, and changed a number of grounds for deportation under Immigration Act 1971 s 3(5) into grounds for removal.

In the 1971 Act as originally passed, breach of condition and overstaying were grounds for deportation (the old s 3(5)(a)). Deportation carried a full right of appeal while summary removal attracted a right of appeal only from out of the UK, i.e., after the event. There was a rationale for that distinction as the original target of the removal provisions was those who were refused entry at the port and people who had arrived clandestinely but were apprehended soon after arrival. People who had overstayed or breached their condition have had some period of residence, and some connection with the UK, perhaps brief, but perhaps of many years. It would therefore be legitimate to treat them differently. However, in practice this rationale broke down because the courts developed the category of illegal entrant to include a person who had entered using deception. This could include a person whose original leave had been gained years earlier. This put a person deemed an illegal entrant and an overstayer in a much more similar position.

Parliament's response to this was to level down the rights of overstayers to those of illegal entrants, influenced no doubt by the policy imperative of moving people though the system more quickly. The levelling down happened in two stages. First, as discussed in chapter 16, the Immigration Act 1988 s 5 limited appeals for people who had overstayed or breached condition, and had been in the UK for less than seven years, to the grounds that that there was 'in law, no power to make the deportation order for the reasons stated in the notice'. In other words, they could only appeal on grounds that they had not, in fact, overstayed or breached their conditions. This took away the right to be heard on all other circumstances of their case.

The second stage of levelling down came with the Immigration and Asylum Act 1999 s 10 which made those who had overstayed, breached condition, or obtained leave by deception (a ground for deportation added by the Asylum and Immigration Act 1996) subject to removal and not deportation. Appeal rights would therefore only be on the restricted grounds, however long the person had lived in the UK, and could only be exercised from outside the UK. These provisions and the changes are discussed in more detail below.

17.2.3.1 *Obtaining leave to remain by deception*

This ground for removal was introduced into 1971 Act s 3 as a new ground of deportation by the 1996 Act but was changed into a ground for removal along with overstaying and breach of condition by 1999 Act s 10.

It refers to situations where, for instance, a person obtains indefinite leave to remain by misrepresenting at the end of their first year of leave that their marriage is still subsisting whereas in fact it has broken down, as for instance in *R v SSHD ex p Chaumun* CO/3143/95 (unreported). The 2002 Act s 74 has tightened this provision further by substituting a new s 10(1)(b): 'he uses deception in seeking (whether successfully or not) leave to remain'. It is difficult to see what is achieved by this attempt to cast the net even wider, as a person who did not succeed in obtaining leave to remain would presumably be without leave and so removable on another ground, probably overstaying. The words 'uses deception in seeking' revive the debates about the role of the deception in seeking leave. As phrased here, the intention would seem to be to catch *any* level of deception, no matter how material it might or might not be to the application. In application this provision should be treated as analogous to the illegal entry provisions, given that the consequences are similar. It does not cover third party deception; the words 'he uses' refer only to the applicant, so a person who was not aware for instance of the falsity of some evidence could not be removed under this provision.

17.2.3.2 *Overstaying and breach of condition*

As mentioned above, these two grounds, related to breaches of limited leave, were formerly grounds for deportation and are now, under Immigration and Asylum Act 1999 s 10 grounds for removal.

Staying beyond the time allowed by a grant of limited leave is a factual matter. There may be issues of proof, for instance of the duration of the leave, but there is little scope for legal interpretation. The only issue of interpreting the statute is a matter of making sense of what would otherwise be nonsense, making use of the golden rule of interpretation. The statute says 'having only a limited leave to enter or remain, he . . . remains beyond the time limited by the leave' (1999 Act s 10). This must mean 'having had', otherwise the leave has not yet expired and no overstaying has taken place (Macdonald 2001:756). It is strange that the opportunity was not taken in the re-enactment of this provision in the 1999 Act to correct the wording of the 1971 Act, which was the same.

A person does not stay beyond the time allowed and become an overstayer by applying for a variation of their leave and then staying for that application to be heard, provided they applied during the currency of the original limited leave. Immigration Act 1971 s 3C (as substituted by the 2002 Act s 118) continues the original leave until the end of the period set for appealing against a decision on the variation application. If an appeal is made, the same section continues the leave while the appeal is pending. It is only once these time limits are exhausted and the applicant has been unsuccessful that they may be treated as an overstayer.

Section 10 of the 1999 Act extends removal to the breach of conditions imposed under 1971 Act s 3(1)(c). The only conditions which may be imposed are: restricting employment or occupation, requiring the subject to maintain and accommodate himself and any dependants without recourse to public funds, and registration with the police. The Home Office policy statement (see chapter 9) that short-term recourse to public funds as a matter of necessity will not attract penalties is an appropriate approach in all cases of breach. Where private or family life would be interfered with by a removal, then the removal would in any event have to be proportionate under Article 8, and a trivial breach should not attract the sanction of removal.

The case of *Sabir* [1993] Imm AR 477 held that past breaches of condition could give rise to liability for deportation, but this could hardly be the case when overstaying is in the past and has been in effect cancelled out by a fresh grant of leave. It seems appropriate for breach of condition and overstaying to be treated similarly in this respect, and the statute does use the present tense, suggesting that overstaying or breach should be current to attract the penalty. This should all the more be the case now that the sanction is summary removal.

Where breaches of condition or overstaying are not disclosed in a further leave application, this may constitute obtaining leave to remain by deception and result in removal under s 10. Where they are disclosed, they should simply be taken into account as part of all the circumstances in the decision to grant or refuse leave on this occasion.

Family members of the person removed may also be removed, providing notice of this is given to them no more than eight weeks after the departure of their relative. Immigration and Asylum Act 1999 s 10 makes this provision in relation to s 10 removals. This was extended for the first time to illegal entrants by the Nationality, Immigration and Asylum Act 2002 s 73, inserting a new para 10A into 1971 Act Sch 2.

17.2.3.3 *Breach of conditions of temporary admission*

The High Court in *Yilmaz v SSHD* [2005] EWHC 1068 (Admin) reconsidered the question of whether someone who breaches their conditions of temporary admission becomes an illegal entrant. A person who is on temporary admission is at liberty instead of in detention (see chapter 15), and is awaiting leave to enter. Earlier cases had suggested that someone who breaks their conditions of temporary admission becomes an illegal entrant as they have destroyed the condition which makes them not an entrant at all (e.g., *R v IAT ex p Akhtar* [1993] Imm AR 424). However, when a claimant sought to be treated as an illegal entrant so as to obtain the benefit of a policy which applied to them and not to those awaiting grant or refusal of leave to enter, the court held that there was a discretion not to treat them as such. In *Yilmaz* the claimant argued that discretion should be exercised *not* to treat him as an illegal entrant. However, Beatson J held that becoming an illegal entrant was the normal consequence of breach of conditions of temporary admission. The common thread with cases suggesting discretion was that the claimant sought to have it exercised in their favour, and this would not be allowed.

17.3 **Effect of leave obtained in breach of immigration laws**

When the courts first began to find that leave obtained in breach of s 26(1)(c) was obtained in breach of immigration laws and thus grounds for finding the holder to be an illegal entrant, they also developed the doctrine that the leave so obtained was void. However, as with the doctrine of a duty of utmost good faith, this was to import into immigration law a concept deriving from the law of contract, and was removed in *Khawaja* where Lord Bridge said at 119:

It is for the immigration authorities to decide whether or not to seek to secure summary removal of an illegal entrant by invoking their powers under Schedule 2. If they do not do so, leave to enter stands.

This point, however, is a rather esoteric one, because once notice is given to a person that they are deemed to be an illegal entrant, any leave that they have no longer has effect. Also, leave obtained by deception is obtained 'in breach of immigration laws', and residence in breach of immigration laws is not effective for all purposes.

The House of Lords in *Shah v Barnet London Borough Council* [1983] 2 AC 309 held that residence in breach of immigration laws could not be relied upon to establish ordinary residence. This was in the context of entitlement to a student grant, and not an immigration case, but is applied in the immigration context where ordinary residence is required to establish settlement. The decision in *Shah* could have meant that an illegal entrant could never become settled, but in fact established concessions, which became rules in 2003 (see chapter 6), do give an opportunity for settlement to people who have been resident for many years.

Nationality, Immigration and Asylum Act 2002 s 11 defines residence 'in breach of immigration laws' for the purposes of calculating entitlement to apply for British citizenship by naturalization or registration to include a resident 'who does not have leave to enter or remain'. A clandestine illegal entrant therefore cannot count their residence towards an application for nationality. What of an illegal entrant whose leave was obtained unlawfully? Following *Khawaja* their leave is in existence, but following *Shah* it does not count towards ordinary residence. A letter from Beverley Hughes, Minister of State in the Home Office, to Fiona Mactaggart MP, 18 July 2002, helps to clarify the policy behind the section. Clandestine entrants and overstayers will be treated as in breach of immigration laws. People on temporary admission or in detention will not be treated as being in breach of immigration laws. Therefore, an asylum seeker who has made an illegal entry but then a claim for asylum, will not be obstructed in making a nationality application on account of their illegal entry or time spent on temporary admission.

The case of *Chaumun* applies the principles of *Khawaja* and *Shah* to leave to remain, as distinct from leave to enter. The applicant's leave to remain was obtained by forging a letter from his ex-wife. The High Court held that this was leave obtained in breach of s 26(1)(c) and, thus, was 'in breach of immigration laws'. The residence which followed could therefore not be counted as ordinary residence, and he was therefore not settled. As a consequence his second wife could not apply to remain with him in the UK. Both were liable to be deported, although now they would be liable to removal under Immigration and Asylum Act 1999 s 10, Mr Chaumun for obtaining leave to remain by deception and Mrs Chaumun for overstaying.

17.4 **EEA nationals and removal**

As EEA nationals may enter as of right on production of a passport or identity documents in order to exercise Treaty rights it is rare that an EEA national may be deemed an illegal entrant. In C–215/03 *Oulane* the ECJ held on a reference for a preliminary ruling that detention of a European national with a view to deportation was an unjustified restriction on free movement where his offence was principally lack of documentary proof of his status. So, while an EEA national may be deported as discussed in the previous chapter on public policy grounds, removal is only likely to occur if the EEA national enters in breach of an exclusion or deportation order (*Shingara v SSHD* [1999] Imm AR 257 CA).

17.5 Exercise of discretion to remove

It is fundamental in the process of removal that the decision to remove a person is a discretionary one. An individual may have stayed beyond their leave or entered in breach of immigration laws, but this does not oblige an immigration officer to order their removal. Government pronouncements announcing targets for removal are open to the charge that they have lost sight of the principle that each case is decided on its particular merits.

One practical difficulty in the way of removal may be obstacles to obtaining travel documents. Asylum and Immigration (Treatment of Claimants etc) Act 2004 s 35 makes it a criminal offence for an asylum seeker to fail to comply without reasonable excuse with obtaining a travel document. Guidance to immigration officers suggests that reasonable excuse would be something like a need for emergency medical care or transport problems which prevented a person from getting to an interview. They do not include the claimant's fear of contact with authorities in their home country. There is a possible maximum prison sentence in the UK of two years for failure to co-operate. Most alarmingly, IND guidance contemplates the possibility of using s 35 while a claim is still pending.

There is no guidance in statute on the exercise of the discretion to remove, but principles are found in rules and policies.

17.5.1 Immigration rules

In the case of proposed administrative removals under 1999 Act s 10, i.e., removal for overstaying, breach of condition, obtaining leave to remain by deception, and removal of the families of those people, regard must be had to any compassionate circumstances of the case (para 395B HC 395). This includes all the factors listed in para 364 which were discussed in the previous chapter with reference to deportation.

Paragraph 364 advises that in transitional cases of overstaying, breach of condition, and leave obtained by deception, to which the old law still applies, 'deportation will normally be the proper course'. This guidance is not repeated in para 395B which does not advise what weight should be given to these personal circumstances. They must simply be taken into account before a decision is made. As government policy is to expedite and increase removals, it would be naïve to suppose that the lack of a presumption in the immigration rules where one existed before will have produced a change in practice.

The lack of guidance reveals an ambivalence about the objective at the heart of these decisions. There is no indication of what weight should be given to the person's circumstances, nor any of what the objective is of the removal. These rules do not apply to illegal entrants. Their application to those faced with administrative removal is an inheritance from the greater degree of scrutiny afforded to deportation decisions.

17.5.2 **Policies**

As the use of removal has grown, so has the number of policies which may guide its use in the increasingly complex situations of people faced with removal. Where these policies are relevant they must be taken into account in making decisions to remove (*Abdi v SSHD* [1996] Imm AR 148 CA). Publication of a policy gives rise to a legitimate expectation that it will be applied fairly and rationally in the applicant's case (*Khan v IAT* [1984] Imm AR 68 CA). The policies discussed in this section all refer to the circumstances of the applicant which should be weighed against removal and all of them are now published. Guidance to immigration officers and Home Office civil servants on making removal decisions is in the Operational Enforcement Manual. Some of this has been made available on the Home Office website, though more recently than many other Immigration Directorate Instructions, and some remains undisclosed. Where policies have not been published there can be no legitimate expectation generated. Nevertheless, policy should still be fairly and rationally applied (*R v SSHD ex p Amankwah* [1994] Imm AR 240 and *Rashid v SSHD*).

As discussed in chapter 3, in order to meet the requirement that it is in 'in accordance with the law', a restriction on a qualified right has to be accessible and precise. This has the potential to generate further transparency concerning the use of policies, but does not have implications for how the policy is applied. The Tribunal dealt with this point in *MA Pakistan* [2005] UKIAT 00090 holding that the requirement of Article 8.2 that an interference be 'in accordance with the law' did not (a) mean that the appellant could claim the benefit of the policy or (b) have implications for how a policy is applied. The seven-year policy on children and family life (see below) was applicable to the case, but the terms of the policy itself allowed that where, as here, there was a significant history of abuse of the immigration system then the family would not necessarily obtain the benefit of the policy.

17.5.2.1 *Families*

Where a person faced with removal has a family in the UK, there are Home Office policies which provide guidance on the decision. The principal ones are DP3/96 and DP069/99 concerning marriage and children. Although much of the content of these is overtaken by the Human Rights Act, they still apply, and in certain instances the Act and policies may complement one another.

DP3/96 applies to deportation and illegal entrants, but not to others refused entry. Where the facts permit, this limitation may result in applications for judicial review in which the applicant, as we have seen earlier in relation to *Yilmaz*, seeks to be treated as an illegal entrant in order to receive the benefit of these policies. In *Olawale* [2001] Imm AR 20 and in *Khaled Ahmed* [2002] Imm AR 427 the High Court confirmed that the Secretary of State had a discretion where the facts allowed, and was not obliged to treat the applicant as an illegal entrant. There would be a difficulty for the Home Office in extending the policies to people who have received so-called 'port refusals' as to do this would be to accept the delay in the system as a factor whose effects must be reckoned with, not just cured. Since the implementation of the Human Rights Act 1998 the difference between these groups is less significant.

Strangely, DP3/96 has not been amended since Immigration and Asylum Act

1999 s 10 came into effect on 2 October 2000. However, as it deals with deportation for overstaying and breach of condition, it should be taken to apply to removal under s 10 (confirmed in *MA Algeria* [2005] UKAIT 127). The central advice in DP 3/96 is contained in the following:

As a *general rule*, deportation action . . . in non-criminal cases or illegal entry action should not be initiated in the following circumstances . . .
(a) where the subject has a genuine and subsisting marriage with someone settled here and the couple have lived together in this country continuously since their marriage for at least 2 years before the commencement of enforcement action; *and*
(b) it is unreasonable to expect the settled spouse to accompany his/her spouse on removal.

The guidance goes on to say that it is for the settled spouse to make the case as to why it would be unreasonable for them to leave, and to suggest that the Home Office will take into account strong family ties in the UK, length of residence in the UK (more than ten years), or that significant impairment or danger to life or health would result from removal.

The emphasis indicates that this is general guidance only, and that removal may still take place even when there is a qualifying marriage. This part of the guidance concludes: 'for instance, a particularly poor immigration history may warrant the offender's enforced departure from the UK notwithstanding the factors referred to above.'

In DP3/96 there seems to be an opposite view of seriousness to that suggested in the immigration rules, as in the policy statement the implication is that a person will not normally be removed for overstaying, illegal entry or breach of condition where the family ties are of sufficient strength. In the rules, enforcement is suggested as the norm for those who have breached immigration laws. Conversely, criminal cases (which would result in deportation) are treated as more serious by DP3/96 as there is no presumption against removal, and less serious in the rules where there is no stated presumption of enforcement in criminal cases.

DP3/96 is in any event ripe for change. Not only does it not take account of the 1999 Act, it also refers only to marriages. As rule changes in September 2000 and December 2005 brought applications to join unmarried partners and same-sex civil partners into the immigration rules, an application of policy which does not respect such relationships when it comes to removal cannot be maintained.

DP069/99 (amending DP5/96) gives guidance on removal when the person to be removed has children. The factors to be taken into account are: the length of the parents' residence without leave; whether removal has been delayed by protracted and repetitive representations; or by the parents going to ground; the age of the children; or whether the children were conceived at a time when either of the parents had leave to remain; whether return to the parents' country of origin would cause extreme hardship for the children or put their health seriously at risk. Enforcement will not generally proceed against families where the children were born here and are aged seven or over or where the children arrived in the UK at an early age and have lived here for seven years or more. However, in *R (on the application of Onwumere) v SSHD* [2004] EWHC 1281 Admin the claimant had a child born in the UK who was older than seven when enforcement proceedings began as well as two younger children. He claimed the benefit of DP5/96. The court held that the Secretary of State was correct to treat the scales as starting evenly balanced and to weigh in them the interests of the children and the interests of immigration control. The claimant's poor immigration history could be taken into account according to the terms of DP5/96 and it was not disproportionate to expect him to leave and apply for entry clearance from Nigeria.

Policies on marriage and children are of less importance since the Human Rights Act, as the Act encompasses all family situations as well as the factors set out in DP3/96 and DP069/99. However, the immigration rules para 395 remains relevant as this applies to every removal under s 10, whether or not the person has a partner or children, and some of the factors listed in para 364 are not necessarily encompassed in the concept of private life in Article 8. In relation to *MA Algeria* the editor of *Immigration Law Update* points out that success under the policy would mean that the Secretary of State would have to consider the case again, whereas success under Article 8 would make removal unlawful. Following *Huang*, it could also be argued that success under the policy means success under Article 8 if rules and policies delineate proportionality.

17.5.2.2 *Long residence*

Similarly of continuing importance are the long residence rules. Again, these apply whether or not a person has a family in the UK and so adds a significant protection outside the Human Rights Act in limited circumstances. These rules have been described in detail in chapter 6.

In cases of removal as opposed to deportation, while immigration offences may have been committed, the grounds for removal relate to immigration status rather than to the desirability or otherwise of the individual's continued presence in the UK. While deportation is, in theory, addressed to reducing harm to the public, whether directly or by way of making an example of someone, removal relates only the person's immigration status. They are an illegal entrant, they have overstayed, etc. The only public interest in removing them which may be set against their interest in staying is the interest in maintaining firm immigration controls and being seen to be doing so. As this is the case, the long residence rules have an important application in cases of removal as the objective of showing firm immigration control is, by the very nature of the rules, accepted as being limited.

17.5.2.3 *People over 65*

There was formerly a policy not to remove people over 65. This was revoked on 28 October 2004, and now each case is to be looked at on its merits (*R (app Doka) v IAT, SSHD interested party* [2004] EWHC 3072 (Admin)). Home Office guidance says 'age by itself is not a realistic or reliable indicator of a person's health, mobility or ability to care for themselves'. It is for the individual to show that they should not be removed (EPU 10/04).

17.6 **Removal directions**

The decision to remove takes different forms depending on what are the grounds for removal. Nevertheless, at some point later than the decision to remove, the person who is to be removed receives removal directions. These are instructions by an immigration officer or the Secretary of State to the captain of a ship or aircraft to remove the person in question (Immigration Act 1971 Sch 2 paras 8, 9, and 10). Unlike deportation there is no order which has legal force and duration and is then enforced. The person is notified of their liability to be removed, and then they are told when this will happen. Removal directions have no duration or continuing legal effect beyond the moment when they are put into practice. They are enforceable in the very real sense that a person may be arrested and detained in order to give them effect. However, in law they are themselves a form of enforcement (see, for instance, Burnton J likening them to a bailiff's warrant in *SSHD v Kariharan* [2001] EWHC Admin 1004). This means that by returning to the UK after being removed pursuant to directions a person is not in automatic breach of a legal provision, as they would be when subject to a current deportation order. However, the removal and the reasons for it are discretionary reasons for refusing entry on a subsequent occasion (HC 395 para 320: see chapter 6).

Removal directions could be appealed under the 1971 Act s 16 and the 1999 Act s 66, but only on the grounds that there was no power in law to issue them on the grounds stated. Additionally, this right of appeal could only be exercised from outside the UK unless there was an asylum or, after the 1999 Act, a human rights claim. Deportees and those refused entry also specifically had an appeal against destination.

These limitations on appeals against removal were particularly problematic where a lengthy claim, perhaps for asylum, ended unsuccessfully. If it had taken years to process the asylum seeker could hardly be expected to refrain from making relationships in that time, but their asylum claim would have dealt with the risk in their country of origin, not any developing private and family life reasons for needing to remain in the UK. There would then be no forum for arguing these points as the appeal against removal directions could only deal with the jurisdictional matter, and there would rarely be any dispute that the person was in fact an illegal entrant or perhaps an overstayer. Some further time might elapse before removal directions were set, perhaps giving further time in which relationships could be forged.

An answer seemed to be provided by Immigration and Asylum Act 1999 s 65, which gave a right of appeal on human rights grounds against 'any decision under the Immigration Acts relating to that person's entitlement to enter or remain' in the UK. If the issue of removal directions was such a decision then there could be a human rights appeal against it.

The Court of Appeal in *Kariharan v SSHD* [2002] EWCA Civ 1102 followed the interpretative obligation in HRA s 3 by giving a meaning to s 65 which upheld Convention rights where it interpreted a 'decision . . . relating to . . . entitlement' broadly so as to allow the possibility of a human rights appeal. It found that removal directions were discretionary and, as such, were capable of being determinative of entitlement to enter or remain. It did not consider that the comparison with a bailiff's warrant was altogether apt because of this continuing discretion. The Court of Appeal's judgment therefore gave the right to an appeal on human rights grounds against directions for removal. The Secretary of State appealed to the House of Lords, but even before that could be heard, the Nationality, Immigration and Asylum Act 2002 s 82 reversed *Kariharan* by specifying what was meant by 'immigration decisions' against which appeals can be made. Section 82(2)(g) and (h) permits an appeal against a 'decision that a person is to be removed by way of directions'. This means that all that is appealable is the initial immigration decision which results in the liability for removal, not the removal directions themselves.

As the 2002 Act does not include removal directions in its list of appealable decisions then the former rights of appeal against removal directions have also gone. There is no challenge to validity or destination. Directions are sometimes issued which are actually invalid but now there is no power in the statute to declare them so. For instance, directions must specify a country to which the person can be returned, and must specify the time and date of removal (1971 Act Sch 2 para 8) and there is a problem if these are wrong or non-existent. However, even under the 1999 Act the Court of Appeal in *SSHD v Zeqaj* [2003] Imm AR 298 confirmed that where the destination country was wrong, there was no appeal on the grounds that there was in law no power to give such a direction. It seems that only remedy will be judicial review, though this would also be on the ground of illegality. In *KF (Iran)* [2005] UKIAT 00109 a notice of decision to remove indicated that the appellant would be removed to Iran, though directions had not actually been given to this effect. It was not certain that Iran could receive him. The Tribunal followed *Zeqaj* — the destination was not appealable. However, the destination did have to be stated as otherwise there was no basis for assessing risk to the appellant of return either under the Refugee Convention or the Human Rights Act. If the destination was invalid under the 1971 Act the Secretary of State would have to issue a new removal decision, and this would attract a fresh right of appeal.

17.7 **Human rights appeals**

The argument that removal will breach Convention rights is now the most important basis of challenge. The Convention rights most likely to be engaged by the threat of removal are Article 3 and Article 8. Article 3 protects against torture, inhuman or degrading treatment or punishment, and will most often be engaged when an asylum claim has failed even though it is established that the asylum seeker may face ill-treatment on return. The use of Article 3 in this context has been discussed in chapter 3. There may also be Article 3 issues outside what is, in effect, the substance of the asylum claim. For instance, in *R (on the application of Ahmadi) v SSHD* [2002] EWHC 1897 Admin, the applicants at first alleged that their return to Germany would breach Article 3, not because they feared that Germany would return them to Afghanistan, the country they originally fled in fear of persecution, but because of the conditions in the refugee centres in which they were living in Germany. This part of the claim was ultimately not pursued before the High Court.

Apart from the use of Article 3 in asylum claims, the article most often engaged in removals is Article 8, the right to respect for private and family life, home and correspondence.

17.7.1 **Article 8**

Reference should be made to chapter 3 for full discussion of Article 8. Here we consider the issues arising from removals. The proper approach to an alleged breach as set out by the Immigration Appeal Tribunal in the case of *Nhundu and Chiwera* (01/TH/000613 at para 24) is:

Article 8 is to be analysed according to a step-by-step approach, asking first whether there is an existent private or family life, second whether there is an interference with that private or family life, third whether that interference pursues a legitimate aim, fourth whether it is in accordance with the law and finally whether it is proportionate.

This step-by-step approach, approved by the House of Lords in *Razgar* will be followed here with application to removal.

17.7.1.1 *Private or family life*

Reference should be made to chapter 3 for full discussion of relationships which are accepted as private or family life. In brief, relationships with husband, wife, and minor children are not contentious as being family relationships. Recognition of wider family relationships is more dependent on context and quality of relationship.

17.7.1.2 *Interference*

The most obvious and damaging interference with family life by a removal is the break up of the family. It can also be argued that the upheaval and disruption of support networks, wider family relationships and so on is an interference with family and private life. If other family members are removed the upheaval to the whole family must be considered as the potential breach, though only in relation to the Article 8 rights of a person who is the named subject of removal (see chapter 3).That removal constitutes such an interference was made clear by the tribunal in *Baljit Singh* [2002] UKIAT 00660. The tribunal in that case did not claim to lay down a general rule of this kind, but given the nature and effects of removal only in rare instances could it be otherwise. *Nhundu* makes this point, saying that where a family is established removal will constitute an interference with family life. This is not always the approach taken in tribunals. The Master of the Rolls' judgment in *Mahmood* suggests that he did not consider the proposed removal of Mr Mahmood to be an interference with family life because either his wife and children could go with him or he could apply for entry clearance from Pakistan. Although these points are obiter as the Court was not applying Article 8 for itself, but simply reviewing the legality of the Secretary of State's decision, *Mahmood* is often followed on this point. The implication seems to be that disruption, distress, discomfort and financial hardship do not constitute an interference with the right to respect for family life. In *SS Hussain v SSHD* [2004] EWCA Civ 1190 the children's six to twelve month separation from their stepfather was not considered to be a relevant interference because it would not be long enough to result inevitably in family breakdown.

What respect for family life requires when a family is already living in a country together may be different from what is required before they have made a home together. This does not mean that ultimately the family may not be required to leave, but that it will be a rare case in which the choice of separation or of uprooting and losing support networks, perhaps jobs, schooling, friends, and family cannot be argued to be an interference with family life. Following *Nhundu*, the question then under Article 8 is whether para 2 of that Article permits the interference. With respect to the Master of the Rolls, the opportunity to apply for entry clearance, and its impact in a particular case, is then a matter which goes to proportionality. This matter is discussed with reference to proportionality in a great number of Article 8 cases: see below.

It may be recalled that Article 8 para 2 states:

There shall be no interference by a public authority with the exercise of this right except such as is in accordance with the law and is necessary in a democratic society in the interests of national security, public safety or the economic well-being of the country, for the prevention of disorder or crime, for the protection of health or morals, or for the protection of the rights and freedoms of others.

17.7.1.3 *Legitimate aim*

The identification of the legitimate aim is a necessary first step in applying Article 8.2 (see chapter 3 for full discussion of this point). In the case of deportations it is usually possible to cite 'prevention of disorder or crime' or 'protection of health or morals' as public interests served by the deportation. However, in removals the legitimate aim may be less easy to identify. Removal is directed towards immigration enforcement, but this is not listed in para 2 as a legitimate aim. In *Abdulaziz* the ECtHR accepted that the immigration policy which restricted entry of spouses was for the 'economic well-being of the country'. However, it would rarely be possible to show that the removal of a person who was making an economic contribution fulfilled this aim, particularly where removal would result in the loss of the only income and therefore leave a family reliant on state support.

The approach that is usually taken is to say that the maintenance of an immigration policy *per se* is for the economic well-being of the country. It is therefore not that the individual must be removed for the public good but that they must be treated as one of a group in relation to whom there is a policy that serves that aim. This then has repercussions for the question of proportionality if the harm to the individual is to be weighed against the need for the policy, but not a specific ill that would result from their remaining.

The courts and tribunals commonly hold, as did the Tribunal in *Baljit Singh*, that the family interests must be weighed against the interest of the government in 'maintaining effective immigration control'. While this may sometimes be used as shorthand for the reasoning above, there is a danger in so doing as the discussion all too easily slips into circularity. The reason there is a case before a tribunal is that there is some breach of immigration law. If the maintenance of immigration control is used *per se* to justify an interference with a right, the individual may easily end up with an unwinnable argument. Indeed this is often the case. One of the many examples, illustrating also the limits of the application of Article 8, is *SO (Nigeria)* [2005] UKAIT 00135. Here, the appellant had a substantial life in the UK. He had entered legally, but as his marriage had not worked out he had no right in immigration law to remain. He employed sixteen people and was a well-regarded Christian lay minister. The tribunal gave extended reasons as to why any economic disadvantage to others from his removal was speculative and irrelevant, but did not appear to consider how removing a productive and socially useful person served the economic well-being of the country. Simply the fact he had no immigration right was enough. Even more starkly, in *AY Ivory Coast* [2004] UKIAT 00205 the tribunal held that Secretary of State provisionally discharged the burden of proof to show that the removal was proportionate by 'relying upon the substantial weight to be accorded to a firm and fair immigration policy' (para 22).

In principle, Convention rights should produce the opposite starting position. The rights are protected, and the legitimate interference in para 2 of the qualified rights is the exception. Of course, the Tribunal still must be satisfied that the rest of para 2 is met.

Interferences are nearly always in accordance with the law in immigration cases, though the legal source should be identified. The substantive issue is proportionality.

17.7.1.4 *Proportionality*

This is a matter which can only be decided on a case-by-case basis. The decision-maker must weigh carefully the harm done to the individual by the interference with their right against the public interest pursued. The task of considering proportionality follows on from the application of the test which the European Court of Human Rights has on the whole taken seriously, that of 'necessity in a demo-cratic society', equating it with a 'pressing social need' (*Sunday Times v UK* (1979) 2 EHRR 245). The State must show that the interference is not just useful or desirable but necessary, then argument will centre chiefly on the question of whether the proposed interference with a right is proportionate to the legitimate aim pursued.

The legacy of the case of *R v SSHD ex p Mahmood* [2001] 1WLR 840, which has been discussed in chapter 3, has significantly affected the development of the approach in the tribunals to proportionality of removal. It may be recalled that this was a judicial review in which the Master of the Rolls laid out a six-point summary of the ECHR's approach to Article 8. This draws quite strongly on *Abdulaziz, Cabales and Balkandali* (1985) 7 EHRR 471, which concerned entry rather than removal, and in any event does not constitute structured guidance on the application of Article 8 para 2 or the test of proportionality, which, as now approved by the Court of Appeal in *Huang* and House of Lords in *Ullah and Do* are the principal tasks of an appellate body hearing a human rights appeal. Although the Court of Appeal in *Mahmood* disclaimed that it was applying the test of proportionality, in many removal cases initially the six points were used as a blueprint, not for the approach of the ECHR, which the Tribunal could then take into account (HRA s 2) but for the proportionality test itself. As time went on, the recitation of the six points became less common, but two factors were extracted from *Mahmood* and are being used in the tribunals with the force of a rule of law. One is the comparison with those in the entry clearance queue and the other is the question of insuperable obstacles, which has been elevated into a requirement.

Comparison with entry clearance

In *Mahmood*, the Secretary of State argued that the appellant could return to his home country to make an application for entry clearance as a spouse. The appellant was a failed asylum seeker who qualified for entry under the immigration rules as a spouse in every respect except the possession of entry clearance. The Court of Appeal thought it not unreasonable that the appellant should return to Pakistan to take his place in the queue. Only exceptional circumstances would warrant his not being obliged to go through that procedure. He argued that he would then lose his job, his wife would go onto benefits and he would not be able to show that he would be able to maintain himself and the family and so his application might fail. The Court of Appeal said that the fact that the application might fail was not a reason not to make it. Many cases have followed this approach closely. The Court of Appeal has taken a similar approach. In *SS Hussain v SSHD* it held that the IAT was not wrong to uphold the removal of the appellant who had entered illegally four years before his marriage to a British citizen who had three children. His immigration history (of entering illegally) was relevant to the question of proportionality, and a wait of six to 12 months for entry clearance as a husband would not be disproportionate. The children's rights were only relevant to the extent that they affected his situation.

In *Cetin* [2002] UKIAT 06272 there was a delay in granting refugee status to the appellant's husband. His solicitors intervened and eventually status was granted. However in the meantime he and his fiancée had become distressed by their separation, and she had come to the UK and made a false and unsuccessful asylum claim. They married soon after her arrival and at the time of the threatened removal she was pregnant. It was accepted that there would be a long wait for entry clearance, but the tribunal held that the proper maintenance of immigration control outweighed respect for family life. She should have waited until he had indefinite leave and applied then, and could not be seen to be gaining an advantage from her illegal entry. In *K(Russia)* (see chapters 3 and 12) there was no basis for an application for entry clearance as the appellant's husband only had exceptional leave to remain which carried no right to be joined by a spouse. The tribunal held (as in *Mahmood*) that the poor prospects of success in an entry clearance application were irrelevant to whether refusal of leave was disproportionate.

Difficulties or dangers of travel to make an entry clearance application have also been held not to make the requirement to do so disproportionate. This was the Tribunal's decision in *SA (Iraq)* (CG) [2006] UKAIT 00011. The appellant's asylum claim had failed, and this no doubt influenced the Tribunals' reasoning, not only in this but in many other similar cases. The nub of the matter is in the Tribunal's quotation from Sedley LJ in *ZT v SSHD* [2005] EWCA Civ1421:

> The underlying message of *N* and *Razgar*, and of *Ullah* too, is that the ECHR is neither a surrogate system of asylum nor a fallback for those who have otherwise no right to remain here. It is for particular cases which transcend their class in respects which the Convention recognizes. (*SA* para 35)

The second sentence demonstrates current thinking as set or exemplified by *Huang*. This context is more influential now in courts and tribunals than the reliance on circumstances found in ECHR cases such as *Boultif v Switzerland* (2000) 22 EHRR 50.

Insuperable obstacles
This new quasi-legal test follows on from the previous one. The Court of Appeal in *Husna Begum v ECO Dhaka* [2001] INLR 115 warned against elevating the idea of insurmountable obstacles into a rule of law, but this still seems to have happened.

The concept of insurmountable obstacles is now routinely cited. It amounts to a requirement to show why the claimant's family should not leave the country with them. It may also be used as a requirement to show why the claimant should not leave the country to apply for entry clearance. The sponsor having refugee status would, one might imagine, be a clear case of insuperable obstacles to return. However, it is not always so regarded. In *Kilala v SSHD* [2002] UKIAT 05220 the appellant's wife had been recognized as a refugee from the Democratic Republic of Congo. Only a year after this recognition, the Tribunal said that this did not mean there were insuperable obstacles to the couple returning. The situation there might have changed. In *R (on the application of Doka) v SSHD* the risk to the applicant's family of return to Sudan was one reason that family life could not be established there with them, but this was one among a number of factors. In the case of *Soloot* 01/TH/001366 the tribunal found that there were insuperable obstacles to the couple returning to Iran. The appellant's wife was a recognized refugee, so clearly she could not return as she would be at risk. The appellant himself would face criminal penalties for his manner of leaving Iran, and would not be able to make an application for entry clearance there.

The approach in *Kalila* and *Doka* requires the applicant to argue their spouse's refugee status all over again. It seems that the courts have reversed the burden of proof in Article 8. Although the Court of Appeal in *Huang* adjures immigration judges to assess proportionality for themselves, cases outside the rules, whether failing under a rule or not covered by a rule at all, should, according to the Court of Appeal, succeed only if the circumstances are exceptional. In *Betts v SSHD* the appellant's father had applied over 30 years previously for registration as a British citizen. The application was not acknowledged or dealt with. Once revived it was eventually granted. The appellant's mother and sister were granted asylum under a policy of no-return then in force in relation to Sierra Leone. He at the time had student status, but once this expired, applied under the policy which was still in force. By the time his application was decided the policy had ended and he was refused. The Court of Appeal held, following *Huang*, that this history of 'near misses' did not make his circumstances exceptional, and he should face the normal consequences of a failed asylum claim, namely removal.

In *AY (Ivory Coast)* it was clear that an application for UK entry clearance from Ivory Coast was unlikely to succeed. The further question was whether the appellant's wife, who was Cameroonian, could live with the appellant in the Ivory Coast, or he with her in Cameroon. There was no evidence before the tribunal as to any legal obstacles. The question was, who should have provided it? The Tribunal said that, despite the poor prospects of UK entry clearance, without evidence of obstacles in Ivory Coast or Cameroon, there was no evidence of interference with the right to respect for private and family life. If they were wrong about that, they said that although the Secretary of State had the burden of showing that removal was proportionate, this was done prima facie by the need for immigration control. The burden then shifted to the appellant to show why this was disproportionate in their case. The underlying theme here is, again, that the appellant must show some exceptional reason why immigration control should not apply to them. Not only must the appellant show the effect of the Secretary of State's actions upon them; they must also show that their rights would be violated in any other plausible destination.

17.7.1.5 *Other family members*

Where a removal is proposed, the rights of other family members are also affected. We can take *Mahmood* as an example of a family situation which is not in any way unusual. The appellant had a wife and two children with whom he lived. If he were removed it is most likely he would be separated from them. If they went with him this would interfere with a further dimension of family life, which was his wife's relationship with her parents and siblings, who were also living in the UK.

The question of whether the rights of other family members must be taken into account in a human rights appeal has been discussed in chapter 3, and is now at least temporarily resolved with the result that the rights of other members of the family may only be considered as part of the circumstances affecting the appellant's rights. Family members may pursue separate actions under the Human Rights Act s 7.

17.8 Conclusion

Removal is a major plank of government immigration policy. There are 'targets' for removals, questions by Opposition MPs about number of removals, and promises to do more. The law on removal is a battleground. It is often tortuous and technical and its implementation may cause enormous human distress. It is a major practical challenge for enforcement agencies. Removal began as a mean of administrative enforcement, but its reach has grown to include people who enter by deceit and long term residents of the UK. Some of the tension surrounding removal is explained not only by what is at stake for individuals, but also by what is revealed by the challenges under Article 8, namely that what is at stake for the Government is the maintenance of a firm immigration policy.

QUESTIONS

1   Do you think the Tribunal in *Cetin* made the right decision?

2   Was it appropriate for the courts to develop the definition of 'illegal entrant' to include someone who entered by deception? What would have been the alternative?

3   Mrs Mahmood was a British citizen. Do you think that this should have affected the decision to remove Mr Mahmood?

FURTHER READING

Evans, J.M. (1983) *Immigration Law*, 2nd edn (London: Sweet & Maxwell), Chapter 6.

Fasti, M. (2002) 'The restrictive approach taken by the European Court of Human Rights: deportation of long-term immigrants and the right to family life, Part 1: integrated aliens and family rights: involution versus evolution' (2002) IANL vol. 16, no. 3, p. 166; Part 2: 'Consensus enquiry and security of residence of long-term immigrants in Europe' vol. 16, no. 4, p. 224.

JCWI (2006) Immigration, nationality and refugee law handbook, ed. Seddon, D., Chapter 33.

Macdonald, I., and Webber, F. (2005) *Macdonald's Immigration Law and Practice*, 6th edn (London: Butterworths), Chapter 16.

Rogers, N. (2003) 'Immigration and the European Convention on Human Rights: are new principles emerging?' *EHRLR* 1, pp. 53–64.

BIBLIOGRAPHY

A select bibliography of reading additional to that found at the end of each chapter.

Arnull, A. (1999) *The European Union and its Court of Justice* (Oxford: Oxford University Press).

Ashford, M. (1993) *Detention without Trial* (London: JCWI).

Bogusz, B, Cholewinski, R, Cygan, R. & Szyszczak E. eds (2004) *Irregular Migration and Human Rights: Theoretical, European and International Perspectives* (Leiden: Martinus Nijhoff).

Evans, J. (1983) *Immigration Law*, 2nd edn. (London: Sweet & Maxwell).

Grahl-Madsen, A. (1966) *The Status of Refugees in International Law Vol. I* (Leiden: Sijthoff).

—— (1972) *The Status of Refugees in International Law Vol. II* (Leiden: Sijthoff).

Grant, L., and Martin, I. (1982) *Immigration Law and Practice* (London: Cobden Trust).

Holmes, C. (1988) *John Bull's Island*: *Immigration and British Society 1871–1971* (London: Macmillan).

Hunt, M. (1998) *Using Human Rights Law in English Courts* (Oxford: Hart).

Legomsky, S. (1987) *Immigration and the Judiciary: Law and Politics in Britain and America* (Oxford: Clarendon Press).

Loveland, I. (2003) *Constitutional Law, Administrative Law and Human Rights: A Critical Introduction*, 3rd edn. (London: Butterworths).

Lester, A., and Bindman, G. (1972) *Race and Law* (Harmondsworth: Penguin Books).

Mowbray, A. (2004) *The Development of Positive Obligations under the European Convention on Human Rights by the European Court of Human Rights* (Oxford: Hart).

Starmer, K. (2003) 'Two Years of the Human Rights Act' EHRLR [2003] 1, pp.14–23.

Steyn, K., and Wolfe, D. (1999) 'Judicial Review and the Human Rights Act: Some Practical Considerations' EHRLR [1999] 6, pp. 614–629.

Symes, M., and Jorro, P. (2003) *Asylum Law and Practice* (London: Butterworths).

Tuitt, P. (1996) *False Images: The Law's Construction of the Refugee* (London: Pluto Press).

Willman, S., Knafler, S., and Pierce, S. (2005) *Support for Asylum Seekers* 2nd ed. (London: Legal Action Group).

WING (Bhabha, J., Klug, F., and Shutter, S. (eds)) (1985) *Worlds Apart: Women under immigration and nationality law* (London: Pluto Press).

Zetter, R., Griffiths, D., Ferretti, S., and Pearl, M. (2003) *An assessment of the impact of asylum policies in Europe* Home Office Research Study 259.

INDEX